Ex Libris

This book supplied by

Geoffrey Godden

Chinaman

17-19 Crescent Road
Worthing, Sussex BN11 1RT
Tel. (0903) 35958

Dealer in fine pottery & porcelain, who trusts
that this book will prove interesting and
helpful, giving added pleasure to your collecting

CHAMBERLAIN-WORCESTER
PORCELAIN
1788–1852

Other books by Geoffrey Godden:

CHAMBERLAIN-WORCESTER PORCELAIN
1788-1852

GEOFFREY A. GODDEN, FRSA

BARRIE & JENKINS
London Melbourne Sydney Auckland Johannesburg

Barrie & Jenkins Ltd

An imprint of the Hutchinson Publishing Group
17–21 Conway Street, London W1P 6JD

Hutchinson Group (Australia) Pty Ltd
30–32 Cremorne Street, Richmond South, Victoria 3121
PO Box 151, Broadway, New South Wales 2007

Hutchinson Group (NZ) Ltd
32–34 View Road, PO Box 40–086, Glenfield, Auckland 10

Hutchinson Group (SA) (Pty) Ltd
PO Box 337, Bergvlei 2012, South Africa

Distributed in the United States of America by
Abner Schram, 36 Park St, Montclair, N.J., 07042

First published 1982
© Geoffrey A. Godden, 1982

Set in Monophoto Ehrhardt
Filmset and printed in Great Britain by BAS Printers Limited, Over Wallop, Hampshire
and bound by Wm. Brendon & Son Limited, Tiptree, Essex

British Library Cataloguing in Publication Data

Godden, Geoffrey A.
    Chamberlain-Worcester porcelain
    1788–1852.
    1. Worcester porcelain – History
    I. Title
    738.2′7   NK4395

ISBN 0 09 145860 9

Abner Schram ISBN 08390-0295-5

CONTENTS

This book is dedicated to Henry Sandon
(Curator of the Dyson Perrins Museum at Worcester)
in appreciation of all his very great help and encouragement
during the preparation of this book –
a dedication which I am sure
all collectors of Worcester porcelain
will readily endorse.

LIST OF PLATES

Colour

Monochrome

ACKNOWLEDGEMENTS

First and foremost I must record my gratitude to the Trustees of the Dyson Perrins Museum Trust and to the Directors of the Worcester Royal Porcelain Company Ltd for so generously permitting me unlimited access to the original Chamberlain account books and archives listed on page 369. Without these records and the opportunity to research them this book could not have been written. In this connection I wish to record the very real help given to me by past and present members of the museum staff – initially by the former Curator Cyril Shingler and then by the present Curator, Henry Sandon. Other helpers at the Dyson Perrins Museum include Henry's two sons, John and David Sandon, Mr Frank Laney and Miss Kim Badland.

Apart from the Chamberlain archives, I have been permitted to handle and to illustrate some of the superb Chamberlain porcelains on display in this magnificent museum. I record with great gratitude my debt to all at the Worcester works and at the adjacent museum, remembering as I do so that they occupy the site of the original Chamberlain factory, and that R. W. Binns, the first Director of the Royal Worcester Company in 1862, was probably responsible for the retention of all the accounts relating to the previous periods – documents which under similar circumstances are so often destroyed, as being of no interest or importance.

Others who have so generously helped with research on various facets of the Chamberlain story include Miss Gaye Blake Roberts, Mrs Sheila Davis, Roger Edmundson, Ian Henderson, David Holgate, Miss Helen Ladd (Local Studies Librarian, Libraries Dept, Worcester), M. Lee, Miss Dorothy McCulla (Librarian of Local Studies, City of Birmingham Libraries), Philip Miller, Paul Rado, George Sinclair, Simon Spero, Jeremy Stedman, W. Ramsay Strachan, Dr Bernard Watney and Mr and Mrs C. Wharf.

With the inclusion of over four hundred illustrations in this book, my list of owners, or suppliers of photographs, is long, but without such a wealth of illustrations this book would have been rather dull and relatively unhelpful. The following firms, museums or individuals have kindly enabled me to dress the bare bones of the historical facts and to show the finished products, the success of which enabled the firm to continue for over sixty years. Commercial concerns have the prefix 'Messrs' but examples credited to them may no longer be in stock.

Miss M. Ball
Messrs Sheila & Charles
  Barkman Ltd
The Bath Preservation
  Trust
C. S. Beach
Messrs Beauchamp
  Gallery
Mrs H. Bennett
C. H. Black
Messrs John Bly
Mrs W. Boardman
Mr and Mrs A. Boyce
Bristol Museum
John Broad
W. Browne
Miss J. Carr
E. H. Chandler
Cheltenham Art Gallery
  & Museum

Messrs Christie, Manson
  & Woods Ltd
Miss C. Cooke
Messrs Andrew Dando
Mrs S. Davis
Messrs Delomosne & Son
Messrs John Duncalfe
The Dyson Perrins
  Museum Trust
Miss S. A. Elliott
Anton Gabazewicz
Messrs Geoffrey Godden,
  Chinaman
Messrs Godden of
  Worthing Ltd
Messrs Thomas Goode &
  Co.
Messrs Graham & Oxley
B. Green
Miss H. Greenfield

Messrs Havelock House,
    Australia
Mrs F. M. Hawley
I. T. Henderson
Mrs J. Houseman
Mrs E. Hutchinson
Messrs Martin Hutton
Messrs King &
    Chasemore
Mrs B. Laker
Messrs Lea & Perrins
Messrs Marshall Field &
    Co.
John C. Matthews
Messrs C. May
Mr and Mrs P. Miller
A. Mitchell
Mrs K. Mitchell
A. Morton
Messrs Neales of
    Nottingham, auctioneers
David Newbon
Miss S. Newman
A. O'Connor
Messrs Phillips,
    auctioneers
W. Pitts
Dr and Mrs D. Rice
The Rous Lench
    Collection
Messrs Monty Sainsbury
W. Seabrooke

Messrs Jean Sewell
George Sinclair
H. A. Snell
Messrs Sotheby & Co.
Messrs Sotheby–Belgravia
G. Spencer
Messrs S. Spero (China
    Choice)
Miss L. Steele
Stoke-on-Trent City
    Museums
W. Ramsay Strachan
Mrs P. A. Street
Miss Urwick
Messrs E. D. Vandekar
Messrs Venner's
    Antiques
Victoria & Albert
    Museum
M. A. Wall
Messrs W. W. Warner
    (Antiques) Ltd
E. H. Webster
Mr and Mrs C. Wharf
Messrs D. Whitelaw
Messrs Winifred
    Williams
Miss P. Willmot
Worcester Royal
    Porcelain Co. Ltd
Mr and Mrs Milton L.
    Zorensky

Some of these simple entries cover whole teams of
persons who have helped in the supply of illustrations

and other material; for example, at Sotheby's I was
assisted by the late A. J. B. (Jim) Kiddell, Mr J. P.
Palmer, Mrs Joanna Forester and Sylvia Hunt. At
Phillips the Ceramic Department team comprised John
C. Matthews, Mrs Marshall and John Sandon.

Several other helpful owners have over the years
kindly supplied photographs which, whilst helping with
research and the completion of Chapter 7, have not been
chosen to be featured in this book, but still I
acknowledge my debt to these unnamed helpers.

I am grateful for the professional skill of my local
photographer – Mr A. J. Whitcomb (of Messrs Walter
Gardiner Photography, Worthing), who has posed and
photographed all illustrations credited to Geoffrey
Godden Chinaman, Messrs Godden of Worthing or the
Godden Reference Collection, as well as many other
objects that were lent to me in order that the
photographs could be taken in Messrs Walter Gardiner
Photography's studio. Mr J. M. Beckerley was responsible for the superb photographs of items credited
to the Dyson Perrins Museum at Worcester. I regret
being unable to mention by name the other professional
photographers who are unknown to me, such as those
employed by the great auction houses. In this connection acknowledgements to firms or museums are
necessarily rather inadequate for many persons were
jointly involved in the help given to me.

On a personal note I must offer feeble apologies to my
wife Jean and to our son Jonathan for being such a poor
companion over the all-too-long period this book has
taken to complete. I also apologize for all the eye-strain
inflicted on a team of typists who have made presentable
my various handwritten drafts and numerous corrected
and enlarged typescripts. This team comprised Miss
Janet Belton, Mrs A. Kemp-Potter, Mrs Malwynne
Magness and Miss Rosemary Manley.

PREFACE

This book fills a great gap in the history of English ceramics. For the first time the detailed story is told of one of the largest and longest-lived English porcelain manufactories – the Chamberlain factory at Worcester.

The Chamberlain works remained under the control of members of this family for over sixty years. On the very site, and using some of the old Chamberlain buildings, the present Royal Worcester Company continues the internationally acknowledged tradition of superb-quality porcelain in the city of Worcester.

It could well be claimed that without the Chamberlains the present company would not have been formed in 1862, for when the management of the Flight, Barr & Barr Company (successors to the eighteenth-century Dr Wall partnership) wished to discontinue trading in 1840, it was the rival Chamberlain Company which took over and combined production at the Chamberlain factory.

Strangely, the founder of the Chamberlain Company, Robert Chamberlain, was reputedly the first apprentice taken on by the original Worcester management in the 1750s. He rose to become head of the decorating department at the Dr Wall factory before leaving to establish his own independent decorating establishment in Worcester in the 1780s, previously having mainly embellished porcelain made at the Caughley factory in Shropshire. These basic points are enlarged upon in Chapters 1 and 2.

Within a few years Robert Chamberlain turned to the manufacture of his own porcelains in Worcester. The earliest essays are amongst the rarest of English porcelains, indeed these unmarked porcelains (see Plates 32–40, 44–55) are but poorly represented in the national collections and are unknown to all but a few specialists. Yet the Chamberlain porcelains quickly became firmly established and were soon being exported. The well-potted durable Chamberlain teawares of the 1795–1825 period must have been envied by all other English manufacturers catering for the vast middle-class market for attractive and serviceable useful porcelains. The range of Chamberlain teaware shapes and patterns illustrated in this book will surprise and delight the collector; but the reader will learn that the Chamberlain porcelains were by no means restricted to useful wares. The range of ornamental objects is enormous – from large ornate vases to miniature toys and small animal models, even buttons, studs and tie-pins.

Whilst the Chamberlain porcelain bodies were reliable and the potting capable, the added decoration could be superb. The brothers Humphrey and Walter Chamberlain enjoyed royal patronage and a national, if not an international, reputation. The many Chamberlain painters and gilders formed a decorating team equal in excellence and versatility to any in the land. The reader who may doubt this statement now is unlikely to do so after a glance at the illustrations in this book. But here lies the difficulty, for the excellence of the Chamberlain porcelains is largely unknown; many of the pieces are unmarked, no great collections have been formed, and previously no reference book has dealt in detail with this important factory.

I hope that this pioneer work, based on a mass of original documents, account and order books, will open the collector's eyes to these often superb and nearly always pleasing Chamberlain-Worcester porcelains, which range in period from the early 1790s to 1852, giving ample scope to the collector. The simpler wares should be within the pocket of most collectors and the many facets of the firm's productions permit specialization and indeed further research.

I should point out that the original copies of letters, accounts and the pattern lists were written with many abbreviations, being in some cases merely notes. I have endeavoured to fill out such abbreviations and in general to make these records understandable to the average, non-specialist reader. While the purist may find some minor differences between the original and my quoted version, I am quite satisfied that the meaning is retained and is indeed now rather clearer.

I would suggest that there is still the opportunity of getting in on the ground floor of collecting Chamberlain porcelain. The collector should be well rewarded for his attention to these interesting and decorative Worcester porcelains.

Good hunting!

Geoffrey Godden,
19 Crescent Road,
Worthing, West Sussex

1

GENERAL SURVEY AND MARKS

The basic facts concerning Robert Chamberlain's early career were set out over a hundred years ago by R. W. Binns, that great ceramic historian and the founder of the concern now known internationally as 'Royal Worcester'. Binns, in his *A Century of Potting in the City of Worcester*, a work first published in 1865, wrote:

Mr. Robert Chamberlain, who was the first apprentice of the Porcelain Company, left the establishment shortly after its purchase by Mr. Flight in 1783, and commenced business as a decorator at premises in King Street, St. Peter's, close to the present works. Here he employed workmen of various grades of talent, and also a large number of apprentices. Mr. Robert Chamberlain was associated with his son Humphrey as a partner, while Mr. Richard Nash was for many years a sleeping partner. Messrs. Chamberlain commenced regular business in King Street in the year 1786, and in the present manufactory in 1788, buildings to the value of £700 having been erected prior to the year 1792.

When Messrs. Chamberlain started operations it was in opposition to the new proprietors [Messrs Flight] of Warmstry House, but being only decorators, the firm was compelled to obtain porcelain elsewhere. The works at Caughley were at this time producing, under the management of Turner, a first class material, and the shapes followed exactly those made at Worcester. There was consequently no difficulty in procuring a supply of white ware.

Messrs. Chamberlain having large experience as decorators were also employed by Turner to decorate Caughley wares for his own sale, and considerable quantities were sent for this purpose to be returned to him or to his warehouse in London . . . .

Binns, however, left many tantalizing gaps in the story. He even neglected at that point to say that Chamberlain later started to produce his own porcelain at Worcester, so that he was no mere decorator but also a

manufacturer and destined to become one of the leading producers of English porcelain. In fact this former apprentice to the so-called Dr Wall Worcester factory succeeded to such an extent that in 1840 his own company was able to join with the then owners of the original Dr Wall Worcester factory and to continue the joint concern at his own factory. In 1862 this combination gave birth to the 'Royal Worcester' company which still continues to add prestige to the tradition of fine Worcester porcelain.

First, however, further details of the story as related by R. W. Binns (just quoted) are necessary. Some of the information given by Binns in 1865 can be traced back to Valentine Green, the author of *History and Antiquities of Worcester* (1796). Green was himself connected with the Worcester porcelain factory for a period from 1760, when he was articled to Robert Hancock, the Worcester engraver. Green, perhaps drawing on personal knowledge, stated that Robert Chamberlain was the first apprentice at the Worcester factory, but I have been unable to trace any records to verify this statement. On the other hand, there is no evidence to disprove the tradition, and to support it, there has recently come to light a most interesting family account of Robert Chamberlain's early life. An annotated copy of the first edition of R. W. Binns's *A Century of Potting in the City of Worcester* (1865) has been presented to the Dyson Perrins Museum Trust by his granddaughter, Mrs Bonnet. This unique volume contains additional information which may have been gathered for a proposed enlarged edition; of particular interest here is a letter from Mrs Alice M. Lilly, the granddaughter of Robert Chamberlain, dated 6 March 1862, containing the following passages:

My grandfather Mr. Robert Chamberlain was born in 1737 and died about 1798. He married either in 1755 or 1756. All that we know of him is that he came from Gloucestershire where his family was situated. He was an only child and married in Worcester an only child. She was the infant daughter of an officer who went abroad and was never heard of afterwards.

When they married my grandfather was 19. My grandmother was 18 and when their first child was 1 year old, the united ages of the three amounted to 40!

My father Humphrey Chamberlain, Alderman and Mayor of Worcester in the year 1819, was born in 1762 and died in 1841. His son Humphrey Chamberlain was born in 1791 and died in 1824 aged 33. He was acknowledged to be by even Bone himself [Henry Bone, 1755–1834, the celebrated miniaturist] unrivalled as a china painter . . . .

From this record of Robert Chamberlain's date of birth, 1737, it is obvious that his apprenticeship in his teens was indeed early in the history of Worcester porcelain, and presumably he had completed his apprenticeship and was fully employed by the time he married at the age of nineteen in 1755 or 1756. He died on 19 December 1798 and was buried two days later in St Paul's Churchyard, Worcester.

Valentine Green stated that this first apprentice, Robert Chamberlain, rose to a position whereby 'the ornamental part of the production of that factory and the embellishing of the ware was carried on under the immediate direction of Mr. Chamberlain and his son for many years'. This important statement has not previously caused much comment, but it would seem at least probable that Robert Chamberlain, with his eldest son Humphrey, was in fact wholly responsible for the decoration or gilding of Worcester porcelain in the late 1770s into the 1780s. The diary of John Flight, then joint owner of the original factory, sheds interesting light on the situation. In the summer of 1789 after his return from Paris in March, Flight noted:

. . . I was sorry to learn Chamberlain and his Son had taken our old House [the retail shop at 33 High Street, vacated early in August 1788] and intended setting up a Retail Shop. – This rendered it necessary for me to come immediately to Worcester to consult with my Brother what was to be done. Coud not at all agree with Chamberlain so I returned after making great enquiry. I at last agreed with Mrs. Hampton to come down with us and *teach us the Gilding* [author's italic] and assist us for 3 years. . . . Mrs. Hampton arrived the day before [6 June 1789]. I had been employed in building a kiln. We hired 3 of Chamberlain's men who are now with us. We have fired twice, once on Tuesday and again last night but neither have succeeded very well . . . .

On 21 July 1789 Flight again referred to the position caused by Chamberlain leaving the employment of the company:

While my Brother and I were determining upon opening a shop in London, Chamberlain was treating about taking over our old House . . . what we could have done had we not met with Mrs. Hampton I cannot tell. I see no possible way by which we could have carried on the business . . . .

Mrs Hampton stayed with the manufactory at least until February 1791, when John Flight recorded:

On Friday [18 February] Mrs. Hampton was taken very ill, so I was obliged to manage the burning of the gold kiln; fortunately, by the attention I have paid to this, was able to do it and I hope could without much difficulty in case we were to lose her, but this I hope will not be the case as she is getting better. It would however, I fear put us to some inconvenience.

Other entries in this interesting diary* refer to trouble with the firing of the decorated Worcester wares, the erection of a new enamel kiln 'on the Plan of Chamberlain's' (July 1789) and the engagement of girls to burnish the gilding.

The phrase italicized, referring to the hiring of Mrs Hampton to 'teach us the Gilding', and other passages, suggest most strongly that the loss of Chamberlain left the Flights without any means of decorating or, in particular, gilding their products. If this is accepted, there remain certain possibilities to consider: firstly, that the two Chamberlains had themselves gilded *all* the Worcester porcelains for a period before the parting, though a point against this is that the output of the factory would have been considerable, far greater than two persons could have decorated themselves. Secondly, there is a possibility that other former Dr Wall gilders left at the same time as the Chamberlains to work with them.

There is a further possibility which seems to fit all the slight clues available. This is that the Chamberlains left the *direct* employment of the Worcester factory in, or about, 1786, and that they then decorated and/or gilded the Worcester porcelains by contract, or similar arrangement. This fits the wording used by Binns: 'Robert Chamberlain . . . left the establishment shortly after its purchase by Mr. Flight in 1783, and commenced business as a decorator at premises in King Street . . . . Messrs. Chamberlain commenced regular business in King Street in the year 1786, and in the

---

*See article 'John Flight of Worcester' by Geoffrey Wills, *The Connoisseur*, June 1947. The diary is also quoted at length by Henry Sandon as Appendix III in his *Flight and Barr Worcester Porcelain 1783–1840* (1978).

present manufactory in 1788 . . .'. The Flight diary makes no mention of the Chamberlains leaving their employment, only that they intended setting up a retail shop, and passages such as 'We hired 3 of Chamberlain's men who are now with us' suggest that Chamberlain was already established with a trained staff. The wording 'Coud not at all agree with Chamberlain' and 'agreed with Mrs. Hampton to come down with us and teach us the Gilding' was written in March or April 1789, suggesting that all was well before that date. Further, there is other evidence that Chamberlain was established as an independent decorator before the spring of 1789, as Flight mentions the trouble which resulted from the Chamberlains opening their own retail shop. This evidence lies in the surviving Chamberlain account books, for these start in 1788 and even earlier ones may have existed but have subsequently been lost.* The existing accounts of 1788 and the first few months of 1789 show clearly that the Chamberlains were then working on their own account and were already decorating Thomas Turner's Caughley porcelain. The following are extracts from these records:

September 29th, 1788. Thos Turner Esqr. Caughley, Shropshire.

	£	s.	d.
12 sets of Common red border 5s. 6d.		3	6	0
28 sets of Dresden G^d [gold] edge 6s. 6d.		9	2	0
		12	8	0

January, 1789. Goods Red^d, from Thos Turner Esqr.

	£	s.	d.
2 Sugar Boxes & Covers, Bute [shape] Blue bordered		5	0
1 Ewer do.		2	0
1 Tray do.		1	6
36 Cups New fluted, blue border		2	5	0
2 Pint basons do.		6	0

Many long lists of Caughley porcelain sent to the Chamberlains, both in the completely white state, and also with underglaze-blue borders added, could be cited here but the Chamberlain-decorated Caughley porcelain is not the prime concern at this point, for the subject is covered in Chapter 2. However, the early Chamberlain account books show sales of both Worcester and supposedly Caughley porcelain in 1788, some six months before the shop, mentioned in John Flight's diary, was opened. Sample entries include:

---

*R. W. Binns, writing in 1865, stated that one of the Chamberlain books dated back to 1 April 1786, but I have been unable to trace this book.

September 29th, 1788. Mr. Jn.Higson.Trodsam [Frodsham?], Cheshire.

	£	s.	d.
1 Comp.[complete] set of Pagoda [pattern]	3	3	0
2 half pint mugs, blue bordered [gold] sprigs		14	0

December 24th, 1788. Mr. J. Richardson, Manchester.

	£	s.	d.
1 Comp. set of Royal Star	7	7	0
6 coffee cups, extra do.	1	0	0
1 comp. set of Queens B & Gd [blue & gold] festoon	6	6	0
6 coffee cups, extra do.		18	0
1 comp. set of blue & gd Spike	4	14	6
6 coffee cups, extra		15	0
12 coffee cups, red and white		13	0

Note that these entries relate to sales by the Chamberlains; they were not then, in 1788, decorators in the direct or sole employment of Messrs Flight.

On 28 June 1789 Flight's diary records: '. . . Yesterday, Chamberlain opened his shop, I was rather surprised as I thought they were hardly ready yet, but they talk of making a flaming shew in about 2 months'; and on 5 September Flight reported that he had sold only very little that week but he understood Chamberlain & Sons were 'doing well'.

I had often wondered how a mere painter or gilder at the main Worcester factory came to break away and set up in his previous employer's former shop. This may be partly explained by the suggestion put forward in the preceding pages, that Chamberlain had in fact broken away a few years earlier but that for some time he had painted and gilded the Worcester porcelain under contract. This being so, he would presumably have been in a stronger position financially to open his own establishment than he would have been if he were merely a factory-employed decorator, drawing the normal wage of the period. As suggested on page 23, it is clear from the Flight diary that Chamberlain had a successful kiln in use at least by the time he broke with Flight in 1789.

It is also clear that the Chamberlains had a minimum of two backers and this fact probably indicates that Robert Chamberlain was already a person of some standing, not a mere employed hand. The foremost backer was Richard Nash, as R. W. Binns and subsequent writers have correctly noted, but it is also probable that Thomas Turner of the Caughley factory was himself an early backer of the Chamberlain venture, for in the Chamberlain 'Summary of Accounts' covering the period 17 August 1789 to June 1792 there are balances of £1,400 due to Mr Nash and the same large sum due to a Mr Turner; there are also several payments of interest, presumably due on the loan – 25 May 1793, 'By Bill to Turner for interest £50'.*

It should be understood that after the Chamberlains had opened their new retail shop at 33 High Street, Worcester, there was keen business rivalry between them and the Flights. Again referring to John Flight's diary there are such statements as: 'My Brother has entered into an agreement with Pennington, a very clever painter in London. We heard he was engaged to Chamberlain and this made us first wish to have him . . .'; and 'Father writes me word Chamberlain will lay open to an action if he calls theirs the Original Worcester China Warehouse . . . and has wrote me to give them notice to be cautious what they do . . .'.

This book is concerned with Chamberlain's own work and porcelains, undertaken and made after his break with the main, or original, Worcester factory, and the products of his successors, but it is interesting to discuss first some of the Worcester porcelains of the 1780s, particularly the pieces made in the early years of the Flight management, between 1783 and 1785.

Most collectors think of Flight's porcelains as being thinly potted, sparsely decorated, often with under-glaze blue in conjunction with simple but tasteful gilding on spiral-fluted forms. Wares of this type were certainly produced under the Flight management, but in the *late* 1780s or early 1790s – some seven years after the take-over in April 1783. Such pieces are very different from the well-known Dr Wall porcelains and those in much the same style made under the Davis management after Dr Wall's retirement in 1774.

It is not generally appreciated that the old style continued long after the Doctor's retirement and after his death in 1776; indeed it continued well into the Davis/Flight or 'Middle' period, which Henry Sandon placed at 1773–93 in his excellent *Illustrated Guide to Worcester Porcelain 1751–1793* (1969, 3rd edition 1980).

I believe that many of the pieces which now tend to be attributed to the Dr Wall period or to the 1770s were in fact made in the 1780s during the Flight period. If so, then most of the thinly-potted spiral-fluted wares are later than is often thought, and are of the 1790s. Perhaps all traditional dating of Worcester porcelain after Dr Wall could be put forward some six or seven years.

Evidence to substantiate this belief is hard to find, for dated pieces of this period are extremely rare. Consider,

however, the straight-sided mug shown in Colour Plate I. It has underglaze-blue borders at top and foot, enhanced with rich gilding very much in the style of a large class of Worcester porcelain of the 1770s. In particular, the flower-painting is easily recognizable as that occurring on a large range of Dr Wall Worcester porcelains. The potting, as well, is all that one would expect of Dr Wall porcelain – robustly potted, with a good tight-fitting glaze, free of bubbles. The glaze has been 'pegged' away from the inside of the foot in the accepted manner. The translucency, too, is green and what might be expected of a Worcester mug of the 1770s. In all tests, therefore, this mug links with Worcester porcelains which would be dated to the 1770s. Yet it is actually dated, in underglaze blue, 1784. It is of the Flight period.

Understandably the new management tended to continue the production of the old tried styles produced by the same workforce. On the take-over by Thomas Flight in April 1783 there was apparently no clear new policy put in force right away – any change of taste or technique was gradual, perhaps necessitated by the loss of Robert Chamberlain and his decorators in 1786 or 1788 (see page 24).

Obviously it is impossible to list all the Worcester porcelains which I feel are at present given too early a dating, but the pieces in the style of the so-called Lord Henry Thynne service should be mentioned in parti-cular – such pieces are similar to the dish shown in Colour Plate II and the scenic-centred pieces such as that shown in Plate 1. The flowers found on the latter dish link with the 1784 mug (see Colour Plate I), whilst the fruit and flower groups seen on the dish illustrated in Colour Plate II are found on Chamberlain-decorated Caughley porcelains of the late 1780s or early 1790s (see Plate 21 and Colour Plate III) and are seemingly by the same hand, one who graduated from the Worcester decorating workshop to Chamberlain's new studio. I regard this class of Worcester decoration not as Dr Wall Worcester of the 1770–75 period, but as bordering on the Flight period, about 1780–85. The same characteris-tic type of fruit painting is to be seen on the Worcester teawares shown in Plate 2. Similar 'new fluted' shapes occur in Chamberlain-decorated Caughley porcelain; the Worcester teaset shown in Plate 2 was certainly decorated under Chamberlain's guidance either before his own decorating establishment was set up in the 1780s or soon afterwards by former Worcester painters who joined him.

The Worcester mask-head jug in the Victoria & Albert Museum, seen in Plate 3, again shows the late style of Worcester enamelling and gilding that was to be

---

*The accounts mention only a Mr Turner; the initial or forename is not in fact given and the references may refer to the London retailer. The Chamberlain accounts include references to Thomas Turner of Caughley, to James Turner and to George Turner.

1. *Left:* A dessert service dish from the original Worcester factory decorated and gilded under Robert Chamberlain's guidance and by painters who were later to join his own staff. Crescent mark in underglaze blue. 9¼ in. square. *c.* 1780. *Godden of Worthing Ltd*

2. *Below:* Representative pieces from a Worcester porcelain tea service painted with fruit and flower sprays of a type found on Chamberlain-decorated Caughley porcelain and on Chamberlain's own wares. *c.* 1780. *Victoria & Albert Museum (Crown Copyright)*

3. *Left:* A decorative Worcester mask-head jug, from the Schreiber Collection at the Victoria & Albert Museum, decorated by a painter and a gilder who were later to decorate Caughley blanks and Chamberlain's own porcelains (see Colour Plate III and Plate 21). 8 in. high. *c.* 1780. *Victoria & Albert Museum (Crown Copyright)*

4. *Above:* A fine-quality Worcester deep-lobed dish painted with 'fancy birds in landscape' in George Davis's typical style. This painting is also found on Caughley and on Chamberlain's porcelains (see Colour Plate III and Plate 21). Crescent mark in underglaze blue. Diameter 9 in. *c.* 1775–80. *Godden of Worthing Ltd*

5.   A Flight period Worcester spittoon printed in underglaze blue
with the well-known fence pattern. Crescent mark in underglaze
blue. Impressed name mark 'FLIGHTS'. 4½ in. high. *c.* 1783-8.
Godden Reference Collection

continued by the Chamberlain decorators on Caughley
blanks. Similarly, the superbly painted Worcester dish
illustrated in Plate 4 is almost certainly by the same
hand that later decorated Caughley blanks and then
Chamberlain's own porcelains. I believe this painter to
have been George Davis (see page 192).

Turning for a moment to the blue and white wares, it
is easy to see that the Flight management continued to
use the Dr Wall period engraved copper plates and to
decorate old shapes with well-tried printed designs,
potted in a thick manner unlike the thinner, later Flight
porcelains. The spittoon shown in Plate 5 carries such a
design and, of course, it bears the old blue crescent
mark, as this appeared on the original copper plate.
However, this piece was made in the post-1783 Flight
period as it bears the mark 'FLIGHTS' impressed into
the body during its manufacture.

Although outwardly of a Dr Wall shape and style of
decoration, the glazing of this piece repays study, for it is
quite different from that on the 1784 mug shown in
Colour Plate I. On this marked Flight spittoon the glaze
under the base is very thickly applied and has tended to
bubble; some of the bursting bubbles became discoloured and formed 'black-heads' or 'sanding'. The
Worcester glazing had degenerated from the good, thin

coating applied to the 1784 mug, to this seemingly later
'Flight'-marked piece.

This bubbled, generous glazing can be found on
much blue-printed Worcester porcelain; indeed, most
of the pieces bearing the so-called disguised numeral
marks (samples of which are shown below, see also
Plates 6 and 8) display this characteristic. It is quite

probable that these pieces are also of a later date than has
hitherto been believed.

It is relevant here to note the similarity between some
Worcester porcelain bearing late disguised numeral
marks and the blue-printed porcelains produced at
Caughley. The cups shown in Plate 7, an 'S'-marked
Caughley specimen and a disguised numeral-marked
Worcester example, both have the same type of moulded
handle found on Chinese export-market porcelains and
would have been marketed during the same period – one
by the original Worcester firm, the other by Turner and
his agents such as Chamberlain. The Caughley one on
its own would be dated to the mid 1780s or even later,
yet the two are surely contemporary.

Evidence shows that in 1789 the Flights were still
endeavouring to manufacture blue and white porcelains
and that they were experiencing difficulties in firing the
wares, these troubles seemingly arising after Chamberlain (with his work people) had left and established his
own retail shop. The following extracts are from John
Flight's diary:

Lords Day the 28th June, 1789, 7 p.m.
The last week has indeed been a very trying one to me and
what is worse the coming one will I fear be more so. We burnt
the kiln every day in the week and still the sulphur continues
and spoils the ware. On Monday, I thought it was better.
Tuesday it appeared to continue to mend and was still better
on Wednesday but on Thursday was worse again. We hoped
then it was owing to the rain, which had made the place damp,
but it appeared otherwise by being no better Friday or
yesterday. What we shall do I cannot tell.
We think of trying to erect one upon the plan of
Chamberlains. Wether we can or not I cannot tell. Have rec'd
the smaller kiln from London which they are now erecting.
We must try that in hopes of doing better. . . .

Lords Day the 12th July, 1789.
. . . On Monday when I consulted Kitchen [Edward Kitchen
was seemingly the foreman who materially assisted the Flights
in the mixing and firing of the porcelains] what further could
be done, we sent for the man who built Chamberlains Kiln,

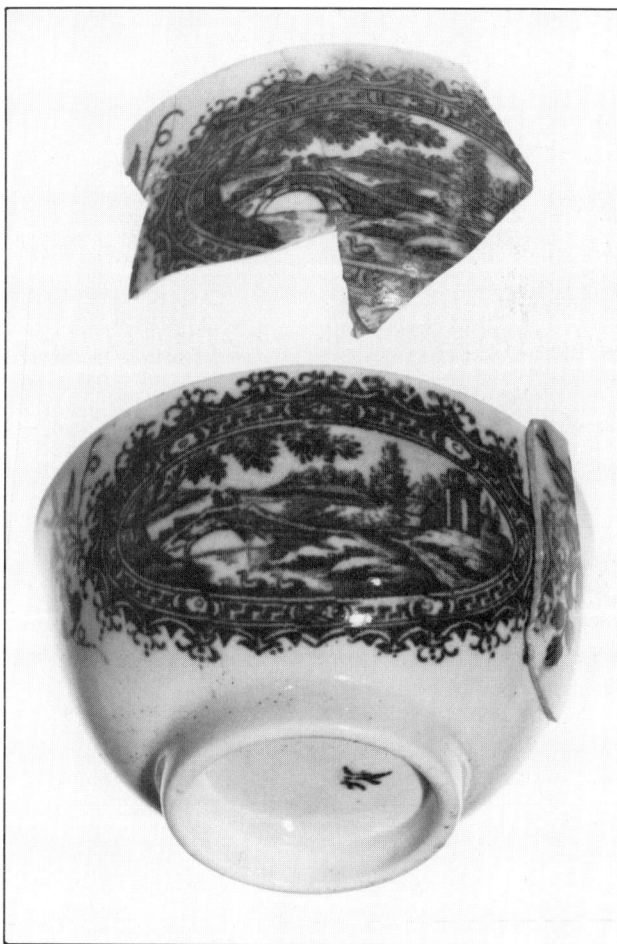

6. Detail of the base of a Flight period Worcester bowl showing one of the disguised numeral marks with the associated bubble glaze. *c*. 1785. *Godden of Worthing Ltd*

7. *Above right:* A Caughley (left) and Worcester (right) blue-printed cup showing the similarity both in shape and in styles of decoration between these two makes. Chamberlain's shop in High Street, Worcester, would have stocked the Caughley porcelains. 'S' and disguised numeral marks respectively. *c*. 1783–8. *Godden Reference Collection*

8. A disguised numeral-marked Worcester blue-printed bowl shown with matching wasters found on the site of the original Worcester factory. These are post-1783 Flight period wares. $1\frac{7}{10}$ in. high. *Godden Reference Collection*

who gave us every necessary dimention and said he could easily build one for us. However, in the interim he proposed burning with saggers [the protective clay boxes traditionally used in the ceramic industry], which we accordingly did, and brought all the ware out good except the top which was exposed to the sulphur from the iron . . .

The mention of the kilns and the spoilt wares probably refers to the glost or glazing kiln and the firing of the glaze or added decoration, not to the main initial firing of the unglazed porcelain. Flight refers to daily firings whereas the main biscuit firing would have taken several days to complete. Flight also mentions building a new kiln on the plan of Chamberlain's, but at this period Chamberlain was not making his own porcelain; he was merely a decorator of Caughley porcelains and as such would not have had a large biscuit kiln. The 'smaller kiln from London' was most certainly a muffle-type kiln used only for firing the added enamel decoration and the gilding. It was the decorating side of Flight's business that was giving all the trouble now that he had lost Chamberlain's services.

In the extract from John Flight's diary just quoted there is, I believe, further evidence that Chamberlain had been decorating Worcester porcelain under contract for a period before he set up his retail shop and made the break which Flight noted in his diary for the week ending 1 June 1789. By the time of the entry of 28 June it is clear that Chamberlain already had a successful kiln, which Flight sought to copy. It could not have been on the Flight factory site for in that case Flight would have had the use of it and would not have sought to build a new one. I therefore consider that the successful Chamberlain kiln was the one which he had been using for a number of years when, as I believe, he was employed under contract, or other agreement, decorating the Worcester porcelains after the Flight take-over in 1783, and before the termination of the arrangement in the spring of 1789 when Flight started to experience all his difficulties and had to resort to bringing Mrs Hampton from London to 'teach us the Gilding'. It must be admitted that this is merely my theory: subsequent excavations on the site may well clarify these troublesome and controversial points on the early period of Chamberlain's activities.

As late as July 1789 John Flight's diary records difficulty with the blue-printing:

Lords Day the 19th July, 1789.

. . . Have had a good deal of trouble the last week about the blue printing, the colours peel off in the burning-in and spoils the vast deal of ware. Every possible attention is payed to it to find out the cause and remedy it, but hitherto without success.

One may well ask what blue-printing was being undertaken by the Flights at this relatively late period. I do not know of any on the Flight spiral-fluted forms but these were not introduced until 1790, as will be shown. The blue-printed porcelains were still most probably in the old style on old forms and may well have included, even at this late period, the wares bearing the disguised numeral marks (see page 22 and Plates 6, 7 and 8). A Chamberlain letter to Caughley written in September 1789 indicates that the Worcester factory was then producing the blue-printed 'Fisherman' or 'Pleasure Boat' patterned teawares (see page 40) which are now found with the disguised numeral marks. The teabowl shown in Plate 8, posed with spoilt factory wasters from the Worcester site, bears one such disguised numeral mark.

At this period, in October 1789, John Flight was still trying to learn the secrets of making his porcelains and the works were still experiencing great difficulties in firing their wares:

I go on trying bodys and Glazes with Kitchen and begin to get a tollerable insight into the process of manufactory, but I must want to do more in this myself. I must contrive some method to do it. . . .

. . . Our kiln of bisct-ware [biscuit or unglazed porcelain] yesterday sennight was so bad that I determined to examine it to know the cause. . . . When I returned [from the grinding mill] the Kiln was burning. . . . It was then drawn much better than the last because better fired but much inferior to what the ware used to be. . . .

Again in November, whilst John Flight was in London, the firing of the Worcester porcelains was still giving trouble.

Here a strange fact must be recorded. John Flight, one of the partners in the concern which his father had

purchased in 1783, still did not know six years later the recipe for the Worcester porcelain body which was seemingly the sole concern of one Shaw. John Flight recorded on 21 November 1789:

We have been making some oblong dishes and have had several fly [break] in the glazing which has made me suspect Shaw was making further alterations in the body . . . at least I resolved to talk to Shaw plainly about it. . . . I concluded by telling him I was resolved to know the composition and had my father's orders to demand him to weigh it up with me . . . accordingly on Wednesday I talked with him again and he promised to give it me in writing as it was not convenient just yet to weigh up either body or glaze, and on Thursday morning he gave it me signed with his name. This is a matter which I can no way account for or indeed scarcely believe what I know and yet its possible he may have deceived me tho' hardly probable. However I shall endeavour to get more certain evidence next week by weighing up with him . . . .

John Flight later recorded in 1791:

After some months illness Shaw the manufactory clerk died last September [1790]. This event must have been attended with very different consequences had it happened a year sooner; indeed most probably would have stopped the manufactory but I had obtained the process from him. . . .

. . . I had a great deal of trouble in securing Shaw's Papers which contained the whole process but at last secured them for ten Guineas, paid his Father. Had expected to pay a much larger sum. . . .

The Flight diary does not include further references to trouble with firing their wares. Early in 1790 mention is made of the order from the Duke of Clarence for a superbly rich dinner service, and on the evidence of the surviving pieces from this service, many of which have passed through my hands, it would appear that the troubles had been overcome. One can hardly fault the body, the potting or the decoration. However, it is relevant to point out that the potting is somewhat thick and the pieces are consequently heavy in weight: these 1790 wares still do not link with the light-weight spiral-fluted Flight teawares. A tureen and stand from the Duke of Clarence service is shown in Plate 9. The above remarks also apply to the Order of the Thistle service made in 1789.

Towards the end of February 1791 John Flight made further entries in his diary which are of interest. He at least was now happy that improvements had been made in their products:

By the improvement we have made Chamberlain has been prevented from injuring us. At least we scarcely feel it. Soon after Shaw, Lewis died [in September 1790]. He managed the printing. This was a sudden event, but also instead of being an injury, was the contrary, as we carry on that at less expense.

9. *Above:* A Flight period Worcester tureen, cover and stand from the celebrated service made for the Duke of Clarence, painted by John Pennington and gilded by (or under) Mrs Hampton. Crowned 'Flight' mark and crescent in underglaze blue. *Marshall Field & Co., Chicago*

10. *Right:* A spiral-fluted or shanked Flight-Worcester teapot bearing an overglaze printed design in an earlier style. This shape is typical of the early 1790s. Unmarked. 6½ in. high. *Dyson Perrins Museum, Worcester*

This February entry was one of the last in John Flight's diary as he died in July 1791, aged only twenty-five.

It is not clear from the above quotation if the Flights were still producing in 1791 wares decorated with underglaze-blue printed designs in the old style (see Plates 7 and 8). The printing referred to could well have been overglaze, for there exists a class of very decorative printing on fluted and spiral-fluted teawares. The teapot shown in Plate 10 is an extremely good example of this class. Henry Sandon, in the first edition of his *Illustrated Guide to Worcester Porcelain 1751–1793* (1969), illustrated this piece from the Dyson Perrins Museum Collection and attributed it to the 1770–80 period; but in the third edition (1980) he amended the dating to 1780–90 and this shows the growing realization of the late date of such pieces. For the first time in the present book a piece of Flight period porcelain of the characteristic thinly-potted, light-weight type is illustrated. This overglaze class of printing could be that which Flight had in mind when writing his diary entry in February 1791. Other representative pieces of the same type and period are illustrated in Plate 11, and one teabowl of this type in the Godden Reference Collection is dated 22 December 1795.

These spiral-fluted teawares were called in the contemporary Chamberlain account books 'shankered', a description sometimes abbreviated to 'shanked' or

'shank'd'. Under the date 15 July 1790, Chamberlain recorded the purchase for Thomas Turner at Caughley of '1 complete sett, Worc. new shankered gold edge and line, except [tea] cannister and [spoon] tray, £2 17s. 0d.'. Note the description 'new' shankered and the abbreviation 'Worc' for Worcester, a description indicating that the teaset had been purchased from Flights, for Chamberlain was not producing his own porcelains at that date. It will be seen later that Turner closely copied these shanked shapes in his Caughley porcelain and supplied blanks for Chamberlain to decorate, and within a few years Chamberlain was producing a fine selection of his own shanked or spiral-fluted porcelains.

It should be realized that any 'Flight'-marked specimens will fall within the period 1783–92, when Martin Barr joined the concern. A crown over the word 'Flight' suggests a date after the granting of the Royal Warrant in March 1789, but it seems to be the case that a large proportion of the Flight products were unmarked – especially the simple tablewares – or that they bore either the old traditional mark of the crescent painted in underglaze blue, or one of the series of disguised numeral marks associated with the blue-printed designs (see page 22). Note that the 1784-dated mug is not marked in any way, nor are most of the Lord Henry Thynne type wares shown in Colour Plate II. If marked, such pieces bear the old crescent device.

It is important to remember that there was no tradition of name-marking Worcester porcelain – Dr Wall never used his name nor did Davis in the 1776–83 period; indeed there was no need to when there was only one porcelain factory at Worcester. The need to differentiate only arose when Chamberlain started up in competition.

The difficulties which faced the Flights subsequent to the break with Robert Chamberlain have been described

at some length, and it is relevant that a few of the porcelains which I consider to be of the post-1783, Flight period are illustrated, for it is vital to know something of the wares being decorated by the Chamberlains before Robert set up on his own account. It is also relevant to understand what was being produced by Chamberlain's rivals in the trade at Worcester.

The later dating suggested for much of the blue-printed Worcester porcelains, into the 1780s if not the early 1790s, shows that Thomas Turner at Caughley did not have the blue-printed market entirely to himself (see Plate 8) and that the porcelains he was supplying to Chamberlain at Worcester had competition. Consideration is given in the next chapter to these Shropshire porcelains, or at least the proportion of them that were decorated, or sold, by Chamberlain at Worcester.

The surviving account and sales books show clearly that the Chamberlains were decorating and selling large quantities of Thomas Turner's Caughley porcelains from at least 1788, the period of the earliest available account book. This is not surprising, especially if Thomas Turner had loaned a substantial sum of money to Chamberlain, as suggested on page 19. Certainly a large part of Chamberlain's business consisted of decorating and gilding Thomas Turner's own porcelain for him, which was either sent to Turner's London warehouse, or shipped back up-river to the Caughley factory for redistribution from there. Notwithstanding this fact, the Chamberlains had several causes of complaint against Turner and the goods he was supplying to them to stock the Chamberlain shop. In August 1789 Chamberlain wrote to Turner at the Caughley works:*

I unpacked three casks yesterday and was much surprised to find such a small quantity of blue goods – can only say we are every day disobliging our customers and injuring ourselves for want of them – in reality we find more difficulty in getting the goods than we do in selling them, must beg you to forward the Temple [pattern].

The handled cups that you have sent us are so much out of date . . . that I am sure we shall find great difficulty to sell them at the second price, indeed my opinion is we never shall. Believe we have about 6 or 7 basons in the House instead of as many gross. Hardly a pint or quart jug.

Hope I have seen the last of Raddish dishes and centres the last is a most terrible shape to my taste & what is worse have often the mortification to have my opinion confirmed by a general dislike.
Beg you not send any more 2nd Shropshire & Temple [pattern tewares] they will not do, at any rate at 7s. per set.

Many such complaints about shortages of saleable wares or the surfeit of unsaleable lines sent down to Worcester from Caughley could be cited from the original records, but the point has been made. But it must not be thought that the Chamberlain letters contained only complaints, as this was not the case. However, the position was such that Chamberlain must soon have considered manufacturing his own porcelain, once he had built up and established his own markets with little financial risk, by selling in the interim the Caughley porcelain.

It is difficult to determine the exact date when the Chamberlains ceased to be only decorators and turned to manufacturing their own porcelain. The purchases of Caughley porcelain continued for many years, well into the 1790s; they did not cease overnight when Chamberlain established his own factory. Unfortunately there is no convenient evidence to show exactly when Robert Chamberlain commenced to manufacture his own porcelain. He was not doing so in September 1789, for in a letter of this date he explained that he was sending to Caughley a quantity of crown-glass which he had had to take from a customer; this would have been used in the china-glaze, and if he had been producing his own porcelain in September 1789 he would probably have used this crown-glass himself. A further batch of over 4 cwt of scrap-glass or cullet was sent up to Caughley on 4 May 1790 and the same point applies.

On the other hand, there is firm evidence that the Chamberlains were making their own porcelains in Worcester by 23 December 1793, for a stocktaking inventory of this date refers to not only quantities of biscuit or unglazed ware, but also 1,606 saggars for firing the porcelain, a 'dipping tub for Glaze', 'sundries in modelling room', and the contents of the 'Throwing room'. The latter (which would not have existed in a decorating establishment, only a manufactory) contained items such as a throwing wheel, lathe, screw box and implements; a drying-horse for moulds, shelves, stools and chairs; also models and shapes, a stock of clay and a large number of biscuit coffee cups. The 'yard' held 50 tons of Cornish stone and thirty-three casks of clay.

11. Representative pieces from a Flight period Worcester shanked tea and coffee service painted in the typical simple style of the 1790s. Unmarked. Coffee pot 10 in. high. *Godden of Worthing Ltd*

* Some of the early Chamberlain account books contain copies or drafts of letters written to Turner at Caughley, or at least notes of the main contents of such letters.

This is clear evidence that the Chamberlains were then manufacturing their own porcelain. It is necessary, therefore, to narrow the gap between May 1790 and December 1793 to determine when porcelain was first made by the Chamberlains. The available records include some relating to letters sent or received; one such entry made on 15 February 1791 reads: 'Mr.Jos^h. Goodwin, Truro for advice of Soap rock'. This material was a vital constituent of both Worcester and Caughley porcelain, but the brief record of this letter is inconclusive evidence as it may refer to raw material ordered by Chamberlain for resale or forwarding to the Caughley factory, for there is a letter showing that the Chamberlains did supply such materials to Turner at Caughley. There is also a reference to Chamberlain's purchase of glaze in October 1790 but again this need not have been for his own use.

On 4 March 1791 the following entry occurs: 'Settled owner Oakes's bill, 5½ ton of Coals to the kiln, £3 3s. 0d.'. This note is of great importance – even more so if it had stated when the coal was ordered or delivered, but in any case there is the use of the words 'the kiln' suggesting that this was a biscuit kiln, for there would have been more than one enamelling kiln; indeed the small enamelling kilns would hardly have warranted the ordering of 5½ tons of coal at one time.

It may also be significant that in July 1791 two payments were made to James Norris of Burslem, a millwright, because a grinding mill would have been needed to grind the raw materials required by the Chamberlains once they were embarking on the manufacture of their own porcelains.

A reference under the date 16 July 1791 reads: 'Wrote to Mr. Norris Burslem – the clay charged too high' (later notes refer to Daniel Norris and the supply of other raw materials, including plaster for mould-making). In October 1791 payment was being made for special fire-bricks from Stourbridge, and the Chamberlain cash book in 1791 records payments to workpeople who would only have been employed in the actual making of porcelain, rather than in the decoration of purchased blanks. Such entries include:

		£	s.	d.
October 17th	Thrower, lent	1	6	0
November 3rd	To Mr. Boot, modeller [This name is indistinct; however, a Derby-trained modeller named Jonathon Boot signed and dated a Derby vase in 1764. A Thomas Boot modelled for Wedgwood in the 1769–73 period.]	3	3	0

December 3rd	Mr. Lewis on account for models		6	0
December 5th	Thrower	1	1	0
December 8th	Mr. Lewis on account for models		6	0
December 24th	Mr. Lewis modeller on account		10	6

These records are of vital importance and seem to show that by at least October 1791 workmen were employed forming and modelling Chamberlain's own porcelain. Other slightly earlier entries, however, are perhaps less conclusive – 3 August 1791, 'To S. Pilcher for John Giles of London, for sundries for the manufactory, £7 4s. 0d.' and on 28 September 1791, 'Materials for the manufactory, 1s. 6d.'. The term 'manufactory' most probably meant the new factory rather than the old decorating studio, but this point is uncertain.

Early in 1792 the cash book entries show other payments relating to a porcelain manufactory rather than just a decorating establishment. On 6 January Mr Goodwin of Cornwall had been paid for 2 tons of Cornish stone – which cost 3d. to weigh three days previously. In the same month Mr Norris of Burslem was paid £15 for clay; transport was extra for there is an additional entry for payment made – 'Received for carriage of clay from Burslem to Worcester, £5 13s. 0d.' (this clearly was not for resale to Caughley for if this were the case it would have been delivered direct) – and in March a further 6 tons of coal were purchased at a cost of 12s. a ton.

It seems highly probable that the Chamberlains were making their own porcelain by the autumn of 1791 or by March of that year when coal for the 'kiln' was paid for, but it must be stated that all was not plain sailing. Troubles undoubtedly arose as is shown by the surviving drafts of two letters written by young Ann Chamberlain, who acted as the Company Secretary or Clerk.

These original copy letters, or perhaps the drafts of such letters, are now very difficult to read and interpret. I am further indebted to Henry Sandon, the Curator of the Dyson Perrins Museum, for his careful copying of these original documents. The letter quoted below, dated 12 July 1792, records Chamberlain's ill health, the shortage of porcelain for the painters to work up, and the lack of clay for its manufacture:

Worcester. July 12th, 1792.

To T. Turner Esqr. London.
Sir,

The 4 Jugs and 1 bowl for the Duke of York, hope you have this day receiv'd safe and shall be glad to know who we are to make the bill of parcels to.

Mr. Chamberlain's late violent illness and his present weak state of health has prevented his writing the disagreeable situation we are in, indeed I may say that reflecting on the certain loss which must attend our having no ware for our hands, has in a great measure aggravated his feverish disorder. Few people can look with apathy on absolute ruin, and there appears to me but little difference when scarcely a post passes that does not bring a countermand for some orders. Our shop is unfurnish'd and we have long been oblig'd to turn customers away for half they ask for, and it will be unnecessary to observe to you that the other shop which supplys their present wants, will claim their future recommendation. I have written to the Manufactory and can only hear they have not one pound of clay to work, and that its impossible to complete our Goods; to you therefore we must now apply, and trust we shall receive some acct. more satisfactory than the above as it is an excuse we cannot tender to our customers. Your answer by return of post will oblige a whole family, who desire I will present their respectful compts. to Mrs. T., for whom I am yr most obedt. Hble servt.

A.C.

P.S. Mr. Barnes has just been up to say he can no longer find ware for the boys to work on, a circumstance too distressing for to bear writing upon longer – pray write what we are to do.

This letter presents several problems to us. By Ann Chamberlain's expression, 'I have written to the Manufactory', it could be that she was referring to the Caughley factory (which would indicate strongly that the Chamberlains were still dependent on the Caughley porcelains), but it should be remembered that the Chamberlain manufactory was separate from their retail shop and even if Ann Chamberlain sent a messenger to their works, she would probably have still written a note. There is, however, the question of why Ann Chamberlain should need to write to Turner in London asking 'pray write what we are to do' and saying that 'your answer by return of post will oblige' as if Turner in London had the answer to all their troubles.

The dearth of goods had apparently been partly rectified by October 1792, for a further draft letter from Ann Chamberlain to a retailer is obviously seeking business, although she acknowledges a shortage of ware:

. . . A regular assortment of enamelled [wares] shall forward in a short time and trust no person can serve upon more honourable principles. Our utmost order is 6 months and we allow 20 per cent discount [4s. in the pound] on receiving the payment. We will likewise send you a sett of cups and saucers of different patterns, handsome, if agreeable, and tho we charge them at the time shall have no objection to give you credit for them in cash when returned perfect in 6 months.

Will likewise send you a smart sett or two upon the same plan, as many shopkeepers find they can sell capital china when they have it to show.

Messrs. Chamberlain wish me to observe their offer proceeds from respect to Mr. Ballard's recommendation and no wish to force the sale of goods being at present so short of coloured china that we must beg of you to excuse our sending the whole of your order for a few weeks when we hope to merit a continuance of your obliging favours to Messrs. Chamberlain for whom I am Sir your most obedient and obliged Humble Servant,

Ann Chamberlain.

The mention in this letter of sets of cups and saucers of different patterns is interesting, for the account books record the despatch of many pattern sets. A typical example of such a record is given below; the amount in the last column represents the cost of the complete teaset.

November 28th, 1792.

Sent as patterns.	s.	d.	£	s.	d.
Plain French sprigs, 1st size	2	0	3	3	0
New Shankered gold edge, 2nd size	2	4	3	13	6
do. do. Angouleme do.	4	2	5	5	0
do. do. Landscape do.	6	8	8	8	0
Plain enamelled blue & gold sprigs	3	0	4	4	0
Broseley make Amitie pattern	5	0	6	6	0
New fluted Birds-eye border & sprigs	4	2	5	5	0
do. do. Fawn & gold curtain, 2nd size	7	6	9	9	0
do. do. Doves, new wreath, 2nd size	5	0	6	6	0
do. do. Princes circle, 2nd size	7	6	9	9	0

Most of these patterns were quite simple, and at least two separate examples refer to Caughley porcelains – the two prefixed 'Broseley' (the name of the nearest town to the Caughley works, often given to its wares). Indeed it is probable that all these samples were still Caughley porcelains bearing Chamberlain's embellishments, but they will be discussed in the next chapter.

The mention of 'new shankered' wares in this November 1792 list of samples or pattern pieces leads on to another interesting letter written by Humphrey Chamberlain to Thomas Turner at Caughley (quoted in full on page 44. This is dated 12 January 1793 and was written in answer to Turner's letters dated four and two days previously. The letter commences by mentioning shanked tea-canisters but later on Humphrey Chamberlain responds to the Caughley packers' complaints of harassment and to Thomas Turner's request for cash: '. . . I really think after we have suffered so very materially for many months past the very attempt to defend on any other ground than unforeseen events is an aggravation of our misfortunes'. This most likely relates to the apparent shortage of goods to decorate or sell, as reported in the letter dated 12 July 1792 – 'the certain loss which must attend our having no ware for our hands . . .'.

Humphrey Chamberlain's 1793 letter to Thomas Turner continues:

. . . you desire [us] immediately to remit you cash – which request will be comply'd with in a few days, and still further can't help remarking the unmerited acrimony that the letter is wrote with. Have only to repeat once more, that we have never had the least intention of doing anything to the detriment of yr manufactory, but on the contrary the whole that has been done, or will be, is to the essential interests of both – even if you will for a moment fancy me the most ungrateful person living. . . . Have only room to add that I shall always adhear to the above declaration – unless by receiving a kind of treatment we do not deserve, are forced to seek refuge in a way we have never yet entertain'd a thought of pursuing . . . .

Quite obviously relations between Turner at Caughley and the Chamberlains at Worcester were somewhat strained, as well they might be once Turner discovered that the Chamberlains, whom he had helped to finance as decorators, were now making their own porcelains and were therefore in open competition with his own Caughley wares. Perhaps Humphrey Chamberlain's point was that in order to remain in business they had to make their own porcelains to fill the void left when they could not obtain Caughley porcelains; at first they sought only to produce articles not available elsewhere, but if Turner persisted in being difficult they would be forced to rely solely on their own make of porcelain.

Another very interesting letter, dated 12 June 1794, sets out in a rather lengthy manner some of the difficulties under which the Chamberlains were labouring some two or more years after they entered upon the manufacture of their own porcelains. As will be shown in Chapter 3, the December 1793 stocktaking list included not merely the old staple teaware lines but also a variety of other porcelains. Nevertheless Ann Chamberlain wrote:

June 12th, 1794

Copy of a letter to Mr. John Warwick, St. Austle, Cornwall.

Sir, Mr. Chamberlain's illness since the receipt of yr letter must plead an excuse for not answering the contents sooner – with respect to the stone & clay should have been happy had you wrote previous to its being ship'd as we are very disagreeably situated for want of room to put it in & should have intreated yr keeping it a few months longer – It was on this acct I requested in a former letter their might be no further quantity sent till you heard from Mr. C. We having been oblig'd to trespass upon friendship for a situation to hold the last of our several buildings will not admit of erecting any place till the latter end of the Summer –

12 months agoe the prospects in trade would have render'd 5 times this quantity no object nor wou'd payment at any hour have been exceptionable, but the difficulty we, & I believe every one else, find in procuring remittances obliges us at this time to withold those large orders we should otherwise send.

At the same time our want of sufficient mill room has compell'd us to buy several tons of *ground* stone from Mr. Valentine Close, Hanley (to whom we were recommended by yr relation Mr. Dickens), who assure us he will send us no other than materials purchas'd of you –

Mr. C desires me to say he feels himself greatly oblig'd by your ready attention to his former orders and assures you the moment his present precarious state of health & the times will admit of his enlarging our concerns you may depend on hearing from him with a large demand for the articles you deal in – in the mean time shall be glad to be inform'd at how much pr ton we can be serv'd with soap rock equal in goodness with the sample receiv'd –

Yr draft becomes due tomorrow & will be properly honor'd – times of payment in this country being 6 or 7 months we shall expect yr drawing on us at that time giving us as much time after date as yr friendship can afford us – with most respectful compt's.

I remain for Messrs C,
Your most obed't
Hbl servt.
A.C.

These copy letters without other correspondence are tantalizing, but here at least it is revealed that previous orders had been placed with John Warwick for Cornish raw materials such as china stone, for which payment was becoming due; that trade had declined and payments were slow; and that soap rock was being enquired after.

In a further copy letter, dated January 1796, Ann Chamberlain mentions improvements in their kilns and presumably in the firing of their porcelains:

Sir,

By a late material improvement in our kilns we have been enabled to make much larger quantity of china, in consequence of which Messrs Chamberlain will be now happy in the favour of your orders.

Unacquainted with London prices and having now disposed of any white [undecorated porcelain] we have this day forwarded three complete setts per Smith's wagon, for your inspection and whilst we know it certainly is [the word here is illegible] will leave the charge to mutual consideration.

On every painted teapot we write *Warranted* which never having in one instance failed – think cannot be too much mentioned to customers, flying [cracking in use] being formerly a principle of complaint but that will never happen to the goods of Messrs Chamberlain, for whom I am most respectfully

Sir your greatly obliged
Humble Servant.
A.C.

As the 1790s progressed the amount of Caughley porcelain ordered by Chamberlain diminished. It seems to have ceased altogether in November 1793 and at the same time the range of Chamberlain's own porcelain became more ambitious and the decoration more ornate, so that one finds such items as 'Pair of rich yellow and gold tumblers, with views near London' featured in the sales book of September 1797. Further evidence on the new Chamberlain porcelain is presented in Chapter 3 and information on the artists who decorated these wares with fine-quality ceramic painting is given in Chapter 6.

By the end of the eighteenth century the Chamberlain factory had built up a national reputation and perhaps even international renown, for many orders from foreign countries are recorded in the contemporary accounts. In September 1796 a fine dessert service was made for the Prince of Orange, then in this country, and the account for this service states:

August 13th, 1796.

His Serene Highness The Prince of Orange. Hampton
Court.

2 Ice pails complete
2 Fruit baskets and stands
2 Cream tureens and covers
2 stand to do. and spoons
1 centre dish and stand
4 triangular [shaped] dishes
4 mellon [shaped] dishes
4 shell [shaped] dishes
2 heart [shaped] dishes
36 dessert plates
all Blue & gold with different figures.

This design would appear to have been duplicated for other customers and similar descriptions are to be found several times in the account books; indeed this royal order was not of a special new design, for the brief initial order reads: 'Prince of Orange, Hampton Court. I complete with figures same as Bowens'. The latter was Henry Bowen of Bath, a dealer who purchased vast quantities of fine Chamberlain porcelain.

In August 1802 Lord Nelson visited Worcester and inspected the Chamberlain factory and retail shop, apparently disregarding the rival works of Messrs Flight & Barr. A contemporary account records this visit:

On Monday morning his Lordship and friends, preceded by a band of music, and attended by Mr. Weaver, of the Hop-pole Inn, and Messrs. Chamberlain, visited the china factory of the latter, over the door of which was thrown a triumphal arch of laurel. . . . For more than an hour his Lordship viewed with the minutest attention every department of this highly improved works, so much the object of general curiosity; and on inspection of the superb assortment of china at the shop in High Street, honoured Messrs. Chamberlain by declaring that . . . he had seen none equal to the productions of their manufactory, in testimony of which he left a very large order for china, to be decorated with his arms, insignia, etc. Sir William and Lady Hamilton also favoured the proprietors with liberal purchases.

(See page 109 and Plates 117 and 118.)

In September 1807 further honour was bestowed on the Chamberlains when the Prince of Wales visited the establishment after previously patronizing the works and granted them the honour of the style 'Porcelain Manufacturers to His Royal Highness the Prince of Wales', an honour reflected in some post-1807 marks. At a later date the style was, of course, changed from the Prince of Wales to that of Prince Regent, and Messrs Chamberlain continued to supply ornate and costly porcelains to the Royal Household. The Prince Regent was also connected with another landmark, the introduction in 1811 of a new porcelain body called 'Regent China' which was whiter and more glassy than the standard body. However, this new ware proved very expensive to produce and specimens are consequently quite rare. The body appears harder than the standard one and the covering glaze is rather prone to 'crazing', that is, hair-line cracks can occur.

Accounts of the ornamental wares of this period and of the artists who decorated them are given later, and a glance at Plates 32 onwards will show how diverse and decorative were these Worcester porcelains which, from about 1795, were generally marked with the firm's name. Although the Chamberlains had always supplied retailers in most large towns as well as providing finer porcelains for London houses, the decision was made in 1813 to open a London establishment under their own name. This was at 63 Piccadilly, but in July 1816 new premises at 155 New Bond Street were taken. The original Chamberlain records show not only the contents of the cases sent down to the London shops but also the sales made from them; these unique contemporary records are quoted, in part, on page 103.

The fortunes of the Chamberlain management continued to prosper until in 1840 the two rival firms of Flight, Barr & Barr (successors to the eighteenth-century Dr Wall factory where Chamberlain was apprenticed) and Chamberlain's were united. The marriage, however, was not very successful, for the loss of the old rivalry had its effect on the new concern, and fresh products such as porcelain door-furniture and buttons did not prove to be a lasting success. The two former works were combined at the Chamberlain factory under the trade name 'Chamberlain & Co', but various partners lost interest and sold their share holdings, with the result that by 1850 only Walter Chamberlain and John Lilly were left. Soon John Lilly was succeeded by his son, Frederick, and a new partner, W. H. Kerr, joined the other two, but in 1851 Walter Chamberlain retired, thereby severing the last direct link between the Chamberlain firm and the family. In the same year Frederick Lilly also retired. Further information on the later wares is given in Chapter 5.

The story of the Chamberlains really draws to a close with the 1851 Exhibition, not the 'Great' Exhibition as far as this firm was concerned, for its display failed to arouse much interest; practically the only novelty was the openwork porcelain (in imitation of an earlier Sèvres style, see Plates 209–14) and this permitted the official jury to report: 'Chamberlain & Co of Worcester exhibit some perforated china of agreeable effect'; but no prize medal was awarded and the management must have seen that drastic measures were necessary to rectify the position into which they had drifted.

At this time W. H. Kerr had been left in sole command, very wisely as it was to turn out, since he invited R. W. Binns to join him in an effort 'to exalt the name and to enhance the reputation of Worcester porcelain'. A new partnership, that of Kerr & Binns, was brought into being and for the next ten years, from 1852 to 1862, this new firm successfully re-established the tradition of quality Worcester porcelain; and on the success of these new wares, R. W. Binns formed in 1862 the 'Worcester Royal Porcelain Company', whose subsequent products are known throughout the world as 'Royal Worcester'. The present work is concerned only with the true Chamberlain-Worcester porcelains, not with the superb post-1852 productions of the succeeding firms (see Plates 215–17), but no work on Worcester porcelain would be complete without a tribute to Robert W. Binns, the Managing Director of the Royal Worcester Company, for to him every subsequent author and collector owes a great debt of gratitude for the way in which he built up the Works Collection, recorded the past history of the works, and ensured that so much contemporary material was preserved. The formation of most of the fine early collections of Worcester porcelain owes much to his enthusiasm.

Marks

The Caughley porcelains which were enamelled and gilded by Messrs Chamberlain in the 1780s and 1790s were *not* marked and do *not* bear even a pattern number. The only exception I know to this is the dish shown in Plate 23, which bears this painted name mark:

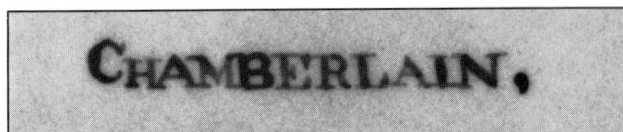

Mark 1

Some blanks, however, were impressed-marked with the name 'Salopian' during manufacture at the Caughley works, and a few specimens incorporating underglaze-blue borders, or other features, bear the initial 'S' (for 'Salopian') in underglaze blue (see Colour Plate III and Plate 2). It has been previously suggested that these porcelains, even if decorated at Worcester, should be regarded as Caughley, for in many cases the decoration was added to the precise instructions of Turner and was returned to the Caughley factory or sent to their London establishment for sale as true Caughley ware.

The very early specimens of Chamberlain's own porcelain made in 1791 and 1792 were completely unmarked, but it would appear that from at least the beginning of 1794 the patterns were entered in a pattern book and given fixed numbers, to facilitate reordering and to simplify the book-keeping. It is evident that by February 1794 these consecutive pattern numbers had reached 32, for the order book contains such entries as the following:

Patterns sent Messrs. Nickin & Company, King Street, Birmingham.

			£	s.	d.	
1 cup and saucer.	No.2.at		1	16	0	[the service]
A	do.	No.3.at	2	2	0	,,
A	do.	No.25.at	4	4	0	,,
A	do.	No.27.at	6	6	0	,,
A	do.	No.32.at	8	8	0	,,

whereas previous written 'orders' described the design in words, for example:

January 25th, 1794. Mr. Crane.
Blk [Black] & gold sprigs & border with rose colour dot in border. £4 4s. 0d.

Once the order books listed the patterns or wares sent, by reference to a fixed pattern number rather than a description, it is reasonable to assume that the pieces themselves also bore the same number, for otherwise greater confusion than before would have arisen. It is probable that at this period also the handwritten name and address marks began to be used. These normally take the form:

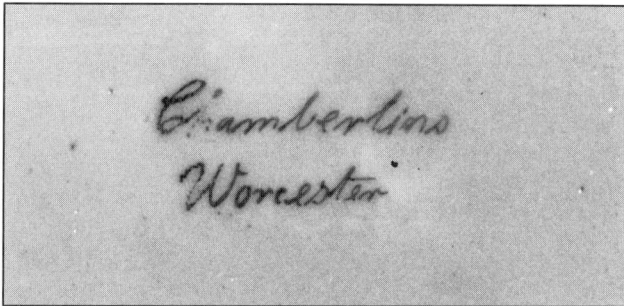

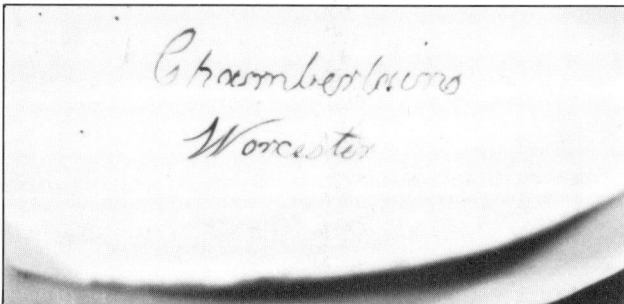

Marks 2 and 3

To these basic marks the pattern number was often, but not always, added, as well as the word 'Warranted' or various abbreviations such as 'Warr^d'.

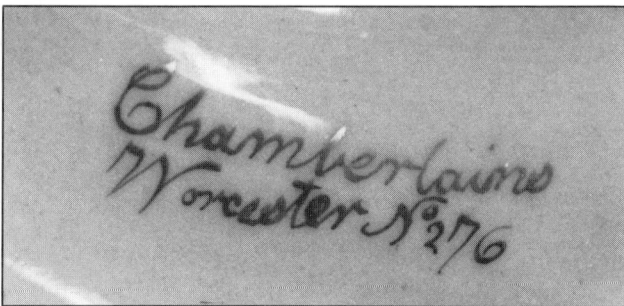

Marks 4 and 5

Spelling errors were by no means rare, even with these basic name and address marks. The significance of the word 'Warranted' is illustrated by the letter quoted on page 30. On tea services these written name marks were added inside the cover of the teapot and the sugar bowl. The Chamberlains were apparently the first to paint their marks in this position but on reflection it is a better place to advertise one's name than the normal position under the base, for while one does not turn up a full teapot, one can easily take off the cover to stir the tea or refill the pot and, of course, the cover of the sugar bowl is lifted off every time sugar is taken. For many years up to about 1820 these Chamberlain name and address marks (and many later variations) were only painted inside the lids of the teapot and the sugar bowl; they do *not* occur on other pieces in the teaset. However, the pattern number alone does very often appear on the remaining pieces, such as the creamer or waste bowl, and this is written in small, neat numerals often without any prefix such as 'N' or 'No.' (see the example shown, Mark 5); but some specimens do not even carry this helpful reference. The correct attribution can nearly always be made, however, by close comparison of the shapes illustrated in this book or by reference to the list of patterns given in Chapter 8 between pages 312 and 359.

On rare occasions the standard name mark was not added, for some retailers requested that the manufacturer's name should not be shown on wares supplied to them. For example, an order dated May 1800 has the request:

The names to be left out of teapots and sugar boxes and only numbered. . . . Be sure no name appears, nor Worcester or any thing else and to be in London by 25th instant. . . .

Some rare early pieces are recorded with the relief-moulded initial 'T' (which would have been incised into the original mould) and this could well relate to the modeller John Toulouse (see page 208).

In 1807 the Chamberlain firm was appointed manufacturer to the Prince of Wales, and this fact was incorporated in some rare marks such as the written mark shown on page 34, which happens to use the post-1811 term 'Prince Regent'.

From 1811, when the Prince was appointed Regent, a crown was added to several marks and from the same time the prefix 'Royal' was sometimes added, giving the description 'Royal Porcelain Manufacturers'. The year 1811 was also important because the new white, glassy body called 'Regent China' was introduced, and a description of this was incorporated in some marks from this date.

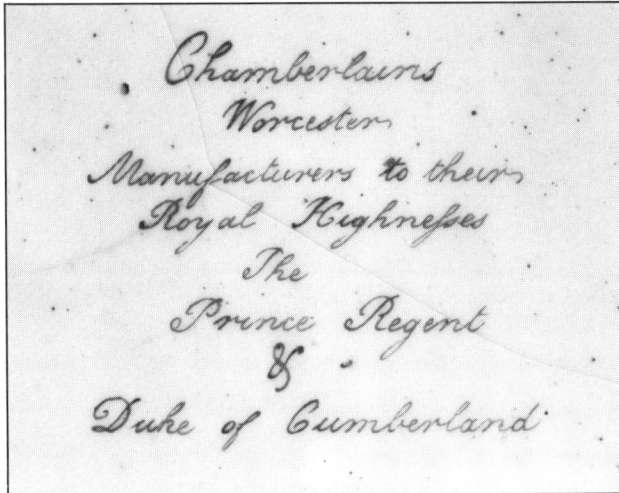

Marks 6 and 7

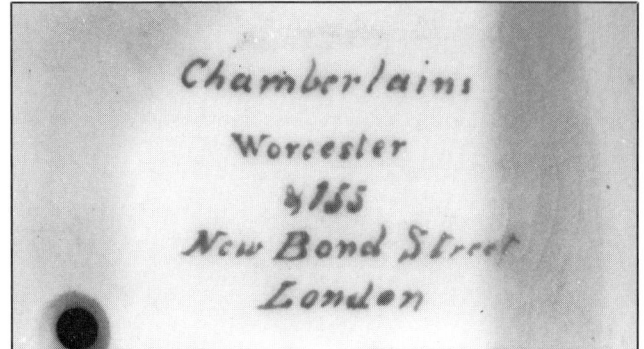

Mark 8

Mark 9

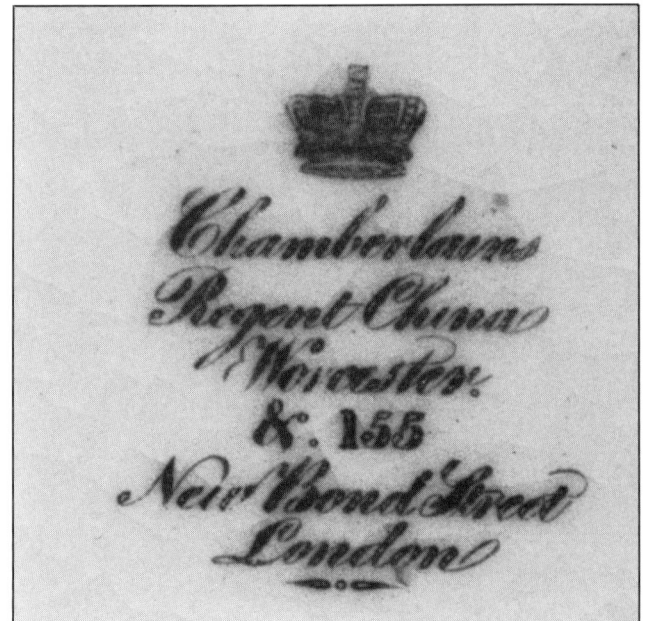

Mark 10

shop was sold in December 1845 so items produced after this date do not bear any mention of a London address. The New Bond Street address marks take several forms, both painted and printed, and some typical examples are shown here:

In the later part of 1813 wares were being made to stock the Chamberlains' new London retail shop at 63 Piccadilly (see page 102). From this period, and until May 1816, most marks incorporated the address of this shop (see Plate 306). However, such marks are now quite rare.

An event which is recorded in some rare marks occurred in May 1814 when Messrs Chamberlain were appointed porcelain manufacturers to Princess Charlotte. This appointment was advertised in *The Courier* in May and July, for the following entry occurs in the factory records: 'By advertisement in Courier of the Appointment, Princess Charlotte of Wales, 10s. 6d.'.

From July 1816 the shop at 155 New Bond Street was open and the new marks incorporated this address. On porcelain after 1840 another address mark, stating 'No.1. Coventry St. London' (Messrs Flight, Barr & Barr's retail shop), may be added. The New Bond Street

Mark 11

A rare form of mark sometimes found incised under cottage pastille-burners and figures comprises the name 'H Chamberlain & Sons' in script (see Plates 247 and 288).

Some rare porcelains are to be found bearing the impressed, crowned mark 'F.B.B.' of the Flight, Barr & Barr partnership (1813–40) as well as a painted Chamberlain mark. The explanation of this is that, as explained on page 31, the two rival firms combined in 1840 and some undecorated Flight, Barr & Barr porcelain, which already bore their impressed initial mark, was taken over by the new company which traded as 'Chamberlain & Co' and, of course, the mark of this firm was applied over the glaze. From about 1840 the new style 'Chamberlain & Co' replaced the old name 'Chamberlain' or 'Chamberlain's' (sample marks are given below), but it must be remembered that many pieces were unmarked. From *c.* 1847 to about 1852 the impressed mark 'CHAMBERLAINS' (Mark 14) oc-

Mark 12

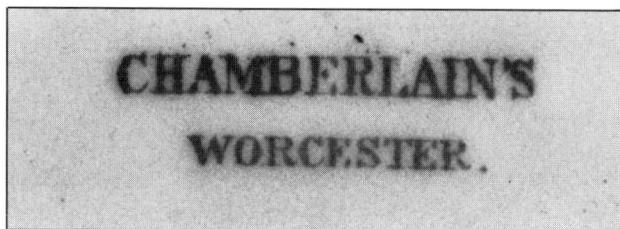

Mark 13

curs in capital letters (sometimes 'WORCESTER' appears below the name) on plates and, on rare occasions, on figures or animal models.

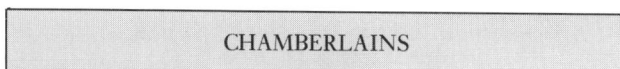

CHAMBERLAINS

Mark 14

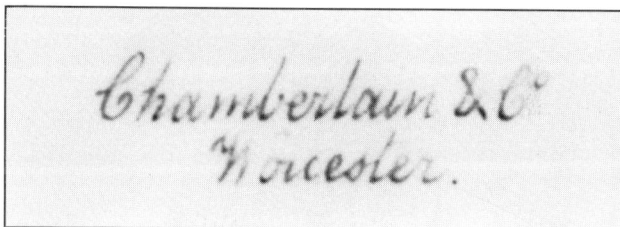

Mark 15

Some post-1840 marks include the two London addresses, 155 New Bond Street and 1 Coventry Street, and the period of these written or printed marks is self-evident, as the Coventry Street shop was sold in December 1844.

In the 1830s and 1840s Messrs Chamberlain also produced limited quantities of useful wares in an Ironstone-type body as popularized by the Mason firm. The marks on such wares can take two forms; firstly:

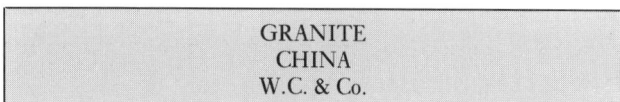

GRANITE
CHINA
W.C. & Co.

Mark 16

This mark is sometimes encountered with the standard mark 'Chamberlain & Co., 155 New Bond Street, London'. The second mark incorporates the description 'Stone-China' as follows:

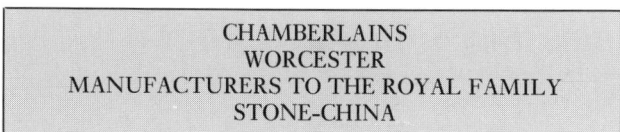

CHAMBERLAINS
WORCESTER
MANUFACTURERS TO THE ROYAL FAMILY
STONE-CHINA

Mark 17

This basic mark has been reported below the name and address of a New York importer, showing that Chamberlain's enjoyed an export market for such wares.

After the Chamberlain partners had sold the New Bond Street shop in December 1845, the well-known china dealers W. P. & G. Phillips employed for a period a printed mark incorporating the words 'LATE CHAMBERLAINS', but this printed name and address mark probably appeared on an assortment of pieces, not all of which would have been of Chamberlain's make.

The printed mark reproduced right was used in the last few years of the Chamberlain Company's period, *c*. 1850–52, but it is rarely found. It was, however, adopted by the succeeding Kerr & Binns partnership with the words 'Royal Porcelain Works' replacing 'Chamberlain & Co'.

Mark 18

2
THE CHAMBERLAINS AS RETAILERS AND DECORATORS

The earliest available records of Robert Chamberlain operating on his own account date from July 1788, leaving perhaps a slightly earlier period unaccounted for; but once the Chamberlain archives commence in the summer of 1788 it can clearly be seen that the blanks he was decorating at Worcester were mainly of Caughley make sent by wherry down the River Severn by Thomas Turner, the owner of that Salopian manufactory. In many cases the decoration was added to Turner's specifications and often the embellished Caughley porcelains were then forwarded to Turner's London warehouse. It was almost as if Turner did not have at his Caughley factory any means of enamelling and gilding his own porcelains, which were consequently shipped down to Worcester. However, the majority of Turner's Caughley porcelain was wholly decorated in underglaze blue, and these wares, representing Turner's main concern, were certainly made and decorated at the Caughley factory.

Although this chapter deals mainly with the trade and correspondence between Turner at Caughley and the Chamberlains at Worcester concerning the more important identifiable examples that were enamelled or gilded in the Chamberlain studio, it would be wrong to suggest that these finer wares represent the whole story; indeed Ann Chamberlain's letter of 1792 quoted on page 29 refers to boy painters, who would be employed on the simplest of designs. Most of the early records relate to very simple designs sold to Chamberlain's own customers. Many of these were standard Caughley or Worcester blue-printed teawares to which the Chamberlains may only have added gilt-line borders. Take,

for example, two sales entered in the account books in September 1788:

Mr. Thos. Whitby, Cheshire.
1 Complete set of Pagoda, gilt £3 3s. 0d.

Mr. John Higson, Trodsam [Frodsham?], Cheshire.
2, ½ pint mugs blue border, gold sprigs 14s. 0d.

In November 1788 a varied and interesting range of designs was sent to William Taylor of Warrington, perhaps as samples of the teaware designs that could be supplied by the Chamberlains. The selection comprised:

Setts of birds, blue
Setts of Landscape, blue edge
Setts of Ruins
Setts of New Temple
Setts of fruit, blue edge
Setts of birds, brown & gold edge
Setts of Milk Maid, gold edge
Setts of Red border Dresden
Setts of Dresden gold edge

I believe that most of these designs were of Worcester make and of the type which sometimes bear the disguised numeral mark, if not the Worcester crescent device. Especially noteworthy are the 'Ruins' and the 'Milk Maid' designs, both of which are well known in Davis-Flight period Worcester porcelain (see Plate 12) but are unknown in Caughley. Other designs such as 'birds, blue' or 'fruit, blue edge' were made at both factories and it is not now possible to tell if these 1788

12. Three typical blue-printed Flight period Worcester tea service porcelains of the type sometimes enriched with gilding by Chamberlain's and sold in their High Street shop. Crescent marks. Diameter of saucers 4¾ in. *c.* 1790. *Godden of Worthing Ltd*

samples were all from Worcester or from the Caughley factory as well. However, a few of the Chamberlain records clearly indicate Worcester as the source:

	s.	d.
8 saucers Worc.^r. Temple	3	8
2 cups do. do. [as in Plate 7?]		11
1 pint bason do. do.	1	0
[24 February 1790]		

Also, in July and November 1791 there is a cash book entry for '. . . China b.^t at Flights' and '2 Tumblers white & gold from F-ts 5s.'.

By 1789, however, there is firm evidence of the supply of Caughley porcelain to the Chamberlains. One such early list is headed: 'Goods Rec^d. from Thos Turner Esq. Caughley with a copy of all orders & remarks'. This is followed by a very long list of articles received from Caughley or of items ordered by the Chamberlains in 1789. Large quantities of underglaze-blue bordered teawares were required for the Chamberlain artists or gilders to embellish. Such goods included 'new fluted festoon for gilding, new fluted broad blue border, and new fluted fly pattern'.

The term 'new fluted' related to the straight-fluted teawares of the shapes shown in Plate 25. An interesting plate, probably from a dessert service, is shown in Plate 13; this design may or may not represent the 'Fly' pattern mentioned in the Chamberlain correspondence with Turner – 'Dessert plates Fly particularly wanted' – but it certainly shows how these blanks were delivered to

Chamberlain already laid with the underglaze-blue border and other blue portions of the pattern, which was then finished with a gilt outer border (covering the ragged blue edge) and other details to complete the design.

13. An 'S'-marked Caughley plate showing only the underglaze-blue part of the decoration. Chamberlain's received porcelains in this half-finished state and completed the design with the gilt portions and edges. Diameter 8¾ in. *c.* 1790. *Godden Reference Collection*

Some Caughley teaware shapes were ordered in a completely white state and these would have been wholly decorated in the Chamberlain workshops, such as one order for 'Bute white and Broseley white'. The terms 'Bute' and 'Broseley' refer to the shapes required.

The Chamberlains opened their retail shop in the High Street on 27 June 1789 and as their rival John Flight remarked, they talked 'of making a flaming shew in about 2 months'. At this period the porcelain stock would have almost entirely comprised Caughley wares, either standard objects sold as manufactured, or special patterns added to the Caughley blanks by the Chamberlain gilders and painters. In November 1789 the Chamberlains were charged £11 8s. 0d. for two enamelling stoves, and a later account of £12 9s. 0d. was paid to the Dale (i.e. Coalbrookdale) Company for '2 enamelling stoves' in November 1791.

Very soon the order books record requests by the Chamberlains' own customers for individual special pieces or sets such as the following examples:

A Scarlet and gold Japan [pattern] dessert set of centrepiece, 2 tureens, covers & stands, 6 dishes and 10 plates.
    [July 1789]
1 complete set of toy china blue & gold sprigs, 10s. 6d.
    [September 1790: see Plate 14]
Three half pint mugs with Comedy.
    [January 1791]

There now follows a selection of 'orders and remarks' sent from Chamberlain in Worcester to Caughley. These records start in August 1789, but from the wording 'no more' or 'before ordered' it is obvious that earlier orders had been placed. The orders quoted, in condensed form, relate merely to one year – 1789 – and concern only Caughley articles ordered by the Chamberlains for their own shop and customers.

August 13th, 1789.

The saucers 2nd [size] new fluted, fine blue borders to the cups sent, are very much wanted.
Plain cups & saucers common are much wanted, with pint or ½ pint basons both best & seconds.*
4 dozen pint Dutch jugs [mask-head cabbage-leaf jugs] white. The cups with the large handles before ordered of the Bute shape – very much wanted.
Temple [pattern] best teas wanting next Saturday in complete sets if possible (Must be sent next week).
Teapots of both sizes and pint and ½ pint basons.
Shrewsbury plain ware as above much wanted.
Pleasure Boat etc. etc. different sizes. ['Fisherman' pattern]
No more common chocolate cups old make in blue, rather a few French or Bute shape in white.

_____

* 'Seconds' were slightly faulty wares sold at a reduced rate.

14.   Representative pieces from a Caughley child's tea and coffee service of the type enamelled and gilded at the Chamberlain studio in Worcester. Perhaps this is the 'complete set of toy china blue & gold sprigs, 10s. 6d.' mentioned in the Chamberlain accounts in September 1790. Unmarked. Coffee pot 3½ in. high. *Godden of Worthing Ltd*

_____

The teapots to be most of them Barrel shape of all patterns plain or fluted.
Wanted immediately 3 or 4 complete [tea] setts of Shropshire [shape]
1st size Plain [shape] with Barrel teapot, 2nd or 3rd size for gilding.

August 20th, 1789.

Dutch jugs [mask-head cabbage-leaf jugs] common, best & seconds – 24 Quart [size] without [blue] border.
24 Quart mugs, wine measure.
24 very small ½ pint.
3 or 4 dozen of very small sauce boats, sorted.
A few dozen small Chelsea [shape] ewers in blue at 8d. each.
    do.   do.   do. gadroon boats   do.   at 6d. each.
A few egg drainers in blue.

August 23rd, 1789.

We want at this time fifteen or twenty complete sets of teas Pleasure boat & Shrewsbury plain ware [not fluted?] with some Shropshire [shape].
The teapots to be principally 3rd or 4th [sizes] barrel [shape], if the cups are but a little larger it would be a great advantage in the sale.
A great quantity of the 2s. 6d. Teas with basons, milk ewers & teapots, best and seconds, if my father can settle the business with Mr. Turner.
We sold a great number of the 2nd [size] teas, seconds at 2s. 8d. with 5 per cent for ready money so that you will easily see our Profit is on the wrong side of the Post – I think unless Mr. Turner can allow us fifteen per cent shall not be able to clear ourselves as we certainly must sell on the same terms as our neighbours [Messrs Flights] or not at all.

No more mustard pots, those that we have, there is no spoons sent to them.

Wanted some egg strainers, blue & white and a few Dresden flower & border do. & [egg] stands do.

24 Caudle cups & stands, Shanked bell fluted, white.

The $\frac{1}{2}$ pint Crucibles of the excellent Cobalt promised.

No more best teas Pleasure Boat 2nd [size] unless they can be sent at 5s. 6d.

September 4th, 1789.

I am sorry to inform Mr. Turner it is now three months since I ordered 8 cups & saucers 2nd long handled Bute shape white.

4 coffee do. and 2 cream ewers with large handles on them and slop basins & sugar do., they are for a lady in Gloucester who I am apprehensive must by this time be greatly offended at our delay.

The teapot Barrel shape Temple [pattern] we are likewise in very great want of.

Basons of every sort blue wanted particularly $\frac{1}{2}$ pint Image.

I own myself disappointed upon opening every cask, to find such a large quantity of those high priced 2nd [size] Teas which we cannot sell and so few of the first size which we can sell.

Must request you will not send any more basket Chantilly [bordered] sprig [pattern] nor Dresden flower & border, except the saucers to the last 3rd size cups.

No more 2nd teas Shropshire & Temple [patterns] to be sent, as 7s. is a charge we cannot sell them at. Wanted teapots, Plates etc. to make those sets we have complete.

No more 2nd teas Pleasure Boat ['Fisherman' pattern], unless they can be sent at the Worcester price 5s. 6d.

Please to send no more white seconds until further orders as at present we really want room to put them.

October 5th, 1789.

We are greatly distressed for want of new fluted white – short of every article but [teapot] stands, [spoon] trays & sugar boxes.

Quart Dutch [mask-head cabbage-leaf jugs] jugs and pint do., white, pint and $\frac{1}{2}$ pint mugs white.

Second plain white plates by the wherry. [This request shows that the goods were sent down the River Severn.]

A few wash-hand basons & ewers blue & different sizes as soon as possible – with their prices.

3 Dozen chocolate cups, new fluted white.

From these few extracts from the original Chamberlain-Turner accounts or copies of the orders, it can be seen that the Chamberlains wanted – presumably mainly to stock their retail shop – a wide range of standard Caughley porcelains. Indeed the vast majority of Salopian wares illustrated in my book *Caughley and Worcester Porcelains, 1775–1800* (1969) would have been represented in the Chamberlains' Worcester shop in the 1788–93 period, after which the new Chamberlain

porcelains would have largely replaced the Caughley wares.

Some of the Caughley porcelains sent down to the Chamberlains at Worcester were not for sale, but were sent purely to be decorated for Thomas Turner's account, a fact evidenced by numerous contemporary accounts such as the following:

November 9th, 1789.

Orders from Thomas Turner Esq.

1 Complete set of New fluted Birds Eye		
1	do.	gold wreath
1	do.	plain, fine blue & gold sprigs
1	do.	Broseley Nankin, bridge border

December 30th, 1789.

Thomas Turner Esq., at the Salopian China Warehouse, No. 5. Portugal Street, Lincoln Inn Fields, London.

1 complete set, Broseley white & gold festoon		
1	do.	gold wreath
1	do.	Birds Eye
1	do.	Blue & gold festoon
1	do.	white & gold festoon
2	do.	new Royal festoon
1 set of patterns		
1 Dessert service, full Nankin edge and line		

Chamberlain's gilding trade for Thomas Turner was evidently extensive and some of these accounts are especially interesting. They are given here (opposite) to show not only the relative cost of the basic white porcelain (first column) and the added decoration (second column), but also to illustrate the types of pattern decorated and gilded by the Chamberlains. These lists occur under the page headings 'THOS TURNER ESQR. TO CHAMBERLAIN & SONS' in the Chamberlain records.

From these costings for both the basic object and the added gilding, one can gauge the amount of decoration added. Purely gilt designs cost far more to embellish than to make – just over £3 to gild the gold festoon teawares which themselves cost a mere £1 13s. 3d.; whilst the designs already half-completed with areas of underglaze blue cost nearly as much to gild as to produce – a 'Royal Star' teaset was invoiced at £2 17s. 0d. with an extra £2 14s. 0d. for Chamberlain's gilding. The blue-printed designs which were all but completed at Caughley and needed only slight additional gold borders and gilt knobs cost much less to embellish than to make, £2 2s. 6d. against £1 7s. 0d. for Chamberlain's gilding.

It is interesting to see that Chamberlain returned faulty pieces to Turner – one such selection (entered on 15 July 1790) appears under the heading 'GOODS

July 22nd, 1789.	cost of ware	gilding charge
	£ s. d.	£ s. d.
1 complete set of Broseley Bridge border	2 2 6	1 7 0
1 cup & saucer Jett [black enamel] festoons	1 1	1 10
1 do. with gold star	1 1	1 10
1 do. Blue & gold birds-eye	2 1	1 10
1 do. Royal Jessamine	2 1	1 10
1 do. Jett [black enamel] flowers	1 1	1 1
1 do. Green & gold Royal Wheel	1 1	3 0
1 do. Purple & gold	2 1	2 6
1 do. white & gold sprigs	5	1 2
1 do. fine blue & gold sprigs	5	1 4
1 do. Tulip with gold edge	5	1 8
1 do. Green & gold sprigs	5	9
10 Setts of teas [cups & saucers] red bordered	1 5 0	1 10 0
24 Dessert plates, Dresden flowers, gold edge & ring	1 16 0	1 5 0
1 Centrepiece do.	10 6	4 1
2 Sauce tureens do. complete	18 0	8 4
4 Richmond [shape] shells, Dresden flowers	16 0	8 0
10 Dishes do.	2 0 0	1 5 0

January 28th, 1790.

TO CAUGHLEY

	£ s. d.	£ s. d.
1 Complete sett of Royal Star	2 17 0	2 14 0
1 do. Gold wreath	1 11 9	2 6 0
1 do. new fluted gold festoon	1 11 9	2 18 0
1 B & B plate 1st [size] new fluted gold festoon	1 3	2 4
1 do. 2nd [size] do. do.	1 9	2 11
1 Teapot stand do.	1 0	1 9
1 [spoon] tray do.	1 0	1 9
1 [tea] cannister do.	1 6	2 4
12 cups & saucers, new fluted, Blue & gold	1 5 0	18 0
1 Slop bason do.	2 6	1 6
1 sugar box & cover do.	2 6	1 10½
1 Teapot 4th [size] do.	3 6	2 7½
1 Ewer do.	2 6	1 1½
1 complete set, Dagger border edge & line	1 14 0	1 1 0
1 do. new fluted festoon in colours	1 11 9	4 0 0

RETURNED NOT FIT FOR GILDING'. The following list, therefore, shows the Caughley goods, some of which were apparently partly decorated with blue-printed designs, in the state that they were received from the factory. The prices quoted are the prime costs of the unembellished porcelains.

	£ s. d.
10 Milks & covers, Broseley Nankeen border	1 5 0
2 Ewers, Birds Eye	5 0
6 Cups do.	6 3
5 Saucers do.	5 2½
2 Coffees do.	2 8
1 [tea] cannister & cover, Birds Eye	2 6
1 Sugar box & cover Shropshire Nankeen	1 9
1 Teapot stand	2 0
1 Saucer dagger border	5
1 Cup Broseley Nankeen border	10
12 Sugar boxes to have lids	18 0

Whilst considering Chamberlain's gilding it should be noted that it was not only Caughley wares they embellished. One order for 20 February 1793 records that about one hundred cups and saucers, as well as some pint and half-pint basins, were to be gilded and returned to a Mr B. Pollard of Gloucester. In 1802

Chamberlain also added gold enrichments to some blue and white Chinese porcelains, but this trade was apparently not large – merely an individual order.

In the 1790s the Chamberlain gilders also added initials and other decorations to glasswares (see also page 55), mainly decanters, some of which were made in the then fashionable blue glass of the type which is normally attributed to Bristol, in the erroneous belief that all such blue glass originated from there. The Chamberlain accounts show the source of some such wares as Stourbridge:

Received from Mr. Witton, Stourbridge.

19 blue quart decanters to be gilt	8 'B', 8 'R', & 3 'G'	
20 blue pint decanters do.	8 'B', 8 'R', & 4 'G'	
7 blue quart decanters do.	3 'B', 3 'R', & 1 'G'	

[6 July 1791]

Individual costs are shown in other entries relating to goods from Messrs Witton & Co. of Stourbridge:

	£	s.	d.
12 blue quart glass decanters gilt	1	4	0
4 green do.		8	0
11 blue pint do. at 1s. 9d.		19	3
9 blue rose foot scallop'd salts at 1s.		9	0
9 blue, round bowl, square foot 9d.		6	9
10 blue jars & beakers 6d.		5	0

[26 July 1791]

A further entry for Messrs Witton & Co. in September 1791 shows that white glass decanters were also supplied, and it seems that such purchases continued over several years. There was also intertrading in glass, for in November 1794 an entry appears in the Chamberlain account books referring to the sale of several smelling-bottles, jars and beakers to a Mr Brown, glass gilder, of London.

The Chamberlain accounts relate chiefly, however, to their trade as china decorators, referring mainly to the embellishing of white or partly-finished Caughley wares laid with underglaze-blue borders etc., or the gilding of Caughley blue and white designs to smarten them up for the London trade.

One Chamberlain account book which was commenced in 1788 includes detailed lists of Caughley porcelains, enamelled and gilded by Chamberlain's at Worcester, which were then either forwarded to London or returned to the Caughley factory. On the first page of this account book the prices of standard enamelled and gilt patterns of the period are listed with the piece-rates. The original order of the list has been retained here, as it is possible that the first designs were the earliest to be introduced. Unfortunately it is difficult now to link the known designs to these very brief descriptions.

New fluted shape	s.	d.
Plymouth	2	8
Plymouth festoon	1	6
Royal Fly	1	1
Royal Jessamine	1	3
Royal Weel [*sic*] border	[no price]	
Blue & gold festoon		9
White & gold festoon	1	2
Blue & gold Birds eye		11
White & gold wreath		11
Blue & gold chain, bridge border, No.4.		9

Bute shape	s.	d.
Blue & gold chain with sprigs		9
Shrewsbury bridge border		7
Shrewsbury edge & line		5
Broseley edge & line		5
Broseley simple edge		4
Broseley bridge border		7
Shropshire edge & line	[no price]	
Temple edge & line*	[no price]	
Dagger border, edge & line		5
Pleasure boat, edge & line*	[no price]	

[Blue-printed 'Fisherman' pattern]

Broseley shape	s.	d.
White & gold sprigs		8
Gold chain border		11
Plain [shape] fine blue spots upon the glaze		8
Blue spots		11
Plain [shape], white & gold sprigs		7
New fluted [shape] Fawn & gold	1	3
do. white, gold edge		4
do. white, & gold spangles	1	3
do. jet [black] sprigs	[no price]	
do. Royal Curtain	[no price]	
plain [shape] white & gold wreath	[no price]	
plain [shape] blue edge, gold chain & bridge border		8
plain [shape] green & gold sprigs	[no price]	
plain [shape] link & gold	[no price]	
Dresden gold edge		4
Tulip gold edge		4
Dresden red border		3
plain [shape] blue & gold festoon		8
Bell fluted [shape] Iron Bridge [border]		10
Ladys sprig		9
Sprig & border	1	6
New fly festoon	1	2

---

*The 'Temple' and 'Pleasure Boat' designs are standard Caughley underglaze-blue printed designs. The 'edge & line' refers to the gilt edge and inner line sometimes added to these patterns.

The above prices refer to the cost of decoration, but as a teapot, for instance, would involve more work than a cup, the following scale of piece-rates was used:

	Times basic cost
Teapot 4th [large size]	$3\frac{1}{2}$
Teapot 3rd & 2nd [sizes]	3
Teapot stand	$1\frac{1}{2}$
Spoon tray	$1\frac{1}{2}$
Cream ewer	$1\frac{1}{2}$
milk pot & cover	2
sugar box and cover	$2\frac{1}{2}$
Slop bason, pint	2
do. $\frac{1}{2}$ pint	$1\frac{1}{2}$
tea cannister & cover	2
Plate 2nd [large size]	$2\frac{1}{2}$
Plate 1st [size]	2
Saucer	1
teacup	1
coffee cup	1

For example, a 'Royal Fly' teapot listed at 1s. 1d. would cost three and a half times this piece-rate, i.e. 3s. $9\frac{1}{2}d.$,

whilst the spoontray would cost 1s. $7\frac{1}{2}d$. A spoontray such as this is shown in Plate 15, but this particular design required much more high-quality gilding than was needed to complete the 'Fly' design seen in Plate 13. (The description 'Fly' in the Chamberlain accounts was probably an abbreviation for 'Butterfly'.)

Only a very small percentage of the Chamberlain accounts as they reflect the trade with Thomas Turner at Caughley can be quoted, and in the main references in this book are confined to 1789, the year that the Chamberlains opened their retail shop; but in 1792 the Chamberlains purchased goods to the value of £2,076 11s. 6d. from Turner, with a 25 per cent discount permitted. In the same year the Chamberlains charged Turner at Caughley for goods valued at £848 2s. $6\frac{1}{2}d$. (less 25 per cent discount) plus gilding charges of £572 18s. $9\frac{1}{2}d$. (less a mere 5 per cent discount), making a total of £1,180 7s. $9\frac{1}{2}d$.

The next balance, for 1793, did not continue up to 31 December as would have been normal but was struck on 27 November 1793. The amount of goods purchased

15.   A Caughley porcelain spoontray from a tea service. This would have been sent down-river from Caughley with only the underglaze-blue border, for gilding and finishing by the Chamberlains. This design is perhaps the 'Royal Fly' of the Chamberlain accounts. $6\frac{1}{2} \times 3\frac{1}{2}$ in. c. 1790. *Godden of Worthing Ltd*

from Caughley was then worth only slightly more than half that for the previous year ($£1,054$ $13s$. $0\frac{3}{4}d$. against $£2,076$ $11s$. $6d$.), whilst the Chamberlain charges to Turner were given as $£843$ $17s$. $0\frac{1}{2}d$. It is not known why these accounts were drawn up in November rather than at the end of the year: it could be that the Turner-Chamberlain trade had ceased after a disagreement. It certainly appears that all was not well between the two firms. Turner mistrusted the Chamberlains and the Chamberlains had long complained about the goods, or service, received from Turner.

At this period, too, the Chamberlains were manufacturing their own porcelains and had less and less need of their former supplier of blanks, a fact shown by the considerable drop in the value of goods purchased from Caughley in 1793. It may also be significant that Chamberlain's order for Caughley porcelains placed on 15 June 1793 was countermanded on 17 September 1793.

I have been unable to find in the available Chamberlain records evidence of new goods purchased from Turner at Caughley in 1794 or in subsequent years. Furthermore, I have not traced any later records of Chamberlain gilding Caughley wares for Turner, and consequently I think the two-way trade between the Chamberlains and Turner ceased in about November 1793. From this period onwards the Chamberlains were fully committed to their own business – they were porcelain manufacturers in their own right, not mere decorators of other firms' goods. Turner's loan also seems to have been repaid as no payments of interest are recorded in later accounts, except to Richard Nash (see page 19).

These Chamberlain porcelains will be discussed in subsequent chapters, but there follows an interesting letter, mentioned earlier (see page 29), which underlines the conflict between the Chamberlains and Turner. Unfortunately only a few copies of letters sent by the Chamberlains to Turner at Caughley are available – these were sometimes entered into the accounts books as a record, but there is no knowledge of the incoming letters from Turner. However, one letter written in January 1793 does show the general troublesome state of affairs into which the Chamberlain-Turner trade had drifted by the beginning of 1793.

The entry is headed 'Copy of a letter from Hump. Chamberlain to Mr. Thos. Turner, Caughley, being an answer to 2 letters, dated 8th & 10th Jany.93'.

Sir.   Worc. January 12th, 1793.

I received your two letters and in answer to the first respecting the shank'd cannisters, have to say that the order

stood last Xmas settling /92 when both the books was put alike by your Clerks as under.

Blue ribbon Shank'd Cannisters on order	16
Blue bord[r] do.	10
White do.	30
	56

Received May 30th No. 22 [case number?]	
Shank'd Canis.[rs]	66
June 14th No. 23 do. do.	8
July 13th No. 25 do. do.	2
Exclusive of them returned which was	29
	105

I believe they will find a difficulty in producing an order for shank'd cannisters since the time mention'd above as I well know there has been no alteration in the order given then, except desiring them to send the whole order entire – thus far I fancy will be found tollerable satisfactory and serve to prove we are not always in the wrong.

The next thing that presents itself is the excuse set up by them as a reason for our not having goods, 'that we have been continually checking and harrasing them, sometimes under one pretence and at other times on another'. In answer to that we have only to say that if they *will persist* in so *un*founded and erroneous excuse we shall not be content with their saying so, because I really think after we have suffer'd so very materially for many months past the very attempt to defend on any other ground than unforeseen events is an aggravation of our misfortunes. With respect to the assertion in your last letter saying you were convinc'd I meant to deceive you in the quantity of stone and clay coming up – am really astonish'd, what end it answer harrasing my mind with disbelieving all I can say, particularly when you was in possession of Mrs C's [Chamberlain's] two letters which ought to have convinc'd you. The one I well know mention'd 40 ton by mistake but it's really cruel you should take no notice of the other which was solely wrote to contradict the former – however I shall content myself that I am not held in that disrepute where I am *better* known, and am still happy to say *you* have nothing against me but an idea, nor had I ever the least intention, whatever your opinion may be, but in that way which has been so repeatedly explained.

You was pleased to say your rider informed you that we held out incouragement to the country customers by no means expected – for answer – I can't form the least idea what can be meant – we only know that we use everybody as well as we can which I always conceived due to ever . . . [piece missing] but if yr rider is willing to hear and believe . . . [piece missing] will be told by some shopkeepers he will [corner of page torn off] . . . to do, but I should like to inform them we do [not intend?, page torn] answering every story he may pick up. . . .

Shall beg leave to say a few more words . . . [piece missing] to the last part of yr letter wherein you desire . . . [piece missing] immediately to remit you cash – which request will be comply'd with in a few days, and still further can't help remarking the unmerited acrimony the letter is wrote with. Have only to repeat once more, that we have never had the least intention of doing anything to the detriment of yr manufactory, but on the contrary the whole that has been done, or will be, is to the essential interests of both even if you will for a moment fancy me the most ungrateful person living still it is impossible to point it out as my interest which I would be found to prove most clearly and wh is the well known sentiments of the family – that being the case, 'tis very improbable I sho.^{d} be the first to injure myself provided I had not a spark of gratitude in me –

Have only room to add that I shall always adhear to the above declaration – unless by receiving a kind of treatment we do not deserve, are forced to seek refuge in a way we have never yet entertain'd a thought of pursuing.

The family joins me in respects & are happy to hear Mrs. Tr. surprised you in her recovered health.

I rem.^{n} Sir y.^{r} Hble Ser.^{nt}.

P.S.   When you are ready for settling . . . please to give no . . . [words missing] notice.

H.C.

One wonders what were the contents of Turner's two letters which prompted this reply. Almost certainly the fact that the Chamberlains were now manufacturing rivals rather than decorating partners had much to do with this correspondence and the fact that Turner was requesting payment for goods supplied. As previously stated, this intertrading seems to have been terminated in November 1793, with both manufacturers going their separate ways – Chamberlain's proceeding to success, Turner slipping into decline and to the sale of his factory in 1799.

The Chamberlains must have held a sizeable stock of Caughley blanks which they embellished as demand required over several years. Indeed the Chamberlains' December 1795 stocktaking list included three pages headed 'Turners ware, not enamelled' with, for example, 660 white cups, 76 shell-shaped dessert dishes and 27 'new fluted' teapots. It is interesting to observe here that the Chamberlains carried much old stock, for the December 1793 list records:

37 dozen old Worc odd pieces at 2s. 6d. a dozen
180 pieces old Worcester at 2d.
43 coffee pots old Worc, white at 2s.
90 dishes old Worcester dessert white at 4s.

Did the Chamberlains ever get round to decorating and selling these old Worcester porcelains? How old were

16.   A rare impressed-marked 'Salopian' Caughley dessert service tureen and stand, almost certainly enamelled by the Chamberlains at Worcester, and perhaps part of the 'scarlet & gold Japan' pattern dessert service invoiced in July 1789. Tureen 5¾ in. long. *c.* 1789. *Messrs Sotheby & Co.*

17. A Caughley mask-head jug of pint size, decorated at the Chamberlain studio in Worcester, made for Mrs Hooper and initialled (or 'cyphered') in a typical manner. Invoiced in September 1789. Unmarked. 5¾ in. high. 1789. *Godden Reference Collection*

they, and when were they purchased? The answers to such questions would help to solve the mystery of the Chamberlains' break with the Worcester management.

It is noteworthy that the Chamberlains' own new porcelains did not directly emulate the old Caughley shapes but, on the contrary, they introduced new updated forms. This fact is well illustrated by comparing the Chamberlain-decorated Caughley cabbage-leaf jugs of 1789, 1790 and 1792 shown in Plates 17, 18 and 19 with the new Chamberlain shapes of 1795 shown in Plates 39 and 40.

Some of the entries in the Chamberlain account and order books relate to surviving objects, and in this way the type of porcelain (normally Caughley) and the styles of decoration in favour in the late 1780s and early 1790s can be gauged. For example, on 24 July 1789 a Mrs Squire ordered a dessert service to be delivered to her, care of Lady Knollizic, Soho Square, London. This set was described as 'scarlet & gold Japan' and included two 'tureens, complete'. The Japanese-styled Caughley porcelain tureen cover and stand with ladle shown in

Plate 16 certainly fits this description. The lobed oval tureen form was a standard Caughley shape of the period, not copied at any other English factory. On 26 September 1789 a Mrs Hooper of Leigh ordered a 'pint jug, fawn & gold, cyphered SMH . . . with border on ye Belly'. The small mask-head jug shown in Plate 17 bears these cursive initials and has the fawn border dropped from the usual position on the top edge to 'ye Belly' of the pot.

These Caughley mask-head cabbage-leaf jugs were very popular as gifts. The pair shown in Plate 18 can be linked with the original order. They were ordered on 11 March 1790:

Jas. Kindon, Birmingham.

2 Quart jugs gold edge & line with cipher, crest & shield at 15s. £1 10s. 0d.

Many other Caughley jugs and mugs were embellished only with simple gilt floral sprays by the Chamberlain gilders. A typical example is shown in Plate 19. The initial 'B' on the front of this jug suggests that this could have been the article ordered on 12 June 1792 by Thomas Hookham of Coventry: '1 Quart jug, gold sprigs, cyphered 'B', 9s.'. Plate 20 shows a similar Caughley jug decorated in a much richer style. This armorial example reveals the Chamberlain decorators at their best. The floral sprays and the wreath surround show a typical and tasteful combination of gilding with a blue overglaze enamel. The wide dark-blue borders at the top and bottom are under the glaze and were added at Caughley during the manufacturing process. The Chamberlain-Turner accounts show that the cost of the quart-size jug, complete with blue borders, was a mere 3s. for best-quality examples. The Caughley jugs with these underglaze-blue borders very often, as in this case, bear the Caughley factory's 'S' initial mark.*

The typical small groupings of flowers and fruit are seen to better advantage on the 'S'-marked Caughley lobed-edged plate shown in Colour Plate III. The blue border is underglaze, added at the Caughley factory. The centre panel shows well the continuation of the style of painting favoured at the Dr Wall factory and features exotic birds in a landscape, or 'fancy birds' to use the contemporary description. Indeed the artist who painted this Caughley blank in the Chamberlain studio most probably painted the Dr Wall specimens some years earlier, moving with Chamberlain when the break occurred. It is significant that the porcelains made by the succeeding Flight management did not as a general

---

*Other examples of Chamberlain-decorated Caughley jugs are depicted in my book *Caughley and Worcester Porcelains, 1775–1800* (1969) in Plates 67–71, which show wares painted with views of Worcester, exotic birds, animal subjects and royal emblems.

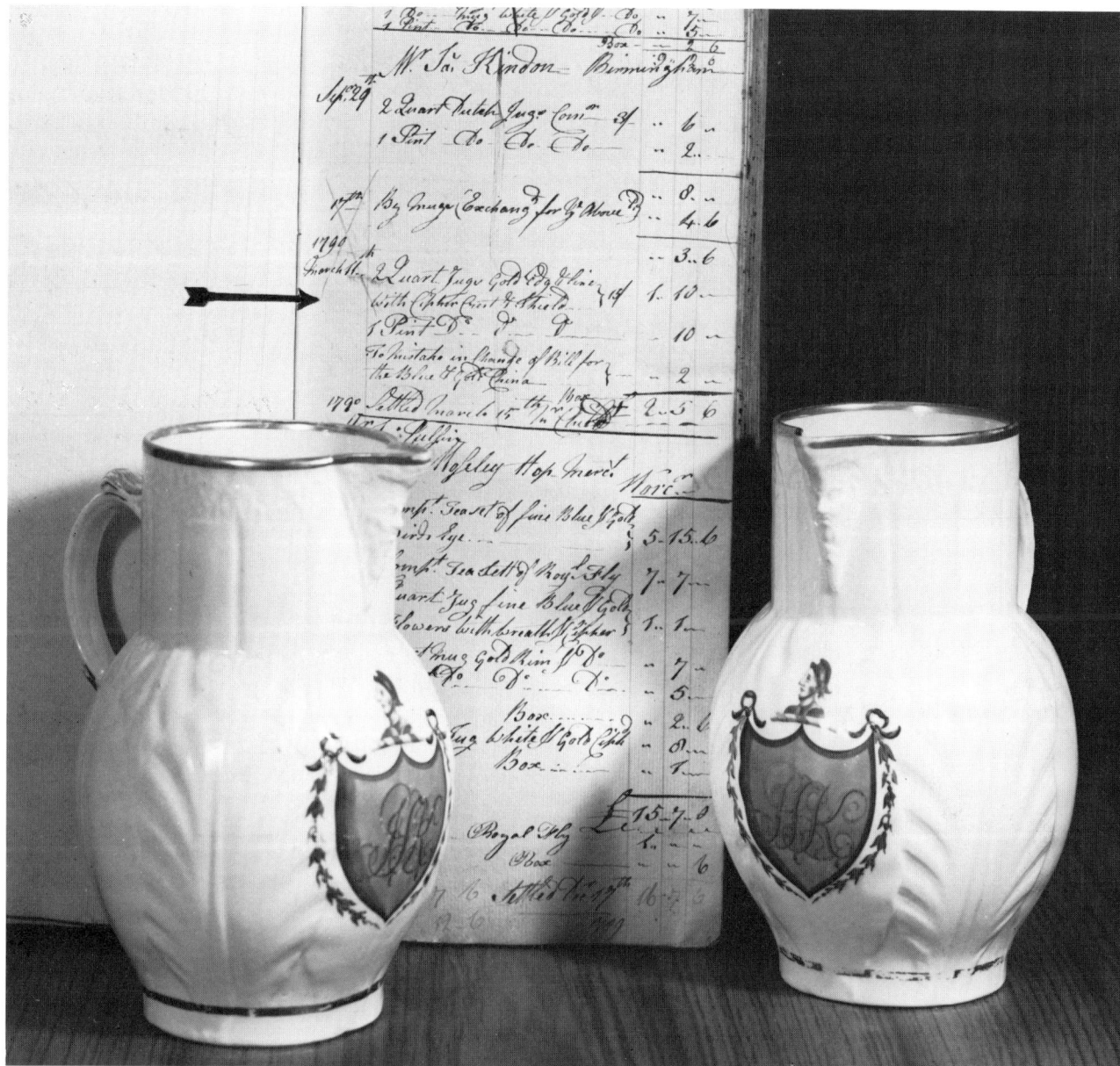

18.   A pair of Caughley quart-size jugs decorated to a special order for James Kindon of Birmingham and invoiced in March 1790 at 15s. each. The relevant page from the Chamberlain records is shown behind the jugs. Unmarked. 7½ in. high. 1790. *Photograph: Dyson Perrins Museum, Worcester. One jug: Godden Reference Collection*

rule continue the colourful old Worcester designs: maybe this was because Chamberlain had taken all the best painters away with him.

The painter of this plate was almost certainly George Davis, a key man in the Chamberlain concern, and the original accounts abound with references to fine pieces decorated with 'Davis's birds' (see pages 193–4). A very fine Caughley 'Dutch' or cabbage-leaf jug is shown in Plate 21; here again one sees the Davis birds and the fruit painting at the side of the jug. The decoration on

the neck is also typical of the Chamberlain-decorated pieces, at least of the richer types. Further information on this artist is given on page 192, but it is interesting to note here descriptions in the factory pattern book such as that under pattern 81, 'Davis's birds with fruit & flowers in festoons, blue & gold border', a description that fits well the example shown in Colour Plate III, as well as pieces such as the jug shown in Plate 21 and indeed the earlier Worcester pieces of the type illustrated in Colour Plate II.

19. *Above left:* A Caughley mask-head jug, gilded at the Chamberlain studio in Worcester; perhaps the 'Quart jug, gold sprigs, cyphered B' which was invoiced in June 1792 at 9s. Unmarked. 7½ in. high. 1792. *Godden Reference Collection*

20. *Above:* An 'S'-marked Caughley mask-head jug of the type supplied to the Chamberlains with underglaze-blue top and bottom borders at 3s. This was enamelled at Worcester to a special order, and the blue enamel in conjunction with the gilding is very typical. 8½ in. high. *c.* 1790. *Godden Reference Collection*

21. *Left:* A Caughley quart-size mask-head jug decorated with birds, fruit and flower subjects at the Chamberlain studio in Worcester, most probably by George Davis, who is associated with earlier Worcester porcelain (see Plates 2, 4, Colour Plate III and page 192). Unmarked. 7½ in. high. *c.* 1788–90. *Godden Reference Collection*

The 'S'-marked Caughley plate shown in Plate 22 with its underglaze-blue border is a most interesting example showing the fine quality of the Chamberlain gilding and classical-figure painting attained by the beginning of 1791. This dating is based on the original entry made in the records on 15 January 1791:

Sent with Mr. Turner to London as pattern . . .

1 Table plate with devices of 2 nymphs adorning Satyr,
    blue and gold festoon [border], 1s. 9d.   £1 5s. 0d.

The Mr Turner referred to is most probably Thomas Turner of the Caughley factory, as the basic cost of his own blank plate, 1s. 9d., is included in the record.

Presumably he called on the Chamberlains on his way from Caughley to his London warehouse in Portugal Street, which opened in 1783 as The Salopian China Warehouse. Turner no doubt took away with him various sample pieces to sell in London. This plate is certainly of London quality, perhaps made to rival the Pennington-decorated Flight-Worcester porcelains (see page 24).

The dessert dish shown in Plate 23 and other parts of the service shown in Plate 24 are highly interesting. The

22. *Right:* An 'S'-marked Caughley plate with underglaze-blue border, decorated at the Chamberlain studio. The factory records list this plate in January 1791 as being 'sent with Mr. Turner to London as pattern'. The design is after an original by Angelica Kauffman. Diameter 9½ in. *c.* 1790. *Godden Reference Collection*

23. *Below:* A Caughley porcelain dessert service dish, made for the Marquess of Donegal, decorated by the Chamberlains at Worcester. Note the classical figures in the border panels and the blue enamel flowers in conjunction with the gilt leafage. This was part of a special service invoiced in September 1793. Painted mark 'CHAMBERLAINS' (see page 32). 10½ × 7¼ in. *c.* 1793. *Godden Reference Collection*

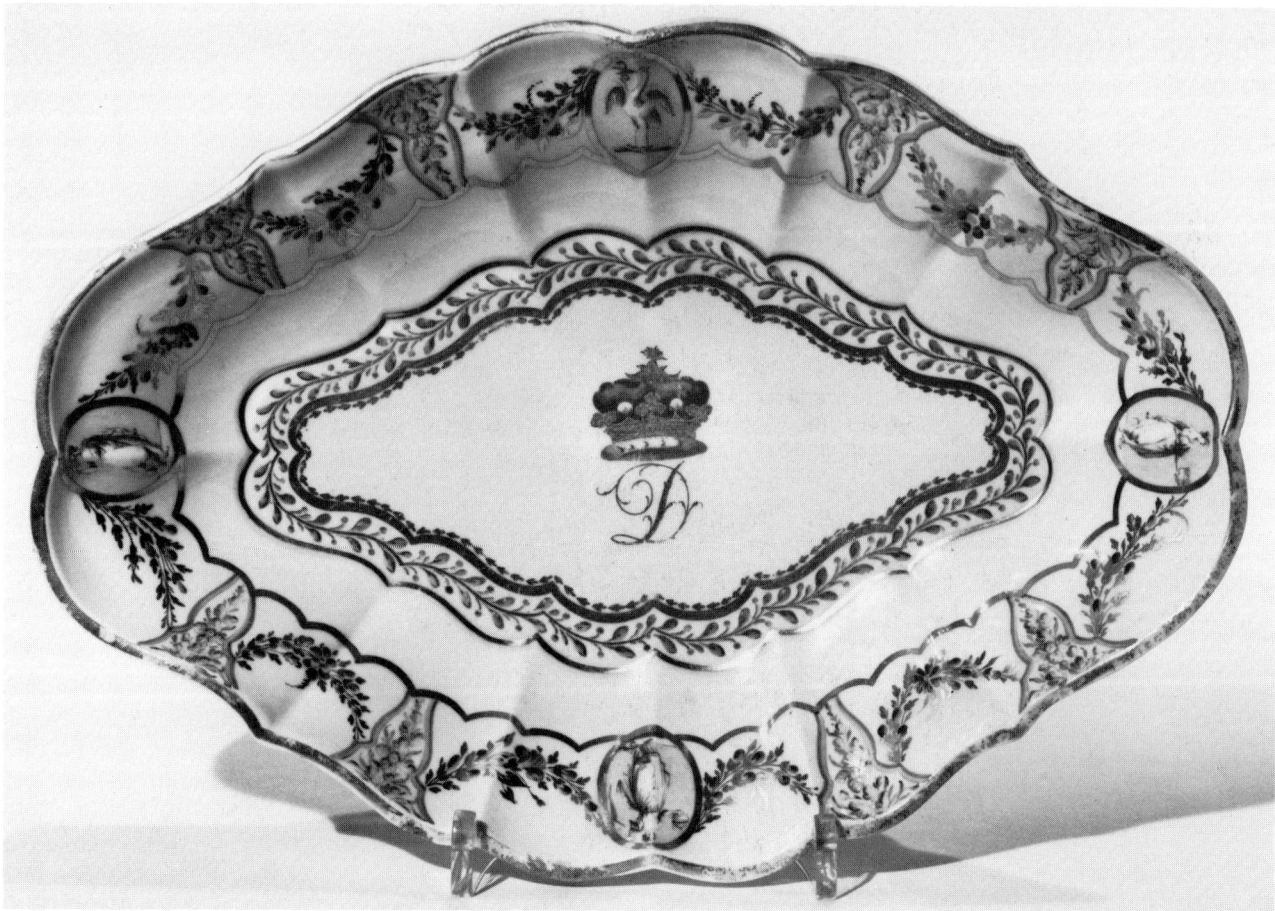

24. Representative pieces of the Caughley dessert service decorated by the Chamberlains and invoiced in September 1793. A single dish from this service is shown in Plate 23. Note the different 'harlequin' border designs. *Messrs Phillips*

large service is in the nature of a 'harlequin' set as the borders are of differing designs – even on the two ice-pails. The constant features – the initial 'D' under a coronet, and the crest in the top border reserve – show that these pieces were made for the Marquess of Donegal and as such they link with an entry in the Chamberlain archives under the date 18 September 1793:

Sold Rt. Hon[ble]. Lord & Marquess Donnegall.

		£	s.	d.
60	dessert plates 3rd [size] Ch.[y] make all different designs, letters D and coronet at 25s.	75	0	0
2	centre dishes do.	8	8	0
8	sugar tureens & covers			
8	stands to do.	21	0	0
8	spoons to do.			
4	ice pails, pans & covers	25	4	0
2	oval scollop dishes [as in Plate 23]	4	4	0
4	mellons [dishes] 2nd size	10	10	0
8	do. 1st size	16	16	0
4	square dishes	16	16	0
8	heart shape [dishes]	16	16	0
8	Shells do.	16	16	0

All the pieces illustrated in Plates 23 and 24 are of Caughley porcelain although the decoration was added in the Chamberlain studio at Worcester. Two of them – the dish shown in Plate 23 and the largest dish in the group pose – bear the very rare painted 'CHAMBERLAIN' mark in red capital letters.

The festoons of flowers linking the border panels show again the use of a bright-blue enamel in conjunction with the gold. The gilt initial is also very delicately picked out in black enamel, a feature which occurs on other initialled Chamberlain-decorated Caughley wares, including the jugs shown in Plates 18 and 19.

In addition to the Caughley pieces shown here, a stand for the centre-dish was made, and this is of Chamberlain's own make although it is not listed in the September 1793 invoice. It would seem that at the period when this considerable order was placed the Chamberlains were not capable of making such a large dessert set in their own porcelain.

As mentioned at the beginning of this chapter, the Chamberlains also decorated and sold large amounts of

Caughley tewares. Up to 1793 one of the most favoured shapes was that known as 'new fluted', which comprised vertical, convex fluting. These 'new fluted' tewares often bore underglaze-blue borders and other features applied at the Caughley factory, the design being completed with gilding at Worcester. Other 'new fluted' blanks were entirely decorated by the Chamberlain hands. One such design which is conveniently easy to identify was called 'L'Amitié' or 'Doves'. An early, perhaps the first, possible reference to this design appears in the Chamberlain records under the date 15 January 1791: 'Sent with Mr. Turner to London as patterns – 1 cup and saucer – blue & gold sprigs and border with Amitie'.

In January 1791, therefore, this was apparently a new design and subsequently many such complete sets were sold at £6 6s. 0d. The first version of this design with the rather fancy blue and gold outer border, and the wreath-like border around the central panel, is illustrated in Plate 25 where typical forms of the period are shown. A simpler, more pleasing version without the fancy outer border was introduced by at least November 1792 when the Chamberlains included in patterns sent to Amsterdam, a cup and saucer – 'new fluted Doves, new wreath'; but within four months the same design was being sent out on a new Caughley shape, known variously as 'shankered' or 'shanked':

Pattern sent to Mr. Miller, Redditch.

A cup and saucer, shanked, Doves new wreath at £6 6s. 0d. the set.

[5 March 1793]

These new shanked wares represent the last Caughley-made tewares to be ordered and used by the Chamberlains before their own porcelains completely obviated the need to purchase blanks from Thomas Turner. These little-known Caughley porcelains of the early 1790s are of great interest especially in the cases, described below, where they bear patterns added by the Chamberlains at Worcester.

The basic feature of the shanked tewares was the spiral fluting, not straight as formerly. These new-fashioned wares were introduced at the Flight factory at Worcester by at least July 1790, at which time Chamberlain sent to Thomas Turner '1 complete sett, Worcr. new shankered'. Turner soon made his own versions, as did the Chamberlains when they commenced the manufacture of their own porcelains. The descriptive word 'shankered' is in fact mentioned in a Chamberlain letter dated August 1789 (see page 40).

Plate 26 illustrates a spoontray of Caughley porcelain,

25. Representative pieces from a Caughley 'new fluted' teaset, decorated by the Chamberlains at Worcester with a version of the 'Doves' or 'L'Amitié' pattern. Unmarked. Tea canister 4½ in. high. c. 1791. *Godden of Worthing Ltd*

which would have formed part of a 6-guinea service painted by the Chamberlain decorators and sold in 1793. At a later period this pattern was applied to the Chamberlains' own porcelains. A related type of pattern, but rather more expensive with a central panel of a coloured landscape replacing the dove motif, first occurs on Caughley porcelain of the early 1790s. The plain, unfluted plate shown in Plate 27 displays the pattern to advantage and this centre panel may well depict a local view of the River Severn.

This basic teware pattern soon appeared on the new shanked or spiral-fluted shapes, as is evidenced by an account dated 28 November 1792 relating to samples sent to a dealer in Amsterdam: 'cups and saucers sent as patterns, new shanked Landscape pattern, £8 8s. 0d. the set'.

In Plate 28 a good selection of these pieces is illustrated – the shaped, oval spoontray (of a form seemingly unique to Caughley), the covered sugar basin,

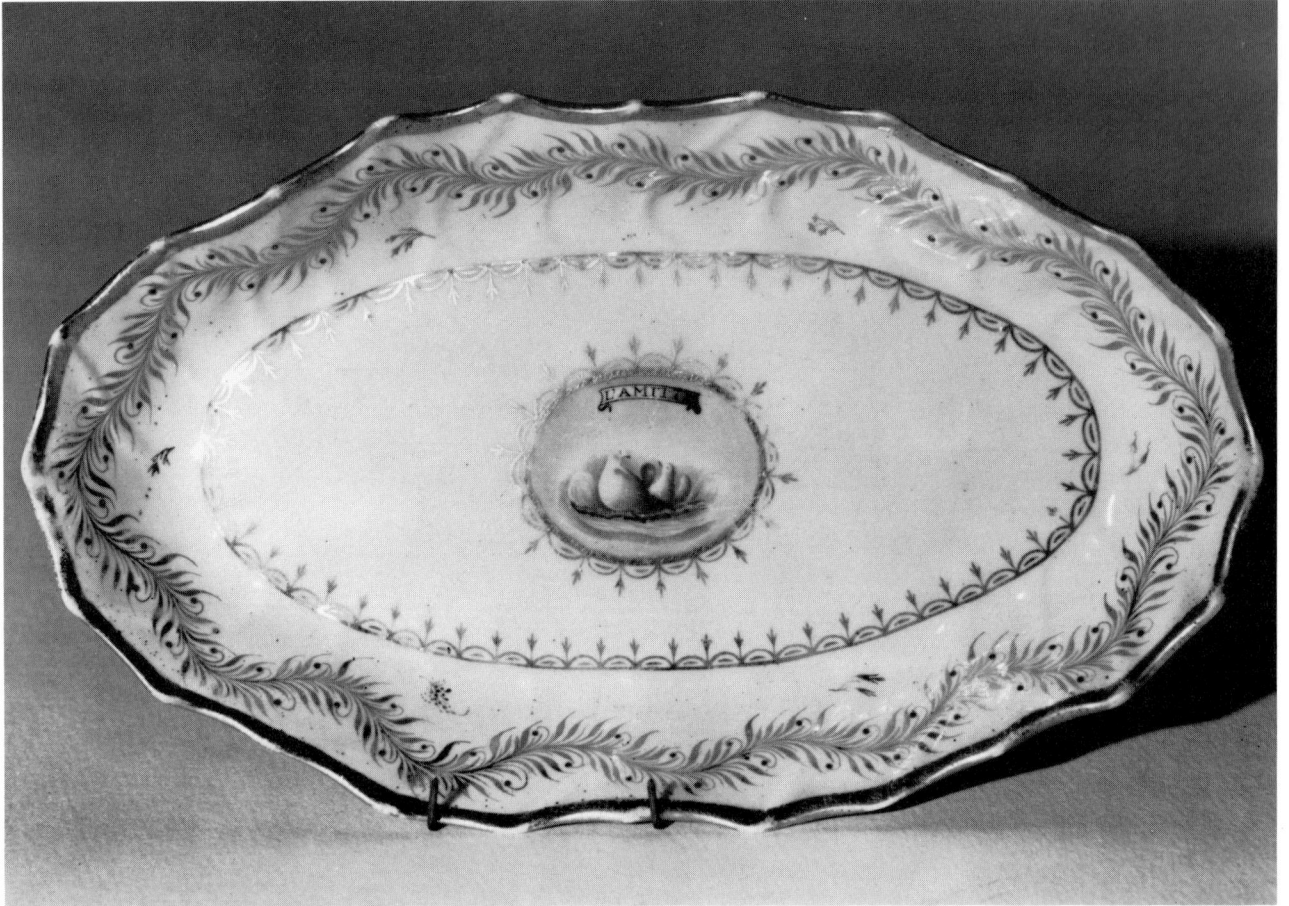

26.   A rare Caughley shanked spoontray decorated by the Chamberlains with a 'new wreath' version of the 'Doves' or 'L'Amitié' pattern. Unmarked. 6¾ in. long. *c.* 1793. *Godden Reference Collection*

27.   A Caughley porcelain bread plate from a tea service decorated at the Chamberlain studio with a landscape pattern. The borders are similar to those of the 'Doves' pattern (see Plate 25). Unmarked. Diameter 8¼ in. *c.* 1791. *Loaned to Clive House Museum, Shrewsbury*

very similar to the Flight version (see Plate 31), the creamer (again seemingly unique to Caughley) and the spiral-fluted teabowl and saucer. The teapot to these sets took the form shown in Plate 29. This simple gilt design shows that inexpensive patterns were applied to these shanked shapes in the 1792–3 period. The Chamberlain records also list teasets at £5 5s. 0d. bearing the little floral sprig motifs, called 'Angoulême' after the French factory which specialized in these sprig designs.

The most interesting example of shanked Caughley teaware has been left to the last. This is the charming tea canister and cover shown in Plate 30. The shape is that referred to in Humphrey Chamberlain's letter to Thomas Turner, dated 12 January 1793 (see page 44),

28. Representative pieces from a Caughley shanked teaset showing Chamberlain's landscape pattern on these new shapes. The complete service was originally sold for £8 8s. 0d. Unmarked. *c.* 1792. *Godden Reference Collection*

when they were in dispute regarding the orders for 'shank'd' canisters. The Chamberlains were then still awaiting thirty white blanks but seventy-six had been received between 31 May and 25 July 1792.

The delicate and extremely talented style of figure painting on this Caughley tea canister and on other pieces from the same tea service does not seem to appear on any other pieces of Caughley porcelain or on any other examples of Chamberlain's own porcelains. Knowledgeable readers may well recognize the style of painting as being extremely similar to signed work by Fidelle Duvivier, a much-travelled ceramic painter who was certainly employed at the Derby factory and at the New Hall factory in Staffordshire. Duvivier wrote to William Duesbury at Derby in November 1790, explaining that his 'engagement in the New Hall manufactory is expired and the proprietors do not intend to do much in the fine line of painting'. Duvivier stated he was taking up a post as a drawing-master but wished to paint porcelain on the spare three days a week. He

29. A Caughley shanked teapot of a rare form, with Chamberlain gilding, shown with a waster knob found on the Caughley factory site. Unmarked. 6 in. high. *c.* 1792. *Godden Reference Collection*

suggested that Duesbury send him Derby porcelain on the weekly wagon to Staffordshire, but not surprisingly Duesbury was not interested in this idea. Duvivier then most probably tried other manufacturers and it seems extremely likely that he worked for a very short period for the Chamberlains at Worcester in October 1792. The reasons for putting forward this new conjecture are given on page 194 in Chapter 6. I deduce that the tea canister shown in Plate 30 was supplied by Thomas Turner between 31 May and 25 July 1792, and that it and the other matching shanked teawares were painted by Fidelle Duvivier in October 1792. Other pieces from this perhaps unique service are illustrated in Plates 238–41.

Whilst reviewing these shanked Caughley teawares of the early 1790s, it is relevant to show how closely they followed the Flight-Worcester shapes of the same period. Plate 31 shows a typical Flight covered sugar

30.   *Left:* A Caughley shanked tea canister from a teaset decorated at the Chamberlain studio in October 1792. Other pieces from this perhaps unique set are shown in Plates 238–41. The painting is attributed to Fidelle Duvivier (see page 196). Unmarked. 5 in. high. 1792. *Godden Reference Collection*

31.   *Below:* A Flight-Worcester (left) and Caughley (right) shanked sugar bowl and cover shown together to illustrate the very similar forms favoured by both these contemporary firms. Unmarked. 5 in. high. *c.* 1792. *Godden Reference Collection*

bowl with the Caughley example on the right. The latter is identified by the discovery of matching wasters on the site, including this knob form which differs slightly from the Flight knob. Also, the Caughley porcelain and glaze is harder and appears slightly more greenish – but still the similarity between the two pieces is remarkable.*

These Caughley shanked tewares represent the last association between Turner and the Chamberlains since, as suggested on page 45, there was a break in their business relationship in November 1793. Chamberlain's own porcelains were taking over and the old forms were being superseded by the new oval teapots – which were to hold sway for the next thirty or so years. The Chamberlains' stocktaking lists of June 1792 included oval tewares, and an account of May 1793 lists '1 large oval teapot new model. 10s.'.

The Worcester *Royal Directory* of 1794, probably prepared in 1793, includes the following mention of the 'Chamberlain & Sons' works:

The Porcelain Manufactory situate near Diglis, where the china – honoured with the approbation of their Majesties – was finished; since which time a considerable improvement has taken place, and a number of hands employed in forming articles upon the Oriental principles of transparency and strength.

This directory also listed the Chamberlain 'China Warehouse' in High Street. Before discussing Chamberlain's own porcelains in the next chapter, it is interesting to return to this retail shop in High Street, Worcester, to see with the help of the old accounts the types of articles that he stocked and which made the 'flaming shew' remarked upon by his rival, John Flight.

The fact that the Chamberlains added gilding to glasswares sent down by the Stourbridge manufacturers has been already mentioned on page 42. The order books also show that they decorated and sold elegant glass in their own shop. Extracts from some of these original orders are quoted below:

Rev. Mr. Faulker.
1 Pair of blue glass decanters, vine border.
Cyphered W.F., Brandy & Rum in full.
[July 1791]
Mr. Thulfall [?] Chorley, Lancs.
A elegant set of blue glass ornaments richly gilt with white pedestals and figures between.
[September 1791]

12 Blue glass finger cups [bowls] with crests and motto in gold. £3 12s. 0d.
[June 1793]
4 pint decanters, Brandy, Rum, Hollands, Shrub, cypher ASG with the crest of Gordon.
[March 1795]
2 Quart decanters, Prince's cut, Port & Sherry. £1 16s. 0d.
2 do. stands, paper. 7s.
[August 1797]

Chamberlain's High Street shop also stocked a good assortment of decorative trays in tôle (tinned metal) and in papier mâché. These goods were purchased from Birmingham, mainly from Frances Byrne 'Japanner', who supplied both metal and paper goods – a fact that shows up the high cost of good papier mâché, for trays, identical in size and pattern, are listed at £1 11s. 6d. in paper compared with 16s. for the same article in decorated iron. Another supplier was John Waring of Birmingham.

The Chamberlains also stocked the decorative and fashionable Derbyshire Spar, or Blue John, ornaments. One order book entry for 26 September 1794 reads: 'Mrs Sayer, Richmond, Surrey. 1 Sett ornaments, Derbyshire spar'. Derby porcelain was apparently stocked as well, if the following descriptions actually relate to the place of manufacture rather than to the shape of the article, although the description 'Derby make' as used in the Chamberlain records does seem to have different meanings at different times – it is now a matter of interpretation.

George Hardinge, Esq., M.P.	£	s.	d.
1 Chocolate [cup] Derby make, Royal Stripe	1	11	6
2 do. do. fawn & gold brown flowers	2	2	0
[September 1794]			

Mr George Stokes.
1 Sett of Derby ornaments with the cup
centre £4 4s. 0d.
[December 1794]

The shop also sold a wide range of decorative figures and groups as well as animal models. The source of these is open to doubt; it would seem that most of them were of Derby porcelain, especially as many were listed in the Chamberlain records as 'biscuit' (unglazed) and the production of such unglazed white figures and groups was the speciality of the Derby factory, but I have been unable to discover any reference to the direct purchase of these figures from the Derby factory in the eighteenth century.

There is, however, evidence that figures and groups

were sent down from Caughley with the standard Caughley useful wares. For example, as early as 1789 a list appears under the heading 'Goods received from Thos. Turner Esq. Caughley':

	s.	d.
A group of Shepherd & Shepherdess &c.	[not priced]	
1 pair of biscuit single figures at	18	6
1 group do.	15	0
2 pairs of figures, damaged	15	0
17 pairs of fancy figures white [with?] a child at	5	0

In February 1791 the Chamberlain order book especially reveals the need for enamelled figures: 'Wanted for the manufactory a few enamelled figures & doggs of all sorts immediately'; and later in the year references to many figure and animal models appear in the Chamberlain-Turner account books. They are listed showing separately the cost of the figures and Chamberlain's gilding charge. For example:

	china			gilding		
	£	s.	d.	£	s.	d.
6 single figures, dancing		15	0		6	0
4 single figures, gardners		10	0		4	0
[February 1791]						

	£	s.	d.	£	s.	d.
10 pair single figures, enamelled	2	10	0	1	0	0
7 double figures do.	1	8	0		8	2
8 women with a child do.	1	0	0		8	0
14 men with a child do.	1	15	0		14	0
2 Greyhounds, killing a hare		3	0		1	6
40 pointer dogs, enamelled	1	10	0	1	0	0
3 French Tarriers, enamelled		2	3		1	6
[March, April and May 1791]						

This Chamberlain gilding of enamelled figures is very puzzling. If, as seems likely to the author, these figures came ready-enamelled from the Derby factory to Turner at Caughley as a middleman or wholesaler, why were they not gilded at the Derby factory? If they were of Turner's own manufacture it is easier to better understand that they were sent to Chamberlain to be gilded, as were Turner's useful wares. I should here mention that a piece of a biscuit (unglazed) female figure or group was found by me on the Caughley factory site and has recently been analysed. It is of a body quite unlike the standard Derby paste of the 1790s for it shows only the merest trace of phosphoric acid, proving it is not a bone-ash porcelain. The fragment from the Caughley factory site has been shown to be of a hybrid hard-paste porcelain, extremely similar in make-up to the later Caughley-Coalport porcelains. This one figure

fragment, at least, appears to be of Shropshire origin.

Could some, or all, of the figures sent from Caughley to the Chamberlains in Worcester have been of Thomas Turner's own manufacture? A perhaps significant fact is that in all the Chamberlain references to these figures, no reference or model number is quoted, all are described in words. The Derby models, however, did bear numbers and it would seem easier to have quoted these references if they related: for example, '10 figures number 101'. On the other hand, several of the described models do seem to match known Derby models, although if Turner was producing figures at Caughley he may well have made copies of popular Derby models.

Some Chamberlain records relating to these figures sold from (or stocked at) their retail shop in Worcester are quoted below. It may well prove possible to trace some of these enamelled and gilt models or to find white unglazed examples of a more compact, harder body than the normal Derby examples.

	s.	d.
1 pair of large gilt figures	18	0
[October 1790]		

	s.	d.
2 Turks, white	1	0
1 Group of figures, large white	14	0
1 double biscuit figure	15	0
[June 1792 stocklist]		

	s.	d.
1 group biscuit figures	12	0
1 do. enamelled	7	6
1 group Fortune Tellers	10	0
[December 1793 stocklist]		

	s.	d.
1 figure white and gold	6	0
[August 1794]		

The Chamberlain records continue to document figures and groups into the nineteenth century, after Turner had sold his factory in 1799 to the partners in the Coalport firm. Figures described as '1 bisquit round ornament 2, lovers' (entry in June 1801), or '1 Figure Falstaff, enamelled £1 18s. 0d.' (December 1813) are almost certainly of Derby origin, but it was not until February 1818, when the London shop in Bond Street was purchasing stock, that a definite reference to the source of the white biscuit figures is found: 'By package of Derby biscuit figures 2s.' – but then they could not have been purchased from the now defunct Caughley factory and the Chamberlains were purchasing stock from all and sundry, including Spode, the Swansea factory and the suppliers of imported French porcelains.

In contrast to such fine porcelains, the Chamberlains also sold Staffordshire earthenwares, purchased from Messrs Daniel & Brown of Hanley. These included blue-printed dinnerwares, the pattern being described as 'Bridge & Temple', and cream-coloured earthenwares. The blue-printed Staffordshire earthenwares replaced the Caughley porcelain sets after the break between Turner and the Chamberlains; indeed the 'Bridge & Temple' pattern is the same as Turner's 'Full Nankin' blue-printed design.

The Chamberlain order book for the 1789–91 period includes at the front the firm's pricing (or costing) code, made up of eleven letters (each representing a figure) forming the words 'GIVE THY CORN'. The pounds were expressed in capitals, the shillings in cursive script and the pence in lower-case letters, so that £5 6s. 8d. would, for example, be written 'T. *H*. c.'. It could well be that some papier mâché or other articles sold at the Chamberlains' retail shop may have such price letters scratched or otherwise marked on them.

This chapter has mainly been concerned with the Chamberlains' trade as decorators of white, or partly-finished, Caughley blanks. When the Chamberlains commenced to make their own porcelains in the 1790s, however, they in turn started to supply white wares to other manufacturers or decorators, although this trade was very small in comparison with that enjoyed by John Rose's Coalport firm. This fact, coupled with the remark 'To be sent at Roses prices' (see page 81), suggests that in general the Chamberlains' prices for white blanks were higher than the Coalport prices.

In 1796 and 1797 large quantities of white Chamberlain porcelains – mainly tearwares – were sent to the London 'chinaman', William Hewson, of 86 Aldgate. Hewson may have had his own decorating staff or alternatively he may have resold the white goods to other London decorators or gilders (see page 104).

In May 1797 Thomas Baxter, the well-known London decorator (see page 184), ordered a white Chamberlain teaset for which he was charged £1 14s. 2d., but apparently this did not suit his requirements and no further orders were placed with the Chamberlains, the Baxters (father and son) subsequently using Coalport blanks as well as lesser quantities of French and Oriental porcelain.

William Billingsley, the famous ceramic artist (see page 101), also placed one order for Chamberlain blanks in July 1799 when he was at Belvedere Street, Mansfield, practising as an independent decorator. The order was not, however, repeated and Billingsley seems to have turned to Staffordshire for his blanks.

Finally, in the nineteenth century the Chamberlains supplied white blanks for amateur painters to work upon (see page 182).

3

CHAMBERLAIN'S PRE-1800 PORCELAINS

It would appear that the production of Chamberlain's own porcelain was on a comparatively small scale for the first few years, and his accounts show clearly that he continued to receive quantities of Turner's Caughley porcelain – mainly teawares – up to the autumn of 1793. It would also seem that the earliest of Chamberlain's porcelain was not marked with his name, for certain early pieces showing typical Chamberlain characteristics, or pieces which appear to link with the contemporary records, do not bear a factory mark. This again is a continuation of earlier practice, for the Caughley porcelains decorated by the Chamberlains do not bear their name mark either, except in the case of the dish shown in Plate 23.

It is necessary in discussing Chamberlain porcelain to examine more closely its characteristics, for it is quite different in make-up from the other contemporary Worcester porcelain and from the Caughley body which was, in both cases, a 'soap-stone' porcelain containing a relatively high proportion of magnesia. A Chamberlain cup of early pattern 55, from the teaset illustrated in Plate 73, was analysed at the Ceramic Testing Laboratory at the North Staffordshire College of Technology in Stoke-on-Trent, with the following results:

	%
Silica (SiO_2)	68.61
Alumina (Al_2O_3)	23.52
Potash (k_2O)	3.61
Soda (Na_2O)	1.27
Lime (CaO)	1.14
Ferric Oxide (Fe_2O_3)	0.34
Magnesia (MgO)	0.16
Titanic Oxide (TiO_2)	0.02
Loss (calcined at 950°C)	0.34
	———
	99.01

The interesting points to note are the high percentage of alumina and the small amount of magnesia (Flight period Worcester porcelain and Caughley wares of the 1790s contained, in contrast, approximately 7 per cent alumina and at least 6 per cent magnesia). In fact the chemical make-up of the early Chamberlain porcelain was very much like the hard-paste New Hall porcelain of the same period, a fact remarked on by Herbert Eccles and Bernard Rackham in their booklet *Analysed Specimens of English Porcelain* (1922). This unexpected discovery led these authors to wonder if the marked example they tested (a 'Dragon' pattern plate, see page 96) was in fact made at Worcester, and they suggested that the specimen might have been a New Hall plate decorated by the Chamberlains. It was, however, a typical example of Chamberlain porcelain of the 1790–1800 period, and modern tests carried out at the British Museum (on a cup from a marked Chamberlain-Worcester tea service of pattern 178) have confirmed that the early Chamberlain porcelain is technically of the hard-paste variety. Indeed in firing tests carried out at the Worcester factory, the earlier Chamberlain body successfully withstood a higher temperature than New Hall porcelain.

The inventory made in, or dated, 1796 includes all the raw materials used in the Chamberlain porcelain mix. The 'manufactory yard' for example contained:

	£	s.	d.
1 cask ground flint, valued at	3	3	0
14 casks china clay do. do.	13	13	0
64 tons stone do. do.	224	0	0
8 Tons Beandon Hill stone do.	4	0	0
Flint & pebbles	3	0	0
1 cask bone ash		10	6
6 tons saggar clay	5	2	0
12 tons coal	9	0	0

There appears to be no mention of soap-rock being in stock at this period. The '64 tons stone' valued at £224, or £3 10s. 0d. per ton, would have been china stone from Cornwall, so that in 1796 the factory held stocks of the main constituents of true porcelain – china clay (kaolin) and china stone (the petuntse of the Chinese potters).

Other raw materials were mentioned in the inventory under different headings. The 'Coach House' was apparently partly used as a store as it held a further fifty-four casks of china clay valued at £56 14s. 0d., as well as a cask of plaster (£1 15s. 0d.) and 4 cwt of fine glass (£6). The 'Slip House' contained 5 tons of sifted china clay (£30) and ½ cwt of lead for the glaze (8s. 4d.). The 'Saggar House' contained 2 cwt of pounded flint, probably for placing in the bottom of the saggar for use as a parting material so that the fired objects did not stick to the bottom of it.

The factory accounts show the sources of most of the raw materials and examples of typical entries follow:

To John Warwick, St. Austle, Cornwall.
For 150 casks of clay at 26s. per cask.
For 10 Ton of [china] Stone at 30s. per ton.
    To be delivered at Bristol.
[For transportation up the River Severn to Worcester.]
    [October 1796]

John Dickins, Plymouth.
For 49 casks of Cornish Clay at 26s. per cask.
Sent Nov. 2nd 97. £63 14s. 0d.
Paid expenses for the ship going to Chepstow £2 9s. 0d.
    [June 1796]

To Palmer & Wright, Shelton, Staffordshire.
For 4 lbs blue to manufactory 21st June [1796] £8 0s. 0d.

Coal came from various sources, sometimes from the Coalport (or Caughley) district:

To William Yates, Madely, Shropshire.
For 33 ton 10 cwt of Coalport Coals at 13s. £21 15s. 6d.
    [December 1797]

The previous reference to the early Chamberlain body appearing extremely hard and to the fact that it was mistaken for New Hall porcelain has additional interest when it becomes obvious from the accounts that apart from purchasing clay (or rather china clay and china stone) from Cornish sources, the Chamberlain management in 1797 purchased 'composition' from Staffordshire:

Valentine Close, Hanley.
For 2 casks for Composition. October 7th, 1797. 19 cwt at 6s.
For do. November 10th, 1797. 25 cwt 3 qts at 6s. £13 8s. 6d.
4 casks and cooperage 17s.
    [November 1797]

It is not certain now what was meant by 'composition', but it was presumably a prepared mix of tried and known quantities and quite expensive at 6s. per cwt compared with the 1s. 6d. per cwt for Cornish china stone. It was also twice as dear as the Cornish clay.

The only other known use of the description 'composition' in the ceramics industry occurs in connection with the New Hall partners' monopoly on the use of hard-paste raw materials up to 1796. Llewellynn Jewitt and other writers have stated that this company sold 'composition' to other potters – 'the most extensive and profitable branch of the New Hall business was the making and vending of the glaze called "Composition", made according to Champion's specification . . .'. However, many problems exist, for a glaze has to be matched to a body and the Chamberlains' purchase of over 2 tons of 'composition' in October and November 1797 implies that (in this case) it was not a glaze. The quantity suggests a ceramic mix perhaps on trial or to be added to their own porcelain body.

Having mentioned the January 1796 inventory, it is interesting to list the various buildings which made up the Chamberlain factory at this period. These are listed here in the order they were originally mentioned as it is probable that this represents a natural progression as one toured the works.

Buiscuit Room,
    [containing the unglazed, once-fired wares]
Painting Room,
Small Burnishing Room,
Burnt ware room,
Enamel kiln,
Burnishing Room,
Glazed warehouse,
Shop backroom,
Shop and room over
Damaged ware room,
Old Burnishing Room,
Coach House,
Manufactory Yard,
Slip House,
Sagger House,
Potters Room,
    [containing the moulds, models, etc., valued at £200]
Biscuit Kiln Stove,
    [containing 2,000 saggars and thousands of straightening rings]
Glazed Kiln Stove,
Enamel Kiln,
Gold Shop,
    [containing muffles, a Dutch oven and air furnace]
Old Burnishing Shop.

The total value given in this 1796 inventory was £4,013 10s. 8d.

The record indicates a rather small output from the Chamberlain factory in the 1796 period, judging from the value put on the monthly record, 'To the manufactory. For Goods received this month', since this recorded value averaged well under £300 per month or about £65 worth per week.

The factory archives which have been so fortunately preserved by succeeding owners of the Worcester factory again assist with the identification of the early Chamberlain porcelains. However, the position is not absolutely clear, because for a period of two to three years from 1791 both Caughley and Chamberlain's own porcelains are listed in the accounts and it is not always apparent to present-day readers which make is listed. One reliable source of information is some of the inventories, for while the completed articles could be either Caughley or Chamberlain, the uncompleted or unglazed biscuit pieces are clearly of Chamberlain's own manufacture. Some earlier stocktaking inventories or lists are mainly unhelpful in identifying the wares: entries such as '1 Kiln white ware, glazed £21', written on 23 December 1793, serve only to show that a glost-kiln of newly-glazed ware had just been, or was about to be fired. However, some indication is given of the early products, as the goods listed below are unglazed and therefore of Chamberlain's own make.

		£	s.	d.
230	dozen pressed and plain coffee [cups], in biscuit	23	0	0
80	half-pint mugs, in biscuit		13	4
40	teapots sorted, in biscuit		6	8
50	[teapot] stands & [spoon] trays, in biscuit		8	4
160	sugar boxes in biscuit	1	6	0
100	ewers, fluted & shanked do.		16	8
70	dozen ewers, sorted do.	7	0	0
20	goblets do.		3	4
100	plates, sugar boxes & basins do.		16	8
13	dozen quarter-pint mugs & egg stands do.	1	6	0
7	dozen tea & coffee pots, toys do.		14	0
117	dozen toy teas [cups] do.	5	17	0
400	dozen teas toys do.	10	0	0
44	teapots, shanked & fluted do.		7	4
8	Bell [pulls] fine blue do.		6	0

The description 'shanked' refers to spiral-fluted wares of the type shown in Plates 70–75. The use of the word 'sorted' after '40 teapots' shows that different shapes or sizes were in stock.

An idea of some of the later productions is contained in the inventory which was made in January 1796. The count was in dozens and the price given in parenthesis is that per dozen, and these amounts give a good comparative indication of the prices for different-size articles of the same type. It must be remembered that these prices are for unglazed, unfinished specimens, not for decorated articles.

Other sections of this inventory mainly list finished, or at least glazed, articles which cannot now be proved to have been made by the Chamberlains, although it is likely that they were. The contents of the 'Burnishing Room', the 'Small Burnishing Room', the 'Old Burnishing Room', the 'Glazed warehouse', the 'Painting Room', the 'Burnt ware room', an 'Enamel Kiln', the 'Coach House' and the 'Yard' are all shown. The contents of the retail shop in the High Street are also listed and details are given on page 92.

In the inventory of the 'Buiscuit Room', containing unglazed, or glazed but unfinished wares, there was a particularly interesting item: '1 Figure Apollo'. This links with an entry in the 'Burnt ware room' – '1 Pickle stand glazed 10s. 6d.' – for in the stocktaking list for Christmas 1795, that is, a few days before the date on the 1796 inventory, there is a slightly more detailed entry for the contents of the 'Burnt ware room', namely: '1 Pickle stand, Apollo, Glazed 10s. 6d.' (a finished example was sold to the dealer Michael Loveley, of Honiton, in November 1797, when it was listed as '1 Rich, 4 shell pickle stand with figure Apollo £3 3s. 0d.').

Such a rare article is illustrated in Plate 32; it is unmarked but displays a body and glaze like that on other Chamberlain porcelains of the mid 1790s and clearly matches the contemporary description. This ambitious specimen, which few collectors would attribute to Chamberlain, was probably modelled by John Toulouse and is in the tradition of similar shell-encrusted stands made at other eighteenth-century factories (see page 209). It is not known if the figure was issued separately as an ornamental figure, or if the '1 Figure Apollo' listed as being in the biscuit room in January 1796 was intended to surmount, and be part of, a shell pickle-stand, such as the one; but it does occur in the form of a Chamberlain watch-stand (see Colour Plate IV and Plate 33). This example, the only one recorded to date, is richly enamelled and gilded, probably in the style of Mr Loveley's 'rich' shell pickle-stand at £3 3s. 0d. This Honiton dealer purchased a large assortment of highly-decorated porcelains from the Chamberlains.

The identification of these two figure-related objects prompts the search for other possible models. Almost certainly the undecorated kingfisher shown in Plate 34 is a Chamberlain-Worcester example of the 1790s as are the two little sheep depicted in Plate 35. Undecorated white sheep and lambs were included in the 1792 Chamberlain stocktaking lists, and later white and gold examples were listed at 2s. per pair. Other factories, like

WORCESTER 1 JANUARY 1796
INVENTORY OF THE STOCK IN TRADE, UTENSILS ETC.
BUISCUIT [*sic*] ROOM.

			s.	d.	£	s.	d.
2 dozen & 3 Teapots	Bell fluted	sorted				no price	
11 sugars	Bell		(16	0)		14	8
11 dozen & 9 Plates	Bell Plain		(12	0)	7	1	0
8 dozen & 6 pint Basons	do.	do.	(12	0)	5	2	0
46 dozen & 6 cups	do.	do.	(8	0)	18	12	0
58 dozen saucers	do.	do.	(5	0)	14	10	0
23 dozen coffee cups	do.	do.	(6	0)	6	18	0
31 dozen & 6 cups 2nd [size]	Bell fluted, handled		(8	0)	14	2	0
4 dozen cups 3rd [size]	do.	do. do.	(10	0)	2	0	0
9 dozen & 6 cups 2nd [size]	do.	do. not handled	(4	0)	1	18	0
26 dozen coffee cups	do.	do. not handled	(6	0)	7	16	0
37 dozen & 6 saucers 1st [size]	do.	do.	(3	6)	6	11	3
40 dozen & 6 saucers 2nd [size]	do.	do.	(4	6)	9	2	8
8 dozen & 6 saucers 3rd [size]	do.	do.	(6	0)	2	11	0
1 dozen & 8 creamers			(12	0)	1	0	0
1 dozen & 11 sugars			(16	0)	1	10	8
4 dozen basins			(12	0)	2	8	0
1 dozen & 6 plates			(12	0)		18	0
67 dozen cups 2nd [size]	Fluted, handled		(5	0)	16	15	0
20 dozen cups 3rd [size]	do.	do.	(6	0)	6	0	0
41 dozen & 6 saucers 3rd [size]	do.	do.	(5	6)	11	8	3
29 dozen & 6 cups 3rd [size]	Fluted, no handles		(5	0)	7	7	6
3 dozen & 6 teapots 4th [size]			(28	0)	4	18	0
3 dozen & 6 teapots 2nd [size]			(16	0)	3	16	0
21 dozen & 6 stands and trays			(8	0)	8	12	0
[These will be teapot-stands and spoontrays, see page 77.]							
16 dozen creamers			(12	0)	9	12	0
10 dozen & 7 sugar boxes Shanked & fluted			(16	0)	8	9	4
1 dozen & 6 coffee pots			(48	0)	3	12	0
33 Tumblers					1	2	0
2 dozen & 6 Muffin Plates & covers			(30	0)	3	15	0
38 Pint mugs					1	18	0
10 dozen Quarter pint mugs			(4	0)	2	0	0
4 dozen half pint mugs			(8	0)	1	12	0
7 Quart mugs			(16	0)		9	4
10 dozen half pint tumblers			(4	0)	2	0	0
5 dozen half pint jugs			(8	0)	2	0	0
5 dozen & 7 pint jugs			(16	0)	4	9	4
2 dozen & 8 Quart jugs			(24	0)	3	4	0
2 dozen three pint jugs			(36	0)	3	12	0
7 two-quart jugs			(48	0)	1	8	0
6 two-quart jugs and covers [see Plate 99]			(54	0)	1	7	0
25 dozen fruit baskets [see Plate 89]			(4	0)	5	0	0
21 dozen stands to do. [see Plate 88]			(2	0)	2	2	0
20 dozen centrepieces, sorted			(5	0)	5	0	0
16 dozen & 9 dessert dishes			(20	0)	16	15	0
3 dozen & 6 dessert plates			(12	0)	2	2	0
7 dozen Table (dinner) plates			(16	0)	4	12	0

			s.	d.	£	s.	d.
2	Table tureens (damaged)				0	0	0
8	dozen & 4 sauce & cream tureens [see Plate 90]	(24	0)		10	0	0
2	dozen & 9 stands to do. [see Plate 90]	(16	0)		2	4	0
2	dozen & 4 spoons	(8	0)			18	8
1	dozen & 2 Fish drainers	(30	0)		1	15	0
3	Table dishes 1st [size]	(2	0)			6	0
11	do. 2nd [size]	(2	6)		1	7	6
11	do. 3rd [size]	(3	6)		1	18	6
9	do. 4th [size]	(4	6)		2	0	6
4	do. 5th [size]	(8	0)		1	12	0
3	dozen & 6 custard cups & covers	(8	0)			16	0
1	dozen & 2 toy baskets	(12	0)			14	0
25	dozen Thimbles	(1	0)		1	5	0
8	dozen ice-pails	(8	0)		3	4	0
3	dozen wine coolers	(8	0)		1	4	0
10	dozen & 7 Large smelling bottles	(8	0)		4	4	8
3	Oil & Vinegar stands	(3	6)			10	6
1	Figure Apollo [see page 60]					2	6
5	Candlesticks					5	0
2	dozen & 10 tobacco-stoppers	(4	0)			11	4
5	dozen ornamental vases	(72	0)		18	0	0
2	dozen ice-pails, mosaic				1	12	0
20	dozen cups – Honeysuckle	(2	0)		2	0	0
32	dozen & 10 egg drainers & cups	(4	0)		6	12	0
5	dozen Asparagus servers	(4	0)		1	0	0
10	Chamber candlesticks	(1	0)			10	0
3	Ink-stands	(5	0)			15	0
1	Muffin plate – Lilley					3	0
	[The underglaze 'Royal Lily' design, see Plate 63.]						
2	wash hand basins					7	0
200	dozen toy teas [cups]	(1	0)		10	0	0
40	dozen toy coffee [cups]	(2	0)		4	0	0
1	dozen toy sugars & milks	(24	0)		1	4	0
1	cask lead				3	3	0

[This cask of lead is a reminder that the articles listed above this entry were in the biscuit room, awaiting glazing.]

MOULD ROOM.

[These articles were presumably in the process of manufacture or drying after being formed in plaster of Paris moulds.]

1	dozen leafage [leaf patterned] goblets [see Plate 38]		12	0
16	dozen low Chelsea-ewers [see Plate 51]	3	4	0
5	dozen small do.	1	0	0
8	dozen stands & trays, shanked & new fluted	3	4	0
18	sugars, shanked & new fluted		18	0
18	teapots 3rd [size]	1	16	0
1	dozen Caudle [cups] & covers	1	16	0

Derby and Lowestoft, made such sheep models but in quite different types of porcelain.

To identify the porcelains made by the Chamberlains between about 1791, when they commenced the manufacture of their own porcelains, and 1796, when the stocktaking lists start to be helpful, only the Chamberlain sales books for the period and the post-1793 marked examples provide information. The following entries are extracted from the factory accounts, orders and stocklists dating from January 1792, but it must be borne in mind that there is no definite proof that these objects were of Chamberlain's

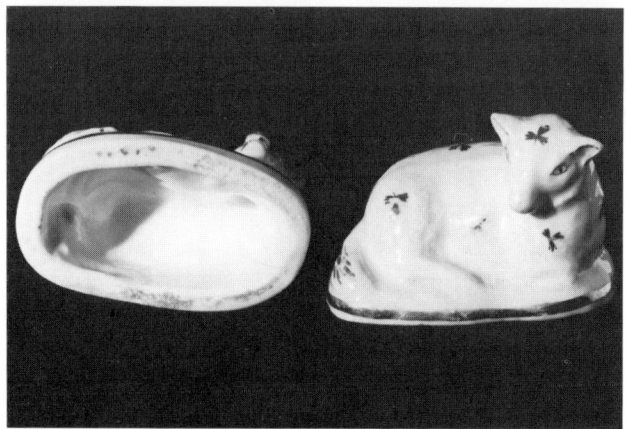

32. *Top left:* A very rare early Chamberlain-Worcester '4-shell pickle stand with figure of Apollo' of the type included in the 1795 stocktaking list. Unmarked. 9 in. high. *c.* 1795. *Godden Reference Collection*

33. *Top right:* The reverse of the rare early Chamberlain-Worcester watch-stand shown in Colour Plate IV. Unmarked. 9 in. high. *c.* 1795. *Godden Reference Collection*

34. *Left:* A rare early Chamberlain-Worcester undecorated model of a kingfisher. Unmarked. 4¾ in. high. *c.* 1795. *Rous Lench Collection*

35. *Above:* Two early Chamberlain-Worcester porcelain sheep after the better-known Derby models. Slightly gilt. Unmarked. 1¾ in. high. *c.* 1795. *Godden Reference Collection*

own manufacture, although this selection of entries, I believe, does relate to Robert Chamberlain's early porcelains.

		£	s.	d.
1	Round Table plate, broad blue border with fine Herculaneum devices, gilt new web border £1 1s. 0d. [February 1792]			
1	Rich enamelled & gilt vase & pedestal £12 12s. 0d. [June 1792]			

		£	s.	d.
1	Pint coffee pot, New fluted, white		3	6
16	Houses, plain white	1	4	0
23	Sheep, plain white		7	8
6	oval teapot stands, white		9	0
12	large Pedestals, embossed, white [see Plate 36]	3	0	0
6	small embossed vases, white		15	0
1	Pint mug Glaze's Map O' the world		10	6
3	Embossed vases & pedestals, birds-eye border & sprigs [Stocklist dated 4 June 1792]	3	0	0

		£	s.	d.
1	Large oval teapot, new model 10s. 0d. [May 1793]			
1	Honey pot, cover & stand, Royal Lily		6	0
1	Complete Toy [tea] set, Davis's flowers		9	0
3	three quart Bowls, rich Muchall's painting	6	6	0
2	jars, 1 beaker, Wood's figures [Stocklist, December 1793]	1	4	0

1 New Shanked coffee-urn, brown & gold sprigs No. 21 £1 [March 1794. Pattern as in Plate 109]

1 Quart coffee pot blue & white, of the Warranted China, as dark as possible [Order dated June 1794]

2 Quart jugs, new make [decorated] JS with the crest and cypher on each side. To have new borders of ermine drapery or something consistent. [Order dated September 1794]

This 'new make' jug was probably of the shape shown in Plate 39.

The May 1793 entry for a 'large oval teapot, new model' is a landmark, showing that by at least this date the oval-form teapot was coming into fashion, replacing the earlier Caughley-type globular pots with their circular plan.

The embossed pedestals, which were sometimes listed with matching vases, were probably of the type seen in Plate 36, which is reminiscent of some Derby designs but of the hard, early Chamberlain body and decorated with gold and blue enamel in the Chamberlain style. The large bowl shown in Plate 37 shows the changing style of decoration coming into favour in the 1790s, with panels of classical figures with a draped border.

From September 1794 some of the entries refer to more ornate styles of decoration, types in the main often associated with post-1800 porcelains. The following entries relate to topographical views, figure subjects and dead game.

		£	s.	d.
7	half pint mugs, sorted, with figures at		7	0
1	Quart mug, with View of Norwich		12	0
1	two-quart bowl with View of Worcester [September 1794]	1	1	0

		£	s.	d.
1	three pint jug [painted] Rivaulx Abbey	1	11	6
1	two Quart jug [painted] Dead Game	1	11	6
1	Pint mug View of Worcester [September 1794]		12	0

		s.	d.
1	set of mugs, with views of Cheltenham – Quart £1. Pint 15s. Half pint 10s.		
1	Pattern Plate with figures (30 guineas a set)	8	0
1	do. (40 guineas a set) [October 1794]	10	0

1 Pair of Goblets, Views of Worcester 10s. 6d. [November 1794]

1 Complete [tea] set, Shanked [pattern] number 48, white & gold. Best white warranted £6 6s. 0d. [December 1794. See Plate 42.]

Estimate of Dessert Service [painted] Birds.

		£	s.	d.
2	ice pails [Perhaps as in Plate 294]	10	10	0
2	tureens	2	16	0
2	stands	1	10	0
2	ladles	1	1	0
1	centre dish	4	4	0
4	mellon [shaped] dishes	7	10	6
4	square dishes	7	10	6
4	shell [shaped] dishes	6	0	0
3	heart [shaped] dishes	4	4	0
24	plates [December 1794]	19	4	0

Plate 38 shows an interesting goblet with relief-moulding to the lower part. This form may be that purchased from the modeller John Toulouse (see page 208) on 4 March 1794 – '2 Goblett moulds 10s.' – for most later goblets were plain and did not necessitate moulds; this spiral-fluted and leaf-moulded shape did need a mould. It is interesting to see, too, that the oval panel is recessed and left unfluted, for painting.

Other objects linking with the original factory records reveal the style of decoration popular in the mid 1790s and some of the shapes then favoured at the factory now that the Chamberlains were producing their own porcelains. For example, the leaf-moulded jug shown in Plate 39 relates to the standard Caughley model (see

36. *Below:* A rare early Chamberlain-Worcester plinth for a vase, typically decorated with blue enamel and gilding. Unmarked. 3¾ in. high. *c.* 1793–5. *Godden Reference Collection*

37. *Bottom:* A Chamberlain-Worcester punch-bowl painted in an early style. Unmarked. Diameter 11¼ in. *c.* 1793–5. *Godden Reference Collection*

38. *Right:* A rare early Chamberlain moulded beaker, the slightly recessed panel painted in brown monochrome. Unmarked. 4 in. high. *c.* 1794. *Godden Reference Collection*

Plates 17–20) but is here up-dated to include a spiral-fluted or shanked top and a new handle. This example would be that listed under the date 14 March 1795:

> Thos. Hookham – Coventry.
> 1 Quart jug, rich brown & gold
> JWW and crest in wreath £1 1s. 0d.
> 1 pair gobletts to match £1 1s. 0d.

The same basic shape of jug but with a different and perhaps slightly later handle form is shown in Plates 40 and 41. This 1795 Chamberlain jug shape would appear to have been produced during a very brief period, as the example illustrated in Plate 98 shows that a new form was employed by at least December 1796 (see page 91).

Another datable example of Chamberlain's own porcelain is shown in Colour Plate V. This shanked teabowl and saucer, in the Dyson Perrins Museum at

---

39. *Left :* An early Chamberlain moulded quart jug decorated to a special order in March 1795 and costed at £1 1s. 0d. Unmarked. 7¼ in. high. 1795. *Godden Reference Collection*

40. *Below left :* A rare early Chamberlain small jug similar to that shown in Plate 39 but here painted in delicate monochrome with a view of Worcester. Painted mark 'Chamberlains Worcester'. 5⅛ in. high. *c.* 1795. *Godden Reference Collection*

41. *Below :* The side view of the jug illustrated in Plate 40 but showing a different handle form from that seen in Plate 39.

Worcester, represents a special order and is dated 1794. The style of decoration is to be seen on the Caughley jug shown in Plate 21, and would be referred to in the Chamberlain accounts as '1 cup and saucer, Davis's birds'. Obviously not all Chamberlain tea services were as richly decorated as this 1794 example; most were quite modestly decorated as can be seen from the dated 1796 oval shanked teapot in Plates 42 and 43. The added pattern is number 48 in the factory records, and the very delicately painted monochrome floral sprays are enriched with gilt leaves. Other gilt enrichments appear dotted over the body and the handle, and the spout and knob are also attractively gilded.

This pattern was introduced on this shanked or spiral-fluted shape by at least December 1794. The contemporary price was £6 6s. 0d. for a complete teaset. An illustration of a similar teapot with a normal painted mark inside the cover is shown in Plate 70. The basic pattern and a very similar design, number 21, proved extremely popular and they are to be found added to several different forms (see Plates 109 and 110).

42. A typical Chamberlain-Worcester oval spiral-fluted or shanked teapot painted with pattern 48. Dated under the base 1796 (see Plate 43). Written name mark. *Formerly Godden of Worthing Ltd, present ownership unknown*

43. The underside of the teapot shown in Plate 42.

Teawares

Having seen in Plate 42 the basic shape of teawares introduced late in 1794, showing the quality of the potting and the added decoration, it is necessary to return to the teawares which pre-date this 1794 pattern, to reveal the great advances made between the introduction of the Chamberlains' own porcelains in 1791, and the 1794/5 products (see Colour Plate V, Plates 42 and 87). Early teawares do not generally bear any pattern number, presumably because they were issued at a date before the pattern numbering system was brought into use. It is convenient to commence our study of the early Chamberlain teawares with pattern 9, described in the factory pattern list simply as 'Hunting pattern in compartments'. This attractive but simple pattern is illustrated in Plates 44–50. The design was based on a Chinese original, was copied on early

Worcester porcelain – I have a charming example of about 1755 – and also occurs on some Liverpool porcelains of the 1770s. The Chamberlain version in the 1790s was priced at £2 12s. 6d., that is, 2½ guineas per complete service, or about half the price of the pattern 48 teawares shown in Plate 42.

The earliest Chamberlain examples of pattern 9 that I have traced are shown in Plate 44. The teapot shape is extremely rare and is the only Chamberlain early teapot form known to me having a circular rather than an oval plan (although lower circular teapots returned to fashion in the nineteenth century, see Plates 136 and 139). The ring knob does not show in this illustration but it is the same as the one on the teapot illustrated in Plate 63.

The teapot-stand shown on the left of Plate 44 is of the same shape as the earlier Caughley and Worcester

44.   Representative pieces from an early Chamberlain porcelain teaset painted with the 'Hunting in Compartments' pattern. The teapot-stand (left) especially shows a link with Caughley porcelains. Unmarked. Teapot 6 in. high. *c.* 1791–3. *Godden Reference Collection*

46. *Below:* A rare early Chamberlain covered sugar bowl from the same service as the teapot illustrated in Plate 45. Unmarked. $4\frac{1}{2}$ in. high. *c.* 1792. *Godden Reference Collection*

45. *Top:* A rare early Chamberlain small oval teapot and stand painted with the 'Hunting in Compartments' pattern. Unmarked. $8\frac{1}{4}$ in. long. *c.* 1792. *Godden Reference Collection*

47. *Above:* An early Chamberlain trio of teabowl, coffee cup and saucer showing the early 'Plain' shapes. Unmarked. *c.* 1792. *Godden Reference Collection*

48. *Right:* A rare large-size early Chamberlain handled teacup of the simple 'Plain' form painted with the 'Hunting' pattern. 2 in. high. *c.* 1792. *Godden Reference Collection*

49. *Above :* A rare early Chamberlain helmet-shaped creamer in the New Hall manner enamelled with the 'Hunting in Compartments' design. Unmarked. 4¼ in. high. *c.* 1792. *Godden Reference Collection*

50. *Right :* A Chamberlain porcelain creamer or milk-jug of a later form than that shown in Plate 49 but bearing the modeller's or mould-maker's initial 'T' (see page 208). Unmarked. 4½ in. high. *c.* 1795. *Godden Reference Collection*

examples. The cream-jug, known at that time as a 'low Chelsea ewer', is also of a shape much favoured at the Caughley and Worcester factories and by other English manufacturers of the 1770–1800 period. The handle-less teabowl indicates an early shape and a modestly priced service.

None of the pieces from this service bears any mark or pattern number, which is suggestive again of an early date before the patterns had been listed or numbered. The body and glaze has a very hard, glassy appearance, quite typical of the early Chamberlain porcelains (see page 58).

To give further examples of this one pattern, Plate 45 shows a delightful, rather small size, oval teapot on its pointed oval stand. With this set was the simple circular covered sugar shown in Plate 46, and also the trio of a handle-less teabowl, handled coffee cup and saucer as shown in Plate 47. This part service is also completely unmarked. In Plate 48 a large handled teacup is illustrated, perhaps from a very early breakfast service.

The attractive Chamberlain helmet-shaped milk- or cream-jug shown in Plate 49 is extremely reminiscent of New Hall examples, a fact that may well link this shape with the so-called silver-shape teapot illustrated in Plates 52 and 55 (see page 72). This example, too, is unmarked and is probably of the 1792–3 period.

A slightly later jug form painted with this 'Hunting' pattern is shown in Plate 50. This example bears the relief-moulded initial 'T' standing, I think, for Chamberlain's early modeller, John Toulouse (see page 208). This jug shape perhaps links with the oval teapot illustrated in Plate 68, and I also have an odd cover of this form bearing this Chamberlain design.

Incidentally, a mention of Toulouse comes in a puzzling reference to early Chamberlain teaware shapes made in the order book in August 1796 but obviously referring back to then superseded forms. The coffee cups were to have 'flat bottoms with the Derby handle before Toulouse'. The 'Derby handle' might be that illustrated in Plate 47 although those in 1796, especially ordered by a Mr E. Joseph of Liverpool, were to be shanked or spiral-fluted. The earliest reference I have traced to the modeller Toulouse appeared in August 1793, so that the 'Derby handle' should pre-date this entry.

The 'low Chelsea ewer' shown in Plate 51 is painted with Chamberlain's pattern 2, 'enamel'd Foreign sprig & Crowfoot border', priced at £2 2*s.* 0*d.* per complete service. The design is again Oriental-inspired and is a simple pattern that could have been painted by the apprentices, hence the low cost. This basic pattern is seen again on the rare early Chamberlain, New Hall-type teapot of the form now known as silver-shape as it emulated contemporary silver examples. This piece (see Plate 52) happens to be a slightly superior version with a little gilding to the edge and spout in place of the enamelled crowfoot border seen inside the cream-boat just shown. This teapot pattern is, I believe, Chamberlain's pattern 1: 'Plain, enamel'd sprigs with

51. An early Chamberlain porcelain creamer of the form known as a 'Chelsea ewer',
as made by most late eighteenth-century
manufacturers. Painted with Chamberlain's
pattern 2. Unmarked. 4¾ in. long. c. 1792.
Godden of Worthing Ltd

52. A rare form of early Chamberlain
teapot of the so-called silver-shape and in
the style of New Hall examples. Painted with
Chamberlain's pattern 1. Unmarked. 8½ in.
long. c. 1792. *Godden Reference Collection*

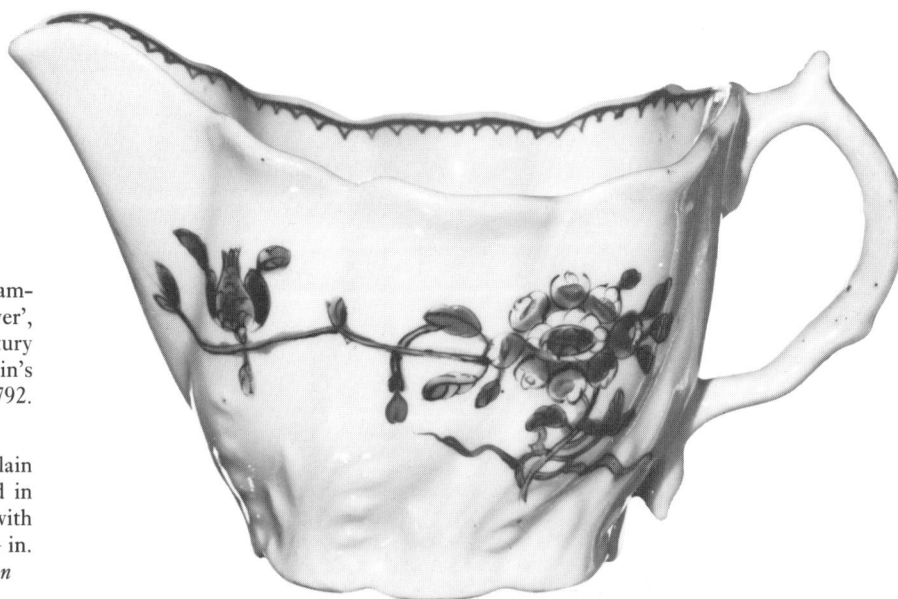

gold edge'. The original price is illegible but the next
pattern, the variations with the painted border, was 2
guineas, so this gilt version may have been £2 12s. 6d. or
thereabouts. The first word of the written description,
'Plain', occurs in several early designations and
probably relates to the plain, unfluted shape, although

the silver-shape teapot is always fluted. I have a teabowl
and saucer of this design which is of this shape (see Plate
54, left). The cup with its simple loop-handle is of
Chamberlain's pattern 24, but serves here to record the
early 'Plain' cup form employed by the Chamberlains.
The plain-shaped teawares were less costly to produce, a

fact that in itself reduced the price of these early teasets, enamelled with simple designs. The manufacturing contrast is seen in the cost of the white cups – 8s. a dozen when fluted, but only 3s. a dozen when plain or unfluted.

The main interest here is to record, in Plate 52, a rare early teapot shape. This may perhaps be that described in the factory records in the mid 1790s as 'organ shape', differentiating these from the oval teapots of the same period. A further, damaged, example is illustrated in Plate 53.

The early Chamberlain silver-shape or 'organ-shape' teapot shown in Plate 55 is larger than that shown in Plate 52; it is also a little later and not as primitive in its potting. The knob and spout forms also differ and the cover is flat rather than domed, showing that there are at least two variations of this early standard shape. The design consists of gilt floral sprays with the typical Chamberlain overglaze-blue enamelled embellishments. The pattern on this teapot is probably number 26, 'blue and gold sprigs', as listed for plain-shape teawares (cup shapes as in Plate 53) at £3 13s. 6d.

The creamer or milk-jug illustrated in Plate 56 is of an extremely rare shape: note the relief-moulded ornate handle, reminiscent of some Caughley handle forms. The other notable feature is the outward-spreading top section, a characteristic also seen in the two cups shown in Plate 57, although the matching teapot form has not

53.   *Top left:* A similar teapot to that seen in Plate 52 but decorated with Chamberlain's pattern 24. This example has the knob missing. Unmarked. 8½ in. long. *c.* 1792. *City Museums, Stoke-on-Trent*

54.   *Above left:* A 'Plain' shape Chamberlain coffee cup (right) of pattern 24 and a 'Plain' teabowl of pattern 1. Unmarked. Cup 3⅛ in. high. *c.* 1792. *Godden Reference Collection*

55.   *Left:* A Chamberlain teapot and cover of slightly different form from those seen in Plates 52 and 53, and decorated with pattern 26. Painted mark inside the cover 'Chamberlains Worcester, Warranted'. 9 in. long. *c.* 1794. *Godden Reference Collection*

56.   *Bottom left:* A very rare form of Chamberlain jug with an intricately moulded handle. It is painted with the 'Dragon in Compartments' pattern which was later given the pattern number 75. Unmarked. 3$\frac{1}{10}$ in. high. *c.* 1794. *Godden Reference Collection*

I.   *Opposite above:* A Flight period Worcester porcelain mug, with underglaze-blue borders, painted and gilded in the manner of the 1770s but dated 1784 in underglaze blue. The decoration was therefore carried out whilst Robert Chamberlain was in charge of decorating at the main Worcester factory and this mug serves to link other pieces of this type and period with the Chamberlains. Unmarked. 3½ in. high. 1784. *Godden Reference Collection*

II.   *Opposite:* A crescent-marked Worcester dish decorated at a period when Robert Chamberlain was in charge of the decorating establishment at the Dr Wall factory. The painter of the fruit was almost certainly later employed by the Chamberlains (see Plates 2, 3 and 21). 10½ × 8¾ in. *c.* 1780–85. *Godden of Worthing Ltd*

III. *Right*: A Caughley plate superbly decorated in the traditional Worcester style by a painter such as George Davis, who moved from the main factory to join Robert Chamberlain's decorating establishment. 'S' mark in underglaze blue. Diameter 9½ in. *c*.1788–92. *D. Whitelaw Collection*

IV. *Opposite*: A very rare early Chamberlain watch-stand incorporating the figure of Apollo, a model mentioned in the factory stocktaking lists. Plate 33 shows the reverse. Unmarked. 9 in. high. *c*.1795. *Godden Reference Collection*

V. *Below*: A finely painted Chamberlain spiral-fluted or shanked teabowl and saucer, almost certainly decorated by George Davis (see pages 192–4). Initialled 'TSG' inside the bowl and dated 1794. Diameter of saucer 5½ in. *Dyson Perrins Museum, Worcester*

VI. An underglaze-blue bordered plate from the service made for A. Heathcott of Bath and invoiced in July 1795. The twenty-four dessert plates, 'Rich blue & gold with Aesops Fables, all different', cost only 10s. each. Other pieces from this service are shown in Plates 87 and 88. Diameter 8 in. *c.*1795. *Photograph: Messrs W. Williams, London. Service: Bath Preservation Trust*

VII. A fine handled dish from a Chamberlain dessert service, with underglaze-blue border. The painted panel and festoons of flowers and fruit were almost certainly painted by the former Dr Wall factory artist George Davis (see page 192, Colour Plate III and Plate 21). This design is perhaps similar to the expensive teaware design 81, 'Davis's birds with fruit & flowers in festoons, blue & gold border £18 18s. 0d.'. Written mark 'Chamberlains Worcester' in gold. 8½ × 7¼ in. *c.*1794–7. *Private collection*

57. *Below:* Two Chamberlain coffee cups of unusual forms, painted with the popular 'Dragon in Compartments' design. Unmarked. 2¾ in. and 2½ in. high respectively. *c.* 1794. *Godden Reference Collection*

58. *Right:* An oval covered sugar basin and a rare form of coffee cup. The enamelled floral design is perhaps number 13, described only as 'Blossom'. Sugar basin marked inside cover 'Chamberlains Worcester, Warranted'. 5½ in. high. *c.* 1794–7. *Godden Reference Collection*

59. Representative pieces from a gilt Chamberlain tea service of pattern 55. Cover to sugar bowl marked 'Chamberlains Worcester, Warranted' in gold and some saucers marked '55'. Sugar 5½ in. high. *c.* 1795. *Godden Reference Collection*

60. *Below:* A small-size waste bowl of the same attractive shape as the set shown in Plate 59 but enamelled with pattern 24. Unmarked. Diameter 4¾ in. *c.* 1794. *Godden of Worthing Ltd*

61. *Right:* The teapot and stand accompanying the gilt tewares shown in Plate 59. This pattern, number 55, was being supplied on shanked shapes by at least November 1796 (see Plate 73). Marked inside cover 'Chamberlains Worcester, Warranted'. 9½ in. long. *c.* 1795. *Godden Reference Collection*

62. One of the two bread and butter plates from a shanked or spiral-fluted teaset of pattern 19, sold at £6 6s. 0d. for the complete service. Unmarked. Diameter 8 in. *c.* 1794. *Godden Reference Collection*

number 75 in 1795. It occurs on Dr Wall Worcester porcelain, on Caughley porcelains probably decorated in the Chamberlains' own decorating establishment, and on a host of other makes.

The cup shown in Plate 58 may be considered a simplified version of the shapes depicted in Plate 57. Unfortunately these pieces do not bear a pattern number, but the design could be number 13, described in the factory list simply as 'Blossom'. It is well painted in red, green and blue with gilt borders.

The matching oval covered sugar bowl has a plain loop-handle affixed with a mock riveted strap like that which a silversmith might employ, a feature seen also in Plates 44 and 63. There is a slight moulding ¼ in. down from the top edge.

The attractively gilt teawares shown in Plates 59 and 61 are of pattern 55 although they are not so marked, probably because this set was made before the numbers were allocated in about March 1795 when this number occurs in the factory records. The official description was 'gold star border with dropping leafage in gold', and by 1795 the complete set, including the standard oval shapes shown in Plate 73, was priced at £7 7s. 0d.

Plate 59 illustrates the same coffee cup form as shown in Plate 58, together with a most attractive teacup with a shaped foot. This shape is followed in the waste bowl and in the oval covered sugar, which has a leafage-moulded handle contrasting with the ring-handle on the previous example. A similar elegant waste bowl, painted with pattern 24, is illustrated in Plate 60; this bowl in particular shows spiral wreathing in the porcelain body,

yet been traced. The shape of these pieces must have been only a short-lived transitional one leading on to the teawares with the same cup-handle form shown in Plates 58 and 59.

The painted pattern on this jug and cup was called 'Dragon in Compartments' before it was given the a throwing characteristic normally associated with the hard-paste Bristol and Plymouth wares. The matching teapot to the set illustrated in Plate 59 is shown separately in Plate 61. This delightful oval pot has the same moulded-leafage knob, a twisted branch-handle with moulded leaf-like terminals. It is seen here sitting on its stand of simple pointed oval form.

This white and gold design on the spiral-fluted shapes of the mid 1790s was priced at £7 7s. 0d., whereas the neatly coloured and gilt tewares of pattern 19 illustrated in Plate 62 were only £6 6s. 0d. One might well expect this latter, quite intricate, enamelled design to be priced at double the gilt one, but instead it was less. It should be remembered that the original buyers had to pay for the gilder's art and, of course, for the almost pure gold that was used.

The teapot shown in Plate 63 is decorated in underglaze blue with slight gilt enrichments. This design is often called the 'Royal Lily' or 'Queen Charlotte' pattern and it also occurs on Worcester porcelains (of all periods) and on Caughley porcelain. It seems to be the only eighteenth-century underglaze-blue pattern issued by the Chamberlains and it does not have a pattern number, only being referred to in the records as 'Lily' or 'Royal Lily'. This teapot shape is closely related to that shown in Plate 61 but the ring knob has a strap attachment.

Whilst the gilt twisted-handled teapot shown in Plate 61 is accompanied by cups with shaped conventional handles (see Plate 59), this 'Royal Lily' teapot with its twisted handle has cups with handles that match (see Plate 64). This Chamberlain cup-handle form is very rare but the similar Flight-Worcester and Caughley examples are more common. In the Chamberlain accounts the Caughley version of this shape is called 'Bell, plain [that is, not fluted or shanked] twisted handle', a description used by at least January 1791. The Chamberlains had apparently introduced a new version by December 1796 as at this period there exist descriptions such as '1 complete sett (except coffees),

63.   An oval Chamberlain teapot painted in underglaze blue with the popular 'Royal Lily' pattern, the borders enriched with gilding. Marked inside cover in gold 'Chamberlains Worc^r. Warranted'. 9¼ in. long. *c.* 1795. *Godden Reference Collection*

64.   A rare form of early Chamberlain teacup and saucer painted with the 'Royal Lily' pattern in underglaze blue and with slight gilding. Unmarked. Diameter of saucer 5¼ in. c. 1795. *Godden Reference Collection*

65.   A very rare form of early Chamberlain teapot painted with the 'Royal Lily' pattern in underglaze blue. Marked inside cover 'Chamberlains, Warranted'. 10 in. long. c. 1795. *Dyson Perrins Museum, Worcester*

New Bell, no. 42. £4 0s. 0d.'. However, both types were being sold at one time, to one customer, as can be seen from an account in March 1797:

	£	s.	d.
1 Complete sett N [New] Bell, handled [pattern] 55.		7	7	0
1 do. O [Old] Bell, handled [pattern] 100.		6	6	0

The rather clumsy teapot illustrated in Plate 65 is again of a very rare, presumably short-lived, shape. The handle form is similar to that on the silver-shape teapots shown in Plates 52 and 59, whilst the knob form resembles that on a slightly later teapot (see Plate 68). This example is on view in the Dyson Perrins Museum at Worcester, where it sits on an unusual oval stand with large moulded handles at the ends, rather like the tureen-stand shown in Plate 90.

As already stated, teawares of the type illustrated up to this point generally bear no pattern number, but those which are featured from now on do normally bear pattern numbers and probably date from 1794. In the earlier factory records each pattern was referred to by name or by description (see page 29), but now a simple number enabled a check to be made and the correct order (or reorder) to be complied with, as a pattern book or pattern list was kept. For example, the order of February 1794 quoted on page 32 under the heading 'Patterns sent, Messrs. Nickin & Company, King Street, Birmingham' simply lists the pattern numbers and the related prices, the pattern pieces being in most cases cups and saucers although the price was for the complete teaset.

The standard 'full' tea service of the better-quality services, priced from about £3 3s. 0d., would have comprised:

A teapot and cover
A teapot-stand
A sugar basin and cover
A jug
A waste bowl
Two bread and butter plates, which were of slightly different sizes
Twelve teacups (some cheaper sets had handle-less teabowls)
Twelve (or less) coffee cups (these were sometimes sold separately)
Twelve saucers

I have not seen a Chamberlain spoontray and these objects were going out of favour in the mid 1790s. However, two orders placed in 1795 do especially include both spoontrays and caddies or tea canisters as extras: '1 complete sett, no 34 shankered, 1 caddee and spoontray do.'. These additional items may have been Caughley examples of the types shown in Plates 26 and 28, although Chamberlain's stocktaking lists of 1793 and 1796 include spoontrays.

The standard teasets did not have matching coffee pots, but this is not to say that they were not made or sold individually. They certainly were and in at least two sizes, as is evidenced by the November 1794 entry: '1, Pint coffee pot, white 2s. 6d. 2, Quart do. do. at 5s. each'. There is also an earlier, unique reference to perhaps a larger, more ornate object: '1 new shank'd coffe urn. Brown & gold. sprigs [pattern] no. 21, £1 0s. 0d.'. A standard-shape shanked Chamberlain coffee pot of the mid 1790s is shown in Plate 66, a plain example is shown in Plate 281, and a later example is depicted in Plate 282.

In about 1795 the Chamberlain teapot shape was beginning to settle into a standard form that was to remain constant into the 1800s. The marks inside the covers now normally included the pattern number as well as the written (in enamel or gold) words 'Chamber-lains Worcester', with or without the word 'Warranted' (see page 33 and Plate 70).

The teapot shown in Plate 67 is an early version of the standard pot with a plain, unfluted body. The ring-handle is as in Plate 63, but the former entwined handle is replaced by a gracefully moulded loop-handle with a slight outward projection two-thirds of the way up the handle, and a balancing, inward projection about one-third from the bottom of the handle: this characteristically Chamberlain handle can be seen on later pots illustrated in Plates 68–74. The low price and the quality of the painting suggest that this pattern was painted by a child, or apprentice painter, a theory also borne out by the spelling of the standard name mark, in this case written as 'Chamberlins'.

A related early teapot is seen in Plate 68, but here the ring knob is replaced by a rather clumsy oval knob, although otherwise this and the previous example are

66. A spiral-fluted coffee pot and cover of a standard form, gilt, with pattern 120. Marked in gold inside cover 'Chamberlains Worcester, N.120'. 9¼ in. high. *c.* 1796–8. *Godden of Worthing Ltd*

67. *Left:* A Chamberlain teapot of pattern 8, 'Common Image', which was priced at only £1 16s. 0d. for the complete tea service. Marked inside cover (in a childish hand) 'Chamberlins [*sic*] Worcester, 8'. 9½ in. long. *c.* 1796–8. *Godden Reference Collection*

68. *Below:* A teapot and cover of the early design number 24, 'Tasker's Chinese Bridge', in the style of Chinese export-market patterns. Marked inside cover 'Chamberlains Worc^r, Warranted, No 24'. 9¾ in. long. *c.* 1795–7. *Godden Reference Collection*

69. *Below left:* A teabowl and saucer showing the enamelled Chamberlain pattern 24, 'Tasker's Chinese Bridge'. Unmarked. Diameter of saucer 5¼ in. *c.* 1796–8. *Godden Reference Collection*

identical. The painted and slightly gilt Chinese-styled design number 24, described as 'Tasker's Chinese bridge pattern, brown edge', occurs listed in March 1795. A more apt description might have been 'Chinese fence pattern'. A teacup decorated with this design is shown in Plate 54, but its 'Plain' early form might pre-date this teapot by a year or more; another teabowl and saucer decorated with pattern 24 is shown in Plate 69 and an earlier teapot in Plate 409.

From about 1795 the standard Chamberlain tewares were very often issued in the shanked style, as seen in Plates 70–75. A characteristic of this moulded fluting is the slight indentation at the highest point which forms the traditionally termed 'tramlines'. In the past these have been cited as a sure sign of Chamberlain origin – this is not the case, for several other makes can also display this feature, including wares from the Flight factory. It can also occur on Grainger tewares (see Plate 112), whereas some of the earliest Chamberlain shanked tewares do *not* show this feature.

The teapot illustrated in Plate 71 is an attractive example of the standard type; note the new knob, the

standard moulded handle and the new fluted spout. The part teaset shown in Plate 72 bears pattern 2, 'Foreign sprig & crowfoot border', which appeared on the earlier shapes shown in Plates 51 and 52 and is now seen on these oval shanked tewares. Michael Loveley of Honiton (see page 60) ordered three complete teasets of this pattern on shanked or spiral-fluted shapes in September 1797, and these cost a mere 2 guineas each, a low price that undoubtedly helped their sale. Standard shapes found with these teapots are shown here although several other shapes of jug or cup can occur, as illustrated by the pieces in Plates 73 and 74 which are of patterns 55 and 69. This standard-shape teapot occurs in a very small size – almost of 'toy' proportions, holding only a single cup of tea – but such examples are very rare.

A spiral-fluted Chamberlain teapot having the same knob form but a new, rare, handle form is illustrated in Plate 75. Note that this shows the 'tramlines' at the top of the fluting as seen in Plate 70. On the rare occasions when a similar type of teapot lacks this feature, as in Plate 76, it is reasonable to question its origin. When

70. *Top:* A standard shape of Chamberlain shanked or spiral-fluted teapot, with pattern 48. The cover is turned to show the usual form of written mark inside the cover. This pattern was £4 4s. 0d. for the complete set on plain shapes, or £5 5s. 0d. on these shanked forms. 10 in. long. *c.* 1796–8. *Godden Reference Collection*

71. *Above:* An attractive standard-shaped Chamberlain shanked teapot decorated with pattern 20, priced at £6 6s. 0d. for the complete set. Marked inside cover 'Chamberlains Worcester, Warranted. 20'. 10 in. long. *c.* 1796–8. *Godden of Worthing Ltd*

72. Representative pieces from a shanked teaset painted with Chamberlain's pattern 2. The bread plate is an unusual form. Unmarked except for the number 2 on some pieces. Diameter of plate 8½ in. *c.* 1797. *Godden of Worthing Ltd*

73. *Top left:* Representative pieces from a shanked Chamberlain teaset of the gilt pattern 55; such a set was sent to the Swansea firm of Coles & Haynes in November 1796. Name mark inside teapot and sugar bowl covers. Diameter of bread plate 8 in. *c.* 1797. *Godden of Worthing Ltd*

74. *Top right:* Representative pieces from a shanked Chamberlain teaset of pattern 69, originally priced at £4 4s. 0d. for the complete service. Name mark inside covers. Teapot 9½ in. long. *c.* 1797. *Godden of Worthing Ltd*

75. *Above left:* A very rare Chamberlain teapot, painted with pattern 69, with a new handle form. Name mark inside cover. 7 in. high. *c.* 1797. *John Duncalfe*

76. *Above:* A shanked teapot in a hybrid hard-paste body, probably a Caughley copy of a Chamberlain standard teapot form painted with an earlier design (see Plates 27 and 28), not included in the Chamberlain pattern list. Unmarked. *c.* 1796–8. *Godden Reference Collection*

77. A 'new fluted' Chamberlain teapot decorated with the early 'L'Amitié' or 'Doves' design (see Plates 25 and 26). Written name mark inside cover, without pattern number. 7 in. high. *c.* 1797–9. *Godden of Worthing Ltd*

78. Representative pieces from a Chamberlain-Worcester 'new fluted' teaset decorated with pattern 34, originally priced at £5 5s. 0d. Such wares were included in the 1796 inventory. Name mark inside covers. Diameter of bread plate 8¼ in. *c.* 1797. *Godden of Worthing Ltd*

compared with marked Chamberlain examples, this unmarked pot reveals several small differences in the mould – the shoulder is more concave than the Chamberlain shoulder, and the foot differs, as does the placing of the grip inside the handle-opening. This is probably an example of a late Caughley copy of a standard Chamberlain teapot: the story has changed, for now Turner is copying Chamberlain rather than the other way about as had previously been the case.

A slight variation of the standard oval shanked Chamberlain teapot occurred with straight fluting and with a new knob form, and this is illustrated in Plate 77. This shape was entered in the pattern list as 'new fluted'. Matching shapes can be seen in Plate 78 which illustrates pattern 34, and the slightly later wares of pattern 193 in Plate 80. The 'Angoulème' sprig teapot of pattern 38 (see Plate 79) stands on an unusual teapot-stand.

It will be noted that the coffee cups in the teaset illustrated in Plate 80 are of a new shape with straight sides. These may represent the shape referred to in an order dated 26 July 1796: '1 complete sett, new fluted, No.69, new shape coffees'.

The last few illustrations have shown standard Chamberlain shanked or spiral-fluted tewares and straight-fluted shapes: the same forms can also occur plain, without any surface moulding. All were available

in the same period, a point well made in an interesting account for white tewares ordered by a London 'chinaman', William Hewson, in February 1797. Chamberlain's clerk added the note, 'To be sent at Rose's prices. These goods are wanted to complete his stock on hand'. The reference to Rose no doubt relates to John Rose of the Coalport factory – the man who was to take over Thomas Turner's Caughley factory in 1799 – and it is interesting in that it suggests that he was undercutting Chamberlain's normal prices. The second part of the note indicates that the shapes wanted were the standard stock lines of the period. The white tewares were sent in July 1797 and comprised three groups – fluted, shanked and plain. The largest quantities required were the shanked tewares, indicating a general preference for these spiral-fluted forms.

It would appear that patterns up to about number 175 had been introduced by the year 1800; pattern 165 was entered in the order books in September 1799 but it is evident that after this some of the old shapes such as shanked wares were still being made and painted with the less expensive patterns. For example, the typical mid 1795 shanked covered sugar shown in Plate 82, uniform in shape with tewares shown in Plates 72–4, is painted with pattern 203 which first appears in the Chamberlain lists in July 1801. This pattern, 'Reynold's bird pattern', is a copy of a Dr Wall period Worcester design.

79. *Left*: A 'new fluted' Chamberlain teapot and stand painted with 'Angoulème' sprigs after a popular French design. The pattern is number 38 in the Chamberlain records, priced at £4 4s. 0d. for the complete set. Name mark and pattern number inside cover. 10 in. long. c. 1797. *Godden of Worthing Ltd*

80. *Opposite*: Representative pieces from a Chamberlain 'new fluted' teaset painted with pattern 193, originally priced at £3 3s. 0d. for the complete set. Painted name mark inside covers, pattern number only on other pieces, as can be seen on the upturned cup. Teapot 10 in. long. c. 1798–1800. *Godden of Worthing Ltd*

81. *Below left*: A rare waisted variation on a standard Chamberlain teapot shape, painted with the popular 'Dragon in Compartments' design, number 75 in the pattern list and originally priced at £7 7s. 0d. per set. Marked 'Chamberlains Worcester' inside cover. 9½ in. long. c. 1797-9. *Messrs Sotheby & Co.*

82. *Above*: A shanked Chamberlain covered sugar painted with pattern 203, an old Worcester design sometimes called the 'Sir Joshua Reynold's pattern'. Painted pattern number 203. 5½ in. high. c. 1801. *Victoria & Albert Museum (Crown Copyright)*

83. *Left*: Chamberlain milk-jugs from tea services of the 1795–1800 period. Right to left: pattern 8 (see page 312); pattern 66 with individual crest and initial motif (see also Plate 412); and pattern 34 matching the set shown in Plate 78. Unmarked. Right example 5¼ in. high. c. 1795–1800. *Godden of Worthing Ltd*

Déjeuner services

Apart from the normal afternoon-tea services, most factories of the 1790–1810 period produced some charming déjeuner services for two persons. The listing for one such service ordered in April 1794 comprised:

	£	s.	d.
2 cups and saucers		12	0
1 teapot		9	0
1 sugar box		6	0
1 creamer		5	0
1 slop basin		5	0
stand for do.		2	2	0
	3	19	0

In this case the pattern was number 20, illustrated on a full-size teapot in Plate 71. Other sets were more richly decorated.

As such sets were intended for only two persons and as all the pieces had to fit on a tray, the teapot and other pieces were only about two-thirds the size of normal tea wares, whilst in some cases special shapes were employed for these expensive services.

Dessert services

Although teawares were the staple of Robert Chamberlain's early trade, he also made a good variety of dessert services. In general these are not as thinly potted as the blanks he would have received from the Caughley factory (see Plate 23) before he commenced the manufacture of his own rather hard porcelain, with its glittery glaze.

Representative pieces from an early Chamberlain dessert service, decorated with the standard underglaze-blue 'Royal Lily' pattern, are shown in Plate 84. A kidney-shaped dessert dish decorated with the popular and highly decorative 'Queen's' pattern, with its areas of underglaze blue with enamel and gilt enrichments, is illustrated in Plate 85.

The 'Dragon in Compartments' pattern dessert service (see Plate 86), number 75 in the Chamberlain records, is a little later in period, being of the late 1790s, but note that in both these standard pattern dessert services the plate edge does not show Coalport-type indentations (see page 184).

Some services were rather more special and as early as August 1794 there are references in the factory order book to sets painted with 'Fable' subjects:

1 complete dessert service, blue border, Fables, consisting of 24 plates 3rd [size], shanked, 17 dishes, do. £30 0s. 0d.

[Order book entry, 25 August 1794]

and in the same year the cash book records the purchase of '2 Volumes Aesops Fables £2 12s. 6d.'. Later order book entries list numbers and page numbers for 'Fables' required by individual customers:

1 Basket & stand Aesops Fables,
Cock & Fox No. 61 page 27 for stand,
Two lots No. 2 page 141 for basket.

The subjects painted on these and similar 'Fable' pieces provide evidence that the two volumes of Aesop's fables purchased in 1794 for use by the Chamberlain painters were those printed and published by John Stockdale of Piccadilly, London, in June 1793, entitled *The Fables of Aesop, with a life of the author*.

One particular 'Fable' dessert set is of special interest here as it was resold in London in recent years. This set was originally invoiced on 31 July 1795:

A. Heathcott, No. 20 Crescent, Bath.

	£	s.	d.
24 dessert plates, Rich blue & gold with Aesops Fables, all different	12	0	0
1 Centrepiece	2	10	0
2 Heart [shaped] dishes	2	12	0
2 Melons [shaped dishes]	2	12	0
4 square [shaped dishes]	5	5	0
4 shells [shaped dishes]	4	0	0
2 cream tureens & covers	1	12	0
2 stands to do.		18	0
2 spoons		12	0

Representative pieces from this set are shown in Colour Plate VI and also Plate 87 with one of the magnificent ice-pails which were purchased later.

Some slightly later services had a pair of elegant oval fruit baskets and stands. One such stand painted with the subject quoted above, 'Cock & Fox No. 61', is shown in Plate 88, whilst one of the baskets is illustrated in Plate 89; the latter is illustrated purely to record this rare Chamberlain shape, for this example does not include the 'Fable' panel.

Plate 90 gives an example of a rare boat-shape dessert service tureen, one of a pair for sugar and cream. These originally had porcelain ladles, and this example bears the standard 'Fable' panels with the underglaze-blue borders and rich gilding. Much the same blue border and over-gilding is seen on the dessert shell-shape dish shown in Colour Plate VII. The enamelled decoration is clearly in a similar style to the Caughley jug shown in

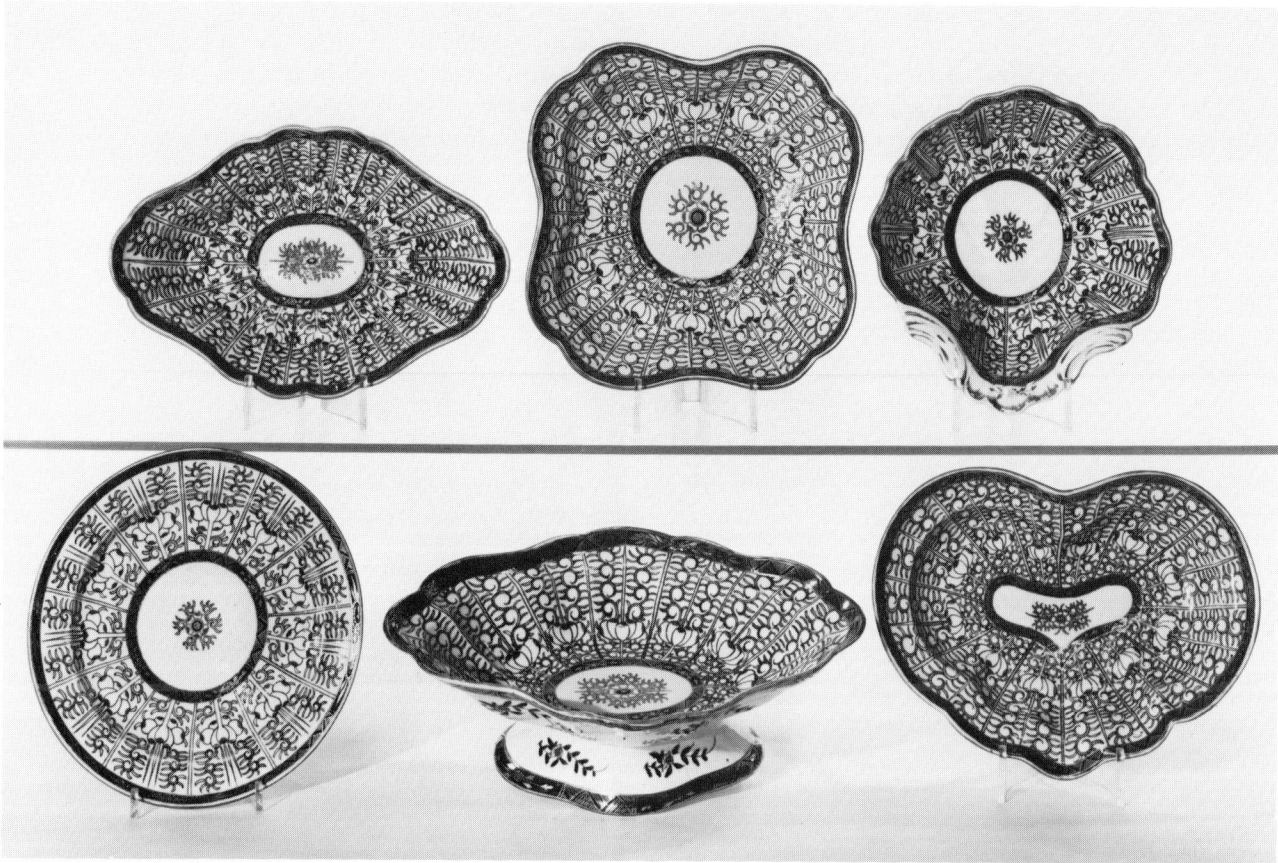

84. *Top:* Representative pieces from a Chamberlain dessert service painted with the popular 'Royal Lily' pattern in underglaze blue. Painted name mark on some pieces. Centrepiece 12¼ in. long. *c.* 1795–8. *Godden of Worthing Ltd*

85. *Above:* A characteristic shaped dish from a dessert service painted with the 'Best Queen's' design, number 78 in the factory records. Unmarked. 10¼ × 7¼ in. *c.* 1795–8. *Godden Reference Collection*

86. Representative pieces from a Chamberlain dessert service painted with the popular 'Dragon in Compartments' design, number 75. Centrepiece 12 × 8¾ in. *c.* 1796–8. *Godden of Worthing Ltd*

Plate 21 and the plate in Colour Plate III, and the decoration is likewise attributed to George Davis (see page 192) in the mid 1790s. However, this version of the standard handled dessert dish is rather more ornately moulded than those in the services illustrated in Plates 84, 86 and 87.

Other designs were also painted within similar blue and gilt borders on Chamberlain dessert wares. In May 1795 there was invoiced: '1 dessert service, rich blue & gold with brown views all different £31 10s. 0d.'. This, in general effect, would have been similar to that shown in Colour Plate VI. In the same period services were also painted with panels of classical figures. Another similar

87. *Below:* Representative pieces from a magnificent Chamberlain shanked dessert service of the mid 1790s painted with panels illustrating various Aesop's fables subjects, within blue and gilt borders. The service was ordered in July 1795. Unmarked. Ice-pail 14¾ in. high. *Photograph: Messrs Phillips*

88. *Right:* An early Chamberlain stand for a dessert basket painted with a scene from fable number 61, 'Cock & Fox', taken from John Stockdale's 1793 edition of these fables. *c.* 1795. *Dyson Perrins Museum, Worcester*

set made for the Prince of Orange in 1796 is listed on page 31, complete with a pair of ice-pails, fruit baskets and stands, cream-tureens and ladles in addition to all the more normal dessert wares.

A few Chamberlain services were especially made to individual order; the one illustrated in Plate 91 is a case in point. This is a truly magnificent service with very

89. A Chamberlain dessert basket with blue and gilt decoration, similar in style to the Aesop's fables service (see Plate 87). Unmarked. 10¾ in. long. *c.* 1795. *Godden of Worthing Ltd*

90. A rare early Chamberlain dessert tureen, cover and stand decorated with panels of Aesop's fables subjects within blue and gilt borders, as the service illustrated in Plate 87. Unmarked. 9½ in. long. *c.* 1795. *Photograph: Messrs Phillips*

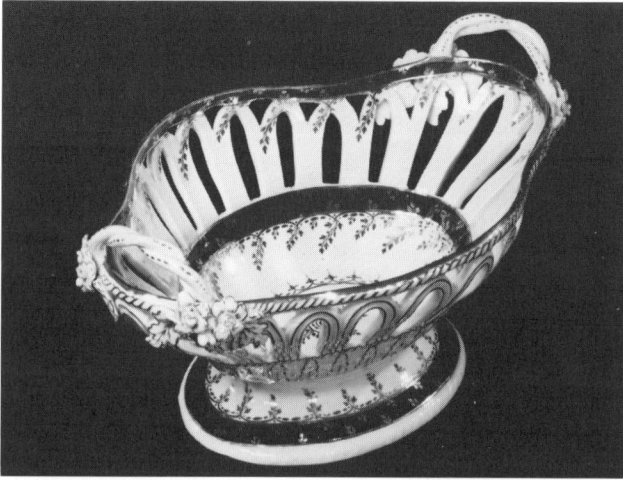

91. Representative pieces from a magnificent special service, the knobs representing the owner's crest, and painted with the armorial bearings of Everett impaling Ellis. The ground is a rich coral colour with elaborate gilding. Painted name mark with modeller's initial 'T' in relief on some pieces (see page 209). Ice-pail 11¾ in. high. *c.* 1796–1800. *Messrs Sotheby & Co.*

92. A rare form of early Chamberlain plate enamelled in a 'harlequin'-style design made up of various neatly painted border patterns incorporating a typical overglaze blue. Written name mark. Diameter 8½ in. *c.* 1796–1800. *Godden of Worthing Ltd*

rich gilding over a coral ground. The painted mark 'Chamberlain Worcester' occurs and also the moulded initial 'T' for the modeller, John Toulouse (see page 209).

Some Chamberlain dessert sets were of 'harlequin' type, each piece having a different decorative subject – landscapes, flowers, figure subjects, or shells, etc. – painted in its centre: the early nineteenth-century service shown in Plate 146 illustrates well this fashion. One unnumbered dessert service pattern of the late 1790s also has a mixture of different border designs repeated on each piece, rather in the manner of pattern plates. An example is illustrated in Plate 92 which serves also to show another rather rare Chamberlain plate shape.

Dinner services

Early Chamberlain-Worcester dinner services, or 'Table services' as they were originally called, are extremely rare, as are Caughley or even Flight-Worcester examples of the mid 1790s. However, they were certainly made, and any plates with a diameter of

9 in. or more and individual soup plates will originally have been part of a dinner service.

The make-up of a dinner service varied somewhat according to the requirements of the purchaser, or the depth of his pocket, and the components also changed at different periods. According to an 'Estimate of a fawn stripe set given to an American gentleman at the Hop Pole', an inn in Worcester, a dinner service in August 1796 comprised:

```
2 tureens and stands
2 sauce-tureens and stands
4 sauce-boats
24 dishes, including vegetable dishes
60 table plates
24 soup plates
24 dessert plates
```

This is the only reference I have noted to Chamberlain sauce-boats, although the earlier Caughley sets had these items. There were always more meat plates than soups. The estimate below for the different matching services is interesting, showing that at this period a dessert service cost three times as much as a teaset, and a dinner service cost five times as much as a dessert service.

Dinner service	150 guineas
Dessert service	30 guineas
Teaset	10 guineas

By 1799 the Chamberlain dinner services were probably very large, as is evidenced by one order for a 'Dragon' pattern service supplied to a Mr Broade of Peover Hall, near Knutsford in Cheshire. This comprised the following:

		£	s.	d.
2 large soup tureens & covers		8	8	0
2 tureen stands		4	0	0
4 sauce tureens, complete		8	0	0
2 vegetable dishes and covers		7	7	0
2 square salad dishes		3	3	0
4 corner covered dishes		8	0	0
8 10 inch dishes	at 18s.	7	4	0
8 12 inch dishes	at 24s.	9	12	0
2 14 inch do.	at 30s.	3	0	0
2 16 inch do.	at 40s.	4	0	0
3 18 inch do.	at 52s. 6d.	7	17	6
3 20 inch do.	at 63s.	9	9	0
72 large table plates	at 10s. 6d.	37	16	0
24 large soup plates	at 12s.	14	8	0
48 dessert size plates	at 7s.	16	16	0
Plus seven damaged dishes				
	Package		15	0
		154	16	6

93. A large shaped-edge Chamberlain dish from a special dinner service, incorporating the owner's armorial bearings and crest with the colourful 'Dragon in Compartments' design. Painted mark 'Chamberlains Worcester. No.75' with the incised size mark '12'. 12½ in. long. *c.* 1796–8. *Geoffrey Godden, chinaman*

94. An early Chamberlain tureen and stand from a special service incorporating the owner's armorial bearings and crest with the 'Dragon in Compartments' design. Unmarked. Stand 8¼ in. long. *c.* 1796–8. *Messrs Phillips*

A 12 in. dish decorated with this basic 'Dragon in Compartment' design (number 75 at the Chamberlain factory) is shown in Plate 93, but in this case the design has been adapted to take the armorial bearings and crest of the purchaser. A further example of this type, a tureen and stand, is shown in Plate 94. Nineteenth-century hard-paste French fakes of this type are known, marked with the Chamberlain written mark.

An oval platter with a similarly shaped edge is seen in Plate 95 painted with classical figures within blue and gilt borders, and this shape appears again in the crested dinner-service pieces shown in Plate 96. The figure-panelled dish represents one of the dinner services of border pattern 66, 'Blue border, gold leafage on the blue dropping border outside', which in September 1796 was listed at £133 15s. 0d. for the set, against £35 8s. 0d. for a companion dessert service.

A magnificent dinner and dessert service of this design is in the collection of Her Majesty Queen Elizabeth the Queen Mother. The large tureen was

95.   A large Chamberlain dish from a dinner service, reputedly made for the 'King of Hanover'. The subject depicts Hamlet, Horatio and Ophelia, within a blue and gold border. 13½ in. long. c. 1795–8. *Messrs Christie, Manson & Woods*

loaned to the 1977 Grosvenor House Antiques Fair and was illustrated in the handbook; the figure-subject panels were attributed to Humphrey Chamberlain and the service dated to c. 1810. The shape of this tureen approximates to the example shown in Plate 94 but I believe that this royal service, reputedly presented to the King of Hanover, slightly pre-dates 1800. Certainly other services of this basic design, but without the gilt Star of the Garter motifs, were ordered or sold in the late 1790s (see page 31). If so, this and the other services of this type could not have been painted by Humphrey Chamberlain as he was not born until c. 1791 (see page 187). Unfortunately this royal service does not appear recorded in any of the surviving factory records.

96.   Representative pieces from a richly gilt coral-ground Chamberlain dinner service bearing the crest of Newton. Written 'Chamberlains Worcester' marks. Oval tureen 13 in. long. c. 1798–1800. *Messrs Sotheby & Co.*

Miscellaneous wares

The Chamberlain factory made a wide assortment of objects apart from the tea, dessert and dinner services previously discussed. Many mugs and jugs were made, and Plate 97 illustrates a charmingly simple, early pair of gilt mugs, one of which has been turned to show the pointed junction of the handle with the body – a feature seen also on early Chamberlain teapots (see Plate 70). These examples are unmarked, but in paste, glaze and style of gilding they are typically Chamberlain and may have been listed in their unglazed, or biscuit, state in the January 1796 inventory (see page 61) as '4 dozen Half pint mugs [at 8s. a dozen] £1 12s. 0d.'. Some other later, more ornate Chamberlain mugs are shown in Plates 328–32.

Many other objects of the period were very richly decorated as can be seen from Plates 98–102. The jug shown in Plate 98 is an interesting dated specimen. The order appears under the date 21 December 1796: 'Moseley Esq., Glasshampton, 1 Quart Jug, rich blue and gold, view of Buildwas Abbey, £2 2s. 0d.'. This jug shape was a standard Chamberlain form used for several years from 1796; it occurs in various sizes and with slightly different handles (see Plates 316–18). The large covered examples as illustrated in Plate 99 were called 'punch jugs' in the factory records.

An idea of the range of Chamberlain's productions in 1795 can be gauged from the stock held in their retail shop situated in High Street, Worcester. This stock is detailed in the inventory of 1 January 1796 under the sub-heading 'Shop and Room over' and 'Shop back Room'. As the list comprises hundreds of articles, all duplicate entries, most repetitive descriptions of tewares, and the glass, metal and papier mâché articles also held in stock have been deleted here. All objects which are obviously of Caughley make are also omitted – for example, '3 Gallon jugs, Pleasure Boat 31s. 6d.' – as these articles are dealt with in my *Caughley and Worcester Porcelains, 1775–1800* (1969); but mention must be made of the fact that the Chamberlain retail shop in January 1796 contained much porcelain from Thomas Turner's factory at Caughley – the ware that the Chamberlain decorators had enamelled and gilded for several years before the Chamberlain factory was established (see page 41). Even allowing for the above-mentioned deletions, the list of porcelains in the Chamberlain shop in January 1796 is lengthy. The various articles have been rearranged in alphabetical order, for easy reference. I have added a few notes, in brackets, to make the meaning clear, or to refer to matching pieces illustrated in this book.

97. Two early Chamberlain half-pint mugs gilded in a simple and characteristic manner and with the owner's initials added. Unmarked. 3⅜ in. high. *c.* 1795–8. *Godden of Worthing Ltd*

98. A fine underglaze-blue striped and gilt presentation jug. The panel is painted in grey monochrome with a view of Buildwas Abbey. Inscribed on the base 'Buildwas Abbey, Shropshire, the property of W. M. Moseley Esqr. 1796' and also 'Chamberlains Worcester'. 6¾ in. high. 1796. *Photograph: Messrs Winifred Williams, London. Ian Henderson Collection*

99. A fine quart-size punch jug and cover painted with a view of London Bridge, copied from an engraving in *The Copper Plate Magazine*, Vol. III, 1796 (see Plate 100). Such a jug was supplied to Henry Bowen of Bath in March 1798. Written mark 'Chamberlains Worcester'. 9¼ in. high. *c.* 1798. *Victoria & Albert Museum (Crown Copyright)*

	£	s.	d.
9 Animals, dogs, cats, lambs, etc.		13	6
9 Bear dogs		22	6
9 Bell handles		22	6
1 Breakfast set	5	5	0
1 pair broth bowls, complete		30	0
5 caddy spoons [? porcelain]		12	6
1 pair Bracket candlesticks	2	0	0
7 pair Chamber candlesticks	5	5	0
7 pair do.	1	8	0
1 pair caskets		16	0
39 chocolate cups		39	0

	£	s.	d.
12 chocolate [cups] and stands	4	0	0
2 coffee pots		21	6
5 pint coffee pots		25	0
3 pint & half coffee pots		31	6
4 quart coffee pots		22	0
4 dessert dishes, Fables & Landskip	3	10	0
9 do. plates	3	12	0
25 gilt egg drainers [perhaps Caughley blanks]		37	6
24 upright ewers	3	0	0
17 Figures	3	8	0
3 Fox heads [perhaps as in Plate 372]		6	0
1 do. gilt		8	0
2 oval fruit baskets [perhaps as in Plate 89]	2	2	0
6 goblets	3	3	0
6 do.	2	10	0
5 Houses		10	0
1 pair ice pails		24	0
1 Inkstand		18	0
30 pint jugs, lettered		9	0	0
16 Quart jugs, handsome – fancy	12	0	0
15 rich pint jugs	9	0	0
10 rich quart jugs	5	0	0
2 three quart jugs	4	0	0
5 three-quarter pint jugs	2	2	6
4 lambs [see Plate 35]			3
16 large Lavender bottles	8	8	0
77 ½ pint mugs, Lettered [see Plate 97]	7	14	0
30 sorted ½ pint mugs & goblets	4	10	0
10 three pint do.	9	0	0
3 Large Blue & gold pedestals [see Plate 36]	1	9	0
1 white do.			
5 Pictures [given as 'Pictures China, Views of Worcester' in the 1795 stocklist]	2	0	0
8 Plates [pattern] number 34 [see plate 78]	2	5	0
101 plates	3	7	4
87 do.	3	12	6
120 do.	7	10	0
59 do.	11	16	0
24 do.	3	0	0
18 dessert plates		18	0
90 Toy plates		11	3
12 pomatum pots	2	8	0
4 rich punch bowls [see Plate 37]	4	4	0
3 rich punch bowls	2	14	0
5 do.	3	15	0
7 do.	4	4	0
21 do.	10	10	0
1 ornamented sheep [see Plate 35]		15	0
8 smelling bottles [see Plate 366]	2	0	0
28 do.	4	18	0
18 white smelling bottles		13	6
1 snuff box [? porcelain]		12	0
3 oval sugar pots Lily [pattern, see Plate 63]		7	6
63 tea [cups] [pattern] No.18	4	14	6
140 tea [cups] [pattern] No. 9 at 9*d.* [see page 68]	5	5	0
200 tea [cups] different patterns	10	0	0

96 teapots, enamelled, sorted	16	16	0
13 teapots, new fluted	2	5	6
1 complete [tea] set, shanked, dragon	3	13	6
8 teasets	54	12	0
2 [tea] sets	12	12	0
1 do.	4	14	6
2 do.	8	8	0
1 do.	12	12	0
66 thimbles	4	19	0
15 tobacco stoppers	1	2	6
54 Lettered, tumblers	6	7	0
2 pair tumblers [these would be richly decorated examples, at this price, perhaps similar in general style to those illustrated in Plate 101]	1	11	6
6 Antique [styled] vases, pedestals, etc.	3	3	0
6 Large vases, different patterns	4	10	0

These inventory records were of necessity extremely brief, but the Chamberlain sales and order books of the same period give more detailed descriptions. From these contemporary entries space permits only a few samples to be listed overleaf as being representative of the Chamberlain porcelains between 1796 and 1800, showing the growing range of richly decorated ornamental wares. The dates of the entries are given in brackets. Fuller details of the Chamberlain shapes are given in Chapter 7.

100. The London Bridge engraving after an original painting by Marlow as published in April 1796 in *The Copper Plate Magazine*, Vol. III, or 'Elegant Cabinet of Picturesque Prints . . .'. The print was soon copied on Chamberlain's porcelains (see Plate 99).

	£	s.	d.	
BEAKERS				
2 large beakers, yellow & gold, View of Worcester, and some others equally good.	5	5	0	[September 1797]
BULB, OR BOUGH, POTS [described as 'Flat chimney pieces' or 'Flat ornaments']				
1 Flat Chimney piece, Queen [see page 96, Plate 337].	2	2	0	[August 1798]
1 Flat ornament, blue & gold, with views of Worcester.	2	12	6	[March 1799]
COFFEE CANS & SAUCERS				
1 Coffee can & saucer, blue border, Davis's birds in the front of the cup & bottom of saucer, yellow between.	1	11	6	[November 1797]
4 Rich coffee cans & saucers, yellow & gold views in Cornwall.	4	4	0	[April 1798]
DESSERT SERVICES				
1 dessert service, Botanical flowers, yellow & gold border.	31	10	0	[September 1797]
1 Complete dessert service [pattern] No. 75 [see Plate 86].	21	0	0	[May 1799]
ICE-PAILS				
2 Ice-Pails complete, Fruit, Birds & flowers.	7	7	0	[November 1798]
INKSTANDS				
1 Inkstand, blue & gold, mosaic, birds etc. in panel.	1	11	6	[January 1799]
1 Inkstand, best Queen [see page 96].	1	11	6	[December 1799]
JARDINIERS [flower pots such as those illustrated in Plates 360 and 362 seem to have been listed as 'Root-pots']				
1 pair rich Queen [see page 96] root-pots and stands.	4	4	0	[August 1798]
JUGS				
1 three pint jug, blue & gold, View of Worcester [see Colour Plate VII for general type].	2	12	6	[September 1797]
2 Quart Punch jugs & covers, rich, London and Blackfriars Bridges.	4	4	0	[March 1798]
MUGS				
1 pint mug, Capt. Buckmer's engagement.		18	0	⎫
1 half pint mug, Westminster bridge, yellow ground.		18	0	⎬ [March 1798]
1 half pint mug, Cepholus & Procius, yellow ground.	1	1	0	⎭
1 pint mug, best Queen [see page 96].	1	5	0	[June 1799]
PLATES				
2 plates [Prince of Orange] border [see page 31] figures. Agrippa on one, Venus & Adonis ye other [see Plate 95 for type].				[October 1798, order not priced]
TEAPOT				
1 teapot, Gen¹ Washington.	1	4	0	[1798 stocklist]
TEA SERVICES				
1 teaset, bell-fluted, Dragon 75 [see page 96, and Plate 56 for basic pattern].	7	7	0	[January 1797]
TUMBLERS				
4 tumblers, views, Worcester, Kennelworth, Hoxton.	2	2	0	[June 1798]
2 large tumblers & covers, 4 half pint do., fawn ground & designs, same as the rich one with beauty.	10	10	0	[October 1798]
2 half pint tumblers & covers, Sappho & Phaon [see Plate 101].				[August 1799, order not priced]
VASES [ornamental vases seem to have been entered as 'Ornaments' in the pre-1800 Chamberlain records]	3	16	0	[August 1798]
3 Ornaments, yellow & gold, View of Worcester on centrepiece.				
1 tall ornament, gold handles, Paris & Oenone.				⎫
2 Flat ones [bulb pots?] Clipping the Wings & Love of Cypheus.	20	0	0	⎬ [May 1800]
2 small handled ones, Beauty & Savius.				⎭
1 large ornament with Triumph of Mercy [see Plate 102].				[May 1800, order not priced]

The popular patterns

Before leaving the pre-1800 wares, mention must be made of some of the popular standard patterns, which are mentioned on numerous occasions in the accounts, for it was the success of these colourful and tasteful designs which formed the foundation of the new company's success and enabled it to branch out and manufacture the expensive 'fancies' which have gained an unduly high esteem with most collectors.

The Chamberlain factory produced very few blue and white patterns, that is, hand-painted or printed designs in underglaze blue. Such wares were successfully produced in large quantities at the Caughley factory and perhaps Chamberlain consequently had little need to produce porcelains in this style, when he could simply order his blue and white 'common' patterns from Turner at Caughley. One of the few exceptions is the 'Royal Lily' or 'Lily' pattern. This formal floral pattern is illustrated in Plates 63–5, but its production is by no means limited to the Chamberlain factory. The original design could well have been copied from an Orien-

tal prototype; it occurs on Dr Wall period Worcester porcelains from about 1765, on post-1775 Caughley porcelain, on post-1783 Flight porcelain, as well as on much nineteenth-century porcelain, and the popularity of the 'Lily' pattern has been continued into the present century by the Royal Worcester Porcelain Company. This design was reputedly chosen by Queen Charlotte when she visited Worcester in 1788, and since then the 'Lily' design has been called the 'Royal Lily' or 'Queen Charlotte' pattern.

101. *Below:* A typical Chamberlain tumbler painted with the figure subjects 'Sappho & Phaon', as invoiced in August 1799. Buff and richly gilt ground. Written name mark. $3\frac{1}{2}$ in. high. *c.* 1799. *Dyson Perrins Museum, Worcester*

102. *Right:* A large three-piece Chamberlain vase, the main panel painted with 'Triumph of Mercy' subject. Salmon-pink ground, richly gilt in a traditional manner. Written name mark. 21 in. high. *c.* 1795–1800. *Messrs Sotheby & Co.*

Another design associated with royalty is popularly called 'the Queen's pattern' (see Plates 85 and 337), one of the most colourful and intricate of the so-called 'Japan' patterns, featuring underglaze blue with over-glaze red and green enamels and gilding. This design is often simply designated 'Queen' or 'Best Queen' in the factory records, but at other times it is referred to as '78', this being the official number in the list of Chamberlain patterns. The contemporary description reads: '78. Best Queen Mosaic, Blue & gold with India work. J. . .' (the page is torn here, but the missing name was almost certainly Spooner, see page 206). Records of articles decorated with this rich design include the following:

	£	s.	d.
1 Pair rich Queen, Root pots & stands	4	4	0
1 Flat chimney piece, Queen [see Plate 337]	2	2	0
1 Inkstand, Best Queen	1	11	6
1 Pint Jug, Best Queen	1	5	0
2 chocolates, two handled, with covers & saucers [1799]	3	3	0

The factory issued several other blue, red and gold 'Japan' patterns: the so-called 'Flower vase' design is illustrated in Plate 118 – it was design number 240 in the Chamberlain records but this pattern is more often found on unmarked Coalport porcelain (see Godden, *Coalport and Coalbrookdale Porcelains*, 1970). A less rich 'Japan' pattern is that which is often called the 'finger-pattern', and number 276 in the Chamberlain numbered list of patterns was originally termed '. . . India, Thumb & finger pattern'. This design is shown in Plates 300 and 420, but these designs belong to the post-1800 period.

A very popular Oriental-styled pattern is the one known as 'Dragon'; it differs from the other 'Japan' patterns in that it does not include any underglaze blue, the whole design being in overglaze enamel and gold. The pattern is shown in Plates 81, 86, 93 and Colour Plate XX. Apart from the original name 'Dragon', it is today often called either 'Tiger' or the 'Bishop Sumner' pattern. It is to be found on Dr Wall Worcester porcelain, on post-1775 Caughley wares, on hard-paste Plymouth porcelains (*c.* 1768–70), on the wares of all post-1783 Worcester partnerships, on some makes of Staffordshire porcelain such as Minton's and Spode's, and it also occurs on unmarked Coalport porcelains of the 1795–1810 period, as well as, more rarely, on Chinese porcelains.

The Chamberlain records in the mid 1790s normally include the written description 'Dragon in pannell' or 'Dragon', but from about 1796 the official pattern

number, 75, was employed. Typical entries taken from the factory records and relating to this pattern are:

	£	s.	d.
1 Large Gallon Punch bowl, Dragon [see Plate 260] [1794]	2	2	0
1 pair of ice-pails, Dragon [1795 stocklist, 'Painting Room']	8	0	0
1 Teaset, bell fluted, Dragon 75 [1797]	7	7	0
Dessert set, pattern No. 75 [see Plate 86] [1798]	21	0	0

In September 1799 a complete dinner (or 'Table') service with this pattern was sold and fortunately the many component parts were listed and priced sep-arately (see page 88):

Other post-1800 Chamberlain porcelains bearing the 'Dragon' pattern include:

			£	s.	d.
2 Quart jugs	Dragon	No. 75	2	2	0
2 Two-Quart	do.	do.	3	10	0
1 Three-quart jug [1801]	do.	do.	2	10	0

		£	s.	d.
1 Sandwich service complete	No. 75	8	8	0
4 Fruit baskets and stands 1st [size]	75	6	6	0
1 Fruit basket and stand 3rd [size]	75	2	12	6
2 Hives [honey pots]	75	1	16	0
3 Gallon Punch bowls Dragon		2	10	0
3 3-Quart Punch bowls do.		2	5	0
3 2-Quart Punch bowls do.		1	10	0
3 3-Pint Punch bowls do. [1803]		1	4	0

	£	s.	d.
1 Dessert centrepiece	1	16	0
2 Hearts [shaped dishes]	1	16	0
12 concave dessert plates at 8s. [1804]	4	10	0

It is possible that Messrs Chamberlain were the first English porcelain manufacturers to produce wares especially for the North American market, painted with American emblems. On 14 May 1795 the order book contained the entry: 'Samuel Guppy Esq., Guppy & Armstrong, Bristol. 1 complete teaset, new-fluted [shape], [pattern] no.18., with the American Arms, etc.'. The contemporary factory description for the standard pattern 18 was: '. . . Brown & gold sprigs & rose coloured border . . .' (the page is torn at this point). Also, in December 1798, when that year's stocklist was being compiled, in the 'Painting Room' there was apparently '1 Teapot, Gen¹. Washington £1 4s. 0d.', and perhaps several other similar examples were made and sold without a record being preserved.

The Chamberlain stocktaking lists and inventories record that the Chamberlains had available articles of undecorated Worcester porcelain: although the period of their manufacture is subject to doubt, they could have been pre-1783 Dr Wall period wares, or alternatively post-1783 Flight period Worcester porcelain. This statement is borne out by the following:

Worcester Ware.		£	s.	d.
3 centres [dessert centrepiece] plain white		1	1	0
13 tureens & covers	do.	1	19	0
36 shells [dessert dishes]	do.	2	12	0
46 hearts [dessert dishes]	do.	6	18	0
9 melons [dessert dishes]	do.	1	2	6
29 squares [dessert dishes]	do.	3	12	6
12 dessert plates 2nd [size]	do.		12	0
36 dessert plates 3rd [size]	do.	2	5	0
215 Table [dinner service] plates	do.	6	0	0

[Stocklist, dated 4 June 1792]

	£	s.	d.
90 dishes, old Worcester, desserts, white	4	10	0
43 coffee pots, old Worcr. white at 2s.	4	6	0
180 Pieces, old Worcester at 2d.	1	10	0
37 dozen old Worcr. odd pieces at 2s. 6d. per dozen	4	12	6

[Stocklist, dated 23 December 1793]

	£	s.	d.
1 old Worcester service	6	6	0
1 do.	9	9	0
1 do.	10	10	0
1 do.	12	12	0

[Stock in 'Damaged ware room', inventory of 1 January 1796]
Sundries old Worcester etc. etc. £30 0s. 0d.
[Stock in 'Glazed Warehouse', inventory of 1 January 1796]

It is therefore quite possible that the Chamberlain decorators painted some 'old Worcester' porcelain in the 1790s. These listed items were probably only the remainders from earlier, larger holdings of Worcester blanks. It has been suggested on page 20 that these decorators had earlier painted Dr Wall Worcester porcelain, either while employed by that company, or under contract; it is further possible that some of this ware was decorated with 'Fable' subjects in the Worcester tradition.

Further puzzling entries in the Chamberlain records refer to 'Houses', which were probably what are now called cottage pastille-burners. However, these entries occur in the 1790s, some twenty years before the period of most porcelain cottages. The 'Front Showroom' at the Chamberlain retail shop contained the following examples at the time of the December 1793 stocktaking: '10 enamelled Houses, 4 enamelled Houses, 2 white Houses'; but there are several even earlier entries, for instance: '15 Houses, enamelled to pattern, Pattern returned' (entry dated May 1790). The following were also probably not of Chamberlain's own make at this early period (although the firm later made their own versions); they might be of Derby manufacture.

17 Houses to Pattern
[April 1791]

1 Toy House, enamelled 4s.
[July 1791]

16 Houses, plain white £1 4s. 0d.
[June 1792 stocklist]

1 China House, enamelled 4s.
[November 1792]

The Chamberlain shop certainly stocked a variety of objects, which sometimes attracted strange customers, for the following is listed in the Day Book:

January 8th, 1796. Mr Ricketts, Surgeon, Droitwich. A cow his property this day came into the shop and broke the door window.

4

CHAMBERLAIN'S PRODUCTS 1800–1820

By 1800 the Chamberlains were very firmly established as porcelain manufacturers. They had built up an international trade and were capable of making useful wares to rival any other English porcelain manufacturer, whilst their ornamental items matched in quality and richness their only serious competitor, Messrs Flight & Barr. In the production of figures and groups, they wisely left this aspect of the trade to the Derby factory.

The standing of the Chamberlains at this period can be illustrated by the fact that when Lord Nelson with Sir William Hamilton and Lady Hamilton visited Worcester in August 1802, they chose to inspect the Chamberlain factory and not those of their two rivals. Not only did they inspect the works but they made purchases and placed a large order for a special, highly decorative service to be made bearing Nelson's arms, crest and orders. R. W. Binns in his *A Century of Potting in the City of Worcester* (1865) gives details of this visit as well as a first-hand account by one of the Chamberlain decorators – Binns quotes Lord Nelson as remarking that, 'although possessed of the finest porcelain the Courts of Dresden and Naples could afford, he had seen none equal to the productions of their [the Chamberlains'] manufactory'. He was surely being rather too flattering, but examples from the service he ordered in August 1802 do bear witness to the quality of the company's productions (see Plates 117, 118 and page 109). The Chamberlain accounts also show that the Corporation of Worcester presented Lord Nelson with a 'half circle ornament, view of Worcester, rich pattern' at a cost of 4 guineas. Such ornaments are now called bulb-pots (see Plates 336–45).

The Chamberlains carried on a vast business with the south-west of England as well as with London. Many pieces will be found, for example, with views of Cheltenham (see Plate 344) and these were presumably ordered and sold there by their agent Isaac Cook, at whose 'china warehouse . . . those who are anxious to decorate their tables with the luxury of the Worcester china manufactory may gratify their keenest appetite by the possession of such articles as Mr. Cook exhibits. . . . The public may be gratified by the constant display of some of the most beautiful and serviceable articles.' (Dr Dibdin's 1803 *History of Cheltenham*). Isaac Cook had the distinction of having purchased in June 1802 the most expensive teaset I have noted up to that period: '1 Complete teaset, rich 200 border and crimson and gold curtain with different figures £52 10s. 0d.'. (Pattern 200 was described as 'yellow ground gold and red diamonds with ovals etc'.) Other fine selections were also consigned to Thomas Rich of Cheltenham.

The following sample entries from the original order and sales books list some of the more standard porcelains supplied by the Chamberlains to these two retailers in Cheltenham between 1800 and 1805.

	£	s.	d.
1 Large half-circle pillar ornament, 240	3	3	0
2 do. tumblers and covers 240	3	3	0
8 Pug dogs, coloured proper at 3s.	1	4	0
2 swans		5	0
2 half pint mugs views of Spa, fancy pattern	1	8	0
3 chocolates yellow ground and views	3	3	0
1 rich chocolate cup, figure from Deserted Village	3	13	6
3 half pint Tumblers, raised covers, Views of Cheltenham	2	14	0
1 half pint Tumbler, figures and gold ground	2	2	0
10 quarter pint mugs, views of Cheltenham, yellow ground at 4s.	2	0	0
2 half pint mugs, painted views of Cheltenham at 12s.	1	4	0

Other, often very richly decorated porcelains of this nature were supplied to Elizabeth Ring to stock her retail shop at 8 High Street, Bristol (see Plate 104). This retailer, like others up and down the country, held a large assortment of earthenwares of all types, as well as glass decanters, wine glasses, fine porcelains, practically anything to furnish the table or to ornament the home.

After the death in 1801 of Robert Chamberlain senior, his two sons Humphrey and Robert in 1804 took as a partner Grey Edward Boulton, who no doubt replaced the original backer Richard Nash (see page 19). From 26 March 1804 the firm traded under the new style 'H & R Chamberlain & Co', although their wares still bore the old simple name and designation, 'Chamberlains Worcester'. At this date the gross amount of stock was agreed at £12,163 18s. 6d., with fixtures, utensils, etc., valued at £3,637 12s. 6d.

It is interesting to quote here the book-keeping arrangements at this time, which no doubt reflect those practised by the earlier partnership:

The Journal of Humphrey & Robert Chamberlain & Grey Edward Boulton; trading under the firm of H & R Chamberlain & Co. In these accounts which commence on the 26th day of March 1804 it is intended to employ the following books – viz.

A Petty or Subsidiary Cash Book to contain an account of all retail receipts and all contingent expenses as heretofore kept by Messrs Chamberlains.

A General Cash Book to contain an account of money or drafts of every kind received and paid on this partnership account, and into which it is intended to transfer once in every month the amount of the Debtor and creditors sides of the subsidiary cash book.

A Journal which is this book; Intended to receive all entries of every kind not belonging to the Cash account.

A General Ledger Into which is to be posted all accounts contained in the cash book and journal – except such as may belong immediately to the personal accounts of the principals themselves and them only, which are to be posted into private ledgers of which each partner is to be furnished with one. . . .

The Chamberlain wage records were made up two weeks to a page for the regular fortnightly payment, a

103. *Below:* Detail from the view painted on the dessert centre-piece to the 1818 set shown in Plate 146, showing the Chamberlain factory with Worcester Cathedral behind. The present Royal Worcester factory occupies the same original Chamberlain site. *Godden Reference Collection*

104. *Right:* The engraved trade card of Elizabeth Ring's retail establishment in Bristol. She was proprietress of the 'Worcester, Shropshire, Swansea and Staffordshire china, glass and earthenware rooms', and one of the Chamberlains' best West Country customers. Clearly the Chamberlain products were in competition in quality and price with many other makes. *Bristol Museum*

system which no doubt helped the company's cash-flow and presumably restricted excessive drinking by the workforce to a fortnightly rather than a weekly occurrence! The wage bill of Messrs Chamberlain for the following nine months, that is, from 25 March to 25 December 1804, totalled £3,407 18s. 6d. R. W. Binns calculated the average wage bill for the 1804–11 period at £4,500 per annum, or approximately £86 10s. 0d. per week. Gold to the value of £640 10s. 0d. was used to gild the porcelains in 1804. Fine grain gold was purchased from Messrs Bateman in London and cost £4 12s. 0d. per ounce, so that nearly 140 oz. of pure gold was used to enrich the Chamberlain porcelains between March and December of that year. The rent amounted to £149 0s. 0d. It is pleasant to learn that Mrs Chamberlain, together with the 'shop-woman', received an allowance which amounted to £147 10s. 0d. in 1805. The customers, too, were looked after – at least, Humphrey Chamberlain drew nearly £100 for entertaining customers over a three-year period. He was also involved in travelling, almost certainly to see customers and take their orders, and Bath, Bristol, Cheltenham and Oxford were favourite calls for the Chamberlains. George Rogers was another traveller at this period: in January 1808 he drew £4 0s. 6d. for expenses to Brighton. Other persons drawing travelling expenses were Thomas Grainger and J. Williams.

During this period the partners invested in a steam engine, purchased from the Coalbrookdale Company for £264 10s. 0d. In 1802 and 1803 numerous expenses were incurred in the purchase and fitting out of a new boat and a barge. The total profit for the period March to December was £1,169 7s. 9d. The profits were to be calculated at 15 per cent of the returns, and were to be divided: 50 per cent to Humphrey Chamberlain, 25 per cent to Robert and 25 per cent to the new, non-working partner, Grey Boulton. By 1807 the partners' capital was set down as follows:

	£	s.	d.
Humphrey Chamberlain	10,677	2	5¾
Robert Chamberlain	4,763	10	2¼
Grey Edward Boulton	3,598	18	8¼
	19,039	11	4¼

The capital credited to the two surviving Chamberlains (£15,440 12s. 8d.) was more than three times that to their credit in January 1796 (£4,581 9s. 1d.), a fact that would indicate their successful trading at this vital period. Humphrey Chamberlain had purchased his late father's share, or capital, for on 31 December 1801 the following entry appears – the only one I have traced relating to the death of the founder and senior partner in the Chamberlain concern:

To Humphrey Chamberlain, Worcester, for the amount of the late Robert Chamberlain senior's capital in this Trade, purchased by him from the executors of the said Robert Chamberlain. Gross £2,325 14s. 6d.

During the period 1804–11 the Chamberlains moved to larger premises at 59 High Street, Worcester, and appointed Messrs Asser of 6 Great Russell Street, Bloomsbury, as their London agent and main stockist, although undoubtedly other china dealers also displayed the Chamberlain porcelains.

Amongst the quantities of Chamberlain porcelain supplied to Asser & Co., a typical page from the factory account books details wares consigned to them on 26 August 1805, and here is a list of some of the more noteworthy items sent in 1805 and 1806:

	£	s.	d.
1 Large Root pots, Landscapes, yellow and gold	2	12	6
2 Root pots, and stands, basket of flowers	4	4	0
2 chocolate [cups] and stands, Wood's figures at	4	4	0
1 pint tumblers, coloured views, raised covers, yellow ground	1	1	0
2 half pint do.	1	12	0
1 large egg-shape ornament, Queen's pattern	4	4	0
2 urns, raised covers, views Malvern and Worcester	3	3	0
12 Thimbles, fancy		18	0
1 Large flat ornament, Charing Cross, fawn	4	4	0
2 small urn shape ornaments, views Malvern and Worcester	3	3	0
3 root pots and stands, shell and horn of plenty	6	16	6
1 Large 3 quart punch jug with cover, 240	5	5	0
1 Large hive [honey pot] 240	1	1	0
1 French [shape] ink, round 240	1	11	6
1 Quart jug 240	1	11	6
1 pair antique griffin [shape] candlesticks	2	2	0
1 pint mug, yellow ground, painted view of Oxford		15	0
2 pair oval Chamber candlesticks, with extinguishers [1805]	1	4	0

	£	s.	d.
1 Round egg-shape ornament, rich gold ground, flowers	8	8	0
1 small egg-shape ornament, yellow ground, view of Malvern, in square [panel]	1	11	6
1 do. Worcester in circle	1	11	6
1 Root pot, 1st size, Etruscan figures in panels red and gold	3	10	0
1 antique [shape] vase, no.403, view of Kirkstall	4	4	0
2 match boxes, French [shape], views of Cheltenham and Malvern Wells	3	0	0
2 End pieces and pint Tumblers and covers, Lesmore Castle and Blarney Castle [1806]	4	4	0

Similar assortments were dispatched to retailers in other towns, such as John Richardson of Cirencester or Henry Bowen of Bath.

The firm's advancement was greatly helped by royal patronage. On 25 September 1807 His Royal Highness the Prince of Wales visited Messrs Chamberlain, an event reported in the local press in glowing terms:

... His Royal Highness, with the greatest affability and condescension desired to see their elegant display of china, which had so particularly and frequently been noticed to him by many of his friends as so much deserving his Highness's attention. While attentively observing the many highly finished services now making for the Duke of Cumberland, Marchioness of Downshire, Marquis Wellesley, Lord Moira, Lord Carberry, &c. &c., his Royal Highness soon discovered and pointed out a piece from his own service made by Messrs Chamberlain some short time since and with which he expressed himself most perfectly satisfied.

... Infinitely pleased with the abundant variety of patterns presented for his inspection, and pronouncing their equal degree of merit did not admit of any decided preference, His Royal Highness desired a large table service, full dessert, breakfast and teaset with every necessary appendage might be made for him, each piece of a different pattern. ...

... His Royal Highness likewise requested that a complete set of superb vases might be painted with Historical subjects by Mr. Chamberlain's son [Humphrey Chamberlain junior, see page 187], whose natural genius and exquisitely finished productions had been named to him, long previous to his visiting Worcester.

In fact Humphrey Chamberlain had received the Royal Warrant as porcelain manufacturer to the Prince of Wales slightly before this visit, the Warrant being dated 3 August 1807, and from this date the factory mark sometimes records this fact (see page 33). On 25 May 1814 the Chamberlains were also appointed porcelain manufacturers to the Princess Charlotte of Wales and richly decorated dessert and dinner services were ordered by the Princess shortly after this. A plate similar to the dinner service pattern is illustrated in Colour Plate IX.

By this period it is possible that the Chamberlain factory was larger than that of their main rival, Messrs Barr, Flight & Barr, for when in May 1811 the city of Worcester was struck by a violent storm, the Barr premises lost 1,311 windows whereas the Chamberlains lost some 2,000. As to their respective output, whilst there are no firm figures, the collector today can expect to find more Chamberlain porcelain than pre-1820 Barr, Flight & Barr or Flight, Barr & Barr porcelain. As each firm was reasonably consistent at this period in marking their productions, the number of present-day findings probably reflect the original output of these two Worcester porcelain factories.

In July 1811 Messrs Chamberlain received an important order from the Prince Regent. This was for a 'harlequin' dessert service – each piece being of a different design. The ninety-six differently decorated dessert plates cost £3 3s. 0d. each (with forty-eight basket-rim ones at £3 13s. 6d. each) and the service included dolphin ice-pails, dolphin-supported cream-bowls, thirty-two dessert dishes in various shapes, and four large mugs painted with dead game (of the type illustrated in Plate 329). For this royal order a special hard body was reputedly introduced at great expense and the marks which occur on this rarely-found porcelain incorporate the description 'Regent Porcelain' (see page 33). The Prince Regent also ordered in February 1813 a superb set of three ornamental vases painted by Humphrey Chamberlain's son, Humphrey junior, and costing 100 guineas. With later orders, the Prince Regent's total order amounted to more than £4,000, but over four years later Messrs Chamberlain were still awaiting payment!

It is interesting to note that under the date 30 May 1812 there is an entry in the account book headed 'Billingsley, Worcester' for a 'Plan of Building a standing kiln, £5 0s. 0d.'. This no doubt relates to the famous and much travelled ceramic painter William Billingsley, who from at least October 1808 to November 1813 was working for Messrs Barr, Flight & Barr at Worcester.

Some superb Chamberlain porcelains were ordered by Lord Nevill in June 1813, and both the original order and some of the items still exist. The first item is illustrated on the jacket of this book and also in Colour Plate VIII and Plate 105, whilst two of the large 'Grace' mugs are shown in Plates 106 and 227 (on view in the Dyson Perrins Museum at Worcester).

The order ran:

Lord Nevill at Earl of Abergavenny's, Berkeley Square. To be sent to 63 Piccadilly and advise his Lordship, to be ready in four months.

5 ornaments.
  1 Regent [shape vase] Henry 8th.
  2 chocolates, King John,
                King Richard 3rd.
  2 Bell shape, Henry 6th, part 1.
                King John.   £60 18s. 0d.
  2 Luminaries.
  2 Graces mugs, Power of Love
    No. 1   and 2.   £42 0s. 0d.

These items, together with '1 new long ink, rich fawn and figures, £15 15s. 0d.', were dispatched (or invoiced) from Worcester on 21 July 1814, over a year after the original order was placed. Other Chamberlain porcelain

105. The reverse side of the 'Regent' shape vase made for Lord Nevill and shown in Colour Plate VIII, showing his armorial bearings and also the fine quality of the gilding. Painted mark. 10½ in. high. Order dated June 1813. *Private collection*

106. One of a pair of large orange- and gold-ground 'Grace' mugs (see also Plate 227), painted by Humphrey Chamberlain and invoiced at £42 the pair in 1813. There are armorial bearings on the side, as on the vase shown in Plate 105. Written marks 'Bacchante, Worcester Porcelain Manufacturers, By appointment to his Royal Highness The Prince Regent'. 6¾ in. high. 1813. *Dyson Perrins Museum, Worcester*

ordered by Lord Nevill in June 1813 included a dinner service for £105 0s. 0d., a dessert service for £50 8s. 0d., plus a pair of dolphin-supported ice-pails at £22 1s. 0d., a Baden-shaped teaset of pattern 298 at £16 16s. 0d. with some extra items such as butter tubs, muffin dishes and egg stands.

In January 1814 Messrs Chamberlain opened their own London showrooms at 63 Piccadilly, moving to 155 New Bond Street in July 1816. These events are of great importance to collectors today – as they were to the Chamberlains' trade at the time – for these addresses were incorporated in the company's marks, so enabling such specimens to be approximately dated. Also, the stylish goods sent down to the London premises were listed, so it is possible to gauge which Chamberlain

porcelains were regarded as the most fashionable at that time.

The sample listings (taken from the thirty-nine cases of porcelains valued at £3,279 2s. 3d. that were sent to London in 1813) given on page 103 include the original prices to show at least the comparison between the various items. When reading these prices, which were probably wholesale prices, one should bear in mind the purchasing power of the pound sterling, or rather the gold guinea, at that period.

The first consignment of porcelains to stock the new London retail shop in Piccadilly was sent on 25 October 1813. The selection included several pieces in the French taste or even of French manufacture (see page 136), and other items painted with the highly fashionable shell or feather motifs (see page 178) similar in style to the then current Flight, Barr & Barr Worcester porcelains. Some of these articles sent down from Worcester in the last months of 1813 before the official opening were:

	£	s.	d.
2 egg-shape ornaments, French handles, feathers	6	6	0
1 small Regent ornament, Feathers	5	5	0
1 egg [shape] vase, shells	4	4	0
2 small inks, Feathers	3	3	0
1 tea set, different feathers	31	10	0
3 Potpourri pots, rich paintings, flowers, feathers and landscapes	31	10	0
1 Quart mug, dogs	2	12	6
1 Dessert service, fawn [ground] Vandyke different paintings. Dolphin creamboats [see Plates 107, 146, 223 and 224]	89	5	0
1 centre ornament, shell and dolphin handles with cattle, fawn ground	5	5	0
4 greyhounds and oak trees	2	0	0
2 two-handle, F [French] cabinets, square foot, [painted] loose feathers	4	4	0
1 Baden [shape] cup and saucer, feathers	2	2	0
2 do. shells	5	5	0
3 large Regent mugs, Dead Game, [pattern] 403 and rich border [see Plates 329–31]	15	15	0
2 rich plates, figures and frames	68	5	0
2 rich French cans and stands, figures	21	0	0
1 plate, Coriolanus	31	10	0
1 Regent ornamental caudle, Timon [see Plate 234]	6	6	0
1 new F [French] ink, Tintern Abbey	2	12	6
1 Regent ornament, Edward & Elinora, fawn marbled [ground] Walters	15	15	0
2 do. King John and Taming the Shrew, Walters	16	16	0

[These last two entries include the very rare mention of the artist's name – Walter Chamberlain – see page 191.]

	£	s.	d.
1 Rich full size Regent ornament – Triumph of Mercy – fawn marbled [ground] Humphrey	31	10	0

[This piece was evidently painted by Humphrey Chamberlain, see page 187.]

	£	s.	d.
2 Regent ornaments, composition marble [ground] Figures, King Henry 6th, Comedy of Errors	31	10	0

Once again the Chamberlains intended to make a 'flaming shew' as their father, Robert, had done with his first shop in High Street, Worcester, in 1789, some twenty years previously. This time, instead of Flight's comments, the manager of Wedgwood's London showrooms wrote on 7 January: 'Mr. Chamberlain of Worcester has just established a very handsome china shop – where there are many very beautiful vases and sets of china. I fear he will prove a dangerous rival in our china trade.'

Concerning the expenses of opening this London shop, one is struck by the relatively high cost of travel – 'expenses three times up and down £53 17s. 0d.' – a very large sum in those days. Other expenses were

107.   A tureen from the fine 1818 dessert service shown in Plate 146 showing the rich gilding and fine-quality flower painting of this period (see also Colour Plate XVII). Name mark inside cover. 8¾ in. high. *Godden of Worthing Ltd*

more mundane: 'Sundry furniture £4 8s. 1d.', 'Shop cloths 16s.', 'Fire Irons £2 8s. 0d.', 'Fancy painting £16 0s. 0d.'.

The opening of the Chamberlains' own retail shop in London afforded them the opportunity to be abreast of fashion and to take special orders direct. It is interesting to follow developments; for example, on 14 February 1814 the manager in London purchased a print of the 'Sleeping Musician' for 12s. and on 8 March a print of a 'Madonna and Child'. On 4 June 1814 expensive porcelains bearing these subjects were invoiced to London:

	£	s.	d.
1 plate, Madonna and Child	10	0	0
1 can and stand, Sleeping Musician	10	10	0

This plate is almost certainly the one signed by Humphrey Chamberlain and illustrated in Plate 235.

The order and sales books continued to be filled with London orders for richly decorated items – in such profusion that only a few sample entries must suffice:

His Royal Highness, Prince Frederick of Orange, Curzon
  Street, Mayfair, London.
1 small dolphin ornament, feathers, etc. £3 3s. 0d.
    [October 1814]

                                                    £   s.   d.

Francis Nalder Esq, London.
1 Large Regent ornament, view of Coniston Lake,
    green ground and fine bronze border   10 10   0
2 new-make side pieces to match, Mercury
    handles, views Burnam Wood and Ragland   10 10   0
    [A vase form seemingly with these new-make
    'Mercury-head' handles is shown in Plates 108
    and 391]
    [November 1814]

Thomas King Esq, London.
1 complete dessert set, drab and embossed union [border]
    different feathers £42 0s. 0d.
    [September 1815]

Lady Somers, London.
2 vase ornaments, Ridley make, fawn ground and gold border
    with different views of Eastnor Castle £10 10s. 0d.
    [October 1815]

These, and all other goods made up to about June
1816, would bear the 63 Piccadilly address as part of the
standard name mark, but from July 1816 the sale book
entries refer to the new shop at 155 New Bond Street.
The fixtures seem to have been rather more costly in
these premises, costing £111 16s. 3d., with 2 guineas for
a desk, the 'fancy painting' costing £24 16s. 0d., and the
charwoman and sweep grouped together at £3 4s. 2½d.
(The later expenses of this shop are detailed on page
140.)

Amongst the fine and decorative porcelain sent to
stock these Bond Street premises was a selection of
charming animal models – dogs, stags, cats, pigs, lambs,
etc. – a grouping of which is illustrated in Plate 246.

Also in this year the royal orders for Princess
Charlotte and the Prince Regent were entered. The
breakfast service included seventy-two 8 in. plates of
which twelve were painted with different views of
Waterloo, priced at £3 13s. 6d. each. The dinner service
was of the design illustrated in Colour Plate IX, the
thirty-six soup plates being charged at £2 each.

Perhaps one should correct any impression the reader
may have gained that all Chamberlain products of
the 1800–20 period were richly decorated ornamental
wares; this is very far from the case, for as with any
porcelain manufacturer his success or failure depends
on the saleability of his standard production – his tea
and dessert services. If these do not compete in style,
taste, price and durability with those of his competitors,

108.   Detail from a Chamberlain 'Mercury-head' vase of a characteristic shape mentioned in an account dated November 1814 (see
also Plates 221 and 391). The panel depicts the Chamberlain factory
with the Bath road toll-gate in the foreground (see also Plate 103).
c. 1814. *Geoffrey Godden, chinaman*

he is soon out of business. The remainder of this chapter
deals with these everyday tablewares.

Again, it must be pointed out that the Chamberlains
in Worcester and London also stocked other wares to
round off their stock or perhaps to meet special orders.
They supplied Staffordshire printed earthenware dinner
services, Swansea earthenwares, Mason's Patent Ironstone China, Bristol glasswares, Derby porcelains,
decorative papier mâché trays, and other Wolverhamp-
ton wares.* There is also very clear evidence that the
Chamberlains purchased French porcelain, some of
which would have been in the white undecorated state.
This was resold to independent decorators such as John
Powell (see page 204), but other French items were
apparently painted by their own artists (see page 181).

The cash book under the date 19 November 1817 also
shows that Humphrey's other son, Walter Chamberlain,
emulated John Flight (see page 18) and visited France.
It is not known if this was to purchase French goods to
resell in London, or whether he went to sell their own
porcelain; his expenses are noted at £22 17s. 6d.

---

*This last aspect of the stock is discussed in my article 'English Paper
Trays, 1790–1815', *The Connoisseur*, August 1967.

Teawares

There was, of course, no complete change of basic shapes or patterns as the nineteenth century commenced; rather, there was a gradual progression and continuation of earlier popular patterns. The porcelain body itself at this period is still extremely compact and hard, covered with a glittery glaze, although it does not have quite as hard or glossy an appearance as the 1792–5 wares.

The teapot shown in Plate 109 serves to link the Chamberlain teawares of the late 1790s with those of the early 1800s. It has the same oval spiral-fluted or shanked body and the same knob as found on the pots illustrated in Plates 70–74. The only amendment is in the 'C'-shape handle with the thumb-rest at the apex; notice also the fact that the 'C' handle is joined to the body by a separate bar, which may be compared with the insulation piece between the body and the handle found on many silver teapots of the period. This same basic shape of teapot was made by most English porcelain manufacturers of the 1800–10 period and has been termed the 'new oval' shape; but this particular specimen is a transitional one between the old standard shanked oval and the new oval which is shown in Plates 110–12.

In considering the new oval shape teawares, observe the change of basic form – the oval globular body without the earlier slight waist, the handle form, in particular, and the new knob shape which is a characteristic feature of the early 1800s. These new oval teawares will be found to span popular early inexpensive patterns such as number 21, seen in Plate 110, to later patterns such as the blue and gold design 385 illustrated in Plate 111, a design number which appears in the order books from 1806. This pattern is listed at £6 6s. 0d. per set on the 'Hambleton-fluted' shape. The differing cup and jug shapes in these two sets are interesting. It is also noteworthy that the cheaper services, even into the early 1800s, had handle-less teabowls rather than handled teacups (compare Plates 110 and 111). The plain version of this fluted 'Bute'-type cup is shown in Plate 426.

Whilst writing of differences, it is as well to remark that in 1801, as far as is known, another Worcester apprentice and former Chamberlain hand, Thomas Grainger, established his own decorating establishment and manufactory in Worcester. In general Grainger tended to copy the Chamberlain shapes and designs rather than those of Barr, Flight & Barr, and these early Grainger wares can quite easily confuse the collector, especially when they do not bear one of the early painted marks: 'Grainger-Wood & Co'; 'Grainger & Co'; or

'New China Works, Worcester'. Plate 112 illustrates a typical early Grainger teapot which should be compared with the Chamberlain examples shown in Plates 110 and 111. Other Grainger porcelains are illustrated in my *British Porcelain: An Illustrated Guide* (1974). Note that this Grainger teapot bears the so-called 'tramlines' or double-line at the top of each flute, a characteristic often quoted as a Chamberlain feature (see page 78).

The Chamberlain teawares illustrated in Colour Plate X unfortunately do not bear a pattern number, indeed they are completely unmarked; but the design reflects earlier Worcester styles with its rich dark-blue ground and superbly painted birds in landscapes – almost certainly the work of George Davis (see page 192). This set, at least, answers the pattern description for number 553, 'Davis' birds in pannel blue & gold ground £25 4s. 0d.'.

109. An attractive shanked Chamberlain teapot decorated with pattern 21, originally listed at £4 14s. 6d. for the complete set. This neat design is painted in brown with gilt enrichments. Name mark and pattern number written inside cover. 7¼ in. high. *c.* 1800–5. *Godden of Worthing Ltd*

The set shows the plain, unfluted version of the standard boat-shaped teapot and covered sugar in Plates 110 and 111. However, the creamer is of a new shape, a progression seen mainly in the new cup shapes and cup-handle forms. Plates 110–11 feature teasets with the same basic form of teapot (spiral-fluted and faceted) but with different classes of decoration and with widely differing cup forms, ranging in period from about 1800 to 1810. Patterns 253, 327 and 342, ordered in February 1807, were to have 'new handles', indicating an as yet unidentified new cup-handle form.

110. *Opposite:* Representative pieces from a shanked Chamberlain teaset of the brown and gilt pattern 21, showing slightly later forms. Written name mark inside cover, pattern number only on some other pieces. Teapot 10 in. long. *c*. 1802–7. *Godden of Worthing Ltd*

111. Representative pieces from a blue and gold Chamberlain tea service of pattern 385, originally priced at £6 6s. 0d. for the complete set. The shapes here are slightly later than those seen in Plate 110. Name mark inside teapot cover. Teapot 6¼ in. high. *c*. 1805–8. *Godden of Worthing Ltd*

112. A shanked teapot and cover from the rival Grainger factory at Worcester; note the slightly different form, particularly the knob. Grainger pattern 209. 10¾ in. long. *c*. 1805. *Godden Reference Collection*

Within this same period it is clear that several other Chamberlain teaware shapes were being supplied with the post-1800 range of pattern numbers, which numbered from about 200. The reader should always remember that at any one period each manufacturer was producing several different teaware shapes, so that the china retailers were able to offer their customers a choice of designs and shapes.

Take, for example, the creamers or milk-jugs shown in the next four illustrations (Plates 113–16). That in Plate 113 is one of the most elegant and trimly potted that I have seen and I long to find the matching tea-pot shape or a covered sugar to match. It would be interesting to discover if the cup-handles follow this jug-

113.   A very well-potted and rare form of shanked Chamberlain milk- or cream-jug painted in blue and gold with pattern 300. Unmarked. 4¾ in. high. *c.* 1801–5. *Godden Reference Collection*

114.   A rather squat shanked Chamberlain jug with yellow and gold border, pattern 221, which was originally sold at £6 6s. 0d. for the complete set. Relief-moulded capital 'T' mark (see page 208) and gilt pattern number. 4 in. high. *c.* 1800–5. *Geoffrey Godden, chinaman*

115.   A narrow-oval Chamberlain shanked milk-jug, with under-glaze blue and gilt design. Relief-moulded capital 'T' mark (see page 208). 4½ in. high. *c.* 1800–5. *E. H. Chandler Collection*

116.   A non-fluted oval Chamberlain milk-jug, decorated with a brown band and gilding. Unmarked. 4½ in. high. *c.* 1800–5. *B. Green Collection*

handle shape. This specimen – the only one known to me – bears the pattern number 300, which agrees with the Chamberlain list of teaware designs: 'Shanked [spiral-fluted shape], enamelled blue & gold wreaths etc. £5 5s. 0d.'. Orders for this pattern span the period October 1801 to January 1803; the pattern on the standard shanked shapes is shown in Plate 422.

The pattern number 221 on the next little jug (see Plate 114) is slightly lower and the potting is rather thicker than on the previous example. Of course, all these non-circular shapes were formed with the aid of plaster of Paris moulds and this jug also bears the relief-moulded initial 'T' under the base, relating to the original modeller or mould-maker – in this case probably John Toulouse (see page 208).

The two jugs in Plates 115 and 116 are of a very narrow oval plan. Unfortunately neither bears a pattern number, but the blue and gold shanked example again has the modeller's relief-moulded 'T' initial mark. The brown and gold example shows the non-fluted version of

this shape, but with two horizontal ribs in the body. I have also seen a creamer of the same shape with upright fluting. Similar jugs accompanied the teasets illustrated in Plates 74 and 80, although these two examples were probably made after 1800.

It is pleasing to be able to illustrate some of the more ornate and expensive designs, especially as one particular set can be approximately dated to 1802–5. This is the tea and breakfast service made for Admiral Lord Nelson at the time of his visit to the works in August 1802 (see page 31). If one can assume that at this period the basic shape of the teawares (see Plates 117 and 118) was agreed upon, then these teaware shapes date to 1802 at the earliest, or at the latest 1805 when the set was finally completed.

117. One of the two teapots from the service ordered by Admiral Lord Nelson in August 1802. The basic design is Chamberlain's 'Japan' pattern number 240, but here it also has intricate armorial bearings and supporters (see also Plate 118). Written name mark inside cover. 10 in. long. c. 1802–5. *Messrs Christie, Manson & Woods*

118. Representative pieces from the service ordered by Admiral Lord Nelson in August 1802 and listed on page 110. The basic design is number 240 – underglaze blue with overglaze red, green and gilding. Name marks and pattern numbers on some pieces. c. 1802–5. *Dyson Perrins Museum, Worcester*

The shape of the teapot is the 'new oval' but it has a ring knob and rather more elegant supporting shapes reflecting, no doubt, the more expensive nature of the order. The background pattern is Chamberlain's popular number 240 'Japan'-style design with its combination of a deep underglaze blue with overglaze red, green and gold. The official description was 'fine old Japan pattern, same as Roses' (John Rose of Coalport) at £12 12s. 0d. for the complete teaset. In my *Coalport and Coalbrookdale Porcelains*, 1970 (Plates 21, 48, 55 and 83) I refer to Rose's version of this design as the flower vase pattern. The design was originally much used on Japanese porcelains of the 1690–1720 period, hence the use by Chamberlain of the description 'Old Japan'. His version of this Japanese design can be seen in the smaller plate on the left of the Nelson grouping (see Plate 118) and in Plates 328, 341 and 360. This pattern number occurs in the Chamberlain orders by April 1802.

The details of the Nelson breakfast service are entered in the order book under the date 26 August 1802. It seems doubtful, however, if His Lordship ever saw the finished service, for the account was not written up until January 1806 after his death at Trafalgar on 21 October 1805; and the matching dinner and dessert services with the decorative vases were apparently never made, although at least one extra plate is known and this may have been part of the dessert service made before

the order was cancelled after his death. This example, similar to the large plate shown in Plate 118, was sold in July 1980 for £3,600 at Messrs Phillips's London auction galleries.

The original account with the individual charges is of interest, but to these should be added the extra payments for adding the arms, crests, etc., to the standard 240 'Japan' pattern. Only the larger pieces, such as the teapot and the bread and butter plates, were embellished with the full armorial bearings at a cost of £1 10s. 0d. each; the smaller items bore only the crests, egrets and coronets as can be seen from the selection in Plate 118. These emblems were charged as follows:

	£	s.	d.
150 Ducal coronets at 1s.	7	10	0
150 crests, San Josif at 2s. 6d.	18	15	0
150 Viscounts coronets at 2s.	15	0	0
5 Egyptian Egrets at 2s. 6d.		12	6

The basic charges for this large breakfast service were listed as:

	£	s.	d.
2 Teapots and stands	2	6	0
2 cream ewers		18	0
2 sugar boxes	1	4	0
2 slop bowls	1	4	0
4 B & B [bread & butter] plates	2	4	0
2 [hot] water plates & covers	8	8	0
2 butter tubs and stands	3	4	0
2 large hives [honey pots]	1	12	0
12 cake plates, 2nd size	5	14	0
6 egg cups and drainers	3	3	0
1 dish, 12 inches	1	16	0
4 dishes, 10 inches	5	8	0
12 half pint bowls and stands	12	12	0
12 quarter pint bowls & stands	9	9	0
12 coffees [and] saucers	6	15	0
6 chocolate cups and stands, complete	6	6	0

119. A French hard-paste large saucer decorated in the fashion of the Nelson service but not of such good quality as the Chamberlain examples. Unmarked. Diameter 6¼ in. *c*. 1880. *Godden Reference Collection*

The twelve half- and quarter-pint 'bowls and stands' as invoiced were almost certainly the large and small teacups and saucers, one of which is illustrated in Plate 118.* Note this 1805 period cup profile and handle shape, later found with some very attractive designs.

In connection with this Nelson service it is relevant to mention that some hard-paste porcelains occur with the Nelson armorial bearings. These appear to be good-quality French reproductions of the second half of the nineteenth century. A very decorative breakfast-cup saucer in the Godden Reference Collection is shown in Plate 119, and a plate of the same class is in the

*Some pieces from this service can be seen at the National Maritime Museum, Greenwich.

120. Representative pieces from a tea service painted with pattern 276, known as 'thumb and finger'. The teapot shape is the same as the Nelson pot shown in Plate 117. Painted name mark with pattern number inside covers. Teapot 6¾ in. high. *c*. 1802–5. *Godden of Worthing Ltd*

Victoria & Albert Museum; but I do not regard these as true Chamberlain products.

Another very popular Chamberlain 'Japan' pattern was numbered 276 and described as the 'Thumb & finger pattern' on account of the two prominent dark-blue features to the left of the all-over design (see Plate 120). This, too, was a popular Coalport pattern (see Plate 40 of my *Coalport and Coalbrookdale Porcelains*, 1970).

This 'thumb and finger' patterned set includes the Nelson shape teapot and creamer of the 1802 period with the matching sugar bowl, but with a different handle form to the cups. This ring or '9' handle is also seen in Plate 123 and was a popular one of the period, being used by most English manufacturers. The Chamberlains' pattern 276 was mentioned in accounts by at least June 1803.

Yet another popular Chamberlain 'Japan' pattern also appears on Nelson shape tewares. This is number 310, priced at 10 guineas for the complete set in June

121. A 'Japan' pattern (number 310) milk-jug. The shape is typical of Chamberlain but the style of decoration is common to most factories of the period. Unmarked. 5¾ in. high. *c*. 1803–6. *Godden of Worthing Ltd*

122. A typical Chamberlain covered sugar bowl form decorated with the popular 'Japan' pattern 310. Painted name mark and pattern number inside cover with moulded initial 'T' (see page 208). 5½ in. long. *c.* 1803–6. *Godden of Worthing Ltd*

123. A trio of coffee cup, teacup and saucer painted with the colourful and popular 'Japan' pattern 310 (as in Plates 121 and 122). Such sets were originally priced at £10 10s. 0d. Painted pattern number only. Diameter of saucer 6 in. *c.* 1803–6. *Godden of Worthing Ltd*

1803. The design, as well as the sugar bowl, creamer and cup shapes, is well illustrated in Plates 121–3, where the slightly tapering shape of the typical Chamberlain coffee can be seen.

Plates 125 and 126 depict a new teapot shape differing in handle and spout forms from the Nelson-type wares. These new 'Dejeune' wares also bear slightly later pattern numbers. The teapot in Plate 125 is decorated with pattern 298 – 'rich blue border of gold with ovals of India work, £14 14s. 0d.'. The description 'India' was very often used to mean Oriental. A coffee can and saucer of this design is shown in Plate 127. Note the tapering can shape with a handle reminiscent of the earlier handle shown in Plates 78 and 80.

Plate 126 shows a truly elegant design, with a finely painted leaf and berry design on a gold ground. This pattern appears to be number 358 – 'Dejeune, holly border on gold ground, Vandike gold border below, £16 16s. 0d.' – which was one of the most highly priced designs of the period. The next design, number 359, was first listed in the order books on 1 January 1806. It is interesting to see that the standard painted mark, 'Chamberlains Worcester Warranted', was still being placed inside the teapot cover (see Plate 70).

In this study of the Chamberlain productions, and in particular the teawares which are under discussion here, it would be satisfying to know that all the Chamberlain shapes are unique. Unfortunately this is not so, since

there exists positive evidence that some teaware shapes, or the basic models, came from a Staffordshire source. There is an entry in the accounts for 30 November 1812 which reads:

	£	s.	d.
Benjamin Bentley. Edmond Street, Hanley.			
For a set of Teapot models, complete including			
sugar and cream moulds	2	2	0
Moulds		15	0

Bentley was paid a further £3 12s. 0d. for sundry moulds on 31 December 1813.

Unfortunately it cannot be proved which basic shape was supplied by this Staffordshire modeller, but it is possible that it was a version of that popular teaware shape now generally known as 'London', although Chamberlain did not use this name. These forms are common to all English porcelain manufacturers of the approximate period 1813–25 but they are comparatively scarce in Chamberlain porcelain and seemingly non-existent in Flight, Barr & Barr wares; at least, the standard 'London' handle form (see Plate 132, left) does not occur.

Plate 128 shows the Chamberlain version of the 'London' shape teapot, alas without the tip of the spout or a pattern number. A further example is shown in Plate 425. The standard covered sugar bowl of 'London' shape is illustrated in Plate 129. Here the early pattern 'Hunting in Compartments', number 9, appears on a shape of approximately 1815. These basic teapot and sugar-box shapes can also occur, at a slightly later date, with an ornate floral wreath knob (see Plates 134 and 427).

The Chamberlain version of the so-called 'London' shape teawares sometimes appears with at least two different relief-moulded floral designs (as seen on the sugar basin illustrated in Plate 130 and on the teapot in Plate 131, with the standard 'London' shape knob). An order dated 19 February 1814 referred to the first embossed tea and dessert services, a description that seemingly relates to these relief-moulded forms (see Plates 130, 132 and 133), and the pattern lists of early 1816 include the description 'embossed' from about

124.   An attractive Chamberlain teapot painted with the early and popular pattern 21 (see also pages 105 and 312). Painted name mark pattern number inside cover. 6¾ in. high. *c.* 1803–6. *H. Martin Collection*

125.   *Centre:* A 'Dejeune' shape Chamberlain teapot decorated with the colourful pattern 298, 'rich blue border of gold with ovals of India work', originally priced at £14 14s. 0d. for the complete set. Painted name mark and pattern number inside cover. 9¼ in. long. *c.* 1803–6. *G. Spencer Collection*

126.   An elegant 'Dejeune' shape teapot painted with pattern 358, 'holly border on gold ground . . .', originally priced at £16 16s. 0d. for the complete set. This example rests on its original stand. Written name mark and pattern number inside cover. 9¼ in. long. *c.* 1803–6. *Geoffrey Godden, chinaman*

128. *Centre left:* A well-painted Chamberlain teapot of the so-called 'London' shape (a name not used by the Chamberlains). No pattern number but perhaps number 634 or 639. Printed New Bond Street mark (see page 34, Mark 10) inside cover. 5¼ in. high. 1816–18. *Mr & Mrs P. Miller Collection*

129. *Above:* A Chamberlain covered sugar basin of the 'London' shape painted with pattern 9, introduced in the early 1790s. Painted pattern number only. 7¼ in. long. *c.* 1813–16. *Geoffrey Godden, chinaman*

130. *Left:* An attractive floral-embossed Chamberlain sugar basin painted with a light green ground. Printed Piccadilly address mark. 6¼ in. high. *c.* 1813–16. *Godden of Worthing Ltd*

number 723 – 'Emboss'd with different flowers & olive ground'.

Two floral-embossed cups are shown in Plate 132. The one on the left is of a characteristic 'London' teacup shape – it is typical in every way of this general popular type. The cup on the right, which bears the same (unnumbered) pattern, is of the same shape as the 1815 Sir James Yeo pieces (see page 116, also Colour Plate XI,

127. *Opposite:* A Chamberlain coffee cup or coffee can and saucer decorated with the rich pattern 298 (as in Plate 125). Marked with pattern number only. Cup 2½ in. high. *c.* 1803–6. *G. Spencer Collection*

131. *Above right:* An orange-ground Chamberlain teapot showing the 'Union' relief design including the national emblems. Unmarked. 10 in. long. *c.* 1816–18. *Mr & Mrs P. Miller Collection*

132. *Right:* Two Chamberlain floral-embossed cups of the same (unnumbered) pattern but different standard shapes. The one on the left is of the 'London' shape as made by most English porcelain manufacturers in the approximate period 1812–20. Unmarked. 2⅛ in. and 2½ in. high respectively. *Godden Reference Collection*

133. *Below:* Representative pieces from a decorative Chamberlain teaset showing the floral-embossed border and hand-painted floral designs. Painted marks 'Chamberlains Worcester'. Diameter of bowl 6¼ in. *c.* 1815–18. *Messrs Delomosne & Son*

134. *Below:* A superbly decorated covered sugar from the service made for Sir James Yeo, ordered in 1815 (see Colour Plate XI). It is surprising that this special piece does not bear a factory mark. 5 in. high. *c.* 1815–19. *Godden Reference Collection*

135. *Bottom:* A breakfast-size cup and saucer from the service made for Sir James Yeo and listed on page 117. The basic design is number 298, charged at £1 4s. 6d. per cup and saucer plus the cost of painting the crests, mottoes and orders. Unmarked. Diameter of saucer 6½ in. *c.* 1815–19. *Godden Reference Collection*

Plates 134 and 135) but has additional relief-moulding. The matching teapot and sugar basin would also have the floral wreath knob of the type seen on the Yeo sugar depicted in Plate 134. These would be the 'Baden embossed' teawares mentioned in the factory records, and representative shapes are shown in Plate 133. The Chamberlain 'Baden' shape teawares are apparently of the 'London' shape but with different forms of cups.

A quite different type of relief-moulding, illustrated in Plate 131, was called 'Union' as it featured the national emblems of England, Scotland and Ireland – the rose, the thistle and the shamrock respectively. This moulding was in use by pattern 702, which reads, 'Union pattern in colours, rose, thistle & shamrock £8 8s. 0d. with gold sprigs £10 10s. 0d.', although it is not clear if these emblems were relief-moulded or merely painted on the surface. However, by pattern 741 the meaning is rather more clear: 'Grey [ground] Union sprigs emboss'd, £10 10s. 0d.'. Relief-moulded 'Union' designs also occur on dessert wares (see page 126 and Plates 149, 150 and 155). In Plate 131 the same basic form of 'London' or 'Baden' shape teapot is illustrated.

The magnificent range of tea and breakfast wares shown in Colour Plate XI and in Plates 134 and 135

represents a most important order placed by Sir James Yeo (1782–1818), for it includes a selection of pieces representing related first quality or expensive shapes of the 1815–20 period.

As with the Nelson service (see page 110), the order was not complete until after the death of the would-be owner, on passage home from Jamaica in 1818. The invoice was submitted to his executor on 8 January 1820, some five years after the order was placed, probably in 1815 when '2 rich pattern plates' were supplied. The basic pattern is Chamberlain's number 298 (see Plate 125) but enriched with Sir James Yeo's crest and orders. The order commenced with a dessert service costing 42 guineas, plus the cost of painting the crests and other personal attainments, but of interest at this point are the

tea and breakfast wares, which were of the 'Baden' shape.

The invoice detailed:

		£	s.	d.
12 breakfast cups and saucers, Baden, No. 298		14	14	0
18 tea cups and saucers,	do.	11	0	6
2 slop bowls,	do.	1	8	0
1 sugar,	do.		14	0
1 cream,	do.		14	0
1 Pint milk [see Plate 321],	do.	1	0	0
2 muffins and covers,	do.	3	12	0
1 egg stand, five cups,	do.	2	12	6
2 butter tubs and stands,	do.	3	12	0
Painting 111 crests, mottoes, Orders &c &c				
at 10s.		55	10	0

Most of these 'Baden' shape porcelains are illustrated in Colour Plate XI. I first observed this shape designation against pattern 441 in the factory list, and pattern 298, mentioned in the Yeo order, was first issued on the 'Dejeune' shape (see Plate 125). The price per cup

136. Representative pieces from a richly decorated Chamberlain tea service of pattern 767, originally priced at £12 12s. 0d.: the factory cost of the various processes is detailed on page 118. Written name mark with pattern number. Diameter of bread plate 8½ in. c. 1816–20. Geoffrey Godden, chinaman

137. A cup from the service shown in Plate 136 showing the attractive handle form; note the little face at the base of the handle. Pattern number 767. 2¾ in. high. c. 1816–20. *Geoffrey Godden, chinaman*

138. A circular covered sugar from a teaset of pattern 1319, 'Baden gadroon, Royal blue & gold leaf & drops of gold £10 10s. 0d.'. Written name mark with pattern number. 4½ in. high. c. 1828–30. *Godden of Worthing Ltd*

and saucer was 12s. 2d., the larger breakfast cups and saucers (see Plate 135) were twice this amount, and the other costs are clearly set out. Remember, however, that they relate to an elaborate, expensive design, a teaset being priced at 14 guineas.

Plate 136 shows representative pieces from a richly, if somewhat fussily decorated Chamberlain teaset of pattern 767 – 'Chinese figures different with temples etc. etc. £12 12s. 0d.'. Unfortunately no shape is indicated in this entry but one of the few remaining pattern books does include a cost estimate for this pattern – the only such costing I have traced. The entry reads:

No. 767 Old Gadroon Chinese figures and rich gold. Figures about 40 in a set.

	£	s.	d.
Ware, making		6	0
biscuit & glaze [firing?]		8	7
Blueing		10	5
Gilding	2	5	9
Figures		14	0
Edging		10	6
gold	1	10	0
enamel and burning		3	0
burnishing 1s. 6d. a dozen		8	6
	6	16	9

On this costing, the selling price of £12 12s. 0d. showed nearly 100 per cent profit on the cost of production. It is noteworthy that the cost of the gold and its application – the gilding – totalled £3 15s. 9d. or over half the total

factory cost of the complete tea service. The making of the complete undecorated set was a mere 14s. 7d.

The approximate date for the introduction of pattern 767 can be estimated from the fact that number 765 is dated 23 May 1816, but these basic shapes probably continued in use for several years.

Note that in this set the teapot is rather squat and of circular plan – a distinct change from the earlier oval or 'London' shapes. The basic cup form is the same as in the Yeo service (see Plate 135) and the cups shown in Plate 132 (right), but with a new handle form. This is very graceful with a griffin's head inside the finger-grip (see Plate 137). I think the term 'Grecian' is suitable for these unnamed shapes, but the point may be clarified when other pattern numbers are reported on these shapes. The description 'Old Gadroon' used in the costing seems unhelpful and probably does not relate to this particular service. The covered sugar shape would be as shown in Plate 138.

The same teapot and sugar bowl shapes are also represented in Plate 139, but here the creamer is different and the plate lacks the gadroon border. The vital difference, however, lies in the cup shapes, graceful reminders of the earlier standard 'London' shape (see Plate 132, left). The patterns reached number 1000

139. Representative pieces from a Chamberlain teaset of pattern 1035, 'New dejeuner Ivory [ground] & Womens flowers in panel & embossed gold', sold for £8 8s. 0d. a set in the early 1820s. Printed New Bond Street marks. Teapot 11 in. long. c. 1822–5. *Godden of Worthing Ltd*

around 1820, so the tewares with these later designs are featured in the next chapter.

Between about 1815 and 1820 the list of patterns includes the shape descriptions 'Grecian', 'Regent' and 'French'. These terms probably relate to the handle shapes or variations, rather than completely new teaware designs.

The dessert service price list illustrated in Plate 147 usefully gives at the head the standard price of the Chamberlain tea services in this post-1800 period.

Dessert services

At the start of the nineteenth century the standard form of Chamberlain dessert service was probably the same as that introduced some five or more years earlier, with individual shapes as illustrated in Plates 84 and 86, since dessert service forms did not change as frequently as tea service shapes. The footed oval comport or centrepiece is shown again in Plate 140. These shapes were the standard ones for the lower- and middle-priced patterns.

The more costly sets, as examples described later show, had dolphin-supported tureens in the same basic style as the 1795 service shown in Plate 87. Indeed as late as October 1818 these shapes are described in the order books: '1 complete dessert service with dolphin cream-bowls, rich fawn and gold, flowers etc. £84 0s. 0d.'.

In the low-priced services the slight change in shape seen during the 1800s is mainly confined to the covered tureens or 'creambowls'. One rather rare shape of about 1800–10 is illustrated in Plate 141: it is part of a yellow and gold bordered service finely painted with botanical specimens (named on the reverse of each piece). Here the style is reminiscent of some contemporary Derby services, but the Chamberlains were carrying out this type of botanical painting by at least October 1798, when such a dessert set was charged to Henry Bowen of Bath for 30 guineas.

The example illustrated in Plate 142 retains the same knob shape but the overall form is different and the side-handles are very similar to the cup-handles seen in Colour Plate IX and in the breakfast service made for Sir James Yeo (see Colour Plate XI and Plate 135). Shown with this cream-boat is the original ladle, a very rare object, as they were so prone to breakage. The basic pattern here is the Chamberlains' number 276, the 'Thumb & finger' design. The other pieces in this service were like the earlier sets shown in Plates 84 and

140.   A standard form of Chamberlain centrepiece from a dessert service, the unnumbered pattern very finely painted in brown and gold. Unmarked. 12 in. long. *c.* 1800–5. *Mrs P. A. Street*

VIII. *Previous page:* The 'Regent' shape vase ordered by Lord Nevill in June 1813 and painted with a scene from Shakespeare's *Henry VIII,* Act 3, Scene 1, with a long quotation inside the cover. The subject is taken from Boydell's 1805 Shakespeare prints (Plate XXVI) – the Queen with Cardinals Wolsey and Campeius – after a painting by Rev. W. Peters, R.A. The piece is typical of Chamberlain's finest production of the 1810–20 period. This special order is painted with armorial bearings on the reverse (see Plate 105). Painted mark inside the cover 'Chamberlains Worcester & 63 Piccadilly, London'. 10½ in. high. *c.*1813. *Private collection*

IX. *Above:* A 'Regent China' soup plate of the pattern made for Her Royal Highness Princess Charlotte in 1816–17; each plate cost £2 at that period. The typical rich Chamberlain gilding and the 'fancy birds' in landscape in the border panels are well illustrated in this example. Printed 'Regent China' mark with New Bond Street address (see page 34, Mark 10). Diameter 10 in. *c.*1816. *Godden Reference Collection*

X. *Right above:* Representative pieces from a Chamberlain teaset decorated with underglaze-blue ground and painted panels of typical 'fancy birds' in landscapes in the style of George Davis (see page 192). The cup-handles are typical of the Chamberlain products. Unmarked. Teapot 5¾ in. high. *c.*1800–5. *Godden of Worthing Ltd*

XI. *Right:* Representative pieces from the tea, coffee and breakfast service made for Sir James Yeo and ordered in 1815. The original prices are listed on page 117. The pattern is number 298 (see Plate 125) with the addition of various special crests, orders, etc., which were costed at 10s. each extra. The breakfast service pieces in the foreground are particularly rare shapes. The jug is shown also in Plate 321, a breakfast-size cup and saucer in Plate 135, and the sugar basin in Plate 134. *c.*1815–20. *Photograph: David Newbon*

XII. A selection of Chamberlain crested or armorial plates from special services made to individual orders. Two of the gadroon-edged plate forms (top and top right) are of the 'new shape gadroon' of the early 1820s, later termed 'Royal Gadroon', and they contrast with the plain edge variety. The raised gilding can be seen around the border panels (bottom left). Various name marks. Diameters 8¾-10¼ in. c.1815-25. *Godden of Worthing Ltd*

XIII. A colourful glazed (as opposed to biscuit, see Plate 247) Chamberlain poodle holding a basket of fruit. This is one of many small animal models made early in the nineteenth century (see page 212). Printed Royal Arms mark with New Bond Street address (see page 35, Mark 11). 4 in. long. c.1820-30. *Geoffrey Godden, chinaman*

141. A tureen and stand from a decorative Chamberlain service painted with botanical specimens within a yellow border. Some pieces with written name mark. Tureen 5 in. high. *c.* 1800–10. *Messrs Christie, Manson & Woods*

142. A tureen, cover and ladle from a Chamberlain dessert service of pattern 276. The ladles are rarely found today. Unmarked. Tureen 5½ in. high. *c.* 1800–10. *Godden of Worthing Ltd*

This service cost 24 guineas so the shapes are not particularly fancy and the broadly painted stock design would have been painted by semi-skilled hands.

In contrast the part dessert service shown in Plate 145 is finely painted with accurately rendered botanical specimens, the work of a leading artist. The cost of the service was therefore higher and the cream-bowls are of the more expensive type with dolphin supports. It should be noted that the top to the cream-boat differs from the more simple form seen on the 1795 set illustrated in Plate 87. A service ordered in April 1810 was to have cream-bowls with 'new knob of dolphin . . .'.

Another aspect of this service contributing to its high price is the sparseness of the decoration which leaves a large area of porcelain showing. This necessitated only the very best unblemished blanks being used, whereas all-over 'Japan'-type patterns, like the 'thumb and finger' design just shown, tended to cover most of the surface with the result that slightly faulty 'seconds' could be used for such designs.

The shaped covered dish in the foreground is one of four segment dishes from a matching supper service

86. This shape of cream-tureen was supplied with a circular stand like a small plate. A part service of this period, of the same shapes but with shell-painted panels, is shown in Plate 143.

This colourful 'thumb and finger' design appears again on the dessert service shown in Plate 144, although this set is a little later, probably about 1810. Note the new centrepiece shape, the mock-ring handles flat on the side of the tureen and the new dish shape (top right).

143. Representative pieces from an orange-ground shell-painted Chamberlain dessert service. Printed mark 'Chamberlains Worcester. Manufacturers to their Royal Highnesses the Prince of Wales and Duke of Cumberland'. Tureen 5½ in. high. *c.* 1800–10. *Messrs Sotheby & Co.*

144. *Opposite:* Representative pieces from a Chamberlain dessert service showing typical shapes and decorated with the popular design 276. Painted name mark and pattern number. Centrepiece 5 in. high. *c.* 1805–10. *Godden of Worthing Ltd*

145. Representative pieces from a Chamberlain dessert service hand-painted with botanical specimens. Painted name marks. Cream-tureen 9½ in. high. *c.* 1805–10. *Messrs Phillips*

(see page 282) while the beehive honey pot is from the matching breakfast service (see page 244).

Plate 146 shows representative pieces from a magnificent Chamberlain-Worcester dessert service of about 1815 variously painted with the popular subjects of the period – shells, feathers, butterflies, birds in landscapes, views and flowers. This was almost certainly the service made for Edwin Stacey, of Maidstone in Kent, costing £84 and featured in the Bond Street account books in October 1815. Nine months later the same buyer came back for the centrepiece: '1 dolphin centrepiece, fawn and view £9 9s. 0d.'. This centrepiece is of a very rare

CHAMBERLAIN'S
WORCESTER CHINA MANUFACTORY.

DESSERT PRICE CARD.

Any Tea pattern at																		
Dessert Plate	2/3	2 6	3	4	4 6	5	6 6	7	8	9 6	10	12	13	15	18	20
24 Plates 3rd Size																
1 Centre																
2 End Dishes																
4 Squares																
4 Shells																
2 Hearts																
2 Cream Tureens																
Complete Set																
Ice Pails Common																

Dolphin Ice Pails, per Pair Extra.   Dolphin Cream Bowls, per Pair Extra.

form, and the view painted in the centre is of the city of Worcester with the Chamberlain factory in the foreground (see Plate 103).

The surviving dolphin-supported cream-tureen bears three panels: the shell-painted one is seen here, the flower panel is shown in Plate 107, whilst the last is painted with a view of Dukinfield Lodge in Shropshire. The shell-painted cream-tureen is shown in Colour Plate XVII, the landscape-painted square dish is illustrated in Plate 223, and the feather-painted dish in Plate 224.

The dessert service price list reproduced in Plate 147 relates to this approximate period showing as it does the make-up of the standard dessert services, which comprised 'a centrepiece, 2 cream-tureens, 4 square dishes, 4 shell-shape dishes, 2 heart-shape dishes, 2 "end" or shaped-edged dishes, 24 plates of the 3rd size'. These ranged in price from £5 10s. 0d. to £62 12s. 0d. for the complete basic set, but the price was increased if the purchaser wanted 'Ice Pails, Common', at £2 12s. 6d. to £21 0s. 0d. per pair depending on the added decoration, or if the dolphin-supported cream-bowls (as in Plates 107 and 146) were required. The 'common' shape ice-pails could also be replaced with the elegant dolphin-supported model (see Plate 293). The varying degree of decoration available is evidenced by the great difference between the cost of a standard dessert plate, a mere 2s. 3d., and the richest standard dessert pattern, £1.

Returning to the examination of basic dessert service shapes, the dish illustrated in Plate 146 (bottom left) is of a form now seen with two variations: firstly, in Plate 148, with an openwork edge, an unusual feature, as is the bird subject painting; secondly, in Plate 149, with the

146. *Opposite*: Representative pieces from a richly decorated fawn-ground dessert service in the 'harlequin' style with different subject panels (see also Plates 223, 224 and Colour Plate XVII). Printed mark as on page 34 (Mark 7). Cream-tureen 9¼ in. high. *c.* 1815. *Godden of Worthing Ltd*

147. *Left*: Dessert service price-list showing the standard prices of the Chamberlain tea services around 1815.

148. *Below*: A rare pierced-edge Chamberlain dessert service dish, the panel hand-painted with a bullfinch. Marked 'Chamberlains Worcester. Manufacturers to their Royal Highnesses the Prince of Wales and Duke of Cumberland'. 9½ × 7¼ in. *c.* 1810. *Geoffrey Godden, chinaman*

149. A Chamberlain dessert service dish embellished with the 'Union' embossments and painted with simple 'womens' flowers. Unmarked. 9½ × 7¼ in. *c.* 1815–20. *Miss H. Greenfield Collection*

relief-moulded 'Union' design (see page 116). It seems that most standard shapes were issued with this popular 'Union' embossing, which remained in demand into the 1820s. It must not be thought, however, that all pieces relief-moulded in this style are necessarily Chamberlain wares – most factories of the period produced their own versions.

Plate 150 shows the 'Union' moulding on a new single vase-shaped cream-boat or tureen from a dessert service. Here the panels are painted in an inexpensive style, perhaps the 'women's flowers' mentioned in the account books. Dessert services with vase-shape cream-bowls were listed as early as March 1816; in fact 'New vase shape' ice-pails were featured in January 1810.

The same shape is seen again in Plate 151, but without the 'Union' embossing, for the customer had a

150. A Chamberlain cream-tureen from a dessert service embellished with the 'Union' embossments. Printed name mark with Piccadilly address. 7½ in. high. *c.* 1813–16. *Miss H. Greenfield Collection*

151. *Opposite:* Representative pieces from a lilac-bordered Chamberlain dessert service showing characteristic shapes which also occur with gadroon edges (see Plate 153). Printed name marks. Ice-pail 10½ in. high. *c.* 1815–20. *Messrs Thomas Goode & Co.*

152. A typical Chamberlain gadroon-edged centrepiece from a dessert service painted with a pale blue border and richly gilt. Unmarked. 12½ in. long. *c.* 1815–20. *C. S. Beach Collection*

154. A decorative gadroon-edged green-bordered dessert dish with costly raised gold surrounds to the panels. Note that the green ground has to be stopped short of the gilt portions. Unmarked. 8½ in. square. *c*. 1815–20. *Godden Reference Collection*

156. A superb-quality Chamberlain plate with a rare and delicately worked relief border, some portions of which are picked out in gold. Printed Royal Arms mark (see page 35, Mark 11). Diameter 8½ in. *c*. 1816–20. *Dyson Perrins Museum, Worcester*

choice of styles as well as of pattern. This vase-shape cream-bowl was included in the dessert and breakfast service ordered by Sir James Yeo in 1815 (see page 117 and Colour Plate XI). In this set there is a new shape centrepiece, a new form of handled dish (middle left) and a lobe-edged plate.

A similarly shaped dessert service centrepiece is shown in Plate 152 and in the service illustrated in Plate 153. Here the edges of the various pieces have rather

153. *Opposite:* Representative pieces from a rich blue-bordered dessert service, each piece of which is hand-painted with a different flower. Name marks. Centrepiece 12½ in. long. *c.* 1815–20. *Messrs Christie, Manson & Woods*

155. Representative pieces from a sage-green ground 'Union' dessert service with Warwick-vase type tureens and ice-pails (see page 245). Printed name and New Bond Street address marks. Ice-pail 11¾ in. high. *c.* 1816–20. *Messrs E. D. Vandekar*

deep nulling with small shell motifs at regular intervals. Another dish of this type is shown in Plate 154, but the reader is warned, however, that this type of border can occur on the products of other factories, including Grainger's Worcester and Coalport porcelains.

Plate 155 depicts the 'Union' embossing on a new range of shapes with the ice-pails and cream-bowls plainly modelled on the famous Warwick vase. Chamberlain dessert services with Warwick-vase cream-bowls were included in the accounts from at least March 1817. In fact they were probably introduced earlier, as 'Warwick vase shape' ice-pails were listed as early as September 1816. Only the more expensive services included the ice-pails or fruit-coolers, which were not part of the standard services.

The superb-quality plate shown in Plate 156 is probably from a dessert service, although it is the only example with this moulded border known to me.

Dinner services

Complete Chamberlain dinner services are rarely found today although the large dinner plates are relatively common; these at least serve to show the diversity of the Chamberlain dinner service designs and the richness of the decoration. Probably most tea service patterns were also available on dinnerwares and many estimates and other records relate to tea, dessert and dinner services of the same pattern.

An order of 1811 for a dinner service of the well-known and long-popular 'Dragon' pattern, Chamberlain's design number 75 featured in Plates 56, 57, 81, 86 and Colour Plate XXV, comprised:

		£	s.	d.
2	soup tureens, covers and stands	12	8	0
4	sauce tureens, complete	8	0	0
2	vegetable tureens, complete	7	7	0
4	square covered dishes	8	0	0
1	salad vessel	1	11	6
1	Fish grate [pierced strainer]	1	11	6
60	plates	31	10	0
24	soup plates	14	8	0
24	pie plates [7 inches]	8	8	0
2	20 inch dishes	6	6	0
2	18 inch dishes	5	5	0
2	16 inch dishes	4	0	0
4	14 inch dishes	6	0	0
4	12 inch dishes	2	14	0
8	10 inch dishes	7	4	0

In addition, this order included a complete sandwich set at £8 8s. 0d., with a wooden tray costing £1 11s. 6d. and a matching dessert service with dolphin-supported cream-bowls (as in Plate 107) at 27 guineas.

At this period the tureens would have been of a shaped oval design, probably rather similar to the forms shown in Plates 157–9. The example illustrated in Plate 159 is particularly ornate and rare. The pieces in these three illustrations, and those shown in Plates 162 and 163, represent special orders, as the owners' crests, initials or armorial bearings are added to standard designs. An assortment of single plates from such services is shown in Colour Plate XII. The plate in the centre (left) has the same border as the service, or rather services, made for The Honourable East India Company's headquarters at Fort St George, Madras, ordered through Chamberlain's customer, Messrs Griffiths Cooke & Co., of that city. The Chamberlains exported a large quantity of fine porcelain to India. The porcelains made for the East India Company, whose earlier trading had brought vast amounts of Chinese

porcelain to Europe,* are entered in the Chamberlain records under various dates in 1817 and 1818. The complete order totalled £4,190 4s. 0d. – a commission of the greatest importance.

The 'dress service' with coloured rendering of the company's arms comprised the enlarged dinner service, a matching dessert service with tea and coffee cups and saucers, as well as twelve ornamental vases.

An idea of the decoration can be gauged from the elegant oval open bowl illustrated in Plate 160. This was perhaps one of the four salad bowls supplied at £1 10s. 0d. each, or £3 0s. 0d. each when the arms were added on each side. The dinner service comprised:

		£	s.	d.
4	oval soup tureens and stands, rich buff & gold	20	8	0
4	large gravy dishes	14	0	0
46	oval shaped dishes in sizes ranging from 22 inches to 10 inches long 3 15 0 to	1	0	6 each
6	Turtle dishes and covers	37	16	0
14	vegetable dishes, divided	73	10	0
20	smaller do.	73	10	0
100	Hot-water plates	95	0	0
100	soup plates	52	10	0
150	Dinner plates	71	5	0
150	cheese plates	52	10	0
4	salad bowls	6	0	0
10	Pie dishes, 12 inches	12	10	0
10	do. 10 inches	10	5	0

To these basic prices must be added the cost of painting the arms at 15s. each, some pieces bearing two or more such arms. As can be imagined, such an order took a considerable period to complete and it was not invoiced until July 1820. Note that this 1817 original order included oval-plan tureens.

I have handled pieces from at least three large services made in the early part of the nineteenth century for the East India Company. A plate from the service made by the rival Flight, Barr & Barr Company in Worcester is shown in Plate 161 by way of comparison. The third service was of Chinese porcelain and served to show how the quality of the Chinese potting and decoration had by then declined whereas the English manufacturers had perfected their techniques and were able to produce pleasing, smooth, pure porcelains.

By about 1820 the tureen forms both for soup and the smaller sauce tureens became circular in plan. Repre-

---

*For details of this massive trade see Godden, *Oriental Export Market Porcelain and its influence on European Wares* (1979).

157. Representative pieces from an apricot-bordered Chamberlain dinner service bearing the arms and crest of Hodges. Printed mark with New Bond Street address. Soup tureen 16¼ in. long. *c.* 1816–20. *Messrs Sotheby & Co.*

158. An extremely colourful Chamberlain soup tureen with printed 'Armada' subject panel on a coral-red ground with rich gilding. 15½ in. long. *c.* 1815–20. *Messrs Christie, Manson & Woods*

159.   A well-modelled Chamberlain soup tureen with red and gilt border, incorporating the owner's crest, Latin motto and initials. Unmarked. 16 in. long. *c.* 1815–20. *Messrs Graham & Oxley*

160.   A rare form of oval salad bowl from the large Chamberlain service made for the Honourable East India Company, ordered in 1817. Printed name and New Bond Street address mark. 11½ in. long. *c.* 1817–20. *Godden of Worthing Ltd*

161. A Flight, Barr & Barr Worcester gadroon-edged plate, part of that company's service made for the Honourable East India Company. Impressed initial mark. Diameter 9¾ in. *c.* 1815. *Godden of Worthing Ltd*

162. A finely painted tureen and stand with blue ground made for the Prescot family and with their armorial bearings. Printed mark with New Bond Street address. Diameter of stand 12¼ in. *c.* 1818–22. *Messrs Christie, Manson & Woods*

163. *Top:* Representative pieces from a richly decorated dinner service incorporating the crest and initials of the Tudway family. Printed name and address marks. Tureen 9½ in. high. *c.* 1818–22. *Messrs Christie, Manson & Woods*

164. *Above:* A richly decorated Chamberlain soup tureen and stand with gadroon edges and extremely well-painted with flowers. Printed marks inside cover. 9½ in. high. *c.* 1818–22. *Messrs Delomosne & Son*

165. A blue-bordered Chamberlain deep circular dish with 'new embossed' border, part of the service made for the Nabob of the Carnatic, and incorporating the Islamic date 1236, relating to 1820. Name mark. Diameter 9½ in. *c.* 1820. *Messrs Sotheby & Co.*

166. A dish from the service made for the Nabob of the Carnatic which comprised over a thousand pieces, each painted with named botanical specimens. Printed mark (see page 35, Mark 11). 10¾ × 9 in. *c.* 1820. *Messrs Sotheby & Co.*

sentative pieces from a crested and initial service made for the Tudway family are shown in Plate 163, whilst an armorial example is depicted in Plate 162.

The very finely floral-painted tureen shown in Plate 164 has the same nulled or gadroon edge as the dessert service shown in Plate 153, but again this edging can also occur on Grainger's Worcester porcelain. Note the same knob as seen in Colour Plate XI and Plate 134. This dinner service shape was probably continued into the 1830s (see Colour Plate XVI).

Many readers may well be surprised to find the circular dish illustrated in Plate 165 featured in this book, for although the relief-moulded border design is well known on several makes of English porcelain of about 1815–25, it is not generally associated with the Worcester factories; yet this example is clearly marked 'Chamberlains Worcester'. Furthermore, the inscription includes the Islamic date 1236 which equates with our year 1820. The order was placed with Griffiths Cooke & Co., of Madras, in that year, but as was always the case with large orders, the porcelain was not delivered for several years. The heading for the order reads, 'Nabob's [His Highness the Nabob of the Carnatic] new embossed blue and gold with Botanicals', giving us Chamberlain's name for this moulded-border design. This order comprised over a thousand pieces – dinnerwares, dessert wares (a dish is shown in Plate 166) and a matching breakfast service – but it was not shipped until 1823.

5
CHAMBERLAIN'S PRODUCTS 1820–1852

This chapter covers a decline in the fortunes of the factory and also a decrease in the amount of porcelain produced, despite the fact that in 1840 the two major Worcester companies, Chamberlain's and Flight, Barr & Barr, combined to form the new firm of Chamberlain & Co. It was not only because the rival Grainger firm was prospering, but rather the result of the rise of the great porcelain manufacturers in the Staffordshire Potteries, who were producing superb bone china porcelains. The Chamberlains after about 1820 gradually lost the market to Staffordshire firms such as Spode, Minton, Davenport or Alcock, which had the advantage of also producing the lower-priced earthenwares. The introduction of Mason's Patent Ironstone China in 1813 and the subsequent rush of other manufacturers to produce durable services in similar bodies must also have had its effect on the trade of the Worcester porcelain manufacturers.

As far as the management of the Chamberlain firm was concerned, Humphrey and Robert continued in command up to the end of 1827, when John Lilly was taken into partnership. It seems probable that at this period Humphrey retired, leaving his son Walter to manage the day-to-day running of the factory with John Lilly, under the style 'Chamberlain & Co'.

The products of the 1820s in fact seem to have changed little from those produced in the previous decade. The management was certainly aware of the prevailing fashion for French shapes and in May 1820 there are entries in the Bond Street cash book concerning the purchase of French porcelain, most probably to serve as models:

	£	s.	d.
By 2 French white vases for Worcester	4	0	0
By 2 French white vases for Worcester	2	10	0

These entries, with others of a similar nature, show that such French porcelains were readily available in London and some were even decorated by the Chamberlain painters. The shop management was also purchasing in London the products of other English firms:

	£	s.	d.
By Messrs Spode & Copeland for china	5	16	0
By sundry pieces of Swansea china	1	3	6
By 4 biscuit figures, I vase, Derby shop	3	6	0

The following sample entries are from the account books kept at the Chamberlains' shop at 155 New Bond Street, an address which was included in the printed marks of the period, and they give some indication of the range of wares stocked at the time:

1 [coffee] can and saucer, fine painting Madonna & child, with blue ground &c. £6 6s. 0d. [probably as in Plate 280] [March 1820]

	£	s.	d.
1 Toy ewer & basin, rich green & gold with birds.	1	11	6
1 complete Table service Marsh's rich Japan pattern.	55	0	0

[January 1821]

	£	s.	d.
1 new rich ornamental chair with biscuit figure &c. [see Plate 167]	10	10	0
A glass shade for do.		12	0

[February 1821]

1 Rich inkstand with biscuit figure &c. £4 4s. 0d. [March 1821]

	£	s.	d.
A complete Table service Marsh's Japan 886.			
[see Colour Plate XVI]	77	4	0
1 two-quart Punch jug and cover, fine			
painting, Pheasant shooting.	7	7	0
[August 1821]			

1 Long ink, maroone & gold with view of Worcester. £3 3s. 0d.
    [November 1821]

1 small basket, biscuit flowers round. £2 2s. 0d.
    [June 1822]

2 small vases, dead-blue [ground] and biscuit flowers.
  £2 10s. 0d.
    [December 1822]

A feature in the Chamberlain sales records during the early 1820s was the diversity of the animal models being supplied, shown, for example, by a few entries from the Bond Street sales journal in the 1821–2 period:

	s.	d.
1 Peacock [glass shade 2s]	10	0
1 small swan	2	6
1 Buck & Doe	7	6
1 Peacock white & gold	8	0

Models such as these are illustrated in Colour Plate XIII and Plates 246–9. Other attractive novelties of the period included cottage pastille-burners to scent a room (see Plate 169).

By no means all the richly decorated goods were being sent to London, however – this was very far from the case. The following are examples of the items supplied to the Cheltenham dealers in 1820:

	£	s.	d.
1 pair of cabinet cups from Thompson	5	0	0
1 pair do. Shakespeare	5	0	0
1 eagle claw ornament, 12th night	2	2	0
2 pastile cottages in gold		16	0
Set fine ornaments, flowers (Baxter)	15	0	0
1 ornament fancy with mermaids	3	10	0
18 rich dessert plates, fine paintings in fruit &c.			
[see Colour Plate XVIII and page 186]	54	0	0
1 dessert plate from Richard 2nd	10	0	0
1 plate, Thomas Cribb & frame	14	14	0
1 box, dead blue and gold, birds &c.	2	0	0

Decorative animals such as '2 pairs stags, dry blue cushions, 15s.', or '12 cats, sorted, at 1s. 6d.', were also being supplied and such goods were being sent to other towns up and down the country. John Yates of Cheltenham, and perhaps other dealers, enjoyed a 5 per cent commission, presumably on orders he had put in the way of Messrs Chamberlain, over and above the

167. *Top:* A rare and colourful Chamberlain model of a 'boy in chair' as included in Humphrey Chamberlain's consignment sent to Birmingham in June 1823. A 'rich chair cupid' was invoiced at £8 8s. 0d. in May 1821. Incised mark as in Plate 168. 5 in. high. *c.* 1821–5. *John Bly, Tring*

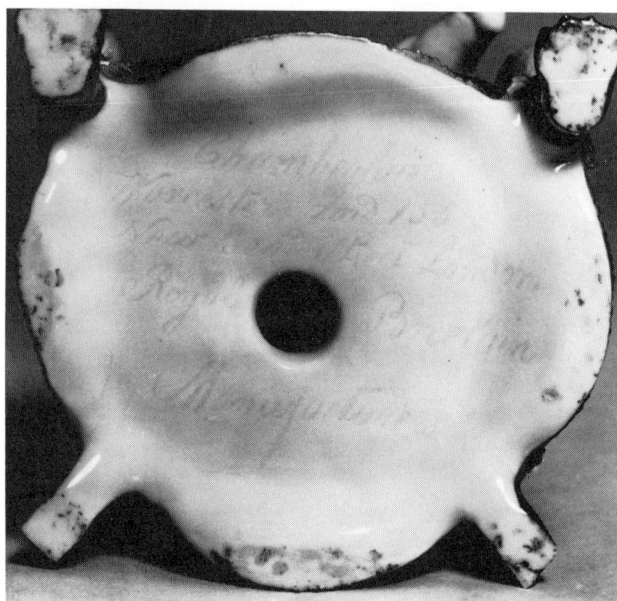

168. *Above:* The underside of the boy and chair model shown in Plate 167, showing a rare incised name and address mark incorporating the Bond Street address. *c.* 1821–5. *John Bly, Tring*

169. A good-quality decorative house pastille-burner for scenting a room (see page 272), the end section withdrawn to show how and where the smouldering pastille was inserted. Unmarked. 6¼ in. high. *c.* 1820–25. *Private collection*

profit charged on stock that he had ordered for his own establishment.

The Chamberlain management was always happy to make special pieces to order, as is evidenced by one entry:

Sir Roger Gresley.

1 pair four bracket candlesticks, made to a silver one, rich. £2 2s. 0d.

Subsequent orders to other people refer to 'new bracket candlesticks' showing how new shapes were added to the factory's list of products.

It is interesting to note that there was a certain amount of intertrading in the ceramic industry. The example below shows one Worcester manufacturer, Chamberlain's, buying from their local rivals to supply a dealer and pottery manufacturer in Bristol:

January 1st, 1822. Purchases from, Barr, Flight & Barr, Worcester.

		£	s.	d.
6	breakfast cups, black shell [printed], gold sprigs		12	0
6	teas and 8 saucers do.	1	2	0
2	coffee cans do.		4	0
1	plate do.		4	6

These were reinvoiced to E. Ring & Co., of Bristol, six days later.

At this period, too, the Chamberlains were supplying several amateur china painters with blanks, together with the ceramic colours to paint on them, and were firing the results in their own kiln. This minor aspect of

their trade is discussed further on page 182. In addition, the firm also supplied at least one of their own staff, who later decorated and sold the finished products under his own name – George Rogers (see page 205). One entry dated June 1822, gives the prices of sundry small items of undecorated Chamberlain porcelain:

George Rogers, at sundry times this month.

	s.	d.
1 small vase, best white	15	0
1 basket	2	6
1 Toy sugar	2	0
1 Toy candlestick	2	0
1 pastile pot	5	0
2 tapers [taper candlesticks]	5	0
2 match pots	4	0

George Rogers apparently did his own gilding, for a little later in 1822 the following entry is listed under his name:

	s.	d.
1 chocolate [cup and saucer] complete, white	5	0
2 Batches of gold	10	0

and at the same period there are references to sales to E. Doe, who was later to work in partnership with George Rogers, as Doe & Rogers.

Reading these detailed accounts one wonders what has happened to these fine porcelains, how many are still in the same family after all this time, or how many are still intact. One strange consignment sold in November 1822 might conceivably still be *in situ*, for in that month the Rev. J. Oldham of Doverdale, Worcestershire, purchased 'Sundry odd covers &c. for Grotto'; not content with these, he then purchased '98 cracked damaged pieces for his Grotto' at 2s. each, followed by a further 112 faulty pieces.

In June 1823 Humphrey Chamberlain was apparently in Birmingham and a selection of the firm's products was sent to him there. These included, according to the order book, the following:

		£	s.	d.
2	seven inch vases, blue and chased gold	4	0	0
1	do. raised gold birds	2	0	0
2	Pastile pots, raised gold birds	3	0	0
2	match pots, raised gold birds	1	16	0
1	Pastile pot, chased gold	1	0	0
1	Gadroon Gordon ornament	1	10	0
2	side do.	2	10	0
1	Regent Bell mouth [vase] and cover biscuit blue	1	1	0
2	match pots do.		16	0
1	small Bell mouth do., Maroon & Birds		18	0
2	small root pots, do. do.	1	4	0

2 small match pots do.	16	0
4 dogs	10	0
2 swans	4	0
A pair pea birds	10	0
A pair cats	3	0
A pair stags, large	7	6
A pair stags, small	6	6
A pair small cupids	1 0	0
A Paris cabinet [cups and saucers] Dry blue, chased gold	1 4	0
A pair tapers [pattern] 582 gold edge	6	0
2 pairs do., Dry blue, chased [gilding]	1 4	0
A pair toy baskets, Dry blue, chased [gilding]	12	0
A pair do., Womens flowers	5	0
A pair water pans do.	12	0
A pair [sweet-water] sprinklers do.	15	0
A pair paste pots, dry blue, chased	1 0	0
4 Toy jugs	16	0
2 do., roses &c.	5	0
4 toy biscuit baskets at 5s.	1 0	0
1 do. at	10	0
1 do.	16	0
1 Cupid in a chair [see Plate 167]	[not priced]	
1 Cupid ink [perhaps as in Plate 308]	4 4	0
1 pair card-racks, flowers	2 0	0
1 pair card-racks, Dry blue &c.	3 10	0
1 pair goblets, Dry blue &c.	3	0
1 pair goblets, Roses &c.	2	0

The reason for Humphrey Chamberlain's presence in Birmingham with such a stock of goods is not known, but perhaps he was opening an agency there – like a present-day Wedgwood or Royal Worcester room in a large store; research in local papers may be helpful on this point. The whole list is headed by four pattern dessert plates indicating that the object was a sales or publicity exercise.

Many of these objects (and others listed elsewhere) are described as 'Dry blue'. This refers to the ground colour, normally a medium light-blue with a matt unglazed surface, rather than the dark glossy blue associated with the colour applied to the biscuit body before glazing. This dry-blue ground was often enriched with thick chased gilding; for example, '2 seven inch vases, blue and chased gold', in the manner of the French porcelains. This dry-blue tended to be a Chamberlain speciality and it is very seldom found on Flight, Barr & Barr porcelains, on Grainger-Worcester wares or indeed on any other English makes. This listing shows that it was an expensive form of decoration for when objects are listed with the dry-blue and gilding they were much more expensive than the same objects decorated in the conventional manner, with hand-painted decoration and the normal gilt edge:

	£	s.	d.
A pair Toy baskets, Dry blue chased	1	4	0
A pair Toy baskets, Womens flowers		5	0
A pair card racks, Dry blue &c.	3	10	0
A pair card racks, flowers	2	0	0

The inkwell illustrated in Plate 170 is similar to one included in a selection of fancy objects sold to Loder & Co., of Oxford, in February 1823: '2 square inks, writing figures in biscuit £4 4s. 0d.'. Other written descriptions of similar pieces show that the prevailing fashion was for such items to have a dry – that is, a matt unglazed – blue ground, with chased gold enrichments. Vases such as the following sold to James Boardman of Liverpool in June 1823 must have been very much in the so-called French Empire style, favoured by the fashionable French manufacturers over a long period:

Two, 12 inch vases French shape, dry blue with chased [gold] Tragic and Comic muses £12 0s. 0d.

A set of similar vases purchased at the same time were of an important size, the centre vase being 31 in. high, the side vases, 21 in. high.

170.   An attractive Chamberlain 'Regent China' inkwell of the type supplied to Loder of Oxford in 1823 at £2 2s. 0d. each. It has a blue-ground base, and the figure is unglazed. Printed 'Regent China' mark with New Bond Street address. 4¾ in. high. c. 1820–25. Messrs Phillips

Other outside influences came from Wales, for not only were Swansea shapes being copied but also Swansea porcelains were being sent down to the Bond Street shop. On 30 April 1824, for example, the following were listed for London:

	£	s.	d.
2 Swansea cup and stands	2	0	0
1 teaset, Swansea ma. 1064	12	12	0

The abbreviation 'ma' presumably stands for 'make', but the pattern was almost certainly a Chamberlain one added to Swansea blanks. The quoted pattern number in the Chamberlain list is described as: 'Swansea make, grey birds eye curtain with 4 groupes of flowers £12 12s. 0d.'. The description 'Swansea make' only occurs against this one design, 1064, and it is unlikely that a set of teaware shapes was made for just one pattern. There is therefore little doubt that this tea-set was of Swansea porcelain. The order books, with their mention of goods sent to the London shop, include several other references to Swansea porcelain – especially cabinet cups and saucers (see page 229). The Chamberlains certainly had Swansea white porcelains available as they were supplying examples of them to George Rogers.

The Staffordshire potteries also had an influence, for the engraving of the Chamberlains' copper plates was carried out mainly by James Kennedy of Burslem. This engraving would have been for overglaze printing, for no underglaze-blue printing on Chamberlain porcelain is known. Some of the engraving would have been for the outlines of standard tableware designs, prints that were later coloured in by the apprentice painters. The dinner service tureen shown in Plate 194 represents such a design.

It is surprising to find that in the early 1820s the wage bill averaged under £100 a week, often totalling only £60 or £70. At this period Humphrey and Walter Chamberlain, the heads of the firm, were drawing an annual salary of only £100 each, although Humphrey was also being paid rent to the sum of £371 5s. 0d. per year. Nevertheless, the low weekly drawing (under £2) does contrast with the costly nature of many of the objects produced in the factory; although some of these objects were small and of a reasonable price, it was in general the upper-class market which the Chamberlain management had in mind for its porcelains.

Pursuing for a moment the subject of accounts, it is interesting to study the expenses incurred in the management of the Chamberlains' London retail shop in Bond Street during the middle 1820s, as extracted from the shop cash books:

	£	s.	d.
Half years Rent	90	0	0
2 quarters Parochial Rates	8	15	0
2 quarters Government Taxes	8	5	3
2 quarters Water Rate	1	11	6
Insurance, Westminster Office	7	10	0
Sewer rate	3	15	0
Watering the street, a quarter		7	6
Subscription to regulate Water Company		10	0
Housekeeping [a month – August 1825]	20	11	9¾
Newspapers from Xmas to June 30th	1	6	8

[A shilling a month was paid to the street-keepers.]

But perhaps the smaller payments are of more interest today. These included:

	£	s.	d.
A large brush for dusting ware		3	6
A set of shoe brushes		4	6
A gallon of sperm oil		5	0
Poison for rats			6
A new hearth rug for Parlour		16	0
Half ream of paper		9	0
A new clock for kitchen		16	0
Dying green curtains		3	6
Monthly payment for blacking		1	0
Repairing water closet		17	0
Beating parlour carpet		2	0
Moore's Almanac		2	3
A new Court Guide		5	0
Burke's Peerage for Worcester	1	11	6
Mr. Dean for Illumination, King's birthday, last April	3	16	6
Reporter for getting Illumination in the newspapers		5	0
A ream of white paper		9	0
Mary Wridgway [sic] for 7 months [housekeeping] wages to Xmas last [1828]	7	7	0
Booting, this month		2	8
A new mop for warehouse		2	6
By 3½ lbs. of soap		2	2½
A new leather		11	3
A knot hat for the Porter		2	0
A new large Porter's basket		6	0
Porter [per week]	1	0	0
Wafers [for sealing letters]			2
Stamps		9	0
A chaldron of coals for show rooms	2	6	0
Omnibus to City [from Bond Street]		1	0
By sweep for wareroom chimney		1	0
R. Jerome for night work, emptying closet below stairs & repairing closet	3	8	6
Subscription towards erecting the elevation of Kings Cross in London in honour of His Late Majesty George the Fourth, agreeable to an order received from Worcester	5	5	0

Each year Christmas-boxes were given at the following rates:

	s.	d.		s.	d.
Dustmen	1	0	Canal men	1	0
Paper boy		6	Scavengers	1	0
Carrier	1	0	Watchman	1	0
Sweeps	1	0	Lamplighter		6
General Postman	2	6	Twopenny Postman	1	0
Mail porter	2	6	Patrol	1	0
Beadle	1	0			

The Bond Street shop also served as an important forwarding post for sending materials or patterns to the factory at Worcester. Each month 8 oz. of gold was forwarded; it was purchased from G. F. Allcock & Co., usually costing £34 8s. 0d., but on occasions the gold was purchased in coin form: 'By gold coins 4.7 oz at 75s. per ounce, for Worcester £16 6s. 3d.' (November 1831). Other items sent up to Worcester included:

1 ounce of Chrome green, for Worcester, 5s. 6d.
By eight engravings, the King's pleasure grounds in Windsor Park, for Worcester, 6s.
Mr. Ackermann for views, for Worcester [no price]
By a bust of the late Duke of York sent to Worcester, 5s.
    [A Worcester example of this subject is illustrated in Plate 171.]
Mr. Cummings for Glass shades, for Worcester, 9s.
By French shapes &c. purchased by Mr. Lilly and the china forwarded by canal to Worcester, £13 14s. 0d.
    [This entry emphasizes the point that at this time all goods were carried by water between Worcester and London, and various payments were made to the Birmingham Canal Company. By the mid 1840s, however, Chamberlain's were regularly sending their porcelain by rail.]
A china watch frame purchased by Mr. Lilly as a pattern and sent to Worcester, £1 15s. 0d. [March 1830]

It is surprising to see from this cash book the rather small amounts of money taken. In 1826, for example, the credit side shows a total of £4,084 10s. 4d., or £340 7s. 0d. per month. Over a longer period, from 1823 to June 1833, the income is recorded as £3,577 4s. 5d., or approximately £64 per week.

The cash book can hardly tell the full story; many important orders must have been taken, and certainly the quality of customers attracted to the Bond Street showroom was extremely high – necessitating the purchase of the *Court Guide* and *Burke's Peerage* previously mentioned. In this connection it is interesting to see that the future Queen Victoria took a very early interest in the Chamberlain porcelains – she in fact was seemingly purchasing porcelain at the age of nine.

171.   A biscuit-porcelain bust of the Duke of York (1763–1827) after a model sent to Worcester from the London shop in February 1827. Incised mark 'H. Chamberlain & Sons, Manufacturers to His Majesty. Worcester & 155 Bond Street, London'. 9½ in. high. *c.* 1827–30. *Dyson Perrins Museum, Worcester*

The Bond Street cash book records such dealings in simple form:

May 7th, 1828	To Princess Victoria, payment received £25 11s. 0d.
November 26th, 1828	To The Princess Victoria for trinkets 13s.
February 4th, 1829	To The Princess Victoria £29 12s. 6d.

She also paid an official visit to the Chamberlain factory in Worcester in 1832, whilst in her early teens (the Princess was born on 24 May 1819). Some fine Chamberlain porcelains are still in the Royal Collections, including, at Windsor Castle, examples with the Prince Regent marks and a service made for William IV in, or soon after, 1830.

Returning to the Chamberlain porcelains or 'trinkets', I cannot resist quoting another reference to the Chamberlain animal figures of the mid 1820s, in this case examples which were sent to a retailer in Yorkshire (home of the rival Rockingham factory):

			s.	d.
4	Rabbits and 3 with young	at	4	0
2	do. young, single	at	2	0
2	single rabbits	at	2	0
4	rabbits with trees	at	4	0
4	rabbits with young	at	4	0
4	do. common	at	3	0
1	cat and kitten		3	6

Messrs Chamberlain also produced human figures – a line almost entirely neglected by the Flight, Barr & Barr partnership. Several models are listed in Chapter 7, but

Plate 172 here shows a most interesting set of figures revealing the quality of the Chamberlain models, and the speed with which the management sought to capture topical events. These fine figures represent the four Rainer brothers and their sister – a musical ensemble from the Ziller Valley in the Tyrol who had a triumphant tour of Great Britain in 1827, performing before King George IV in August. These figures were almost certainly copied from a coloured lithograph by E. Wilson, seen here behind the porcelain copies. The set was included in the Chamberlain records in January 1828, at a mere £2 10s. 0d. This particular set was sold for 1,400 guineas (£1,470) at Christie's in June 1971 and with the generous help of a local benefactor, and of various donations, the Rainer family are back in the factory of their ceramic birth, available for all to see at the Dyson Perrins Museum in Worcester.

172.   A very rare set of Chamberlain figures representing the Rainer brothers and their sister, the famous Tyrolese singers (see page 242). These are posed in front of a print from which the porcelain models were almost certainly copied. Unmarked. 6 in. high. *c.* 1828
Dyson Perrins Museum, Worcester

It is necessary at this point to review the situation concerning the two other Worcester porcelain manufacturers in the early 1840s. The separate Grainger company seems to have prospered and to have continued its progress without any apparent difficulty, but this was not the case with Messrs Flight, Barr & Barr, the partnership which now managed the Dr Wall factory. Unfortunately no documents relating to this partnership are known to have survived, but the minutes of the joint meetings between the Flight, Barr & Barr partners and the Chamberlain management on the proposed merger* show that the Barrs, after the death of Joseph Flight in 1838, were declining the business and that the Chamberlains were the senior partners in the proposed amalgamation:

Martin Barr and George Barr having determined to relinquish the business of Porcelain manufacturers, have agreed to sell and dispose of their manufactory, stock in trade both manufactured and unmanufactured goods, implements and utensils in trade unto the said Worcester Royal Porcelain Company, for the sum of £13,000 of which £5,000 is considered as the value of the Works and £8,000 as the value of the stock. . . .

The company minutes covering this difficult period contain several interesting points. Firstly, the stock of materials owned by the Flight, Barr & Barr concern included 30 tons of soap-rock, suggesting that their standard porcelain body still contained this traditional Worcester ingredient. Indeed their porcelains all have that compact, slightly greasy appearance, and the wares tend to be rather heavy in weight. In contrast, the Chamberlain body by the 1840s appears to have changed to the bone china type and is rather whiter, more open or floury, and therefore rather light in weight.

It is also interesting to see that in 1840 it was proposed to call the new firm The Worcester Royal Porcelain Works, a term not in fact used until 1862. However, James Yates, the manager of the London shop, suggested 'that it would be more advantageous to the Company that the business should be carried on under the style of a Firm in preference to that of a public company'. In consequence, a compromise was arrived at and it was resolved 'that the Manufactory shall be styled The Worcester Royal Porcelain Works but that the business shall be carried on under the Firm of Chamberlain & Co.'.

James Yates in London enjoyed an annual salary of £500, and had in the previous year purchased all the

stock at 155 New Bond Street from the company. On 1 June 1840 the stock held at the Bond Street premises was bought back from James Yates for £4,310 19s. 2d. However, he declined to continue serving the new partnership and the more usual method of payment was proposed for his successors, namely £100 per annum plus a 2½ per cent commission on sales, after the first £5,000 of sales from the London shop.

The proceedings for the new partnership continued over many years. In September 1842 it was resolved to sell by auction all the surplus Flight, Barr & Barr stock, and in December 1844 the decision was made to sell Messrs Flight, Barr & Barr's retail shop at No. 1, Coventry Street. The porcelains bearing the addresses of both shops are therefore very rare and can be dated to the 1840–44 period. The relief-moulded dish of the so-called 'Blind Earl' pattern (see Plate 173) shows that after 1840 the Chamberlains lost no time in producing the designs and shapes of their former rivals. The design first occurred on Dr Wall Worcester porcelain of the First Period made in the 1760s, and the same relief-moulded design is still being produced by the present

173. A Chamberlain & Co. dessert dish of the so-called 'Blind Earl' pattern (the design is moulded in relief), copied from a Dr Wall period design. Printed mark incorporating both London addresses. 12¼ × 9 in. c. 1840–45. A. O'Connor Collection

*A summary of these minutes is contained in Henry Sandon's *Flight & Bar Worcester Porcelain (1978)*, Chapter 5.

Royal Worcester firm in the 1980s. This Chamberlain piece provides the link – the continuation from the eighteenth-century porcelains up to the present time.

In August 1843 the Worcester firm sent a very rich selection of porcelains to its two London showrooms, showing clearly that it was then capable of producing extremely decorative porcelains and that contrary to what may have been suggested they were not concerned only with buttons, door-furniture or tiles. Some of the goods sent to New Bond Street are listed below:

	£	s.	d.
1 China slab fine painting flowers & imitation oak frame	18	7	6
2 China slabs fine paintings fruit	31	10	0
1 do. antique frame and painting of The Queen, in red morocco	6	6	0
1 China slab, painting Brighton Pier	5	5	0
1 Cabinet cup and stand, fawn [ground] with gilding. Painting of London	2	2	0
2 rich plates, Prize Cattle	6	6	0
1 card tray, raised shells, [painted views of] Bournemouth	6	6	0
1 do. no shells, [view of] Windermere	6	6	0
1 tall vase, white ground with landscapes both sides, surrounded with Dresden flowers &c.	8	8	0
2 Fish-tail flower vases, Celeste ground, raised [gold], panel painted birds both sides. Raised flowers &c.	10	10	0

In addition, the following selection was sent to Coventry Street, to Messrs Flight, Barr & Barr's former retail shop:

	£	s.	d.
2 large vases, garter blue and paintings Constantinople and Smyrna, with 2 shades and stands	47	5	0

[A pair of vases painted with these subjects was shown by Chamberlain's at the 1851 Exhibition, see page 147.]

	£	s.	d.
1 Warwick vase, half biscuit and panels	7	7	0
1 oval shade and stand for do.	1	11	6
2 bottles celeste ground and flowers	2	10	0
4 small mounted bottles, green ground various paintings, priced from 5s. 6d. to £1 5s. 0d. each			
2 Frosted glass vases mounted	1	0	0
1 set 3 celeste glass vases, enamelled	2	5	0
1 centre do. odd		17	6

[It is interesting to see that in the 1840s as well as in the 1790s the Chamberlains were also selling glass wares.]

	£	s.	d.
1 set 3 china vases, fawn ground & painted views	5	5	0

	£	s.	d.
2 ornamental cups and stands, green ground and painted figures (F B & B)	2	8	0

[The initials F.B.&B. in parenthesis suggest these were old Flight stock.]

	£	s.	d.
1 ornamental cup and stand, garter blue and painting Duke of Wellington	3	3	0
1 Dessert plate, Garter blue bands, richly gilt and painted Watteau centre		15	0
1 do. Sèvres style, Celeste, gold band and painted flowers in embossed gold panels	1	10	0
1 small oblong ink, green ground, gold gadroon [edge] and painted flowers (F & B)		18	0
2 small round inks painted feathers and fawn ground (old stock)		18	0

[This note 'old stock' and the references to F & B for Flight & Barr indicate that some former products were being sent to London.]

	£	s.	d.
1 open card basket green ground and painted flowers	3	3	0
3 small seal trays, various. White gadroon edges	1	11	6
1 do. cross-handled same shape mat blue and figure centre (F B & B)		18	0
1 large cross-handled basket white and gold, vermicular and flower centre	1	5	0

In December 1843 all was not well with the new company. A motion was proposed by Mr St John, and seconded by Mr Lilly, 'That the accounts as well as the present state of the business being unsatisfactory, the following Gentlemen, viz. Mr. W. Chamberlain and Mr. F. St. John do form a committee to consider the present state of the affairs of the Proprietors and what arrangements can be made for the future . . .'. Their report, presented on 10 January 1844, was not all that constructive:

Upon consideration of the whole matter and referring to the state of the assets and liabilities the Committee are of the opinion that the business cannot be advantageously carried on under the present arrangements. They take into consideration, the proposed retirement from the partnership of Mr. Jabez Allies. The Notice from Mr. Carden to sell his shares and a similar notice just received from Mr. Hyde . . . . They suggest this as a favourable opportunity for a General arrangement whereby the affairs of the present Partnership may be wound up. . . .

In consequence of this, a new decision was made early in 1844 with Walter Chamberlain and John Lilly taking the Diglis Street factory (that is, the Chamberlain factory), all the stock and fittings (except the tile business) of this concern and that of the High Street shop. It also became apparent, as a result of new stock figures, that instead of a previously reported profit, the

Chamberlain partnership had suffered a trading loss for the year 1842–3.

In January 1844 George Barr and Fleming St John travelled to London to make an accurate stocktaking at the two London shops. This was set down as follows:

1, Coventry Street [the former Flight, Barr & Barr premises]

	£
Worcester Porcelain	4163
Bought china and earthenware	2839
Glass	2219
Encaustic Tiles	15

155, New Bond Street [the Chamberlain shop]

	£
Worcester Porcelain	5437
Bought china and earthenware	2012
Encaustic Tiles	3

[Amounts are given to the nearest pound.]

It is interesting to see here that the amount of glass-ware and the non-Worcester porcelain* and earthenware at the Coventry Street premises exceeded in value the Worcester porcelains, the totals being £5,058 against £4,163. The minutes also make it plain that much of the stock at these London premises was 'old fashioned' and that it 'still hangs on hand even at these greatly reduced prices'. The point was also made 'that a considerable portion of the china and earthenware at Coventry Street consists of broken sets which must be made up in order to become saleable'.

The partnership between the two Worcester firms had not prospered, rather it seems to have declined further. The last links with the old Flight, Barr & Barr concern were severed in 1848, when Martin Barr died, to be followed by the deaths of his brother George and their sister Maria in the same year.

A separate Appendix (see page 360) gives an interesting account of a visit to the Chamberlain factory in 1843. If the line engravings are accurate and truly relate to that visit, the methods of manufacture and the equipment used cannot have altered much since the days when the Chamberlains first commenced porcelain manufacture in the eighteenth century – indeed they were probably much the same as when the original partners established the industry in Worcester in 1751. The text supports the first engraving in stating that the power to the potter's wheel was supplied by a young lad or 'wheel turner' – and this only a decade before the

Great Exhibition. However, the descriptions of the various ceramic processes are of great interest to all collectors and lead to a better understanding and appreciation of all specimens that are coveted today. One can also marvel at the relatively low cost of the fine porcelains, despite the many complexities and risks involved in the manufacturing process.

In the early 1840s various changes were taking place at the Chamberlain factory – old buildings were being pulled down and new ones erected. Nevertheless, a real decline came after the amalgamation of the two firms. R. W. Binns in his excellent book *A Century of Potting in the City of Worcester* (1865), written within some thirty-five years of the event, stated:

The year 1840 was specially noteworthy in the history of the Royal Porcelain Works, as the hitherto rival establishments were then united. We fear that the union was a marriage 'de convenance', not of love; for the proprietors had been conducting their businesses on different principles, and had been activated by widely different motives, both equally delusive and without prospect of success.
. . . it was proposed to form a joint stock company, to consist of the members of the two firms . . . and adding to their number several of the most influential gentlemen in the city to subscribe the necessary capital, which, including the valuation of plant, stock &c. amounted to about £40,000.
. . . Some large workshops and warehouses were now erected on the manufactory of Messrs. Chamberlain, whither the plant of Messrs. Barr had been conveyed, and every attention was given to the business with the determination of making the re-commencement both creditable and prosperous. Unfortunately the branch of manufacture which was chosen was in no way adapted for the leading business of the works.

R. W. Binns continued by describing the innovations, which took the form of porcelain door-furniture (see page 238) and porcelain buttons (see page 224); but such ventures could hardly solve the problems of the failing company and in December 1845 the retail shop in New Bond Street was sold to Phillips, the china dealer of Oxford Street, so that from 1846 the New Bond Street address does not appear in the Worcester printed marks.

The book of copy-letters of this period suggests a general shortage of funds, or cash-flow difficulties in today's parlance. The company was writing to their customers in the following terms: '. . . we will therefore thank you to send us a cheque for £50 on account per return of post as we have some heavy bills to meet'.

Messrs Chamberlain also resorted to the practice of selling surplus stock by auction, as Bloor of Derby and other manufacturers had previously done. In March 1848 arrangements were in hand to hold the first of a

---

* The 'bought china and earthenware' included goods purchased from H. & R. Daniel, Samuel Alcock & Co., John Rose & Co. of Coalport, John Ridgway & Co., William Ridgway & Co., Davenports, and Thomas Dimmock & Co. Much of the glass was purchased from Thomas Webb of Stourbridge. In 1842 specimens of Dresden porcelain were also purchased and the company even bought wares from its rival George Grainger & Co.

series of sales in Ludlow and Mr Davis, the local auctioneer, was told 'it is our intention to send frequently to your town'.

However, at least one local retailer seems to have taken exception to Chamberlain's action and his un-recorded complaint was answered on 23 March 1848 in the following manner:

Dear Sir,

We have seen the circular and think it is every way correct. Mr. Saunders will instruct you or Mr. Davis respecting them but we trust no time will be lost in getting them out and distributing them and we should feel obliged if you would yourself make the thing so well known as possible amongst your customers and friends in Ludlow and neighbourhood as all depends on this.

After a sale in a town like yours there will be a great deal of matching etc. required for a long period and we should be happy to allow you a third on every order you may send us. . . .

P.S.   There will be useful articles of every description in the sale. . . .

The serious times for Messrs Chamberlain are also reflected in the following letter written on 1 May 1848 by Frederick Lilly, one of the partners:

I have been accused of spoiling the China Trade in mortice furniture [door-handles, finger-plates, etc.] by so reducing it in price and I feel confident that it has been done by others. I should therefore feel particularly obliged if you would inform me per return the lowest price at which Kennedy [William Kennedy of the Washington Works at Burslem] offers his white and black mortice furniture per sets mounted with his spindle.

At this period, too, the company was producing the less expensive Granite China, an Ironstone-type ware sometimes termed Opaque China: 'The dinner ware sent you is our opaque ware and it is never so white as china although it is much more durable' (4 July 1848).

However, the Chamberlains were also bringing out new simple designs on their porcelains obviously in an effort to meet competition for the less expensive wares. The company informed the important Dublin retailers, W. H. Kerr & Son (Kerr was four years later to become a partner in the new Kerr & Binns company at Wor-cester, see page 32): 'We are about bringing out some new patterns at earthenware prices. . .' (30 August 1848). It is not clear if these new inexpensive patterns were on porcelain blanks, earthenware, or 'Stone China', but it may be relevant to mention that the pattern list in the late 1840s makes a few references to a '22 body': '2429. Coburg, 22 body, pink lines vine leaves in gold, Meigh's style'. Meigh would have been Charles Meigh of the

Old Hall Works at Hanley (c. 1835 onwards), a leading producer of earthenware dessert and dinner services. I cannot at present offer any explanation of the special '22 body' and I have not seen this designation included in any marks.

Apart from stock Chamberlain patterns, in their own style or that of other successful manufacturers such as Charles Meigh, the Chamberlains also made replace-ment pieces for earlier existing services of various makes. Such special orders gave rise to unusual patterns and to non-standard shapes and even special bodies made to match the original. Plate 174 is a classic case. This plate is printed in underglaze blue with armorial bearings (of Earl Annesley) and a border design in the style of a Chinese export-market dinner service of the 1795–1805 period. The plate shape, too, is a special one, and the body and glaze were also made to emulate the Oriental original. Without the underglaze-blue Cham-berlain name mark, this workmanlike replacement could not be correctly identified – it has no Chamberlain characteristics.

R. W. Binns's review of the period continues:

We have learned from many quarters that the partners . . . could not and did not work harmoniously, that the concern was in fact a house divided against itself; it is not surprising therefore, to find that, in 1848, all partners had withdrawn except Mr. Chamberlain and Mr. Lilly. In 1850 Mr. Walter Chamberlain and Mr. John Lilly were the sole proprietors and the establishment was confined to the Worcester house.

In the latter part of the year Mr. Lilly retired from the business and his son Frederick, together with Mr. W. H. Kerr, were taken into partnership, the title of the firm remaining 'Chamberlain & Co'.

The new firm, thus created, used their best exertions to raise the credit of the house; a handsome show room and new kilns were built, whilst a series of alterations and improve-ments were commenced by Mr. Kerr. Had the Great Exhibition of 1851 taken place at a later period, we have no doubt that a respectable position would have been obtained, but that great display was a trying ordeal for the Worcester Porcelain Works.

With some creditable specimens of their own manufacture, backed by a few of the glories of former years, which although old fashioned, bore the evidence of taste and Royal character of their workmanship, the establishment passed muster and received the compliment (rather slight) of honourable mention.

It is a source of much regret that we should have to record the centenary celebration of this establishment under such depressing circumstances especially as the occasion was possibly without parallel. In May 1751, the Worcester Porcelain Works were established and in May 1851 after an extraordinary career of a hundred years, they were painfully reminded of past triumphs and present deficiences.

174. An unusual Chamberlain blue-printed plate in the style of Chinese export-market dinner services of the 1800 period, perhaps made as a replacement piece as it matches a Chinese shape with a narrow high flange and has an unusual porcelain body. Blue-printed mark 'Chamberlain & Co., 155 New Bond Street'. Diameter 8¾ in. c. 1820. *Godden of Worthing Ltd*

The official catalogue of the 1851 Exhibition lists Chamberlain's exhibits:

Tea service of egg-shell china, with a medallion of Shakespeare on each cup.
Communion and dejeune services, of pierced or honey-comb china [see Plates 212 and 214].
Pierced jugs, bottles, chalice, cups and stands [see Plates 209–13].
Portfolio china slabs, with views of Malvern and scene from 'Twelfth Night'. Slabs and frames with paintings [see Plate 356].
Adelaide [shape] vases, gilt &c. with views of Constantinople and Smyrna, and paintings of various kinds [see page 144].
Snake-handle vases, with views of Worcester and Malvern.
Coventry vases with medallions of Shakespeare and Milton.
Large inkstand.
Dresden [shape] basket; china bracelets and brooches.
China mortice door-furniture.
Vegetable dishes and covers. Sauce tureens and stands.
Breakfast cup and saucers. Tea cups. Dessert and table plates.
Portion of dessert service – biscuit – blue band with views, crests and coats of arms.
Gold and white Dresden baskets with paintings.

The jury's report was brief: 'Chamberlain & Co of Worcester exhibit some perforated china of agreeable effect'. But even this was no new invention, for they were rather poor copies of Sèvres examples of the 1840s. Of the major British porcelain manufacturers, the Chamberlains were alone in not exhibiting Parian wares at the Great Exhibition.

As related on page 32, in 1852 the new, highly successful partnership of Kerr & Binns (also known as W. H. Kerr & Co.) continued the Worcester tradition up to 1862. R. W. Binns in his *Worcester China 1852–1897* (1897) writes of this transitional period:

In 1850 Mr. W. H. Kerr of Dublin, who had become connected by marriage with the Chamberlain family, entered into a partnership with Mr. Walter Chamberlain and Mr. Frederick Lilly, but in 1851 both Mr. Chamberlain and Mr. Lilly retired from the concern. Mr. Kerr being then alone in the establishment, invited Mr. R. W. Binns to join him and to undertake the artistic direction of the manufactory. His invitation was accepted and the new firm began their work of renovation with much energy. Mr. Kerr being particularly anxious to repair the old buildings and to add to the manufactory such improvements as were called for by an extending business. A new mill, new ovens and new workshops were put in hand. The art department was found to be in a most unsatisfactory condition and some far reaching alterations were made. These were rendered the more necessary from the fact that the Great Exhibition had opened the eyes, not of the manufacturers alone but of the public.

Purchasers were no longer content to buy only what the dealer had to sell, but made enquiry for the productions of certain manufacturers which had attracted their attention. The immediate result of this was that a name and a reputation became of the highest importance and it was to exalt the name and to enhance the reputation of Worcester porcelain that the new proprietors applied themselves. They felt at the same time that if this work were to be accomplished it must be upon new lines; to revive old styles by old hands would neither show progress nor meet the requirements of a newly educated and critical public. . . . A change was imperative. . . .

With the conviction that reputation was the first thing to be gained, the partners determined that everything they undertook should be well done and that no pains should be spared to achieve success. . . . Lax discipline, imperfect machinery, inferior mixtures of body and glaze – in a word, a degenerate and almost moribund establishment had to be revived and endowed with a new vigour, new ideals and new aims.

Perhaps even more troublesome than these difficulties was the lack of artistic knowledge amongst the staff. The old proprietors had lost the enthusiasm of their youth and had allowed matters to drift, with the consequence that the powers of modeller and decorator had waned for want of a central inspiration and their work, while technically of good quality, was deficient in style. . . .

Perhaps Binns as the new proprietor was rather overstating the situation that he took over and endeavoured to set on new lines, but certainly the basic points are correct, as is his belief that the new styles were tasteful and of the finest quality. Unfortunately the superb Kerr & Binns period porcelains have so far been rather neglected by ceramic historians, but some sample illustrations have been included in this work (see Plates 215–17), pending a new detailed book on this period of Worcester ceramic history which is to be written by Henry Sandon.

There seems to have been a surprising lack of publicity over the termination of the Chamberlain firm and the take-over by the new partnership. Binns himself does not give a precise date, only the year 1852. Unfortunately the copy-letters of the period are extremely indistinct, but one which I read to be dated 16 February 1852 is signed for 'W. H. Kerr & Co., late Chamberlains', and one which is clearly dated 14 June 1852 and written under a printed Chamberlain & Co. heading, has the added device of 'W. H. Kerr & Co. – proprietors'.

On the general success of the 1852–62 Kerr & Binns productions, the present world-famous Worcester Royal Porcelain Company was formed on 24 June 1862. This company continues to the present day under the familiar name 'Royal Worcester' although since the amalgamation of the Staffordshire firm of Spode and Royal Worcester in the summer of 1967, the official group title has been Royal Worcester Spode Ltd. Both companies, however, use their own individual name marks and follow their own traditional styles.

In accordance with the scheme of previous chapters the standard tablewares of the period, that is, from the 1820s to the closure of the Chamberlain period in 1852, are discussed and illustrated here.

Teawares

The later Chamberlain teawares are surprisingly difficult to find, perhaps because so many examples were unmarked and are unattributed to their true source, but at the same time it is true to say that the concern was in decline (or rather their commercial rivals were increasing). One must remember that when the Chamberlains commenced production in about 1790 there were less than ten porcelain manufacturers in the British Isles. Now, in the 1830s and 1840s, there were probably nearly a hundred. Porcelain was no longer a novelty, it was a standard product.

Many of the designs followed the old traditional lines. The description which follows could well have been written in 1800 or even before but in fact it is taken from

the order book under the date 22 March 1824 and relates to an export order for Madras:

A teaset porr [porringer shape] blue ground, gold shell and Davis's fancy birds in panels and flies. Consisting of 18 tea cups and saucers, 12 coffees, teapot and stand, creamer, sugar-bason and 3 plates. £29 7s. 0d.

One of the difficulties of identifying and dating the later Chamberlain porcelain lies in the strange lack of pattern numbers on the great majority of pieces. However, the pattern book was still written-up and the pattern numbers allocated. By the early 1820s the sequence had exceeded 1000, or to be more exact, pattern 870 was listed in April 1820 and number 880 in May 1820. Pattern 1000 appears on invoices in September 1822. Typical entries of the period in the pattern book include:

918   Ivory ground with rose wreath etc. in colours, gold key border with lines £10 10s. 0d.
1009 New make [shape] squat grey and wreath of flowers on the grey £8 8s. 0d.
1023 Rose embossed with small carnation pattern
       seconds £1 4s. 0d.
       best   £2 2s. 0d.

[This last entry is a rare reference to the two grades of porcelain – the cheaper 'seconds' with slight manufacturing faults or blemishes, and the perfect or 'best' porcelains at nearly double the reduced price.]

1038 New Dejeunne [shape] green and flowers in panel embossed gold £12 12s. 0d.
      without gold   £10 10s. 0d.

[Several sets at about this period were embellished with embossed or raised gilding and with this design the buyer could have a cheaper set without the intricate gilding.]

1040 New Dejeunne [shape] rich blue and embossed gold, flowers finely painted £21 0s. 0d.

[This design was obviously a very fine quality one and the flower painting would have been carried out by a leading painter, not an apprentice – the standard of finish is reflected in the high price of 20 guineas. Contrast this with pattern 1067, 'Embossed, womens cheap flowers' at £1 2s. 0d. for the complete teaset.]

1090 New squat dejeunne green and wreath of flowers, gold dontel border and lines   £14 14s. 0d.
      with pink, ivory or grey ground £12 12s. 0d.

[It is interesting to see here that the chrome-green ground was more expensive than other colours, and certainly it is rarely found.]

1205 Plain Baden [without gadroon edge], grey and gold with roses etc. £10 10s. 0d.

[The part breakfast service illustrated in Colour Plate XIV may be regarded as a continuation of the popular 'Baden'

Fig. 1

Fig. 2

shape. The extra-large cup and saucer are shown and also one of the very rare egg-cups.]

Pattern 1235 introduces a series of tewares designated 'new gadroon'; for example, '1240 New gadroon, Dresden flowers in groups & sprigs printed and filled in, £4 4s. 0d.'. This is a rare reference to sprays of flowers printed in outline and coloured in by the apprentices or young painters – a fact reflected in the low price of this set.

From pattern 1351 the description 'New Ham'n' or 'New Hambledon' is occasionally used for an updated shape, but still the 'Baden' teaware forms appear to be those most in demand in about 1830. New names such as 'Berlin', 'Kent', 'New Flanged' or 'French shape' also occur during this period. The 'Kent' cup shape is shown

in Fig. 1, reproduced from one of the few surviving pattern books.

The shape name 'New Adelaide' appears against pattern 1650, closely followed by the simple description 'Adelaide'. It is not known if this meant that there was just one shape, or if there were two differing versions. The teacup shape was drawn against pattern 1799, reproduced in Fig. 2; the coffee cup is illustrated in Plate 176 and a trio is shown in Plate 429.

The trio of teacup, coffee cup and saucer shown in Plate 175 is from a very well-decorated teaset which, whilst it bears the printed Royal Arms mark (see page 35, Mark 11), does not unfortunately bear any pattern numbers. The ornate shape of the cup-handle is related to the 'Adelaide' shape as shown in design number 1799, which may be the 'New Adelaide' shape.

The covered sugar basin illustrated in Plate 177 is of a related but not identical shape. The contemporary factory name for this shape is not known, but it could be 'Victoria', a name which first occurs against pattern 1785 for dessert wares or plates, and against 1823 on teawares. The date incorporated in the printed garter motif, 1837 (see Plate 176), is the year of Queen Victoria's coronation, but this may be coincidence.

At the same period the descriptions 'Windsor' and 'New Windsor' appear in the Chamberlain list. Two typical examples are:

2239 Windsor shape, two pannels of flowers on each cup & saucer, marone ground gilt etc.

2243 New Windsor shape, two pannels of flowers on cup & saucer, blue ground & gilt.

[N.B. Prices are not given against the later entries in the pattern list.]

Another description, 'Gotha', also occurs occasionally in this list of patterns, from number 1879. The cup shape is helpfully drawn against pattern 2449 and is reproduced in Fig. 3. Also during this period a strange shape designation, 'Half orange', appears, as in pattern 2241: 'Half orange shape, two pannels of flowers on cup & saucer, pink ground gilt etc. . .'.

One of the few later designs that I have been able to link with the pattern list is illustrated in Plates 179 and 180. These pieces do not bear a manufacturer's name, or a pattern number, only a neatly written retailer's name, 'Rollason & Burman, Birmingham'. The quality of the decoration on these pieces, however, is superb and the moulded forms and cup-handle shape are identical with

175.   *Top:* A trio of teacup, coffee cup and saucer well decorated with an unnumbered design. Printed Royal Arms mark (see page 35, Mark 11). Diameter of saucer 5¾ in. *c.* 1830–40. *Geoffrey Godden, chinaman*

176.   *Below:* A thickly potted Chamberlain teapot bearing a garter and motto printed motif encircling the date 1837. The cup, which may not match this teapot, is of the 'Adelaide' shape. Printed Royal Arms mark (see page 35, Mark 11) inside teapot cover. Cup 3 in. high. *c.* 1837–45. *Dyson Perrins Museum, Worcester*

177.   *Centre:* A covered sugar bowl related in shape to the teapot shown in Plate 176, decorated with a gilt seaweed design. Unmarked. 5¾ in. high. *c.* 1840–45. *C. May, London*

178. A blue-bordered plate of the 'new registered' shape, a form first registered on 6 June 1846 and subsequently much used for dessert services. Oval printed mark (see page 36, Mark 18). Diameter 10½ in. *c.* 1846–50. *Dyson Perrins Museum, Worcester*

179. *Above right:* One of two bread and butter plates from a finely decorated Chamberlain service supplied to a Birmingham retailer. Painted name mark 'Rollason & Burman, Birmingham' (see page 150). 11½ × 10 in. *c.* 1846–9. *Geoffrey Godden, chinaman*

180. *Right:* An attractive form of Chamberlain teacup and saucer, part of the service supplied to Rollason & Burman of Birmingham and so marked. Diameter of saucer 6 in. *c.* 1846–9. *Geoffrey Godden, chinaman*

Fig. 3

the marked 'Chamberlain & Co' example illustrated in Plate 181. Although the pattern is unnumbered, it is obviously an expensive design and it is probable that the relevant reference to it is that listed under pattern 2382: 'Malta shape, gilt roses as Rollason's [teaset] £14 14s. 0d.'. The name Rollason & Burman appears written on the tewares; perhaps the pattern was a special one made specifically for this Birmingham retailer, maybe to his own design. This pattern can be dated to the 1846–7 period, as a registered plate of June 1846 first appears against pattern 2250 and design 2443 has the date June 1847 entered against it. The pattern number of these tewares falls neatly between these two designs.

The dating of this service and these shapes is further helped by the retailer's written name mark, for this partnership is listed in the local directories only between 1846 and 1849. The partnership then succeeded Thomas Rollason junior at 30 Union Street, Birmingham. The Rollason firms (T. Rollason and G. Rollason) were very good customers of the Chamber-

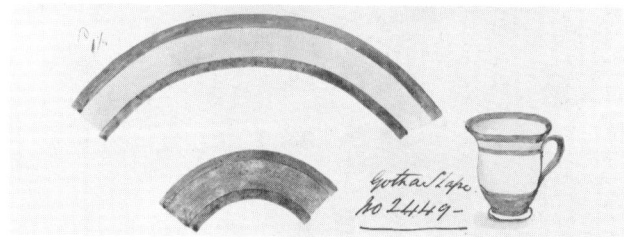

lains in the 1830s and 1840s, and other pieces bearing this name mark could well prove to be of Chamberlain make as well.

The attractive cup and saucer illustrated in Plate 182 are probably of Chamberlain make of about 1850 and are related in style to those shown in Plates 180 and 181.

Design number 2387 introduces a new shape name – 'Besborough' – and pattern 2388 is listed: '2388 Besborough shape, bat-printed figures in gold pannel richly gilt £7 17s. 6d.'. This last entry serves as a reminder that printing was still practised, and when

Bluewing Gelding 4½

3 of these in Saucer
and 3 in the Cup
No 2452.

Fig. 4

181.   A teacup and saucer of the same basic shape as that shown in Plate 180, hand-painted with flowers on a pale yellow ground. Written marks 'Chamberlain & Co., Worcester'. Diameter of saucer 6 in. *c.* 1845–50. *Geoffrey Godden, chinaman*

compared with the previous pattern, which cost £14 14*s*. 0*d*., the relative cheapness of this mass-production technique can be seen. A half-page from a pattern book showing the 'Besborough' shape cup, with pattern 2452, is illustrated in Fig. 4.

From pattern 2403, of the late 1840s, there is mention of 'Melon' shape tewares: '2403 Melon shape, blue & gold edge & stripes £2 7*s*. 3*d*.'. In general, all designs on the 'Melon' shape tewares were inexpensive. Fig. 5, from a factory pattern book, shows teware designs 2493

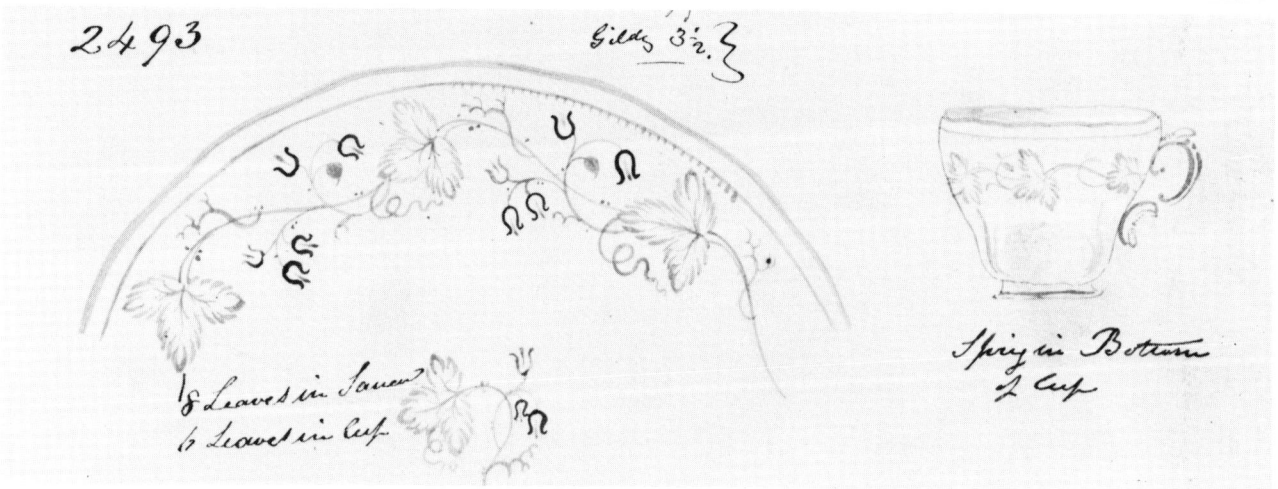

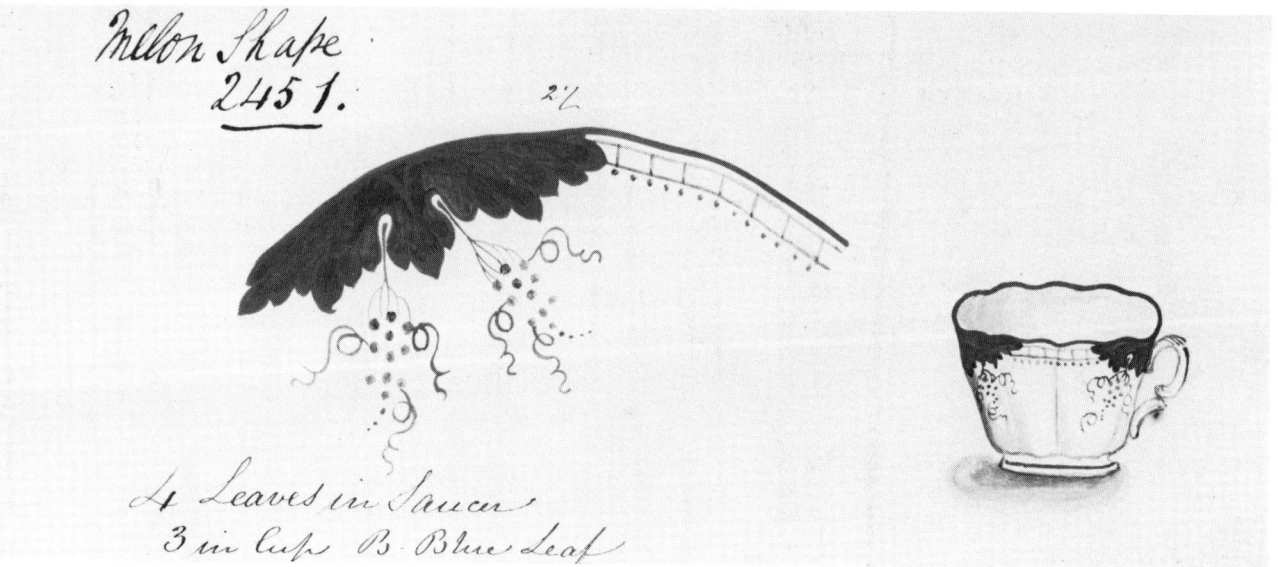

2494

Gilding ⁴ Flower 1½ Running

3 of them in Saucer
2 of them in Cup

Stars in bottom of Cup

2493

Gilding 3½

8 Leaves in Saucer
6 Leaves in Cup

Sprig in Bottom
of Cup

Melon Shape
2451.

2/

4 Leaves in Saucer
3 in Cup B. Blue Leaf

Fig. 5

Fig. 6

and 2494 with drawings of the 'Melon' shape cup. It would appear, however, that the handle form was the key feature of this shape, for design 2451 is also described as 'Melon' in the factory list, although the drawn cup shape is slightly different.

The old 'Baden' shape tewares are no longer mentioned in the list. Against pattern 3014 the shape name 'Albert' appears for the first time, but by then the

182.   An attractive cup and saucer, related in general form to the marked Chamberlain example illustrated in Plate 181 and probably of that make. Unmarked. Diameter of saucer 5½ in. *c.* 1850–52. *Geoffrey Godden, chinaman*

Chamberlain period was fast drawing to a close, for against design 3082 there appears the important note: '. . . as Lord Ward's March 19th, [18]52. . .'.

The 'Albert' shape cup is shown in Fig. 6, reproduced from a pattern book, but this French-style double-twig handle was used at several factories apart from Chamberlain's.

The sequence of pattern numbers breaks at 3099 and restarts at 4000, but this jump may be pure error. Another break in the numbering (or rather in the available records) occurs between patterns 5019 and 6000, and I have taken this to mark the end of the long Chamberlain management of the factory that was subsequently continued by the Kerr & Binns partnership in 1852. The list of Chamberlain designs from 1 to 5019 is given in Chapter 8.

It is unfortunate that the later shape names cannot be linked to the illustrations in this book. The main reason for this is that most of the surviving specimens that I have handled do not bear a pattern number and therefore cannot be related to the original list of patterns. It is to be hoped, however, that some numbered examples will be reported and that in subsequent writings the correct designations can be given.

Dessert services

The situation regarding the later Chamberlain dessert services is even more complex than that of the tea-wares. Complete services are rarely found and many examples of dessert wares – the odd plates, dishes or comports – are unmarked or do not bear a pattern number.

The magnificent plate shown in Plate 183 is part of a service made for King George IV, who acceded to the throne in January 1820 and was crowned on 19 July 1821. The plate form is a popular one and was perhaps reasonably new at this period. The rich green border is very well 'ground-laid' – a tricky process – and the gilding is also of the finest quality, with raised scroll-work. The flower painting is of royal quality, by an unknown painter (but perhaps Webster), one whose work occurs on much of the finer Chamberlain products of the 1821–30 period (see Plates 186, 187, 195, 392 and 394). The quality of the painting and gilding of the Royal Arms speaks for itself: justification indeed of the Chamberlains' status as porcelain manufacturers to the Royal Family.

Soon after this plate was made for George IV, a new plate form was introduced, for orders in 1822 refer to square plates:

6 new square plates, black views and gold edge and line £1 10s. 0d.
    [January 1822]

6 new square Gadroon [edge] plates, best white £1 1s. 0d.
    [June 1822]

This plate shape is shown in Plate 184 but it seems to have been a short-lived novelty, and one which was not wholly confined to the Chamberlain factory, for some very similar examples were made at Charles Bourne's factory in the Staffordshire Potteries.

The dessert service shown in Plate 185 is interesting, not only on account of the different dessert dish shapes illustrated but because the pieces bear a pattern number, 1621. The set is not priced. These shapes were also

called 'Royal Gadroon', and the plate is similar to the royal plate shown in Plate 183. The name Ashcroft is bracketed after pattern 1621 and this occurs after several designs of this period (1830–32), mostly flower patterns. The same shapes were produced without the moulded gadroon edge, as is shown by the dessert dish illustrated in Plate 187.

The gadroon-edged dessert plate shown in Plate 186 is of the same shape as the pattern 1621 service but is very much richer in style, with a fine maroon ground, richly gilt and finely painted with flowers. This unnumbered design has not been traced in the factory list, but the porcelain bears the name mark

183. A superb green-bordered plate, the centre finely painted and gilded with the Royal Arms, as used by George IV who acceded to the British throne in January 1820. Printed name mark with Bond Street address. Diameter 10 in. *c.* 1820. *Dyson Perrins Museum, Worcester*

184. *Top:* Representative pieces of a Chamberlain 'Regent China' dessert service including the square plates mentioned in 1822 orders. Printed name and address marks. Tureen 7¼ in. high. *c.* 1822–5. *Messrs Christie, Manson & Woods*

185. *Above:* Representative pieces of a Chamberlain gadroon-edged dessert service of pattern 1621, described in the list as 'Gadroon, dessert, lace gilding & group of birds in centre, varied (Ashcroft)' (see page 183). Name mark. *c.* 1830–32. *Messrs Christie, Manson & Woods*

186.   *Left :* A fine-quality 'Regent China' gadroon-edged plate with maroon ground and floral-painted panels. Impressed mark 'CHAMBERLAINS' (applied twice in cross fashion). Diameter 9 in. *c.* 1830–35. *Geoffrey Godden, chinaman*

187.   *Above :* A richly decorated blue-bordered and cream-ground Chamberlain dessert service dish without the gadroon edge seen in Plate 185. Marked 'Chamberlains Worcester'. $12\frac{3}{4} \times 9\frac{1}{2}$ in. *c.* 1825–35. *C. Barkman*

Fig. 7

'CHAMBERLAINS' impressed twice into the body, which is of the rather compact glassy 'Regent China' type.

At this period the Chamberlain management was especially prone to copying other firms' shapes and designs. For example, pattern 1661 reads: 'Ridgways shape dessert, celeste green & drab views & color'd birds'; and pattern 1686 is described: 'New flanged, drab & gilt view under (as Coalport)'. Chamberlain's version of Ridgway's dessert service plate is probably that reproduced in Fig. 7 with the number 1637, a design described as 'Ridgways dessert' in the Chamberlain list.

Names given to the post-1825 Chamberlain dessert ware shapes include 'Adelaide', 'Victoria', 'Chantilly' or 'Royal Chantilly', 'Coburg', 'New Gadroon', 'Royal' or 'Royal Gadroon'. The edge shape for 'Adelaide' was very ornate, as can be seen from design 1793 (see Fig. 8) which was described as 'Adelaide, drab scroll as Daniels'. The moulded edge for a 'Victoria' shape plate is illustrated in Fig. 9, reproduced from the pattern book, and the approximate date of this design, number 1798, is 1840–45. The 'Royal' shape of the late 1840s is represented by the drawing of pattern number 3033 from one of the Chamberlain pattern books (see Fig. 10).

A new dessert shape was introduced in the first half of 1842, with the shell-shaped handled dish, raised on feet.

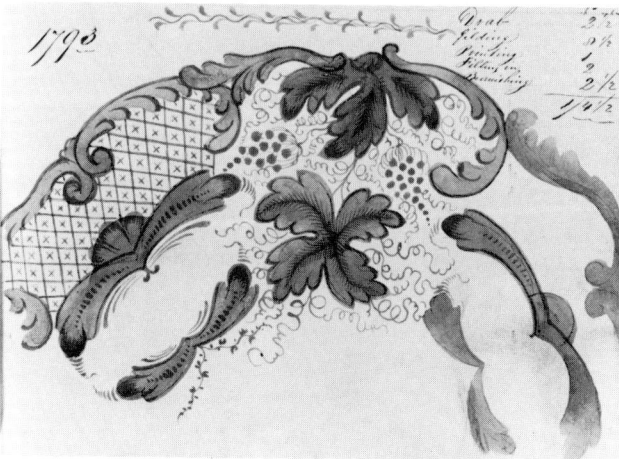

Fig. 8

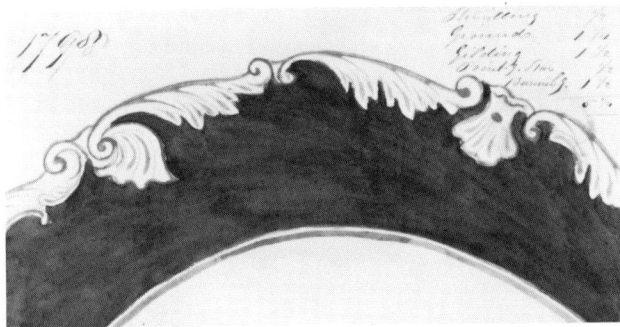

Fig. 9

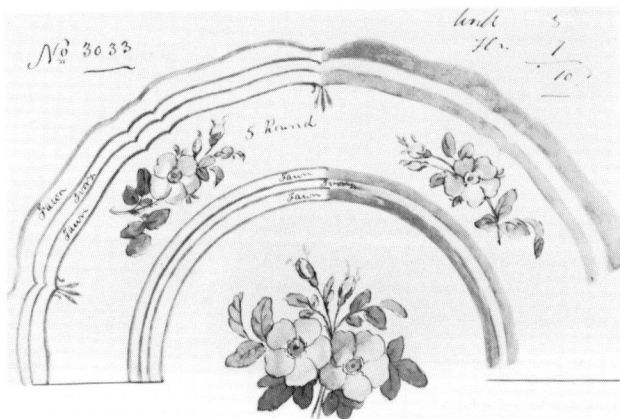

Fig. 10

188.   A Chamberlain gadroon-edged dessert plate of an unusual form, decorated with a dark blue band with gilt borders. Name mark. 9½ in. *c.* 1830–40. *Geoffrey Godden, chinaman*

189.   A particularly elaborate four-footed centrepiece from the blue-bordered dessert service represented in Colour plate XV and Plate 190. Unmarked. 16 in. long. *c.* 1840. *Geoffrey Godden, chinaman*

It is not clear from the following entry if the other dishes were footed or not, nor is a name given to this shape:

24 dessert plates stone [colour] and gold with flowers on new shapes.
4 shells on feet do.
2 square [dishes] 2 oval [dishes] and centrepiece. £9 4s. 0d.
    [May 1842]

'Harlequin' services were still being ordered and apparently replacements were made for old services. At this period, too, very soon after the amalgamation of the two companies, the new concern was producing services, or at least replacements for services, in the old Barr, or Flight, Barr & Barr, forms:

60 Table [plates] pink banded and brown line to Barr's Windsor shape £7 10s. 0d.
    [December 1842]

A Chamberlain dessert plate shape (quite rare) of the 1835–45 period is shown in Plate 188 but it does not bear a pattern number.

By the mid 1840s new names such as 'Dessert new vine emboss'd' (patterns 2185 +) are listed, and against pattern 2250 there is the important description 'New Registered embossed', the introduction of which can be dated to June 1846, although it remained in use until at least 1850. This registered shape is illustrated in Plates

178 and 191 and the pieces should bear on the back the diamond-shaped Design Registry device. The particular (unnumbered) design shown in Plate 191 is an inexpensive one, the central floral spray being a printed outline which was then coloured in by the boys or apprentices. This design could be number 2258 of June

191.   *Above:* A 'new registered' Chamberlain dessert plate of the post-1846 period decorated in an inexpensive style with coloured-in printed floral centre. Impressed mark 'CHAMBERLAINS. WORCESTER' and printed 'Chamberlain & Co.' name and address mark. Diameter 9¼ in. *c.* 1846–8. *C. H. Black Collection*

190.   One of four handled dishes of this form from the dessert service represented in Colour Plate XV and Plate 189. Impressed-marked 'CHAMBERLAINS'. 10¾ × 9¼ in. *c.* 1840. *Geoffrey Godden, chinaman*

192.   An attractive turquoise-blue bordered Chamberlain plate of a form similar to the 1846 registered shape (see Plate 191). The garden scene is hand-painted. Impressed mark 'CHAMBERLAINS. WORCESTER' with written name 'Chamberlain & Co. Worcester'. Note that in the late 1840s the London address was no longer used. Diameter 9¼ in. *c.* 1846–52. *Mrs K. Mitchell*

or July 1846: 'New registered embossed, blue & gold traced edge & filled in Dresden group & sprigs'. The term 'Dresden group' was often used for flower sprays.

The dessert plate shown in Plate 192 is slightly different in outline from the registered shape but it is clearly of the same period, that is, the mid to late 1840s. Here, however, the decoration is very much richer. The wide border is a hand-laid turquoise and the centre is hand-painted. Such a service would have cost four or five times as much as the floral-printed set.

Dessert shape names of this later period include 'Scroll embossed', 'Chelsea rosebud', 'Ward', 'Malta', 'new Grass edge', 'new Leaf Edge' (or 'new embossed leafage') and 'London embossed', in addition to the former shapes such as 'Royal', and 'Coburg'. The 'new embossed leafage' edging is shown in Fig. 11.

However, not all Chamberlain dessert services were of porcelain in the mid 1840s. The pattern list shows

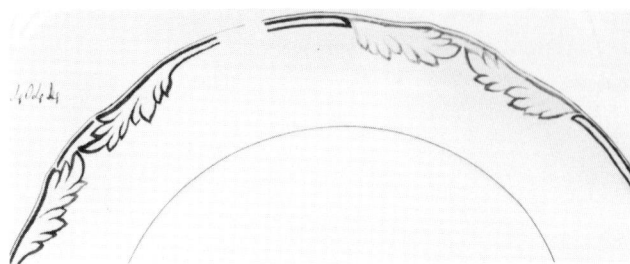

Fig. 11

that many were of the Granite body, a type of Ironstone, and pattern 4044 is an example of this kind of ware (see also page 146).

By at least the mid 1840s the old shaped-edged dessert dishes gave way to plate-shape comports on stems of varying heights – approximately 6 in., 4 in. and 2 in. high, judging from contemporary Staffordshire sets and from the later Royal Worcester services.

Dinner services

The Chamberlain dinner services of the early 1820s continued the styles and shapes favoured in the previous decade. The tureens were of a circular plan as shown in Colour Plate XVI.

This dinner service soup tureen bears pattern 886, a popular form of 'Japan' pattern, which was ordered by at least June 1820. The full pattern is shown on the plates illustrated in Plate 193. The basic shape of this tureen is similar to the one shown in Plate 164, except that this is of the plain-edged variety without the moulded gadroon edge. The knob forms match the Yeo service pieces (see page 117 and Colour Plate XI).

The same tureen form, but with a new and slightly later knob, is seen in Plate 194. The decoration here is not as colourful as the rich 'Japan' pattern and comprises a printed outline coloured in by the younger, or female, painters. This design was issued in several variations which were introduced during 1824 and 1825.

Some sets of this period cost nearly twice this price; for example, pattern 1120, which was simply described as Dr Shuttleworth's pattern, 'drab & gold', cost £84 0s. 0d., whilst other sparsely decorated dinner sets were priced at only 15 guineas.

A complete Chamberlain dinner service of the post-1820 period comprised the following items:

60	dinner plates
24	soup plates
24	side or dessert plates
2	soup tureens covers and stands
4	sauce tureens covers and stands
4	vegetable dishes and covers
1	salad bowl
1	fish drainer
2	platters 20 ins long
2	do. 18 do. do.
2	do. 16 do. do.
2	do. 14 do. do.
4	do. 12 do. do.
4	do. 10 do. do.

A buyer could, of course, purchase lesser amounts to suit his personal requirements or the depth of his pocket.

Some Chamberlain dinner services matched the tea and dessert services in that they had embossed, or relief-moulded, floral edges. Such a design was number 1021: 'New embossed with enameled womens flowers in panels Gold edge. £31 10s. 0d.'. The matching teaset was a mere £3 13s. 6d.

The Victorian service represented in Plate 195 by the large gadroon-edged platter must have been a very costly set. I have been unable to trace the pattern

193.   *Opposite above:* The front and reverse of Chamberlain dinner plates painted with the colourful 'Japan' pattern number 886, as the tureen shown in Colour Plate XVI. This design was also favoured at the Coalport and Derby factories. Printed name and address mark, as shown. Diameter 9½ in. *c.* 1820–25. *Godden of Worthing Ltd*

194.   *Opposite:* A tureen and dinner plate decorated with a popular printed design coloured-in by hand. Several variations of this standard design occur. Printed mark inside tureen cover. Tureen 9 in. high. *c.* 1826–35. *Godden of Worthing Ltd*

195. A large gadroon-edged dinner service dish with blue border, embossed gilding and finely painted flowers, reputedly part of a service presented by Queen Victoria to the Grand Duchess of Hesse. Impressed mark 'CHAMBERLAINS'. 14 in. long. *c.* 1837–42. *Messrs Sotheby & Co.*

196. An outline drawing of a Chamberlain soup tureen form of the mid to late 1840s, reproduced from a factory pattern book. Size noted as 13 in. high. *Worcester Royal Porcelain Co. Ltd*

number but it was part of a set reputedly presented by Queen Victoria to the Grand Duchess of Hesse. Apart from the finely painted flower group and the ground-laid border, the other obvious sign of quality lies in the superb raised gilding, where each of the flowers and leaves is in effect modelled in slight relief. The cost of this painstaking gilding can be gauged by comparing two similar tea service designs – one with raised gilding, the other without.

1308 Baden gadroon, glaze blue & embossed gold ornamental
£18 18s. 0d.

1460 Baden gadroon, Kings blue as 1308 but not rais'd
£12 12s. 0d.

If it were assumed that the price reflected the degree of decoration, then the teaset cost 50 per cent more when embellished with the raised gilding; but as the basic porcelain articles themselves represent perhaps a quarter of the cost, say £4 4s. 0d., the less expensive decoration cost £8 8s. 0d. against £14 14s. 0d. for the same decoration but with raised gilding. This high cost of quality gilding should be borne in mind when looking at all ornamental pieces gilded in this manner.

Chamberlain dinnerware shapes of the 1830s and 1840s were termed 'New Chantilly', 'Coburg' and 'Reed edge'. Of these, 'Coburg' was the most popular judging from the pattern list (see Chapter 8), but all these shapes were continued up to the end of the Chamberlain period. The 'Coburg' dinnerwares were made both in the Granite Ironstone-type body and in porcelain. The collector today will, however, find few Chamberlain dinner services complete, and not even the main pieces such as the tureens. The plates, too, are surprisingly difficult to trace, perhaps because so few examples bear a Chamberlain mark.

From May 1839 dinner services included tureens described as 'new round soup tureens and stands, with rose knobs'. The smaller sauce-tureens were scaled-down versions of this form.

Illustrated in Plate 196 is a drawing of a tureen from the Chamberlain design book. On stylistic grounds this would date to the 1840s, but similar soup tureens were made by most English manufacturers of that period.

Ornamental wares

The ornamental porcelains produced in the last period of the Chamberlain concern are quite diverse, as will be seen from the main coverage of shapes which are listed in Chapter 7; but nevertheless there was a decline in their manufacture, particularly in the 1840s.

A few general points should be made regarding the main styles. The Chamberlain management certainly sought to produce floral-encrusted porcelains in the so-called Coalbrookdale manner. The covered cup and stand shown in Plate 197 is a rare but typical example of its type, but it must be borne in mind that most manufacturers of the 1820–40 period were producing such pieces and the general style emulated the Dresden porcelains.

The charming little footed bowl and saucer shown in Plate 198 must be regarded as an ornamental or cabinet piece. This fine-quality example is very much in the Flight, Barr & Barr style, but the flower painting is obviously by a hand which had decorated many other Chamberlain pieces. Whilst the Chamberlain factory is not generally known for its flower painting, several superb flower painters were employed, such as Ashcroft, George Davis and John Webster, and their work bears comparison with the most famous names.

The way that the manufacturers rang the changes is well illustrated in Plates 199–201. Plate 199 shows a good-quality dish, or shallow bowl, or tray with a leaf-

197. *Below left:* A marked Chamberlain floral-encrusted covered cup and stand in the Coalbrookdale style. Printed Royal Arms mark (see page 35, Mark 11). Covered cup 4½ in. high. *c.* 1820–30. *Godden of Worthing Ltd*

198. *Below:* A rare Chamberlain small footed bowl and stand painted with a deep-blue ground, richly embellished with raised gilding. A similar shape was made at the rival Flight, Barr & Barr factory. Painted mark 'Chamberlain & Co. Worcester'. Diameter of saucer 4½ in. *c.* 1840–45. *Godden Reference Collection*

199. A fine-quality and attractive leaf-bordered dish. Printed 'Chamberlain & Co' mark with both London addresses. Diameter 9½ in. *c*. 1840–45. *Private collection*

moulded edge; the centres of such dishes were painted in several different styles. This example was made after the amalgamation of the two companies in 1840, as the mark incorporates the addresses of the two London retail shops at 155 New Bond Street and 1 Coventry Street. Indeed a similar shape appears in pre-1840 Flight, Barr & Barr marked porcelains. The same basic shape appears in Plate 200, filled with delicately hand-modelled flowers in the manner of Dresden, Coalport or Minton examples. Plate 201 shows the same shape adapted to a basket by the addition of feet and a handle. Such baskets might again be decorated with different coloured grounds and painted with various views or other motifs.

The Chamberlain management's love of views continued right up to the closing years of the firm – if all the pieces painted with Worcester views were intended for sale in their High Street shop, these premises must

200. A leaf-bordered dish similar to that shown in Plate 199 but here filled with hand-modelled flowers. Painted mark 'Chamberlain & Co. Worcester'. Diameter 11 in. *c*. 1845–50. *Messrs Sotheby & Co.*

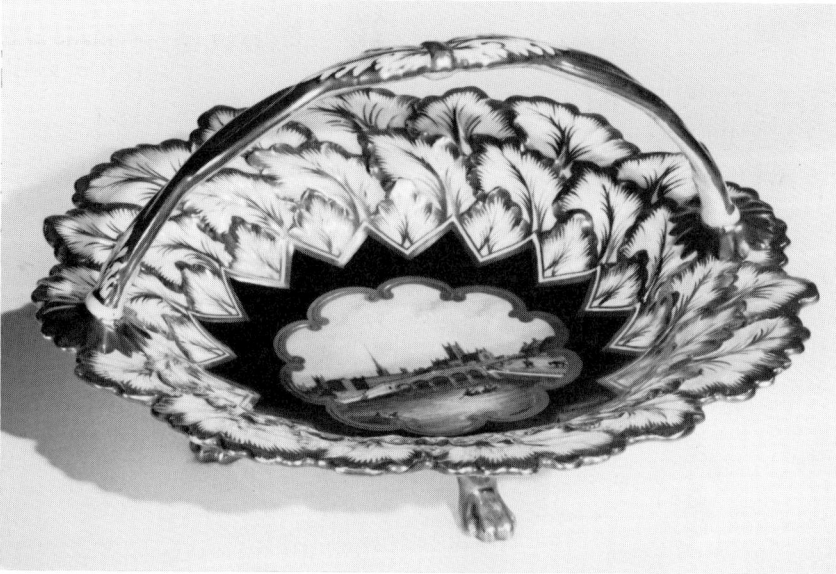

201.   *Left*: A Chamberlain handled basket of the same basic leaf-bordered edge as in Plates 199 and 200. The centre is painted with a standard view of Worcester. Marked 'Chamberlains Worcester'. Diameter 8 in. *c*. 1840–50. *Private collection*

202.   A green-ground mug turned to show the moulded handle form. The panel shows a standard view of Worcester. Printed 'Chamberlains' mark. $3\frac{1}{4}$ in. high. *c*. 1840–45. *Miss S. Newman*

203.   A decorative tray hand-painted with a view of the new Houses of Parliament within a relief-modelled shell border. Such a specimen was invoiced at £5 5s. 0d. in July 1841 (see page 264). Painted mark 'Chamberlains Worcester'. 13 in. long. *c*. 1841. *Messrs Christie, Manson & Woods*

have enjoyed very good business. The green-ground mug shown in Plate 202 bears the same local view as the basket discussed above. It has been turned to show the handle form which is helpful in distinguishing between unmarked Chamberlain mugs and those produced by other concerns.

In the 1840s a decorative class of porcelain was enriched (but not necessarily enhanced) with applied porcelain shells. Two typical examples are illustrated in Plates 203 and 204, and several different views were painted on such objects.

The heavy, over-ornate, taste of the 1840s is well seen in the set of Chamberlain vases shown in Plate 205.

Much work obviously went into the manufacture of such pieces, which are representative of their period, but a little less work might well have ensured a more lasting popularity.

The next illustration also shows a specimen of which the management of the time was no doubt very proud. The ornament shown in Plates 206 and 207 forms an inkstand when the dog top is lifted off. This rare example is shown together with the outline drawing from the factory shape book, and is very reminiscent of French porcelains of the 1830–50 period; several types of late Chamberlain porcelain were probably inspired by the popular continental porcelains which were then

204. A decorative Chamberlain basket, the edge of which is encrusted with porcelain shells. The centre is painted with a view of 'Malvern Abbey'. Painted mark 'Chamberlains Worcester'. $10\frac{3}{4}$ in. long. *c.* 1840–45. *Messrs Phillips*

205. A selection of five Chamberlain covered vases embellished with raised flowers. The side vases are marked with the addresses of both London retail shops. Centre vase $19\frac{1}{2}$ in. high. *c.* 1840–45. *Messrs Christie, Manson & Woods*

206. A drawing from a Chamberlain design book of a large continental-styled inkstand of the mid 1840s (see Plate 207). *Worcester Royal Porcelain Co. Ltd*

207. A claret-ground Chamberlain inkstand, containing three inkwells under the dog cover. Script name mark inside cover. 9¾ in. long. *c.* 1845. *Messrs Christie, Manson & Woods*

available and competing with British wares. Many Chamberlain vase forms are very French in style, and the point has already been made that Chamberlain purchased and decorated French blanks. Chamberlain cup-handles often betray a French origin, the standard handle shown in Plate 208 being a case in point: it would

have been introduced in about 1820 but was still being employed by Chamberlain's in the 1840s.

A few other drawings of late Chamberlain shapes have survived in the factory archives, but no finished examples have been traced to match the drawings, underlining the fact that the later Chamberlain porcelains are scarce.

The openwork porcelains noted in the magazine *Art Union* in March 1846 were featured in many subsequent reviews, indeed they seem to typify the later Chamberlain porcelains – rather heavy-looking garish objects which were derivative – in this case, poor imitations of Sèvres porcelains which were themselves probably taken from Eastern prototypes.

Rather surprisingly some of the openwork pieces appear in the list of tableware patterns, with the original prices:

208. A pale turquoise-ground Chamberlain cup and saucer, the panels painted with the traditional birds in landscape design. Painted mark 'Chamberlain & Co. Worcester'. Diameter of saucer 6¼ in. *c.* 1840–45. *Miss J. Carr Collection*

	s.	*d.*
2456 Bottle 5⅜ inches high. Three compart-ments pierced and three solid with painted birds. Canary finish (see pattern book). [See Plate 209]	25	0 each
2457 Ditto with painted flowers. Biscuit blue ground and pearls and gilding. [See Plate 209]	23	0

209. *Below left:* Two drawings of Chamberlain's openwork-bodied bottles of patterns 2456 and 2457 showing the different manufacturing costs. *c.* 1846. *Worcester Royal Porcelain Co. Ltd*

210. *Below right:* A drawing from the Chamberlain design book showing the basic form of a pierced double-walled jug. These were very popular in the mid 1840s. *Worcester Royal Porcelain Co. Ltd*

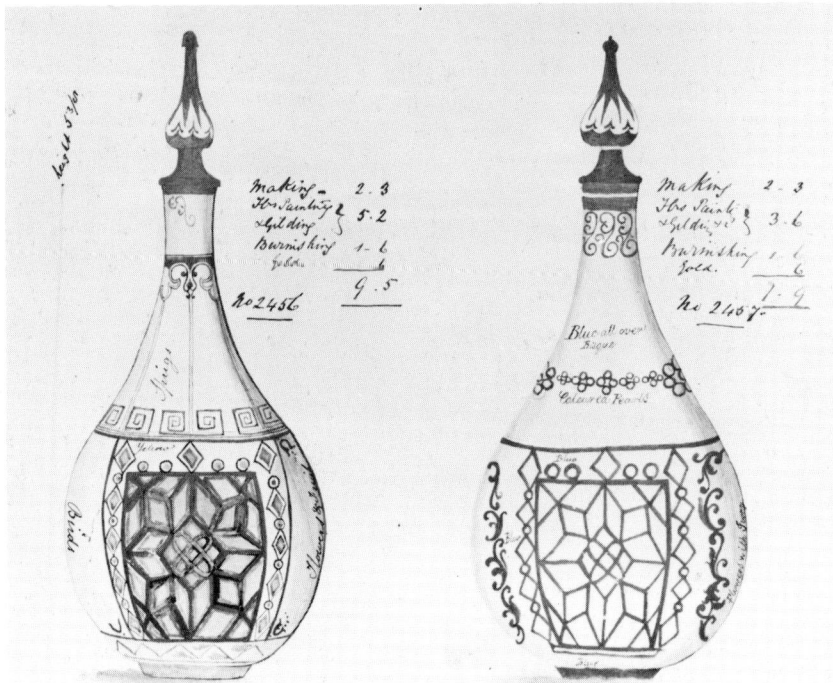

211.   A selection of Chamberlain's pierced double-walled porcelains as engraved in *The Illustrated London News* of 17 February 1849, representing a proposed gift to Jenny Lind.

212.   A rare Chamberlain cabaret or early-morning teaset, all except the tray being of the pierced honeycomb type. The jug is seen drawn in Plate 210. *c.* 1846–50. *Mr & Mrs Milton L. Zorensky*

213. An elegant Chamberlain yellow-ground pierced double-walled scent-bottle. This is a rather more elaborate version of those shown in Plate 209. Also a cup and saucer in the same technique. Written mark 'Chamberlain & Co. Worcester'. *c.* 1846. *Messrs King & Chasemore, Pulborough*

However, these entries would have been entered well after the date of the *Art Union* article as the numbers are some two hundred higher than the entry for the first registered plate design of June 1846.

In 1849 the celebrated singer, Jenny Lind, visited Worcester where she was presented with a fine selection of Chamberlain pierced porcelains (see Plate 211). She courteously declined the gift, however, explaining that her services were to be purely charitable.

The Chamberlain openwork wares were featured in the *Art Journal* of October 1849. The company's stand at the Great Exhibition in 1851 included 'Communion and dejeune services, of pierced, or honey-comb china. Pierced jugs, bottles, chalice cups [see Plate 214] and stands'. These exhibition pieces are preserved at the Dyson Perrins Museum at Worcester. Not all Worcester pierced or openwork designs are of Chamberlain make, however – rather later in the nineteenth century the Grainger management specialized in such wares, although the ultimate in reticulated porcelain was produced by George Owen* working for the Royal Worcester Company – on the old Chamberlain factory site.

_____

*For these George Owen masterpieces see Henry Sandon's *Royal Worcester Porcelain* (1973, 3rd edition 1978).

214. *Left:* A fine-quality Chamberlain chalice in the pierced honeycomb style. This was one of this firm's exhibits in the 1851 Exhibition. Written mark 'Chamberlain & Co. Worcester'. 8¾ in. high. *c.* 1851. *Dyson Perrins Museum, Worcester*

215. *Above:* An engraving of a group of Messrs Kerr & Binns's essays in the style of the Limoges enamels, painted in white enamel on a dark blue ground. *Art Journal, January 1857*

216. *Left:* A superb-quality Kerr & Binns Worcester vase painted by Thomas Bott with white enamels on a deep-blue ground. Shield mark with year numbers for 1857. 12¾ in. high. 1857. *Godden Reference Collection*

217. *Above:* A good-quality Kerr & Binns small basket in the general style of some earlier Chamberlain examples. Printed mark. Diameter 4¼ in. 1855. *E. H. Webster Collection*

The final illustrations in this chapter, Plates 215–17, show a small selection of Worcester porcelains of the succeeding Kerr & Binns period made between 1852 and 1862. In shape and general style these usually differ greatly from the late Chamberlain porcelains; the forms in particular are less fussy, although some models such as the little basket in Plate 217 are related to Chamberlain shapes (see Plate 257). The Kerr & Binns porcelains in the style of Limoges enamels (see Plate 216) are particularly noteworthy for their superb quality.

6

THE CHAMBERLAIN ARTISTS, MODELLERS AND GILDERS

Hitherto, very little has been known about the Chamberlain porcelain decorators, apart from a simple list of names recorded by R. W. Binns (*A Century of Potting in the City of Worcester*, 1865, 2nd edition, 1877), and attributions are made difficult since the painters were not permitted to sign their work. However, some information can be gleaned from the contemporary records which include the original wage books and the pattern and sales books; but very little is known about the Chamberlain decorators of the 1820–40 period and still less about the painters employed from 1840 (when the rival Chamberlain and Flight, Barr & Barr firms combined) to the termination of the Chamberlain partnership in 1852. The names of a few Chamberlain decorators are, however, given in rare lists of painters' 'stops', which apparently record fines, or monies to be stopped from their wages.

I have endeavoured to trace some of the later artists of the 1840–52 partnership by extracting the names of 'China painters' from the Worcester census returns of 1841 and 1851, and from these names I deleted those known to have been employed earlier at the old Chamberlain factory, or those connected with the rival Grainger factory. This leaves the names of china painters who were presumably employed by the only other Worcester factory, Messrs Flight, Barr & Barr, before 1840 and who continued under the new firm of Chamberlain & Co. The names of these painters are: Samuel Astles, John Barry, Joseph Brock senior, Joseph Brock junior, Thomas Carwardine (or Caradine), Richard Dighton, John Lead, James Lowe, William Morrison (or Manason), Charles Richards, John Rider, James Tomlins and Thomas White. All these are discussed in this chapter, but it must be remembered

that there is no *definite* proof that they were Chamberlain artists. A list of Flight, Barr & Barr artists, many of the pre-1840 period, is given in *Chaffers's Marks & Monograms* (15th edition 1965), but I have been unable to discover the source of this information. In more recent times information on the Flight decorators has been given in Henry Sandon's, *Flight and Barr Worcester Porcelain 1783–1840* (1978).

In December 1800 one hundred and nineteen persons were on the wage books of the Chamberlain factory; this number was made up of forty-seven 'Painters' (a term which includes gilders as well as painters), sixteen 'Potters', twenty-four 'Daymen', thirteen 'Burnishers of the gilding', four girls and nineteen boys. Their hours of work and required conduct are set out in Plate 218. Apart from the wage books, there is a most interesting letter available, written by Sarah Billingsley to her mother in October 1808 (first quoted by John Haslem in his book *Old Derby China Factory*, 1876). It describes the wages, conditions and some of the living expenses which William Billingsley and his two daughters found prevailing at Worcester in 1808. They were employed by Barr, Flight & Barr, not the Chamberlains, but one assumes that the rates and conditions were reasonably consistent at the two rival factories in Worcester.

... wages very low for a good hand, indeed he has not any more at present than the Common hands. ... My father's wages being so low and everything so extremely high here that with every frugality we could not subsist on it, and now Lavinia and myself have begun to go to work. I don't know what we are to have a week but it is I believe very little at first, it is not burnishing, it is a kind of work you never saw.

You may judge of the low wages here when I tell you that when a young woman first goes to Burnishing she has not

RULES AND REGULATIONS

TO BE OBSERVED BY ALL

PERSONS EMPLOYED IN THIS MANUFACTORY.

TIME.

1.

All Persons employed in this Factory to assemble at HALF-PAST SIX O'CLOCK throughout the year.

2.

BREAKFAST TIME, HALF-PAST EIGHT to NINE.

3.

DINNER HOUR, ONE to TWO, P.M.

4.

Every day's work reckoned to terminate at SIX, P.M.

5.

All work not ready to be passed through the Warehouse by SIX O'CLOCK, P.M., on Friday, not reckoned for until the week following.

6.

Half an Hour allowed for assembling in a Morning, after which the Entrance Door will be locked ; and a Quarter of an Hour at Breakfast and Dinner (except to day men.)

7.

On Saturdays, Manufacturing labour to cease at FOUR, P.M., from which time to hour for paying Wages, hands to employ themselves in cleaning rooms and benches, putting tools, &c., in order throughout the Works.

8.

Wages commence paying at FIVE O'CLOCK, P.M., on Saturdays throughout the year.

CONDUCT.

1.

SWEARING and BAD LANGUAGE strictly forbidden at all times.

2.

During work hours SILENCE and ORDER are required, and at all time steadiness and propriety of conduct recommended.

3.

SOBRIETY, CIVILITY, and PUNCTUALITY, are indispensable for length of service.

4.

Useful reading at proper times approved. All immoral Publications and Prints found in the Works DESTROYED, and their Owners DISCHARGED.

5.

"ON NO PRETENCE WHATEVER" is intoxicating drink, of any description, allowed in the Works, and smoking is strictly prohibited.

6.

Such of the hands as take meals on the premises, are required to do so in their respective workshops, or in the case of Girls in the room appropriated to their exclusive use.

7.

Any Person found loitering in another Working Room will be fined unless he can give satisfactory reasons.

8.

Boys are not allowed to play on the Premises.

CHAMBERLAIN AND CO.,

Royal Porcelain Works, Worcester.

MARCH 1st, 1851.

218.   The manufactory's rules and regulations concerning hours and conduct, 1851.

more than 3*s*. 6*d*. a week for the first year and never more than six shillings when they have worked 4 or 5 years. Lodgings and House rent is uncommonly dear, we pay six shillings a week for two rooms, and they are reckoned the cheapest rooms in the Town, we cannot get a bit of Bread flour under 3*s*. 6*d*. a stone and everything dear in proportion.

We go to work at 7 in the morning and leave at seven at night. . . .

It is possible that Messrs Chamberlain paid rather higher rates than their rivals. In 1819 Thomas Baxter, who had earlier been employed as a leading painter with Barr, Flight & Barr* and was now with Chamberlain's, wrote:

. . . It is not very likely that I shall ever paint anything more for them, as the people I am now engaged with are more liberally minded. . . .

However, Thomas Baxter may not have been referring specifically to scales of payment, but rather to their attitude towards the Arts in general. Nevertheless, the different porcelain manufacturers within the city of Worcester must have paid much the same rates, although according to Solomon Cole, who had been employed by Flight, Barr & Barr, the basic methods of remuneration employed by the Flight and the Chamberlain concerns differed. Cole wrote:

There were several peculiarities connected with the manufactory of Messrs. Flight, Barr & Barr, one of which was that of paying the painters by time and not by the piece. This plan was wholly confined to them. . . .

By implication Cole stated that the Chamberlain painters were paid on a piece-rate scale, although it is difficult to judge now how this system worked with all the different patterns involving varying amounts and types of decoration. The situation is also complicated by the lack of any personal marks, signs or signatures on the individual pieces. However, notes in the front of some Chamberlain wage books do tend to confirm Solomon Cole's statement, as the hands had to render 'accounts' once a fortnight:

January 1st, 1801.

It is expected everyone in the manufactory will close their accounts once a fortnight – any person not complying with the above necessary rule will not be permitted to draw any money till the next fortnight's settling. Everyone who has an account against him must be stop'd regularly according to the proportions sett down and agreed upon without any alternative whatever.   Henry Chamberlain
                                                        Robert Chamberlain

---

*The Barr, Flight & Barr trading-style gave way to Flight, Barr & Barr in 1813, and this partnership then continued until the combination of the two firms in 1840 (see page 143).

It would seem that piece-rate payment was the general system within the industry at that time, for a Chamberlain wage book includes the following notation:

Staffordshire dozen's in painting.

cup and saucers	36 [to the dozen]
coffees [cup]	36
pint basons	24
half-pint basons	30
B & B plates	12
teapots 2nd [size]	24
do. 4th [size]	18
small ewers	30
large ewers	24

The rate obviously takes into account the different amounts of decoration necessary to complete the various component parts of a tea service, depending on the area to be covered. The more work involved, the fewer items to the dozen count.

In the list of artists and gilders starting on page 183 some idea of their wages is given as an indication of their talent or standing. The average adult weekly wage in the 1790s was under £1; only the very senior hands were receiving more than this, and a new young hand or apprentice drew only a few shillings per fortnight. There seems no point in reproducing any of the wage lists as the amounts varied slightly at each payment and the names are all recorded in alphabetical order in the following pages. The wage lists are by no means complete and stop in 1809, although some later lists of 'painters' stops' have been preserved.

It is possible that not all the workers were paid on a piece-rate basis; indeed against John Toulouse's name one often finds notes such as 'and over work 9*s*.', suggesting that a fixed sum was paid with additions. If he was employed on a piece-rate basis no over-work would have been shown, just the total amount as indicated by his output.

It cannot be claimed that all the very fine-quality decorations found on the more decorative Chamberlain porcelains were original compositions, indeed probably very few were. However, the fact that most subjects were copied from published sources would have enabled the customer to choose a painting to suit his or her own taste from the prints or illustrated books that were available in the retail shop and in the factory (see page 176). It would also have enabled the painters to reproduce exactly the subject required, or to match or replace sold stock. In fact the number of different figure compositions produced before about 1810 was surprisingly small. The list below is of some of the main Chamberlain figure subjects from 1791 into the early years of the nineteenth century. The dates cannot necessarily be considered the earliest for each figure as many orders do not detail specific subjects. For example, the 1796 order for the Prince of Orange's large dinner service (see Plate 95 and page 31) reads only 'Blue and gold with different figures' and the seventy-four figure panels on this one service may well have borne all Chamberlain's classical-figure subjects although they were not then separately listed. The more ornamental wares, too, were often only described in general terms, as in the order of 18 July 1795: '2 vauses & covers . . . with Emblematical figures, £3 3s. 0d.'.

Some Chamberlain classical-figure subjects

AGRIPPA   Listed in October 1798

ARIADNE   Listed from June 1799

BEAUTY   'Beauty directed by Prudence rejects with scorn the solicitations of Folly'. Engraving by J. M. Delattre, after Angelica Kauffman, 1783

BELESAUIS   Listed in September 1797

CALYPSO WEDDING   Listed from June 1791

CORNELIA MOTHER OF GRACCHI (Mother of Grace)   Listed from August 1799

CREONE   Listed from September 1799

CUPID & CEPHISA   See Plate 220

DEATH OF ELOESA   Listed from June 1791

EUROPA   Listed from December 1798

EXTREME & UNCTION   Listed from December 1800

FORTITUDE   Listed from November 1795

MEEKNESS   Listed in April 1798

MIRANDA   Listed from June 1791

MUSIC & SAPPHO   Listed from February 1802

ORPHEUS & EURYDICE   Listed from April 1807

PARIS & OENONE   Listed from December 1800

PAULAS & OEMELIUS   Listed from November 1804

PENELOPE   Weeping over the bow of Ulysses (see Plate 228)

RINALDO & ARMIDA   After Tasso

SAPPHO & PHAON   After Angelica Kauffman, engraved by T. Kirk – pub. 1794. Listed from August 1799 (see Plate 101)

SILVIA   Listed from September 1799

TRIUMPH OF MERCY   Listed from May 1800 (see Plate 102)

VENUS & ADONIS   Listed in October 1798

Many of these Chamberlain classical-figure paintings have in the past been attributed to Thomas Baxter (see page 184), yet most examples were produced some twenty years before he was employed at the factory in July 1819. Thomas Baxter was born in February 1782 but the Chamberlain decorators were producing classical-figure subjects from at least January 1791, when there is mention of: '1 Table plate with devices of 2 Nymphs adorning satyr, blue and gold festoon, £1 5s. 0d.' (see Plate 22). Several of these figure subjects were taken from Angelica Kauffman's paintings, or rather from engravings of such originals. In one case the original order makes this point: '1 centre jar to pattern. Penelope from Angelica Kauffman's design . . .' (October 1812).

Late eighteenth-century prints of the type and subject copied on to porcelain by the Chamberlain artists form one source for students wishing to trace the original inspiration for the decorators. One such print is illustrated in Plate 219. This subject was meticulously copied on to pieces like that shown in Plate 220. Other types of figure subject were taken from such works as *The Deserted Village* as is evidenced by many orders, including one dated October 1798:

219.   A late eighteenth-century print (unfortunately now lacking the title and artist's credit) of the type copied by the Chamberlain figure painters (see Plate 220). $12\frac{1}{2} \times 10$ in. *c.* 1785–95. *Godden Reference Collection*

220. A typically well-painted Chamberlain tumbler with orange and gold ground. The panel is painted with the named subject 'Cupid & Cephisa', taken from a contemporary print (see Plate 219). Painted mark in gold 'Chamberlains Worcester'. 4¼ in. high. *c*. 1795–1800. *Mrs B. Laker Collection*

Two Quart Punch jugs and covers. Snake twisted on top of ye cover. Group in front of one. The Dance in the Deserted Village . . . ye other something to answer [to match?].

By about 1811 figure subjects from Shakespeare were being copied on to Chamberlain's porcelains as is shown by the orders quoted on pages 101 and 191 as well as the pieces illustrated on the jacket of this book and in Colour Plates VIII, XXIV and Plates 230, 268, 269, 279, 326, 385–7 and 389. Such subjects remained popular for the more expensive pieces into the 1820s, and in many cases quotations from the plays were neatly painted on the wares (see Plate 306). Some orders relating to Shakespearian subjects include:

1 small Regent ornament, painted from Shakespeare, Henry 8th. Act 3, Scene 1. £16 16s. 0d.
     [February 1813]
2 cabinet [cups] and stands from Richard 2nd and Henry 8th. Green marble ground. £8 8s. 0d.
2 Regent ornaments, . . . Figures, King Henry 6th and Comedy of Errors. £31 10s. 0d.
     [December 1813]

1 Regent [shaped vase]. Taming Shrew £7 7s. 0d.
1 do.   Richard 2nd.   £7 7s. 0d.
2 Bell-mouth [vases]. Merry Wives of Windsor and Richard II.
     [August 1817]

I am grateful to Mrs F. Wharf for suggesting where these subjects were taken from and the significance of the full detailing in some instances of the precise act and scene of the play. Many of these Shakespearian subjects were taken from the prints and engravings published by John and Josiah Boydell of London. These printed sources take two forms; the 1805 *Collection of Prints from Pictures painted for the purpose of illustrating the dramatic works of Shakespeare by the artists of Great Britain* (Vols. I and II); and the nine-volume 'National' edition of Shakespeare's works by George Stevens and published by the Boydells in 1802.

John Boydell (1719–1804) established a gallery of original paintings, all depicting Shakespearian subjects, by leading artists of the day. The Boydell Shakespeare Gallery was situated in Pall Mall and was opened to the public in 1789. Boydell was a very successful printer and publisher, reputedly employing about 250 engravers at one period, and his catalogue listed nearly 4,500 subjects.* He was Lord Mayor of London in 1790 and obviously at the height of his profession.

For comparison Plate 390 shows part of the original Boydell illustration XLVIII, 'Shakespeare nursed by Tragedy and Comedy', engraved by B. Smith after the original oil painting by George Romney, and also the Chamberlain porcelain vase bearing this fully coloured subject. In this instance, the artist has in fact combined two Boydell subjects into one continuous band encircling the vase. The other side, shown in Colour Plate XXIV, is taken from Sir Joshua Reynolds's painting illustrating *A Midsummer Night's Dream*, Act 2, Scene 2 (see also Plate 233).

The student should be able to find many other examples of John Boydell's finely engraved prints copied on to Chamberlain porcelains by their leading figure painters.

A few orders mention the name of the artist who decorated the object. For example: 'Three ornamental pieces, enamelled blue and marble [groundwork] and Walter's figures. £7 7s. 0d.' (September 1813). This reference is to Walter Chamberlain (see page 191). Other entries have the name 'Walter's' bracketed against them, such as the items sent to London in

*Readers wishing to check the Boydell engravings with the Chamberlain renderings will probably find it most convenient to consult the recent American reprints under the title *The Boydell Shakespeare Prints*.

December 1813, detailed on page 103; whilst on page 188 are listed some of the few orders which have Humphrey Chamberlain's name written against them.

I have mentioned on page 103 that prints were purchased in London in 1814 and that very soon the same subjects were being added to the invoiced Chamberlain porcelains. Many of these superb figure-painted Chamberlain porcelains were being supplied to influential persons and these orders obviously gained the company much prestige. Unfortunately pieces of this kind seldom come on the market today, but it is to be hoped that, if still existing, they give enjoyment to descendants of the original owner. One such order simply reads:

Her Majesty the Queen of England, Buckingham Palace.

One pair Cabinet cups, two handles, Paintings from The Lady of the Lake. Drab ground, gilt borders, £16 16s. 0d.
 [June 1816]

Many of the early scenic paintings, especially those featuring country houses, were copied from engravings found in *Picturesque Views of the Principal Seats of the Nobility and Gentry in England and Wales, by the most eminent British Artists*, published by Harrison & Co., of 18 Paternoster Row, London, in about 1790. A copy of this work is still at the Worcester factory and this was almost certainly the very book used by the customers to choose a view to enhance their porcelain, or by the artists to render an exact representation. This one book – and there were many other of a like nature – contains ninety-one English views and nine in Wales. Some of the engravings are dated 1788. Several other views were taken from the popular part-work *The Copper Plate Magazine*, the second series of which was published from 1792 onwards, which was a source of inspiration used by many manufacturers but particularly the Chamberlains.

The vase shown in Plate 221 is interesting in several regards. Firstly, the panel is painted with a distant view of Magdalen College, Oxford, which was almost certainly taken from the first engraving in Volume 1 of *The Copper Plate Magazine*. This indicates the long period over which these popular designs were employed, for this vase (in the Allen Collection at the Victoria & Albert Museum) is marked inside the cover 'Chamberlains Worcester and 155 New Bond Street, London', signifying a date subsequent to July 1816; in fact this basic shape, with 'Mercury-head' handles, dates from at least September 1816 and was probably used into the 1820s, as suggested by an order dated 28 February 1820: '1 Mercury ornament, Ivory & gold, view from Iffley. £3 3s. 0d.'.

221. A Chamberlain 'Mercury-head' vase with the panel painted with a view of Oxford copied from an engraving in *The Copper Plate Magazine* of 1792. Chamberlain's name mark with New Bond Street address. 8¾ in. high. *c.* 1816–25. *Victoria & Albert Museum (Crown Copyright)*

It is also interesting to observe the general fine quality of the Chamberlain wares of this period and to note how well they competed with the Flight, Barr & Barr products, which are generally conceded to represent the ultimate in English ceramic quality at this period. Yet Henry Sandon, in *Flight and Barr Worcester Porcelain 1783–1840* (1978), illustrates this very Chamberlain vase form as a Flight example (see his Plate 146). His slip, and Messrs Christie's before him, stresses the point concerning the quality of the Chamberlain decoration. This form of vase with the 'Mercury-head' handles is also seen in Plate 108, in this case bearing a view of the Chamberlain factory.

Many of the popular sporting subjects to be found on Chamberlain's porcelains were taken from, or at least inspired by, W. B. Daniel's *Rural Sports*, the first edition of which was published in 1801. A typical entry from the Bond Street shop accounts of July 1818 reads:

Col. Fitzgerald, 12, Hereford Street, London.
1 Quart Jug, fine painting, Greyhounds running vide Daniel's Rural Sports. £3 3s. 0d.

In December 1815 the purchase of 'Hunting Prints' at a cost of 1 guinea is listed, but unfortunately no details are given in the account books. The dead game subjects were extremely popular but expensive. One entry reads:

His Grace the Duke of Norfolk.
2 Two quart mugs, rich blue ground, with gold marble [marbling in gold over the blue]. Dead game [in panel] £12 12s. 0d.
    [January 1815]

Another source of inspiration for the Chamberlain artists were the popular prints by, or after, George Morland, again as shown in an account: 'Two bell [shape] vases, subjects from Morland. £8 8s. 0d.' (August 1817).

Some printed designs were apparently not used at once, or were reused over a number of years, for in March 1814 an employee in London purchased a print of 'an old woman reading, for Worcester', at a cost of 8s. 6d., but it was not until December 1817 that a sales entry for '1 can and stand, Old Woman reading £10 10s. 0d.' is found.

---

222. A Chamberlain jug decorated with the popular 'Best Queen's' pattern, number 78 in the factory list (see page 315). Unmarked. 6¾ in. high. c. 1795–1800. *Mrs W. Boardman*

Botanical studies, especially those where the name of the specimen was written on the reverse, were copied from printed sources such as *The Botanical Magazine or Flower Garden Displayed* (1787–1820).

Whilst discussing styles of decoration, it is useful to take two classes of object popular in the 1795–1815 period – the decorative bulb pots and the 'harlequin' dessert service datable to 1815 – as showing the standard forms of Chamberlain decoration, the fashionable ornamental styles at that time.

The earliest bulb pot that I have traced is shown in Plate 336. The central panel bears a very finely painted 'fancy bird' posed against a landscape background. This type of painting, in the style of George Davis (see pages 192–4), appeared on the earlier Worcester porcelains and on the Caughley wares decorated by the Chamberlain painters before that partnership commenced to make its own porcelains. This type of 'fancy birds in landscape' decoration remained popular with the Worcester firms at least into the 1830s.

By December 1798 the orders were listing bulb pots and other objects painted with the popular 'Queen's' pattern, which was given the number 78 in the factory list. This is an extremely rich design usually very well painted and gilded. In quality of decoration it rivals the earlier Dr Wall Worcester porcelains in a similar style. Plate 222 illustrates a jug of this pattern which is also shown on a bulb pot in Plate 337.

Other, slightly later, colourful 'Japan' patterns were also fashionable, including the flower-pot design taken from a Coalport original, which was Chamberlain's pattern 240 (see page 110 and Plates 118 and 341). Fine classical-figure subjects of the type previously discussed were also popular at the end of the eighteenth century and appear on these rich bulb pots. Other examples bear less expensive printed designs, both figure subjects (see Plate 342) and landscape or scenic views (see Plates 344 and 345). Some even less expensive pieces bore simple patterns similar to teaware designs of the pre-1810 period.

The 1815 dessert service, representative pieces of which are illustrated in Plate 146, displays a slightly different style of birds in landscape, finely painted views in the Flight, Barr & Barr style (see Plate 223), and also an extremely well-painted group of tightly bunched flowers (see Plate 107) – all traditional types of ceramic decoration in favour over a long period. However, this 'harlequin' service also includes other new, but now fashionable, motifs – shells, feathers and butterflies. The first mention of shell subjects in the available Chamberlain archives occurs in April 1808 – a 'harlequin' dessert service with shell and feather subjects at 100 guineas. Thereafter for about ten years shell motifs were painted, meticulously, on a variety of rich Chamberlain porcelains (see Colour Plate XVII). Unfortunately the name of the painter is not known. Certainly it was not the famous Thomas Baxter, who was elsewhere at this period (see page 184), but any of the top-ranking Chamberlain artists – particularly the figure, the flower and the landscape painters – could have painted shell subjects, and certainly several illustrated books were available should the painter require exotic specimens to copy.

Probably the earliest record of Chamberlain's feather-painting occurs in July 1807, a little before the date for shell decoration. These motifs were used on several different types of articles and often in association with shells: '2 cup and saucers, feathers and shells £3 3s. 0d.' (July 1809).

The owners of Chamberlain's porcelains or the reader of this book can hardly fail to be impressed with the quality of the gilding. The reason for this high standard probably dates back to the days when the Chamberlains were responsible for decorating the Dr Wall period

223.   A dish from the service shown in Plate 146 painted with a view of Ludlow Castle, probably copied from an illustrated book of the period. Name mark 'Chamberlains Worcester'. 8 in. square. *c.* 1815. *Godden of Worthing Ltd*

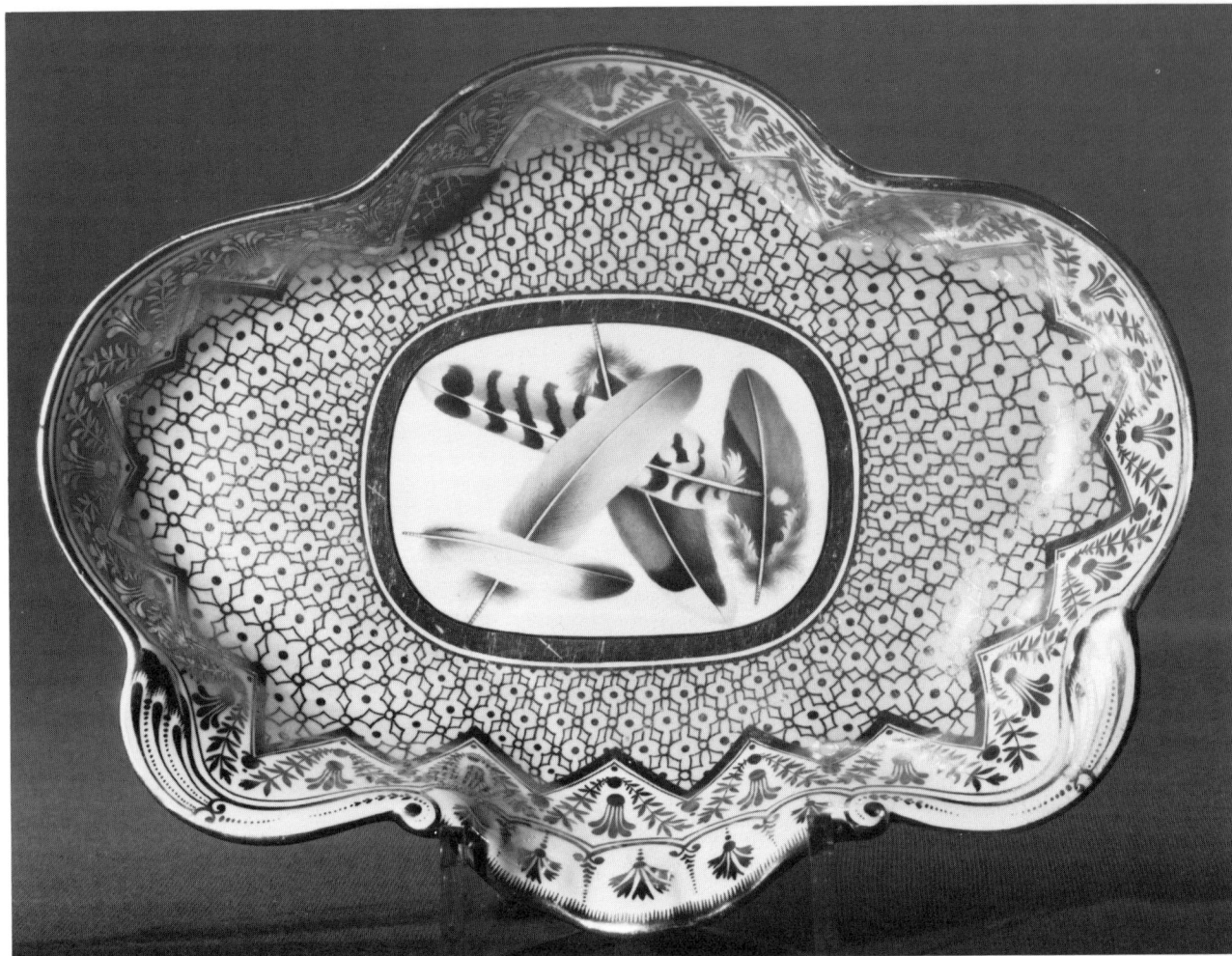

224. A dish from the service shown in Plate 146, the centre finely painted with feathers in the style of the period. Printed mark. $9\frac{1}{2} \times 7\frac{1}{2}$ in. *c*. 1815. *Godden of Worthing Ltd*

225. *Opposite*: A Paris hard-paste porcelain vase with a wreath of raised hand-modelled flowers. Such wares were available in London and in many cases set fashions which British manufacturers copied. Unmarked. $10\frac{1}{2}$ in. high. *c*. 1810–20. *Godden of Worthing Ltd*

Worcester porcelains and to the fact that when the Chamberlains started up in competition they took all the gilders from the main factory with them, as is revealed by the entries in Flight's diary quoted on pages 18–24.

Some rich examples were embellished with raised and tooled gilding, a very expensive process. Typical entries include: 'A gallon jug very rich . . . fine borders of raised gold. £31 10s. 0d.' (December 1819). This raised gilding appeared particularly effective on the matt blue grounds. In style these wares emulated the fashionable French imports. The French-style inkstand shown in Plate 307 illustrates this taste very well.

Whilst imitation jewelling is quite well known on Flight, Barr & Barr porcelains, it is extremely rare on Chamberlain objects. This technique can be seen to perfection on the charming spill-vase shown in Colour Plate XXI. Jewelling is mentioned in the Chamberlain books in January 1818 but it must have been very costly and it was therefore seldom employed.

Another mode of relief decoration comprised raised, hand-modelled flowers applied to the porcelain body. Again, the basic style came from the Continent, but the technique had been practised at various English factories for a long period. At Chamberlain's these floral reliefs were in biscuit or unglazed porcelain, often on a light, matt blue ground:

Two tripod blue & gold dolphin Warwick ornaments with white biscuit flowers. £4 10s. 0d.
[February 1819]

One box biscuit flowers on top and hunting subjects. Unpriced order.
[September 1820: see Plate 369]

Two Coronet baskets, fine biscuit flowers, dry blue &c. £5 5s. 0d.
[February 1823]

The Times of 1 December 1813 carried an advertisement for a sale of 'a large and elegant assortment of French Porcelains' at the London Commercial Salerooms, and there were several other contemporary advertisements for French porcelains. Chamberlain's even sold French porcelains encrusted with flowers: 'Two French make Luminaries with handles, embossed with flowers £1 10s. 0d.' (April 1818). In Plate 225 one of a pair of fine-quality French vases shows this type of white unglazed flower decoration arranged under the *lip*.

By at least November 1824 the raised flower work was sometimes naturally coloured in a style generally associated with the Coalport factory, and as such was

often sold as 'Coalbrookdale'. However, most English factories copied this fashionable style; in fact the Minton examples are more often found than the Coalport ones. The Chamberlain floral-encrusted porcelains are scarce, if not rare, but examples of the 1824–40 period do exist (see Plate 197), perhaps giving way later to the Chamberlain speciality of raised shell decoration on trays and similar objects (see Plate 203).

Apart from the French hard-porcelain blanks the Chamberlains also, for a short period, seem to have decorated Swansea porcelains. Whilst most of the available records relate to the sale of Swansea wares, there is one entry showing the purchase of goods. This occurs under the date 15 May 1821:

T & J Bevington, Swansea

	£	s.	d.
For goods as per bill	7	16	8
25% discount 6 months	1	19	2
	5	17	6

The subsequent use of the description 'Swansea', therefore, clearly relates to the make of the article listed, rather than the shape: indeed some entries actually read 'Swansea make' or 'Swansea ma'.

The original bill of the account mentioned above has not been preserved, but four days later a selection of 'Swansea ware' was invoiced to John Richardson of Cirencester and the goods listed below could have formed part of this consignment:

Swansea Ware		£	s.	d.
8 Breakfast cups & saucers [decorated] to pattern		1	10	0
6 Teas & Saucers	do.		15	0
2 Muffin Plates & Covers	do.		12	6
2 Basins, two sizes	do.		7	6
2 × 10″ Dishes	do.		13	0
12 Breakfast plates	do.	1	7	0
2 Jugs, two sizes	do.		8	0
Painting 50 crests @ 10d.		2	1	8
	Swansea package		5	0

It must be conceded that these wares could have been of Swansea earthenware rather than porcelain, and there is also the possibility that these wares were ordered ready-decorated from Swansea, but as the cost of painting the crests was added separately, it would suggest that this decoration was applied at Worcester. Certainly other Chamberlain records make it quite clear that the firm had available white and biscuit Swansea porcelain.

The earliest entry that has been traced relating to Swansea wares occurs in the cash book kept at Messrs Chamberlain's London retail shop in Bond Street. The simple entry, 'By 2 Swansea match pots £1 1s. 0d.', was written on 21 July 1816, and on 22 January 1818 another entry records, 'By sundry pieces of Swansea china £1 3s. 6d.'. There is no proof or indication that these pieces were decorated at Worcester, but these cash book entries do, however, indicate that some of them could have been purchased through the London shop – from other London 'chinamen' and not purchased direct from the Swansea factory – and in fact many of the entries are of a period after production of porcelain at Swansea is believed to have ceased. It would appear that Messrs Bevington & Co. at Swansea, and other dealers, had stocks of blanks available and that these stocks lasted for several years.

Collectors of Swansea porcelain like to attribute figure-subject painting (and recently scenic designs) to the much-travelled ceramic artist Thomas Baxter. Baxter certainly painted at Swansea but for a relatively short period, from the summer of 1816 to the winter of 1818–19. It is relevant in this account of Chamberlain-decorated Swansea porcelain to remind collectors that Thomas Baxter was employed by Chamberlain's from at least July 1819 until his death in April 1821, so that Baxter's paintings on Swansea porcelains could well have been added at Worcester. An entry in the Chamberlain records under 10 November 1819 records that a Mrs Lingham of Broad Street, Worcester, was charged for 'Painting a figure on a Swansea cup and gilding, 18s.'.

The existence of this Worcester-decorated Swansea porcelain serves to show the superior qualities of the Swansea body and the fashionable 'Empire' forms, especially of the cabinet cups and saucers. One even wonders if other porcelain manufacturers were alive to the fact that Swansea porcelain was the best of the period and if they, like Chamberlain, purchased blanks to decorate for their own customers.

As yet it is not possible to state if these Worcester-decorated Swansea porcelains bear a Chamberlain mark added over the glaze at the time of decoration. It would seem at least possible that Swansea porcelain sent to Chamberlain's New Bond Street retail shop for sale there, bore a Chamberlain mark.

In contrast with such finely decorated porcelains, some Chamberlain blanks were painted and gilded by amateur painters in their own homes. This was quite a fashionable pastime and several factories, notably the one at Coalport, did a large trade in supplying the undecorated blanks.

The Chamberlain records are quite full in this regard. Take, for example, these two entries:

Mrs. Blake, St. James's Square, Bath.
2 Candlesticks, black & orange 15s.
    To be sent to Bowers [the dealers] with some brown and black for the lady to paint figures with and two or three pieces of broken china.
        [July 1800]

Prince Bariatinsky, Cheltenham	£	s.	d.
A complete set of colours	1	1	0
Pencils [thin brushes] oil, knifes		8	0
A batch of Bronzes		10	0
Regilding a plate and 3 candlesticks		19	0
Eight lessons in painting	6	16	6
Expenses to Cheltenham	5	16	0
[June 1806]			

The Chamberlains' most prolific amateur painter was a Mrs Hayton, of Moreton near Hereford, and many entries in the Chamberlain account books of the 1820s relate to her purchases of blanks, or to the gilding and firing of her ceramic painting. As a general rule these amateur-painted porcelains are obviously not factory work, for the painting appears laboured, the colours dull or dirty. Often, too, such works are fully signed and dated, a practice frowned on at this period by the porcelain manufacturers. Of course, other blanks supplied by the Chamberlains were for professional independent decorators such as their former artist, John Powell (see page 204).

Specialist subjects of the leading factory artists

Armorials and crests
John Bly
James Plant
George Rogers

Bird subjects
Ashcroft
George Davis
James Doe
James Rogers

Flowers
Ashcroft
Thomas Baxter
George Davis
Thomas (?) Steel

James Taylor
John Webster

Figures
Thomas Baxter
Humphrey Chamberlain
Walter Chamberlain
George Davis
Enoch Doe
James Lowe
John Powell
John Wood

Fruit
Thomas Baxter
Thomas (?) Steel

'Japan' patterns
William Marsh
Robert Mills
J. Spooner

Landscapes
Thomas Baxter

Enoch Doe
John Muchall
John Powell
Thomas Rogers
John Smith
Joseph Williams
John Wood

The following list is arranged in alphabetical order and contains information gathered from the sources mentioned earlier. In many cases only the names are given, without supporting facts, and these are recorded for the benefit of future students or in case further evidence is forthcoming.

Chamberlain decorators, gilders and modellers

ROBERT ACRILL (or Ashrill and other spellings) Listed as a painter, *c.* 1800–1.

JOHN ADAMS Listed as a painter in the wage records, *c.* 1795–1809.

ASHCROFT Listed as a painter, *c.* 1830–32. Patterns numbered 1469, 1474–7, 1483, 1494, 1496–8, 1500, 1503 and 1504 and some later designs have the name Ashcroft entered in brackets after the description. Most of these patterns are of a floral nature, but number 1621 is painted with bird subjects (see Plate 185). The possibility exists that Ashcroft was also a gilder as some of his patterns do not appear to have painted decoration.

SAMUEL ASTLES This very talented flower painter, who was born in about 1792, is mainly known for his work on Flight, Barr & Barr porcelain, but it is possible that he continued to work for Chamberlain & Co. for a few years after the amalgamation in 1840. Astles was reputedly trained under Thomas Baxter in the 1814–16 period. Although authorities spoke highly of his flower painting, his factory work was not signed. However, a signed and dated porcelain plaque was exhibited in the Royal Academy Exhibition of 1827. This important and superbly painted plaque was sold recently and is illustrated in colour on the cover of *The Antique Dealer and Collectors Guide,* June 1954, showing clearly the skill of this Worcester ceramic artist. A rather similar example is illustrated in colour by Henry Sandon in his book *Flight and Barr Worcester Porcelain 1783–1840* (1978). His name is included in the 1841 census

returns, but there is no trace of it in the 1851 list, a fact which indicates that he had left the city between these two dates. A descendant in America, Geoffrey C. Astles, says that Samuel died of typhoid fever on 13 April 1853, at Spoon Lane, Smethwick, and that he was then aged 61. During his period at Worcester he was probably one of the finest flower painters employed in the ceramic industry.

RALPH BALL R. W. Binns includes this name in his list of Chamberlain painters or gilders of the early 1800s, but there appears to be no trace of him in the contemporary records.

THOMAS BARMORE R. W. Binns included Barmore in his list of Chamberlain painters or gilders and the name is mentioned in the wage books during 1792–4.

GEORGE BARNES Listed as a painter for many years from 1799.

JOHN BARNES Listed in the wage records from 1804–9. A John Barnes 'China-painter' is also mentioned in the 1841 Worcester census returns. It is unlikely, however, that this painter is the same one referred to in the available wage records, although it is possible that he was the son of the earlier John Barnes.

SAMUEL BARNES He was one of the earliest of the Chamberlain hands, and also seems to have been the foreman of the painters, as from 1791 the Chamberlain cash and wage records include payments made to Samuel Barnes 'for ye men'. In addition, there is the postscript to Mrs Chamberlain's letter dated 12 July 1792 (see page 29) which reads: 'Mr. Barnes has just been up to say he can no longer find ware for the boys to work on . . .', which suggests that he held a position of responsibility.

JOHN BARRY   This person is listed in the Worcester 1841 census returns as a 'China painter' and was probably formerly employed by Messrs Flight, Barr & Barr as his name is not recorded as a Chamberlain, or a Grainger, artist. This being so, Barry may have been employed by the new Chamberlain company after 1840.

THOMAS BAXTER senior   Born about 1760. Little is known of his early career but he may have received his ceramic training at the Worcester factory, for his son Thomas was born in that city on 18 February 1782. By 1797 the Baxters had established a London decorating studio at 1 Goldsmith Street, Gough Square, Clerkenwell. The relevant sewer-rate records show Baxter at this address from the Michaelmas quarter of 1797 to the Christmas quarter of 1814. The first recorded transaction of this concern occurs in the Chamberlain account books under the date 16 May 1797: 'Baxter. No. 1, Goldsmith Street, Nr. Gough Square, London. 1 Teaset (except coffees) Bell plain, white. £1 14s. 2d.'. This is the sole reference to Chamberlain supplying white porcelains to the Baxter London studio, which seems to have relied later on Coalport blanks.

THOMAS BAXTER junior   This extremely talented artist is one of the most famous of the English porcelain decorators, but his name is often associated with finely painted Chamberlain ware that was manufactured entirely outside the period when he was employed at this factory.

He received his basic training in ceramic colours and painting in his father's studio in Goldsmith Street, London, when he was only in his mid-teens in 1797. He also studied at the Royal Academy School and later exhibited work submitted from this decorating studio at Royal Academy exhibitions between 1802 and 1812. His exhibited works included fruit, flower and shell compositions as well as figure subjects.

Between 1800 and about 1810 signed or initialled examples of Baxter-decorated porcelains occur, mostly on Coalport porcelains. It is often difficult to state with certainty if these are the work of father or son, for both had the same name and therefore the same initials. It is most likely that all signed or initialled specimens are the work of Thomas Baxter junior, who was certainly a publicist as is indicated by the watercolour drawing of his father's studio as it appeared in 1810 (exhibited at

the Royal Academy in 1811 and now to be seen in the Victoria & Albert Museum), two self-portraits and various ceramic portrait medallions.

The early signed specimens of his painting and unsigned examples thought to be by him are often attributed to the Chamberlain factory. However, the Chamberlain records show only one sale to Baxter – a white teaset in 1797. The signed vase shown in Plate 226 has in the past been attributed to the Chamberlain factory whereas in fact it is of Coalport porcelain and shape, and was painted well before Thomas Baxter returned to Worcester in about 1814. It should be mentioned also that the lobed-edged plates on which Baxter often painted are Coalport not Worcester, and the jardinières illustrated by Henry Sandon in Plate 51 in his book *Flight and Barr Worcester Porcelain 1783–1840* (1978) are likewise of Coalport manufacture.

The connection between the Baxter studio and the Coalport-Caughley factory is underlined by the 1810 watercolour drawing showing the interior of the studio. On the wall hangs a notice, only the heading of which is reproduced in the drawing and this reads: 'New Price List. Coalport White China'. The teawares shown on the studio work-bench, moreover, are of a particular type which match unglazed factory wasters found on the Coalport-Caughley site.

In 1814 Baxter moved to Worcester and is said to have established a school for painting where several of Messrs Flight, Barr & Barr's foremost artists were trained. It should be noted that Thomas Baxter was not, therefore, at Worcester during the Barr, Flight & Barr period, 1807–13, although plainly marked specimens of this period are often attributed to him in error. Baxter decorated for the Flight, Barr & Barr partnership when he was at Worcester.

In the summer of 1816 Thomas Baxter junior moved to Swansea where he was employed on a part-time basis by Messrs Dillwyns, the celebrated porcelain manufacturers, and after September 1817 by their successors, Bevington & Co. He also painted portraits and drew and

---

XIV.   *Opposite above:* Representative pieces from a richly decorated tea and breakfast service showing the typical large-size breakfast cup contrasted with the normal teacup. The rare egg-cups were supplied only with breakfast cups. Note the moulded gadroon border on all pieces – the same basic shapes also occur without this edging. Printed Royal Arms mark with New Bond Street address. (see page 35, Mark 11). Diameter of plate 9 in. *c.* 1825–35. *Geoffrey Godden, chinaman*

XV.   *Opposite below:* One of a pair of covered tureens from the marked Chamberlain floral-painted dessert service shown also in Plates 189 and 190. Printed mark with New Bond Street address inside covers. 7 in. high. *c.* 1840. *Geoffrey Godden, chinaman*

XVI. A typical shape Chamberlain soup tureen and cover from a dinner service of pattern 886 (see also Plate 193). This popular 'Japan' pattern was originally priced at £63 (60 guineas) for the complete service. Printed Royal Arms mark (see page 35, Mark 11) inside cover. 10 in. high. *c.*1820–30. *Godden of Worthing Ltd*

XVII. A cream- or sugar-tureen from the 'harlequin'-type dessert service shown in Plate 146, turned here to show the shell-painted panel, the typical ground colour and the rich gilding. The floral panel is illustrated in Plate 107. 8¾ in. high. *c.*1815. *Godden of Worthing Ltd*

XVIII. *Left:* A 'Regent China' plate almost certainly painted by Thomas Baxter and perhaps one of the thirty dessert plates, 'gadroon and gold with fine paintings of fruit', supplied to John Eversley in June 1820 at £2 17s. 6d. each. Crowned 'Regent China' mark with New Bond Street address (see page 34, Mark 10). Diameter 8½ in. *c.*1820. *Private collection*

XIX. *Below:* An attractive Chamberlain cup and saucer, the titled panels depicting 'The Seat of the Duke of Montrose, Stirlingshire' and 'The Seat of Earl Cowper, Herts'. Written mark 'Chamberlains Worcester'. Diameter of saucer 5¾ in. *c.*1810–20. *Godden of Worthing Ltd*

XX. *Overleaf:* One of a pair of Chamberlain ice-pails, with liners and covers, painted with the popular 'Dragon in Compartments' design, Chamberlain's pattern 75, much used on teawares, dessert and dinner services and a host of other porcelains. This colourful design is not by any means confined to the Chamberlain factory. Written mark 'Chamberlains Worcester'. 14 in. high. *c.*1810–20. *Messrs Sotheby & Co.*

226. A Coalport covered vase painted in Thomas Baxter's London decorating studio, signed and dated 1802. Unmarked. 13½ in. high. 1801–2. *Victoria & Albert Museum (Crown Copyright)*

engraved local views: 'six views in or near Swansea by T. Baxter, Portrait Painter. . . . Portraits drawn from one guinea upwards' (*The Cambrian*, July and August 1818).

Examples of Thomas Baxter's supposed painting on Swansea porcelains of the 1816–18 period are illustrated in Plates CXIX–CXXV of E. Morton Nance's *The*

Pottery & Porcelain of Swansea & Nantgarw (1942). The subjects include garden scenes, landscapes, flowers, figures, cupids, shells and birds, but examples of his painting on Swansea porcelains do not appear to have been signed.

In the winter of 1818–19 he returned to Worcester. A contemporary, and a pupil, of Baxter's at Worcester, Solomon Cole, related: 'Thomas Baxter, who was first employed at Worcester in 1815, may be said to stand unrivalled in the country as a classical-figure painter on porcelain . . . and was esteemed one of the best draughtsmen of his time. . . . His fine productions on porcelain elevated the taste, and his tuition cultivated the talent of several others of that period. . . .' (quoted from *Chaffers's Marks & Monograms*, 15th edition 1965).

Solomon Cole continued: 'Soon after Baxter arrived at Worcester and was engaged by Messrs Flight Barr & Co., he painted a cabinet plate, the subject of which was Mrs Siddons in the character of the "Tragic Muse", which the then Marquis of Stafford purchased for fifty guineas. A second plate was afterwards painted by Baxter, precisely the same in all respects. . . .' This plate is now in a private collection in Sussex, but fine as it is, it does not bear Thomas Baxter's signature which will only be found on his earlier London painting. In 1980 the first Mrs Siddons plate, now alas damaged, was purchased for the Dyson Perrins Museum at Worcester, where this magnificent example of Baxter's painting is now on display.

This 'Tragic Muse' plate led to a most interesting correspondence. A review of Flight, Barr & Barr porcelain was published in Vol. IV of the *Annals of the Fine Arts*, 1819. The writer noted: 'the enamel paintings from well known pictures are beyond any china painting we remember. They are more fit for framing as pictures than for plates, or cups, or vases. One of the plates with a miniature copy of Mrs Siddons as the Tragic Muse, would grace the cabinet of a prince. . . .' This review prompted a letter from Thomas Baxter to his friend B. R. Haydon. It is dated 21 July 1819 and was written from Edgar Street, Worcester. The relevant parts of the letter (which is quoted in full in Henry Sandon's book on Flight porcelains) show that he had left London five years previously and that he was employed by the Chamberlains in July 1819.

Five years banishment from all that is great [presumably a reference to London life] has rather increased if possible my love of the Arts. . . . I am employed here on little things and the 'littler the prettier' the *dear* little things and the dearer they are made the better . . . in the last number [of the *Annals of the Fine Arts*] I was very much surprised to find myself indirectly mentioned in an article respecting Flight & Barr's china works . . . the two plates which are noticed are my painting, and their [Flight, Barr & Barr] figure painting is now done by a pupil of mine named Lowe. It is not very likely that I shall ever paint anything more for them, as the people I am now engaged with are more liberally minded. . . .

Baxter's views are perhaps not shared by all but they are the contemporary remarks of an artist employed by the firm and on the evidence of them Baxter was perhaps more than a painter, for he seems to have had his own opinion on shapes. Writing of the editor's views Baxter stated that 'perhaps he does not know that they are not the designers of the forms, nor the painters of the subjects nor even the improvers of the porcelain. The forms which are mentioned are as near to antique forms as I could persuade their obstinacy to have executed for they have an antipathy to everything that is simple.'

Here Baxter was referring to the Flight management, but it would be interesting to know the extent of his influence over the Chamberlains in the two years from July 1819 to his death in April 1821. Perhaps he did some designing or modelling, for the wholesale order book contains the following description, '2 Baxter vases, blue, gold and flowers £2 2s. 0d.' (May 1823), so that some two years after Baxter's death a vase shape was being associated with his name. Indeed in December 1824 it is used again when the description 'mercury' handled vase is crossed out and 'Baxter' inserted to read '1 Baxter handled vase, blue & flowers, £1 10s. 0d.'.

There is another reference to Baxter at the time he was employed at the Chamberlain factory, in the diary of Michael Faraday who visited Worcester in 1819. On 2 August, after a quick visit to the Flight, Barr & Barr factory, he noted:

From thence I went to seek out Mr. Bagster [Baxter] an artist employed at Chamberlains to whom I had words of introduction from several friends. I had found out at Barr's manufactory that he lived in Edgar Street. . . .

I went with him to Chamberlains, the manufactory of porcelain, where I believe he superintended the painting department . . . the place looked much fitter and more lively than Flight & Barr's had done.

At home he showed me various paintings and drawings of his own admirably done and a specimen of porcelain entirely the work of his own hands. After lunch he again walked with me and set me on the river side where we parted having promised to meet together in the cathedral in the afternoon, he to draw and I to see. . . .

Sadly, his period of work with Chamberlain's was very brief, probably less than two years, for he died on 18 April 1821. The above-quoted diary entry suggests he also painted and drew in his own time, and one

wonders if such examples of his art still exist. The reference to a 'specimen of porcelain entirely the work of his own hands' implies that in this case at least he also added any gilt enrichments – he was obviously a capable gilder as well as a superb painter.

During the eighteen-month period of the Chamberlain factory sales book there is only one specific reference to an artist: that is Baxter, and the subject is flowers. It would therefore seem certain that Thomas Baxter was employed as a flower painter at Chamberlain's; the expensive fruit pattern plates (see Colour Plate XVIII) are also likely to be from his hand. Presuming that Humphrey Chamberlain reserved for himself the fine figure painting, it is probable that Baxter painted some of the scenic objects such as the 'rich vase with view of Walterton Hall, Nottinghamshire, £52 10s. 0d.', or some of the several Swansea cabinet cups included in the Chamberlain books – '2 two handled Swansea make cups, Views. £3 0s. 0d.'. Baxter certainly painted views when he was at Swansea in the 1816–18 period and he would have been familiar with the Swansea porcelain body.

BAYLIS This name occurs in the wage book as a painter or gilder in 1799.

RALPH BELL Listed in the wage records as a painter or gilder from August 1800 to March 1801.

BEVINGTON R. W. Binns listed a painter or gilder of this name and the factory wage records also list him from 7 July 1796 to September 1796, but the remuneration was low, at 6s. per week.

GEORGE BEVINS Listed as a painter or gilder in about 1800.

BENJAMIN BIRBECK Listed as a painter or gilder in the 1800–1 period.

JOSEPH BIRBECK At least three male decorators with the name Birbeck were employed at Chamberlain's factory. Joseph Birbeck was perhaps apprenticed to the works in the late 1780s or early 1790s, for in September 1792 the following entry appears in the factory records: 'Warrant for apprehending E. Ellis and Josh. Birbeck, 1s. 6d.'. This suggests that Ellis and Birbeck were absconding apprentices. Joseph Birbeck's name is subsequently entered in the Chamberlain wage book in the 1800s and one entry also has the notation 'Gilder' added.

A flower painter of the same name was employed at the Coalport factory from the 1820s, but it seems unlikely that he was the same person as that mentioned in the Chamberlain records, although he may have been his son.

MRS BIRBECK   A Mrs Birbeck was occasionally employed on printing, at 2s. per day.

WILLIAM BIRBECK senior   The wage books list William Birbeck from 1792 to at least 1809, and there are other entries relating to this painter or gilder: 'Wm. Birbeck has 29 pieces of [pattern] 34 in this weeks bill agreed 5d. each' (17 January 1795). His name is also mentioned in 1796 against patterns 228 and 487 and in the cash book in May 1801 the entry 'I sett, red, yellow and black. W. Birbeck' is entered.

WILLIAM BIRBECK junior   The Chamberlain wage book for the 1801–9 period lists William Birbeck junior from 29 November 1806.

BLOORE   Listed in the wage book in 1802 and 1803 and R. W. Binns includes this name as a painter or gilder. A Benjamin Bloore was employed at the Coalport factory in the 1820s: he was born in London in about 1782 but there is no information on whether this gilder is the same person as the one recorded in the Worcester records.

JOHN BLY   This gilder and crest painter was one of several hands who came from the Lowestoft factory, in Suffolk, to Worcester in 1799. He was born at Lowestoft in September 1779 and was subsequently apprenticed to the local porcelain factory, which employed various members of his family. The Chamberlain wage records include John Bly's name from 28 September 1799 until December 1802 when he presumably left to join the rival Flight & Barr works, for there is contemporary evidence of his employment there. There is, however, a complication in that he appears again in the Chamberlain records from March 1808 to the end of 1809.

Solomon Cole, a fellow artist, commented on John Bly's work:

John Bly, who came from Lowestoft, excelled in shading the gold in arms, and was unequalled in giving a natural expression to the lion in the Royal Arms, or where ever it occurred, and took that part in the grand service made for his Majesty William IV.

It appears likely that Bly had been engaged on similar armorial work at the Chamberlain factory from 1799 to December 1802 and during the 1808–9 period. He died in 1833, but his son (born in October 1814) of the same name, was employed as a landscape painter on Flight, Barr & Barr porcelain. John Bly junior died in December 1873.

BOOT   In the Chamberlain cash book covering the period June 1789 to October 1792, the entry 'To Mr. Boot, modeller £3 3s. 0d.' is included on 3 November 1791, at the time when the first entries related to the

Chamberlains establishing their manufactory for the production of their own porcelain. The written name is indistinct but I read it as Boot, and a Derby vase sold at Sotheby's in April 1967 bore an incised inscription 'Jonathon Boot, 1764'. He is believed to have been a Derby-trained modeller, but details are lacking. A Thomas Boot modelled for Wedgwood in about 1769–73.

GEORGE BOWKER   This artist was born in about 1800, for the 1851 Worcester census returns list him as an 'artist, china painter' aged 51, who was born at Bletchington, Sussex. His name is also included in the 1841 and 1861 census returns for the city of Worcester. George Bowker was employed by Chamberlain's by at least 1820 when his name is included in a list of debits, and his name occurs again in contemporary records in 1823, 1830 and 1832.

JOSEPH BROCK senior   This gilder worked at the Derby factory for several years early in the nineteenth century before moving to Worcester in about 1815. He was born in London in the 1780s and his name is included in the Worcester census returns of 1841, 1851 and 1861. He is believed to have been employed first by Flight, Barr & Barr, then after 1840 by the new Chamberlain & Co. partnership, by Kerr & Binns, and finally by the new Royal Worcester Company. He died, at Birmingham, in 1870.

JOSEPH BROCK junior   This artist was born in Worcester in about 1816, and his name is included in the 1841 census returns as a 'china enameller', as well as in the 1851 returns. He is believed to have been employed first by Flight, Barr & Barr and later by the new Chamberlain & Co. partnership.

BRUNTON   R. W. Binns listed Brunton as a Chamberlain painter or gilder and the name appears in the wage records from May 1807 to the end of 1809, that is, the last available wage book.

THOMAS CARWARDINE   Born in about 1794. Chaffers listed a Flight, Barr & Barr painter named Caradine but the entries in the census returns appear to read Carwardine. The return of 1861 is interesting as it gives his age as 67, with the description 'formerly china painter', showing that he had then retired. It is, however, probable that this artist worked for Chamberlain & Co. for a period after the 1840 amalgamation.

HUMPHREY CHAMBERLAIN   The son of Humphrey Chamberlain senior, he was himself a talented figure painter, and the quality of his painting is of the same high standard as Thomas Baxter's compositions. As the son of the proprietor, Humphrey Chamberlain's name does not occur in the wage books (although yearly salaries of £100 are recorded), but on the other hand he was allowed to sign, prominently, at least some of his work (see Plates 227–30 and 235), a practice not permitted to the other artists.

Humphrey Chamberlain was painting by at least 1810, as his work is mentioned in a book published in that year, the *History of Worcestershire* by Laird. Writing of this artist, Laird noted: 'Some of his works, on a service for the Prince Regent, being copies from historical engravings of English History, are quite exquisite both in the outline and brilliancy of the colouring.' Binns noted that Chamberlain's figure compositions were copied from engravings or other sources and he tends to disparage this fine work; but for sheer quality of brushwork they can hardly be bettered – signed specimens are very rare and today command high prices.

It is regrettable that the descriptions of Chamberlain porcelain sent from the Worcester factory to the London shop do not, except in one instance, include Humphrey's name as the painter. For example, in May 1951 Sotheby's sold a magnificent plate which was described in the following manner:

A very fine Chamberlain's Worcester plate, superbly painted by Humphrey Chamberlain with a full-length portrait of Thomas Cribb, 'The British Champion', standing in an attitude of defence, naked from the waist up, in a ring marked out in the forefront of a landscape with lowering sky, within a grey marbled and gilt line border, signed H. Chamberlain pinxt, $9\frac{3}{4}$ ins. Script marks in puce. Inscribed on the back with a list of the Champion's Victories from 1805 to 1811.

This plate can be traced in the contemporary records, for on 31 January 1816 the following item is listed as being sent to the London shop: '1 Plate with Painting of Cribb, £21 0s. 0d.'.

Incidentally, this 'British Champion' became a coal merchant in London, and by at least April 1816 he was supplying the Chamberlain shop with coals. He was paid cash, not with a plate depicting himself in his former glory. His coal merchanting, however, was not successful and he eventually became a publican at the Golden Lion in Southwark.

The high price of this Cribb subject plate and the lack of mention of the artist is interesting. Against two items sent from the works to the Piccadilly retail shop in December 1813 someone has added the margin note 'Humphrey's', and against two others 'Walter's', presumably indicating that these objects were painted by the young Chamberlains. The items attributed to Humphrey Chamberlain were two ornaments called 'Triumph of Mercy' and 'Taming the Shrew'. This

227. One of a pair of large orange- and gold-ground mugs (see Plate 106 for the companion). The panel is entitled 'The Power of Love' and the mug is signed under the base by Humphrey Chamberlain. Marked 'Chamberlains Worcester Manufactory. By appointment to H.R.H. The Prince Regent'. $6\frac{3}{4}$ in. high. *c*. 1815. *Dyson Perrins Museum, Worcester*

228. A well-painted Chamberlain blue-ground coffee can and saucer. The painting is signed by Humphrey Chamberlain in the special mark (see Plate 229). Can $2\frac{5}{8}$ in. high. *c*. 1815–24. *Martin Hutton, Esq.*

229. The base of the coffee can illustrated in Plate 228 showing the special mark and Humphrey Chamberlain's signature under the Prince of Wales's plume. *Martin Hutton Esq.*

230. *Below left:* A superbly painted plate by Humphrey Chamberlain; the subject is taken from Shakespeare's *King John* (see also Plate 232). Painted mark. Diameter 9¼ in. *c.* 1815–20. *Messrs Winifred Williams*

231. Detail from the Shakespeare-subject plate painted by Humphrey Chamberlain and illustrated in Plate 230. *Messrs Winifred Williams*

232. *Below:* Detail of the reverse of the plate shown in Plate 230. The written quotation is typical of the finer products of this nature. *Messrs Winifred Williams*

233. *Right:* Detail from the engraving taken from John Boydell's Shakespeare-subject prints, the source of Humphrey Chamberlain's rendering shown in Plate 230. (Reprinted by Benjamin Blom Books, 1968; distributed by Arno Press Inc.)

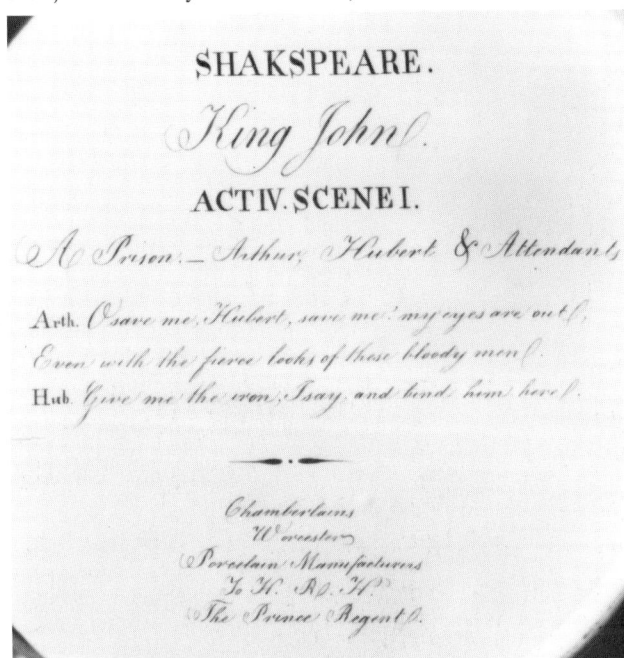

SHAKSPEARE.

King John.

ACT IV. SCENE I.

234. *Left:* A fine-quality Chamberlain cup and saucer, perhaps that returned to Worcester from the London shop in July 1816: 'A chocolate [cup] with fine cover and stand Timon. Blue and black marbled ground. £7 7s. 0d.'. The painting is attributed to Walter Chamberlain (see page 191). Cup base inscribed with a quotation from *Timon of Athens*, Act 4, Scene 3. *c.* 1815–18. *Dyson Perrins Museum, Worcester*

235. *Opposite:* A finely painted plate signed by Humphrey Chamberlain. A print of this 'Madonna and Child' subject was purchased in March 1814 and a plate invoiced at £42 0s. 0d. in June 1814: on account of the high price this plate is almost certainly the same one. Written mark similar to the one in Plate 232. Diameter 9¾ in. *c.* 1814. *Dyson Perrins Museum, Worcester*

margin note is the exception rather than the rule, but many of the fine and expensive figure-painted porcelains listed must be by his hand, although modern practice is to attribute such pieces to Thomas Baxter (q.v.).

Humphrey Chamberlain junior died in 1824 at the early age of 33, so that he probably only painted on his father's wares for some fourteen years from about 1810.

WALTER CHAMBERLAIN   The brother of the better known Humphrey Chamberlain junior (q.v.). In the 1810–20 period Walter painted some Chamberlain porcelains with figure subjects and the contemporary factory records include a few relevant entries, although many other pieces were probably painted by this artist without his name being listed in the available records. The rare named entries include:

3 Ornamental pieces enamelled blue, marble and Walter's Figures. £7 7s. 0d.
    [September 1813]

	£	s.	d.
1 Regent ornament Edward & Elinora, fawn marble.	15	15	0
2 do. 1st size King John & Taming the Shrew.	16	16	0
[December 1813]			

These prices are not as high as some pieces attributed to Humphrey Chamberlain, and judging by the covered cup and saucer shown in Plate 234, Walter's style is not as meticulous as that of the pieces signed by his brother. There is in the Allen Collection at the Victoria & Albert Museum a floral-painted porcelain plaque, the reverse of which is inscribed in pencil 'Walter Chamberlain Esq. China Factory'.

It is not known how long Walter Chamberlain continued to paint on Worcester porcelain, but it may have been only a passing phase as he was later concerned with the day-to-day management of the factory after his brother's death and the retirement of his father, Humphrey Chamberlain senior. Walter continued as proprietor until the Kerr & Binns partnership was formed in 1852.

CHETWYNE   R. W. Binns listed Chetwyne as a Chamberlain painter or gilder in 1808 and the wage records list 'Chetwin' from August 1802 to the end of the last available book, in 1809. He continued working, however, at the factory, for his name, sometimes with the initial 's' added, occurs in 1820, 1823 and 1830 records.

COFFEE   The cash book for the Bond Street retail shop has the following two entries:

By Mr. Coffee for a model, Worc. £8 10s. 0d.
   [November 1818]
To Mr. Coffee, modeller, for a breakfast cup & saucer 10s.
   [November 1822]

but it is not known if the man referred to was a London modeller or one employed at the factory at Worcester; the former is more probable.

John Haslem, the former Derby painter and historian, records that William John Coffee was taken on as a modeller at Derby in 1792. After several moves and a return to Derby, Haslem relates:

On finally leaving Derby he removed to London and opened an establishment in Oxford market, for the making and sale of plaster figures and ornamental castings. After a time he went to America and his son carried on the business in London for some years.

It would seem highly likely, in view of the two named purchases, that this former Derby modeller (or his son) supplied Chamberlain with new models – perhaps in plaster – which were later copied in Worcester porcelain. Other unnamed purchases of models may also have come from Coffee.

DANIEL COOPER⁴   This painter or gilder's name occurs in the Chamberlain wage records in 1800 and 1801.

COTTON   This painter or gilder's name occurs in the Chamberlain wage records from November 1807 to the end of 1809, that is, the last available wage book.

JOHN COURTNEY   This painter or gilder's name is included in the Chamberlain wage book from July 1807 to the end of 1809, the last available wage book, and his name is noted against pattern 481.

GILBERT CRUMP   This painter or gilder's name occurs in the Chamberlain wage book from February 1800 to the end of the last available book, in 1809, but the name is also included in debt lists dated 1820 and 1823, showing that he was still employed at that period.

DANIEL   R. W. Binns listed a painter or gilder of this name and it occurs in the factory wage records from 7 August 1802 to 23 July 1803.

GEORGE DAVIS   Probably born in about 1768, this artist was one of the most talented of the early Chamberlain painters, and his speciality was in the painting of colourful exotic birds in landscape (see Colour Plates III, V, VII and Plates 21, 236, 237, 294 and 336).

The early career of George Davis is somewhat clouded in mystery; he may have been engaged in painting Worcester porcelain before Chamberlain left in the 1780s but there is evidence that an artist of this name was at Hanley in the Staffordshire Potteries in 1788. This evidence takes the form of a letter written by George Davis in Hanley to William Duesbury of the Derby factory:

Sir,

I was informed by my wife some time back that Mrs Gould recommended me to you as an enameller in which I shall be happy to serve you. . . . I shall be disengaged in two months time. . . .

George Davis
March 17th, 1788

It is not known if Duesbury took advantage of this offer but it is unlikely, for there are no references to Davis working at Derby. If this Hanley artist *was* the superb Worcester bird painter it is difficult to know for whom he was working in Staffordshire in the 1780s. There is, however, firm evidence that the Chamberlain artist George Davis was employed at Worcester by at least May 1793, for the factory cash and wage books make many references to him from this period. There is

an intriguing note in the cash book for 16 November 1790 – 'Letter from Geo. Davis' – but typical entries after 1793 read:

	£	s.	d.
By Cash Mr. Geo Davis [May 1793]	5	5	0
By Geo. Davis for the men	2	3	10
G.D. [September 1793]	15	15	0 men
By Geo. Davis, four days wages [October 1793]		16	0

The inclusion of the title 'Mr' and the payment of the men's wages to George Davis, coupled with the high wages paid to this artist, suggest strongly that George Davis was the leading artist, or foreman of the painters. He was certainly a person of some responsibility and experience, for in March 1797 he received extra payments for grinding the gold:

	£	s.	d.
For attending the gold grinding from October 3rd 95 to December 31st 96	3	0	0
Dark Brown for 3 years at 21s. a year	3	3	0

236.   *Top:* A spiral-fluted Chamberlain coffee can and saucer, the border of pattern 60 and the centre panels painted with exotic birds in the manner of George Davis. Pattern number in gold. Diameter of saucer 5½ in. *c.* 1795–1800. *Messrs Sotheby & Co.*

237.   *Above:* A pale blue-ground mug, the panel painted in a typical manner and inscribed 'George Davis, Worcester. Jany 28th 1818'. 3½ in. high. 1818. *Messrs Sotheby & Co.*

Also at this time there was a further unexplained payment, 'Contract £1 1s. 0d.'.

Davis was the only artist to be mentioned by name in the early Chamberlain factory records. Such entries include:

1 Pint cup, initial W. only   Birds-eye border
1   do.   P.W.   with Davis's
1   do.   E.W.   Birds, etc.
    [September 1793]

5 saucers, Davis's birds. £1 2s. 6d.
    [account book, January 1794]

12 cups & saucers, Davis's birds & fruit
    [September 1795]

Dessert set, Davis's birds
    [October 1795]

George Davis's name is given against several designs in the original list of numbered patterns; these are 22, 47, 81, 143, 149, 452, 520, 553, 590, 599, 630, 732, 744, 761 and 762. He is also mentioned several times in the stocktaking lists of 1793. The 1795 stock (listed on 1 January 1796) included in the 'Painting Room':

	£	s.	d.
6 Chocolate [cups] & saucers, Davis's birds.	4	4	0
1 plate, dessert, Davis's birds, finished.		12	0

Later entries show the high original cost of these fine-quality Davis-decorated Chamberlain porcelains:

1 [coffee] Can & saucer, blue border, Davis's birds in the front of the cup & bottom of saucer, yellow between. £1 11s. 6d.
    [November 1797]

It is interesting to read in the original accounts that Davis not only painted birds but also fruit, flowers and 'Davis's devices'. It is almost certain that the splendid Caughley porcelain jug illustrated in Plate 21 was painted in Chamberlain's Worcester works by this artist. Indeed the description against Chamberlain's own teaware pattern 81 almost exactly fits such pieces: 'Davis's birds with fruit & flowers in festoons, blue & gold border'.

It would appear that George Davis worked for the rival Flight, Barr & Barr partnership for a period early in the nineteenth century, for one of their artists, Solomon Cole, stated that '... the celebrated bird-painter, George Davis, usually called Dr Davis, added his brilliant colouring in the rich plumage of his birds to the decoration ...'. It is probable, however, that this change of allegiance was for only a short period, perhaps between 1809 and 1813 or between 1817 and 1824, for George Davis's name is included in the Chamberlain wage books until the last available one, in 1809, and

from 1813 his name is found in the Chamberlain records. Of course, the sales book records are not conclusive, as pieces sold in any given year could have been decorated several years previously. Sample entries in the post-1813 order book, however, do suggest that Davis was employed at that period:

12, half pint Baden [shape cups] & saucers, blue ground & Davis's flowers. £10 10s. 0d.
    [London shop sales record, December 1814]

1 Regent [shape] vase, Davis's Birds, blue ground & antique gilding. £4 4s. 0d.
    [Order book, October 1815]

5 blue & gold ornaments, Davis's birds. £15 15s. 0d.
    [Order book, July 1816]

From this point until March 1824 there appears to be a gap in the Chamberlain records which mention Davis by name; this may be accidental, or he may have been with Messrs Flight, Barr & Barr during this period, c. 1817–24. An important signed and dated example of his painting of 1818 is shown in Plate 237, but it does not bear a factory mark. A sales record entry made in March 1824 reads:

A teaset, blue ground, gold shell and Davis's fancy birds in panel and flies, consisting of 18 teas and saucers, 12 coffees, teapot and stand, cream [jug], sugar basin & 3 plates. £29 7s. 0d.

This is one of the latest records that have been traced relating to George Davis and there appears to be no mention of his name in the 1841 census returns, a fact that suggests that he may well have died by this date.

M. DEVIEA   This name is listed in a single Chamberlain wage record in 1792. At first I was unable to link the entry with any known artist, which was strange as a higher-than-average remuneration was recorded against the name, a sum of £3 3s. 0d., which indicated a talented hand. It then occurred to me that this entry could well be a *phonetic* spelling for the well-known artist Fidelle DUVIVIER, the initial 'M' standing for Monsieur.

This being at least a possibility, it is relevant to give an outline of Duvivier's ceramic career as far as it is known. He was born in Belgium in August 1740 and was reputedly employed at the Tournai factory from about 1756 to 1763, after which he came to England and was employed at first in London. In 1769 he worked at Derby – the agreement is dated 31 October. A superbly painted Worcester teapot is signed and dated 1772, but it is not known if he was then employed at the Worcester factory, for his agreement with Derby should have continued until October 1773. Duvivier apparently went to France in the mid 1770s, but was working for

238. *Below:* A Caughley shanked teapot decorated in the Chamberlain studio by Fidelle Duvivier in October 1792. Unmarked. 1792. *Mr & Mrs P. Miller*

239. *Right:* A Caughley cake plate from the tea service here attributed to the former New Hall painter, Fidelle Duvivier. Unmarked. Diameter 7½ in. October 1792. *Godden Reference Collection*

240. A Caughley teabowl and saucer from the service here attributed to Fidelle Duvivier. Unmarked. Diameter of saucer 5½ in. October 1792. *Godden Reference Collection*

the New Hall Company in Staffordshire in the 1780s. A Turner Staffordshire porcelain beaker is signed by Duvivier and is dated 'Lane-End, Juin, 1787'. By November 1790 he had left his perhaps part-time employment at the factory and, in a letter to Duesbury of Derby, he explained that he intended to settle in Newcastle-under-Lyme (Staffordshire), 'being engag'd to teach drawing in the Boarding School at that Place . . .'. He had not, however, given up ceramic painting, for he asked if Derby porcelain could be sent to him for decoration.

It now seems possible that he moved to Worcester in 1792 and was engaged by Chamberlain's. It should be pointed out that at this period the Chamberlains were still decorating Thomas Turner's Caughley porcelain, so that if this 'Deviea' wage entry does in fact refer to Fidelle Duvivier, he could have painted both Chamberlain-Worcester and Turner's Caughley porcelains. Further information on the part tea service shown in Plates 30 and 238–41, here attributed to Fidelle Duvivier, is given on page 54.

There is in the Chamberlain records a further tantalizing brief reference to a 'M Deviea' who, I believe, was the same person who had by then left Worcester, for under 'Letters & to whom wrote', there is an entry, 'M. Deviea do.', under the date 3 April 1793. The ditto mark related to the previous entry, a letter to Mr Norris of Burslem, indicating that M. Deviea had returned to Staffordshire.

The extremely short working-period at Worcester of this artist, who is named in a single fortnight wage list at the Chamberlain factory in October 1792 (see page 194), is perhaps emphasized by the fact that some pieces of the only service known with figure decoration in the Duvivier manner are by a different artist – one who lacked Duvivier's continental touch and flair. Perhaps the original artist left before he completed a single teaset. Fidelle Duvivier is believed to have died in Staffordshire in 1817, aged 77.

RICHARD DIGHTON   This painter is not recorded in collectors' reference books, but the name is included in the Worcester 1841 census returns when he was then in the 45–9 age group and had probably been employed by Messrs Flight, Barr & Barr or by Messrs Chamberlain.

ENOCH DOE   This artist was born at Worcester in about 1795 (his age is recorded as 56 in the 1851 census returns) and he may have been the son of James Doe (q.v.).

An entry dated 21 September 1805 shows that Enoch Doe was engaged that day for one year's service and that he was given 1s. 'earnest' on finishing his apprentice-

241.   A detail of a saucer from the Caughley teaset painted by Fidelle Duvivier (see also Plate 30 and page 53). Diameter of panel 2½ in. 1792. *Godden Reference Collection*

ship. The wage records continue to June 1807, but from then to January 1808 there is a gap. The name reappears in January 1808 and continues until the end of the last available wage book in 1809. Some of these records include the description 'jun' for junior, showing that both father and son were employed, but it has proved difficult to differentiate between the two.

One artist of this name reputedly also painted for the rival Worcester factory, and the Chamberlain painter certainly left the factory to work as a decorator in the High Street, in partnership with George Rogers (q.v.) from the 1820s. A marked jug dated 1828 is in the Worcester Works Museum, and typically marked 'Doe & Rogers' porcelains are illustrated in Plate 241 of my *Illustrated Encyclopaedia of British Pottery & Porcelain* (1966, 2nd edition 1980). An 1835 Worcester directory lists Enoch Doe of 17 High Street (an address incorporated in several marks) as a landscape artist, and one superb signed saucer is shown in Plate 242. But Doe's display at the 1851 Exhibition mainly featured figure subjects: 'Enoch Doe. High Street, Worcester. Designer. Specimens of enamelling upon porcelain plates, scenes from Shakespeare's Richard the second, Royal Arms, Tilting'. Plate 243 illustrates a plate which was almost certainly one of his 1851 exhibits, showing the fine quality of his work, not only in the figure

242.   A superbly painted saucer-shaped dish painted with a landscape subject and signed 'E Doe'. Unmarked. Diameter 6¼ in. *c.* 1820–25.
Mr & Mrs Wharf

painting but in the armorial details and especially in the rich gilding.

Many signed examples of Doe's ceramic painting are recorded but these are pieces painted after he had left Chamberlain's, while painting independently or in partnership with Rogers. There appears to be no trace of Enoch Doe's name in the 1861 census returns.

JAMES DOE   When this much-travelled ceramic painter committed suicide, near Bristol, on 14 September 1797, the contemporary *Monthly Magazine* gave a good account of his career:

James Doe was born at Lambeth in Surrey. . . . He served an apprenticeship at Lambeth to a painter in the china and earthenware line, . . . he worked some years at Mr. Wedgwood's manufactory in Staffordshire. He worked at Mr. Baddely's in Staffordshire for six or seven years. About three years ago he came to London, and finding little or no employment, he was obliged to leave town, he embarked on a ship for Newcastle, and from thence went to Glasgow. He then went to Ireland, and, after stopping there a short time, he embarked on board a vessel bound for Swansea, in South Wales, where he worked some time, and then went on to the Worcestershire China Manufactory, which was, I believe, the last place he worked at.

243.   A blue- and gold-bordered Worcester plate. The scene is taken from *Richard II* and is signed 'E Doe'. This, or a similar example, was shown by this artist at the 1851 Exhibition. Painted inscription and signature. Diameter 9¼ in. *c.* 1851. *Godden Reference Collection*

Taking up the reference to the Worcestershire China Manufactory, it appears that a person named Doe was employed at the Flight factory in 1789, for mention is made of him in John Flight's personal diary (see 'John Flight of Worcester' by Geoffrey Wills in *The Connoisseur*, June 1947):

Having been informed a man at Derby woud be very useful to us I consented to let Doe write to try to get him here. . . . Yesterday, Doe received a reply to his letter. . . .

But the Chamberlain wage records include James Doe from 9 January 1796 to 17 June 1797, and against one entry of March 1797 someone has pencilled the note 'bird painter'.

MATTHEW DOUGHTY   This china painter was born in Worcester in about 1781, and was employed by Chamberlain's for a long period from 5 April 1800 (the first entry in the wage records). His name occurs in other documents up to at least 1831 and is included as a 'china painter' in the 1841 Worcester census returns, although there appears no trace of it in the next census in 1851. A Joseph Doughty was apparently apprenticed to Martin Barr of the rival firm.

JOSEPH DUTTON   Little is known of Dutton, although the name is included in the Chamberlain factory wage records from 17 December 1796 to 10 June 1797, and against one record the description 'gilder' has been pencilled. A Thomas Dutton (or Ditton) is recorded as a Flight, Barr & Barr decorator.

DUVIVIER   See M. DEVIEA.

RICHARD DYER   R. W. Binns, in his *Century of Potting in the City of Worcester* (1865), wrote of the closing of the Chelsea factory and the opportunity then afforded to the Worcester management to engage artists trained to paint in the then popular style. Binns continued:

As to who these men were, or what was their number, no particulars remain, but three of them named Dyer, Mills and Willman survived to be known and well remembered by a workman lately employed on these works, named James Plant, who has been nearly sixty years in the manufactory; the account he had from themselves was that they had served their time at Chelsea under a Frenchman, was very particular in keeping them all within doors so that they might not disclose the secrets outside of the manufactory; and that they came to Worcester on the closing of the Chelsea works.

Fortunately, the original apprentice document has lately been discovered, showing that Richard Dyer (son of John Dyer) was apprenticed to Sprimont, the proprietor of the Chelsea factory, on 7 February 1750

for a term of seven years to learn the art of 'painting in enamel'. As most apprenticeships were taken in the early teens, it seems likely that Richard Dyer was born in the mid 1730s. The Chelsea factory closed in 1769, at which time, according to Binns, Dyer transferred to the Dr Wall Worcester factory.

It would appear, however, from the original Chamberlain records, that Richard Dyer transferred to this factory at least by 6 September 1794, when a remuneration of 13*s*. 6*d*. is recorded for four and a half days' work, and subsequent wage records go up to 1 March 1800. There is an interesting note in a cash book in September 1798: 'By Rd Dyer colours from Daniel & Co. £1 8*s*. 0*d*.'. Details of Dyer's apprenticeship indenture were discovered amongst papers belonging to Messrs Daniel & Co. (also styled Daniel & Brown up to June 1806), who were enamellers and colour makers in the Staffordshire Potteries. For a period up to 1822 the Daniels decorated all Spode's porcelain (see Leonard Whiter's *Spode*, 1970) and the Chamberlains purchased blue-printed earthenware dinner services from them according to the factory records.

WILLIAM ECCLES   Mentioned in the Chamberlain wage records in 1793 and 1794. Nothing is known of him but he may have been a gilder, rather than a painter.

EDWARD ELLIS   Mentioned in the Chamberlain wage records in 1792 and 1793, he apparently was not happy at the works, for the cash book contains the following two related entries:

Warrant for apprehending E. Ellis & Jos^h. Birbeck.
    [5 September 1792]
Paid Mr. Hook for expenses – Bringing Ellis & Birbeck from Bristol. £1 13*s*. 0*d*.
    [13 September 1792]

These suggest that at this period Ellis was an apprentice, but no other records relate to this person.

JAMES FARNSWORTH   Little is known about this early Chamberlain employee; his name appears in the factory wage records from 29 October 1796 and continues to 7 July 1798. He was apparently an important person, for although only a few names appear in the early order books, Farnsworth's occurs twice:

1 can & saucer, Rose border, yellow (Farnsworth).
    [November 1796]
6 or 8 fancy Pint mugs, Farnsworth.
    [December 1798]

A James Farnsworth is recorded as a Derby-trained flower painter, who was discharged in about 1821 to find employment at the Coalport factory; but there is no reference to him at Coalport and it seems unlikely that this Derby flower painter is the same person as the Worcester artist, for the Derby historian, John Haslem, stated that Farnsworth was apprenticed at the Derby factory.

JOHN FREEMAN   His name is included in the Chamberlain wage records from September 1792 into 1793. He was perhaps a gilder, rather than a painter, and a Joyce Freeman is later recorded as a burnisher of gold.

THOMAS GRAINGER   R. W. Binns included the name Thomas Grainger in his list of Chamberlain painters and gilders. Elsewhere he is referred to as a Chamberlain apprentice who left in 1801 to set up his own factory (at first a decorating establishment) at Worcester, but the Chamberlain records do not help to clarify the position.

Very low wages of 1s. per week were recorded against his name from 1796–8, adding weight to the belief that he was an apprentice, and from then until June 1805 occasional payments, some large, were recorded. Some records confuse the issue and suggest that Thomas Grainger was decorating on his own account in the 1790s when he was purchasing white porcelains from the Chamberlains; other records suggest that he was not an apprentice in the 1790s but an established and known person to whom payments were made and who made purchases from Chamberlain's in 1788, if not before.

Mr. Grainger, New Street,
     1 Teapot to match
     1 ½ pint bason do.
[Entry dated 7 September 1788 but crossed through, either because the order was cancelled, or perhaps because it had been fulfilled.]

Mr. Thos. Grainger, New Street,

		s.	d.
1 3rd size teapot, Blue spots.		7	6
1 Stand	do.	3	0
1 Plate	do.	4	6
1 Sugar box	do.	4	0
1 spoon tray	do.	3	0
1 2nd size ewer	do.	3	0

[It is very likely that these blue-spotted tewares, with a spoontray, were really Caughley porcelains, not Chamberlain's own make: see Godden, *Caughley and Worcester Porcelains, 1775–1800* (1969), Plate 8.]

Sold Thos. Grainger, Worcester, Sundries damag'd. China, white thirds. £1 1s. 0d.'.
     [February 1794]

To Thos. Grainger, Worcester. For the entrance of Wm. Birbeck 10s. 6d.
     [February 1795]

To Thos. Grainger, Worcester. For entrance of Jno Hood, Nov. 91. 10s. 6d. For entrance of J. Birbeck, Apl. 90. 10s. 6d.
     [March 1795]

Thomas Grainger, Worcester.

	s.	d.
6 cups & saucers, shanked white	3	6
6 coffees	3	0
2 slop basons	2	0
[May 1799]		

Entries in the Chamberlain records continue after 1801, the claimed date for the establishment of Thomas Grainger's own works in Worcester, and some of these entries suggest that Grainger was a traveller, not a painter:

	£	s.	d.
By J. Williams & Grainger's expenses to Bristol, Bath, Oxford etc, including chaise.	16	3	3
[July 1803]			
By T. Grainger's expenses 22 days.	15	8	0
[August 1803]			
By T. Grainger's expenses to Bristol.	6	14	0
[December 1803]			

One entry of 30 January 1804 in the sales book perhaps gives a clue to the complex picture of Grainger's activities:

Thomas Grainger, Senr. Worcester.
     Teawares, Irish [shape] 2nd. Rose 16 £1 10s. 0d.

It is, of course, the addition of the description 'Senr' (for senior) that is the vital link, suggesting that there was both a senior and a junior Thomas Grainger.

It is difficult to know which of these two persons broke away from Chamberlain's to establish his own works (with a partner named Wood). Chamberlain's still employed a traveller of this name in 1803 and Thomas Grainger senior was still buying Chamberlain porcelain in 1804, but this fact is inconclusive, for as a decorator Grainger would need to purchase porcelains from one source or another. The Thomas Grainger who is recorded as purchasing Chamberlain porcelain, some of it white or partly decorated (such as the blue-spotted teawares purchased in 1789), must have been a decorator, and perhaps a gilder, and from the dates it can be assumed that he was the senior Thomas Grainger, the son being employed by Chamberlain's as a traveller or salesman. This son would have joined his father in the early 1800s once the Grainger wares had been successfully launched; the Chamberlain records do not include the name after September 1804.

George Grainger, presumably the son of Thomas Grainger junior, was born in about 1813, and he was to continue the rival Grainger factory for most of the century. The Grainger company was taken over by the Royal Worcester Company in 1889.

It is interesting to note that the name Grainger has a lengthy connection with Worcester porcelain, for a George Grainger was apprenticed to the first (or Dr Wall) company on 11 August 1767, and it is possible that Thomas Grainger senior was his son.

GREATBATCH   R. W. Binns listed a painter or gilder of this name, and the wage records from August 1802 to August 1803 include this name; but there is no further information.

HANCOCK   The name Hancock is included in a debt list of 1820, and in painters' 'stops' in the 1830–32 period, but there is no further information although several artists of this name were engaged in the ceramic industry.

C. HAYTON   Chamberlain and other porcelains of the 1820s may be found bearing the name Hayton, with or without a date. These are examples of amateur decoration. Between May 1821 and March 1825 Chamberlain's supplied blank porcelain and various ceramic colours to Mr and Mrs C. Hayton of Moreton, near Hereford, and such pieces were returned to Worcester for firing and gilding. These sales of white blanks give an idea of the basic costs:

	£	s.	d.
2 Swansea cabinet [cups] & stands, white		5	0
2 F [French] cans do.		1	6
2 ewers and basins do.		5	0
2 second [size] Regent bell-mouth ornaments	1	4	0
1 Ridley [shape] Ice vase do.	2	0	0

Related entries for gilding and firing were:

	£	s.	d.
Burnishing and burning 6 plates	1	1	0
Gilding, burnishing & burning a gadroon			
Baden [shape] chocolate cup		10	6
do. a 8 inch plate		3	6
Batches of prepared fine gold		5	0

EDWARD HAYWARD   R. W. Binns listed a painter or gilder of this name and the factory wage records from April 1800 to the end of 1809 (the last available book) include this name.

WILLIAM HAYWARD   Binns also listed this painter or gilder who is included in the wage records from September 1799 to the end of 1809 (the last available book).

MRS HEWITT   The head of the female burnishers of the gilding, before September 1799 she was referred to as Mary Glaze. Several members of the Hewitt family were employed at the Chamberlain factory: an interesting cash payment was made in July 1802 and refers to one of the Hewitt sons 'for release of John Hewitt from the military, under an indenture of apprentice £4 18s. 6d.'.

HOPKINS   The Chamberlain wage records include a Thomas Hopkins from 23 April 1796 to June 1797; one entry dated 4 March 1797 has the description 'crest painter' pencilled in.

THOMAS HURD   R. W. Binns listed a painter or gilder of this name and it occurs again in the factory wage records from 11 October 1800 to 7 November 1801.

NATHANILL JOHNSON   The Chamberlain wage records include a Natll Johnson senior from 30 July 1796 to 23 September 1797. One entry, dated 4 March 1797, has the description 'ground layer' pencilled in.

JAMES JONES   R. W. Binns listed a painter or gilder of this name and it occurs in the factory wage records from 31 May 1800 to the end of 1809 (the last available wage book). He apparently continued for many years, for the name Jones occurs in debt lists of 1820 and 1823, and again in 1830 in a list of 'stops'. A John Jones 'china painter' is included in the 1841 Worcester census returns – at this period he was in the 50–54 age group, and was most probably employed at the Flight factory.

JOHN KEELING   R. W. Binns listed a painter or gilder of this name and it occurs in the factory wage records from 5 April 1800 to the end of 1809 (the last available wage book).

ALEXANDER LANGDALE   R. W. Binns listed a painter or gilder of this name and it occurs in the factory wage records from 20 September 1800 to the end of 1809 (the last available wage book).

JOHN LEAD   This china painter was born in Derbyshire in about 1786 and, according to John Haslem, was employed at the Pinxton factory. According to the 1841 Worcester census returns he had been in that city from at least 1821 (for his eldest daughter, Sarah, was born at Worcester and was then aged 20, and a succession of children show that the family remained there). He had been employed by Messrs Flight, Barr & Barr (he is included in the 1819 list) and then by the succeeding amalgamation of Chamberlain & Co. John Lead 'china painter' was also included in the 1851 census returns, when he was aged 65.

LEWIS   The Chamberlain cash books include such entries as: 'Mr. Lewis, on account of models. 6s.' (December 1791). Another record mentions 'Mr. Jas. Lewis £5 5s. 0d.', but it is not now known if this James Lewis is the same as that listed as supplying models, for this surname is included under very low, apprentice wages.

JAMES LOWE   Little is known about this Flight, Barr & Barr painter. A Thomas Lowe is better known as a talented figure painter who had been trained by Thomas Baxter (q.v.) and then succeeded this famous figure painter. Chaffers's list of Flight, Barr & Barr artists includes both James Lowe's and Thomas Lowe's names, but the 1841 and 1851 Worcester census returns list only James Lowe. From these sources it appears that this artist was born at Burslem in the Staffordshire Potteries in about 1775. The 1841 returns list him as a 'china painter', but ten years later he was entered as a 'Retired china painter', so that he may only have worked for the firm of Chamberlain & Co. for a few years after the amalgamation with Flight, Barr & Barr in 1840. I have a very well-painted figure-subject plaque (see Plate 244) signed and dated, Thos Lowe, 1841. Thomas Lowe exhibited painted porcelains from a London address at the 1851 Exhibition.

THOMAS LOWE   See JAMES LOWE.

WILLIAM MANASON   This artist is listed by Chaffers as a Flight, Barr & Barr painter, but as William Manason is given in the 1841 and 1851 census returns as a 'china painter', it is probable that he was retained by the new firm of Chamberlain & Co. after the amalgamation in 1840. He was born at Worcester in about 1797.

WILLIAM MARSH   The Chamberlain wage records include this name from September 1802 to the end of 1809 (the last available wage book) and the name Marsh occurs in later lists of painters' 'stops' in the 1830–32 period. It would appear that Marsh was responsible for some of the colourful 'Japan' patterns, such as in Colour Plate XVI, as the sales book for the London retail shop includes the following records:

The Hon^{bl}. Colonel Locks, Reigate.

60 Table plates, rich Japan, Marsh's [at] 18s.
    [September 1820]

J. Young Esq. 27 Bedford Square, London.

A Complete Table service, Marsh's rich Japan pattern.
    £55 0s. 0d.
    [January 1821]

244.   A porcelain plaque signed by the Worcester artist Thomas Lowe and dated 1841. Unmarked. $7\frac{1}{2} \times 6\frac{1}{4}$ in. *Godden Reference Collection*

There were apparently two painters of this name, for one entry includes the abbreviation 'senr' (for senior), and the 1841 census returns include William Marsh 'china p^r' in the 60–64 age group and a son in the 35–9 age group. This William Marsh junior was born at Worcester in about 1805 and was described as a 'china painter' in 1841. He was probably employed from the early 1820s.

MATTHEW MASON   R. W. Binns listed a painter or gilder of this name and it occurs in the factory wage records from 21 December 1799 (but this full entry 'Math. Mason' is a continuation of an earlier simple entry 'Mason') to 13 June 1807. There are, however, several Masons included in the factory records. Samuel Mason was a traveller, head clerk or foreman in the 1790s, as suggested by several notations in the order book, such as 'Per Hoppole Coach, Oct. 9th [signed] Sam Mason'. There was also an apprentice or boy named John Mason who was employed from September 1797.

A Mr Mason was employed at the Chelsea factory from about 1751, and he later worked for Duesbury at Derby. According to William Chaffers, he and his son, 'also a china painter', later worked for Flight's at Worcester.

JAMES MEIGH The name Meigh occurs in the Chamberlain wage records from March 1808 and in 1832 the name is included in a list of painters' 'stops'. The local census returns show that there were two china painters of this name, father and son. James Meigh is listed as a 'china painter' in the 60–64 age group in 1841. His son was born in London in about 1805, for the 1851 census returns give the age of this 'china painter' as 46. A painter named Meigh was also working at the rival Grainger factory.

THOMAS MEREDITH R. W. Binns listed a painter or gilder of this name and it occurs in the factory wage records from November 1799. He is also included in a debt list of 1820 but there is no trace of the name in the 1841 census returns.

ROBERT MILLS senior This person is included in the available Chamberlain wage records from 22 December 1798, sometimes with the prefix 'Dr' added, but he had apparently died or left by 25 April 1807.

ROBERT MILLS junior Born at Burslem in the Staffordshire Potteries in about 1783, his name appears with his father's from 22 December 1798. Robert Mills junior was apparently a gilder and perhaps a painter of 'Japan' patterns, for the name is linked with both these skills in the sales books:

Mr. East, Adelphe, West End, London.
 1 Desert service. No. 75, Mills.
  [June 1801]

1 Root pot & stand & 2 half circle small ornaments, Queen [pattern] & Mills gilding.
  [August 1801: see Plate 337]

Cup & saucer, Mills, Japan.
  [September 1815]

The following designs also have Mills's name added in the numbered list of patterns – 316, 608, 645, 845, 1161, 1256, 1389–92, 1456, 1462, 1490–92, 1499, 1513, 1529, 1623, 2225. Robert Mills's name was still included as a 'china painter' in the 1851 Worcester census returns. A son, Thomas Mills, was born in about 1823 and in the 1841 census returns he too was described as a 'china painter'.

EDWARD MITCHELL R. W. Binns listed a painter or gilder of this name, it appears in the Chamberlain wage records from at least January 1800, and in 1805 a record of the yearly engagement appears: 'Engaged for one year at 31s. 6d. per week'. In the same year the following note occurs in the order book, relating to tewares: 'New Vine pattern, Mitchells, £14 14s. 0d.'.

JOHN MITCHELL A person of this name is included in the Chamberlain wage lists from 1792, but it is not known if he was a painter or not.

JOHN MUCHALL The name Muchall occurs many times in the Chamberlain records of the early 1790s; several indicate that he was a landscape painter. The name is unusual and one is tempted to wonder if it is an incorrect spelling of Mitchell or possibly Muckell.

It is, however, apparent that Muchall was an employee of some importance, at times entrusted with purchases; at others he was away from Worcester but sending back letters, as might a traveller taking samples and receiving orders. Sample entries include:

Paid out in different articles by Mr. Muchall, at Birmingham. £8 3s. 2d.
  [February 1791]
To Muchall for wages. 15s. 1d.
  [March 1793]

The 1793 stocktaking lists include:

	£	s.	d.
14 dessert plates, Muchalls Landscapes Fancy border	6	8	0
1 centrepiece do. do.	2	2	0
6 dessert plates Muchalls Landscapes	2	8	0

An early book mentions:

	s.	d.	s.	d.
2 squares Muchall Landscape	5	0	8	0
1 Plate Muchall Landscape	1	3	3	6

The first price is for the undecorated porcelain, or 'blank'; the second charge is the cost of decoration. Such double entries usually indicated that Thomas Turner's Caughley porcelain was being decorated at Worcester by special order, so that these two entries, coupled with the early date of Muchall's work, c. 1791–5, indicate that this artist probably painted Caughley as well as Chamberlain's own porcelain. The Caughley plate illustrated in Plate 27 may represent this artist's work.

CONINGSBY NORRIS This Worcester china dealer decorated Worcester and other porcelains in the 1840s and 1851, and such specimens sometimes bear his name mark. His name occasionally occurs in the Chamberlain order books of the 1840s, but almost certainly he obtained his stock from several sources.

His name appears in Bentley's 1840–1841 Guide under the heading 'China, Gilding and Enamellers'. In Lascelles & Co's 1851 Directory and Gazetteer, his advertisement reads:

C. NORRIS,
55, TYTHING, WORCESTER.
MANUFACTURER OF BURNISHED GOLD
CHINA TEA & BREAKFAST SETS,
Desserts, Ornaments &c.

Matchings executed on the Premises, at the shortest notice.

Although this advertisement uses the description 'manufacturer', he may correctly be considered an independent decorator and retailer.

THOMAS PEGG   R. W. Binns listed a painter or gilder of this name and it occurs in the factory wage records from December 1798 to June 1801 and from January 1802 to August 1805. Haslem lists a Derby gilder of this name but it is not known if this is the same person.

JOHN PERRENS   R. W. Binns listed a painter or gilder of this name and the factory wage books include a John Perrens from 20 April 1799 to 7 February 1807, but no further information on this person has been discovered.

SAMUEL PETTYGROVE   R. W. Binns listed a painter or gilder of this name and it occurs in the Chamberlain wage records from 10 November 1793, at first drawing very low, apprentice-like wages. This first set of entries ceases on 11 July 1801, but the name reappears in September 1803 until February 1804.

JAMES PLANT   This artist was born in Staffordshire in the early 1780s (the 1841 Worcester census returns gave his age then as between 55 and 59), and the name appears in the factory wage records from 5 April 1800. In 1864 he recollected to R. W. Binns the occasion of Lord Nelson's visit to the works in 1802. Plant was employed for many years (at least forty) and he is believed to have specialized in heraldic work. A son, Alfred, was born in about 1813 and he followed his father's calling. A James Plant is well known for his charming figure painting on Nantgarw porcelain, which is believed to have been carried out at Sims's London decorating establishment, but it is unlikely that this is the same artist as the one employed at Worcester by the Chamberlains. According to Binns, a heraldic painter named Plant was employed by Chamberlain & Co. in about 1852 when Messrs Kerr & Binns succeeded the earlier firm, but there are no means of telling if this was James Plant, who must then have been in his seventies, or his son Alfred.

JAMES POWELL   R. W. Binns listed a painter or gilder of this name and it occurs in the Chamberlain wage records from 17 September 1796 to 11 June 1801 and again from 19 December 1801 to 30 January 1802, but no further facts on this artist have been discovered.

245. A porcelain plaque signed by the Worcester artist John Powell, who also practised his craft in London. Unmarked. $5\frac{1}{2} \times 4\frac{1}{2}$ in. c. 1820–30. *Godden Reference Collection*

JOHN POWELL   R. W. Binns listed a painter of this name and it is included in the factory wage records from 1792 to 29 May 1802. Apart from factory work, John Powell would appear to have painted Chamberlain porcelain in his own time, for the factory records include sales to him of undecorated porcelain, the last record for this whilst he was in Worcester being dated 2 June 1802.

It was this independent work that was to bring Powell lasting fame, for in 1802 he moved to London where he established himself as a decorator, of various porcelains. On 18 December 1802 Chamberlain's invoiced a selection of white wares, which included twenty sets of cups and saucers, to John Powell in London. Such sales continued for many years and on occasions included white French porcelain.* It is also known that Powell decorated (or at least added his name to) Swansea porcelains. The address '91 Wimpole Street, London'

*A pair of French porcelain vases bearing a long Powell name and address mark is illustrated in Plate 467 of my *Illustrated Encyclopaedia of British Pottery & Porcelain* (1966, 2nd edition 1980), and a signed plaque is shown here in Plate 245.

occurs on some signed examples painted by this decorator and some figure subjects are known. However, in 1812 Chamberlain was addressing him at 53 Great Marylebone Street.

WILLIAM POWELL   R. W. Binns listed a painter or gilder of this name and it occurs in the Chamberlain factory records. He would appear to have been apprenticed in 1792 – 'Paid for enrolling Wm. Powell's Indenture. 2s. 6d.' – and for some years low wages are recorded against his name. The wage records for him continued to 1809 (the last available wage book).

JOHN PRIDDEY   R. W. Binns listed a painter or gilder named Priddey and the Chamberlain wage records include a John Priddey in the 1792–4 period, but no further information on this person has been discovered.

CHARLES RADCLIFFE   R. W. Binns listed a painter or gilder named Radcliffe and the Chamberlain wage records include this name from 1792 (when he drew very low wages) to July 1797.

JOHN REDGRAVE   This artist was christened at Lowestoft on 3 July 1775. In July 1792 he married and in July 1799 his wife, Ann, gave birth to a daughter at Lowestoft. John Redgrave is one of the Lowestoft hands recorded as moving to Worcester on the closure of the East Coast factory (see Godden, *The Illustrated Guide to Lowestoft Porcelain*, 1969), and the Chamberlain wage records list this painter from 16 November 1799. His wife was also employed by the Chamberlains, as a burnisher of gilding. John Redgrave was still employed in 1815 when the accounts record 'Jhn Redgrave, extra work done at the manufactory £1 7s. 5d.'.

CHARLES RICHARDS   Chaffers, in his list of Flight, Barr & Barr artists, includes Thomas and William Richards (flower painters) and Charles Richards, but only Charles is to be found in the Worcester census returns of 1841, 1851 and 1861. These returns show that Charles Richards was born at Worcester in about 1792. The 1861 census returns gave his occupation as 'china gilder' rather than a painter, and it would appear that Richards gilded Flight, Barr & Barr porcelains before 1840 and Chamberlain & Co.'s wares after the 1840 amalgamation.

JOHN RIDER   The 1841 Worcester census returns include a 'china painter' named John Rider, in the 35–9 age group, but there appears to be no other information on this person, who may have been employed by Messrs Flight, Barr & Barr prior to 1840 and perhaps for the new firm of Chamberlain & Co. for a few years after 1840.

THOMAS ROBERTS   R. W. Binns listed a painter or gilder of this name and the Chamberlain wage records include him from September 1799 to at least June 1803.

GEORGE ROGERS senior   Again Binns listed this painter or gilder and the name occurs in the factory wage records from December 1799; patterns numbered 271, 272, 282, 308, 343, 362, 416, 567, 570, 782 and 1138 have his name added. The situation is complicated, however, by the fact that there were, it appears, two persons of this name employed, for pattern 782 (introduced in about June 1816) was by George Rogers junior (q.v.). George Rogers senior was apparently a crest painter, for an entry in May 1803 reads: 'Teaware, No. 298 and crest, a Bear, G. Rogers'; and in August 1805 a margin note reads: 'See Geo Rogers for crest'.

The name is included in the wage records to the end of the last available book in 1809 and it also occurs in an 1823 debt list; but these later entries may relate to George Rogers junior.

George Rogers senior was probably the person listed in directories of the 1840s as a China Glass and Earthenware dealer, but he had died by the time of the 1851 census when his wife Nancy was described as 'Head of family' and a widow.

GEORGE ROGERS junior   This Chamberlain and independent artist was born at Worcester in about 1805, being aged 45 at the time of the 1851 census, when he was described as an 'artist in stained glass'. At this period he apparently left Chamberlain's employment, but he was almost certainly trained at the factory, probably under his father: as previously mentioned pattern 782 of about June 1816 has the name George Rogers junior noted against it, although he could only have been about 11 at the time this pattern was introduced.

By the early 1820s a George Rogers (probably the son although this is not certain) was decorating white porcelains on his own account or in partnership with Enoch Doe (q.v.). The Chamberlain sales books include references to much white porcelain sold to a George Rogers, and typical entries made in 1822 read:

		s.	d.
Small vase, white		15	0
Toy sugar do.		2	0
Toy candlestick do.		2	0
1 chocolate cup do. complete	[no price]		
2 batches gold	[no price]		

These and similar objects would have been decorated by the Doe & Rogers partnership (see page 196) and would bear their name and address mark.

George Rogers junior died in 1877. Examples of his work, which until recently were in the possession of members of the family, are illustrated in an interesting article by Mrs Audrey Wildish in the *Antique Collecting* journal (Antique Collectors' Club), April 1981.

JAMES ROGERS   R. W. Binns listed a painter or gilder of this name and he mentioned one Rogers as a bird painter. The name is included in the Chamberlain wage records from 1792 and he was employed until at least November 1813.

THOMAS ROGERS   This painter is included in the Chamberlain wage records from July 1796 and one entry of March 1797 has a pencilled note 'Landscapes'. The entries cease in June 1806.

WILLIAM RUSSELL   R. W. Binns listed a painter or gilder of this name and the Chamberlain wage records include him from December 1796 to May 1808.

SCARRAT   See SKARRATT.

SHAPLEY   R. W. Binns listed a painter or gilder of this name but I have only been able to trace, in the wage records, a William Shipley, during the period July 1802 to December 1806.

SHEELE   R. W. Binns listed a painter or gilder of this name and the Chamberlain wage records include a George Sheate (who, presumably, is the person referred to in Binns's list) from 1792 to 10 June 1797.

JOHN SKARRATT   R. W. Binns listed a John Skarratt and a John Sherrett in his list of early Chamberlain painters and gilders, but it is difficult to know if these were two persons with similar names or one person – the clerks often used different spellings, for many irregular spellings of even simple names are to be found in the old lists and accounts. John Skarratt is listed from 16 November 1799 to at least 1809, the date of the last available wage book.
   The 1841 and 1851 Worcester census returns include a china painter of this name. The latter gives his place of birth as Hanley in the Staffordshire Potteries and records his age as 70, giving a date of birth of *c.* 1781.

JOHN SMITH   The Chamberlain wage records include a painter of this name from 1796 to at least April 1798. One entry of 4 April 1797 has the pencilled note 'Landscapes' added. A painter of this name was also employed at the Flight factory.

GEORGE SPARKS   This entry is included here because several written 'Sparks-Worcester' marks occur on well-painted porcelains. In most cases, however, the porcelain is of Coalport manufacture as some of his marks make clear. One of George Sparks's advertisements from Lascelles's 1851 *Directory of Worcester and Neighbourhood* shows that in the city of Worcester the buyer had a wide choice of ceramics available, not only the Chamberlain and Grainger porcelains made locally. The marked Sparks porcelains are well worth studying and collecting but they will not be of Chamberlain make.

An Advertisement in Lascelles & Co's *Directory and Gazetteer for Worcester & Neighbourhood.* 1851.

By Appointment to her late Majesty the Queen Adelaide.

Her Royal Highness the Duchess of Kent and the Nobility of her Majesty's Court.

SPARKS'S
ROYAL PORCELAIN HOUSE,
BROAD STREET, WORCESTER
Established for the sale of
THE CELEBRATED COALPORT CHINA
At the SAME PRICES as charged at the Manufactory

Dinner, Dessert, Tea and Coffee Services always in stock from the lowest description up to the most costly patterns upon the fine old Dresden and Sèvres shapes, so much admired by connoisseurs of really fine transparent Porcelain.

The Nobility, Clergy and Gentry, are respectfully informed that orders are taken at this Establishment for Services got up with Arms, Crests, Mottos &c., on the most reasonable charges – Crests from Sixpence each.
Hotels, Boarding Houses, Schools &c. supplied at Wholesale Prices at

SPARKS'S
GENERAL CHEAP FURNISHING WAREHOUSE
In China, Glass, Semi-China, Ironstone, Pearl White Ware &c. from the first Manufacturing Houses in the Kingdom.

Parties are respectfully invited to inspect the Showrooms and Warehouse, whether as purchasers or parties in search of amusement, which will be found to contain, in addition to the above, some beautiful specimens of the newly introduced Parian Statuettes, Ladies Bracelets and Brooches, from 2s. 6d. each; Papier Mache Tea Trays, Inkstands &c.
LAMPS, LUSTRES, BOHEMIAN VASES &c.
SOLE AGENTS FOR MINTON'S WAX FLOWERS & MATERIALS, FOR MODELLING THEM.
Price same as London.
FRENCH GLASS SHADES, WITH GILT AND PLAIN STANDS.

J. SPOONER   This painter was apparently concerned with the colourful 'Japan', or as they were originally called, 'India' patterns. One entry of November 1814 reads: 'Spooners full India pattern, 1 ornament

£3 3s. 0d.'; and pattern 668, which was introduced in about October 1813, was described as 'India, red, gold & green, Spooner £8 8s. 0d.'.

STEEL senior and junior R. W. Binns noted a fruit painter named Steel, but there are no surviving wage records for the period during which he was employed, only some few lists of painters' 'stops'. Steel senior had 'stops' entered against his name in 1830 and in 1831. These 'stops' ceased on 21 January 1832, but for Steel junior they ceased on 24 December 1831 with an added note, 'left 8s. in debt'.

It is tempting to link these entries with the famous fruit painter Thomas Steel and one of his several sons, but there were other ceramic artists and gilders with this surname. But Binns did list the Worcester artist as a fruit painter and this was one of Thomas Steel's specialities. For this reason a brief resumé of Thomas Steel's ceramic career is given here.

He was born in Staffordshire in about 1771 and although little is known of his early life he was probably employed in the late 1790s and early 1800s at one of the Staffordshire manufactories such as Davenport's or Minton's. By about 1815, however, he was working at Derby and his work there is highly prized. He was subsequently employed at the Rockingham factory in Yorkshire, at a period just prior to 1830. His name is included in the wage books of Minton's in Stoke-on-Trent from 17 March 1832, and he remained at Stoke until his death in 1850. The records from 1830 to January 1832 of a painter named Steel employed by Chamberlain's at Worcester, therefore, fit into this picture of Thomas Steel's ceramic career. (A fuller account is given in Godden, *Minton Pottery & Porcelain of the First Period, 1793–1850*, 1968.) The fruit-painted basket shown in Plate 255 is very much in the Steel style.

JOHN STEPHAN The Chamberlain cash book contains the following entry, under the date 26 January 1793: 'Cash for models, John Charles Stephan £6 5s. 0d.'. One may then assume, perhaps, that Stephan was a modeller in the early days of Chamberlain's own production of porcelains. A modeller named Pierre Stephan was employed by Duesbury at Derby (also at Bristol), and was reputedly later employed at Coalport and in the Staffordshire Potteries, as a son, Peter, was born at Stoke-on-Trent in about 1796. John Charles Stephan may have belonged to the same family of modellers.

G. STERRY The Chamberlain cash book contains two entries in 1802 referring to engraving work by G. Sterry:

	£	s.	d.
By G. Sterry on acct of Engraving	2	2	0
By G. Sterry on acct of Engraving	1	1	0

No further references to this engraver have been traced.

JAMES STEVENSON This name is recorded in lists of painters' 'stops' in the 1830–32 period, but there appear to be no further details, although James may have been the son of either John or William Stevenson who came from the Lowestoft factory in 1799 and were employed as 'Potters' by the Chamberlains.

THOMAS STEVENSON This name is recorded in a list of monies lent to painters in 1830, and the Worcester 1841 census returns include a 'china painter' of this name, then in the 60–64 age group. The name Stevenson is entered against pattern 1468.

ROBERT TASKER This painter or gilder was one of the earliest Chamberlain employees and was probably the foreman of the decorators. Early entries in the factory records include:

Teawares to be decorated Tasker's pink border
    [April 1791]
Paid Mr. Tasker senr on acct of Robt. Chamberlain £15 0s. 0d.
    [May 1794]

The prefix 'Mr' indicates a highly respected, leading employee (the addition of the abbreviation 'senr' implies that a son of the same name was also employed), and the name consistently heads the list of painters and gilders in the wage lists. One entry of March 1797 has the pencilled note 'gilder' added. Tasker's name is given against designs 24 (see Plates 53, 60, 68, 69 and 409), 227 and 697 in the list of patterns.

The available wage books do not continue after 1809, but two later sales records include Tasker's name:

1 violet-basket, Dragon scarlet, Tasker's £1 1s. 0d.
    [October 1815]
12 cups & saucers, same as desserts by Tasker
    [October 1816]

It is not known, however, if these later entries refer to Robert Tasker or to his son.

JAMES? TAYLOR R. W. Binns listed a painter or gilder named Taylor and the Chamberlain wage records include a Taylor from September 1796, but no Christian name is given and he was at first drawing very low, apprentice wages. In the 1815 period there are references to a flower painter of this name:

1 Breakfast cup & saucer, Taylor's best Dresden 8s. 8d.
  [June 1815]

1 Table plate, blue ground, Taylor's flowers 14s.
  [November 1815]

It is not known if this 1815 flower painter was James Taylor, or the Taylor listed from 1796, who may well have been James's father, especially as there are records of a William Taylor employed both at Derby and by Chamberlain's, and James was born at Derby in 1793. There are some references to a Taylor in the 1798 stocklist but no mention of a Christian name or the type of work done, except for '2 sauce tureens, complete, Taylor's' and '9 Table plates, Taylor's, finished and burnished'. Pattern numbers 1145, 1393 and 1454 have the name Taylor entered.

The 1851 Worcester census returns list a Derby-born china painter named James Taylor, then aged 58, giving a date of birth of about 1793 (his son Henry, born at Worcester in about 1824, was also listed as a china painter). R. W. Binns recorded that when the new partnership of Kerr & Binns succeeded Messrs Chamberlain & Co. in 1852, the artists then included a flower painter named Taylor. This may well have been the aged James Taylor, whose flower painting was mentioned in 1815 or, alternatively, his son Henry.

JAMES TOMLINS According to the Worcester artist, Solomon Cole, James Tomlins was a ground-layer for Messrs Flight: 'Before grounds were dusted upon the border of the plate or upon vases, they were laid of one uniform even tint with a large flat brush. This was very skilfully done by James Tomlins, who excelled all others in this peculiar branch . . .' (see *Chaffers's*, 15th edition, 1965, Vol. 2, p. 149). This ground-layer is included in the 1841 census returns, where his age is recorded in the 40–44 age group, giving a date of birth of about 1800. There seems to be no trace of the name in the 1851 returns, but it is possible that James Tomlins continued to work for the new firm of Chamberlain & Co. for a few years after 1840.

CHARLES TOULOUSE Born at Worcester in about 1780. He is described as a potter by Binns and this is confirmed by the 1841 census returns, so it is certain that he was not a painter or gilder. Nevertheless it is interesting to see that the family was at Worcester in 1780. Charles Toulouse's name is included in the wage records from January 1794 and a cash book entry dated 7 September 1795 reads: 'By an Indenture for Chas. Toulouse 7s. 3d.'.

JAMES TOULOUSE senior This painter or gilder was included in the wage records from October 1799 to at least 1809, the date of the last available wage book. He was more likely to be a gilder than a painter for an order book entry made in February 1795 reads: '1 Teapot Toulouse gold traceing'.

JAMES TOULOUSE junior The 1841 census returns include a James Toulouse 'china painter', aged 26, giving a date of birth of about 1815, so that there can be no confusion between this artist and that listed in the 1790s. James Toulouse's father had apparently died by 1841 for only his mother, Ann, was listed in the census returns, with James's wife, Mary.

JOHN TOULOUSE senior This person was apparently a modeller and was employed from the early 1790s. The Chamberlain cash books include several interesting references to him:

Jno Toulouse on account £7 7s. 0d.
  [August 1793]

Toulouse for models
  [January 1794]

By Toulouse, modeling, coffee pot etc 10 s.
  [August 1794]

Toulouse, moddilling £2 15s. 0d.
  [September 1794]

There are also several payments for 'overwork' and these give rise to an agreement, the rough notes of which are written in one of the wage books: 'Agreement between Toulouse and Messrs. Chamberlains. Toulouse not to be paid any more than 12 shillings overwork in a week and that only in proportion to the number of Days he shall [work?].'

This undated draft agreement would suggest that Toulouse undertook a great deal of 'overwork' or overtime, and this is perhaps due to the fact that during his normal hours he was fully employed in forming the everyday productions, the special modelling work being largely undertaken in his own time. This would account for the fact that the payments for modelling were made separately, rather than being incorporated in his weekly wage.

Some rare pieces of early Chamberlain wares bear the relief-moulded capital letter 'T' (see Plates 50 and 114) and it is reasonable to attribute the moulds for such pieces to John Toulouse senior.

It is interesting to turn for a moment from pure facts and put forward a theory that could well prove to be extremely important. Collectors of eighteenth-century porcelains will be familiar with an impressed, or relief-moulded, mark 'To' (rarer alternatives are 'T' and 'I T') which has for many years been attributed to a modeller, mould-maker, or 'repairer' (a skilled work-man who assembled the finished article from the different moulded parts needed to form the whole) called 'Tebo', which is believed to have been an anglicized version of the name Thibauld.

Very little is really known about Tebo and it is possible that these 'To', 'T' or 'I T' marks really relate to John Toulouse.

The initial marks of this modeller or repairer are found on the following wares:

Bow porcelains	*c*. 1755–65
Worcester porcelains	*c*. 1765–9
Bristol porcelains	*c*. 1770–73
Caughley porcelains	*c*. 1776–85

It is difficult to give precise dates for his stay at each factory but the above periods are approximately correct. It must be remembered that the initial marks occur on only a few models from each of the above factories, and if the mark is relief-moulded it cannot even be certain that the modeller or mould-maker was at the factory, for he could merely have supplied the moulds, which would subsequently have reproduced his personal sign on all pieces made from such moulds. I do not know of any clear evidence that Tebo was employed at any of the above listed factories, although there are several references to 'Tebo' in the Wedgwood correspondence in 1774 and 1775 to show that such a person did exist. In a letter dated 5 November 1774, Josiah Wedgwood wrote to his partner, Bentley, in London: '. . . Mr. Tebo, our new modeller, did not return here of some days after me, and I am glad he did not for he would have made a shocking ugly thing of the lamp if he had been left to himself. But he has sprained his arm, and has done very little work at present. . . .' From these Wedgwood references to Tebo, various authorities seem to have related the 'To', 'T' and 'I T' marks to this person. In this they may be correct, but consider the possibility of John Toulouse being this porcelain modeller.

Firstly, John Toulouse would seem to have been known to the Chamberlains in 1793 but was apparently not then at Worcester. These ideas are suggested by the fact that Chamberlain paid him on account, and perhaps in advance, £7 7s. 0d., a large sum in August 1793, and in October he received a letter from Toulouse. The 'To' modeller could well have been known to Chamberlain, for he had previously been employed at the Dr Wall factory where Robert Chamberlain was apprenticed and where he worked until the 1780s. Chamberlain may also have known the 'To' modeller because he was apparently employed at Turner's Caughley works and

Chamberlain had close ties with this factory and visited it on several occasions.

It should be remembered that the Chamberlains were originally purely decorators and that once they had started to produce their own porcelain they urgently needed a good modeller and mould-maker, and it is reasonable to assume that they approached one already known to them. The 'To' modeller had been at the Worcester factory and at Caughley; and it is known that Chamberlain employed John Toulouse.

The rare mark 'I T' is of importance, for given the fact that the initial J was very often written as I in the eighteenth century, one can deduce that the 'To' modeller's initial might in fact have been J and, while Tebo's Christian name is unknown, it is known that Toulouse's was John. While Tebo would have had little need to abbreviate his short name, Toulouse would have needed to shorten his when he sought to 'sign' his work. Having made the above comments, I will leave more detailed study of this intriguing theory to other students of eighteenth-century ceramics. There is, admittedly, one drawback to this theory, that is, that 'To' marks are found over a probable period of some forty years, ranging from Bow porcelains of the 1750s to the Caughley pieces of perhaps the 1780s, and the mention of Toulouse in the Chamberlain records is of 1793 and 1794. However, the Chamberlain shell-centrepiece shown in Plate 32 is very much in the style of Tebo's earlier work at Bow and Bristol.

John Toulouse obviously worked into the nineteenth century, and the wage book under the date 10 January 1801 shows that he was still supplying models then, for in addition to his normal wage there is the following: 'John Toulouse, extra bill for lamps £1 16s. 0d.'. A loose sheet dated 4 July 1807 uses the term 'old Toulouse' indicating that this old hand was still employed by the Chamberlains. His death is reasonably well fixed by a simple entry in the factory wage book for the two weeks beginning 18 March and 23 March 1809: 'Toulouse 22nd Dead £1 1s. 0d.'.

Unfortunately Henry Sandon and I have been unable to discover any other facts about this Chamberlain modeller, who was obviously a key figure in the building up of the firm as a porcelain concern. If I am correct in linking this person with the 'Tebo' modeller or repairer associated with the Bow, Worcester, Bristol and Caughley factories, then he was obviously an aged employee on his death in 1809, and the clerk correctly described him as 'old Toulouse'. Further research on John Toulouse should prove rewarding.

JOHN TOULOUSE junior The 1851 Worcester census returns list a Worcester-born 'china painter' named

John Toulouse, then aged 39, giving a date of birth of about 1812. The name appears in painters' 'stops' lists in the 1830–32 period and these entries probably relate to John Toulouse junior, not to the older modeller of this name.

EDWARD TYRER   R. W. Binns listed a painter or gilder of this name and it occurs in the factory wage records from 1792 to the end of the available records in 1809, but no other relevant facts have been discovered.

SAMUEL VAUGHAN   R. W. Binns listed a painter or gilder of this name and it occurs in the factory wage records from 28 September 1799 and continues to at least 1808. The 1841 and 1851 Worcester census returns list a 'china painter' of this name who was born in Worcester in about 1785, a fact which would account for the very low apprentice wages originally paid to him. These census returns indicate that Samuel Vaughan was still working in 1851, but there are no means of telling if this was for the Chamberlain company or for Messrs George Grainger. A Vaughan occurs in the earliest Chamberlain records, and one entry indicates that he was a turner of fluted wares at the Caughley factory; this person may have been the father of Samuel Vaughan.

JOHN WEBSTER   This artist appears in the factory wage records from 2 September 1800 and by about 1814, at least, he had built up a reputation as one of the leading flower painters, if one can judge from the several named references to his work in the sales and order books:

1 set three ornaments, drab, Websters flowers £5 5s. 0d.
    [January 1815]
Set of 5 ornaments, best flowers, Websters £32 0s. 0d.
    [January 1815]

The Chamberlain pattern records, including the official description, also mention Webster's name under design number 733, which had been reached by October 1814:

Webster's roses & rose buds, Table set £130, Dessert set £31 10s. 0d., Tea set £10 10s. 0d.

R. W. Binns listed a painter named Webster as being employed by the rival firm of Flight & Barr, but this may have been the Derby flower painter, Moses Webster, who according to Henry Sandon came to Worcester in 1821, after the period of the Chamberlain entries. Pieces which were perhaps painted by John Webster are illustrated in Plates 164, 186, 187, 195, 392 and 394.

THOMAS WHITE   The name of this 'china painter' is given in the Worcester census returns of 1841, 1851 and 1861, and in the later year his age is given as 69 so that he would have been born in about 1792. Nothing further is recorded about this painter but he may have worked for Messrs Flight, Barr & Barr before 1840 and subsequently for the new firm of Chamberlain & Co.

JOSEPH WILLIAMS senior   R. W. Binns listed as foreman of the Chamberlain painters and/or gilders one Williams, without giving a Christian name. The early factory records list a Joseph Williams from 1791 but this person would appear to have been a clerk or traveller for the firm, as the shop 'day book' contains notes signed 'J Williams' or with the initials 'J.W.'. A 1794 expense account is for £4 paid to J. Williams for expenses incurred on a trip to Bath and Bristol. Other payments relate to commission paid to Williams and yet others refer to the burnishing of the gilding, but in this respect it should be noted that a Sarah Williams (perhaps the wife or daughter of Joseph Williams) was engaged in this occupation, which led to such entries as: 'By Sarah Williams, burnishing from 26th July, £1 2s. 0d.' (13 September 1794).

JOSEPH WILLIAMS junior   R. W. Binns mentioned a landscape painter named Williams, but this is unlikely to be the Joseph Williams listed above. The 1851 Worcester census returns list a Worcester-born Joseph Williams, 'china painter', then aged 45, but again this artist could not be the Joseph Williams mentioned in the Chamberlain accounts of the 1790s, although it could be his son. A Joseph Williams was still employed in the early 1830s as his name is included in painters' 'stops' in 1830, 1831 and 1832. R. W. Binns in his *Worcester China, a record of the work of forty-five years 1852–1897* (1897), states that when the new firm of Kerr & Binns succeeded Chamberlain & Co. in 1852, the painters included Williams, a landscape painter, and it is quite possible that this was the Joseph Williams who was born in about 1806 and included in the 1851 Worcester census returns as a 'china painter'. His work is illustrated in Henry Sandon's *Royal Worcester Porcelain from 1862* (1973, 3rd edition 1978).

JOHN WOOD   One of the leading early Chamberlain artists, Binns lists him first in a summary of specialist artists: 'The principal painters besides Mr. Humphrey Chamberlain, were Wood and Doe for landscapes and figures . . .'. The wage records include the name from 1792 and several entries in other records mention him, a rare occurrence in the 1790s. The 1793 stocklist included a reference to '2 Jarrs, 1 beaker, Wood's figures £1 4s. 0d.'. Other records include:

1 complete [tea] sett, princes circle with John Woods gold border as on ye birds. £10 10s. 0d.
     [December 1794]

2 chocolate [cups] & stands, figures, Woods, 4 guineas each.
     [August 1805]

The 1798 stocktaking records include the entry 'Books & prints valued by J. Wood, £1 1s. 0d.', indicating that Wood was a person of some standing, entrusted with valuing the books. It is of some interest to see that these included '63 numbers of Copperplate magazines, 1 Vol. Edmonson's Heraldry, 1 do. [Vol.] Aesops Fables'; these were no doubt used by the painters as the sources of many of their compositions (see Plates 99 and 100).

A painter named Wood later joined Thomas Grainger in establishing an independent decorating workshop and manufactory under the style 'Grainger, Wood & Co' during the 1801–12 period, and later a John Wood was employed by Grainger as a flower painter. In the 1820s and later, a William Woods was employed as a painter, or gilder, by the Chamberlains, and his name appears against patterns 1478, 1495 and 1510.

JOSEPH YARNOLD   This painter or gilder was born in Worcester in about 1778. The name occurs in the Chamberlain records from December 1793 and one wage entry of March 1797 has the pencilled notation 'gilder' added. The name appears again in 'stops' and 'monies lent' lists in 1830.

JOSEPH YEATES senior   R. W. Binns listed a painter or gilder of this name and it occurs in the factory wage lists (sometimes with the alternative spelling 'Yates') from at least 1792. He drew a relatively high wage, which continued into the nineteenth century.

JOSEPH YEATES junior   The Chamberlain wage records also include Joseph Yeates junior from 31 December 1796 and into the nineteenth century. A pencilled notation against a March 1797 entry includes the description 'blue-print'.

In conclusion it must be stated, to clarify the position regarding several names quoted in Mr Fisher's book *Worcester Porcelain* (1968) as being Chamberlain painters and gilders of the 1799–1804 period, that all records I have examined indicate that those not included in my list were in fact 'potters' *not* painters or gilders, and as such they were engaged in the making of the porcelain, not in its decoration. In this belief I am in the good company of R. W. Binns. The names of the persons about whom such discrepancies arise are: John Ash, George Chamberlain, John Hewitt, William Hewitt, John Rickhus, John Stevenson, William Stephenson (or Stevenson), Charles Toulouse (see page 208), John Toulouse, James Turner and Richard Walthall. Of these, John and William Stevenson had been previously employed at the Lowestoft factory as modellers or finishers of undecorated porcelain (see Godden, *The Illustrated Guide to Lowestoft Porcelain*, 1969).

THE CHAMBERLAIN ORNAMENTAL FORMS

This chapter comprises a list of the known or recorded Chamberlain ornamental shapes, arranged in alphabetical order. It also serves to show the many differing styles of decoration, but in general the decorative treatments are discussed in the earlier chapters dealing with the trends in each period. The tablewares are illustrated in the preceding chapters.

In most cases sample extracts from the contemporary factory order, or sales book, are quoted to confirm that such objects were made at the Chamberlain factory, and to show the original cost.

It is regretted that this list of Chamberlain shapes cannot be considered to be complete, but it does show a good cross-section of the factory's output between 1790 and 1852.

ANIMAL MODELS

References to small animal models appear in the Chamberlain records from the late 1780s, that is, before the Chamberlains commenced to make their own porcelains. There is some doubt as to whether these non-Chamberlain examples, almost certainly ordered through Thomas Turner at Caughley, were of Derby or Caughley manufacture, or from other less obvious sources. Some of the early references are given below:

1 pair of lambs 1s. 6d.
         [July 1789]
4 dozen lambs, white
         [1789 order headed 'Goods ordered by Chamberlain from T. Turner of Caughley'.]
An assortment of enamelled figures, Dogs &c. all sorts immediately
         [Entry in order book relating to goods ordered from Turner at Caughley, February 1791.]

Other orders for goods from Caughley under the date 30 April 1791 included:

12 Pointer dogs and partridge
12 Greyhounds and hare
12 Foxes
12 French Tarriers
12 Dogs a fighting
12 Cats at play

The June 1792 stocktaking records listed:

		£	s.	d.
1	Greyhound and hare, enamelled		1	6
4	Pointers white		3	0
2	do. enamelled		4	0
4	Cats enamelled		9	0
12	Bear dogs enamelled	1	10	0
3	Foxes enamelled		6	0
3	Pointers and partridges		9	0

The retail price of some of these models is indicated in the following account, dated 15 June 1792:

Mr. Richard Winnall, Bromsgrove.

			s.	d.
2	small Pointer dogs, enamelled		3	0
1	Pointer and Partridge	do.	2	6
1	Greyhound and hare	do.	2	6
2	Foxes	do.	5	0
2	Bear Dogs	do.	5	0
2	Cats at Play	do.	5	0

At, or soon after, this date the Chamberlains were making simple, small animals themselves in their heavy, hybrid, hard-paste porcelain (examples are shown in Plate 35). It would appear likely, however, that more elaborate models, as well as figures, were being ordered from Turner at Caughley until at least 1794.

246. *Top*: A selection of marked Chamberlain animals, mostly mounted on matt-blue bases. Written mark 'Chamberlains Worcester'. Rabbit 2¼ in. high. *c*. 1810–25. *Dr & Mrs Rice Collection*

247. *Above*: A biscuit-porcelain model of a poodle and a glazed greyhound on a blue base. Biscuit example has an incised mark 'H. Chamberlain & Sons. Worcester'. 4 in. long. *c*. 1815–25. *Miss M. Ball*

The following models were almost certainly of Chamberlain manufacture and some later examples bear clear factory name marks: '3 Pairs lambs, white & gold at 2*s*.' (June 1798). The painting shop contained eleven white lambs at Christmas in 1798.

Other references to Chamberlain animal models include:

	s.	*d.*	
4 Squirrels	12	0	[March 1802]
2 Geese	5	0	[July 1802]
2 Parrots	8	0	[October 1802]
8 Pug doggs, coloured proper at	3	0	[November 1802]
3 small birds with their bills to the left, gilt	6	0	
1 Kingfisher	4	0	[December 1803]
1 Swan	2	6	[August 1805]
2 large Swanns, white & gold	14	0	[June 1806]
4 Swanns and 4 Pelicans, large at	4	0	[October 1811]
Stag and goat at	4	0	[February 1812]
4 Greyhounds and oak trees			[December 1813]

248. A pair of Chamberlain pug dogs of the type listed at 5s. each in 1816. Green bases. Written mark 'Chamberlains Worcester'. *Mr & Mrs A. Boyce Collection*

In December 1816 the following animal models were sent down to the London shop: '2 Does, 2 Stags, 2 Canarys, 6 Cats, 2 Pugs, 4 Lambs, 6 Canary birds coloured'.

Later references include:

	£	s.	d.	
2 stags with ornamental trees	1	0	0	[April 1819]
1 Pair plain stags		7	6	[May 1820]
1 Tortoiseshell cat		2	0	[February 1821]
2 Pairs stags, dry blue cushions		15	0	

[This entry on 25 April 1821 is the first to mention the dry, or matt, blue base or cushion, a colour so typical of the post-1820 Chamberlain animals models.]

New small stags, unpriced order   [December 1821]

	£	s.	d.	
13 Lions	[no price]			
17 Pea hens	10	10	0	
18 Cats	1	7	0	
9 Peacocks	3	6	6	[February 1822]
1 Peacock, white & gold		8	0	[April 1822]
3 small Spaniel dogs at		2	0	[January 1823]
6 large stags, gilt horns at		4	6	[January 1824]
2 New Poodles at		3	0	[June 1824]
2 Poodles on blue cushions at [see Colour Plate XIII]		2	6	
2 Greyhounds at		4	0	[July 1824]
A pair of Rabbits with small trees				[July 1825]
2 Rabbits with bush at		5	0	[August 1825]
4 Rabbits and 3 with young at		4	0	
1 cat and kitten [see Plate 249]		3	6	[April 1826]
A pair of stags with green cushions		7	6	[April 1826]

A toy biscuit poodle	5	0	[September 1828]
A pug dog	2	6	[January 1829]
Elephant	2	6	
To a biscuit poodle and shade	15	0	[February 1829]
A fox	[no price]		[July 1829]

In the 1830s the demand for Chamberlain's animal models seems to have decreased and there appears to be no trace of any orders for them in the 1840s.

A very well-modelled small figure of a cow, mounted on a green painted base, is in the Hove Museum and Art Gallery. This specimen, like most of the Chamberlain animal models, bears the painted mark 'Chamberlains Worcester'.

The Grainger factory also made animal models, but they tend to be rather larger than the Chamberlain examples and normally have the impressed Grainger mark.

ARTICHOKE BUTTER CUPS

It is possible that the items referred to below were of Caughley manufacture, rather than early Chamberlain porcelain, but the full description – artichoke butter cups, rather than artichoke cups – is interesting and most probably links with the covered handle-less bowls of the type shown in Plate 85 of my *Caughley and Worcester Porcelains, 1775–1800* (1969).

May 12th, 1795. William Bartfield, Esq. Dawley.
6 Artichoke butter cups.
1 Stand.

249. A rare Chamberlain cat and kitten and a model of a mouse. Written mark 'Chamberlains Worcester'. Cat 2½ in. high. *c.* 1820–30. *Private collection, on loan to the Dyson Perrins Museum, Worcester*

ASPARAGUS SERVERS

Caughley wedge-shaped asparagus servers are well known (see Plate 86 of Godden, *Caughley and Worcester Porcelains, 1775–1800*, 1969) but I do not recall having seen Chamberlain examples. The 'Lily' pattern is the underglaze-blue (and often also gilded) 'Royal Lily' pattern as illustrated in Plates 63–5.

May 7th, 1799. 2 Asparagus servers, Lily 2s.

BADGES

This may have been a special order, for a single badge. I do not know of such an example.

November 16th, 1815. Wood Esq., Heralds Cottage, London. A China badge with Regent's Arms and Lodge of Antiquity.

BANISTER RAILS

I have never seen such items, but an article on a visit to Chamberlain's factory in the early 1840s mentions banister rails, for staircases, being turned on a lathe (see Appendix, page 364).

BASKETS

The Chamberlain order and sales books include many references to baskets. Several of these descriptions are interesting in that they indicate the original use of the objects – 'jewell basket' – or that some were made purely for decoration – '1 oval biscuit basket and [glass] shade'. Some early dessert services of the 1790s included fruit baskets and stands, and the circular pierced bowl or basket shown in Plate 250 is a rare early example. Frequent references to baskets include the following:

7 round fruit baskets with stands, rich burnished gold all over, inside and out, 4 at £10 10s. 0d., 3 at £12 12s. 0d.
 [October 1800]

250. A very rare form of early Chamberlain pierced-edged circular basket showing the written name mark under the base. Diameter 7½ in. *c.* 1795–1800. *Godden Reference Collection*

2 large roll baskets, old make £6 6s. 0d.
[September 1812]

2 Jewell baskets [painted with] loose feathers £1 16s. 0d.
[May 1814]

2 Violet baskets [painted with] feathers at 30s.
[January 1815]

2 New rich shell baskets at 18s.
[December 1815]

2 biscuit baskets of flowers £3 3s. 0d.
[August 1819]

It is not clear if the description 'shell' relates to the shape (see Plate 251), to the painted decoration, or to the fact that the basket may have been encrusted with applied modelled porcelain shells (see Plate 204), although these are normally later in date. The term 'biscuit' here and in similar contexts refers, of course, to unglazed porcelain.

251. A rare and colourful Chamberlain shell basket. Written mark 'Chamberlains Worcester & 155 New Bond Street, London'. 5 in. long. c. 1816–20. *Godden of Worthing Ltd*

2 biscuit baskets upon gilt pedestals £2 2s. 0d.
[January 1823]

A fine fancy coronet [shape] basket, pink ground, biscuit flowers &c. with a shade £2 12s. 6d.
[January 1823]

12 toy baskets with blue flowers and shades £2 12s. 6d. to £3 3s. 0d. each
[July 1823]

1 square basket & cover, pink and flowers, painted and raised £2 2s. 0d.
[August 1824]

2 violet baskets, pink at 8s.
[October 1824]

A pair large bow-handled flower-baskets, blue ground & flowers £3 0s. 0d.
[January 1826]

1 basket 10 inch, with shells and birds £1 7s. 6d.
[July 1838]

1 basket 10 inch, shells, maroon [ground] and [view of] Clifton £2 2s. 0d.
[March 1839]

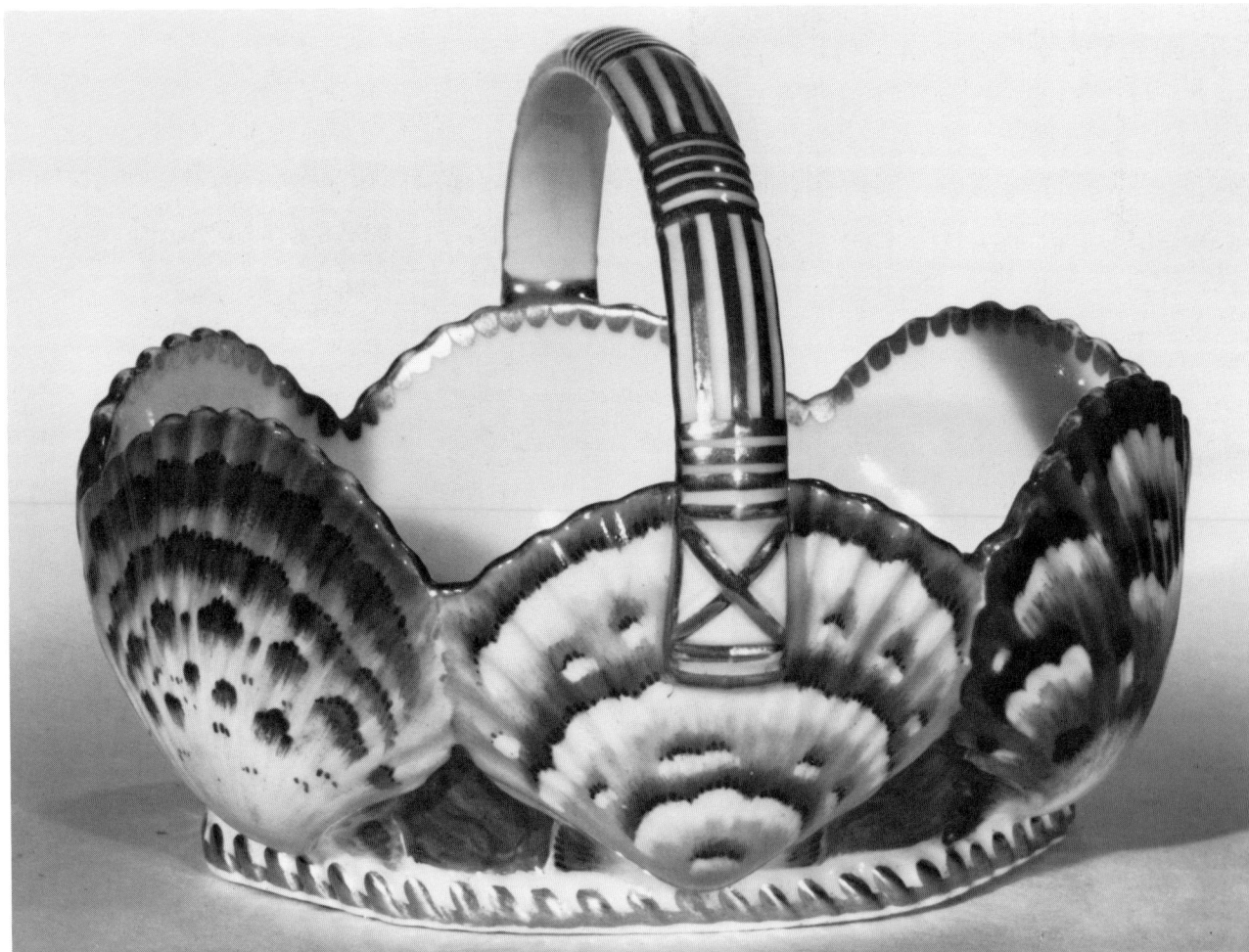

252. A circular blue-ground Chamberlain basket, the cover encrusted with blossom and leaves. Written mark 'Chamberlains Worcester' inside cover. Diameter 5 in. *c.* 1815–25. *Messrs Sotheby & Co.*

253. A biscuit-porcelain ornamental basket, perhaps the '1 Biscuit basket, Love among roses 16*s.*' as listed in April 1822. Unmarked. 8¼ in. long. *c.* 1822–5. *Geoffrey Godden, chinaman*

254. An attractive pale blue-ground Chamberlain basket and pierced cover. Written mark 'Chamberlains Worcester' inside cover. 6¼ in. high. *c.* 1815–25. *Mrs J. Houseman*

255. A very decorative and well-painted Chamberlain open basket. Written name mark. 10½ in. long. *c.* 1830. *Messrs Sotheby & Co.*

Basket, 4 inches, raised flowers in the middle biscuit 5*s.*
    [August 1841]

1 square, bow-handle, basket 10 inches, view Malvern, maroon ground, gilt, £1 10*s.* 0*d.*

6 baskets, 4 inch, handled, Views of Worcester, white and gold seaweed £1 19*s.* 0*d.*
    [September 1841]

1 ten inch basket, celeste ground, raised gold and panels of fruit £3 3*s.* 0*d.*
    [November 1841]

1 Large canoe basket, best blue and gold, grass edge, painted shells £1 5*s.* 0*d.*
    [March 1842]

1 Sherriff basket, richly painted flowers and mounted in best ormolu £10 10*s.* 0*d.*
    [June 1842]

6 Dresden [shape] baskets, mounted, at 5*s.*
    [July 1842]

1 open work Dresden [shape] basket, figures £1 10*s.* 0*d.*
    [December 1842]

1 round leafage basket green ground, basket of flowers in centre, mounted handle £1 11*s.* 6*d.*
    [May 1843]

256. *Left:* A large and elaborate Chamberlain two-piece basket of flowers, the base of which is encrusted with shells. Unmarked. 9 in. high. *c.* 1840–45. *Dyson Perrins Museum, Worcester*

257. *Above:* An attractive dark blue-ground small basket painted with a view of Worcester. This form was also used by the succeeding Kerr & Binns partnership (see Plate 217). Printed mark 'CHAMBERLAIN'S WORCESTER' (see page 35, Mark 13). Diameter 4⅛ in. *c.* 1840–50. *M. A. Wall Collection*

1 Basket with view of Witley £2 12s. 6d.
   [August 1843]

1 Dresden [shape] oval basket with Watteau figures £1 10s. 0d.
   [October 1843]

1 Adelaide card basket, Dresden form pierced, richly gilt £1 8s. 0d.
   [October 1844]

2 four inch baskets filled with shells at 5s.
   [November 1844]

2 small Dresden baskets, raised flowers all over outside and Dresden group [of flowers] inside, at 12s.
   [July 1845]

Chamberlain & Co.'s stand at the 1851 Exhibition included decorative baskets simply described as 'Gold and white Dresden baskets, with paintings'.

It should be noted that some of the more expensive early nineteenth-century Chamberlain breakfast services included one or more 'square sugar baskets' in addition to the normal sugar-box. These sugar-baskets had the usual, stock, teaware patterns and not the special fancy designs found on the ornamental type of basket.

BEAKERS   See TUMBLERS

BELL-ROPE HANDLES

These simple objects were of egg-shape, a little smaller than a hen's egg. They were pierced down the middle to take the bell-rope or cord. A good example is in the Dyson Perrins Museum at the Worcester Works. Early references to such items include:

1 pair of blue and gold bell handles 9s.
   [July 1791]

1 enamelled and gold bell handle – egg shape 4s. 6d.
   [May 1792]

At this date it is possible that these bell-pulls were of Caughley porcelain; alternatively, if they were of Chamberlain make, they must have been very early specimens. But an entry in 1797 shows that some were of Derby make, or of Derbyshire Spar.* Other references include:

1 Bell handle, Royal Stripe [pattern] ware 1s. gilding 1s. 6d.
   [December 1794]

1 pair bell rope balls, Dresden flowers 3s.

1 pair bell rope balls, fawn and gold stripe, very light colours twisted shape
   [January 1796]

*The Chamberlain retail shop also sold Blue John or Derbyshire Spar bell-pulls, which in May 1797 were purchased from Richard Parkes.

1 Bell ball. Queen's [pattern] 7s. 6d.
[An example of such a 'Queen's' pattern bell-pull is shown in Plate 258]

The basic cost of white, undecorated bell-rope handles in January 1796 was 2s.

In the mid 1840s 'bell pulls' were being listed, but these were probably porcelain handles for the Victorian metal lever-type bell-pulls.

BLOTTING CASES

In the late 1830s and early 1840s the company made blotting books, or blotting pads, with the front covers containing a painted porcelain plaque. Examples are in the Dyson Perrins Museum, Worcester. One typical entry reads: '1 Blotting book, dark ground and group of flowers richly painted. £5 5s. 0d.' (June 1839). Other references are given under PLAQUES.

BOTTLES

The Chamberlain accounts contain many references to bottles of various types, but in general these are quoted under scent-bottles or as vases. Most large bottles seem to have had a purely ornamental purpose; for example: '2 large bottles, dragon stoppers solid gilt, scarlet ground white figures. £1 16s. 0d.' (October 1844).

258. A rare 'Queen's' pattern bell-pull of typical egg-like form. 2 in. high. c. 1800. *Chantonbury Gallery, Sussex*

259. A superbly painted and gilded bowl, perhaps from a tea service, inscribed under the base 'A view of the Water of Leith near Edinburgh'. Written mark 'Chamberlains Worcester'. Diameter 6½ in. c. 1815–20. *Geoffrey Godden, chinaman*

260. *Top:* A Chamberlain punch-bowl painted with the colourful and popular 'Dragon in Compartments' design, number 75. A twelve-inch bowl of this pattern was invoiced at £3 0s. 0d. in 1800. Written name mark and pattern number. Diameter 9¾ in. *c.* 1795–1805. *Godden of Worthing Ltd*

261. *Above:* A well-decorated large Chamberlain-Worcester dark green-ground punch-bowl with hunting subject panels. Written mark 'Chamberlains Worcester'. Diameter 15 in. *c.* 1815–25. *Messrs Sotheby & Co.*

262. *Opposite:* The interior view of the punch-bowl shown in Plate 261; note especially the fine quality and costly gilding. *Messrs Sotheby & Co.*

BOWLS

Small bowls with a diameter of under 7 in. were originally the waste or slop bowls from tea services, and such examples are illustrated with their matching teawares in Plates 44, 59, 72, 73, etc. A single example is shown in Plate 259. Some of these can be of very fine quality and are decorative and useful items in their own right. The printed price-card also listed with the breakfast-service wares 'milk basons' of pint and half-pint size.

Larger bowls are traditionally called punch-bowls and four standard sizes are included in Messrs Chamberlain's printed price-list: 'Punch Bowls, 2 Quarts, 3 Quarts, 4 Quarts and 6 Quarts'.

Sample entries from the earlier order books are quoted here:

3 three-quart bowls, rich Muchall's painting £6 6s. 0d.
    [December 1793]

1 12 inch Punch bowl, Dragon No. 75, £3 0s. 0d.
    [February 1800: see Plate 260]

A rich one gallon bowl, no. 299 patt. with figure Hope and three views. Brown. £15 15s. 0d.
    [August 1802]

1 six-quart Punch bowl, rich vine pattern with a Venus painted in bottom
    [August 1806]

A three-quart Punch bowl with white setter, plough and cypher and implements of Husbandry with motto – Speed the plough. Gold vine border, a painting of grapes proper in bottom, £4 4s. 0d.
    [July 1814]

263.   A spiral-fluted large-size breakfast cup and saucer, the gilt design incorporating the owner's initials and crest. Diameter of cup 4¼ in. *c.* 1794. *Godden of Worthing Ltd*

264.   *Opposite :* A marked Chamberlain butter tub, cover and stand decorated to a Dr Wall period design. The flower painting is probably by George Davis (see page 192). Written mark 'Chamberlains Worcester'. Diameter of stand 6½ in. *c.* 1810–15. *Messrs Christie, Manson & Woods*

Other rich punch-bowls were made after the period for which records still exist, and the following entry shows that ornately decorated bowls were made into the 1840s: '1 bowl and stand. Baden [shape] solid gold inside and view Witley on Royal blue and pearls. £4 4s. 0d.' (September 1843). All large bowls, however, are very rare.

BREAKFAST SERVICES

These magnificent sets are a feature of the more expensive early nineteenth-century orders. They are, in effect, enlarged tea services, but with extra large-size cups and saucers (see Colour Plates XI and XIV), and other rare items such as muffin dishes and covers, egg stands and bee-hive shaped honey pots (see Plate 145).

The Prince Regent's order in 1816 (see page 104), for example, included a massive combined tea and breakfast service, listed below, of the 'harlequin' type:

	£	s.	d.
72 Breakfast cups and saucers	106	4	0
72 Tea cup and saucers	82	16	0
72 Coffees and stands	82	16	0
60 8 inch plates	60	0	0

12	do. fine views of Waterloo	44	2	0
12	Muffin dishes and covers	31	10	0
2	Slop bowls	1	10	0
4	Teapots and stands	6	12	0
4	Coffee pots and stands	12	12	0
4	Cream ewers	3	0	0
4	Milk Jugs	6	0	0
4	Egg stands, six cup each	14	0	0
4	Roll baskets, richly painted	29	8	0
6	Butter tubs & covers with stands	15	15	0
6	Hive [shape] honey pots	11	8	0
6	Square sugar baskets	5	11	0

Other breakfast-service pieces made for Sir James Yeo are discussed on page 117 and illustrated in Colour Plate XI. The following details of a standard tea and breakfast service of pattern 831 ordered in 1818 give a more realistic idea of the current prices at that time, and of the make-up of such a service.

	£	s.	d.
12 Tea cups and saucers	4	4	0
12 Coffee cups (no saucers)	2	8	0
12 Breakfast cups and saucers	7	0	0
8 Plates	2	8	0
1 Teapot and stand		16	0

1 Sugar box	7	0
1 Slop bowl	7	0
1 Cream jug	6	0
1 Pint jug	12	0
2 Muffin dishes & covers	2 0	0
2 Butter tubs & stands	2 0	0
2 Loaf plates, 9 inches	1 3	0
2 Egg stands, 3 cup each	2 8	0
1 square sugar basket	7	0
	26 6	0

Although most of the magnificent Chamberlain breakfast services are of the nineteenth century, some earlier examples were apparently made. The cup and saucer shown in Plate 263 is such an example, with the cup twice the size of an ordinary teacup. Here the decoration is in gold with the owner's initials and crest appearing in the centre of the saucer and inside the cup.

Whilst today these large-size cups are usually called breakfast cups, they were not always so designated. In the case of the example shown here, John Sandon has traced the original order and cups and saucers like this one – described as '$\frac{1}{4}$ pts and stands, hand^d' – were listed with seemingly normal-sized teawares:

29th December 1794.
James Nind, Overbury – by the water to Tewkesbury.
12 cups and saucers 2nd Shank^d.
 9 coffee cups   do.
 6 Chocolate cups and saucers
 2 plates   do.
 1 slop basin
 1 sugar box
 1 cream ewer
 1 teapot and stand
 6 $\frac{1}{4}$ pts and stands, hand^d.
 2 small plates
Border to match the pint tumblers, Cypher J S N. Gold border as directed by Mrs C.

Delivered to Hodges by Mr. Groves, 7th February 1795.

This order is repeated in another order book where these large cups are described as: '6 cups and saucers, large size, $\frac{1}{4}$ pints and stands'.

Certainly such quarter-pint cups and saucers, or breakfast cups and saucers, are very rare. The one illustrated in Plate 263 can be conveniently dated between the date of the order, 29 December 1794, and the date of delivery, 7 February 1795.

BROTH BOWLS

As is evidenced from the orders below, the broth bowls originally had covers and stands, and probably also had two side handles.

	£	s.	d.
1 Broth bowl, cover & plate, dragon in compartment	1	1	0
1 do. Scarlett dragon	1	1	0

[November 1794]

1 Broth, bowl & stand [pattern] 240. £2 2s. 0d.
     [August 1806]

BULB OR BOUGH POTS   See ORNAMENTS

'BUMPERS'   See STIRRUP-CUPS

BUTTER TUBS

All porcelain butter tubs are rare, but a Chamberlain circular butter tub and stand, in this case richly decorated in an early Worcester style of the 1765–75 period, is shown in Plate 264. This particular pattern seems to match that of a dessert service order placed by the 'Marquis of Donigall' in May 1813 – 'Blue ground with flowers (Davis's) and antique gilding'. If this old-style flower painting does in fact reveal George Davis's hand, then he could have been responsible for the Dr Wall and Flight period flower painting found on Worcester porcelains from about 1765 onwards (see Colour Plate I and page 192).

2 round butter tubs & stands Royal Lily [pattern] gilt £1 1s. 0d.
     [July 1793]

1 butter tub & stand, white 4s.
     [January 1814]

BUTTERFLIES

The Bond Street cash book shows sales of objects described simply as 'a Butterfly 5s.' or 'a Butterfly and shade, 3s. 6d.'. These could be small covered boxes made in the form of a butterfly, but the sale of one with a glass shade suggests that they were ornamental objects.

BUTTONS

The buttons referred to below were almost certainly made at the Caughley factory and gilded by the Chamberlains at Worcester. Many porcelain button wasters of various types and designs were found on the Caughley factory site (see Godden, *Caughley and Worcester Porcelains, 1775–1800*, 1969, Plate 94), as well as on the Flight factory site (see Henry Sandon, *Worcester Porcelain 1751–1793*, 1969, 3rd edition 1980).

2 dozen coat buttons, white & gold, ribbed ware 18s.,		gilding		9d.
12 buttons, 1st [size] sorted patterns	9d.		do.	$\frac{3}{4}d.$
18 do. 2nd		do.	1s. 6d.	do.	1d.
18 do. 3rd		do.	1s. 10½d.	do.	1¼d.
18 do. 4th		do.	2s. 3d.	do.	1½d.

     [April 1790]

In the late 1830s Messrs Chamberlain commenced the manufacture of buttons produced under pressure from dies. R. W. Binns, writing in his *A Century of Potting in the City of Worcester* (1865), rather decries this innovation:

. . . we fear that the button trade, in the composition of its bodies (agate, cornelian &c) and the special care required in the making and firing departments, absorbed more time than was profitable and engaged attention which ought to have been devoted to the more legitimate works of the manufactory.

The button business yielded a good profit on its own separate account, but it was scarcely generally profitable for the manufactory. The lawsuit [between Richard Prosser and the Chamberlains concerning Prosser's 1840 patent for his pressed dry clay process] disgusted the patentee and he no longer cared to protect his licencees from the competition of the French manufacturers who had improved upon the invention and were introducing a superior article at lower prices; the trade was therefore shortly afterwards given up.

The cost of manufacture for these buttons must have been extremely low – a button press purchased from W. Elliott of Birmingham cost a mere £3 15s. 0d. The quarterly accounts for the production of buttons in 1849 have been preserved. These broken-down costings are of interest and the production costs for the period 1 January to 30 March 1849 are given below. Surprisingly, in all periods the cost of 'carding', or mounting the finished buttons on cards ready for sale, exceeded all other production costs.

	£	s.	d.
Wages of Makers	33	10	2
Wages of Kiln men	16	1	3
Wages of tool men	25	5	10
Agate clay	3	16	0
Bats and saggers	5	0	0
Cost of cards	5	2	0

Cost of boxes	2	8	0
Cost of carding	49	15	2
Cost of coal	10	0	0
Royalty	45	10	0
Blue clay bauks	14	5	0
	210	13	5

The total costs for the production of buttons in 1849 amounted to £1,253 1s. 8d., but these buttons showed a very good profit calculated at £1,915 2s. 11¼d. on a gross sale of £3,713 4s. 7¼d. The two basic types of ceramic buttons produced by Chamberlain's at this period were described as 'Agates' and 'Cornelians'. Some of these Chamberlain buttons, still mounted on their display-cards, are to be seen in the Worcester Works Museum collection. The production of Chamberlain's buttons continued to at least September 1850.

CABINET CUPS

As the name suggests, these very ornately decorated cups were intended purely for ornamental purposes, rather than for drinking from. Some of these cabinet cups were very expensive single pieces priced in keeping with complete tea services of quite fancy and complicated painting. Cabinet cups were also some-times made in pairs for use as small vase-like ornaments, such as those referred to in the following royal order, dated 29 June 1816:

Her Majesty the Queen of England, Buckingham Palace.

    1 Pair cabinet cups, 2 handles, painted from the Lady of the Lake, Drab ground, gilt border. £16 16s. 0d.

Most examples were equipped with saucers or stands, and some also had covers. More typical entries from the factory records are given below:

2 Cabinet cups and stands, Othello & Desdemona. £10 10s. 0d.
    [October 1811]

1 Cabinet cup and saucer, composition marble and feathers. £2 12s. 6d.
    [March 1812]

English Cabinet cup, cover & stand, beaded, white. 10s.
English Cabinet cup and stand, white. 8s.
    [October 1812]

The description 'English' may perhaps indicate a non-Chamberlain blank; alternatively, it may refer to the shape, especially as some of the following examples were French or of French shape.

2 two handle F. [French?] cabinets, square foot [painted with] loose feathers £4 4s. 0d.
    [November 1813]

2 Cabinets and stands from Richard 2nd & Henry 8th, green marble ground £8 8s. 0d.
    [December 1813]

Cabinet and stand, Madonna & child £10 0s. 0d.
    [February 1814]

2 Cabinet cups and stands, subjects from Lady of the Lake £21 0s. 0d.
    [January 1815]

1 Cabinet cup and saucer, snake handle, Coburgh shape. Views £2 2s. 0d.
    [July 1816: perhaps as in Plate 271]

2 Rich Cabinet cups and saucers, gold snake handle, one blue and gold, ye other green and gold, with flowers &c. £3 3s. 0d.
    [July 1818]

2 Upright French cups with three feet, Waterloo Church and Claremont with ivory ground
    [November 1818. These are called chocolate cups in the Spode shape book. Chamberlain cups on three feet are shown in Plate 270, but those in Plate 266 are more French in style.]

2 French cups and saucers, one handle, without feet
2 New Baden cup with one handle and three ornamental feet
    [November 1818]

2 Cabinet cups, Shakespeare, Tempest and King Lear, £6 6s. 0d.
    [May 1819]

265. A typical Chamberlain marbled-ground cup and saucer, the panels depicting 'Pike Fishing' and 'Cock Shooting', taken from W. D. Daniel's *Rural Sports*. Written name mark. Diameter of saucer 5¾ in. *c.* 1803–8. *Messrs Sotheby & Co.*

266. A pair of three-footed French-style Nantgarw cups and saucers of a form also made at Swansea and copied, or decorated, at Worcester; for example: '2 Swansea cabinets, views at £1 10s. 0d.' (April 1820: see also page 140). Unmarked. Diameter of saucer 5¼ in. c. 1817–20. *Messrs Sotheby & Co.*

267. *Left:* A fine-quality Chamberlain 'Regent China' cup with raised gold border to the panel, which was perhaps painted by Thomas Baxter (see page 184). Very neatly written mark 'Chamberlains Regent China Worcester & 155 New Bond Street, London'. 3½ in. high. c. 1816–20. *Messrs Phillips*

268. *Above:* A marbled celeste-ground Chamberlain cabinet cup and saucer; the cup is painted with a scene from *King Henry VI, Part 1*. Written name mark 'Chamberlains Worcester'. Diameter of saucer 5¾ in. c. 1815–20. *Dyson Perrins Museum, Worcester*

2 Swansea ma [manufacture?] cup, 2 handles & stands, grey £2 10s. 0d.
[September 1819]

2 Cabinet cup on feet, grey and gold with paintings from Thompson £5 5s. 0d.
[February 1820]

1 Cabinet & stand, Swansea ma. Old Well Walk [Cheltenham] unpriced order
[October 1820]

2 Cabinets, Hop Pickers £1 16s. 0d.
[October 1821]

A pair of 2-handled cabinets on feet, maroon and gilt, Cheltenham & Leamington at £1 5s. 0d.
[August 1822]

1 set of three cabinet cups, painted groups and raised flowers, rich (two at 18s., one at 21s.) £2 17s. 0d.
[July 1839]

2 Cabinet cups and stands, French shape, Sèvres wreath, richly gilt £5 5s. 0d.
[March 1842]

1 Cabinet cup and stand, biscuit blue with painting of the Duke of Wellington £1 10s. 0d.
[June 1842]

1 Pierced cabinet cup and stand, gold, etc. £3 13s. 6d.
[December 1842]

1 Cabinet cup and stand, fawn and rich gilding, painting of London £2 2s. 0d.

2 Rich cabinet cups and stands beaded, celeste, raised [gold] panels views Malvern & Windsor, at £3 3s. 0d.
[September 1843]

269. *Top:* A very richly decorated buff-ground cabinet cup and saucer. The panel is painted by Humphrey Chamberlain (see page 187) with a scene from *Love's Labour Lost*, Act 1, Scene 2. Signed 'H. Chamberlain. Pinsit' with inscription and name mark. *c.* 1815–20. *Dyson Perrins Museum, Worcester*

270. A very rare pair of Chamberlain cups mounted on three feet, a form which could not have been very practical. The scenic panels are of Cheltenham and Worcester. Three-legged 'French cups' were invoiced in 1818. Written mark 'Chamberlains Worcester'. 4½ in. high. *c.* 1815–20. *Dyson Perrins Museum, Worcester*

271. A rare cup form, maybe one of the snake-handled cabinet cups of the 1818 period. The style of landscape painting is perhaps in the manner of Thomas Baxter (see page 184). Written name mark with New Bond Street address. Cup 3 in. high. *c.* 1816–20. *Private collection, on loan to the Dyson Perrins Museum, Worcester*

2 Cabinet cups and stands, biscuit blue and views, Witley & Malvern £6 6s. 0d.
  [December 1843]

2 rich cabinets and stands, Brunswick shape, Garter blue band and broad gold lines and border. Watteau figures, at £2 16s. 6d.
  [March 1844]

6 Rich cabinet cups and saucers, Baden Gadroon [shape] groups [of flowers] and richly gilt with Royal views £12 12s. 6d.
  [June 1845]

The following references to white examples give some indication of the shapes and again emphasize the low cost of the white blanks.

2 New Cabinets and stands under, with ornamental handles, beads etc. White. 10s.
  [May 1824]

4 Cabinets on feet white, 10s.

272. A richly decorated cabinet cup and saucer of dark-blue ground with coral-style gilding. The panel is painted with a view of Frogmore. This is a particularly finely gilt example. Written mark 'Chamberlain & Co., Worcester'. Cup 4½ in. high. *c.* 1840–45. *Dyson Perrins Museum, Worcester*

2 Upright do. one handle, white 2s.
[December 1826]
1 Cabinet, two handle, on claws [feet?] white 3s.
[March 1826]

The reference under the date 9 September 1819 (see page 227) to two Swansea cups is interesting and, with the earlier references to French cups, shows that the Chamberlains were still content to act as decorators, when their own shapes did not meet the customer's requirements. Further references to Swansea blanks are given on page 140.

CADDY SPOONS

It is not known if the caddy spoons referred to in the Christmas 1795 stocktaking lists were of porcelain, or of silver or silver-gilt:

5 Caddy spoons gt [gilt] at 2s. 6d.
6 dozen of caddy spoons 6s.

CANDELABRA

In September 1844 the New Bond Street shop was supplied with a pair of candelabra described in the following terms: '2 china double-light candelabras china pillar and branches. Celeste and traced gilding, mounted &c &c'. No price was given. A further pair was sent to London in February 1845 and these were described as: '2 candelabra Celeste, richly gilt and flowers, 2 branches and top [or centre] for flowers or light. £16 16s. 0d.'

Such pieces are extremely rare in any porcelain, and these are the only records I have come across.

CANDLESTICKS

Candlesticks are normally divided into three classes: the low chamber candlesticks which were equipped with a carrying-handle; the taller standing sticks which were sometimes termed 'bracket candlesticks' and which could be very decorative objects; and the very small taper candlesticks for the desk, table or inkstand. These taper sticks held a taper or small candle for melting sealing-wax.

274. An important large-size pillar candlestick of dark-blue ground richly gilt in the French taste. Name mark with New Bond Street address. 15¼ in. high. c. 1816–20. *In the possession of a branch of the Urwick family, directly descended from Henry Chamberlain, of Bredicote Court, near Worcester*

273. *Top:* A rare pair of candlesticks, perhaps the 'white and gold boys' of 1807. Others of the same period are listed as 'Griffin'. Unmarked. 7 in. high. *c.* 1805–10. *Messrs W. W. Warner (Antiques) Ltd*

275. *Above:* A small chamber candlestick of typical flat handled form, the edge encrusted with porcelain shells. Written mark 'Chamberlains Worcester'. Diameter 4 in. *c.* 1840–45. *Dyson Perrins Museum, Worcester*

Many of the Chamberlain sales entries, however, are so brief that one cannot tell which type was being sold. For example, in January 1807 there appears listed:

2 pairs Mermaid Candlesticks, rich
Pair Griffin candlesticks in gold, large
Pair   do.   in bronze, small
Pair bronze boys
Pair white and gold do.
Pair chamber candlesticks, dolphin handles.

The candlesticks shown in Plate 273 are perhaps the white and gold boys. A tall pair of Chamberlain pillar candlesticks is illustrated in the Allen Collection Catalogue, Plate 68, and a superb example is shown here in Plate 274.

Chamber (or hand) candlesticks

1 Chamber candlestick & extinguisher, blue border 10s. 6d.
    [July 1795]
10 Chamber candlesticks at 1s.
    [Stock in biscuit-room, Christmas 1795]
1 small candlestick & extinguisher [pattern] 240   12s.
    [March 1803]

2 Antique [shape] candlesticks, dolphin handles, gold
£3 3s. 0d.
[October 1805]

2 Pairs oval chamber candlesticks gold edges with extinguisher £1 4s. 0d.
[November 1805]

Standing (or bracket) candlesticks

1 Bracket candlestick, Davis's birds 4s.
[Christmas 1793 stocktaking list]

Pair of candlesticks, Queen's pattern £1 1s. 6d.
[February 1796]

2 Griffin candlesticks with high nozzles and pedestals
£3 0s. 0d.
[September 1806]

Pair three-dolphin candlesticks, rich red & gold £3 3s. 0d.
[August 1812]

8 Rich Turks candlesticks, Brackets £11 8s. 0d.
[April 1816]

1 new rich candlestick, gadroon [edge], dry blue and gold,
flowers in panels £1 10s. 0d.
[August 1822]

1 Candlestick figure £1 1s. 0d.
[August 1822]

Pair tall candlesticks, white & gold and printed flowers
£1 10s. 0d.
[September 1841]

Taper candlesticks

1 taper candlestick 4s.
[May 1811]

4 tapers, feathers and grey £3 12s. 0d.
[November 1813]

2 tapers pattern 276 at 5s.
2   do. pattern 240 at 6s.
[November 1821]

2 tapers, gadroon border and extinguishers at 2s. 6d.
[June 1822]

2 Nasturtium tapers at 5s.
[August 1844]

2 pierced shell tapers and extinguishers at 2s.
[November 1844]

2 taper candlesticks, sea green ground, broad gold edge and
fine line and painted groups of flowers on ground, shell
shape at 10s. 6d.
[April 1846]

Candlestick, or candelabra, bases

3 pairs stands for glass candlesticks
[June 1797]

Very small, or toy, candlesticks were also made.

CARD CASES

These objects probably held visiting-cards.

1 card case, with tablet, rich 16s. 6d.
[December 1838]

2 canoe [shape] card cases, Malvern & Cheltenham and
flower reserves £2 12s. 6d.
[March 1842]

CARD RACKS

Card racks were probably for holding visiting-cards (see
Plate 276). The Coalport company made similar articles
at the same period (see Godden, *Coalport and Coalbrookdale Porcelains*, 1970, Plates 166–7).

2 card racks, flowers £1 16s. 0d.
[November 1820]

2 card racks, Dresden flowers £2 2s. 0d.
2   do.   views £3 3s. 0d.
[April 1821]

Small card racks on feet, unpriced order
[August 1822]

1 pair card racks, pink and gold and flowers £3 3s. 0d.
[August 1824]

CAUDLE CUPS

Caudle cups normally have two handles but some, such
as the Regent ornamental caudle priced at £6 6s. 0d. (see
Plate 234), were for ornamental purposes rather than for
use.

It is difficult to distinguish between caudle cups and
chocolate cups (q.v.) which normally had covers.

1 Caudle cup and stand, one handle. Arms in front. . ., crest a
griffin head. . . . The ornamental part to be left to Mr.
Chamberlains judgement.
[June 1791]

		£	s.	d.
2 caudle cup & saucers, French sprigs			16	0
2 do.	Lord Coventry's green		15	0
2 do.	Royal Lily		18	0
2 do.	Royal Fly	1	4	0
[July 1793]				

1 Caudle cup, pink cupids etc. 10s. 6d.
[December 1806]

1 Regent ornamental caudle, Timon £6 6s. 0d.
[December 1813: see Plate 234]

1 Pair Prince's Caudles, painted loose feathers £5 5s. 0d.
[April 1814]

CENTREPIECES

Centrepieces were the largest components of dessert services, but as is evidenced here they were sometimes sold separately.

1 Centre piece, new model, Royal Lily £1 5s. 0d.
    [August 1791]

1 Centrepiece, pattern 55 £1 12s. 0d.
1 low   do.   top & bottom £2 10s. 0d.
3 low centres, without ears
    [June 1796]

On some occasions they were purchased slightly later to supplement existing matching services, as is the case with that shown in Plate 277:

1 Rich Dolphin centre, View of man.y [manufactory] fawn
    and gold £9 9s. 0d. [see Plate 277]
    [July 1816]

Typical Chamberlain dessert centrepieces are shown in Plates 84, 86, 140, 144 and 151–3.

CHAMBER POTS

The examples below were probably of Caughley make but Chamberlain decoration. I have not seen any true Chamberlain chamber pots.

12 Chamber pots, full size, Chantilly sprigs
12 Chamber pots, full size, Dresden flowers and border
    [Supplied to the Earl of Oxford in August 1796]

CHEESE TRAYS

Cheese trays may well have been of papier mâché, not porcelain: '2 Cheese trays, round.' (August 1796). However, the following, with a reference to a pattern number, could well have been a porcelain example: '1 Cheese tray, 880, £1 5s. 0d.' (July 1820).

CHELSEA EWERS

Chelsea ewers were made in two distinct varieties: the low Chelsea, and the much rarer, high Chelsea ewer.

These creamers were made at most pre-1810 English porcelain factories, notably at the Worcester and the Caughley works.

The June 1792 Chamberlain stocklist included:

72 low Chelsea ewers, valued at £1 16s. 0d.
21 tall Chelsea ewers, valued at £1 1s. 0d.

but these were probably of Caughley make, available at Chamberlain's establishment for decoration and resale.

Certainly, however, the Chamberlains made low Chelsea ewers when they commenced to produce their own porcelains (examples are shown in Plates 44 and 51), and firm evidence to support this is to be found in the Christmas 1795 Chamberlain stocklist where, under the sub-heading 'mould room', this entry appears: '16 dozen of low Chelsea ewers, biscuit best at 4s.' (per dozen). These were obviously half-finished examples, still in the mould-room and as yet unglazed. Chamberlain examples are very rare.

CHOCOLATE CUPS

References to chocolate cups include the following:

Rt. Hon[bl]. Lord Courtney, Powerham Castle, Devon.
4 Antique [shape] chocolate cups and covers and saucers fine
    blue & gold, Royal Stripe &c. £8 8s. 0d.
    [February 1794]

Mrs. Powys, Berwick House, Shrewsbury.
2 Chocolate cups, covers and saucers, Diamond pattern, with
    arms and views £4 4s. 0d.
    [February 1795]

6 chocolates and saucers, Davis's birds £4 4s. 0d.
    [Christmas 1795 stocktaking, painting-room]

Viscount Ashbrook, Woodstock, Oxfordshire.
6 Rich figured chocolates, complete with covers and stands,
    pattern 305 without fawn ground at £4 4s. 0d.
    [May 1803]

	£	s.	d.
Pair chocolates, gold ground with flowers	2	12	6
Pair do. fruit and flowers in colours	2	12	6

    [October 1803]

1 chocolate cup, rich fruit etc. £2 12s. 6d.
    [November 1803]

1 Rich chocolate, figure from Deserted Village £3 13s. 6d.
    [June 1804]

Pair of chocolate cups, covers and stands, yellow ground, with
    brown figures £1 10s. 0d.
    [March 1805]

2 chocolates, mosaic blue and gold, flowers in panel £3 0s. 0d.
    [September 1805]

2 chocolates and stands, best white 5s. 4d.

---

276. A rare hanging card rack painted with a distant view of Worcester in the stippled manner of Doe (see page 196). Written name mark. 7½ × 5 in. c. 1820–30. *Cheltenham Art Gallery & Museum*

277. A 'rich dolphin centre' of the type supplied with the more expensive dessert services in about 1815. The centre of this example bears a standard view of Worcester and Chamberlain's factory (see Plate 103). It was invoiced at £9 9s. 0d. in July 1816. Unmarked. 10½ in. long. c. 1815. *Godden Reference Collection*

278. A rare spiral-fluted or shanked Chamberlain salmon-bordered covered chocolate cup and saucer decorated in a simple style for use rather than purely for show. Unmarked. Cup 4½ in. high. c. 1795–1800. *Godden of Worthing Ltd*

This last entry is interesting as it shows the low cost of the basic undecorated object. The following examples were invoiced in the same month, October 1805, but with their fine decoration, the prices had risen to about sixteen times the cost of the white examples.

2 chocolates, enamelled views. Rich red and gold stripes £4 4s. 0d.
   [October 1805]

1 chocolate complete, feathers, gold bead £2 12s. 6d.
   [July 1811]

1 Ornamental chocolate and cover with stand, fawn and gold Paintings of dogs &c. £3 13s. 6d.
   [April 1817]

2 double-handled, Baden chocolates, complete, white 6s.
   [March 1824]

COFFEE CANS

The term 'can' is used to describe the continental style of straight-sided coffee cup. These were in fashion at most English factories from the mid 1790s to about

1815. Earlier examples are likely to be individual small mugs and not coffee cups from tea services.

The early Chamberlain coffees were conventional shaped-sided cups, as shown in Plates 47, 54, 58 and 59. A prototype coffee can is to be seen in Plate 57 (right). The typical Chamberlain coffee can had a slightly tapered form, as illustrated in Plates 72, 74, 80, 111, 120, 123 and 127, although some sets still had conventional coffee cups (see Plates 73 and 78). By the time of the introduction of the 'London' shape and the embossed floral-bordered teawares (see Plates 132 and 133), the straight-sided or tapered coffee can had gone out of fashion.

One might expect Chamberlain teasets to have as many coffee cups or cans as there were teacups, but this was not always the case. The company's printed price-card lists '12 cups and 12 saucers', followed by '8 coffee cans'.

Some coffee cans and saucers were decorated in a very ornate manner – these were made as cabinet pieces rather than as parts of standard tea and coffee sets. Some of this type are listed below, taken from the factory accounts:

Dowager Lady Ely, Bristol.
1 can & saucer, yellow & gold, views of Port Eliot £1 1s. 0d.
   [February 1797]

279. A superb-quality coffee can and stand with blue ground marbled in gold. The panel is painted by Humphrey Chamberlain (see page 187) with a scene from *King Henry VIII*. Written name mark with 63 Piccadilly address. *c.* 1815. *Dyson Perrins Museum, Worcester*

280. A magnificent Chamberlain coffee can and saucer with dark-green ground. The 'Madonna and Child' panel is by Humphrey Chamberlain (see pages 187–91). In May 1815 '1 can and stand, Madonna &c.,' was invoiced at 10 guineas. Written name mark with 63 Piccadilly address. *c.* 1815. *Dyson Perrins Museum, Worcester*

	£	s.	d.
1 quarter pint can – Othelia, & stand	10	10	0
1 can and stand, Sleeping Musician	10	10	0
[June 1814]			

1 can & stand, Madonna &c. £10 10s. 0d.
[May 1815: the subject is shown in Plate 280]

	£	s.	d.
1 Can & stand, Windsor	1	10	0
1 Can, Love	3	3	0
[July 1819]			

2 F [French make or shape?] cans and stands. Rustic figures
£1 10s. 0d.
[June 1821]

COFFEE JUGS

Chamberlain's printed price-card of the 1820s includes reference to 'Quart coffee jugs', bracketed with break-fast service components – muffin dishes, and butter tubs and stands.

COFFEE POTS

Chamberlain coffee pots are rarely found and are usually of the pre-1810 period. They were not supplied with the standard tea and coffee service.

1 Pint coffee pot, white 2s. 6d.
2 Quart do. at 5s.
        [November 1794]

A shanked gilt coffee pot or coffee jug is shown in Plate 66, and a plain example in Plate 281. 'New fluted' (vertical-fluted) coffee pots were included in the January 1792 stocktaking list, but these were probably of Caughley make. The true coffee pot with its long curved spout shown in Plate 282 is an extremely rare piece and probably dates to about 1805.

CORAL (IMITATION)

In July 1812 there was invoiced to James Taylor of Birmingham (see page 284) '61 dozen and 8 imitation corals. 1s. 3d. a dozen, £3 17s. 1d.'. It is not known if these

---

281. *Above:* A standard-shape Chamberlain coffee pot and cover painted with the inexpensive pattern number 258 (see page 319). Written name mark inside cover. 9¾ in. high. *c.* 1795–1805. *Messrs Sotheby & Co.*

282. *Left:* A rare form of Chamberlain coffee pot painted with a simple (unnumbered) sprig pattern in puce and gold. Written name mark inside cover. 10¼ in. high. *c.* 1805–10. *Geoffrey Godden, chinaman*

were porcelain imitation corals of Chamberlain's own make, but such copies were being advertised in *The Times* in 1813:

BEADS. The finest substitute for coral ever offered for inspection, being fully equal in appearance, hardness and durability of colour, can be had only at Mr. Reilly's, 12, Middle Row, Holborn, 7s. 6d. the necklace, 12s. the set.

In January 1822 there was a further entry in the Chamberlain records relating to ceramic jewellery: 'China necklace and ear drop to match, mounted in gold. £4 14s. 6d.'. The gold mounts were undertaken by G. Walker at a cost of £2 4s. 6d.

CORNUCOPIA

These are exceedingly rare, and very few references to such items exist:

2 cornucopia, celeste & rich [gilding] £8 8s. 0d.
[October 1841]

1 Large cornucopia, garter blue and raised gold &c. £8 8s. 0d.
[September 1842]

2 Small cornucopia, shells &c at 5s. 6d.
[August 1844]

COTTAGES   See PASTILLE-BURNERS

CREAM-BOATS OR EWERS

Small low creamers such as referred to below, with a gadrooned edge, were probably Caughley examples at this period. Such an item is illustrated in my *Caughley and Worcester Porcelains, 1775–1800* (1969), Plate 108.

88 Gadroon boats, £2 4s. 0d.
[June 1792 stocklist]

However, the Chamberlains were making small creamers or ewers by 1795, for in the December 1795 stocktaking list it appears that the mould-room contained:

5 dozen small ewers   at 4s. per dozen
8 dozen new fluted do.   at 12s. per dozen

The normal cream-jugs used as part of standard tea services are shown in Plates 72–4, 80, 83, and the later ones in Chapter 4.

CREAM-BOWLS

These, in the following connection, are what would now be called dessert service tureens. The full set has two tureens, with covers and stands, originally used for cream and for sugar.

Creambowls to have new nob of dolphin and handles of shells
[April 1810]

Further mention of dolphin cream-bowls and other models is given under TUREENS.

CRUETS

At the time of the 1798 stocktaking, the glazed-ware room contained: '1 Vinegar stand and cruets, white'. This rare object was seemingly of Chamberlain's make.

CUPS AND SAUCERS

Teacups and saucers of the conventional forms are shown with their matching tewares in the illustrations to Chapters 3, 4 and 5.

In general, teasets made before about 1795 have handle-less teabowls rather than handled cups. Nevertheless this is not an inflexible rule, particularly with rather special costly sets where the buyer might be expected to be willing to pay the higher price for a service with handled teacups. Such a case is shown in Plate 283 where each piece has a finely painted panel depicting a basket of flowers.

More ornate cups still are listed under CABINET CUPS but these, of course, were not part of a tea service.

283.   A fine-quality spiral-fluted teacup and saucer, unnumbered, and perhaps a special order. Diameter of saucer 5¼ in. *c.* 1798. *Godden of Worthing Ltd*

CUSTARD CUPS

The records overleaf show that most custard cups were originally sold with a matching stand – in the continental fashion. Chamberlain custard cups are very rare.

12 custard cups, gold linings, covers and stands, new make.
[November 1803]

		£	s.	d.
3 custard cups, fine shape, scarlet & gold.			1	1	0
6 do. do. oval, handled white & gold.			1	10	0

[December 1806]

1 custard stand, with seven cups, grey and gold, Union
[design]. £3 3s. 0d.
[August 1820]

1 stand, with seven custards, green ground with growing
flowers in panels. £6 6s. 0d.
[September 1825]

DÉJEUNER SETS

These most attractive tea services for two persons were
supplied with a matching tray. The teapot and other
pieces were usually of a smaller size than normal.

Lady Hurd, estimate for Dejeuner, no. 20 pattern.

	£	s.	d.
1 teapot		9	0
1 sugar box		6	0
1 creamer		5	0
1 slop basin		5	0
2 cup and saucers		12	0
Stand for do.	2	2	0

[April 1794]

1 Dejeuney, fawn and gold, views etc.
The stand to have a view of the Oatlands. £6 6s. 0d.
[November 1797]

1 double Dejeune, feathers. £12 12s. 0d.
[December 1813]

A Dejeuney set consisting of a tray, 2 cups and saucers, small
teapot, creamer, sugar basin with one plate. Lady Loftus
pattern. £4 4s. 0d.
[August 1815]

See also TOYS and Plate 374.

DENTISTS' BASINS

The following article was invoiced to the New Bond
Street retail shop in April 1845 but this was probably a
one-off special order: '1 Dentist's basin, Garter blue
border and gold coral, groups of flowers in centre.
£2 2s. 0d.'.

DISHES

Most dishes found today were originally part of dessert
services and a selection of the various standard shapes
are illustrated in this book. Occasionally, however, one
finds unusual shapes with rather special decoration and

these may have been made for ornamental purposes
only, in the same way that richly decorated cabinet
plates were made. Such a dish is illustrated in Plate 284.

A dessert service dish of an unusual shape is
illustrated in Plate 285. Although the pattern (number
1473), 'drab tree pattern with rose color flower in
centre', is not of the finest quality or the most attractive,
it does serve to make the point that these odd dishes,
especially the handled ones, could be used for festive
occasions.

DOG PANS

Only a single entry referring to this unlikely porcelain
object seems to exist in the records: '2 dog pans,
[patterns] 701 and 582, gold edge with the pattern in and
out. £2 0s. 0d.' (September 1816).

DOOR-FURNITURE

In the 1840s, after the amalgamation of Flight, Barr &
Barr with Messrs Chamberlain, the manufacture of
porcelain door-furniture – finger-plates, door-knobs,
etc. – was undertaken (or rather increased, as some
door-handles and similar objects were sold as early as
September 1838), probably to emulate the fine productions of Staffordshire firms such as Copeland &
Garrett. Of this branch of Chamberlain's later trade, R.
W. Binns wrote:

A great demand has arisen both at home and in America for
china door furniture and the facilities offered for mounting,
&c, by contiguity to Birmingham, induced the proprietors to
enter very extensively into the business, and a large
proportion of the hands of the manufactory were engaged
upon it, so that at one time the manufactory may be said to
have been employed in making door furniture alone. This was
a branch of work which we cannot recognize as suited to the
establishment, particularly to so absorbing an extent, and we
are not astonished therefore to learn that after some time a
heavy financial loss ensued.

Although Binns stated that large quantities of such
products were produced, a view borne out by the sales
and order books of the 1840s, they are certainly
extremely scarce today. Examples were included in the
Chamberlain display at the Great Exhibition of 1851,
and earlier references include:

	s.	d.
1 Finger plate, white & gold	12	0
1 door knob & rossettes	6	6
1 key hole escutcheon	3	0

[April 1842]

284. A rare-shape dish with dark-green border, the panel well painted with a 'Land Raike'. Printed name mark with Piccadilly address. 10½ × 9 in. *c*. 1813–16. *Private collection*

285. An unusual form of handled dish from a dessert service of pattern 1473, with gadroon edge. 9¼ × 9 in. *c*. 1830. *Godden of Worthing Ltd*

Examples are on view in the Dyson Perrins Museum at Worcester.

During this period many handles and similar objects were probably mounted in metal and vast quantities were supplied to various Birmingham firms.

DRAINERS

Small saucer-shaped, pierced egg-drainers were apparently made by the Chamberlains as they were included in the August 1802 order for Lord Nelson's breakfast service (see page 110); such specimens have been sold by me. They had handles and were similar to the eighteenth-century Caughley and Worcester egg-drainers.

EGG-CUPS

The superb breakfast service ordered by Lord Nelson in August 1802 included six small egg-cups (without a stand), and these were accompanied by the small, handled, saucer-shaped, pierced drainers such as Robert Chamberlain had stocked when he was selling Caughley porcelain in the late 1780s and early 1790s.

The printed price-card includes three sizes of egg-cup stand, which would hold either three, five or six egg-cups. A three-cup stand is shown in Plate 286, and Lord Nevill's order of June 1813 (see page 101) included egg-stands for three cups. An interesting reference to egg-

286. A gilt Chamberlain stand for three egg-cups. Similar stands were often included in breakfast services; they took various forms and were for differing numbers of egg-cups. Unmarked. 6 in. high. c. 1810–15. Geoffrey Godden, chinaman

cups on a fixed, small, saucer-shape stand occurs listed in May 1821: '2 New egg cups on fixed stands [pattern] 904 16s.'.

The egg-cups themselves came in a low or high form. The low examples in their white state were priced at 4d. each in 1796. A conventional egg-cup is shown in Colour Plate XIV. All antique porcelain egg-cups are rare and highly collectable.

ESSENCE POTS

Some references to these items are included for general information, but I cannot link the descriptions with known objects.

1 collum [column?] essence pot [pattern] 403. £2 2s. 0d.
    [March 1808]
1 stand with 4 essence bottles, roses and heartsease. £4 4s. 0d.
    [February 1814]

EWERS

Although these objects are described as ewers, they were seemingly a form of ornamental vase, probably with a single handle.

2 rich fancy ewers, flowers and gold £3 3s. 0d.
    [August 1821]
A pair new rich ewers, blue ground £10 10s. 0d.
    [March 1825]
1 rich blue & gold ornamental ewer, chased and flowers in panels £5 5s. 0d.
    [January 1826]

EWERS AND BASINS

Ewers and basins in porcelain are rare; most were made in less expensive pottery and the majority of the more utilitarian examples suffered damage and were discarded. The desirable miniature or toy examples (see page 289) are more common than the full-size Chamberlain ones; the following entries probably refer to the former:

1 water ewer and basin, damaged. French sprigs. 18s.
    [June 1796]
1 water ewer and wash bowl all burnished gold except the outside of bason, which is scarlett and gold. £21 0s. 0d.
    [October 1800]
1 elegant rich oval water ewer & bason. £6 6s. 0d.
    [December 1806]
2 ewers and basins, small at 2s. 6d.
    [November 1823]

EXTINGUISHERS OR CANDLE-SNUFFERS

I do not recall having seen Chamberlain candle-snuffers, although Spode and Minton examples are known. They are small in size and of a conical form with a handle at one side.

2 extinguishers, dry blue and 'Bon Soir' 12s.
[October 1821]

2 extinguishers, Worcester, Malvern, wrote in gold 'Bon Soir' £1 1s. 0d.
[November 1821]

5 snuffers on pen trays at 15s.
[October 1822]

1 Tray with two extinguishers, green scroll and flowers 18s.
[December 1838]

EYE BATHS

This example could have been a Caughley blank, rather belatedly sold by the Chamberlains: '1 eye bath, gold edge' (June 1798). I have not seen any early Chamberlain examples, but they may have been made at a date before 1800. However, some were of a later date and can be considered as being of Chamberlain's own make, for the Bond Street sales book includes items such as: '1 eye cup – 2s.' (February 1828).

FIGURES AND GROUPS

The various Chamberlain records include many references to figures and groups, but most of those before about 1810 seem to relate to Derby examples which in many cases were supplied by Thomas Turner at Caughley; some, however, may have been decorated in the Chamberlain studios.

This somewhat confusing subject is discussed on page 55. Certainly some figures were made by the Chamberlains in their hybrid hard-paste body during the 1790s, for, as related on page 60, the 1795 stocktaking list included: '1 Figure Apollo 2s. 6d.' in the biscuit-room, showing that it was in a half-finished state, not yet glazed. This figure was incorporated in watch-stands (see Colour Plate IV and Plate 33) and in pickle-stands (see Plate 32 and page 60), and may also have been sold as a single ornamental figure. At this period in the 1790s the Chamberlains were also making animal and bird models (see Plates 34 and 35 and pages 212–13).

By 1806 the accounts mention figures with a bronze-like finish. These were probably of Chamberlain's own make, as the style was used on other objects; but apparently it was not favoured by the Derby manage-ment. Later there are references to the same models with two styles of decoration:

	£	s.	d.
2 boys, white and gold	3	0	0
2 do. bronze	4	4	0

[October 1813]

In 1817 and 1818 the management of Chamberlain's London shop in Bond Street purchased biscuit figures from the Derby shop, but by this period the Chamberlains were almost certainly producing their own figures, although on a modest scale. It is, however, noteworthy that their competitors in Worcester, Messrs Flight, Barr & Barr and Messrs Grainger, made practically no figures.

Between 1810 and 1825 the French influence was quite strong, and matt white biscuit figures were contrasted with glazed and decorated porcelain – in the manner seen in the Paris-style inkstands illustrated in Plates 307 and 308.

A selection of references relating to Chamberlain's figure models, as gleaned from the factory records, is given below:

	£	s.	d.
2 Figures, biscuit on plinths, blue & gold	2	2	0
2 Figures, biscuit on plinths, ivory & gold	2	2	0
1 biscuit figure and [glass] shade	2	2	0

[1819]

1 Biscuit female figure with lace cap £3 3s. 0d.
[1820]

The last example is an interesting reference to lace-work on figure models (a craft practised at an earlier date on the Continent and at Derby). In October 1821 Chamberlain's paid £14 11s. 8d. to a Mr Arnoux for his 'procedure for making lace in china'.

1 New rich ornamental chair, with biscuit figure (1 glass shade for do. 12s.) £10 10s. 0d.
[This model is illustrated in Plate 167.]

2 Biscuit cupids £1 10s. 0d.

2 small biscuit cupids on blue pedestals £1 0s. 0d.
[see Plate 287]

1 cupid and dog £1 1s. 0d.

1 biscuit figure & shade £2 2s. 0d.
[August 1819]

In January 1820 Chamberlain's very good customers, Loder & Co. of Oxford, requested 'some small biscuit figures same as sold at Woodcocks, 42, Lincolns Inn Fields, at 5s. a shade 2s.', but it is not now known what the origin of these was, or if Chamberlain's copied these presumably small models. The Chamberlain examples were normally more expensive:

1 rich chair cupid £8 8s. 0d.
[May 1821: see Plate 167]

2 small cupids at 10s.
[December 1821: subsequently sold in pairs]

2 biscuit reading figures & shades £4 4s. 0d.
[1821: perhaps the model adapted as an inkstand and shown in Plate 170]

2 reading figures, dry blue, plinths £3 0s. 0d.
[See note above. 'Dry' colours are matt enamels]

	£	s.	d.
1 Candlestick figure	1	1	0
By a set of painted Bull-fighters	3	9	6
[1822]			

	£	s.	d.
1 milk maid [see Plate 290]	2	2	0
1 biscuit do.	1	1	0
[1826]			

In April 1827 the London shop purchased elsewhere a figure of the 'Broom-Girl', as depicted by Madame Vestris (see Plate 291), which cost 7s. 6d. Within two months the shop was selling other examples which were presumably Chamberlain's copies of the original (Derby?) model. New brooms for these figures were supplied at 6d. each.

By August 1827 the Chamberlain shop in Bond Street was selling figures described as 'school boy & girl' at £1 1s. 0d. and £1 5s. 0d. These were probably the models shown, in biscuit, in Plate 288. They are also known in the glazed and decorated state, the boy being titled 'Just Breeched'. Figures of this type are sometimes incised with the name mark 'H Chamberlain & Sons, Worcester'.

Twice in the Bond Street sales book, under the date September 1827, the sale of 'A biscuit poodle and cupid' is recorded at a price of 15s., but it is uncertain if this represents one group or two separate pieces.

In July 1829 the Bond Street staff sold 'A Tyrolese woman' at 8s. This may have been one of the singers discussed on page 142 and illustrated in Plate 172, or it could have been a new model. Models mentioned in the 1830s included:

A cupid and shade 6s.
[February 1831]

1 bust in wax of Queen Victoria, with shade and stand £1 11s. 6d.
[September 1838. This entry serves to remind us that not all the items sold in the New Bond Street retail shop were of Chamberlain's own make, or even of porcelain.]

2 biscuit figures of Brigand Chiefs with glass shades and stands £16 16s. 0d.
[These costly examples were possibly of continental origin, perhaps in coloured biscuit rather than in white.]

287. *Top:* A charming pair of very small unglazed cupids on blue and gilt plinths, of the type invoiced at £1 the pair in August 1819. Written name mark. 2½ in. high. *c.* 1819. *Private collection, on loan to the Dyson Perrins Museum, Worcester*

288. *Above:* A rare pair of marked Chamberlain biscuit figures, probably the school boy and girl mentioned in August 1827. Incised marks 'H Chamberlain & Sons, Worc' and 'Chamberlain's China Works, Worcester'. 6¼ in. high. *c.* 1825–30. *Messrs Phillips*

Later examples include:

2 bisque Queens on black plinths at 4s.
   [October 1844]

3 large bisque groups   at 1s. 6d.
4 less   at   9d.
   [These were probably flower-pieces]
2 light sprigs do.   at 1s.
   [November 1844]

FINGER-CUPS

The Chamberlain accounts include references in 1814 to 'finger cups'. However, these finger-bowls or 'finger cups' may well have been of glass, not Chamberlain's porcelain, sent for sale in the London shop.

FRUIT BASKETS

Many of the finest dessert services included fruit baskets and stands, but these are now very rare (see Plates 88 and 89). An entry of November 1803 shows that these baskets were made in at least three sizes:

	£	s.	d.
4 pint baskets 1st[size] [pattern] 75	6	6	0
1 do. 3rd[size] do.	2	12	6

GARDEN SEATS

The following entry almost certainly represents a one-off special order, but it does show that the Chamberlain management was game to try its hand at almost anything.

Sir Francis Shuckbury.

Three garden seats to represent Bath Stone with crest embossed £4 8s. 6d.
   [December 1843]

A letter dated 5 June 1848 shows that Chamberlain's were still willing and able to make such wares, for it states: 'we can make the garden seats'.

289.   An important Chamberlain glazed, coloured and gilt figure. 8¼ in. high. *c.* 1820–30. *John Broad Esq.*

290.   *Left:* A glazed and coloured Chamberlain figure of a milkmaid, complete with two buckets. At least two versions were made of this model which was invoiced at £2 2s. 0d. in 1826. 7¼ in. high. *c.* 1825–35. *Godden of Worthing Ltd*

291.   *Above:* A small Chamberlain figure of the 'Broom-Girl' (see page 242), made in several sizes. This example lacks the loose non-porcelain brooms. 5½ in. high. *c.* 1827–35. *John Broad Esq.*

GOBLETS

An elegant goblet of this period is shown in Plate 38, and this model might well be the leafage goblets listed at 1 January 1796 (see page 62).

In later Chamberlain records the designation 'tumbler' is used rather than 'goblet' (see page 64).

Pair of Gobletts, views of Worcester at 10s. 6d.
    [November 1794]

1 Dozen of leafage goblets 12s.
    [Christmas 1795 stocklist of items in the mould-room]

'GRACE' MUGS (CUPS)   See MUGS

HONEY POTS

Honey pots were often included in the more expensive breakfast services (see page 222), but they were also sold separately. Specimens are today very rare. The stocklist of December 1793 records: '1 honey pot, cover and stand. Royal Lily 6s.'. Beehive-shaped honey pots were invoiced as early as August 1801 and the idea was probably taken from silver examples.

1 large hive, Etruscan figures, Trafalgar emblems £1 10s. 0d.
    [May 1806]

Bee-hive, rich landscapes £1 5s. 0d.
    [August 1810]

292.   An attractive honey pot in the form of a beehive. Other simpler forms were made, without the relief-moulded bees, and various styles of decoration were added. Painted mark 'Chamberlains Worcester'. 5½ in. high. c. 1805–10. Messrs Phillips

Others were decorated in a simpler style, as witnessed by the relatively modest price of the following example: '2 hives honey-pots at 10s.' (January 1818: see Plate 292).

HOT-WATER PLATES

Some services included a double-walled hot-water plate, the interior of which was filled with hot water to heat the plate, or to help retain existing heat. The relatively high cost of these articles is reflected in the following account:

72 table [dinner] plates, [pattern] 925 at   3s. 6d.
24 water plates   do.   at 10s. 6d.

Here the difference in price is almost entirely due to the relative difficulties of manufacturing these objects.

'HOUSES'

'Houses', or 'toy houses', are mentioned surprisingly early in the Chamberlain records, by May 1791. It is probable that they were the hollow objects normally used for burning scented pastilles in a room, but they were not so designated in the available records before February 1813 – one bill reads: '1 house for Pastiles, bloom ground 14s.'. It would appear that these early 'houses' were not of Chamberlain make, for the following entry appears in the Turner-Chamberlain accounts under the date 25 May 1791: '15 Houses enamelled to pattern £1 2s. 6d.', with a margin note 'Pattern returned'. It is not now known if these pieces were of Caughley or Derby make or perhaps of continental origin, but seemingly they were in their finished state and Chamberlain's were asked to decorate to this pattern-piece.

1 Toy house, enamelled 4s.
    [July 1791]
16 houses, plain white £1 4s. 0d.
    [June 1792]

In December 1793 the stock at the High Street retail shop included in the front showroom:

14 enamelled houses at 3s. and 2 white do. at the same price

Later references are given under PASTILLE-BURNERS.

HYACINTH POTS

I have not traced any Chamberlain examples of these objects, but the general form should be like the well-known glass examples – a slightly tapering cylinder with a bowl at the top to hold the bulb.

2 Hyacinth pots, views all round vermicelli [gilding]
£2 12s. 0d.
   [October 1806]

2 hyacinth pots, Etruscan figures and gold bands £2 2s. 0d.
   [July 1808]

ICE BUTTER TUBS

These were probably butter tubs with a separate container or walled surmount to hold crushed ice for cooling the butter. Such an item is listed in July 1821: '1 Ice butter tub, best white 16s.'.

ICE-CUPS

The Christmas 1795 stocklist included in the mould-room: '2 dozen of ice cup and covers 16s.'. This is probably a reference to small covered cups for ice-cream.

ICE-PAILS

The first reference in the factory records to complete ice-pails decorated with the Dresden flower patterns could well relate to Caughley examples (see Plate 125 of Godden's *Caughley and Worcester Porcelains, 1775–1800*, 1969), but the linked reference to others for decanters is interesting, showing that not all were for fruit and complete with the inner bowl and cover.

2 Ice pails, complete, Dresden flowers
4   do.   for decanters with plated pans
   [April 1792]

At the time of the Christmas 1795 stocktaking, Chamberlain ice-pails were in the biscuit-room, also in the glazed-warehouse. The painting-room included a pair bearing the 'Dragon' pattern, valued at £8 0s. 0d.

The gold-decorated example shown in Plate 293 is one of a marked pair that was sold by Messrs Phillips late in 1980. They are undoubtedly of early Chamberlain manufacture of approximately 1795. They are of an elegant form which I have not previously seen, and the pattern number is 44.

Whilst most ice-pails formed part of the larger more expensive dessert services (see Plates 87 and 91), others were supplied separately:

Sir Christopher Sykes, Heldmere Milton.

1 Pair of Ice Pails to match with his views of Milton and two of Medmere. £9 9s. 0d.
   [January 1795]

1 Pair rich Ice Pails, mosaik blue & gold, pheasant in pannell. £10 10s. 0d.
   [April 1795]

293.   A rare early form of Chamberlain ice-pail decorated in gold and marked 'Chamberlains Worcester. No 44'. 11¼ in. high. *c.* 1795. *Messrs Phillips*

1 Pair ice pails, complete, rich birds and fruit in pannells, with yellow ground, richly gilt £18 18s. 0d.
   [January 1800]

Pair Ice Pails, new vase shape
   [January 1810: perhaps as in Colour Plate XX]

Pair rich blue and gild Dolphin Ice Pails, birds, &c. &c. £31 10s. 0d.
   [July 1815: see Plate 294]

2 Warwick vase shape, ice pails £21 0s. 0d.
   [September 1816]

The basic cost is indicated in the first entry below:

1 Pair Ice Pails, new make [shape], white £2 8s. 0d.

G. Dowdswell, Esq., May Place, Little Malvern Wells.
Pair Ridley ice pails, [pattern] 995, with a view on each. £10 10s. 0d.
Taking view of the House &c and a fine drawing of the same. £3 3s. 0d.
   [November 1822]

The model shown in Plate 295 is the nearest to the massive Roman marble open vase now known as the Warwick vase, recently purchased for £253,000 by the Glasgow Art Gallery and Museum, for display in the

294. *Left:* A superb Chamberlain dolphin-supported ice-pail decorated with rich underglaze-blue ground overlaid with gilt marbling and a panel of George Davis's 'fancy birds' in landscape. 14¾ in. high. *c.* 1800–10. *Photograph: Beauchamp Gallery*

297. *Below:* An apricot-ground Chamberlain ice-pail, richly gilt and part of a service ordered in 1813 by Felix Booth of Russell Street, London, and bearing his arms. Painted name mark. 11¼ in. high. *c.* 1813. *Messrs Sotheby & Co.*

295. *Above:* A rare marked Chamberlain open ice-pail or wine cooler modelled on the famous Warwick vase (see page 247) and embellished with gilding. Printed 'Chamberlain & Co.' mark with New Bond Street and Coventry Street addresses. 9 in. high. *c.* 1840–45. *Dyson Perrins Museum, Worcester*

296. *Right:* A fine Chamberlain covered ice-pail, based on the Warwick vase, with apple-green ground and a painted view of Malvern. Name mark with New Bond Street address. 11½ in. high. *c.* 1816–25. *Messrs Delomosne & Son*

Burrell Gallery, Pollok Park, Glasgow. This model was in production by at least March 1818 when the following was supplied to Lady Portsmouth in Portland Place, London: '2 Warwick Ice Pails with embossed heads, fine grey ground &c. &c. £31 10s. 0d.'. Lady Portsmouth also ordered a pair of grates and two pedestals to accompany the ice-pails at an extra 6 guineas.

However, this design, with the relief-moulded heads around the body, did not permit the conventional ceramic decoration to be added: most examples are of a simplified design – as in Plates 296 and 297 – and usually covers and liners were added so that the vases could be used as ice-pails. (Simple vases of this form were not provided with the bowl-like liner and were sometimes issued without covers as shown in Plate 393.)

2 Ellenborough ice pails complete, chrome green with mixed groups of fruit and raised gold sprays and butterflies. £14 14s. 0d.
[July 1838]

By about 1838 ice-pails seem to have largely gone out of fashion; certainly they were no longer being supplied with dessert or dinner services.

INCENSE POTS

In May 1980 a pair of objects matching the second description below appeared in Sotheby's, still with their wood bases and glass domes. One, now in the Godden Reference Collection, is shown in Plate 298; the other is in Australia. The reference to raised white flowers on objects protected under glass shades suggests that they were purely for ornamental use.

1 Warwick [shape] incense pot, handled with white flowers and glass shade £2 10s. 0d.
[March 1819: the basic Warwick-vase shape is shown in Plates 295–7]

2 Incense pots, dolphins, white raised flowers and glass shade £5 0s. 0d.
[May 1819]

The quality and design of these quite small objects is superb, and the general style of decoration was probably taken from the popular French porcelains. It is, however, possible that they were violet-pots, as a July 1819 description also seems to fit them: '2 Dolphin violets, blue and gold with biscuit flowers £4 4s. 0d.'.

INKSTANDS

Chamberlain inkstands took many forms, from the basic drum shape (see Plates 299 and 300) to the very elaborate later ornamental forms.

298. One of a pair of superbly potted small dolphin-supported incense pots (or possibly violet pots) with raised white flowers, as invoiced at £5 in May 1819, complete with the original glass shade. Painted 'Chamberlain's Regent China Worcester' mark. 4½ in. high. c. 1815–20. *Godden Reference Collection*

1 white & gold, inkstand 12s.
[November 1793]

2 inkstands, Davis's birds &c. £2 2s. 0d.
[December stocktaking at High Street shop]

1 inkstand, white, new make 7s. 6d.
[August 1794]

1 inkstand, blue & gold, mosaic birds in panel £1 11s. 6d.
[January 1799]

1 round ink, best white 3s.
[July 1805]

1 Grecian shape ink, bronze handles, rich white & gold £3 3s. 0d.
[August 1806]

1 oval crane-neck ink, bronze [pattern] 403 £1 10s. 0d.
[November 1806]

1 long ink, with sand box [pattern] 183 £2 2s. 0d.
[December 1806. For basic shape see Plate 107 in *The Illustrated Encyclopaedia of British Pottery and Porcelain*, 1966, 2nd edition 1980.]

299. *Below:* Two small round or drum inks, one on its separate stand, the other bearing a printed view of Worcester. This was the cheapest form of Chamberlain ink and was made over a long period. The floral-painted example bears pattern 582. 1¾ in. high. *c.* 1810–20. *Godden of Worthing Ltd*

300. *Right:* A Chamberlain drum ink decorated with the popular 'thumb and finger' pattern (number 276, see page 319). 2½ in. high. *c.* 1805–15. *Geoffrey Godden, chinaman*

301. *Bottom left:* A rare and unusual 'eagle' inkstand with underglaze-blue ground and a panel showing a 'fancy bird'. 3½ in. high. *c.* 1805–15. *Godden of Worthing Ltd*

302. *Bottom right:* A rare 'eagle' inkwell and cover. This is a slightly different version of the form shown in Plate 301, painted with feathers on a pale pink ground. Painted mark 'Chamberlains Worcester'. 4 in. high. *c.* 1810–15. *Messrs Sotheby & Co.*

1 mermaid tripod ink [pattern] 276 £1 10s. 0d.
  [February 1812: see Plate 305]

1 triangular ink, dolphin top, grey ground with feathers, gold
  beads £3 3s. 0d.
  [February 1813]

1 new French ink, brown figures £2 12s. 6d.
  [October 1813]

1 new long ink, rich fawn and figures £15 15s. 0d.
  [July 1814]

1 ink on three feet and double covers [pattern 240]
  £1 10s. 0d.
  [November 1816]

3 round fine fluted fancy inks, at 12s.
1 oval   do.   18s.
  [September 1817]

1 square F [French shape?] laylock ground and flowers with
  biscuit figure at top £2 12s. 6d.
  [May 1819]

1 cupid ink, ornamental £4 4s. 0d.
  [November 1820]

---

304. A French-style ink in the form of a boy on a dolphin, with
matt colours and slight gilding and probably of Chamberlain's
manufacture. 5½ in. high. c. 1805–15. *Godden of Worthing Ltd*

303. A rare Chamberlain 'Mermaid tripod ink', a form invoiced in
February 1812. This is a quaint but hardly graceful model although
it is painted here with feather subjects. Painted 'Chamberlains
Worcester' mark. 4½ in. high. c. 1810–15. *Dyson Perrins Museum,
Worcester*

305. A very well-painted Chamberlain drum ink made in the
'Regent' body and painted with a scene from *Paradise Lost*, perhaps
by Walter Chamberlain. Painted mark as in Plate 306. 2½ in. high.
c. 1813–16. *Godden Reference Collection*

306.   The underside of the ink illustrated in Plate 305 showing a
typical written name and address mark and also the neatly written
quotation which inspired the design.

307.   A rare and fine-quality Chamberlain ink in the French style
combining matt colours and gilding with a biscuit-porcelain figure.
This figure may have held a garland of flowers as a description of
1821 reads: '1 cupid ink and shade, the one with a wreath of flowers
£4 4s. 0d.'. This distinguishes this model from the similar one shown
in Plate 308. Painted name mark with New Bond Street address.
5½ in. high. c. 1816–25. Geoffrey Godden, chinaman

	£	s.	d.
1 rich ink stand with biscuit figure &c.	4	4	0
1 glass shade to do.		12	0

[March 1821: see Plate 307]

1 long new gadroon ink and stand with sand and waffer pot, complete £3 3s. 0d.
[June 1831]

1 cupid ink and shade, the one with wreath of flowers £4 4s. 0d.
[April 1821: see Plate 307]

	£	s.	d.
1 saucer ink, roses etc.	1	1	0
2 vine inks, green, blue & gold	3	3	0
1 rich cupid ink and shade	4	4	0

[November 1821]

2 small inks and stands at 12s.
[December 1821: see Plate 299]

1 boat ink 15s. (gilt 12s., white 7s.)

1 F. ink with writing figure £1 11s. 6d.
[June 1822]

1 cupid ink, glazed figure £3 3s. 0d.
[August 1822]

1 ornamental square ink, view Malvern, dry blue & gold cupid top £2 12s. 6d.
[January 1823]

2 square inks, writing figure in biscuit £4 4s. 0d.
[February 1823: see Plate 170]

It is interesting to see from one order that matching writing equipment was ordered, for on 24 March 1823 John Yates, the Cheltenham dealer, ordered:

	s.	d.
1 Bosom ink	25	0
1 pen tray	12	0
1 small taper	6	0

Dry blue, with birds.

Also listed were the following:

2 new pen tray inks, roses and chased [gilding] £3 0s. 0d.
[July 1823]

A shoe 3s. 6d.
[January 1833. This entry probably relates to one of the small shoe-shape inkpots, after a French model; in October 1833 the description 'a china slipper' was also used – the cost was 2s. 6d.]

To an inkstand square shape on feet, gold weed and view of Worcester £1 0s. 0d.
[September 1833]

1 ink tray imperial blue and flowers, with cornucopia [shaped] fittings £2 10s. 0d.
[May 1838]

To 2 rich inkstands, model of King John's Tomb in Worcester Cathedral £4 4s. 0d.
[January 1841]

308. *Top:* A similar French-style ink to that shown in Plate 307 but here the biscuit-porcelain cupid is writing in a book. Perhaps this is the 'F. ink with writing figure £1 11s. 6d.' listed in June 1822 (but see also Plate 170). The base is matt blue. Incised name mark with New Bond Street address. 5½ in. high. *c.* 1816–25. *Private collection*

309. *Above:* A good-quality orange-ground three-welled Chamberlain ink. The side-panels are painted with shells and feathers. Written 'Chamberlains Worcester' mark. 7½ in. long. *c.* 1810–20. *Messrs Sotheby & Co.*

The price for white examples was £1 8s. 0d., but some richly decorated specimens were invoiced at £5 5s. 0d. (see Plate 312).

Later, slight amendments were apparently made, as shown by a sales entry dated 25 October 1843:

1 King John tomb, stone colour with covers altered to form a paper weight, £2 2s. 0d.
1 do. richly finished £4 4s. 0d.
    [October 1843]

Other references include:

1 tray [shape] ink, celest & flowers with tulip top £1 15s. 0d.
    [July 1841]
3 shell inks, 1st size £1 11s. 6d.
    [November 1841]
4 handled Dahlias or inks at 5s.
    [March 1842]
4 Ward's Dahlias, green and gold at 6s. 6d.
2   do.   new shape on feet at 7s. 6d.
    [September 1842]
1 Dog ink on cushion £5 5s. 0d.
    [October 1843]
1 Large sporting ink, biscuit blue and flowers.
    [February 1845: see Plate 313]
1 Bulldog ink without the dog. Garnet ground with gold panels of flowers and chequered stripes, the interior plain white and gold £3 3s. 0d.
    [December 1845: see Plate 207]

310. *Below:* An extremely well-painted ink, the view of Worcester featuring the Chamberlain factory in the foreground. Written name mark with New Bond Street address. 5¼ in. long. *c.* 1816–25. *A Morton Esq.*

312. *Opposite above:* A drawing of the 'King John's tomb' inkstand, taken from the factory drawing book. The inkwells are under the lift-off cover. This popular novelty model was issued in several forms (see left). A historical account of the tomb usually appears inside the cover. The written name mark normally includes the addresses of both London shops. *c.* 1840–45. *Worcester Royal Porcelain Co. Ltd*

313. *Opposite below:* A drawing from the factory records of an elaborate inkstand, perhaps the 'Large sporting ink' as listed in February 1845. *Worcester Royal Porcelain Co. Ltd*

311.   A footed table inkstand enriched with porcelain shells and richly gilt. Written name mark. 11 in. long. *c.* 1835–45. *David Newbon Esq.*

INSTANTANEOUS LIGHTS

The Times carried the following advertisement on 27 December 1813 and on 4 January 1814:

NEW INSTANTANEOUS LIGHT MACHINES

The general construction of this machine is so simple that anyone may understand the management in five minutes. Light is produced in an instant, upon any emergency during the night. . . . These machines may be used for several months, and renovated at a very trifling expense.

The Chamberlains were very quick to produce articles made for or adapted to suit the new 'Instantaneous Lights', the machine itself apparently costing 16s. References in the order book include:

2 violet pots for Instantaneous lights [pattern] 240. £3 12s. 0d.
  [February 1814]

1 Instantaneous light fitted up with matches and small bottle of liquid. £1 11s. 6d.
  [July 1814]

1 Pagoda ornament or Instantaneous light. £2 2s. 0d.
  [August 1815]

The Spode shape book includes references to 'Phosphorous Pots' which may be similar to the Chamberlain 'Instantaneous lights'.

JARS AND BEAKERS

Sets of vases were sometimes described in the contemporary accounts as 'Jars and beakers'. Some of the early examples may well have been of Caughley manufacture.

5 jarrs and beakers, French sprigs £1 11s. 6d.
  [March 1792]

	£	s.	d.
5 Jarrs and beakers, D's [Davis's] birds	2	0	0
2 Jarrs and 1 beaker, Wood's figures	1	4	0

  [December 1793 stocklist, front showroom, High Street Shop]

2 Hexagon – 13 inch jars and 2 beakers, no. 240 £21 0s. 0d.
  [December 1804]

2 Hexagon jars, French green ground, solid gilt dolphin handles, plants £8 8s. 0d.
  [November 1811: shape as in Plate 314]

1 13 inch jar, gold dolphin handles, 240 £5 5s. 0d.
  [May 1812: perhaps the form shown in Plate 314]

2 large rich jars, blue & gold with flowers all round £42 0s. 0d.
  [December 1817]

314. One of a pair of Chamberlain covered jars with dark-blue ground and dolphin handles, probably of the type invoiced in November 1811: '2 Hexagon jars . . . solid gilt dolphin handles . . . £8 8s. 0d.'. Written 'Chamberlains Worcester' mark. 13 in. high (but these were made in several different sizes). c. 1810–20. *Messrs Delomosne & Son*

JEWEL TRAYS

The Bond Street sales book includes several references to jewel trays, such as: 'A pierced jewel tray £2 2s. 0d.' (January 1828). Trays like this were also being sold in the 1840s (see ORNAMENTAL TRAYS): '2 Jewel trays on feet, raised flowers at 18s.' (September 1841).

JEWELLERY (see also CORAL)

In the nineteenth century Messrs Chamberlain produced many different types of porcelain jewellery which needed mounting in gilt metal or gold. Typical orders include:

China necklace and ear drops to match mounted in gold £4 14s. 6d.
> [January 1822. The charge for mounting these pieces was £2 4s. 6d.]

a pair bracelets, 12s.
> [August 1833]

3 Brooches, mounted, 15s.
> [September 1841]

2 Celeste and gold hair pins at 4s. 6d.
34 Hair pins, mounted at   4s. 6d.
> [April 1842]

2 Pairs ear rings, Royal blue £2 2s. 0d.

4 Pairs glove bands at 1s. 6d.
> [April 1842]

7 square brooches, mounted at 12s.
3 large slides at 10s. 6d.
> [September 1842]

6 glove studs and bands, large 4s. 6d.
> [September 1842]

2 hair pins, white and flowers at 9s.
2 do.   white only   do.
2 do.   green & flowers   do.
> [November 1842]

2 sizes of square brooches 8s. 6d. and 18s.
2 sizes of crescent shaped do. 7s. 6d. and 8s. 6d.
> [December 1843]

4 Dresden tinted groups for brooches at 10d.
3 single Dresden flowers on blue and black at 1s. 3d.
6 pin heads, wreath of flowers at 6d.
> [October 1844]

24 Brooches apple blossom at 14s. a dozen
24 do.   apple blossom and rose bud at 10s. a dozen
> [December 1844]

There is a possibility that these seemingly relief-modelled floral brooches in biscuit china or Parian were not of Chamberlain's own make. Each month the 'Bought Goods' records included small sums paid to Messrs Samuel Alcock & Co., of Burslem, a likely maker of such brooches.

	£	s.	d.
1 oval brooch, view Worcester	1	1	0
1 new Garter brooch, Worcester		12	6
1 oval do. rich mounting		10	6
[May 1845]			

Other items made by Chamberlain may perhaps be grouped in the category of gentlemen's jewellery: these included studs, cravat pins, and shirt buttons.

315. A small Chamberlain brooch with gilt-metal mount, the panel painted with a view of Malvern. Unmarked. $1\frac{3}{4} \times 1\frac{1}{2}$ in. c. 1840–45. *Godden of Worthing Ltd*

The Chamberlain stand at the 1851 Exhibition included 'China bracelets and brooches', and I have seen some attractively painted porcelain brooches mounted in gold, the porcelain bearing minute views of Worcester and Malvern (see Plate 315).

JUGS

The first two entries of 1790 must refer to Chamberlain's decoration of Caughley blanks:

1 Quart jug, cyphered 'S' with the Free Mason's Arms.
1 Pint mug do. £1 6s. 0d.
> [January 1790]

and possibly the next two which are similar to known examples:

1 Quart jug, blue and gold sprigs, Arms of Earl of Bristol.
1 3 pint do.
> [September 1790]

The early Chamberlain jug forms are shown in Plates 39 and 40.

	£	s.	d.
1 Quart jug, Davis's birds	1	1	0
1 3-Quart jug, Davis's birds	2	0	0
[December 1793 stocklist, front show-room, High Street shop]			

Sayer, Esq., Richmond, Surrey.
2 Quart mugs, new make, J S with arms in front and the crest and cypher each side. To have new borders of ermine drapery or something constant.
> [September 1794]

316. *Below:* A blue and gilt jug, one of two decorated to special order, and painted with a portrait of Mrs Catherine Hawley. The other jug bears a portrait of Colonel Francis Hawley. Painted 'Chamberlains Worcester' mark. 6¾ in. high. *c.* 1795–1800. *Mrs F. M. Hawley Collection, on temporary loan to the Dyson Perrins Museum, Worcester*

317. *Opposite*: A large-size jug of this standard shape, neatly painted with an elaborate version of a standard teaware design – number 21. Written mark 'Chamberlains Worcester' with pattern number. 8½ in. high. *c.* 1795–1800. *Godden of Worthing Ltd*

318. *Opposite below*: Two matching blue-bordered small-size jugs with a different handle form from the two previously shown (see Plates 316 and 317). Unmarked. 5 in. high. *c.* 1797–1805. *Geoffrey Godden, chinaman*

319. *Above left*: An unmarked Chamberlain jug simply decorated with bat-printed designs. The central panel has a view of Cheltenham (as in Plate 344). The figure prints are also seen in Plate 342. 6¼ in. high. *c.* 1805–15. *Godden of Worthing Ltd*

320. *Above right*: A pink-ground Chamberlain jug, the central panel painted with a view of Worcester. Inscribed under the base 'S. Hartley. March 1824'. 7 in. high. 1824. *Private collection*

321. *Left*: The one-pint milk-jug from the service made for Sir James Yeo and ordered in 1815 (see page 117 and Colour Plate XI). This example cost £1 0s. 0d. plus 10s. for painting the crest, etc. Unmarked. 5¼ in. high. *c.* 1815–20. *Godden Reference Collection*

322. A documentary orange and gilt election jug commemorating the election of William Gordon in February 1807. In June and July 1807 'Gordon jugs' were invoiced to different people at £1 1s. 0d. each. The full wording on the jug reads: 'To record the memorable Triumph of Liberty in the Return of Wm. Gordon Esq. 17 Feby. 1807, by a glorious majority of 352'. Gilt mark 'Chamberlains Worcester'. 6¾ in. c. 1807. *Private collection*

The 1794 'new make' shape was probably that illustrated in Plates 98, 99, 316–18 and Colour Plate VII. Jugs of this type were sometimes made in pairs, or even sets of three, in graduating sizes.

		£	s.	d.
1	Pint jug, gold border and sprigs with views		15	0
1	3 pint jug, Rivals [sic] Abbey	1	11	6
1	2 quart jug, dead game	1	11	6

[September 1794]

1 Quart jug, with [painted] figure, Fortitude £1 4s. 0d.
[August 1796]

2 Quart Punch jugs & covers, London and Blackfriars Bridge £4 4s. 0d.
[March 1798: see Plate 99]

1 rich Punch jug & cover with sea-piece &c. £6 6s. 0d.
[October 1800]

1 3-pint jug, coursing and vermicelli [gilding of seaweed type, see Plate 345] £4 4s. 0d.
[November 1806]

Rt. Hon. Earl of Hardwick.
1 three pint jug, hunting piece, rich fawn and gilt £5 5s. 0d.
[September 1813]

1 Quart jug, Worcester, French grey [pattern] 403 £2 12s. 6d.
[July 1815]

323. A salmon-ground jug richly gilt with a fine-quality painting titled 'Breaking Cover'. Written mark 'Chamberlains Worcester. Manufacturers to Their Royal Highnesses the Prince of Wales and Duke of Cumberland' (see page 34, Mark 6). 7¼ in. high. c. 1805–10. *Messrs Sotheby & Co.*

1 three-pint jug, grouse shooting, blue ground gold marbling £7 7s. 0d.
[August 1815]

1 Quart jug, fine painting, Greyhounds running, vide Daniels – Rural sports £3 3s. 0d.
[July 1818]

Of course, most jugs are of a more ordinary nature than these, being decorated with standard designs to match the breakfast services or other tablewares. The printed price-list includes two sizes of jugs – quart and pint size – priced according to the standard design they bore.

The jug shown in Plate 325 is reminiscent in form to the Mason Ironstone examples and its octagonal shape can be dated to the late 1830s or the 1840s. In November 1842 one finds listed:

2 half pint jugs, Octagon, white & gold at 2s.
2   do.   drab and gold   at 2s.

324. A magnificent-quality 'Regent China' large-size jug laid with a lilac ground and with rich raised gold borders. The superbly painted panels are probably by Humphrey Chamberlain. Painted mark 'Chamberlain's Worcester. Regent China and 155 New Bond Street, London'. 9¾ in. high. *c.* 1816–25. *Messrs Sotheby & Co.*

325. A Chamberlain porcelain jug in the style of the well-known Mason's Ironstone examples, perhaps the 'Octagon' jugs of the early 1840s. These were made in various sizes including miniature examples. Painted mark 'Chamberlains Worcester'. 4¼ in. high. *c.* 1835–45. *W. Browne Collection*

KETTLE HANDLES

Amongst the mundane objects supplied to Birmingham firms in the 1840s were hundreds of white kettle handles of various forms; such pieces were, of course, not marked.

Other similar utilitarian objects were fire-iron heads and various knobs.

KINDLE ENGINES OR LAMPS

In March and April 1843 there occur references to the following items:

1 Kindle lamp, green ground & gold 12*s.* 6*d.*
2 Kindle engines 16*s.* 6*d.*

The engine referred to may well be the working parts for the porcelain lamp.

KNIFE AND FORK HANDLES

These porcelain handles are now extremely rare, although they were made by most of the eighteenth-century porcelain factories. Examples do not bear factory marks.

24 dessert knife and fork handles, blue & gold, pheasant in panel at 3*s.* 6*d.*
    [April 1796]
18 knife handles, white & gold, crested £1 16*s.* 0*d.*
    [February 1817]
20 knife and fork handles, embossed white at 2*s.*
    [March 1821]
13 pairs dessert knife handles, gilt
29 pairs table do. embossed, white
    [May 1822: examples sent to Mr Crowley of Birmingham, probably to be mounted]

KNIFE-RESTS

Knife-rests are normally of silver, silver-plate, glass or pottery. In their simplest form they are merely bars or slabs which raise the knife-blade about an inch from the table top.

4 knife rests 6*s.*
    [May 1817]
2 knife resters
    [April 1822]

Later references to 'asparagus knife rests' at 1*s.* 4*d.* each, as invoiced in 1844, most probably relate to porcelain sticks of asparagus, naturally coloured, for use on the table as novelty knife-rests, similar to the half-open pea-pods made by other firms.

LAMPS

Most of the major early nineteenth-century porcelain manufacturers made attractive antique-shape lamps, normally for ornamental purposes rather than for use.

1 Grecian [shape] lamp, [pattern] 240. 18s.
    [June 1808]

In November 1842 there was a reference in the records to a 'Nurse Lamp, blue & coral at 5s. 6d.' – this may have been a type of night-light.

LANTERNS

The following entry probably relates to a one-off special order: '1 Bright painted lantern, Louis Quatoize style £7 17s. 6d.' (March 1842).

LAVENDER BOTTLES

The Christmas 1795 stocktaking list of Chamberlain's retail shop included: '16 large handsome Lavender bottles, average price 10s. 6d. £8 8s. 0d.'. This is about twice the cost of the normal smelling-bottle as listed on page 283 and shown in Plates 366 and 367. These objects must have been very imposing.

At a later period one finds listed 'Lavender water pots':

1 Rich chas'd gold, Lavender pot £1 0s. 0d.
    [June 1820]

2 Lavender water pots, pattern 865 at 12s.
    [November 1821]

LUMINARIES

These objects were probably what are now called spill-vases, but they were apparently also described as (and listed under) 'match pots'.

Pair spill mugs or Luminators 12s.
    [September 1801]

2 Luminators, view Rivolx [sic] Abbey & Matlock
    [October 1802]

2 Luminaries, rich view, new shape, damaged £1 8s. 0d.
    [October 1804]

	£	s.	d.
2 Luminaries, French shape, Queen Elizabeth pattern		2	2	0
2 do. common shape		1	16	0

[September 1805]

2 Luminaries, best white 2s.
    [October 1805]

Pair Luminaries yellow ground, figures in octagon panel 16s.
    [May 1806]

2 large F. [French shape] Luminaries, grey [ground] and shells £3 3s. 0d.
    [February 1815]

1 antique [shape] Luminary, blue and gold with biscuit wreath of flowers £1 5s. 0d.
    [January 1821]

4 large rustic Luminaries and covers, raised flowers & gilt at 35s.
    [November 1841]

MATCH BOXES

The form of the Chamberlain match boxes is not now known. However, the Ridgway shape book does include oblong boxes rather like a Swan Vesta box, under the description 'Lucifer box'.

Matches boxes, pattern 240 and 292
    [July 1803]

2 Match boxes, views of Worcester £2 2s. 0d.
    [July 1807]

At a later date the description 'match cases' was used: '2 match cases, round, 1st size, Biscuit blue raised [gold] panels and figures. £1 5s. 0d.'.

MATCH POTS

The objects which are now called spill-vases were called 'match pots' early in the nineteenth century, a fact shown by the named drawings in the Spode factory shape book (see L. Whiter's *Spode*, 1970, pages 100–7). The Ridgway shape book also describes these items as match pots. It is possible that the objects called 'Luminaries' in the Chamberlain records and listed under that heading were also what are now called match pots.

Typical references from the Chamberlain sales and order books include:

2 match pots, Etruscan figures £1 1s. 0d.
    [August 1810]

2 fine match pots, fancy – jewell'd £3 0s. 0d.
    [January 1818: perhaps as in Colour Plate XXI]

6 match pots, full size views of Oxford £6 6s. 0d.
    [July 1820]

2 F [French shape or make] M.pots best white 4s.
    [May 1822]

	£	s.	d.
Pair 2⅝ inch M.Pots, blue embossed gold and flowers	1	1	0

326. Two finely painted marked Chamberlain match pots, the panels taken from Shakespeare's *King Henry VIII* and *The Merry Wives of Windsor* and so marked with quotations. A perhaps similar pair was invoiced in April 1819: '2 small match pots, Henry and King John £4 4s. 0d.'. Written mark 'Chamberlains Worcester. Manufacturers to Their Royal Highnesses the Prince of Wales and Duke of Cumberland'. 3¼ in. high. *c.* 1815–20. *M. Sainsbury Collection*

327. An unusual marked Chamberlain match pot or spill-vase in the Coalbrookdale manner. Printed Royal Arms mark (see page 35, Mark 11). 5¾ in. high. *c.* 1835–40. *Mrs E. Hutchinson*

Pair 2½ inch M.Pots, marone do. and views	1	10	0
2 M.Pots bell-mouth, blue & birds	1	0	0
[June 1822]			

	£	s.	d.
1 bell-mouth M.Pot, ivory and gold, view	1	1	0
Pair do. dry blue and birds	1	16	0
[October 1822]			

From October 1823 sets of fine tall match pots were being ordered, painted with a blue ground and flowers; for example: 'Two square-foot match pots, gold weed 16s.' (June 1833).

MINIATURE PIECES   See TOYS

MUFFINS

The circular muffin dishes were sometimes included in breakfast services, but today they are very rarely found complete with covers. One example from the Yeo service is included in Colour Plate XI.

2 Muffin plates and covers. Royal Lily, gilt, £1 4s. 0d.
  [July 1795]

MUGS

Some of the earliest references no doubt relate to Chamberlain's decoration on Caughley blanks:

3 half-pint mugs with [figure of] Comedy.
  [January 1791]

1 pint mug, Glaze's map of the world. 10s. 6d.
  [1792 stocklist]

The earliest Chamberlain mugs that I have traced are illustrated in Plate 97 – the handle-joints match tewares such as the teapot shown in Plate 70. The Chamberlain accounts include references to many gilt mugs with initials, as well as rather more ornate examples such as the following:

1 half pint mug with science 2s. 6d.
  [May 1793]

1 pint mug, Davis's birds 10s. 6d.
  [October 1793]

1 pint mug, blue and gold, Trollop's Engagement £1 1s. 0d.
  [November 1796]

1 half-pint mug, yellow ground, view of London Bridge 18s.
1 half-pint mug yellow and bloom, figure of Mistress £1 1s. 0d.
  [May 1798]

3 half-pint mugs, Loyal Bristol volunteers at 9s.
  [October 1798]

328. A marked Chamberlain mug with the popular 'Japan' pattern number 240 in underglaze blue with overglaze red, green and gold. Written marks 'Chamberlains Worcester. 240'. 3¼ in. high. *c.* 1800–5. *W. Seabrooke Collection*

329. An imposing blue-ground mug, the blue overlaid with gold marbling. The vine border and the central game subject are very finely painted. Painted Chamberlain mark 'By appointment to H.R.H. The Prince Regent'. 6¾ in. high. *c.* 1811–15. *Private collection*

1 Quart mug, rich fawn & gold, with figure of Ariadne £3 3s. 0d.
   [June 1799]

1 half-pint mug, Warwick castle 12s.
   [August 1801]

2 half-pint mugs, views of spar [Cheltenham] fancy £1 8s. 0d.
   [May 1804]

10 quarter pint mugs, views of Cheltenham, yellow ground at 4s.

2 half-pint mugs, painted views of Cheltenham at 12s.
   [August 1805. The first item may have borne printed views, but not the more expensive version.]

The low initial cost of the undecorated mugs is witnessed by the selling price of the following:

1 quarter pint mug, white 6d.
1 half-pint   do.   white 1s.
   [August 1806]

Mug, two-handles, with yellow ground and gold border. Caricature arms on one side, Jesus College on the other £1 11s. 6d.
   [December 1809]

4 large mugs [pattern] 403 with dead game and rich gold border inside £29 8s. 0d.
   [ordered for the Prince Regent in July 1811]

330. A detail showing the handle shape of the mug shown full-face in Plate 329.

331.   A large four-pint blue-ground Chamberlain mug with gilt marbling. The panel is finely painted with the popular dead game subjects of the period. 7¾ in. high. *c.* 1805–10. *Private collection*

332.   A fine large-size mug, the figure-subject panel signed by Humphrey Chamberlain, and similar to the Lord Nevill examples shown in Plates 106 and 227. Written name mark. 7 in. high. *c.* 1813–15. *Private collection*

Two quart mugs, fox hunting, marbled ground. Breaking
  cover and the death £7 7s. 0d.
    [August 1812]

2 mugs at 20 guineas – Triumph of Ariadne and marriage of
  Bacchus with Satyres and attendants
    [August 1812]

2 Grace mugs, Power of Love and no. 2. £42 0s. 0d.
    [June 1813. These were part of a special order for Lord
    Neville with His Lordship's armorial bearings etc. on the
    sides; see page 101 and Plates 106 and 227, and Plate 105
    for the arms.]

'Grace' or 'Toast' mugs were large examples, having a capacity of over four pints. Dr Johnson defined a 'Grace' cup as 'The cup or health drank after grace'. The large capacity is explained in James Woodford's famous *Diary of a Country Parson* under the date 25 December 1770:

We had a grace cup before the second course. . . . Mr. Adams drank to me out of it, wishing me a Merry Xmas. I then took it of him and drank wishing him the same and then it went round three standing up all the time. . . .

	£	s.	d.
1 rich two-quart mug, hunting subjects with crests and top border inside	18	18	0
Two quart mug, coursing and pheasant shooting	8	8	0
6 large Toast mugs, blue and white with Cocks, etc.	3	0	0

    [December 1821]

The normal one-handled mugs were produced right up to the end of the Chamberlain period; many were painted with local views, for example: '1 half pint mug, view Worcester, 18s.' (September 1842: see Plate 202).

OIL AND VINEGAR STANDS

At the time of the Christmas 1795 stocktaking list, the Chamberlain biscuit-ware room contained three un-glazed 'oil and vinegar stands' valued at 3s. 6d. each. These were obviously of Chamberlain's manufacture, but I do not know of any surviving examples.

OPENWORK OR PIERCED WARES

These openwork porcelains are also discussed and illustrated in Chapter 5 (see page 168).

The first two references to such pieces that have been traced appear in the account books in August 1842:

1 pierced jug, £2 12s. 6d. [see Plate 210]
1 openwork bottle, £3 13s. 6d. [see Plates 209 and 213]

ORNAMENTAL TRAYS

Many trays of various types occur listed in the nineteenth-century Chamberlain records. They were mostly of an ornamental type although sometimes the intended use is indicated, such as a 'jewel tray'.

Those of a general nature include:

A tray openwork edge. Imperial blue and gold with flowers £3 13s. 6d.
    [August 1830]

A tray raised flowers and fruit £2 10s. 0d.
    [February 1832]

---

333.   A richly decorated maroon-ground Chamberlain tray painted with a view of Buckingham Palace from the gardens. Painted name mark. 12 × 9 in. c. 1840–45. *Dyson Perrins Museum, Worcester*

1 square tray with view New Houses of Parliament £2 10s. 0d.
    [July 1838]

1 Jewell tray on foot, raised flowers, gilt 18s.
    [July 1841]

Some very richly decorated ornamental trays were made in the 1840s, variously encrusted with relief-moulded shells around the edge. Typical examples are shown in Plates 334 and 335. Sample entries in the account books include:

1 shell tray, view Houses of Parliament £5 5s. 0d.
    [July 1841: see Plate 203]

1 tray, view Houses of Parliament, coloured shells and solid gold edge £5 5s. 0d.
    [May 1843]

Some of these ornately decorated trays were intended to hold cards (visiting-cards?) and the addition of the raised shell-work border added a guinea to the cost.

1 card tray, raised shell & painting of Buckingham Palace in centre. [No price]
1 card tray, raised shells, Bournemouth £5 5s. 0d.
1 do., no shells, Windermere £4 4s. 0d.
    [August 1843]

Other shell-decorated trays were of a less costly nature:

1 shell tray, 10 inch, gold vermicelli and groups [of flowers]
    Raised shells round £2 12s. 6d.
        [January 1842]

Some trays were apparently made purely for show, as decoration. For example: '1 oval cabinet tray, [painted with] fruit £10 10s. 0d.' (February 1842); but others had a named use:

3 small seal trays, various with gold gadroon edges at 10s. 6d.
        [August 1843]

3 card trays, Dresden style with a wreath of raised flowers, &c &c pierced, at £2 12s. 6d.
        [November 1845]

ORNAMENTS

The description 'ornaments' was generally used in the Chamberlain records for those flat-backed, half-circular pots which are normally called bulb or bough pots. These were very popular articles made by most por-

celain manufacturers and by many potters. Bulb pots were being made at the Sèvres factory by at least 1756, and examples occur in Chelsea and in Dr Wall period Worcester porcelain.

Josiah Wedgwood, as might be expected, took great trouble over his examples. In a 1772 letter to his partner, Thomas Bentley, Wedgwood noted:

I have had a visit from Mr. & Mrs. Southwell, they like our new flower and bough pots, ... We fixed our general principles, and then examin'd every flowerpot we had by those principles, & we found all those which we had hitherto made, & which have not sold, to be very deficient in some of these first principles. I have now much clearer ideas of bow-pots &c. than before, and believe I can now make them to please your customers.

This morning I have had an opportunity of consulting with Lady Gower & Lady Teignham, & their two Lords, upon the subject of Bough pots, & find they prefer those things with the

334.   A Chamberlain card tray of the same shape as that shown in Plate 333 but here embellished with shells and painted with a view of Bournemouth. This is perhaps the '1 card tray, raised shell, Bournemouth' invoiced in August 1843 at £5 5s. 0d. Painted name mark. 13¼ in. long. c. 1843. Messrs Sotheby & Co.

335.   A similar shell-encrusted Chamberlain card tray of the type painted with various well-known resorts and places of interest – in this case the suspension bridge over the Avon Gorge at Bristol. Painted name mark. 13¼ in. long. *c.* 1840–45. *Messrs Phillips, New York*

spouts, much as the old Delph ones, they say that sort keep the flowers distinct & clear. Vases are furniture for a chimney piece. Bough-pots for a hearth, under a slab or marble table. I think they can never be used one instead of another; & I apprehend one reason why we have not made our dressing flower-pots to please has been by adapting them to chimney-pieces.

[29 July 1772]

However, by the 1790s these decorative ornaments seem to have been used on the mantle or on the tops of side tables. Christie's in April 1810 were selling (probably new) examples in sets of three: 'A set of three semi-circular vessels for bulbous roots, English manufacture, £2 6s. 0d.', although most examples were sold in matching pairs.

Representative entries gleaned from the Chamberlain accounts are quoted below and the typical shapes and decorative styles are illustrated in Plates 336–45.

3 rich ornaments and covers, figures &c. yellow ground £3 13s. 6d.
[July 1798]

1 Flat ornament, rich blue & gold, with Gooder's view of Worcester £2 12s. 6d.
[September 1798]

2 Flat ornaments, with new covers. The bust of Pope on one and Cornelia on ye other.
[August 1799]

2 ornaments, 1st [size] oval, handled, Beauty & Sarvius, gilt handle

2   do.   Flat, clipping the wings of Love & Orpheus
[May 1800: subject as in Plate 339]

2 half-circle pillar ornaments, white £1 10s. 0d.
[November 1801]

1 ½ circle pillar-ornament large, three views of Cheltenham
[1802: see Plate 344]

1 large pillar ornament, yellow and gold, pine top. Central view of Worcester from Henwick. Small side views of Kenilworth – Warwick, Bosham Abbey, Sussex. The names of the views to be put under the bottom of the ornament. £4 7s. 0d.
[June 1803. The description 'pillar ornament . . . pine top' would seem to fit those shapes shown in Plates 342–5.]

337. A rare early
form of Chamberlain
bough pot with typical
pierced cover.
Decorated with the
'Rich Queen's' pattern
(see also Plates 85 and
222). $7\frac{1}{2}$ in. high.
c. 1798–1805. *Godden
of Worthing Ltd*

336. A very rare early Chamberlain bough pot or bulb pot with the
typical flat back to fit on a mantel but with an unusual recessed
pierced top. It is painted with the typical 'fancy bird' in landscape
design on a pale salmon ground with gilt borders, etc. Written mark
in gold 'Chamberlains Worcester'. $5\frac{1}{2}$ in. high. *c.* 1795–1800. *Victoria
& Albert Museum (Crown Copyright)*

338. A flat-backed bough pot decorated in a typical Chamberlain
style with orange ground. (For details of the figure subject see Plates
219 and 220.) However, a marked Chamberlain example of this form
has yet to be found and its origin is therefore open to some doubt.
$8\frac{1}{2}$ in. long. *c.* 1800–5. *Messrs Christie, Manson & Woods*

339. *Above left*: A rare form of Chamberlain flat-backed bough pot decorated in a typical style. The panel is titled 'Orpheus & Eurydice': in December 1800 the Chamberlain records listed '1 do. [ornament] figures – Orpheus & Eurydice, ½ circular shape'. At this period other bough pots were described 'with pillars', but the same basic form also occurs on rare occasions without the pillars. Gilt written mark 'Chamberlains Worcester'. 8½ in. high. *c*. 1800. *Victoria & Albert Museum (Crown Copyright)*

340. *Above right*: A typical Chamberlain orange- and gold-ground bough or bulb pot, the large panel painted with 'Venus attired by the Graces', probably by John Wood. This example never had the feet that are found on slightly later examples. Title and mark 'Chamberlains Worcester' in gold under the base. 8 in. long, 7¼ in. high. *c*. 1795–1800. *Geoffrey Godden, chinaman*

---

1 large half-circle pillar ornament, View of Cheltenham, small views of Cheltenham on each side [see Plates 344 and 345]

3 new claw-foot ornaments, drab and gold with view of Oxford £7 7s. 0d.
    [January 1818: see Plate 345 for possible shape]

PAINT-STANDS

The paint-stands referred to on page 271 may well have been of Caughley make – certainly in 1789 Chamberlain received from Thomas Turner '24 paint stands white to pattern' at 3*d*. each. The Caughley factory site yielded several wasters of flat oblong slabs, usually with three circular depressions and a long trough, some of which are shown in my book *Coalport and Coalbrookdale Porcelains* (1970), Plate 81, and these were presumably paint-stands.

341. A colourful Chamberlain covered bough pot on three bun-feet, decorated with the popular 'Japan' pattern number 240. Written name mark 'Chamberlains Worcester 240'. 7½ in. high. *c*. 1800–10. *Messrs W. W. Warner*

342. *Opposite*: A rare matching set of bough pot with two spill-vases. These were probably the ones invoiced in August 1805: '1 half-circle small 31*s*. 6*d*. 2 match boxes 10*s*. 6*d*. Brown figures red [ground] and gold stars'. The figure motifs are printed and may also occur on other objects such as the jugs shown in Plate 319. This bulb pot with pillars is a standard shape and a variation of that shown in Plate 340. 8 in. high. *c*. 1800–10. *Private collection*

343.   A rare set of Chamberlain ornaments for a mantel. The bough pot is of a standard shape, and the red and gold design is pattern 211. Written mark 'Chamberlains Worcester, 211'. 8 in. and 8½ in. high. *c.* 1800–10. *Messrs Christie, Manson & Woods*

344.   A standard-shaped Chamberlain bough pot with bat-printed views, the central one titled 'Cheltenham Spa'. In August 1805 a 'Large half circle pillar ornament, view of Cheltenham, small views of Cheltenham on each side' was listed. Written name mark. 8 in. high. *c.* 1805. *Messrs Christie, Manson & Woods*

345.   A variation of the standard-shaped Chamberlain bough pot with bat-printed views of Worcester, Cheltenham and Malvern set on a gilt seaweed-type ground. This is perhaps one of the 'new claw-foot ornaments' as invoiced in January 1818. 8 in. high. *c.* 1818–20. *Geoffrey Godden, chinaman*

Sold William Higgin, Gloucester.

			s.	d.
1 paint stand,	1st [size] white			9
1	do.	2nd	1	0
1	do.	3rd	1	3
1	do.	4th	1	4

[October 1793]

PAPERWEIGHTS

In May 1824 '2 Lion paper presses, pink & gold at 6s.' were listed. The heavy-based object illustrated in Plate 346 answers this description.

The following items were most probably of porcelain, the description 'marble' referring to the form of decoration, rather than the material: '2 Paper weights, marble and white top at 3s. 6d.' (June 1842).

PASTE-POTS

These were probably the low circular covered pots of the type shown in Plate 347.

2 Almond paste pots, blue and gold with flowers £3 0s. 0d. [January 1818]

	£	s.	d.
Almond paste pots, 2 each, roses		10	0
dry blue,	1	0	0
pattern 865	2	6	0

[September 1822]

PASTILLE-BURNERS

These necessary and decorative objects took many forms and examples were made by most manufacturers of the period. The Chamberlain records include the following:

1 Mermaid tripod pastile pot [painted] feathers £2 2s. 0d. [December 1813: perhaps similar to Plate 303]

1 Dolphin pastile, feathers £2 2s. 0d. [August 1815: see Plate 348]

1 Pastile burner, biscuit cover £3 3s. 0d. [September 1819]

1 conical pastile, rich blue and birds £1 11s. 6d. [April 1821]

			£	s.	d.
1 conical pastile ornamental, blue and birds			1	5	0
1	do.	flowers, black ground	1	5	0
1	do.	rich India pattern	1	1	0
1	do.	dead-blue and birds with embossed gold	1	11	6

346. *Top:* A marked Chamberlain lion ornament, perhaps one of the 'lion paper-presses, pink and gold' invoiced at 6s. in May 1824. Written name mark. 4¼ in. long. *c.* 1824. *Godden of Worthing Ltd*

347. *Above:* A marked Chamberlain covered box, perhaps one of the 'Almond paste pots' as invoiced in the 1818–22 period. Printed Royal Arms mark (see page 35, Mark 11). Diameter 5 in. *c.* 1820–30. *A. Mitchell Collection*

1	do.	French sprigs	12 0

[November 1821]

1 Pastile pot, white 5s.
2 conical pastiles biscuit flowers round and shades £4 4s. 0d. [June 1822]

A standard-shape conical pastille-burner is illustrated in the Allen Collection catalogue, Plate 68, and another is shown here in Plate 349.

PASTILLE-BURNERS – COTTAGES AND HOUSES

The early Chamberlain records, from July 1791, contain puzzling references to 'houses' (q.v.) or 'toy houses',

348.   A marked Chamberlain pastille-burner, perhaps the 'Dolphin pastile, feathers £2 2s. 0d.' as invoiced in August 1815. Written name mark. 7¼ in. high. c. 1815. *Messrs Sotheby & Co.*

349.   A standard-shape light blue-ground 'conical pastile' as listed in the early 1820s. However, other factories also produced similar shapes. 4¾ in. high. c. 1820–25. *Geoffrey Godden, chinaman*

but it is not until 1813 that the use of the word pastille confirms the purpose of these objects – to contain a smouldering pastille to scent a room.

1 house for pastiles, bloom ground 14s.
    [February 1813]

2 Pastile houses, bloom £1 1s. 0d.
    [September 1814]

2 Eware pastile houses at 2s. 6d.
A box of Richardson pastiles 7½d.
another kind at 2s. 6d.
    [The reference to earthenware examples is strange but some occur very similar to that shown in Plate 352.]

1 pastile house 12s.
1 box, French pastiles 5s.
    [October 1815]

1 pastile cottage 6s.
    [April 1817]

3 cottages, white and gold, Thatched covers 10s. 6d.
    [February 1820]

A 'Swiss Cottage' was sold from the Bond Street shop in October 1829 for £1 11s. 6d. and it must have been a very large or richly decorated item judging by the high price – other 'cottages' were being sold at 8s. at the same period. It would appear that these cottages were also sold purely on their decorative merits: 'A Swiss Cottage and shade, £1 16s. 0d.' (March 1830).

PATCH BOXES

These were probably small circular boxes, but few have been identified as Chamberlain examples with certainty.

3 Patch boxes, pattern 120, cyphered. £1 2s. 6d.
    [April 1804]

1 small patch box, view of Worcester. 5s.
    [July 1805]

Plate 354 illustrates a small covered box which recently appeared in Messrs Phillips's London auction

350. *Left:* A finely modelled biscuit-porcelain 'cottage' or 'pastile house'. Incised mark 'Chamberlain's Royal Porcelain Works'. 4½ in. high. *c.* 1815–20. *H. A. Snell Collection*

351. A decorative marked Chamberlain cottage pastille burner on a green base with gilt embellishments (see also Plate 169). Written name mark. 5¾ in. high. *c.* 1815–25. *Messrs Sotheby & Co.*

352. *Left:* A simple Chamberlain 'pastile cottage' of the type invoiced at 6*s* in 1817 (earthenware examples were only 2*s.* 6*d.*). These, like other cottages, were decorated in various styles. Written name mark. 3½ in. high. *c.* 1815–25. *Messrs Sotheby & Co.*

353. *Below:* A rare form of Chamberlain cottage or bungalow decorated with printed motifs. Printed name mark with New Bond Street address. 7¾ in. long. *c.* 1820–30. *Private collection*

rooms. Although unmarked, its Chamberlain origin is in little doubt. The darker portions are in underglaze blue with added gilding, and the title of the figure-subject top, 'Venus & Adonis', is inscribed in gold amid the gilt design on the underside of the cover. In general style this very rare example is similar to the early scent- or smelling-bottles shown in Plates 366 and 367.

PEDESTALS

The Bond Street cash book under the date 14 June 1827 lists the sale of 'A Pedestal with biscuit flowers on top, 25*s.*'.

354. A rare and early Chamberlain patch-box and cover decorated in underglaze blue and with intricate gilding. The cover is painted with 'Venus & Adonis' subject (named inside). Unmarked. Diameter 1¾ in., 1 in. high. *c.* 1800. *Geoffrey Godden, chinaman*

	£	s.	d.
12 large pedestals, embossed, white	3	0	0
8 small do. do.	1	0	0

[June 1792 stocktaking: see Plate 36 and page 64]

PEN TRAYS

These narrow trays need no description, but Chamberlain examples seem to be very rare.

1 Pentray, marbled ground, rich gold handles, £1 5s. 0d.
[September 1805]

1 Pentray, Etruscan figures outside, rich marble work inside, £1 10s. 0d.
[May 1806]

1 Pentray on feet, Dresden flowers, £2 2s. 0d.
[November 1811]

1 Pentray, grey ground, feathers and gold bead, £2 2s. 0d.
[February 1813]

1 Shell and canoe [shape] pentray, £1 16s. 6d.
[February 1821]

The Chamberlain factory apparently copied at least one Derby model, for the Bond Street cash book includes the entry, 'By a pen tray from Derby warehouse for Worcester 21s.' (May 1828).

4 pen rests, raised flowers at 3s. 6d.
[December 1841]

1 Pentray, fly handle 12s.
[July 1824]

PICKLE-STANDS

On the evidence of the Chamberlain records and one surviving example, these items were the ornate shell-supported centrepieces which were made by most of the English porcelain manufacturers of the 1760–80 period. The Chamberlain references given below are later in date than any others known for these objects.

1 Pickle stand, Apollo, glazed 10s. 6d.
[Christmas 1795 stock, 'burnt ware' room]

Michael Loveley, Honiton, Devon.
1 Rich 4-shell pickle stand with figure of Apollo £3 3s. 0d.
[November 1798]

1 Pickle stand, Apollo, white
[December 1798 stock, 'glaze ware' room: see Plate 32 and page 60]

PIERCED, OPENWORK OR HONEYCOMB CHINA

See plates 209–14 and page 168.

355. A blue and gold advertisement plaque with a typically ornamental moulded frame. 12 × 10 in. *c.* 1840–45. *Dyson Perrins Museum, Worcester*

PIN TRAYS

Some small trays, intended for pins, were presumably made for a lady's dressing table.

1 eight-inch pin tray, white 7s. 6d.
[December 1825]

	£	s.	d.
Pair four-inch Ladies pin trays with fruit and flowers		14	0
Pair nine inch do.	1	10	0

[January 1826]

1 pin tray, view of Windsor 14s.
[February 1839]

PIPE HEADS

It is not clear what the form or purpose of these porcelain pipe heads was. Were they the bowls of

tobacco pipes? Probably not, as they were too costly. The 1825 example in particular might be the ornamental head of a water drain pipe on the outside of a building.

2 Pipe heads 4s. each
[March 1822]

A pipe head, figures &c. to pattern £2 10s. 0d.
[December 1825]

A pipe bowl, to pattern 3s. 6d.
[November 1831]

PLAQUES, 'TABLETS' OR 'SLABS'

Early plaques would almost certainly have been plain slabs richly painted in the manner of an oil painting.

356.   A decorative Chamberlain plaque. The moulded and gilt porcelain frame design is similar to that on the advertisement plaque in Plate 355. The hand-painted view of Malvern is in the manner of Doe (see page 196). 'Chamberlains Worcester' mark. $8\frac{1}{4} \times 7$ in. *c.* 1840–45. *Cheltenham Museum & Art Gallery*

	s.	d.
3 pictures, china, views of Worcester	18	0
3 tablets do.	9	0

[Christmas 1795 stock in painting-room]

Some fine plaques, or 'slabs' as they were termed, were produced in the 1840s and these would have been painted by the leading artists.

1 Large slab, rich subject of flowers on dark ground £10 10s. 0d.
    [July 1841]

2 Portfolios white slabs of rich views Doe's at £6 6s. 0d.
    [July 1842: see page 196 for the painter named Doe]

1 Slab 7 inches long and 5 wide painted fruit £1 15s. 0d.
    [December 1842]

	£	s.	d.
1 china slab, fine painted flowers & imitation oak frame	18	7	6
1 small china slab painting Miser, in red morocco cover	6	6	0
1 Blotting book and china slab painting of Windsor Castle, in purple morocco & gilt	6	6	0
1 do. antique frame and painting of the Queen, red morocco			

[Some of these porcelain plaques were sold ready mounted in blotting cases (q.v.)]

| 1 china slab celeste and raised gold, panel with painting Buckingham Palace in centre | 3 | 13 | 6 |

[August 1843]

The example shown in Plate 356 is much later in period and has a gilt porcelain frame. It may have been exhibited in the 1851 Exhibition, as Chamberlain & Co.'s stand included:

Slabs and frames with paintings.
Portfolio china slabs, with view of Malvern and scene from Twelfth Night.

A similar, but not identical, moulded porcelain frame is seen on an advertisement slab (see Plate 355) which can be dated to the early 1840s by the inclusion of both London retail addresses.

		£	s.	d.
1 Round slab, view Washington		2	12	0
2 Round do. American Rustic scenery, larger size painting	at	1	5	0
2 slabs 10¼ ins, view of America	at	1	3	0
2 do. 12 ins, views of America	at	1	3	0
[December 1845]				

Payment for two flower-painted 'slabs' at 15 guineas each, and two painted with fruit, were made in July 1845 – but these do not seem to have been of Chamberlain make. Similar examples were made at the Grainger factory:

PLATES

Whilst most plates found today were originally part of dessert or dinner services and are therefore of standard designs, some were very richly decorated purely for ornamental purposes – as cabinet plates.

In the main these decorative plates were made in the nineteenth century and some of the relevant factory records are quoted below. The reference 'Table plate' refers to the larger plates with a 10 in. diameter, rather than the smaller plates of dessert size.

1 Table plate, Venus attired by the Graces, the figure with red hair, to be painted with much darker hair than any of the others
 [January 1810]   [unpriced order]

2 rich plates, figures & frames £68 5s. 0d.
 [December 1813]

1 Plate Madonna & child £42 0s. 0d.
 [June 1814: see Plate 235]

1 Plate with painting of Cribb £21 0s. 0d.
 [January 1816: see page 188]

	£	s.	d.
18 rich dessert plates, fine paintings in fruit &c. at £3 [see Plate 357 and Colour Plate XVIII]	54	0	0
1 Dessert plate, from Richard 2nd [1820]	10	0	0
1 Table plate, Madrass [see Plate 358]	4	4	0

		£	s.	d.
1 do.	Lord Boyne [1821]	2	10	0

A plate, a fine painting from Henry 8th & frame £31 10s. 0d.
 [October 1823]

These very expensive examples would have been painted by the best artists, and the references to frames may suggest that such pieces were intended as wall decoration. In contrast to these masterpieces, it should be noted that the richer types of the more ordinary standard plates were quite inexpensive; for example:

48 Table plates, fine blue ground and Davis's flowers at 14s.
 [March 1824]

18 Plates, fawn pattern 403 with fine views at £1 1s. 0d.
 [February 1818]

Richly decorated plates were being produced into the 1840s:

1 Plate blue border and compartment of flowers and imitation of pearls to plate £5 5s. 0d.
 [December 1842]

1 Dessert plate, celeste ground, Fancy gilding with group of fruit & flowers 11s.
 [May 1843]

357. A magnificent Chamberlain 'Regent China' plate with gadroon edge almost certainly painted by Thomas Baxter (see pages 184–6). Eighteen such plates were invoiced in 1820 (see also Colour Plate XVIII). Painted 'Regent China' name mark with New Bond Street address. Diameter 9 in. c. 1820. *Dyson Perrins Museum, Worcester*

358.	A superbly painted yellow-bordered gadroon-edged Chamberlain 'Regent China' plate painted with a view of the Government House and Council Chamber at Madras, India. This is perhaps the 'Table plate, Madrass' invoiced at £4 4s. 0d. in 1821. Written 'Regent China' mark with New Bond Street address. Diameter 9½ in. c. 1820. *Dyson Perrins Museum, Worcester*

359. A simple green and gold Chamberlain plate with relief-moulded edge. This is a plate from a service, rather than a purely decorative display item, as illustrated in Plates 357 and 358. Written name mark. Diameter 8½ in. *c.* 1810–20. *Miss L. Steele Collection*

6 rich plates, 4 at £2 12s. 6d., 2 at £1 10s. 0d.
2 do. Prize cattle at £3 3s. 0d.
1 Dessert Plate, Garter blue band, richly gilt and painted Watteau [figure] centre 15s.
1 do. Sèvres style, Celeste & gold band, painted flowers in embossed gold panel £1 10s. 0d.
　[August 1843]

See also TEA PLATES.

POMATUM POTS

Pomatum pots, as drawn and described in the Spode shape book, are cylindrical covered pots with a simple turned knob; they were also called 'toilet pots'.

The Chamberlain examples often have a coloured ground and panels of flowers or other painted motifs, and are sometimes marked inside the cover.

				s.	d.
7 pomatum pots	1st [size]	white	at		6
6	do.	2nd	at		9
12	do.	3rd	at	1	0

　[1792 stocklist]
1 Pomatum pot and cover, gold stars and blue dots, birds eye border 9s. 6d.
　[October 1793]

Pair pomatum pots 1st [size] birds and landscape 12s.
　[November 1793]
Pair pomatum pots with figures 12s.
　[March 1794]

POT-POURRI JARS OR VASES

Pot-pourri bowls, jars or vases normally had a pierced outer cover and a solid inner cover to retain the aroma when it was not being used to scent a room. These decorative items took many forms and were made in various sizes.

			£	s.	d.
1 Popery [sic] jar,	figures		15	15	0
1 do.	flowers		10	10	0
1 do.	landscape		10	10	0

　[June 1813]
3 Poperrea pots, rich painting, flowers, feathers and landscape £31 10s. 0d.
　[October 1813]
1 rich Ellenborough [shape] poterra vase, maroon and gold with views, Hope End, Eastern and Great and Little Malvern £14 14s. 0d.
　[October 1821]
2 large hexagon poperie jars, white £2 0s. 0d.
　[January 1826]
2 Pot pourri jars and covers and stands, Imperial blue ground, ormolu & gold subjects one side & flowers the other £16 16s. 0d.
　[August 1843]

PUNCH-BOWLS　See BOWLS

RING STANDS

Although the stand referred to below had only one panel, other examples were decorated with two.

1 Ring stand, one panel and flowers matt blue 4s. 6d.
　[March 1842]

ROLL TRAYS

The printed price-card includes references to both roll trays and roll baskets decorated to standard designs, presumably as part of large breakfast services. Certainly the Prince Regent's order in 1816 included '4 roll baskets richly painted' at 7 guineas each.

2 roll trays [pattern] 880. £1 0s. 0d.
　[July 1820]

ROOT POTS

The objects described in the original Chamberlain records as 'root pots' were probably what are now called jardinières or cache pots. The general shape is similar to that of a garden flower-pot and most examples had separate stands to retain the surplus water draining from the pot.

1 pair rich, Queen's [pattern] root pots and stands £4 4s. 0d. [August 1798]

---

360. A decorative Chamberlain root pot, jardinière or cache pot decorated with the colourful 'Japan' pattern number 240. Most other factories of the period made similar bucket-shaped jardinières. Written name mark with pattern number. 5¼ in. high. c. 1800–10. *Photograph: Beauchamp Galleries*

361. A fine set of orange and gold Chamberlain ornaments comprising a covered jardinière or root pot (made in four pieces) and a pair of tumblers with two-piece pierced covers and with stands. The figure panels depict 'The Triumph of Mercy' (centre); 'Cornelia Mother of Gracchi' (left); and 'Orpheus & Eurydice' (right). Written marks 'Chamberlains Worcester'. c. 1800–10. *Victoria & Albert Museum (Crown Copyright)*

1 pair root-pots, brown and gold with flowers £2 2s. 0d.
  [May 1800]

	£	s.	d.
2 root pots and stands, 2nd size, basket of flowers	4	4	0
3 root pots and stands, shell and horn of plenty	6	16	6
[August 1805]			

	£	s.	d.
2 root pots, 1st size, broad gold bands, black etruscan figures	2	2	0
1 centre ornament, root pot shape with pierced cover, 276	2	2	0
[May 1806]			

2 root pots and stands, white £1 1s. 0d.
  [November 1807]

1 ornamental root pot, with cover and stand, rich fawn and gold with Orpheus and Euridice £9 9s. 0d.
  [February 1813: see Plate 361]

1 root pot and stand, view Earl Bathurst £1 5s. 0d.
  [April 1817]

Root pots of the simple shape illustrated in Plate 360 were also made at the Coalport factory and by most other porcelain manufacturers of the 1795–1825 period, but the forms shown in Plate 362 and 363 are more often of Coalport manufacture.

ROSE-WATER BOTTLES

Several forms of small bottles were probably used to hold sweet-smelling rose-water, but few entries specifically include this description. In April 1842, however, the following entry appeared: '3 Rose water bottles at 3s. 6d.'.

ROUGE POTS

These little dished-topped rouge pots may have been of Caughley or Coalport manufacture; certainly many wasters of such objects were found on that factory site (see Plate 81 of Godden's *Coalport and Coalbrookdale Porcelains*, 1970).

6 dozen plain white china rouge pots
6 dozen   do.   gold sprigs
3 dozen   do.   Royal stripe
  [October 1797]

39 rouge pots, white & gold sprigs at 1s. 2d.
19   do.   blue & gold, Royal stripe 1s. 8d.
  [February 1798]

362. A decorative Chamberlain root pot or jardinière on a loose base, enamelled and gilded in a typical manner. A similar form was made at Coalport, by Spode and at the Herculaneum factory at Liverpool. 7½ in. high. *c.* 1800–10. *Geoffrey Godden, chinaman*

363. A marked Chamberlain root-pot or jardinière of a form also made at the Spode factory, at Coalport and at the Herculaneum factory at Liverpool. The named view is of 'Hillington House, Middlesex'. 7¼ in. high. *c.* 1805. *Messrs Sotheby & Co*

RUSHLIGHT STANDS

The form that these articles took is not clear. The entries below are for the late 1830s and early 1840s:

3 Rush light burners, different colours, maroon, Imperial blue and green and gilt at 8s. 6d.

3 Rushlight burners £1 2s. 6d.

SALAD DISHES

While usually salad dishes or bowls formed part of all standard dinner services, this example appears to have been a special order: '1 square salad on 4 gold dolphins £5 0s. 0d.' (October 1811).

SALTS

Porcelain salts are extremely rare and I have not seen any Chamberlain examples, although judging from the following entries they were made:

1 pair rich salts and stands with gold linings £4 4s. 0d. [October 1800]

2 pairs salts and stands, white and gold at 16s. [March 1800]

2 double salts, flowers £1 16s. 0d. [May 1819]

4 scollop shells on high rock feet to pattern £6 0s. 0d. [February 1844]

SANDWICH SETS

Sandwich sets consist of four matching segment dishes (see Plate 364), normally with covers, surrounding a central bowl or tureen. These were usually equipped with a handled mahogany tray, and often such sets were sold with matching plates. The complete sandwich set could form a circle or an oval. Today such sets are often incorrectly called breakfast or supper sets.

1 sandwich set with 12 plates [pattern] 124 £7 17s. 6d. [November 1799]

	£	s.	d.
1 centre sandwich, best Queens	3	10	0
4 dishes and covers do.	12	12	0
24 plates do.	17	8	0

[February 1800]

1 Sandwich service, centre covered [pattern] 88 £1 17s. 0d. [July 1800. The oval-footed dish shown in Plate 365 was probably the centrepiece to such a set but it has now lost its cover.]

	£	s.	d.
1 complete sandwich [pattern] 224	10	10	0

364. A Chamberlain segment dish and plate from a sandwich service of pattern 582. Four such covered dishes fitted into an oval mahogany tray. Written name mark. Diameter of plate 7¼ in. c. 1810–15. *Messrs Sotheby & Co.*

365. An oval dish, without its cover, of pattern 258, probably the centre component of a sandwich service. 4½ in. high. c. 1805–10. *Miss S. A. Elliott Collection*

1 mahogany tray with plated handles	1	4	0

[September 1802. The trays were purchased from Richard Dean of Birmingham and Thomas Corbett of Worcester.]

1 complete oval sandwich, with a grate to fit the centre to hold eggs occasionally and a cover. 1 extra dish and cover each shape £4 4s. 0d. [August 1804]

1 tray with partitions £1 12s. 0d. [December 1813]

SCENT-BOTTLES   See SMELLING-BOTTLES

SCENT-POTS

2 scent pots, blue ground and flowers £5 5s. 0d.
  [August 1820]

	s.	d.
2 Dahlia boxes	5	0
6 Dahlias, dry flowers at	6	6
2 do. pink at	5	0
2 do. green at	5	0
8 white Dahlias, raised flowers at	3	6

  [July 1843]

SHELL-SHAPED DISHES

Most eighteenth-century porcelain factories produced small shell-shaped dishes, but it is very rare to find later examples.

2 oyster shells [pattern] 982, no gold 8s.
  [February 1823]

This, in fact, is the only Chamberlain entry regarding these oyster-shaped dishes, although one must remember, however, that all pre-1840 dessert services had some side dishes which could loosely be described as shell-shaped (see Plates 84, 86 and 87).

In November 1842 there was listed: '1 shell on rocks feet, white and gold at £1 5s. 0d.'. At such a price this must have been a large imposing article, perhaps a centrepiece.

SLABS   See PLAQUES

SMELLING-BOTTLES

These are amongst the most attractive of the early Chamberlain porcelains and fortunately they are well covered by the surviving factory records. Typical examples are shown in Plates 366 and 367.

  Smelling-bottles were being made by at least April 1794. The Christmas 1795 stocktaking records list:

Biscuit Room
127 Large smelling bottles, at 8d.

Painting Room
 53 smelling bottles, five blue, at 1s.
    [These would have had the underglaze-blue portions laid on and glazed.]

Shop

	s.	d.
8 smelling bottles, retail price	5	0
28 do. do.	3	6

366.   A Chamberlain smelling-bottle with underglaze-blue border. The centre is painted with a named view of Worcester, and the reverse with a figure-subject panel. It is shown here with the exterior of its original morocco case. Such examples were sold for 2 or 3 guineas. Bottle 4½ in. high. *c.* 1798–1802. *Godden Reference Collection*

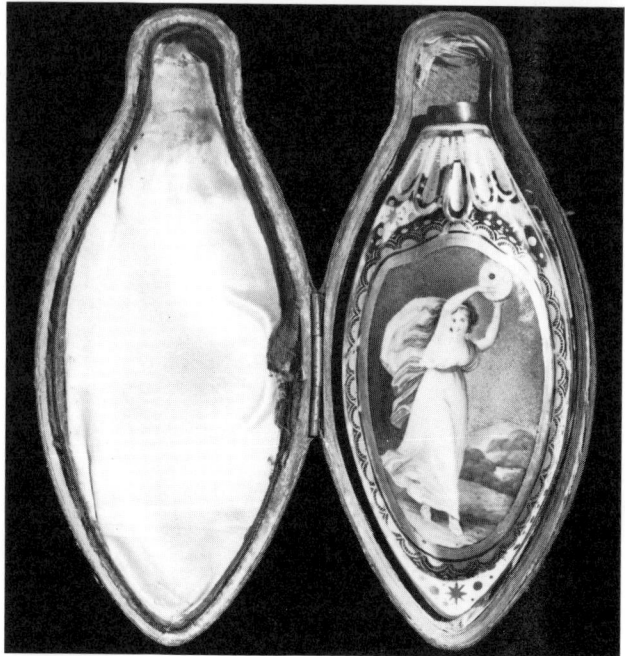

367.   The reverse side of the Chamberlain scent-bottle shown in Plate 366, here seen in its open case. This example has lost the original stopper and gilt-metal cap, which were added in Birmingham. *c.* 1798–1802. *Godden Reference Collection*

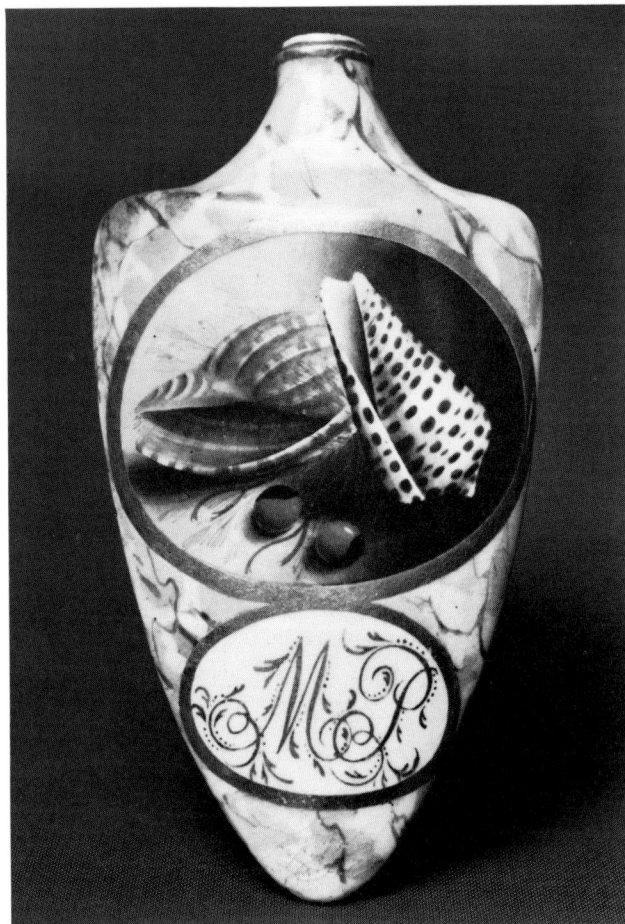

368. A Chamberlain scent-bottle with painted mock-marble ground and painted shell panel. Cyphered to a special individual order. 3½ in. high. *c.* 1810–15. *Dyson Perrins Museum, Worcester*

To the basic glazed porcelain bottle, the glass stoppers and gold or gilt-metal cover or mounts had to be added. For this the bottles were sent to James Taylor & Co. of 35 New Hall Street, Birmingham, or to Isaac Bedford of Birmingham. References in the order book include:

J. Taylor & Co. Birmingham.
Mounting 23 smelling bottles, glass stoppers and gilt mounts £1 16s. 10d. (approximately 1s. 7d. each)
2   do.   gold mounted at 6s.
    [June 1797]

A bill from Isaac Bedford of Birmingham in September 1797 shows that at least two sizes of scent-bottle were then being made:

		s.	d.
Mounting 8 large smelling bottles, screw and gilt cap	at	1	0
Mounting 14 small do.	at		10

Accounts for finished specimens include:

1 smelling bottle, Worcester view 12s.
    [August 1795]

3 rich new make smelling bottles, view of Worcester on one side with the different cyphers C.J.S. and S.S. Gilt metal caps with cork stoppers £2 0s. 0d.
    [October 1795]

4 rich smelling bottles, gold mounted in morocco cases at £2 2s. 0d.
    [May 1800: see Plates 366 and 367]

1 smelling bottle, figure and view 15s.
    [January 1801]

2 large rich smelling bottles, figures &c. gold mounts and morocco cases £3 3s. 0d.
    [June 1801]

Chamberlain's retail shop also stocked glass smelling-bottles listed at 1s. 9d. each.

Scent-bottles continued to be made into the 1840s, and examples mentioned in the records include:

1 second size scent bottle, French green and flowers, richly mounted £1 11s. 6d.
    [October 1841]

4 smelling bottles, Dresden flowers, mounted at 5s.
    [July 1842]

3 double dome bottles, mounted at 8s. 6d.

2 tall bottles & spiral top, blue coral at 15s.
    [November 1842]

1 double dome bottle, scarlet with solid gilt eagle stopper £1 1s. 0d.
    [May 1843]

SNUFF-BOXES

These rare porcelain snuff-boxes are of superb quality. Typical ornate examples are illustrated in Plates 369 and 370.

1 snuff box, gilt mounted 6s.
    [November 1795]

1 china snuff box, metal gilt mounted 15s.
    [April 1797: the mounts were added or supplied by J. Taylor & Co. of New Hall Street, Birmingham.]

1 snuff box, with hunting subjects finely painted, biscuit flowers on cover £5 5s. 0d.
    [October 1819: see Plate 369]

1 Box, dead blue and gold, birds etc. £2 0s. 0d.
    [November 1820]

GOING ALONG A SLAPPING PACE

GOING IN AND OUT CLEVER

369. *Above left*: A marked Chamberlain 'Regent China' snuff-box, painted with titled hunting scenes. This is perhaps the example invoiced in October 1819: '1 snuff box, with hunting subjects finely painted, biscuit flowers on cover £5 5s. 0d.'. Name mark with 'Regent China' and New Bond Street address. Diameter 3¾ in. *c.* 1819. *Private collection*

370. *Above right*: A well-painted Chamberlain snuff-box, the sides painted in a similar style to that illustrated in Plate 369. This is perhaps one of the '2 snuff boxes with sporting subjects' invoiced at 10 guineas in October 1819. Diameter 3¾ in. *c.* 1819. *Dyson Perrins Museum, Worcester*

371. Two green-ground Chamberlain spill-vases, with costly raised-gold surrounds to the panels. Examples of this type were invoiced at 18s. each in December 1841. Spill-vases, like other items, were made in various sizes and were normally sold in pairs or sets of three with a large central example. Written mark 'Chamberlain & Co. Worcester'. 3¼ in. high. *c.* 1840–45. *Dyson Perrins Museum, Worcester*

SPHINX

It is not certain if this sale entry relates to a paperweight such as the lion shown in Plate 346: '2 finx's £4 14s. 6d.' (February 1812). The price is too high for the small animal models such as those illustrated in Plate 246; indeed the cost may indicate a pair of ornamental sphinx-form mantle ornaments, perhaps adapted for use as candlesticks.

SPILL-VASES

The objects which are now called spill-vases were apparently originally called luminaries (q.v.), luminators, match pots (q.v.), spill-mugs and perhaps also match boxes (q.v.). For example:

2 pairs spill mugs, neat and low price with small birds etc. to form two sets for the chimney, 5s. each
[July 1803]

4 match boxes, printed figures, yellow ground at 8s.
[August 1805]

2 match boxes [pattern 403] Cheltenham and Malvern Wells £3 0s. 0d.
[December 1806]

However, some few entries in the 1840s relate specifically to spills:

			s.	d.
4 spill pots, canary colour and flowers			18	0
2	do.	raised flowers	11	0
2	do.	Chinese figures	11	0

4 do. Indian pattern [July 1841]	10	0

	£	s.	d.
1 spill 'Grosvenor' Celeste & flowers	1	10	0
1 spill, green & plain raised gold and panel of birds		18	0
1 do. biscuit blue raised gold and figures [December 1841]		18	0

STIRRUP-CUPS OR 'BUMPERS'

Silver stirrup-cups in the shape of a fox's head are very well known and were made from at least 1769 into the nineteenth century. Several porcelain manufacturers made similar pieces, including the Derby factory and the Chamberlains, from a surprisingly early date.

Apart from fox-head stirrup-cups, examples were also made in the form of a hare's head and some were especially embellished with initials or crests. A couple of the Chamberlain entries refer to these cups as 'bumpers'. Two exceedingly rare Chamberlain examples are shown in Plate 372.

1 fox head [inscribed] Tally-ho
   [September 1791. This early example might well have been of Derby manufacture.]

2 foxe's heads, enamelled 2s. (ware) 5s. (decoration) [April 1794]

2 hares heads enamelled proper, handsome [April 1795]

1 pair fox heads, letter L and crest with rich blue border [July 1795]

	s.	d.
3 foxes heads, white at	2	0
1 do. gilt [Christmas 1795 stocklist]	8	0

6 fox heads, proper at 7s. 6d. [April 1814]

4 fox heads, bumpers at 7s. 6d. [August 1821]

TEA PLATES

Whilst it is true that English tea services before about 1860 did not originally have place-plates, the complete sets did have two bread and butter plates (see Plates 62, 72, 73 and 78) which were of slightly different sizes, and of a shape following that of the saucer.

However, some of the larger breakfast services were equipped with small plates which may be taken for tea

372.   Two very rare and early Chamberlain stirrup-cups or 'bumpers'. The lefthand example has an underglaze-blue border and such items were invoiced at 10s. 6d. each in April 1795. Unmarked. $4\frac{7}{8}$ in. and $3\frac{1}{2}$ in. high. c. 1795–1805. *Messrs Sotheby & Co.*

plates. The printed price-card lists breakfast plates of three sizes – 6 in., 7 in. and 8 in.

Most plates were originally from dessert or dinner services, rather than from tea or breakfast services.

TEA SERVICES

The Chamberlain teawares are fully covered in Chapters 3, 4 and 5, and the tea service patterns are listed in Chapter 6.

However, one estimate given in October 1793 does serve to list the standard components and to show that the fluted shape (or any other moulded shape) was more expensive than the plain shapes.

Estimate of china, white as under.

	Plain		Fluted	
	s.	d.	s.	d.
Teapot [3rd size]	2	6	5	0 oval
Stand	1	0	1	6
Creamer	1	0	1	6
Plate 1st size	1	0	1	9
Sugar box	1	0	1	9
Slop bowl	1	0	1	6
Irish [large size] cup	3	0 dozen	8	0 dozen
do. saucers	3	0 dozen	8	0 dozen
Coffee cups		7 each		10 each

Most sets would have included a second bread and butter plate. The coffee cups were probably not quoted at the dozen price as many sets had only eight coffee cups (see page 234) or none at all. Coffee pots were not part of standard sets.

THIMBLES

It is readily apparent that the Chamberlains made porcelain thimbles from at least 1795, as in the Christmas stocktaking list it is recorded that in the biscuit-room there were three hundred unglazed examples estimated at a penny each. In the same list completed examples in the shop are listed priced at 1s. 6d. each. Other references include:

2 thimbles at 2s. 6d. each
    [March 1794]

1 thimble cyphered P.L.
    [April 1794]

1 thimble, white 9d.
    [October 1806]

6 rich thimbles £1 1s. 0d.
    [October 1821]

48 thimbles £2 8s. 0d.
    [April 1841]

Most of these porcelain thimbles would have been sold in small protective cases which were purchased from a Mr Graves.

TILES

From about 1836 to 1848 Messrs Chamberlain produced a quantity of encaustic tiles. R. W. Binns, in his *A Century of Potting in the City of Worcester* (1865), gives an account of this branch of the business, undertaken at

373. A Worcester inlaid earthenware tile of the type that was being produced at a separate works in the late 1830s and in the 1840s. Impressed mark 'WORCESTER'. 6 in. square. *c.* 1840–45. *Dyson Perrins Museum, Worcester*

a time when trade was bad and when the company was seeking – unsuccessfully – to compete with the Staffordshire manufacturers in utilitarian lines, such as toilet wares, door fittings or buttons.

R. W. Binns wrote of these times:

One of Mr. Chamberlain's schemes was to reproduce the encaustic tiles of the middle ages. This most interesting branch of manufacture had in olden times been carried on in the County and the enterprising proprietors consequently hoped that prestige as well as profit would result if the speculation could be brought to a successful issue.

The undertaking was successful and was carried on for many years by the wet clay process, as well as by the dry, the latter being worked under Prosser's patent.

When the two establishments were united a few years later, the tile business was removed to the old manufactory [Warmstry House] and there worked by the firm, special attention being given to it by [George] Barr and [Fleming] St. John. Subsequently [in 1850] it was given up to Messrs. Maw and about 1853 was finally removed by them to the Benthall works near Ironbridge in Shropshire.

The Chamberlain accounts include payments for laying the tiles in churches, but presumably such payments were recharged to the purchasers.

The surviving records also show that the tiles, or rather the basic patented process, were giving trouble respecting the rights. For example, in February 1844 Fleming St John travelled 'to Shelton to see Mr. Wright respecting his claim on renewing Patents', and claimed £2 16s. 9d. for his travelling expenses.

On 30 June 1844 payments are recorded showing that a 5 per cent royalty was also made to Herbert Minton:

To Messrs. Samuel Wright & Herbert Minton. For Royalty on £61 10s. 4d. amount of encaustic tiles sold from the 26th January to 29th April £3 14s. 6d.

To Messrs. H. Minton & F. St. John. For Royalty on £180 10s. 4d. amount of do. [encaustic tiles] sold from 29th April to 30th June £9 0s. 6d.

These entries show the relatively small amount of tiles sold in the period 26 January to 30 June 1844 – under £250 worth. They also reveal that Fleming St John seems to have taken over Samuel Wright's royalty rights, from 29 April 1844, although Herbert Minton was still paid his share of the 5 per cent.

An interesting first-hand account of the manufacture of Chamberlain tiles is contained in *The Penny Magazine* of February 1843 and is reproduced in the Appendix.

Most Chamberlain tiles bear the mark 'Chamberlain & Co', impressed into the reverse side.

'TOAST' MUGS

'Toast' mugs sometimes had two handles and on occasions a cover as well. An early reference in the records reads: '1 Pint toast mug, two handles, white and gold with crest and cypher. 15s.' (December 1793). (See also page 263.)

TOAST RACKS

Toast racks are rare in old porcelain as they suffered a high casualty rate. Two Chamberlain entries of 1801 read:

Toast rack, pattern 53
    [April 1801]

1 Toast rack, white & gold, 12s.
    [July 1801]

TOBACCO BURNERS

A puzzling entry of August 1821 relates to three 'tobacco burners' at 4s. each, but it is not certain what these were – perhaps ornate pipe bowls. The order originated from John Yates, of Cheltenham, and reads: '3 Tobacco burners if can be done in 10 or 12 days, 4s. each'.

TOBACCO STOPPERS

The Chamberlains made tobacco stoppers, for compacting the tobacco within a pipe, from at least 1795, as uncompleted examples in the biscuit-room are recorded at the time of the Christmas 1795 stocktaking, priced at 4d. against a valuation of 1s. 6d. each for completed items in the shop.

Unfortunately, it is not known what form they took (a Dr Wall Worcester model was in the shape of a female head, taken from one of the rare figure models), but a record of May 1795 relates to the gilding of tobacco stoppers. I do not know of any surviving Chamberlain examples.

TOILET POTS

It is difficult now to know exactly what form toilet pots took, but in November 1793 a pair were described in the following way: 'One pair toilet pots and covers, fancy sprigs and gold borders 12s.'. See also POMATUM POTS.

TOYS

Miniature items of all types are included under this heading, as this is the description used in the Chamberlain archives, and it is one which clearly makes the point that such pieces were *not* travellers' samples.

The early entries relate to Caughley blanks decorated by the Chamberlains – these are mainly teasets, such as: '1 complete set of Toy china with gold sprigs, to be done this week' (September 1789). This may well have been similar to the pieces shown in Plate 14.

However, the Chamberlains' 'flaming shew' at their new High Street retail shop in Worcester included, by December 1793, miniature wares that were possibly of their own make. Under this date, for example, there is listed as being in the front showroom: '1 complete sett, Toys, Davis's flowers, 9s.'. The stocktaking list for that year includes toy tea and coffee pots and 517 dozen toy cups.

By Christmas 1795 ornamental items were also being produced, as is evidenced by the listing in the biscuit-room of '14 Toy baskets at 1s.'.

Later, in the nineteenth century, it appears that some toys were quite expensive, being made for a good class market; for example, in April 1813 there was invoiced:

1 Rich Harlequin Regent Toy set consisting of 12 shankered tea cups and saucers, 8 coffee cups, coffee jug, creamer, bason, sugar and 2 plates – six inches. £5 5s. 0d.

The size given against the bread and butter plates suggests that this set was on a somewhat larger scale than most miniatures.

The little ewers and basins were a very popular toy line, and they were also made by other firms such as Spode. Four 1819 entries for these give Chamberlain's prices:

			s.	d.
1	Toy ewer & basin, pattern 562, gold edge		6	0
5	do.	painted roses at	8	0
4	do.	rich India pattern	12	0
2	rich Toy ewers and basins		30	0

In the 1820s miniature déjeuner teasets on trays were produced and sold at about £1 10s. 0d. (see Plate 374), as were toy cabinet cups and saucers, jugs and goblets, candlesticks, ornamental baskets and vases. The Bond Street sales book includes references to toy pieces, of which some are as follows:

1 pair Toy vases, views Cheltenham &c. pattern in gold £1 4s. 0d.
  [September 1822]

A rich toy tea set £2 12s. 6d.
  [May 1828]

To 2 toy ornamental ewers £2 0s. 0d.
  [March 1829]

A toy teapot, raised flowers 7s.
  [February 1832]

A toy kettle 10s. 6d.
  [August 1833]

A toy basket gold weed and raised flowers 5s.
  [September 1833]

			s.	d.
8	toy jugs	at	1	6
6	Toy mugs	at	1	6
12	toy goblets	at	1	0
	[November 1842]			

374. A rare toy or miniature tea and coffee service on its tray. Painted name mark with New Bond Street address. Teapot 2¼ in. high. c. 1816–25. *Godden of Worthing Ltd*

4 toy jugs, green ground and gilt at 3s. 6d.
        [March 1842]

	s.	d.
12 toy mugs, assorted, large	1	6
12 do. small	1	0

[May 1843]

6 toy baskets, shells, flowers &c. 3s.
        [October 1847]

TRANSPARENCIES

The Chamberlain invoice books contain two entries in
October 1841 and February 1842 relating to the sale of
'transparencies': '5 Transparencies, biscuit, "Our
Saviour", at 3s.'. It is not known, however, if these 'Our
Saviour' transparencies were of Chamberlain's own
make.

These thin press-moulded slabs were variously called
'Berlin Transparencies' or 'Lithophanes'. Most were of
continental make but the Grainger factory at Worcester
made some ornaments incorporating Lithophane-type
panels. These need to be held to a light to see the effect
produced by the relief-moulded design. (Further
information is given in Chapter 4 of my book *Antique
China and Glass under £5*, 1966.)

TRAYS   See JEWEL TRAYS, ORNAMENTAL TRAYS, TRIFLE TRAYS

TRIFLE TRAYS

The reference below comes from the Chamberlain sales
records.

One 12 inch trifle tray, flowers etc. £1 10s. 0d.
        [January 1826]

TUMBLERS

These simple and useful objects offered a good surface
for decoration and they proved exceedingly popular.
Many were made to special order and bear the owner's
initials. The basic cost of the undecorated tumblers was
1s. for the half-pint size and 2s. for the pint size.

A very rare early moulded example is shown in
Plate 38. The standard later shape is as illustrated in
Plates 376–8, but different sizes – pint, half-pint (4¼ in.
high), and quarter-pint (3½ in. high) – were made, and
some were equipped with covers (see Plate 361), being
more ornamental than useful. Several, in fact, were
described as 'Ornamental Tumblers'. In some 1794 and
1795 accounts the description 'Goblet' is used rather
than 'Tumbler' (see page 244).

375. A blue-bordered spiral-fluted tall cup or perhaps a 'handled-
tumbler' as listed in 1795. The front panel bears the monogram
'A M W' relating to a special order. Unmarked. 4¼ in. high. *c.* 1795–
1800. *Godden of Worthing Ltd*

Typical entries from the factory records include:

1795. 2 Three quarter pint tumblers, blue and gold with urn
          at 10s.
       1 do. handled, Gooder's view of Worcester
          [The example shown in Plate 375 may represent a
          handled tumbler]

1796. Half pint tumblers with figures and cyphered J E W

1797. 1 Pair rich yellow and gold tumblers, views of
          Worcester and Blackfriars bridge £1 10s. 0d.

	£	s.	d.
1798. 2 Tumblers with views – Norwich Gate & Cathedral and Salisbury Cathedral	1	1	0
1 Pint Tumbler, Nelson's Victory, yellow & gold	3	3	0

	£	s.	d.
1799. 3 rich ornamental Tumblers, fawn & gold with figure Ariadne	6	6	0
3 do. with views	5	5	0
3 pint Tumblers and covers, birds and yellow ground	3	12	0

	£	s.	d.
1800. 2 pint Tumblers & covers, Birds, dogs &c.	2	10	0
2 do. do. Best Queen's [pattern]	2	10	0
1 Half pint Tumbler, yellow & gold pattern 151 with figure of Venus	1	1	0
1 Ornamental half pint Tumbler, figures, blue bell border	2	2	0

376. A superb-quality Chamberlain tumbler delicately painted with a view of Worcester and with gilt borders. Unmarked. 3½ in. high. *c.* 1800–10. *I. T. Henderson Collection*

377. *Above right:* A typical Chamberlain tumbler, the panel of which is painted with a figure subject titled 'Music'. Written mark 'Chamberlains Worcester'. 4¼ in. high. *c.* 1798–1803. *Geoffrey Godden, chinaman*

	£	s.	d.
1802. 3 rich ornamental Pint Tumblers with new covers, with emblems of Peace &c.	15	15	0
2 Tumblers with raised covers, views of Worcester	2	10	0

	£	s.	d.
1804. 3 Half pint Tumblers, raised covers, views of Cheltenham	2	14	0
1 Pint Tumbler, yellow ground with figures		12	0

	£	s.	d.
1805. 2 Pint Tumblers with covers, best white		5	0
2 Half pint Tumblers, best white		2	0
2 Pint Tumblers, covers and stands, Beauty rejecting Folly and Cleopatra (with a half circle ornament)	16	16	0

[A pair of covered tumblers and stands is shown in Plate 361]

378. A peach-ground Chamberlain tumbler with bluebell border motif, a form of decoration mentioned in accounts in 1800. The figure panel is titled 'Cymon & Iphigene'. Written name mark in gold. 3½ in. high. *c.* 1800–3. *Messrs J. Sewell*

		£	s.	d.
1806.	2 Half pint Tumblers, printed views		8	0
	4 Half pint Tumblers & covers, yellow-ground painted church views	4	4	0
1808.	2 Half pint Tumblers & covers without the small tops, Gold sprigs and painted views, Henwich Church, Bridge View, Cheltenham	[unpriced order]		

TUREENS

Covered tureens, with their stands, originally formed part of dinner or dessert services. The large ones were soup tureens from dinner services, whilst the smaller examples were either sauce tureens from dinner services or sugar and cream-tureens from dessert services. Tureens matching standard dessert services are shown in Plates 145 and 146.

However, some examples were sold on their own and two entries made in 1811 relate to the attractive dolphin-supported tureens as illustrated in Plates 107 and 145:

1 pair Dolphin cream & sugar pieces
1 pair rich cream bowls, Dolphins, with birds &c.

Tureens of this shape did not have separate stands.

The date of introduction of one shape can be more exactly pinpointed by an entry under the date 14 April 1810: 'Cream bowls to have new nob of dolphin and handles of shells'. However, most examples do not have the shell-shaped handles.

URNS

Most urns were seemingly entered in the records under the general descriptions 'vases' or 'ornaments', but the following was listed in August 1805: 'Two urns, raised covers, views Malvern & Worcester £3 3s. 0d.'.

VASES

The Chamberlain factory produced some magnificent vases from the 1790s onwards, rivalling if not surpassing the main competition from the Derby factory and the Flight-Worcester factory prior to about 1810.

One very interesting order is dated 17 June 1791 and relates to vases supplied to Richard Walker in Manchester. A small clue to the style or type of such vases may be afforded by the single plinth or 'pedestal' shown in Plate 36.

The entries below, gleaned from the factory records, refer to objects which were termed 'Ornaments', as well as vases.

	£	s.	d.
1 Rich centre vase, blue & gold, device – Calypso weeping	2	12	6
1 do. end vase do. device Miranda	2	5	0
1 do. end vase do. device Miss Hardy	2	5	0
2 antique [shape] embossed vauses, blue & gold	2	2	0
2 smaller do.	1	11	6
7 Pedestalls to do.	3	3	6
5 Plain jars and beakers for sitting room, new pattern	2	2	0

The set or garniture of five plain 'jars and beakers' was most probably of Caughley porcelain and certainly such Chinese-form sets are known from that factory. The low cost of this complete set, £2 2s. 0d. against £2 5s. 0d. for the richly decorated Chamberlain end-vases, emphasizes the decorative nature of the first item invoiced.

The 1792 stocktaking list includes other vases:

	£	s.	d.
6 small embossed vases, white		15	0
3 embossed vases and pedestals, bird's eye border & sprigs	3	0	0
3 do. rich	4	4	0
2 vases with figures – antique	4	14	6

Invoice descriptions in 1792 give some indication of the degree of decoration:

	£	s.	d.
5 rich blue and gold vases & pedestals	5	2	0
5 rich vases and pedestals, with devices	15	15	0
1 rich enamelled and gilt vase & pedestal	12	12	0

By the year 1795 the fashion for vases mounted on separate pedestals had passed, and the following types of vases appear in the records:

2 vases and covers, pierced tops with emblematical figures £3 3s. 0d.
    [see Plate 379]
2 vases and covers, with emblematical figures of a young lady's death just on the point of marriage
    [unpriced order]
1 ornamental vase and cover with figure – science £1 10s. 0d.

In 1797 and 1798 some vases were being painted with views:

	£	s.	d.
1 sett rich ornaments, blue & gold with views	10	10	0
3 ornaments, yellow and gold, views of Worcester	3	16	0
Pair ornaments, fawn and gold, views	4	4	0

In September 1799 there appears an unpriced order for '1 flat ornament – Cornelia'.

The oval covered vase illustrated in Colour Plate XXI is seemingly of the 1790s in style, with spiral fluting

379. A rare and early yellow-ground Chamberlain covered vase. The figure panel is titled 'Cephalus & Procris', and the spiral-fluted body is picked out with gilt enrichments. Unmarked. 12½ in. high. *c.* 1795–1800. *Photograph: Sotheby & Co. George Sinclair, Australia*

380. A fine-quality three-piece Chamberlain salmon-ground vase richly gilded, with a figure panel titled 'Paulus Amelius'. Written mark 'Chamberlains Worcester' in gold. 14¼ in. high. *c.* 1800–5. *Godden Reference Collection*

382. A small-size Chamberlain vase with gilt marbling over an orange ground. The panel is painted with a feather motif – popular at this period. This and most other vase shapes were made in three or more sizes. Written name mark 'Chamberlains Worcester'. 5¼ in. high. *c.* 1805–15. *Geoffrey Godden, chinaman*

381. *Opposite:* An important Chamberlain vase with gilt marbling over an orange ground. The figure panel depicts 'Orpheus & Eurydice'. Written name mark 'Chamberlains Worcester'. 11¼ in. high. *c.* 1800–5. *Messrs Andrew Dando, Bath*

383. A marked Chamberlain-Worcester orange-ground urn-shaped vase. This form was also made at the Coalport factory but with a thinner base. Written name mark. 9⅛ in. high. *c.* 1805–15. *Victoria & Albert Museum (Crown Copyright)*

matching the shanked tewares of the mid to late 1790s (see page 78). Another rare example of the same period is shown in Plate 379. The style of these two vases is clearly of an earlier period than the post-1800 vases with their flat curved surfaces and rich painted motifs (see Plates 380–88).

In 1800 these rich and costly pieces were listed:

	£	s.	d.
1 large rich ornament, figures, Triumph of Mercy	31	10	0
1 large round ornament, rich fawn & gold, with figures Extreme and Unction	12	12	0
1 large rich ornament at	21	0	0
2 next size do. the pair	31	10	0

2 Ornaments 1st size oval, handled Beauty & Savius			
2 do. flat – clipping the wings of Love and Orpheus, gold handles	20	0	0

Within a few years of 1800 there appear references in the Chamberlain records concerning richly decorated vases and ornaments, probably of standard shapes and with figure-subject panels, which might be linked with recorded examples.

1 Ornament with double handle, fawn and gold all over subject Orpheus & Eurydice, 2nd size [unpriced order] [1803: subject as in Plate 381]

1 rich vase, with figures, Paulus – Amelius £13 13s. 0d. [1804: see Plate 380]

1 rich large centre ornament, no 299 with figures 21 0 0
2 rich side pieces to match 31 10 0

    [1805. The reference to 299 refers to the basic ground colour and gilding which in this case is illustrated in Plate 421.]

1 vase ornament gold bands with paintings Othello and Desdemona £4 4s. 0d.
    [1811]
1 small Regent vase, blue marble [ground] Venus presenting Helen to Paris. Damaged. £8 8s. 0d.
    [1813]
The Prince Regent.
Three rich ornamental pieces figure paintings £52 10s. 0d.
    [February 1813]
1 small Regent [shape] ornament, painted from Shakespeare's Henry 8th Act 3. Scene 1 £16 16s. 0d.
    [1813]

1 large Regent ornament, gold bands with Satyrs – head knobs 2 2 0
2 middle size   do. 3 3 0
    [1813]

In April 1813 the following were supplied to Powell, the London decorator (see page 204):

384. A rare form of large Chamberlain vase with typical gilt seaweed ground. The panel is painted with a rather rare landscape subject. Written name mark. 14¼ in. high. c. 1805–15. *Messrs Sotheby & Co.*

385. A 'Regent' shape Chamberlain covered vase with gilt marbling over a salmon ground. The panel depicts a scene from *The Taming of the Shrew*, Act 3, Scene 2, and is so inscribed. A vase of this type with *The Taming of the Shrew* panel, painted by Walter Chamberlain, was invoiced at 8 guineas in December 1813. Printed name mark under the Prince of Wales feathers (see page 34, Mark 7). 9 in. high. c. 1813–18. *Dyson Perrins Museum, Worcester*

CORNELIA MOTHER OF THE GRACCHI

XXI. *Opposite page* 296 : A superbly decorated spill-vase or 'match pot', perhaps such as the 'fine match pots, fancy-jewell'd' at £1 10s. 0d. each invoiced in January 1818. The figure-subject panel is titled 'The Mother's Hope' and the same subject occurs on Flight, Barr & Barr porcelain. The quality of this piece is very fine and the mock jewels are most unusual. Written name mark with New Bond Street address. 3½ in. high. *c.*1818. *Godden Reference Collection*

XXII. *Opposite* : A rare early spiral-fluted or shanked Chamberlain vase and cover with typical gilding. The figure panel, 'Cornelia mother of the Gracchi', was probably painted by the early figure painter John Wood (see page 210). Painted name mark 'Chamberlains Worcester' in gold under the cover. 12¼ in. high. *c.*1795. *Godden Reference Collection*

XXIII. *Above left* : An attractive and typical pair of Chamberlain vases. The background and gilding relate to pattern 299, one often used for decorative items in the early 1800s. The figure-subject panels are titled under the base 'Maid of Corinth' and 'Love Sleeps'. Painted marks 'Chamberlains Worcester. 299'. 9 in. high. *c.*1804. *Geoffrey Godden, chinaman*

XXIV. *Left* : A finely painted 'bell-shape' vase, a standard Chamberlain form made at the same period as the 'Regent' vases (see Colour Plate VIII and Plate 385). The subject is taken from Boydell's illustration to *A Midsummer Night's Dream* (see page 176), and the body is painted in a continuous manner (see Plate 389 for the reverse side). Unmarked. 7½ in. high. *c.*1813–18. *Geoffrey Godden, chinaman*

XXV.   A superbly painted teapot and stand from a service painted with Chamberlain's 'Dragon in Compartments' pattern (number 75 in the factory list), but adapted here to take the arms of Sir Charles Malet (quartering Hache) who was created a baronet in February 1791. This popular pattern was often chosen to accompany individual armorial bearings, crests or initials (see also Plates 93 and 94). Written mark 'Chamberlains Worcester, Warranted. No 75' inside the cover. 10 in. long.
*c.*1802–5. *Messrs Sotheby & Co.* (*from the Estate of the late Nelson A. Rockefeller*)

	£	s.	d.
3 large Regent ornaments	3	0	0
4 do. Unicorn head	4	0	0
2 bell shape, large do. Lion head	2	0	0
2 egg [shape] ornaments, Dolphin & shell	1	10	0

In June 1813 there is an entry which gives an indication of the really superb quality which Chamberlain's own decorators could achieve. The order for the Marquis of Abergavenny simply reads:

5 Ornaments, 1 Regent [shape] Henry 8th
2 chocolates, King John
　　　　　King Richard 3rd
2 Bell shape, Henry 6th. Part I £6 18s. 0d.
　　　　　King John
2 Luminaries
2 Grace mugs, Power of Love and number 2 £42 0s. 0d.
Fawn and gold
Arms on the back of each piece

386.   A superb-quality orange-ground Chamberlain vase with rich gilding. This form is probably the 'unicorn-head' vase associated with the 'Regent' shape (see Plate 385). The central panel, titled 'Horace', is painted in a dark grey monochrome. Painted name mark. $7\frac{1}{2}$ in. high. c. 1810–20. *Private collection*

387.   A fine set of three Chamberlain ornamental vases of standard shapes. The side vases are painted with figure panels from *King John* and *Julius Caesar*, and the centre vase depicts Falstaff. Written name marks. $7\frac{1}{2}$ in. and $6\frac{1}{4}$ in. high. c. 1810–20. *Messrs Sotheby & Co.*

388. *Opposite left:* A good Chamberlain wide-mouthed urn-shaped vase of a characteristic shape (see also Colour Plate XXIV and Plates 387 and 389), with a gilt seaweed design over a peach ground. The panel depicts 'Tintern Abbey'. This vase shape seems to be contemporary with and complementary to the 'Regent' ornaments (see Plate 385) featured in the factory records during the 1810–20 period. It is probably the 'Bell-shape – lion head' listed in the white at £1 each in April 1813. In 1815 the description 'Regent bell-mouth' probably relates to the same shape. Written name mark. 7½ in. high. *c.* 1810–20. *Messrs Sotheby & Co.*

389. *Opposite:* A finely painted characteristic Chamberlain bell-shape vase. The other side is shown in Colour Plate XXIV. Unmarked. 7½ in. high. *c.* 1810–20. *Geoffrey Godden, chinaman*

390. *Opposite below:* Detail from the engraving taken from John Boydell's Shakespeare-subject prints, the source of two designs on the vase shown in Plate 389 and Colour Plate XXIV (see also page 176). (Reprinted by Benjamin Blom Books, 1968; distributed by Arno Press Inc.)

391. *Below:* A decorative Chamberlain light blue-ground covered vase, probably one of the 'new make . . . mercury [head] . . .' vases invoiced from 1814. This vase shape, like others, was made in various sizes and is found embellished in many different styles (see Plates 108 and 221, and page 104). In April 1819 a vase answering this description was invoiced at £4 4s. 0d. Written name mark. 8½ in. high. *c.* 1814–20. *Messrs Sotheby & Co.*

Colour Plate VIII and Plate 105 show the 'Regent' shape vase decorated with scenes from *Henry VIII*, and Plates 106 and 227 illustrate the 'Grace' mugs.

In December 1813 some superb vases and other items were sent down to stock the London retail shop (see page 103). In two cases the pieces were important enough to warrant the listing of the artist responsible for the fine figure painting:

	£	s.	d.
2 Regent ornaments, 1st size, King John & Taming of the Shrew. Walter's [Walter Chamberlain's painting: as in Plate 385]	16	16	0
1 rich full size Regent ornament, Triumph of Mercy (Humphrey's) fawn ground marbled [Humphrey Chamberlain's painting]	31	10	0
1 Regent ornament, Edward & Elinora, fawn marble	15	15	0
2 Regent ornaments, figures King Henry 6th, Comedy of Errors. Composition marble ground	31	10	0
1 Regent 1st size Taming the Shrew [as in Plate 385]	12	12	0

In July 1814 a magnificent set of these 'Regent' shape vases (see Colour Plate VIII and Plate 385) was ordered:

1 Rich set Regent ornaments, fawn & gold and different painting from Shakespeare. Seven pieces £60 18s. 0d.

Also recorded were:

	£	s.	d.
2 new shape ornaments, griffin handles [1814: perhaps the shape shown in Plate 394]	[unpriced order]		
1 large Regent ornament, View of Coniston Lake green ground and fine bronze border	10	10	0
2 new make side pieces to match, Mercury handles & views Burman Wood and Ragland [1814: for this handle form see Plate 391]	10	10	0
1 new ornament 15 inches. Dragons head, maroon & gold, with flowers all round [1814]	12	12	0

By no means all the fine vases were painted with figure-subject panels – other motifs were certainly in fashion at that time. In 1815, for example, the following appear among items recorded:

	£	s.	d.
1 set three ornaments – Webster's flowers	5	5	0
1 Regent bell-mouth [vase], view Warwick Castle fawn [ground] pattern 440	5	5	0
1 centre [ornament] Grouse shooting. Ridley shape with pierced cover	5	5	0
2 End [vases] mounted Pheasant & Fox & Terrier	8	8	0

392. *Below:* A small blue-ground Chamberlain urn-shape vase, the flower panel by a known hand, perhaps Webster's (see page 210). Written name mark. $4\frac{1}{4}$ in. high. *c.* 1820–25. *Geoffrey Godden, chinaman*

393. *Right:* A magnificent pair of open vases, showing a continuation of the Flight, Barr & Barr shape and style of gilding but made after the 1840 amalgamation. They have a rich blue ground with scenes of London and superb gilding. Written mark 'Chamberlain & Co. Worcester'. $7\frac{1}{2}$ in. high. *c.* 1840–45. *Messrs Sotheby & Co.*

394. One of a set of three Chamberlain vases decorated with a rich underglaze-blue ground and gilt embellishments. The flower painting is probably by Webster (see page 210). Written name mark. Centre vase 9 in. high, side vases 7 in. high. *c.* 1820–30. *S. Arnold Collection*

395. A superb French-styled tall Chamberlain vase decorated with a characteristic matt-blue ground. The finely painted London-view panel is surrounded by a raised gold border. Written name mark with New Bond Street address. 15¼ in. high. *c.* 1825–35. *Messrs Sotheby & Co.*

396. A fine pair of Chamberlain urn-shape vases, rather in the prevailing French taste, with an apple-green ground, painted views of Berkeley and Warwick Castles, and richly gilded. Written name mark with New Bond Street address. 10½ in. high. *c.* 1825–35. *Messrs Neales of Nottingham*

397. An elegant French hard-paste porcelain vase decorated by Chamberlain's at Worcester with a blue ground and a view of Greenwich Hospital. Chamberlain's purchased several hard-paste French blanks which were subsequently decorated and resold under their own name (see page 181). Written name mark. 13 in. high. *c.* 1825–40. *Messrs Phillips*

	£	s.	d.
2 Bell vases, subjects from Morland	8	0	0
2 small Bell mouth [vases] & stands	4	0	0

For subsequent years, other entries include:

	£	s.	d.
1 Mercury handled vase view of Oxford from the London Road [see Plate 221]	4	4	0
1 do. blue ground & birds [see Plate 391]	4	4	0
[April 1819]			

1 Mercury ornament, Ivory & gold, Iffley £3 3s. 0d.
      [February 1820: see Plate 221]

	£	s.	d.
1 ornament & shade, white and gold, biscuit flowers	3	0	0
2 new ornaments, 10½ inches high, finely painted in flowers with ivory ground and raised gold &c.	21	0	0
[1820]			

1 F [French] vase, view of Worcester & Malvern £8 8s. 0d.
      October 1821]

1 Warwick vase, centre ornaments, Worcester, marone & gold, rich £5 5s. 0d.
      [1822: shape as in Plate 393; see page 247]

	£	s.	d.
1 small French shape ornament, dead blue ground and view, with wreath of biscuit flowers	3	3	0
1 new shape ornament marone ground with Warwick handles, view Alnwick	4	14	6
[1823]			

A vase Dresden raised flowers &c £4 4s. 0d.
      [March 1830]

2 Bachanalian vases, green ground, gilt rich with views of Tintern Abbey, & Warwick Castle £16 16s. 0d.
      [July 1841]

1 set of 3 Barr's shape [vases] gold vermicelli and groups of flowers £3 13s. 6d.
      [September 1841]

1 vase, Barr's egg shape, maroon ground raised gold, panel Malvern £3 3s. 0d.
      [November 1841]

1 vase, richly gilt with painting of Shelley £10 10s. 0d.
      [May 1842]

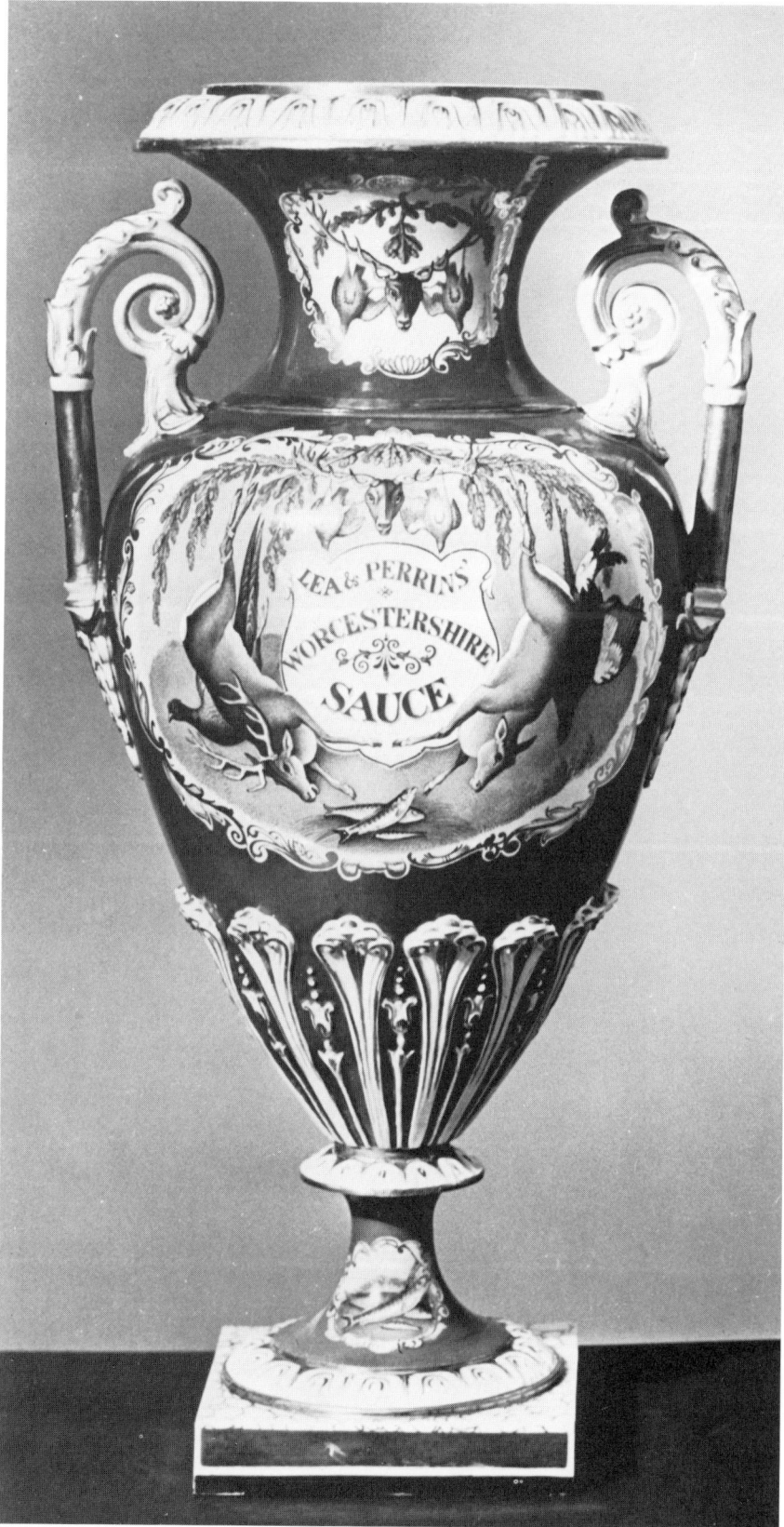

398.   *Left:* A very large Chamberlain vase made for another great world-famous Worcester firm – the sauce manufacturers Lea & Perrins. This was perhaps intended as a window dressing or even for their stand at the 1851 Exhibition. Written mark 'Chamberlain & Co. Worcester'. 20½ in. high. *c*. 1840–51. *Messrs Lea & Perrins*

399.   *Above:* A blue-ground Chamberlain oval vase of a popular shape, one produced also by other manufacturers including Minton's. This is probably one of the 'flat-sided vases . . . solid gold dolphin handles' as invoiced in May 1844. This form occurs in several sizes and with many different styles of decoration. 'Chamberlain & Co.' mark with both London addresses. 12 in. high. *c*. 1840–45. *Miss H. Bennett Collection*

		£	s.	d.
2	vases Windsor [shape?] French green ground and full painted flowers all round	5	5	0
1	Tall vase, white ground with landscape both sides, surrounds with [raised?] Dresden flowers [General style perhaps as in Plate 402]	8	8	0
2	Fish tail flower vases, Celeste ground raised [gold] panel painted birds both sides, raised flowers &c. at	5	5	0
1	set 3 ornaments, pink ground, ormolu & gold, flowers on both sides	3	3	0
1	set 3 do. painted cupids and flowers [August 1843]	7	7	0

2 large flat-sided vases, white, broad gold bands and finely painted single flowers on each side. Solid gold dolphin handles £8 8s. 0d.
[May 1844]

This basic shape of vase would appear to be that shown in Plate 399 but Minton and other makers also employed this form. The entry below shows that the Chamberlains would make vases to order.

Mrs Hodges.

	£	s.	d.
2 small vases, biscuit blue, raised gilding	5	10	0
modelling above	1	1	0
[June 1844]			

Subsequent references to Mrs Hodges's shape vases suggest that this new form became a standard factory shape.

Chamberlain's vases were shown at the 1851 Exhibition and were described in the following manner in the official catalogue:

Adelaide vases, gilt &c. with views of Constantinople and Smyrna and painting of various birds.
Snake-handle vases, with views of Worcester and Malvern
Coventry [shape] vases with medallions of Shakespeare and Milton.

These 'Adelaide vases' may have been those first listed on 29 August 1843:

2 large vases. Garter blue &c. Paintings of Constantinople and Smyrna.
2 shades and stands for do. £47 5s. 0d.

The later Chamberlain vases, of the 1840–52 period, are in general rather heavy-looking objects (see Plates 401–4), typical of their age, but not to everybody's liking today.

400. An important Chamberlain vase and cover decorated with an underglaze-blue ground, richly gilded and with a panel of typical 'fancy birds' in landscape. Written name mark with New Bond Street address. 21 in. high. c. 1825–45. *Messrs Sotheby & Co.*

401. A tall marked Chamberlain vase and cover, typical of the 1840s and of a type often encrusted with relief-moulded flowers, as in Plate 402. Written mark 'Chamberlains Worcester'. 14 in. high. *c*. 1842–50. *Messrs Sotheby & Co.*

402. An elaborate floral-encrusted Chamberlain covered vase in the Coalbrookdale manner, but described as 'Dresden flowers' in the factory records. An ornate set of five floral-encrusted vases of a similar type is shown in Plate 205. 21 in. high. *c*. 1842–50. *Messrs Sotheby & Co.*

403. A restrained Chamberlain vase form as drawn in the factory shape book with other objects of the mid 1840s. *Worcester Porcelain Co. Ltd*

404. A richly decorated blue-ground Chamberlain covered vase with raised gilding. The painted panel is in a typical early Victorian style. 'Chamberlain & Co.' mark with both London addresses. 18¾ in. high. *c.* 1840–45. *Victoria & Albert Museum (Crown Copyright)*

VINAIGRETTES

The following entry may not relate to porcelain vinaigrettes but it occurs with other Chamberlain products: '2 large vinegarettes at 6s. 6d.' (November 1842).

VIOLET POTS

Violet pots in the Spode factory shape book were small vases with pierced covers, or two-handled vase-shaped cups on stands also with pierced covers – violets were presumably inserted into the water-filled body. I have not traced any Chamberlain examples although obviously they were made, as the following accounts show:

	£	s.	d.
Four violet pots and stands, feathers	6	6	0
Two violet pots 403 [ground] and Love sleeps and Venus and Cupid [December 1813]	5	5	0

Two violet pots and stands, Webster's flowers £3 0s. 0d. [January 1815]

1 Warwick [shape] violet 2nd size blue and gold with raised flowers £2 12s. 6d. [November 1818]

2 Dolphin [shape] violets, blue and gold with biscuit flowers £4 4s. 0d. [July 1819: perhaps as in Plate 298]

Some articles were also listed as 'violet baskets' or 'violet plates':

1 violet plate with shells £1 10s. 0d.
   [May 1838]

1 Grape handle violet plate £1 10s. 0d.
   [July 1841]

1 violet plate and cover, small, Barr's shape, buff ground and
   gilt, gadroon [edge] 10s. 6d.
   [October 1841]

However, covered violet pots were still produced:

2 sarcophagus [shape] violets and covers, blue celeste
   £2 2s. 0d.
   [April 1845]

2 violets and covers, biscuit blue ground and gilt on three feet
   and pierced cover £1 5s. 6d.
   [July 1845]

WAFER STANDS

These were not dishes to hold edible wafers, but stands
to hold the letter-sealing wafers in use at the time; they
were part of the equipment used on a writing-desk.
Sample references to these stands include:

1 ornamental waffer stand £1 10s. 0d.
   [May 1821]

Pair waffer stands, dry blue & birds [unpriced order]
   [October 1822]

2 tall wafer stands, Dresden raised flowers and birds, at 15s.
   [August 1842]

WASH BASINS

Some large bowls were probably intended as wash
basins, rather than ornamental bowls or punch-bowls,
as suggested by the following sales entry: '1 wash hand
basin with figure of Fortitude £1 11s. 6d.' (September
1796).

WATCH-STANDS

The earliest Chamberlain watch-stand is undoubtedly
the one shown in Colour Plate IV featuring the standing
figure of Apollo, but this model is not mentioned in the
available records.

Other models, however, were made in the nineteenth
century, as is evidenced by the two following entries:

2 greyhound watch stands, £1 1s. 0d.
   [November 1812]

1 ornamental watch stand, £12 0s. 0d.
   [May 1821]

The Bond Street cash book contains an interesting
reference in March 1830: 'By a china watch frame

purchased by Mr. Lilly as a pattern and sent to
Worcester, £1 15s. 0d.'. We have no knowledge, how-
ever, of the source of this pattern piece or of the model.
Further items include:

1 Watch stand, traced in blue with a rose knob £1 0s. 0d.
   [July 1838]

	£	s.	d.
1 new watch stand.	1	5	0
1 old shape do.		18	0

   [August 1841]

2 watch stands, raised flowers £1 16s. 0d.
   [December 1841]

WATER- (OR WATERING) POTS

Some small water-pots were intended for sprinkling
lavender- or rose-water on to linen or other articles. These
items were mainly fashionable in the 1815–25 period
and entries from the Chamberlain records include:

2 water pots, roses £1 1s. 0d.
   [November 1818]

2 watering pots, Dresden flowers £1 0s. 0d.
   [November 1821]

A pair water pans, Women's flowers 12s.
   [June 1823]

The Spode shape books depict such items as scaled-down
watering-cans.

WHISTLES

Messrs Chamberlain also made, or at least sold, dog
whistles, as one sales entry shows: '8 coloured dog
whistles at 9d.' (August 1841). The following entry is
rather clearer, indicating that these were in the form of a
dog's head, and that they were made in at least two sizes.

	s.	d.
12 dogs-head whistles, large coloured & gilt	18	0
12 smaller do.	12	0

   [October 1841]

Other factories apart from Chamberlain's may have
made such whistles, and these are normally unmarked
and apparently earlier than this entry. Other Chamberlain dog's-head whistles were listed in August 1844.

WINE CISTERNS

Several wine coolers were very ornately decorated
objects. However, one pair, described as wine cisterns,
were of a form not known today:

Lord Melbourne, Whitehall, London.
One pair wine cisterns, Queen Elizabeth pattern, £14 14s. 0d.
    [October 1803]

WINE COOLERS

Whilst ice-pails of standard shapes were included in the various dessert or dinner services supplied, wine coolers were sold separately. Some were so ornately decorated as to serve as table centrepieces in their own right.

Unglazed examples included in the December 1795 stocktaking were entered at a mere 8s. each, but those listed below are altogether very elaborate examples, some of which were extremely costly.

A distinction must be made between the three-piece ice-pails (see page 245) for cooling fruit, etc., and the more richly decorated and generally smaller wine coolers. This distinction is made in an entry of September 1810:

2 ice pails complete
4 wine coolers, rather smaller than ice pails

Other references include:

E. Ellice Esqr. 19, Upper Grosvenor Street, London.
Two large ornamental wine coolers, with Baccanelian figures painted all round. £170 0s. 0d.
    [December 1811]
1 rich ornamental wine cooler with a fine hunting piece. £63 0s. 0d.
    [March 1816]
1 ornamental wine cooler, rich with fine painting of Cardinal Woolsley and the Abbey of Leicester. £150 0s. 0d.
    [February 1818]

WINE LABELS

It is not clear from the original records if the several labels or wine labels mentioned were of porcelain, or of silver or plate or even enamel. In November 1794, for example, a reference to '2 oval labels Port and Madeira' is listed, but other entries in January 1802 certainly did not refer to silver or plate – '1 label blue and gold', '4 do. [label] white and gold'. These were almost certainly made of porcelain or pottery, although they could have been bin labels, for use in a cellar, rather than decanter or bottle labels.

8

THE CHAMBERLAIN PATTERNS

This chapter comprises the original Chamberlain pattern list. This is a unique written record of a porcelain factory's tableware designs ranging in period from the 1790s to the early 1850s.

It is not known if there were also the more normal illustrated pattern books, where each design was carefully drawn; certainly such a record was used for at least some patterns, in the 1840s, but the survival of the written list is of vital importance in enabling the collector to check if a numbered design is a Chamberlain one or not, and in many cases it also gives the original price of a complete tea service or, occasionally, of the matching dessert or dinner service.

The list commences at or shortly after the period when Robert Chamberlain started the manufacture of his own porcelain – pattern number 1, for example, is shown in Plates 52 and 54, and pattern number 2 in Plates 51 and 72. The list does not include the patterns added at an early date to porcelains purchased in the white from the Caughley factory. Therefore, designs such as 'Doves' or 'L'Amitié' (see Plates 25 and 26) are not included in Chamberlain's list of his own patterns supplied to customers after about 1791.

The original documents are now in a bad state of repair – several entries or groups of entries are illegible. The original descriptions were written without punctuation, with many odd spellings, and the meaning of some words is not now clear, whilst others are unreadable. Apart from some minor amendments to clarify a description, and some simple punctuation to aid reading, the following list of over 2,500 patterns remains as it was written. The old spellings include, for example, several variations on 'dentil' for the tooth-like edging to many designs, such as the Princess Charlotte plate

shown in Colour Plate IX, a detail of which is reproduced in Plate 405.

Different spellings also occur for descriptions such as 'vermicelli', which denotes the seaweed-type gilt continuous worm lines found on so much Worcester porcelain (shown in detail in Plate 406).

References to Plates or pages where designs are illustrated or mentioned in the main text have been added, and a few notes on the approximate dating of some patterns are also included.

Very few references occur in the list to factory artists, but where they are mentioned cross-references will be found in Chapter 6, which is devoted to the decorators. For example, the Davis bird patterns will be found listed under that artist's name on page 194.

In most cases the first word of the description relates to the basic shape of the blanks to which the pattern was added. To clarify this point I have added a comma after the shape description. In general the less expensive designs were painted on the cheapest shapes, plain being cheaper than the shanked or spiral-fluted shapes. However, the situation is confused when an early pattern such as number 2 (see Plate 51) was added to a later and more fashionable form replacing the original unsaleable shape (see Plate 72). The shapes named in the pattern list are those to which the pattern was first applied.

The identified shapes are listed below. They are given here in the order in which they appear in the pattern list.

'*Plain*' This designation appears to relate to the simple cup forms, for several different early teapot shapes appear under this heading (see Plates 44, 55 and 68). Two early cup forms of this type are shown in Plates

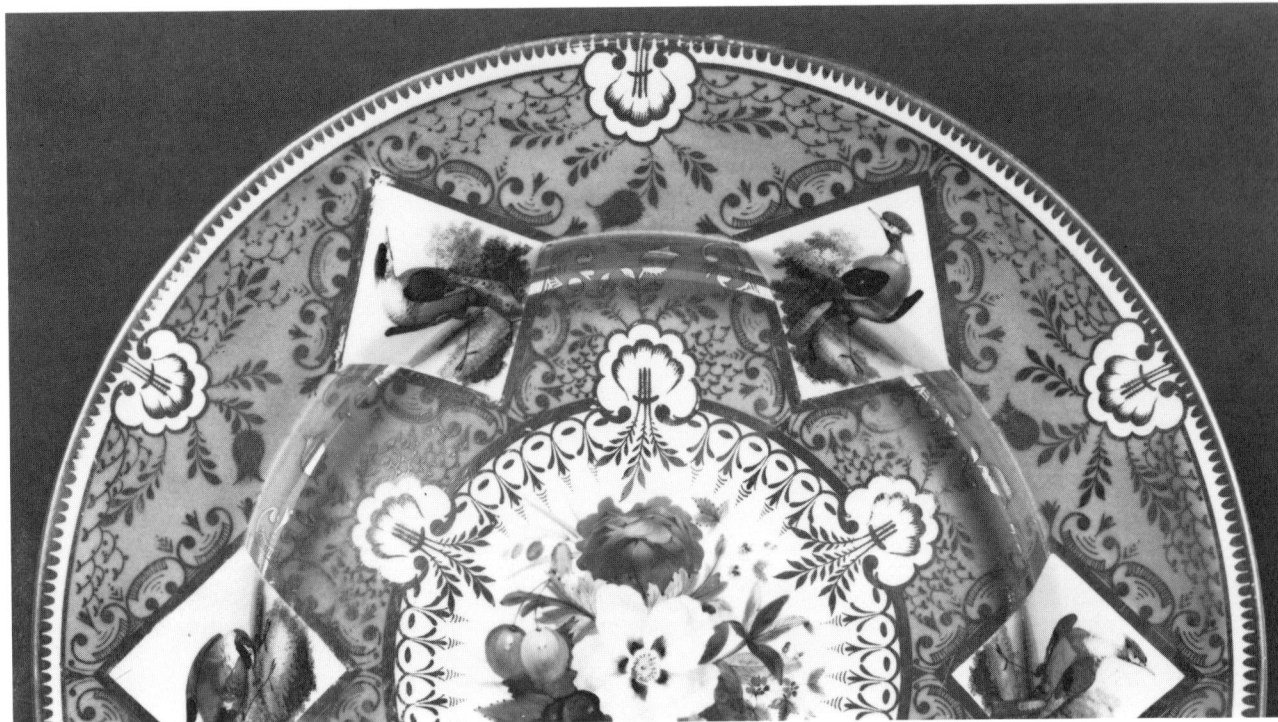

405.   Detail of the soup plate illustrated in Colour Plate IX which was made for Princess Charlotte in 1816–17. *Godden Reference Collection*

406.   Detail of the seaweed-type gilt decoration known as 'vermicelli' which is found on much Worcester porcelain.

47 and 54, but most cups were teabowls without the handle, as in Plates 54 and 69.

'*Common*'   It is not clear if this word relates to a simple standard shape, or to an inexpensive design to be painted by apprentices. It seems likely to have been an early simple shape, for against pattern 8 there are two prices – £1 16s. 0d. for 'Common' and £2 2s. 0d.

for 'New fluted shapes' (see Plate 67). The two terms 'Plain' and 'Common' were only used prior to 1800.

'*Shanked*' or '*Shankered*'   The term relates to the spiral-fluted forms so fashionable between approximately 1792 and 1810 (see Plates 42, 66, 70 and 75). The wares were more costly than the 'Plain' or 'Common' shapes (see also page 312). However, there appear to have been two grades of shanked teawares – 'Common' and 'Fine' (see patterns 153 and 154) – but these terms may refer to the more normal descriptions, 'Best' and 'Seconds', for the grades of ware as they came from the kiln.

'*New fluted*'   These forms are embellished with vertical flutes (see Plates 77–80 and 83, left). The basic type occurs in earlier Caughley and Worcester porcelains. These Chamberlain 'new fluted' shapes are contemporary with shanked wares.

'*Bell*', '*Bell plain*', '*Bell fluted*'   It is not clear what forms are indicated here but those shown in Plates 56, 57 (left), 59 (teacup) and 64 seem likely contenders.

'*Dejeune*' (several different spellings)   The Nelson teawares of pattern 240 are of the 'Dejeune' shape (see Plates 117 and 118), as are the teawares of pattern 276, illustrated in Plate 120 (see also Plates 125 and 126).

'*Seconds*'   This description refers to slightly faulty blanks, and such items were of an inexpensive nature.

Against pattern 928 is the notation 'Seconds half price' (see also page 148).

'*Bute*' This description first occurs against pattern 76, and against 94 there is the description 'Bute or can shape'. However, the cup forms shown in Plates 58 and 59 and bearing earlier patterns are similar to 'Bute' shape cups made later at other factories – at Caughley and in Staffordshire. The standard 'Bute' shape cup is shown in Plate 426.

'*Irish*' The reference to 'Irish' against patterns such as number 153 most probably relates to the size rather than shape. The Staffordshire Potters' 1814 price agreement uses the term in this manner: 'Irish or first size'. On the evidence of design 258 the Irish tewares were plain, not fluted.

'*Hambleton*', '*Bute Hambleton*' The description 'Bute Hambleton flute' appears against design 314. Pattern 385 on the 'Hambleton' shape is illustrated in Plate 111; the teacup is of the basic 'Bute' form. The approximate period of this shape is 1802–4.

'*Porringer*' This description is a rare one, first occurring against design 421 in about 1805. As yet no shape is linked with this name.

'*Baden*', '*Baden gadroon*' The name 'Baden' first occurs under pattern number 441 of about 1809. It subsequently occurs very frequently and over a surprisingly long period, up to pattern 2418 of the late 1840s. It would appear to have been introduced with a plain border but by pattern 1071, in 1822–3, the description 'Baden gadroon' was used to indicate a moulded gadrooned edging. The 'Baden' shapes appear to have been popular over so long a period that various amended shapes or combinations of shapes were so designated (see page 116).

'*Grecian*' The designation was rarely used but first appeared against design 604 in about 1812. The form might be that shown in Plate 136, although the general style of these pieces might also be described 'French' or 'Regent'.

Later known shapes are illustrated in the following pages with the help of some drawings in the surviving factory pattern books.

The list of patterns quoted for the Chamberlain period from 1791 to 1852 runs to number 5019, but taking into account some blank numbers or breaks in the sequence, the total number of Chamberlain designs is reduced to about 2,670, giving an average of just over forty-three patterns a year.

In the mid to late 1840s a few references appear in the list to another series of numbers bearing the prefix B. For example: '2263. Windsor, celeste band & gold lines (as B333. Feb 3rd, 1846)'. Such 'B'-numbers may relate to an inexpensive non-porcelain body, or perhaps to an order placed at the Bond Street retail shop.

It is apparent that some entries refer to special orders for a single service, or to items matching other firms' designs. Some patterns did not find favour with the dealers and their customers, and were discontinued after a short period, so that only a very few sets were produced. Other designs, such as number 75, remained popular over many years; indeed this design was reissued in 1979 by the present Royal Worcester Company.

It is interesting to see that the rival Grainger firm, which had been established in 1801, had in its early days a larger number of new patterns per year than the Chamberlain company with its ten year start. This fact is indicated by two interesting cross-references in the Chamberlain list in the summer of 1813, for Chamberlain's pattern 638 was listed as 'Grainger's 972' and Chamberlain's pattern 640 as 'Grainger's 930'. The rival firm's pattern sequence, therefore, was then up to at least 972, giving an average of some eighty patterns per year. The reason for this may have been that the Grainger firm was at that time almost entirely concerned with tableware designs.

It is noteworthy that the rival Flight firm, and the Barr, Flight & Barr and Flight, Barr & Barr managements appear to have managed without a pattern book or pattern list, for their porcelains do not seem to have been marked with pattern numbers.

The surviving Chamberlain list was probably only intended as a guide to the prices to be charged for each design, as in many cases the written descriptions are not detailed enough to have been a positive guide to the painters – for example, '325 Rich blue red & gold £12 12s. 0d.'. The original pricing was mostly in guineas ('gs').

I gladly acknowledge the help given to me by Jeremy Stedman in preparing the initial draft of this list from the handwritten original pages. The result is a most valuable aid to the identification or confirmation of the source of a huge range of Chamberlain tablewares, where these bear a pattern number. All references are to tea services but in some cases the prices for dessert sets are added, as well as for dinner services, which were termed 'Table'.

Note: Unless otherwise stated, the prices relate to tea services. In many cases, however, particularly in the later patterns, no teaware prices are given in the original list.

£ s. d.

1. Plain, enamel'd sprigs with gold edge
   [see Plates 52 and 54]   [price not clear]
2. Plain, enamel'd Foreign sprig & crowfoot
   border [see Plates 51 and 72]   2 2 0
3. Plain, enamel'd, new Dresden [flowers] gold
   edge   2 2 0
4. Broad blue borders, gilt, Chain border & sprigs 3 3 0
5. Blue & green sprigs, gold edge   6 6 0
6. Common enamelled, purple chain etc.   [price not clear]
   [Perhaps as in Plate 408]
7. Common enamelled, rose coloured border &
   enamelled sprigs   2 2 0
8. Common image [Chinese figures] white edge,
   no border [see Plate 67]   1 16 0
   On new fluted shapes   2 2 0
9. Hunting pattern in compartments [see Plates
   44–50 and 129]   2 12 6
10. Gold sprigs   [price not clear]
11. Sable & gold border & sprigs, Gold edge   3 3 0
12. Foreign wreath [of flowers]   [price not clear]

13. Blossom [see page 74 and Plate 58]   3 3 0
14. French sprig without border [plain forms]   3 3 0
    On fluted tearwares   4 4 0
15. Gold edge & neck'd on edge   3 3 0
16. Plain, rose colour & gold sprigs, Mr. H C's
    pattern   2 12 6
17. Shanked & New fluted do.   do.   3 13 6
18. Do.   Brown & gold sprigs
    & rose coloured border ...   4 4 0
19. Do. brown ribbon intermixed with Dresden
    flowers [see Plate 62]   6 6 0
20. Do.   black & gold border & bottom without
    sprigs, black dots & leafage [see Plate 71] 6 6 0
21. Do. brown & gold flowers with small rose
    colour & gold sprigs, double edge [see Plates
    109, 110 and 124]   4 14 6
22. New fluted, Temperance [blue] border,
    Davis's birds   [price not clear]
23. Shanked, jett [black] S...rd [word indistinct]
    border outside   6 6 0
24. Plain, Tasker's Chinese bridge pattern, brown
    edge [see Plates 53, 60, 68 and 409] [price not clear]
25. Shanked, birds eye border with line outside &
    new fluted   4 4 0
26. Plain, blue & gold sprigs [see Plate 55]   3 13 6

407.   A decorative yellow-ground Chamberlain cup and saucer from a tea service, painted with Worcester views in brown monochrome. The American eagle and shield motif are worked into the border to a special order. This cup profile is a characteristic Chamberlain one. Cup 2½ in. high. c. 1805–10. *Private collection*

27. New fluted, birds eye — 6 6 0
28. [Illegible] Birds eye border & wreath — 5 5 0
29. [Illegible] — 4 4 0
30. [No pattern recorded but account book states 'New fluted festoon'] — 6 6 0

[The first few words of patterns 31–53 are missing.]

31. Gold Royal Star — 7 7 0
32. Plymouth birds eye bottom — 7 7 0
33. Brown & gold feather border with a neat husk wreath in gold outside the upright pieces — 5 5 0
34. New fluted, gold feather border with a neat husk wreath in gold outside the upright pieces [see Plates 78 and 83] — 5 5 0
35. [No pattern recorded, but a shanked shape] — 6 6 0
36. Shanked, with wreath outside & sprig — 6 6 0
37. Shanked with edge & line [gold spray design] [see Plate 410] — 4 4 0
38. Shanked [Angoulème sprigs] also new fluted [see Plate 79] — 4 4 0
39. [Illegible] Birds eye border — 4 14 6
40. [No pattern recorded] — 4 14 6
41. [No pattern recorded] — 10 10 0
42. [Illegible] shanked shape — 4 14 6
43. [Illegible] Fruit enamelled, gilt, the pattern of Dr. Beadman[?] — 10 10 0

44. [Illegible] with brown & gold sprigs in the bottom — 3 13 6
45. Shanked [?] festoon border, with neat chain inside cup etc. — 6 6 0
46. Shanked[?] [illegible] border straw [illegible] & sprigs in the bottom, all gold — 7 7 0
47. Shanked [illegible] oval, brown & gold flowers, Davis's — 9 9 0
48. Shanked [illegible] full pattern on best white Plain [see Plates 42 and 70] — 5 5 0 / 4 4 0
49. [Illegible] Dresden flowers first size — 6 0 0
50. Bell shape, sprigs in compartments — 6 6 0
51. Bell shape, Two panell Dresden flowers — 12 12 0
52. Blue & gold, Royal stripe — 12 12 0
53. New fluted [illegible, but a white and gold design] — 3 3 0
54. Plain, rose colour border in compartments — 1 4 0
55. New fluted, gold star border with dropping leafage in gold [see Plates 59 and 61. Also supplied on shanked shapes by at least November 1796 – see Plate 73] — 7 7 0
56. [Illegible] & spray — 1 16 0
57. Plain, rose colour border & sprig — 1 16 0
58. Plain, enamelled 4 roses in border & flowers, gold tracing — 2 2 0

408. A teabowl and saucer of typical early hybrid hard-paste body and glaze, painted in the style of the Chinese imports and of the New Hall type porcelains. This is probably Chamberlain's pattern 6, 'Common enamelled, purple chain etc.'. Diameter of saucer 5 in. *c.* 1795–8. *Godden Reference Collection*

410.   Chamberlain shanked tearwares decorated in gold with pattern 37, originally priced at £4 4s. 0d. for the complete service. Gilt pattern numbers. Teapot 7 in high. *c.* 1796–8. *Godden of Worthing Ltd*

409.   An early Chamberlain oval teapot decorated with pattern 24, 'Tasker's Chinese bridge pattern, brown edge' (see also Plates 53, 60 and 68). Unmarked. 6 in. high. *c.* 1795–7. *Godden Reference Collection*

59. Plain rose festoon & sprigs & red border	1	16	0
60. Shanked. B.B. [blue border]	8	8	0
with views [or figures or birds]	12	12	0
61. Shanked, blue border with gold ovals, gold leafage dropping inside [see Plate 411]	7	7	0
62. Fluted, blue bordered gold ovals & starrs on the border gold sprigs & insects	5	15	0
63. Dejeune, broad gold edge & ring around foot & inside	4	4	0
64. Shanked, 44 [pattern], sprig & brown & gold dropping border	4	4	6
65. New fluted, B.B. [blue border] gold leafage on border, gold sprigs	5	5	0
66. Shanked, Blue border, gold leafage on the blue dropping border outside [This pattern was sent out in August 1795: see Plates 83 and 412]	6	6	0

67. Shanked, B.B. & blue & gold leafage with gold wave from border to leafage	12	12	0
68. Shanked, B.B. The above pattern [reversed?] that is room of blue in place of white	12	12	0
69. Shanked, 44 [pattern] sprig & small border of leafage [see Plates 74 and 413]	4	4	0
70. Plain, black & gold leafage, gold edge & ring with black sprigs	3	3	0
71. Shanked, white & gold Nindi pattern	9	9	0
72. Fluted, new birds eye bordered, enamelled blue & gold bordered outside standing pieces	5	5	0
73. Bell shape, plain, Plymouth bordered inside blue & gold pieces	14	14	0
74. Bell plain, three panels fawn Dresden flowers	14	14	0
75. Bell Fluted [and other shapes] Dragon in compartments [see Plates 56, 57, 81, 93, 94 and Colour Plate XXV]	7	7	0
76. Bute shape, Lord Pontetts border, Brown & gold	8	8	0
77. Shanked, white & gold dropping border	5	5	0
78. Best Queen mosaic, Blue & gold with India work. J [see page 96. This pattern is often found on early ornamental pieces, see Plates 85, 222 and 337]	16	16	0

[The page is torn here and the prices for patterns 79 and 80 are missing.]

79. Dejeune shape, blue & gold border			
80. Shanked, Lord Palett's border with brown & gold festoons			
81. Davis's birds with fruit & flowers in festoons, blue & gold border [Perhaps similar to the dessert dish shown in Colour Plate VII]	18	18	0
82. Bell plain, border inside blue & gold balloon leafage [A pattern cup of this design was sent in January 1796]	16	16	0
83. Seconds, shanked or fluted, sprigs with brown edge			
84. New fluted, B.B., Husk with small drops & 3 sprigs [see Plate 414]	5	5	0
85. Old mosaic & India work with blue and gold	14	14	0

411.   A blue- and gold-bordered shanked sugar basin and teabowl of a pattern often numbered 60 but probably 61 in fact. Written name mark 'Chamberlains Worcester, No.60'. 5¼ in. high. *c.* 1798–1800. *Geoffrey Godden, chinaman*

412.   A teabowl and saucer with underglaze-blue border with added gilding to form Chamberlain's basic pattern 66, here further embellished with the owner's crest and initials. Diameter of saucer 5½ in. *c.* 1796–8. *Godden of Worthing Ltd*

413. A shanked sugar-box and cover from a teaset of pattern 69 in brown and gold, a tasteful inexpensive design, originally sold at £4 4s. 0d. for the set. Painted mark inside cover 'Chamberlains Worcester, Warranted. No.69'. 5½ in. high. *c.* 1797–1800. *Geoffrey Godden, chinaman*

414. A 'new fluted' Chamberlain teapot with underglaze-blue border and slight gilding. This is Chamberlain's pattern 84, priced at £5 5s. 0d. Written mark inside cover 'Chamberlains Worcester, Warranted'. 9¼ in. long. *c.* 1797–1800. *Godden of Worthing Ltd*

86. Shanked, Vandike border brown & gold	14 14	0
or blue & gold	21 0	0
87. French border, green & gold with red, green & gold flowers in bottom	8 8	0
88. Shanked or fluted seconds, gold edge only	2 2	0
89. Do. do. fawn & gold stripe	10 10	0
90. Bute, white & gold with yellow ribbon	8 8	0
91. Poppy border etc. [Perhaps as in Plate 58, but this design does not seem to warrant this high price]	10 10	0
92. Vandike border, red, yellow, etc. with small Dresden flowers	16 16	0
93. Shanked, yellow & gold stripe	8 8	0
94. Bute or can shape, rose border, yellow ground	16 16	0
95. Bell, brown Derby border & festoon	6 6	0
96. Bell plain, Plymouth, Blue & gold border inside	12 12	0
97. Bute, landscape, rich blue & gold leafage & border	24 0	0
98. [No pattern recorded but shanked, with white and gold tassels]	5 5	0
99. Blue & gold border, Fleurs de lis, six sprigs & gold line	6 6	0

[The page here is badly torn and designs up to 108 are difficult to read.]

100. Brown & gold border, festoons & sprigs	6 6	0
101. Brown & gold border, Staffordshire border & brown roses	2 12	0
102. Shanked, Tournay sprigs	4 14	0
103. Shanked, Angouleme sprigs & gold border	4 14	0
104. [Illegible]	5 5	0
105. [Illegible]	5 5	0
106. [Illegible]	8 8	0
107. [Illegible]	7 0	0
108. Bell fluted, blue & gold ribbon	6 6	0
109. New fluted, Plymouth festoon	7 7	0
110. Bute, Dresden flowers, border edge & line	4 4	0

111. New fluted, Gold festoon & wreath	6 6	0
112. Shanked, yellow ribboned & gold border	7 7	0
113. Shanked, fawn ribboned with gold stripes, Roses of gold, wreath inside cup etc.	8 8	0
114. [No pattern recorded]		
115. [No pattern recorded]		
116. Shanked, Diamond border, Roses, black & gold	6 6	0
117. Fluted, blue & gold sprigs	4 4	0
118. [No pattern recorded]		
119. Shanked, purple & gold border outside in a wreath, gold line inside	5 5	0
120. White, & gold star border, old Tyer [see Plate 66]	5 5	0
121. Shanked, blue border gold stripes, Roses with Vandike sprigs	7 7	0

415. A Chamberlain teapot-stand decorated in underglaze blue and gold, showing pattern 126 or 'Sir Charles Talbot's pattern', priced at £14 14s. 0d. for the set. Gilt pattern number only. 6¾ in. long. *c.* 1797–1800. *W. Pitts Collection*

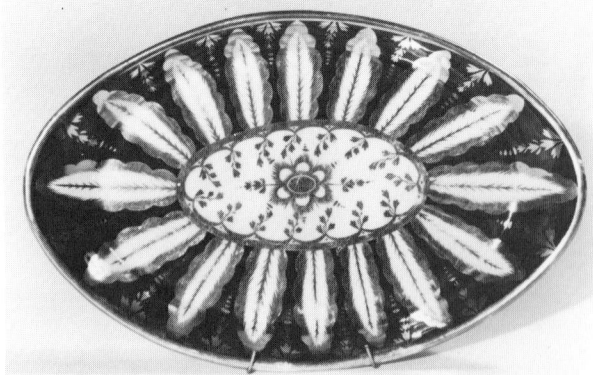

122. Shanked, yellow ribboned & gold bands — 6 6 0
123. Shanked, bloom & gold border — 6 6 0
124. Shanked, yellow & gold border [Sample cup and saucer sent out in October 1797] — 6 6 0
125. Shanked, Bloom border & gold festoons — 8 8 0
126. Dejeuney shape handled [see Plate 415], blue & gold leafage, Sir Charles Talbot's pattern — 14 14 0
  Dessert Service — 42 0 0
127. Dejeuney shape, bloom border sprigs — 6 6 0
128. Shanked, bloom stripe and gold — 9 9 0
129. Shanked, blue stripe & gold, new thumb — 12 12 0
130. Shanked, border of green, gold bands & sprigs — 6 6 0
131. Plain, brown & gold flowers, J. Rogers pattern — 3 3 0
132. Shanked, green & gold border, green & gold band & gold husk — 8 8 0
133. [No pattern recorded]
134. [No pattern recorded]
135. Shanked, Bloom border festoons & gold — 8 8 0
136. Bute, fawn ground, Dresden flowers in compartments, gold stars on the fawn — 16 16 0
137. [No pattern recorded]
138. [No pattern recorded]
139. Shanked, fawn band gold sprigs etc. — 6 6 0
140. Common shanked, Queen — 10 10 0
141. Fine shanked, Queen — 14 14 0
142. Dejeuney handled, brown band, Rich gold border, Robert's pattern — 10 10 0
143. Shanked, enamelled and gold border & lines, Davis's — 6 6 0
144. Fluted, Jassamine — 7 7 0
145. Fluted, Segg[?] — 5 5 0
146. Bell fluted, blue landscape in pannells, blue ground gilt — 7 7 0
147. Shanked, French grey border — 5 5 0
148. Fluted, Princes circle — 8 8 0
149. Davis's birds yellow & bloom — 15 15 0
150. Shanked, Vandike gold border & line — 6 6 0
151. Dejeuney shape, handled yellow ribbon & gold [This basic design was also used for ornamental objects] — 10 10 0
152. Shanked handled, flowers in pannells front different gold border — 12 12 0
153. Irish, fawn & gold bands — 4 4 0
154. Irish, bloom & gold Dejeune — 4 4 0
  Plain — 3 13 6
155. I ish, yellow & gold bands — 4 4 0
156. Shanked, Vandike double border brown festoons of gold etc. — 18 18 0
157. Fluted 2nds, Dresden flowers, gold edge & ring — 4 4 0
158. Shanked, border of flowers in colours etc. — 7 7 0
159. Shanked, brown yellow and gold border with flowers outside — 7 7 0
160. Dejeuney, brown, yellow, same as 151 — 10 10 0
161. Bute, broad yellow views etc. Lord Stamfields — 12 12 0
162. Dejeuney shape, Oak & Acorn border — 9 9 0
163. Dejeuney, yellow ground & brown gold border as 151 with husk — 12 12 0
164. Shanked, Bell, flowers and blue border gilt etc. — 7 7 0
165. Dejeuney shape, brown & gold bands — 7 7 0
166. Do. do. Clutterbuck pattern — 12 12 0
167. Do. Gold wreath from French rouge pot — 6 6 0

168. Do. Orange ground Brown band Bird etc. — 21 0 0
169. Do. Brown & gold. Jas Clutterbuck
170. Shanked, bloom and gold nobb pattern — 7 7 0
171. Fluted, green and gold curtain — 8 8 0
172. Fluted, Royal stripe enamel blue dots etc. — 7 7 0
173. Wedgwood's pattern Bloom ground green & Gold border — 12 12 0
174. Shanked, 151 pattern with views — 18 18 0
175. Dejeuny shape, vine border — 10 10 0
176. Bute shape, yellow ground, brown & gold striped border — 10 10 0
177. Dejeuney shape, Bloom 113 pattern — 8 18 0
178. Shanked, Gold sprigs small & gold bands [see Plate 416] — 4 4 0
179. Shanked, brown feather & gold feather with sprigs [see Plate 417] — 5 5 0
180. Shanked, brown husks with sprigs — 5 5 0
181. Shanked, do. do. no sprigs
182. Shanked, or Bute enamelled blue, green and gold sprigs [roses] — 3 13 6
183. Shanked, red & gold sprigs star centre — 4 4 0
184. Shanked, small red and gold husks small gold sprigs — 4 4 0
185. Shanked, blue, rose colours & gold sprigs narrow red border & gold husks [see Plate 418]
186. Do. Gold edge & stars
187. [No pattern recorded]
188. [No pattern recorded]
189. Shanked, red & gold Well border, roses — 5 5 0
190. Do. blue, red & gold sprigs narrow yellow border and husk — 5 5 0
191. Do. do. do. fawn do. — 5 5 0

---

416. A shanked sugar-box and cover of pattern 178, a simple gilt design priced at £4 4s. 0d. the set. Painted mark inside cover 'Chamberlains Worcester No. 178'. 5½ in. high. c. 1800–5. *Godden of Worthing Ltd*

417.   Part of a shanked teaset of pattern 179, 'brown feather & gold feather with sprigs' at £5 5s. 0d. Painted mark inside cover 'Chamberlains Worcester, Warranted No. 179'. Teapot 7 in. high. c. 1800–5. *Godden of Worthing Ltd*

192. Fluted, panelled edge, plain band	3	3	0
193. Do. small gold sprigs and gold edge and foot line [see Plate 80]	3	3	0
194–8. [No pattern recorded]			
199. Irish double edge and bands			
200. Dejeuny yellow ground gold and red diamonds with ovals etc.	4	4	0
201. Shanked Brown and gold husk neat small gold sprigs	14	4	0
202. Plain Chinese sprigs gold edge, best ware [?]		12	6
203. Shanked enamelled birds do. [see Plate 82]	2	12	6
204–8. [No pattern recorded]			
209. Dejeuny Diamond border with the 157 & Wilkins	21	0	0
210. Do. Yellow & red with gold	10	10	0
211. Do. do. Brown and red diamond border [see Plate 343]	16	16	0
212. Do. do. Red & gold	10	10	0
213. Do. do. White & gold	10	10	0
214. Do. do. Ribboned and double husk & gold	6	6	0
215. Do. do. do. and gold antique drops etc.	12	12	0
216. Dejeuny, brown and gold	12	12	0
217. Do. do. and gold	8	8	0
218. Do. Brown bands red and gold husk	9	9	0
219. Shanked, yellow, red and gold	6	6	0
220. Do. do. do.	6	6	0
221. Do. do. do. bluebell border [see Plate 114]	6	6	0
222. Do. Marble border etc.	10	10	0
223. 105 border in yellow ground, red brown & gold [ordered in November 1800]	10	10	0
224. Dejeuney blue bell border red band & gold husk	10	10	0
225. [No pattern recorded]			
226. Shanked, yellow border with red & gold husk	5	5	0
227. Dejeuney, Rich blue & gold ground with sators [sic] head & flowerpot in pannell, Tasker	21	0	0
228. Do. Yellow & Red ovals with black diamonds. W. Burbeck	16	0	0
229. Do. No. 55 with fawn band	9	9	0

230.	Do. Red bands oval in border cream & blue in festoons [gold] between and gold husks below	12	12	0
231.	Shanked, blue edge & best	1	8	0
232.	[No pattern recorded]			
233.	[No pattern recorded]			
234.	Red, yellow & gold oval border	14	14	0
235.	Dejeuney, star border and red band	9	0	0
236.	Do. blue bell & feather with husk	12	12	0
237.	Do. Vandike border yellow barrs red & gold flowers & gold dots	14	14	0
238.	[No pattern recorded]			
239.	[No pattern recorded]			
240.	Dejeuney shape, fine old Japan pattern same as Roses [see Plates 113–15 and page 110]	12	12	0
241.	Shanked, sprigs, Miss Pools pattern			
242–9.	[No pattern recorded]			
250.	Brown rose border & sprigs see no. 58. pattern plain	3	3	0
251.	Dejeuney, red & gold same as done for Mr. Woodwick	9	9	0
252.	Irish Ware, same as 250 without border	2	2	0
253.	Dejeuney, gold border see pattern from Bristol	6	16	6
254.	Do. strawberry border in brown, see 292	7	7	0
255.	Do. Pegg's blue & gold diamond	12	12	0
256.	Do. Pegg's red & gold diamond	10	10	0
257.	Do. Pegg's gold fanns & blue dots	10	10	0
258.	Irish, brown & gold sprigs & wreath [see Plate 419. It is interesting to see this early-looking pattern introduced after 1800, and that tea-bowls were still employed for the less expensive patterns]	3	3	0
259.	[No pattern recorded]			
260.	Shanked, Nankin, Gold edge and band	3	13	6
261.	Shanked, green leaves & red berries. G. Rogers	7	7	0
262.	Dejeuney, diamond gold border. Star border & ovals inside fawn band & drops	16	16	0
263.	Do. India blue, red & gold, flowers	12	12	0
	Dessert set	37	16	0
	Dinner set	189	0	0
264–9.	[No pattern recorded]			
270.	Dejeuney, Angouleme pattern or French sprig	5	5	0
271.	Do. Green red & gold border. G. Rogers	7	7	0
272.	Do. Roses in colours with fawn & gold festoon. G. Rogers	8	8	0
273.	Do. Blue border gold barley ears	5	5	0
274.	Do. do. do. do.	5	5	0
275.	Shanked, Nankin gilt chain see no. 4.	4	4	0
276.	Dejeuney, India, Thumb & finger pattern [see Plates 120, 142 and 420]	10	10	0
277.	Do. Vandike blue & gold border	6	6	0
278.	Irish, Nankin pattern Best edge line & ring	3	13	6
279.	[No pattern recorded]			
280.	[No pattern recorded]			
281.	[No pattern recorded]			
282.	Dejeuney, laurel border & gold. G. Rogers	12	12	0
283–9.	[No pattern recorded]			
290.	Dejeuney, Plymouth with fawn ground			
291.	Fawn ground Derby small gold diamond relieved with red & gold border			
292.	Shanked, strawberry border inside in brown & gold	6	6	0

418.   *Top:* A shanked teabowl and saucer enamelled and gilded with a simple £5 5s. 0d. design. This is pattern 185 with a red border and blue and gilt sprigs. Pattern number only. Diameter of saucer 5¾ in. *c.* 1800–5. *Miss C. Cooke*

419.   *Centre:* A simple non-fluted teabowl and saucer painted in brown and gold with pattern 258, described as 'Irish' and priced at only £3 3s. 0d. for the complete service. Painted pattern number only. Diameter of saucer 5¼ in. *c.* 1802–5. *Mrs P. Willmot*

420.   *Bottom:* A desert dish from a service of the popular 'thumb and finger pattern', design 276. The dark areas are in underglaze blue. Written mark 'Chamberlains Worcester'. *c.* 1805–10. *Godden of Worthing Ltd*

421. A rare small-size plate, bearing the owner's crest, decorated with the richly gilt fawn-ground design 299, much used on ornamental vases (see Colour Plate XXIII). This teaware design had the extremely high price of 30 guineas. Unmarked except for pattern number. Diameter 7¼ in. c. 1800. *Geoffrey Godden, chinaman*

293.	Dejeuney				
294.	Do.	yellow & gold Vandike border	7	7	0
295.	Do.	Narrow blue border & bands	4	4	0
296.	[No pattern recorded]				
297.	Shanked, same as 66 only red in line of blue		6	6	0
298.	Dejeuney, rich blue border of gold with ovals of India work [see Plates 125, 127, 134, 135 and Colour Plate XI]		14	14	0
299.	Do.	Fawn ground & gold see Bickfords [This rich gilt pattern was much favoured for the ground work of vases, beakers and similar objects – see Colour Plate XXIII and Plate 421]	31	10	0
300.	Shanked, enamelled blue & gold wreath etc. [ordered October 1801 : see Plates 113 and 422]		5	5	0
301.	Do.	French do. border & gold	6	6	0
302.	Do.	Gold wreath & starr centre [see Plate 423]	4	4	0
303.	Do.	Small gold chain & 53 sprigs	4	4	0
304.	Do.	Single 42 border & starrs	7	7	0
305.	Dejeuney, Rich Salmon & gold, Newton [figure subjects]		26	5	0
306.	Do.	Fawn ground gold spangles Wedgwood's border	12	12	0
307.	Do.	Gold border, small as no. 305	12	12	0
308.	Do.	Full border of flowers etc. G. Rogers	8	8	0
309.	Do.	Courant border in cellors [sic]	7	7	0
310.	[No pattern recorded, but as illustrated in Plates 121–3]		10	10	0
311.	Dejeuney, Jet flowers printed gold & foot line		3	3	0
312.	Do.	green festoon & gold leafage with red & purple	8	8	0

423. A shanked trio of teabowl, coffee cup (or can) and saucer, embellished in gold with pattern 302, at £4 4s. 0d. for the complete service. Painted pattern number. Coffee can 2½ in. high. c. 1802–5. *Mrs P. Willmot*

422. Chamberlain's shanked teawares of pattern 300, 'enamelled blue & gold wreath etc. £5 5s. 0d.', as ordered from October 1801. Painted mark inside covers 'Chamberlains Worcester, 300'. *c.* 1802–5. *Messrs Sotheby & Co.*

313. Do.   fawn & gold border with enamelled blue & rose colour drops, small gold — 7 7 0

314. Bute Hambleton flute, Rotton Slick [?] pattern on blue border — 8 8 0

315. Do.   do.   do.   Blue & gold border broad with dagger diaper — 8 8 0

316. Dejeuney, India work Red green & gold, Mills — 10 10 0

317. Do.   New Dresden flowers — 3 3 0

318. Do.   Red festoon & gold — 5 5 0

319. Do.   Green curtain & gold — 5 5 0

320. Do.   Gold grape border etc. — 8 8 0

321. Do.   105 Border & gold leaf — 9 9 0

322. Bute Hambleton, flute Broad blue & gold border — 8 8 0

323. Dejeuney, enamelled blue & gold Chinese Temple — 10 10 0

324. Dejeuney, Red diamond border see 211 without yellow — 10 10 0

325. Rich blue red & gold — 12 12 0

326. Black printed with gold edge & ring — 3 3 0

327. Dejeuney, gold border [illegible] — 5 5 0

328. Do.   Red & gold India work [Similar to a Coalport pattern] — 10 10 0

329. Do.   India flowers & blue dentel edge inside — 10 10 0

330. Dejeuney, Salmon & gold border — 5 5 0

331. Salmon border brown & gold — 6 6 0

332. Dejeune, blue & gold India work flowers without the dontels. — 8 8 0

333. Dejeune, Brown & gold. G.R.'s pattern — 6 6 0

334. Do.   Red ribboned & gold weed, star in bottom — 5 5 0

335. Do.   Gold & red botto[?] in pannel — 6 6 0

336. Shanked, gold festoon & star — 4 14 6

337. Dejeune, 246 border — 9 9 0

338. Shanked, green edge, seconds — 2 2 0

339. Dejeune, oak & ribboned and G. Temple — 10 10 0

340. Do.   Revd. Cliff's Pattern, yellow red & starr border — 10 10 0

341. Do.   Brown ribboned — 5 5 0

342. Do.   running sprigs of gold all over & narrow antique border — 10 10 0

343. Hambleton, blue & gold. G. Rogers — 8 8 0

344. Dejeune, gold feather border. Mitchell — 10 10 0

345. Printed views Yellow border & bands — 5 15 6

346. New Japan girls pattern — 6 6 0

347. Black landscape gold edge & fine line (Printed) — 4 4 0

348. Dejeune, red & Gold — 8 8 0

349. Do.   Fawn & gold ivy border — 10 10 0

350. Do.   Blue border gold edge & lines — 14 14 0

351. Irish, enamelled border & sprigs — 2 12 6
     plain edge — 2 2 0

352. Black chain border — 2 12 6

353. Red green & gold feather border — 10 10 0

354. Hambleton, gold Etruscan border — 6 6 0

355. Hambleton, Orange red & gold stripe — 10 10 0

356. Bute, printed broken flowers — 3 3 0

357. Hambleton, broad blue Etruscan border — 8 8 0

358. Dejeune, holly border on gold ground, Vandike gold border below [see Plate 126] — 16 16 0

359. Bute, red ground etc. with Etruscan border & Etruscan pattern inside — 12 12 0

360. Bute, chocolate colour border pink thorn pattern — 6 6 0

361. Dejeune, small red & green sprigs edge & ring — 4 4 0

362. Do.   Broad fawn border without shells. G.R.'s — 14 14 0

363. Dejeune, fawn gold green & gold Wedgwood with spangles — 10 10 0

364. Do.   Japan border etc. — 10 10 0

365. Do.   or Bute shape, six gold lines & stars — 6 6 0

366. Do.   or do.   red & gold husk wreath — 14 14 0

367. Bute, scarlet & gold border with some [sun?] flower, Chitwins [?] — 8 8 0

368. Dejeune, Corinthian border — 10 10 0

369. Irish, best full gold edge — 2 12 6

370. Do.   2nd enamelled wreath & rose pattern — 1 16 0

371. Do.   Same as 360 only red instead of chocolate brown — 6 6 0

372. Irish, collared pattern without green, brown sprigs — 1 16 0

373. Shanked, purple Paccary [?] — 3 3 0

374. Bute, diamond cornflower & gold border with black dots — 7 7 0

375. Bute Trafalgar with shipping — 16 16 0

376. Broad red & gold border with landscape — 8 8 0

377. Red Etruscan figures in pannells [ordered March 1806] — 10 10 0

378. Brown views with brown line — 2 12 6

379. Dejeune, Brown & gold ivy border — 7 7 0

380. Do.   enamelled blue & red flowers with bold gold work — 7 7 0

381. Bute, red & gold border with four hearts or shells in it & gold sprays — 8 8 0

382. Dejeune, Oak & palm branch in gold, small coloured flowers in pannel — 12 12 0

383. Dejeune, green leaf & gold laurel — 8 8 0

384. Dejeune, Oak border in gold — 9 9 0

385. Hambleton, blue & gold border [see Plate 111] — 6 6 0

386. Shanked, blue & gold border with small gold leaves all over — 6 6 0

387. Dejeuner, ragged Sir Gold [?] — 6 6 0

388. [No pattern recorded]

389. [No pattern recorded]

390. Bute, red border & black key with gold lines — 5 5 0

391. Bute, printed wreath of roses filled up with gold — 7 7 0

392. Bute, printed red India sprigs & gold — 6 6 0

393. Hambleton, red leaf with black shading gold etc. — 7 7 0

394. Shanked, blue bell [?] — 5 5 0

395. Shanked, brown & gold sprigs gold edge & ring — 3 13 6

396. Do.   do.   do.   with border — 4 4 0

397. Bute, brown berries & gold leaves — 4 14 6

398. Bute, Red berries & gold leaves — 4 14 6

399. Bute, brown Etruscan figures in pannell — 10 10 0

400. Irish, enamelled sprigs and border not edged — 1 16 0

401. Bute, and border white & gold shells — 7 7 0

402. Bute, rich salmon ground & gold border with zig zag edge etc. — 10 10 0

403. Bute, gold vermicelli [gold scroll or seaweed-type design] — 8 8 0

404. Hambleton, brown sprigs all over — 2 12 6

405. Dejeune, red ground ground [sic] with ivy all over — 16 16 0

406. Bute, Seaweed in red & gold — 12 12 0

407. Bute, Red & gold holly etc. — 10 10 0

424. A Chamberlain teapot and cover decorated with pattern 419, 'bloom & gold festoons £7 7s. 0d.'. Painted mark inside cover 'Chamberlains Worcester, Warranted. 419'. 10¼ in. long. *c.* 1805–10. *Godden of Worthing Ltd*

408. Dejeune, with blue & gold etc. L. Moriar's pattern	16 16 0		434. White & gold net	9 9 0
409. Do. new brown ribboned broad border	6 6 0		435. Bute, fawn border gold palm & laurel flowers in ovals	12 12 0
410. Bute, vermicelli and 342 border	10 10 0		436. Fawn marble gold bead border	10 10 0
411. Bute, nett pattern	8 8 0		437. Dejeune, fawn net	16 16 0
412. Hambleton, blue border & diamond	8 8 0		438. Hambleton, new weed red & gold	10 10 0
413. [No pattern recorded]			439. Bute, purple stars & gold border solid	8 8 0
414. Bute, Strawberry in red & gold ground	6 6 0		440. Porringer, vermicelli & Diamond border solid	10 10 0
415. Dejeune, red weed ground & gold border	12 12 0		441. Baden, fine brown views all round & bead border	18 18 0
416. Bute, purple & gold wreath border. G.R.'s	5 5 0		442. Black & gold sprigs	2 2 0
417. Bute, brown & gold border & brown & gold rose centre	6 6 0		443. [No pattern recorded]	
418. Any shape fawn border & gold	8 8 0		444. Bute, brown oak & acorn border	6 6 0
419. Do. bloom & gold festoons [see Plate 424]	7 7 0		445. Do. purple zig zag green & gold	4 14 6
420. Bute, gold strawberry & white ground	5 5 0		446. Do. gold zig zag & purple leaves	4 14 6
421. Porringer, brown & gold oval border	4 14 6		447. Do. brown & gold spray border	5 5 0
422. Bute, brown & gold oval border	4 4 0		448. Do. fawn & brown strawberry	6 6 0
423. Bute, white & gold new border	6 6 0		449. Dejeune, blue & gold ivy palm with ovals & sprigs	10 10 0
424. Bute, moss rose border [see Plate 425]	6 6 0		450. Brown views different and gold bead border	7 7 0
425. Do. purple & gold border with oval stars	7 7 0		451. Border on other shape fawn marbled with beaded diamond border and gold	12 12 0
426. Do. Pavellion [?] border	7 7 0		452. Bute, blue ground & Davis's flowers one pannell Gold handle & antique gold	14 14 0
427. Dejeune, red & gold leaf	6 6 0		453. Bute, gold oak & ivy border with fawn marble	12 12 0
428. Do. brown & gold leaf	7 7 0		454. Bute, Enamelled blue red & gold sprigs edge & gold ring	3 13 6
429. Bute, diamond border black & gold	6 6 0		455. Grey marble gold veins & bead border	10 10 0
430. Bute, gold border	5 5 0			
431. Bute, purple ribboned & gold sprigs	4 14 6			
432. Bute, brown & gold wreath border	4 14 6			
433. Fawn ground net & gold border	14 14 0			

425. A teapot and coffee cup of pattern 424, 'moss rose border £6 6s. 0d.'. Painted pattern number. Teapot 10 in. long. *c.* 1813–18. *Geoffrey Godden, chinaman*

426. A Chamberlain cup and saucer of the standard 'Bute' shape (see page 311), decorated with a simple green and gold festoon design. This pattern, number 478, was priced at £3 13s. 6d. for the complete set. Unmarked except for pattern number. Diameter of saucer 5½ in. *c.* 1815. *Godden of Worthing Ltd*

456.	Irish, red border & flowers with red edge	1 8 0	
457.	Irish, red checker & small festoon of flowers coloured sprigs	1 8 0	
458.	Porringer, brown husk & gold (Courtney]	6 6 0	
459.	Gold bell fawn border brown & gold on fawn	4 14 6	
460.	Red husk & slight gold leaves	4 14 6	
461.	Brown & gold Ivy	7 7 0	
462.	Fawn & gold border with black leaves	5 15 6	
463.	Vermicelli border only	6 6 0	
464.	New finger pattern	8 8 0	
465.	New Nelson Pattern	12 12 0	
466.	Blue Ground antique gold border with birds	14 14 0	
467.	Slight gold diamond & red wreath	5 5 0	

468.	Brown husk green wreath & sprigs	2 2 0		
		[price crossed out]		
469.	Green sprigs & dark brown edge	2 2 0		
470.	Yellow band with black edge line & sprigs	1 10 0		
471.	Brown & green border sprigs & brown edge	1 16 0		
472.	Green & red dropping border & sprigs red edge	1 16 0		
473.	Blue birds eye & sprigs with red edge	1 16 0		
474.	Red bead border black edge line & sprigs [ordered November 1809]	1 16 0		
475.	Blue leaves & green & red flowers all over	7 7 0		
476.	Blue red fawn & gold in pannel & basket [?] centre	9 9 0		
477.	Brown basket centre & small sprigs	3 3 0		
478.	Green & gold festoon [see Plate 426]	3 13 6		
479.	Narrow border Vermicelli & gold line	3 13 6		
480.	[No pattern recorded]			
481.	Fawn & gold with white pearls. Courtney [?]	12 12 0		
482.	[No pattern recorded]			
483.	Two rows Vermicelli	5 5 0		
484.	Fawn & gold ovals gold chain top & bottom	10 10 0		
485.	[No pattern recorded]			
486.	Gold band and ring	5 5 0		
487.	W. Burbeck's rich purple & gold diamond	14 14 0		
488.	W. Burbeck's gold & purple Jassamine	6 6 0		
489.	Fawn border marble husk	6 6 0		
490.	Purple & gold border	4 14 6		
491.	Barberry & gold	14 14 6		
492.	Indian blue red & green & gold border	7 7 0		
493.	Porringer, bead border & line outside	4 4 0		
494.	Dejeune, Trafalgar border	8 8 0		
495.	Shanked, red bell	5 5 0		
496.	Blue & gold from 323 Chinese centre enamelled pannell, border birds & India work	10 10 0		
497.	Blue bell & sprig border	5 5 0		
498.	New brown & gold vine leaf border	4 14 6		

499.	French grey with birds eye of different landscape	26	5	0
500.	Rich fawn in and out with 440 & different paintings in feather, birds, shells, landscape	42	0	0
501.	Paris sprigs with gold edge	2	12	6
502.	Brown & gold wreath border something like 416	4	14	6
503.	Three brown berries & gold leafage	5	5	0
504.	Brown & gold barley border	5	15	6
505.	Rose buds in colour & gold sprigs edge & rings	3	13	6
506.	Green & gold rose border	6	6	0
507.	Blue mosaic in pannel with red flower & gold marble on blue	15	15	0
508.	Rich fawn & gold border with white birds eye, see 418 Peacock	8	8	0
509.	Brown & gold leaf with dentell edge	5	15	6
510.	Green rose colour & gold border	5	5	0
511.	Purple rose bud border	6	6	0
512.	Dresden flowers & chain	4	4	0
513.	Dresden flowers & gold edge	3	3	0
514.	Gold oak & ivy slight without fawn	9	9	0
515.	Half vermicelli & diamond border	9	9	0
516.	Best Leeds	9	9	0
517.	Slightly less [?] see 581	8	8	0
518.	Red bands & gold lines	3	13	6
519.	Blue ground Ivy border same as Noweles service	10	10	0
520.	Blue ground Davis's birds			
521.	Red hawthorn berry	5	5	0
522.	Brown oak & gold sprigs	4	4	0
523.	Brown & gold border of leafage	5	5	0
524.	Enamelled blue red & gold border	5	5	0
525.	Hambleton, blue & gold	7	7	0
526.	Fawn & slight gold border	5	5	0
527.	Blue & gold wreath red & diamond lines	6	6	0
528.	Dresden flowers red bead with gold edge	3	3	0
529.	Dresden flowers with donteld gold edge	3	3	0
530.	Bourbon sprigs & gold edge	3	3	0
531.	French shape oak leaf & berry border	7	7	0
532.	Slight oak & ivy fawn marble	10	10	0
533.	Large blue leaves and fawn boss[?]	8	8	0
534.	Gold wave & 120 sprigs	6	6	0
535.	Paris sprigs in brown & gold edge	12	12	6
536.	Blue ground red flowers in pannel owls eyes	10	10	0
537.	Blue tree large blue & fawn leaves	8	8	0
538.	Purple enamel leaves zig zag red bulls & gold dots	10	10	0
539.	Brown leaves and sprigs in bottom same as border	3	13	6
540.	Blue eagles	8	8	0
541.	Blue ground 3 pannells gold ground Leeds India slight	10	10	0
542.	Blue bird [?] & green leaves	10	10	0
543.	Gold oak on fawn	10	10	0
544.	Scarlet with blue & gold curtains	12	12	0
545.	Brown border something like 105	3	3	0
546.	Brown leaves two colours and a little gold	3	3	0
547.	Three brown leaves with edge & line in a border	3	3	0
548.	Scarlet dragon & green border	14	14	0
549.	India pattern blue & enamelled with border compartment & curtains etc.	10	10	0

550.	Blue & red leaves with gold dots	8	8	0
551.	[No pattern recorded]			
552.	Gold views & gold border with fawn in & out	16	16	0
553.	Davis' birds in pannel blue & gold ground [ordered May 1811: see Colour Plate X]	25	4	0
554.	Trafalgar border & gold ivy wreath pale fawn	8	8	0
555.	Girl's green leaf & blue berries coloured edge	2	12	6
		1	16	0
556.	Girl's brown bramble border coloured edge	2	12	6
		1	16	0
557.	Girl's five rose & 4 sprigs gold coloured edge	2	12	6
		1	16	0
558.	Girl's brown leaf border & berries coloured edge	2	12	6
		1	16	0
559.	Girl's green leaf purple & red flower border coloured edge	2	12	6
		1	16	0
560.	Girl's enamelled blue border with small sprigs coloured edge	2	12	6
		1	16	0
561.	Girl's enamel'd flowers in blue red & yellow coloured edge	2	12	6
		1	16	0
562.	Black & gold basket husk & sprigs, gold edge	3	3	0
563.	Black & gold festoons gold edge	3	3	0
564.	Black & gold roses sprigs, crowfoot border	3	3	0
565.	Black band in compartments husk & sprigs	3	3	0
566.	Brown band all round lines with sprigs husks & star centre coloured edge	2	12	6
		1	16	0
567.	Brown & gold leaf border & sprigs. G. Rogers	4	4	0
568.	Gordons border in blue & gold	10	10	0
569.	Birds in pannels in antique style & gilding. G. Davis's	18	18	0
570.	Fawn border with brown leaf and enamelled blue. G. Rogers	8	8	0
571.	French grey with gold P [Prince of Wales?] pattern & gold border	9	9	0
572.	French grey with gold P pattern, no border	8	8	0
573.	Different feathers gold bead & double edge	31	0	0
574.	Fawn ground bordered with brown & gold leaves & 3 blue berries	7	7	0
575.	Fawn 403 & husk border on white with different coloured views	31	10	0
576.	Fawn ground with brown & gold wreath all over brown bell flowers	8	8	0
577.	Fawn Tournay sprigs & gold edge	4	4	0
578.	Blue trees & brown & gold flowers	10	10	0
579.	Boy's India pattern in red & green with brown leaves	6	6	0
580.	Slight scarlet Japan	6	6	0
581.	Slight Leeds	6	6	0
582.	New Dresden with brown edge by the women brown lines [see Plate 299, left]	2	12	6
		1	16	0
583.	Oak & ivy with blue & gold marble	12	12	0
584.	Blue tree with red flowers	7	7	0
585.	Oak & ivy with grey marble ground	10	10	0
586.	Enamel'd blue & gold sprigs	3	13	6
587.	Oak & ivy on blue & gold marble			
588.	Light blue & gold something [sic]			
589.	Light blue with 344 gilding	12	12	0
590.	Blue ground with gold G. Davis's festoons of flowers	12	12	0
591.	Blue ground with India work in pannels	10	10	0
592.	Balloon stripe in fawn & gold	10	10	0

593. 403 gold on light blue ground etc.	12 12 0
594. Dresden flowers Diff't and double edge	
595. Duke of York's Japan	8 8 0
596. Blue ground mosaic [?] pannel & Dresden flowers	14 14 0
597. Marble ground gold border different flowers	12 12 0
598. Different botanical plants & 318 (or 378) rich gold	10 10 0
599. Purple & green border. G. Davis	6 6 0
600. Trafalgar light blue	7 7 0
601. Light blue & diamond gold dontell edge	10 10 0
602. Light blue & gold wreath sprigs in bottom [ordered July 1812]	6 6 0
603. Black views with gold wreath border	6 6 0
604. Grecian with light blue & roses gold marble on blue	10 10 0
605. Drab ground 403 Vandyke border	12 12 0
606. Blue mosaic panneled gold marble & flowers	14 14 0
607. Rose colour & gold border line outside	6 6 0
608. Mill's full India pattern with curtains in blue & gold	12 12 0
609. Zig zag in gold with red spot with gold sprigs	4 14 6
610. Grey leaves & gold lines narrow	3 13 6
611. Fawn & gold all over	6 6 0
612. Rose ribbon & gold border	4 4 0
613. Fawn border narrow one row in gold	
614. Grey borders & brown leaves	
615. Blue ribboned & gold border & ring	4 4 0
616. Brown feather & fleur de lee, gold	5 5 0
617. Enameled blue husk etc.	
618. Light blue ground gold marble & gold husk border	
619. Broad blue border gold scollopes feather & festoons	6 6 0
620. [No pattern recorded]	
621. India spray work with a fly in centre & dontled edge	9 9 0
622. India sprays with red flowers & fly in centre of pannel & dontell edge	9 9 0
623. New Nelson	10 10 0
624. New Wheel	10 10 0
625. Blue eagle & red berries	8 8 0
626. Red flowers & blue & gold leaves	8 8 0
627. Red flowers with green leaves blue ground etc.	8 8 0
628. Blue leaves with enamelled flys etc.	6 16 0
629. Bloom ground with brown views & gold [wave] border	14 14 6
630. Grecian, with Davis's birds flys & dontled edge	10 10 0
631. French shape, Dresden flowers & moulded edge	10 10 0
632. Girls Indian flowers coloured edge Tea	2 12 6
Dessert	8 8 0
Dinner	42 0 0
& Gold edge	52 10 0
633. Fawn ground & gold brambles	6 6 0
634. Rose & gold border, G's [probably 'Girl's'] pattern	3 13 6
635. Blue ground & three pannels of India work	10 10 0
636. Grainger's 302 enamelled gold edge & ring	3 3 0
637. Do. Hop leaf in green & rose colour edge	1 14 6
638. Do. 972 Green leaf border etc.	1 16 0
coloured edge	1 14 6

639. Girls border of roses etc.	5 5 0
640. Grainger's 930 enameled & gold boss border of purple red etc.	5 5 0
641. Green curtain 5 groups Dresden flowers	12 12 0
642. Green ground & black views 1 group Dresden flowers [ordered June 1813]	10 10 0
643. Do. do. 4 groups Dresden flowers	12 12 0
644. Blue enamelled curtain & 1 group of flowers in centre	12 12 0
645. Japan green centre, Mills	8 8 0
646. Do. scarlet centre	8 8 0
647. Border with blue & red bell flower Gr's [probably Grainger's]	6 6 0
648. Red fan with flowers & 3 brown birds	8 8 0
649. Red & black birds eye borders three small pannels of fruit all in India style	
650. Red ribband & gold leaf Gr's [probably Grainger's]	6 6 0
651. Blue & red India sprigs inside & out with flies etc.	8 8 0
Grecian New In & Out	7 7 0
652. Blue red & gold fans with India flowers & fly in bottom in & out	8 8 0
653. Girl's green leaf & purple berries purple edge & ring enamelled	2 12 6
654. Do. Purple & green garland do.	2 12 6
655. Do. do. husk & green dots edge & line	3 3 0
656. Girl's red & green wreath with brown edge line & ring (only)	2 12 6
	1 14 6
657. French make, with gold balls lines & white edge	6 6 0
658. Grecian, red fawn & gold inside & out	10 10 0
659. [No pattern recorded]	
660. French shape, with different feathers, gold band and line	31 10 0
661. Fawn net with Vandyke border, Baden (with views)	16 16 0
different paintings	31 10 0
662. Blue red & gold India basket	11 11 0
(inside & Out)	12 12 0
[This design is reminiscent of a popular Coalport pattern]	
663. Blue & fawn drapery India tree	10 10 0
664. India vine centre	12 12 0
665. Grey ground red balls & gold star	8 8 0
666. Strawberry border with gold chain inside	8 8 0
667. Rich rose colour [border?] & gold border	10 10 0
668. India red gold & green. Spooner [see page 206]	8 8 0
669. India rock & strawberry	7 7 0
670. India blue & gold bridge with flower & trees	7 7 0
671. India tree & birds	7 7 0
672. India rock bridge with flowers	8 8 0
673. India rock with flower in centre trees etc.	8 8 0
674. India Vandyke border in blue, fawn, red & gold	8 8 0
675. Red ground do.	8 8 0
676. Fawn ground & 327 gold	6 6 0
677. Grecian, rose colour wreath & lines with rose edge	1 14 6
gold edge	2 12 6
678. Red & gold	4 4 0
679. Red husk & gold leaves & berries	4 4 0

680. Red brown & gold	4	4	0
681. Hair colour & gold	4	14	6
682. Gold holy [sic] leaves & red berrys	5	5	0
683. Blue husk & gold leaves & berries	4	4	0
684. Gold holy [sic] leaves & blue berries	5	5	0
685. Blue 5 leaves & gold leaves & berrys	4	4	0
686. Blue & gold same as 679	4	4	0
687. Green & gold same as 679	4	4	0
688. Rich red & gold broad border edge lines fine lines	6	6	0
689. Printed views in black & black line	1	14	6
gold edge	2	12	6
690. Enameled common seaweed	1	14	6
691. Enameled shanked green & red sprigs all over & red edge	1	14	6
gold edge	2	12	6
692. Do. purple & red flowers & green leaves	1	14	6
693. Do. yellow & blue green border	1	14	6
694. Do. rose colour & green leaves open border	1	14	6
695. Gold wreath & red berries	3	13	6
696. French with roses & hearts ease	8	8	0
697. Tasker's India trees & red dragon dontled edge			
698. Gold oak & ivy open border	8	8	0
699. Printed black views and gold bead	5	5	0
700. Grecian emboss'd white gold dontled edge & lines [ordered March 1814]	4	4	0
701. Womens new Dresden flowers gold edge	3	3	0
702. Union pattern in colours, rose, thistle & shamrock	8	8	0
with gold sprigs	10	10	0
703. Small roses & hearts ease with gold sprigs three roses	10	10	0
704. French green ground & rose border	10	10	0
705. Grecian, blue & red flowers	7	7	0
706. Grecian, blue & red flowers fine blue line in bottom	8	8	0
707. Dresden flowers womens 5 groups [prices for various sets]	2	12	6
708. Dresden flowers womens 3 groups	2	12	6
coloured edge	2	2	0
709. Green & gold border	4	14	6
710. Small gold border & green ground	5	5	0
711. Grecian, embossed with dontle edge & flowers differ't	7	7	0
712. Mosaics without the brick work	14	14	0
713. French grey embossed	7	7	0
714. Fawn & gold arch border	8	8	0
715. Grey & flowers (Lady Jane Loftus's pattern)	7	7	0
716. Olive & do. do.	7	7	0
717. Purple & rose colour leaf gold sprays & berries	6	6	0
718. Olive ground with gold border & red berries	5	5	0
719. Brown & gold borders in antique style	7	7	0
720. Red & gold border with white leaf purple berries [?] & shade	8	8	0
721. Blue & gold border with flowers different in compartments	10	10	0
722. Red husk gold dots and gold wheel	5	5	0
723. Emboss'd with different flowers & olive ground	8	8	0
724. Enameled flowers and black sprigs edge & ring	3	3	0
725. Border 3 lamps & 3 darts etc. in purple & gold	7	7	0

726. Same in brown & gold	7	7	0
727. Green & red double wreath enameled edge line & ring	1	14	6
728. Rose colour leaf & gold border with 3 green berries Gold line & ring	5	5	0
729. Neat oval blue & green blossoms with 5 sprigs & brown edge	1	14	6
730. Gre [Grecian?] bridge arch red & gold same as 714 fawn	8	8	0
731. Mens best Dresden flowers different	7	7	0
732. Davis's blue ground & flowers with antique gilding	10	10	0
733. Webster's roses & rose buds, Table set	130	0	0
Dessert set	31	10	0
Tea set	10	10	0
734. Womens six small color'd sprigs & centre in colours			
735. Blue fawn & gold rock blue & gold leaves fawn flowers with blue green leaves gold berries	8	8	0
736. Oak & ivy with drab ground	10	10	0
737. Brown & green leaves with red flower border	1	14	6
gold edge	2	12	6
738. Rose colour red & green & black border & blue edge	1	14	6
do. [gold edge]	2	12	6
739. Baden, roses & small blue flower gold bands but edge white French style	10	10	0
740. Green & gold sprigs	4	4	0
741. Grey Union sprigs emboss'd	10	10	0
742. Blue ground & gold shell with border inside	14	14	0
743. Blue grey marble & gold edge & ring	5	5	0
744. Grey ground Davis's birds in pannels	21	0	0
745. Brown feather & gold leafage in a border, Grecian	4	4	0
746. Red ground with black & gold & gold border & centre			
747. Do. do. no border except in cup, no star			
748. Drab ground with brown upon it & gold border			
749. Dark green with saw tooth centre & gold border			
750. Dark green double key on Etruscan border			
751. Dark green single key on Etruscan border			
752. Brown ground & double gold border			
753. Drab ground gold border & berries	10	10	0
754. Embossed with the flowers gold & fawn ground	12	12	0
755. Baden blue ground & gold from top to bottom border inside	12	12	0
no border	10	10	0
756. Grecian emboss'd Drab etc. without flowers see 723	5	5	0
757. Grecian drab & gold slight	5	5	0
758. Do. fawn & gold	5	5	0
759. Mostiyns pattern Grey & flowers union	5	5	0
760. New 14 with French line gold	3	3	0
761. Drab ground Davis's birds	21	0	0
762. Fawn & gold border Davis's birds 3 in the border, fly in centre	14	14	0
763. Baden, oak & ivy drab ground	10	10	0
764. Brown ground rose colour wreath gold bead border & lines	14	14	0

765. Drab, embossed with gold etchings & different flowers May 23rd, 1816 [The date 23 May 1816 would appear to have been added when the original price of £14 14s. 0d. was amended to 12 guineas] — 12 12 0
766. Grey embossed with roses different — 8 8 0
767. Chinese figures different with temples etc. etc. [see Plate 136] — 12 12 0
768. Grecian, embossed French line & foot ring gold — 3 3 0
769. Fawn marble & butterfly border in gold — 14 14 0
770. Three slight wreaths gold & colours edge & ring — 3 3 0
771. Poppy border & gold edge — 4 4 0
772. Blue & gold sprigs French line, womens — 4 4 0
773. Red & gold sawtooth border with large red stars in border, saucer etc. — 5 5 0
774. Baden, slight festoons & gold stars on fawn ground bead inside cup & centre saucer — 12 12 0
775. Gold oak & ivy border [?] no ground — 8 8 0
776. New Waterloo pattern in fawn & gold Grecian something like Trafalgar — 7 7 0
777. Bourbon sprigs gold edge — 4 4 0
778. Rich blue ground old lining & 299 gilding gold honeysuckle border beaded stands [?] — 42 0 0
   without gold lining — 31 10 0
779. Baden, with different views & 344 border — 31 10 0
780. Baden, F [French] grey, gold festoon & birds in pannel [finches?] — 18 18 0
781. Grecian embossed blue gold & red rich border of roses — 21 0 0
782. Poppy & blue sprigs & gold edge. G. R. junior — 3 3 0
783. Blue ground (Earl of Fifes pattern) with fine Japan gilding, teaset — 10 10 0
784. Gold curtain border cross & dots of blue fawn gold etc. — 8 8 0
785. G. Rogers junior brown border & gold edge — 3 3 0
786. Gold honeysuckle border etc. — 8 8 0
787. Fawn band & gold lines — 3 3 0
788. Grey & gold narrow border — 4 4 0
789. Small French blue & gold sprigs — 3 3 0
790. Cobourg green border & roses — 18 18 0
791. Border of roses & gold lines — 14 14 0
792. York & Lancaster roses — 16 16 0
793. Roses & yellow Jassamine — 16 16 0
794. Green curtain border with India flowers — 10 10 0
795. Wreath of flowers & gold bands — 16 16 0
796. Green antique border & gold shell with festoons of flowers — 14 14 0
797. Green border & pannels of flowers gold bead & lines — 12 12 0
798. Green border & wild roses gold diaper & dots — 18 18 0
799. Green & gold border on Grecian — 7 7 0
800. Drab embossed gold etchings without flowers gold honeysuckle border — 10 10 0
801. Green band & gold bell border French gold line — 6 6 0
802. Derby pattern in India style in blue, red & gold narrow blue border Zig Zag gold — 10 10 0
803. Blue ground with fawn enamel gilding etc. in compartments New Trafalgar — 10 10 0
804. Yellow ground border flowers white — 8 8 0
805. Yellow ground border & flowers, Fleur de Lis — 8 8 0

806. Yellow ground border & flowers white & gold chain — 6 6 0
807. Grey ground border & flowers white & gold — 8 8 0
808. Spode's pattern in India style Blue green red etc. etc. — 10 10 0
809. Grecian, blue & gold broad border [ordered July 1817] — 7 7 0
810. Grecian, white & gold border & wreath inside
811. Small purple flowers & gold festoons etc. — 5 5 0
812. Printed views gold edge — 2 12 6
813. Bourbon sprigs [?] white edge Seconds — 1 2 0
   Best — 2 2 0
814. Embossed with grey or lilac ground drab etc. without gilding, best — 3 3 0
815. Grecian rose colour leaf & gold border inside — 5 5 0
816. Rose drops and small coloured drops between gold bead inside cups [ordered May 1818] — 6 6 0
817. Regent, Green [?] gold bands & lines
818. Regent, gold border & grey ground with small gold sprig centre gold lines
819. Regent, rose wreath inside & straw ground etc.
820. Baden, grey band & enamelled flowers (Womens) — 5 5 0
821. Baden, Regent barbos[?] & gold line — 3 3 0
822. Baden, blue & gold (from 298) with antique gilding & roses in pannels — 12 12 0
823. Baden, rose wreath & sprig gold lines — 6 6 0
824. Baden, rose & red flower grey ground & gold drop inside cup [ordered May 1818] — 10 10 0
825. Grecian rose border & grey ground gold border inside cups etc. — 12 12 0
826. Baden, black border below the embossed part & black edge — 4 4 0
827. Baden, Grecian band with gold drops — 5 5 0
828. Grecian, gold lines & arch & bell drop border gold — 4 4 0
829. Grecian, drab & flowers (Loftus) — 8 8 0
830. Grey ground & Union gilding — 12 12 0
831. New union, grey ground and white flowers — 8 8 0
832. From 240 blue & India work with flower pot centre — 9 9 0
833. Grecian Ivory band of gold bell drop, husk inside upright pieces — 5 5 0
834. Grecian Grey band of gold bell drop plums [?] etc. husk inside the upright pieces — 5 5 0
835. Grecian lilac band of gold bell drop gold F [French] lines [see Plate 427] — 5 5 0
836. Baden, drab & gold with different flowers full gold bell drop — 10 10 0
837. Baden, grey band & black lines — 2 2 0
838. Broad blue border on Grecian with gold festoons etc. on the blue — 6 6 0
839. Ivory band & gold bell drop F [French] line — 5 5 0
840. Ivory with 3 pannels of flowers without spangles, Bell gold border — 18 18 0
   with spangles — 21 0 0
841. Green with   do. do. do. do. do. — 21 0 0
842. Grey with   do. do. do. do. do. — 21 0 0
843. Blue with 3 pannels of flowers, Bell gold border — 21 0 0
844. Narrow blue with gold lines & blue daggers (Col Bailley patt'n India) — 5 5 0
                                    [price crossed out]
845. Orange ground & Union gilding (R. Mills) — 14 14 0

427. A 'Regent China' teapot of pattern 835, 'lilac band of gold bell drop gold F [French] lines £5 5s. 0d.'. Printed crowned 'Regent China' mark and New Bond Street address inside cover. 10 in long. c. 1813–18. *Messrs C. Barkman*

846.	Grey ground & rose border (Lady Price's pattern) [ordered January 1819]	10 10 0	
847.	Union drab & flowers	8 8 0	
848.	Baden, & gre S[?]. Gold drops as 833 but enamel blue band	6 6 0	
849.	Grecian, gold acorn etc. Sprigs	3 13 6	
850.	Rose & red jassamine wreath	6 6 0	
851.	Grecian, brown & gold strawberry	7 7 0	
852.	Grey with white roses any shape	6 6 0	
853.	India blue & gold & enamel in & out with blue etc [?] border [ordered April 1819]	8 8 0	
854.	India rock & bridge in & out the cup	10 10 0	
855.	Blue rock & India flowers	8 8 0	
856.	Broad blue & gold border with 193 sprigs	7 7 0	
857.	Loose roses & blue flowers gold line [crossed out]	6 6 0	
858.	Red & gold border in pannels gold line	7 7 0	
859.	Bloom band & gold lines No drops as 835	4 4 0	
860.	Ivory & gold with roses in the border in pannels	8 8 0	
861.	India flowers Vandyke border (printed)	6 6 0	
862.	Blue Regent sprigs printed Best	2 2 0	
	Seconds	1 8 0	
863.	Baden, lilac & gold with roses in pannell	10 10 0	

864.	Baden, 298 Blue with raised gold [antique] roses in pannel	21 0 0	
865.	Spode's India flowers in blue & gold border inside & out	10 10 0	
866.	Same as 863 without the gold drops	9 9 0	
867.	Blue & white birds with gold edge & foot ring or blue eagle	2 12 6	
868.	Grey band & gold lines	4 4 0	
869.	Ivory band & gold lines	4 4 0	
870.	Roses & blue flowers any shape	6 6 0	
	Dinner 50 gs		
	Dessert 12 gs		
871.	Embossed with single rose Gold lines	6 6 0	
	Dinner 50 gs		
	Dessert 15 gs		
872.	Ivory band & gold festoon in & out	5 5 0	
873.	Very rich India fan & star pattern	10 10 0	
874.	Very rich India F B & B pattern bridge etc. etc.	14 14 0	
875.	Old enamelled partridge pattern	8 8 0	
876.	Light blue & rose Loftus with small festoons of gold in & out	12 12 0	
877.	India rock & bridge with flowers & birds & also a red & gold border, temple etc.	12 12 0	
878.	Green & rose Loftus with festoon of gold inside & out	12 12 0	
	Single . . .	10 10 0	
879.	Gold S border	6 6 0	
880.	Printed India flowers with gold ['Sidmouth' Japan pattern] [ordered May 1820]	3 3 0	

881.	Painted blue Dresden sprigs	1	14	0
	Dinner service	26	5	0
882.	Old pink pattern & flies done in purple	2	2	0
883.	Womens purple & green flowers & gold edge	3	13	6
884.	Blue pink & flies see 882	2	2	0
885.	Stock gold line Dessert Set	12	12	0
	Dinner Service	42	0	0
886.	Blue & gold Sir E. Denny's pattern from Derby blue gold & red etc.			
	Dessert service	15	15	0
	Dinner service	63	0	0
887.	Naylor's pattern teas no gold [ordered May 1820]	2	2	0
	Dinner service	21	9	0
	Dessert set	6	6	0
888.	Flowers dropping from the edge gold line	4	4	0
889.	Baden, rose Loftus blue & gold	10	10	0
890.	India blue & gold with red purple etc. 3 birds downwards	10	10	0
891.	Grecian blue pannel border & rose Loftus with raised gold leafage & gold wreath [ordered October 1820]	12	12	0
892.	[Crossed out pattern]	10	10	0
893.	Baden, long blue Dresden sprigs. Best ware	2	2	0
894.	Crome green & rose Loftus with bell drops inside	10	10	0
895.	880 pattern in black & gold at same price	3	3	0
896.	880 and Vandyke border and Green blue red & yellow			
	Dinner set 30 gs			
	with gold 40 gs			
897.	Sidmouth 880 Centre Vandyke red, blue etc. no gold			
	Dinner set 30 gs			
	with gold 40 gs			
898.	Same with gold			
	Dinner set 40 gs			
	Dessert set 12 gs			
899.	Vandyke green & gold border with 880 centre			
	Dinner set 40 gs			
900.	Ivory ground border with biscuit blue & gold flowers gold edge tea set	9	9	0
901.	Lilac & rose Loftus without the drops	8	8	0
902.	Orange border & gold with gold sprigs [ordered February 1821]	5	5	0
903.	880 done in brown & gold	3	3	0
904.	Roses disposed all over & barley corn gold line & dontle	6	6	0
	Dessert 15 gs			
	Dinner 50 gs			
905.	Dresden roses, buds & hearts ease & gold line. Prices as 904	6	6	0
906.	Brown border & roses etc.	9	9	0
907.	Ivory band gold wreath & sprigs with gold line	5	5	0
908.	Drab & white jassamine gold wreath outside	6	6	0
909.	Lilac band with narrow blue bold border above and below gold wreath inside cups	5	5	0
910.	Ivory band with narrow blue bold border above & below gold wreath inside cups	5	5	0
911.	Straw colour & gold border & sprigs	5	5	0
912.	Brown & gold groups of flowers French line & dontel	5	5	0

913.	Green ivy brown berry & gold & gold lines	5	5	0
914.	Brown & orange Turban Lilly & gold wreath outside	5	5	0
915.	Green leaf & red berry & green & red sprigs	5	5	0
916.	Ivory & gold wreath small sprigs in gold	4	14	6
917.	Gold wreath & gold sprigs & lines	4	4	0
918.	Ivory ground with rose wreath etc. in colours gold key border with lines	10	10	0
919.	Brown & gold hopp border with gold wreath outside & gold lines etc.	8	8	0
920.	Green leaf & black berry & gold wreath	6	6	0
921.	Shamrock leaf & clover flowers Sprigs of same outside. Royal	6	6	0
922.	Hearts ease	6	6	0
923.	Black & gold with ivory & slight flowers in pannels	16	16	0
924.	Princess Charlottes gadroon. Rose & hearts-ease wreath of gold, rich	31	10	0
925.	Indian jar in brown & gold [ordered May 1821]			
	Dinner set 35 gs			
	Dessert set 12 gs			
926.	Grey border & Union white flowers			
927.	Indian stork in brown & gold	3	13	6
	Dinner 35 gs			
	Dessert 12 gs			
928.	India stork in brown & yellow instead of gold	3	3	0
	Dinner 30 gs			
	Dessert 10 gs			
929.	Womens rose border. Rose centre sprigs enameled etc.			
	Dinner 50 gs			
	Dessert 18 gs			
930.	Union grey & white flowers gold lines border inside	5	5	0
931.	India stork in red blue & gold & gold line			
	Dinner set 40 gs			
	Dessert 15 gs			
932.	India stork in blue red & gold No line	3	3	0
	Dinner 30 gs			
	Dessert 12 gs			
933.	India stork in blue red & gold without gold	3	3	0
	Dinner 21 gs			
	Dessert 6 gs			
934.	Grey & white jassamine [ordered June 1821]	6	6	0
935.	Vandyke in green blue red & orange. Without gold			
936.	Antique border with gold			
	Dinner service 30 gs (without any gold 25 gs)			
	Dessert without gold lines 8 gs			
937.	Chatham pattern French sprigs small, gold edge	3	13	6
938.	Baden, grey & gold with wreath border of flowers finely painted			
939.	Garland pattern [ordered July 1821]	5	5	0
	Dessert 15 gs			
	Dinner Set 50 gs			
940.	Rich blue & gold with roses & passion flower border on ivory ground, gold bells etc.	25	4	0
941.	Ivory ground with blue & gold bell flowers	8	8	0
942.	Embossed, roses without gold	2	2	0
	Dessert 6 gs			

943. Embossed & roses with goldline   3 3 0
     Dessert 8 gs

944. Full groupes of womens flowers   2 12 6

945. Blue painted French border & sprigs Best tea
ware   2 2 0

946. Blue painted French border & sprigs with gold
key & edge reduced from £5 5s. 0d. to   3 13 6

947. New embossed Panel border with roses different
     Table set 40 gs no gold

948. New embossed panel border with small Dresden groups
     Table set 40 gs no gold

949. Tea set blue ground and rich gold pattern India work in panel Red & gold star centre [ordered July 1821]   10 10 0

950. Embossed with gold lines   3 13 6

951. Blue & gold border style of 941 with fine line inside upright pieces   8 8 0

952. Small brown & gold sprigs or flowers & brown lines   3 3 0

953. Small brown & gold sprigs or flowers with gold lines   3 13 6

954. Same as 909 only on blue   6 6 0
     Dessert 18 gs
     Table 60 gs

955. New Hop border
     Dessert 15 gs
     Table 50 gs

956. Marone & Bell drop (as 835)   5 5 0

957. Slight 906   8 8 0

958. Antique border same as 936
     with gold lines 35 gs

959. Sidmouth in red blue & white
     no gold 25 gs

960. Red & gold border (without centre) see 932
     with gold 30 gs
     without 25 gs

961. Union embossed dessert with 4 different flowers & gold dontle
     Dessert 15 gs

962. Four antique compartments with different flowers Blue border antique gilding as Scarbro & new ball drops – varied groups of flowers in centre   37 16 0

963. Basket rim flower pot or India jar in red blue & gold   3 13 6

964. Gadroon grey birds eye border & small centre groups of flowers   10 10 0
     Dessert 24 gs

965. Gadroon blue rings & star
     Dessert 20 gs

966. Union with gold line different flowers [ordered December 1821]
     Dessert 15 gs

967. Gadroon, grey bird's-eye [crossed out]

968. Rich scarlet blue & gold diamond etc. border & India centre
     Table 60 gs
     Dessert 18 gs

969. Chinese temple, boat etc.   6 6 0
     Table 60 gs
     Dessert 18 gs

970. Chinese scrowl [?] & shell in blue & gold, red etc.
     Table 60 gs

971. India basket of flowers & flowers in same style for border
     Dinner 40 gs
     Dessert 10 gs
     Gold edge 60 gs
     Dessert 12 gs

972. India flowers in blue & gold enamel & gold edge
     Dinner set 50 gs
     Dessert 15 gs

973. New embossed green & gold ground border with flowers
     Dessert [?] 30 gs

974. New embossed lilac   do.   do.   do.
     Dessert 30 gs

975. Rose & gold running border with small blue flower in border   6 6 0

976. Brown & enameled rose wreath etc.   2 2 0
     Dessert 6 gs

977. Do. do. do. with gold lines   3 3 0
     Dessert 9 gs

978. Grecian with groups of flowers & gold rich & gold net work   10 10 0

979. Chinese figures and temple with gold [ordered April 1822]   3 13 6
     Dessert 10 gs

980. Blue & gold common womens rose, Loftus   4 4 0

981. New embossed & flowers
     Dinner set 35 gs
     with gold lines 40 gs

982. New enameled flowers in India style printed in red blue etc.
     Dinner set 25 gs
     Dessert 8 gs

983. Rich blue 3 fans Red Green & gold
     Dessert 20 gs

984. Blue & green India tree centre with border to corrispond
     Dessert 10 gs

985. With 982 pattern biscuit blue & gold leaves
     with gold lines 35 gs

986. Enameled India stork green etc. Damaged ware no gold
     Dinner set 15 gs

987. Gadroon Princess Charlottes shape Dresden flowers different [?] & Dontil [white ground]   8 8 0

988. Brown & gold sprigs in Brunswick with gold line   4 4 0

989. P. Charlottes shape green ground & flowers   12 12 0

990. Blue & white with gold border. Old Mosaic pattern   4 4 0
     Dessert 12 gs

991. Gadroon Ivory & birds eye border & flowers in style of 964 and same price   8 8 0

992. Half basket India jar enameled red, blue & gold & gold line
     Dessert set 12 gs
     Dinner set 40 gs

993. Brown stork
     2nds Dinner set 15 gs
     Dessert 5 gs

994. Slight roses & hearts ease with gold lines [ordered May 1822] — 5 5 0

995. Roses small blue flower & small gold leafage — 5 5 0
Table 50 gs
Dessert 15 gs

996. Gre 909 pattern without the gold lines above & below the border — 5 5 0

997. Blue convolvulus etc. etc. — 6 6 0

998. Lilac border with white flowers and lines gold wreath outside — 5 5 0

999. Green Jassamine border on ivory gold lines do. — 5 5 0

1000. Poppy border with black shade do. do. [ordered September 1822] — 6 6 0

1001. Green & gold border & lines do. do. — 5 5 0

1002. Green leaves & white flowers, gold lines etc. — 5 5 0

1003. Morone border & roses in panel, gold lines etc. — 8 8 0

1004. Chantilly table set 982 pattern with biscuit blue & gold etc.
Dinner Service — 26 5 0

1005. Light blue ground gold border & different flowers [ordered August 1822]
Dessert Service — 21 0 0

1006. Tea set ivory & gold with a little red star — 5 5 0

1007. India border & panels of blue hearts & fawn red green etc. — 8 8 0

1008. Red ground border & gold wreath of white roses — 7 7 0

1009. New make squat grey & wreath of flowers on the grey — 8 8 0

1010. 982 in colours
Dessert 10 gs
Dinner set 30 gs

1011. 964 in blue etc. (With full groups of flowers 12 gs) — 10 10 0

1012. India border blue green fawn gold etc. — 6 6 0

1013. New embossed, with enameled blue groupes of flowers
Dinner 20 gs
Dessert 6 gs

1014. Shamrock border green
Table set 30 gs
with gold lines 36 gs

1015. New embossed white and six groupes of flowers
in black 30 gs
with gold 36 gs

1016. Do.   do. with   do.   do.
in brown 30 gs
with gold 36 gs

1017. Do. Rich blue with gold embossed flowers white, three groupes of flowers. Centre rose buds. 3 others [?] small
Table set 80 gs

1018. Rich [?] border in blue, red, green & gold & gold
Dinner set 60 gs
Dessert 18 gs

1019. New embossed with enamelled blue & 9 small groupes of flowers in Dresden style
Dinner set 60 gs

Dessert 20 gs

1020. Derby Garland border with 5 sprigs & gold lines
50 gs dinner

1021. New embossed with enameled womens flowers in panels Gold edge [ordered February 1823] — 3 13 6
Dinner 30 gs

1022. Dark brown flowers with a little gold 30 gs with gold edge 35 gs

1023. Rose embossed with small blue carnation pattern (2nds Teaset 28s.) — 2 2 0

1024. New embossed, with gold seven groups of flowers on cup & five on saucer

1025. New embossed, Rose & gold weed with gold lines

1026. New dejeunner shape, Womens French sprigs & border without gold

1027. Do.   do.   do. coloured border & sprigs do. do.

1028. Do.   do.   Broad blue & womens flowers

1029. New dejeunner, Cookes pattern in purple & gold wreath

1030. Do.   Blue & gold with groups of flowers by women

1031. Do.   Pink & gold with flowers & embossed gold

1032. Do.   Grey & flowers & embossed gold

1033. New dejeunner, flowers in panel & embossed gold

1034. Do.   Ivory & flowers in panel & embossed gold

1035. Do.   do.   do.   Womens do.   do. [invoiced at £8 8s. 0d.: see Plate 139]

1036. New pattern, Womens

1037. Gadroon pink border & flowers as 964

1038. New dejeune, green & flowers in panel embossed gold & (as 1031) without dontil gold 10 gs — 12 12 0
[ordered August 1823]

1039. New Dejeunne, Fine blue Dresden flowers & dontiled lines (with raised [?] gold dontel 6 gs) — 4 14 6

1040. New Dejeunne, Rich blue & embossed gold flowers finely painted — 21 0 0

1041. Do.   do.   pink do.   do.   do. — 12 12 0

1042. Per 976 pattern in purple — 2 2 0

1043. Per 933 border only — 2 2 0

1044. Wild Strawberry (or Cranberry) colours green & gold

1045. Brown (& light colour) Stork

1046. India sprigs

1047. [?] blue & gold spots [?] flowers

1048. Japan pattern in light & dark blue & gold [ordered November 1823]

1049. Womens roses & gold leaves

1050. [?] border in red blue & gold
Table 60 gs
Dessert 18 gs

1051. New brown & gold oak & brown border & sprigs — 6 6 0

1052. Morone or claret gadroon gold dontel & line scollop edges

428. A small–size teapot from an early-morning teaset of pattern 1054, after a Flight, Barr & Barr design. Unmarked. 4¾ in. high. *c.* 1824–8. *Geoffrey Godden, chinaman*

	Dinner service 40 gs			
	full gilding 50 gs			
1053.	Embossed chrome green sprigs	2	12	6
	Dinner service & gold line 30 gs			
	without gold 25 gs			
1054.	F. B. & B.'s gold bramble gadroon 12 gs or new weed with flowers plain [see Plate 428]	10	10	0
1055.	Dessert gadroon & womens flowers, blue & embossed gold	18	18	0
1056.	Do. do. green do.	23	2	0
1057.	Green & gold shamrock [ordered February 1824]	5	5	0
1058.	Baden, rose & blue flowers with gold lines	6	6	0
1059.	New Dejeunner, green in style of 1030	8	8	0
1060.	Do. do. with panel of flowers growing			
1061.	Do. flowers thrown over & gold antique border	12	12	0
1062.	Do. do. in groups & large gold dontel line	6	6	0
1063.	New Dejeunner, grey & gold & border in panel	8	8	0
1064.	Swansea make, grey birds eye curtain with 4 groupes of flowers	12	12	0
1065.	Antique border, Partridges & flower pots in colours			
	Dessert service 15 gs			
	Dinner service 45 gs			
1066.	Antique border, Partridges & flower pots in brown & gold			
	Dessert service 14 gs			

	Dinner Service	47	5	0
1067.	Embossed womens cheap flowers [ordered June 1824]	1	2	0
1068.	Same as 1035 only green			
1069.	Gadroon with groups of flowers and gold line only			
	Dessert Service	12	12	0
1070.	New embossed, [?] flowers blue gold line	4	14	6
1071.	Baden, gadroon, gold edge & ring & different Dresden flowers	7	7	0
1072.	Gadroon dessert service green & Chelsea gold wreath & flowers in centre	42	0	0
1073.	Do. do. flowers & gold jassamine (small groups 16 gs)			
	full groups	21	0	0
1074.	New embossed, biscuit green & gold flowers	3	13	6
1075.	Do. small pink & gold sprigs in & out	3	13	6
1076.	Ivory ground & wreath of flowers & double chain gold border etc.	10	10	0
1077.	Groups of flowers finely painted gold wreath outside & dontled lines	7	7	0
1078.	Small & curtain border green etc. Dessert service			
1079.	Antique border in red etc. etc. flower pot centre & panels			
	Dessert service			
1080.	New Dejeunner, birds eye Tea set	6	6	0

1081. New Dejeunner, in style of 1059 in green Embossed gold etc.   9 9 0

1082. Bis't green sprigs Black line etc.   2 12 6

1083. Dinner service groups of flowers all [illegible] & gold lines   52 10 0

1084. Dinner service blue & gold curtain border partridge centre & 3 flower pots 50 gs
Dessert 16 gs

1085. Dark brown shamrock on ivory   Tea set   6 6 0

1086. Light brown do. do. do.   6 6 0

1087. New squat, fluted pink & key borders as 909   5 5 0

1088. Do. do. do. with arches of flowers   12 12 0

1089. Do. do. do. Crome green 1030 etc. [ordered September 1824]

1090. New squat dejeunne, green & wreath of flowers Gold dontel border & lines gold   14 14 0
with pink ground ivory or grey   12 12 0

1091. New squat, antique flute York Japan   7 7 0

1092. New embossed, enameled blue flowers gold line   2 12 6
Dinner service 30 gs

1093. Gadroon morone border dead imitation chas'd gold wreath
Dessert service   42 0 0

1094. New Gadroon Tournay shape, pink band [?] with gold flowers diff't
Dessert service 20 gs

1095. Do. do. do. green do. do.
Dessert service 20 gs

1096. New Gadroon Tournay shape, blue ground & flowers 6 panels basket flowers etc.
Dessert service 30 gs

1097. Tea set new make antique fluted, pea green diamond border of flowers   8 8 0

1098. Do. do. do. blue do. do.   9 9 0

1099. Antique flute, birds eye border & gold sprigs   4 4 0

1100. Do. India blue tree & flowers with blue fawn & gold antique border   6 6 0

1101. Embossed black & gold sprigs gold lines [ordered January 1825]   2 12 6

1102. Antique flute, blue bell border   4 4 0

1103. New embossed, girls black & gold sprigs gold [ordered January 1825]

1104. New squat antique flute, ivory & basket or flower pots in panels

1105. J. Phillips pattern

1106. Antique flute border and blue flower & red berry etc.

1107. Scroll & curtain border with gold line red etc. Any shape
Dinner service   47 5 0
Dessert   15 15 0

1108. Slight mens flowers without any gilding gadroon 35 gs   5 5 0

1109. Womens flowers in colour 1013 Done in colours
Dinner service   31 10 0

1110. Gadroon, & womens flowers with gold & enameled blue lines
Dinner Service   37 15 0

1111. New embossed scroll etc. in green blue red etc. [ordered April 1825]

Dinner service   26 5 0
Dessert   8 8 0

1112. New dejeune, boy's small sprigs in pink & gold gold husk outside   3 3 0

1113. New embossed table ware, scroll & antique border
Dinner Service   37 15 0

1114. Antique flute, new blue bell border etc.   4 4 0

1115. Do. gold border & red dots   4 4 0

1116. New embossed dinner set, brown flowers in style of 1092
Dinner Service   21 0 0

1117. New gadroon, painted pink & brown flowers
Dinner Service 35 gs
Dessert Service   12 12 0

1118. Baden, lilac gadroon & white flowers gold bell drops

1119. New dejeuner, morone & gold tea set   6 6 0

1120. Dr. Shuttleworths pattern [dinner] drab & gold
Dinner Service   84 0 0

1121. Royal shape, oval gold border   9 9 0

1122. New dejeuner, green & gold tooled border   6 6 0

1123. Do. light brown & gold & bands [?]   4 4 0

1124. Royal flute, grey & gold antique border as 1087 [?]   6 6 0

1125. Round gadroon, in 982 in Brunswick, Covers gilt only
Dinner Service   21 0 0

1126. Round gadroon, the stork in Brunswick
Dinner Service   31 10 0

1127. Rose & green vine border   2 12 6

1128. Royal purple vine   2 12 6

1129. Royal brown husk border   2 12 6

1130. Royal 979 border in red & brown

1131. Chantilly table set, 5 printed sprigs as border in 204 brown no gold
Dinner service   21 0 0

1132. Royal shape, blue & panels flowerpots & diff't flowers   12 12 0

1133. Royal green ground & panels growing flowers etc.   14 14 0

1134. Plain round India border

1135. India spray centre & border blue dark & light with red & gold etc.
Dessert service   12 12 0

1136. Royal shape, light & dark blue & flowers etc. [ordered June 1826]   8 8 0

1137. Royal shape, green bands & gold lines   4 4 0

1138. Baden, Ivory ground of diff't flowers (G. Rogers)   7 7 0

1139. Royal flute, green & chased gold wreath & flowers   14 14 0

1140. Do. as 1087 in green   5 5 0

1141. Do. brown flower border inside & out without gold

1142. Pink band & gold lines Royal   4 4 0

1143. Baden, gadroon blue rose wreath and gold borders (Major Blackers)   10 10 0

1144. Ivory ground all over outside and deep border inside with promiscous [?] Spriggs in the Dresden style   10 10 0

1145. Chantilly, Corinthian border by Taylor
Dinner service   52 0 0

1146. Chantilly, enameled blue & red wreath border & 3 sprigs
Dinner service   31 10 0

1147. Do.   do.   red & gold border & drops
Dinner Service   42 0 0

1148. Do.   lilac band & gold lines as 610
Dinner Service   36 15 0

1149. Do. pink do. do. do.
Dinner Service   36 15 0

1150. Do.   Fawn blue & gold border of 3 sprigs (per Spodes toys)
Dinner Service   36 15 0

1151. Do.   Fawn white & gold flower border sprig centre
Dinner service   36 15 0

1152. Royal shape, ivory wreath of flowers   10 10 0

1153. Do.   ivory band & brown flowers gold lines   5 5 0

1154. Chantilly, biscuit green & gold star & blue & gold enameled border & centre
Dinner service   47 5 0

1155. Chantilly, blue & gold ground & yellow etc wreath with 3 sprigs
Dinner service   36 15 0

1156. Royal flute, gold tooth single border & line   3 13 6

1157. Do.   ivory band & gold line   4 4 0

1158. Gadroon, India flowers no gold on seconds.
Dinner Service   15 15 0

1159. New embossed union, blue finely painted & gold line
Dinner Service   36 15 0
without gold   30 0 0

1160. Round gadroon, brown stork in Brunswick no gold
Dinner Service   21 0 0

1161. Blue as 1030 with fawn & gold etc. (R. Mills)   8 8 0

1162. Royal, small roses Blue birds eye gold dotts & sprigs gold line inside & out   5 5 0

1163. Bramble sprigs blue & white   1 2 0

1164. Royal, enameled blue & gold draping flowers   4 4 0

1165. Royal, grey with roses etc.   5 5 0

1166. Do.   drab with roses etc.   5 5 0

1167. Baden, gadroon, green over outside Birds eye no gold inside   10 10 0

1168. Royal gadroon, Lord Rolls blue pattern
Dinner service   42 0 0

1169. Do.   Mr. Lilly's pattern without gold
Dinner service   21 9 0

1170. Royal shape, marone band & gold lines   4 4 0

1171. Do.   thistle border & sprigs under the glaze & gold line   4 4 0

1172. Royal shape, printed purple flowers & gold line
Dinner service   26 5 0

1173. Baden gadroon, new imperial blue & gold shell etc. ivory etc.   8 8 0

1174. Do.   do.   do.   gold drops & star & wheel gold   8 8 0

1175. Royal gadroon, marone & white hawthorn gold border different centre flowers
Dessert service   25 4 0

1176. Do.   blue border & pink flowers Jones's pattern   6 6 0

1177. Royal, with blue running border and sprigs without the brown line   1 14 0

1178. Baden Gadroon, rich blue & gold stripes & different single flowers in blue   12 12 0

1179. Royal, grey with 12 small roses in panels & white & gold stars   7 7 0

1180. Royal, G. Rogers grey & rose & gold wreath   9 9 0

1181. Do.   Imperial blue & roses & gold as 1179   8 8 0

1182. Do.   marone & gold flowers small as in last number   8 8 0

1183. Baden, imperial blue & gold balloon stripes & small groupes flowers   10 10 0

1184. Baden, marone & gold   do.   do.   do. do.   12 12 0

1185. Do.   grey   &   gold do. do.   different single flowers   10 10 0

1186. New Dejeune, grey border with wreath roses etc. on grey & bold husk border   10 10 0

1187. Gre[?] ivory ground & jasmine wreath in colours gold lines etc. gold wreath   5 5 0

1188. New Dejeune, ivory & rose wreath as 918 only with gold husks   10 10 0

1189. Royal, blue French border with gold line

1190. Royal Chantilly gadroon, Dresden flower group & fancy sprigs with gold line.
Dinner service   36 15 0

1191. Do.   do.   do. 4 groups
Dinner Service   42 0 0

1192. Royal, green rose buds & gold leaves & gold line   3 13 6

1193. Royal, broad green border & gold wreath on green gold border outside   6 6 0

1194. Royal, blue border & gold beaded below the blue & gold sprigs   6 6 0

1195. Do.   pink & brown & gold border gold sprigged outside cups   7 7 0

1196. Do.   pink & gold border with groupes of flowers   8 8 0

1197. Do.   do.   with square panels flowers in the border & gold border outside   10 10 0

1198. Do.   marone & gold 3 gold stands with flowers etc. in the border and gold border   10 10 0

1199. Do.   Grey with Horn gold panels & groupes flowers   do.   10 10 0

1200. Do.   imperial blue horn with rose at top & panels of flowers beaded gold etc.   10 10 0

1201. Baden, gadroon grey etc. with rose at top & panels of flowers beaded gold etc   12 12 0

1202. Do.   Kings blue & do. do. do. do. do.   12 12 0

1203. Do.   Marone with gold horn, flowers & flies beaded gold etc.   14 14 0

1204. Do.   marone square panels flowers & gold outside   14 14 0

1205. Plain Baden, grey & gold gold [sic] stands with roses etc.   10 10 0

1206. Do.   Imperial blue etc.   do.   10 10 0

1207. Do. Marone & gold S & large gold flowers outside	7 7 0	
1208. Do. grey & gold slight border outside	5 5 0	
1209. Do. blue & gold drops etc. do.	5 5 0	
1210. Do. do. do. do.	6 6 0	
1211. Do. grey & gold slight bell on the grey outside	5 5 0	
1212. Do. grey & gold thistle border do.	6 6 0	
1213. Royal, pink & gold thistle border inside	6 6 0	
1214. New Dejeune, pink & gold border Diff't sprigs of flowers in bottom	8 8 0	
1215. Royal, grey & gold S with brown intermix'd inside. Gold wreath outside	7 7 0	
1216. Do. grey & gold honeysuckle on grey & gold wreath outside	5 5 0	
1217. Royal gadroon, 982 in purple & gold	3 3 0	
1218. Chantilly curtain & scroll in purple & gold Dinner service	31 15 0	
1219. Royal, India blue gold & enamel panels & flower pot centre	10 10 0	
1220. Royal bamboo (in enamel blue 42s.) with gold line	3 3 0	
1221. Royal shape, Imperial blue with white & gold stars & oblique white bals[?] & gold stripe	8 8 0	
1222. Rose embossed, Gold line with purple & gold flower in single flowers in bottom	2 12 6	
1223. Chantilly, gold line & printed purple flowers & gold Bishop of Chester Dinner Service	36 15 0	
1224. Rose embossed, green purple & gold flowers printed, gold line & foot line	3 3 0	
1225. Royal shape, Thistle sprigs & gold line	2 12 6	
1226. Blue bamboo under glaze, with gold line	3 3 0	
1227. Old Gadroon, Imperial blue 3 groupes flowers in ground & gold sprigs	12 12 0	
1228. Royal shape, from 1161 (but slighter) No sprigs but small square centre	7 7 0	
1229. Gadroon Baden, Pink ground & gold leaf	10 10 0	
1230. Royal, printed purple flower border & groups gold line	2 12 6	
1231. Do. 3 curtains in purple in 3 baskets & centre printed not gilt	2 2 0	
1232. Do. Chinese temple & border in purple	2 2 0	
1233. Do. do. do. in do. gold line	2 12 6	
1234. Royal gadroon, Imperial blue & slight gold & flowers Dessert service	31 10 0	
1235. New gadroon, pink band gold lines & wreath of French sprigs outside	5 5 0	
1236. Do. ivory do. do. do. do. do.	5 5 0	
1237. Do. new blue do. do. do. do.	5 5 0	
1238. Do. new Imperial blue & stencilled bell in centre of ground	6 6 0	
1239. Do. stencilled new marone & gold border etc. & line outside	6 16 0	
1240. New gadroon, Dresden flowers in groups & sprigs printed and filled in	4 4 0	
1241. Baden, Imperial blue ground & small groupes flowers crowfoot [border] inside	10 10 0	
1242. New low shape gadroon, Imperial blue band small groups flowers & gold	10 10 0	

1243. Do. groups flowers, gold line (printed & coloured) no gold	3 13 6	
1244. Do. pink band gold lines	4 14 6	
1245. Do. Imperial blue band gold drops & lines & do. sprigs outside	5 5 0	
1246. Do. Ivory blue band gold drops & lines & do. sprigs outside	6 6 0	
1247. Do. Ivory band & gold line [ordered October 1828]	4 14 6	
1248. Do. Moroone band & gold line	4 14 6	
1249. 1 coat of green band with three groups flowers		
1250. Do. marone band with three groups of flowers		
1251. Do. ivory band with three groups of flowers		
1252. Royal Chantilly gadroon, chrome green & star Dinner Service	36 0 0	
1253. New Gadroon blue flowers & gold line (in blue not gilt 30s.)	2 12 6	
1254. Royal Chantilly gadroon blue & gold curtain 3 red India star flowers India flower centre Dinner Service	47 5 0	
1255. Do. India pattern in biscuit blue border & flowers, & flower centre Dinner service	52 10 0	
1256. Do. do. Mill's draggon & wheel border no centre Dinner service	63 0 0	
1257. Do. India flower border & blue line broad blue & fine lines in bottom, India centre Dinner service	63 0 0	
1258. Do. India blue & old flower pot & rich flowers all over & gold lines etc. Dinner service	63 0 0	
1259. Do. India blue & gold 3 curtains and flowers gold line etc. Dinner service	63 0 0	
1260. New Gadroon, 1222 centre & small flowers in and out 2nds 34s. set with gold lines	2 12 6	
1261. Do. 939 green & blue garland & two fine gold lines	4 4 0	
1262. Royal Chantilly gadroon Imperial blue band gold lines & star. Baden gadroon	4 14 6	
1263. New gadroon, gold weed & gold line on the gadroon	9 9 0	
1264. Do. ivory border with antique gilding below	6 6 0	
1265. Do. imperial blue do. do. do.	6 6 0	
1266. Royal flute, pink diamond & arches flowers (no centre) pink band outside cup	8 8 0	
1267. New gadroon union & gold line Dinner Service	36 15 0	
white edge corners gilt	3 13 6	
1268. Old gadroon, Ivory band & slight gilt with different single flowers	8 8 0	
1269. Border shell gadroon Morone birds eye all over & groups of flowers	12 12 0	
1270. Royal Chantilly gadroon, Biscuit blue bramble & gold India work Dinner Service	36 15 0	
1271. Do. do. bold flowers Dinner Service	42 0 0	

1272. Royal, loose flowers in colours & gold line	3	3	0
1273. Do. biscuit & green & gold wreath	6	6	0
1274. New Gadroon, 1036 Blue single flowers & slight gilding	5	15	6
1275. Number wrong: green 982 with gold line	2	12	6
1276. New gadroon, green groups & gold line (without gold 42s.)	3	3	0
1277. Do. morone & gold	6	6	0
1278. Baden gadroon, blue rose etc. border & gold lines (not gilt £2 0s. 0d.)	3	3	0
1279. Royal Chantilly green & gold flowers & gold line (not gilt) [ordered June 1829] Dinner Service	36	15	0
1280. New gadroon, pink band & gold escollope			
1281. Do. do. & gold border			
1282. Do. two pink bands & blue & gold border between	6	6	0
1283. Do. grey & gold honeysuckle	5	5	0
1284. Blue & gold vine border	6	6	0
1285. Zig Zag border	6	6	0
1286. Grey & gold border			
1287. New Gadroon, chrome green & gold honeysuckle			
1288. Do. light blue & gold	5	5	0
1289. Do. Imperial blue & gold with purple beads etc.	6	6	0
1290. Do. Light blue & honeysuckle above & below	5	5	0
1291. Royal, blue & gold diamond	4	14	6
1292. Do. do. curtain border	5	5	0
1293. Blue & gold stripe on New Gadroon (Baden 8 gs)	7	7	0
1294. Blue & gold drop border, New Gadroon	5	5	0
1295. Green & ivory border with brown & gold drop border [?]			
1296. New emboss, biscuit blue & gold flowers	4	4	0
1297. New gadroon, morone in arches & gold roses etc.	6	16	0
1298. Do. light blue & gold lines with dots of pink blue & gold	4	14	6
1299. Do. two narrow borders biscuit blue & gold with gold border & blue line in Dresden style			
1300. Do. double blue border & gold with morone band between			
1301. Do. antique gold border & blue line in Dresden style			
1302. [Crossed out, and 'see 1278' inserted at end of the line]			
1303. New Gadroon, No.66 drops or leafage & Imperial blue bands	6	6	0
1304. Royal, blue & gold with arches & diff't flowers	10	10	0
1305. Do. rich blue & gold antique border with beads & drops below	8	8	0
1306. Baden gadroon, green & embossed gold ornamental	18	18	0
1307. Do. maroon do. do. do.	18	18	0
1308. Baden gadroon, glaze blue & embossed gold ornamental	18	18	0
1309. Do. white do. do. do.	16	16	0
1310. Do. chrome green do. do. do.	18	18	0
1311. New gadroon, new Dresden flowers & gold line	3	13	6
1312. Double green vine border & gold line Dinner Service	31	10	0
1313. Royal Chantilly gadroon blue bamboo & basket edge gilding Dinner Service	42	0	0
1314. Do. as 1279 red in lieu of green Dinner Service	36	15	0
1315. Do. small green groupe & G small sprigs Dinner Service	21	0	0
1316. Gadroon, green rose wreath & gold line	3	3	0
1317. Do. Baden gadroon, as 1312 with basket or open gilding on gadroon	4	14	6
1318. Baden red ground & gold wreath with white rosets	8	8	0
1319. Baden gadroon, Royal blue & gold leaf & drops of gold [see Plate 138] Dinner service	10	10	0
1320. Royal Chantilly gadroon morone & gold lines with 3 white jasmine flowers Dinner Service	63	0	0
1321. Royal Chantilly gadroon Bishop of Chester pattern large centre Dinner service	36	15	0
1322. Green vine with open gadroon gilding	4	4	0
1323. New gadroon, new bell border inside cup & stripe handle & lines outside	5	5	0
1324. New Gadroon, new bell border inside cup & stripe handle biscuit blue	6	6	0
1325. New Gadroon, marone blue border & gilding with stripe handle & lines outside	8	8	0
1326. Baden, rose embossed Womens roses & gold line	2	12	6
1327. New Gadroon, Imperial blue & gold to cups as 1318	7	7	0
1328. As 1171 in colours thistle pink instead of blue	4	4	0
1329. Blue curtain & fawn the strong colour	5	5	0
Dinner Service	60	0	0
Dessert Service	15	15	0
1330. Green & gold stripe	10	10	0
1331. Gadroon, Ivory & gold jasmine border	7	7	0
1332. Baden gadroon, Morone & gold stripe etc.	12	12	0
1333. Blue curtain & fawn pale fawn	14	14	0
1334. New Gadroon, Ivory & gold border Lady Godfrey's pattern	7	7	0
1335. Slight sea weed without flowers (with flowers 10 gs)	8	8	0
1336. King's blue & embossed gold	18	18	0
1337. Imperial blue raised	18	18	0
1338. Green curtain & flowers raised & chased gold	12	12	0
1339. Chrome green with urns in gold raised spangles & lines	12	12	0
1340. Chinese bridge & black & gold rock	4	4	0
1341. Blue & gold Chinese temple boat etc.	4	4	0
Dessert Service	12	12	0
1342. Glaze kiln green curtain & flower red & gold flowers Dinner service	63	0	0
1343. Swiss gown[?] gilded flute	7	7	0
1344. Printed curtain & scroll enamelled & gold & gold line Dessert service	10	10	0
1345. Biscuit green & fawn curtain with red flowers etc.			

Dessert service	18	18	0
1346. Baden gadroon, morone & shell gold star	8	8	0
1347. New gadroon, green band inside & gold lines	4	4	0
1348. New gadroon, imperial blue & 3 panel shell gold & 3 gold drop centre	8	8	0
1349. Do. green & 4 panels fawn & gold in saucer 3 in cups sprig centre	7	7	0
1350. Do. 6 curtains in saucer 4 in cup Imperial blue & gold small group flowers in centre	7	7	0
1351. Hambledon, green border with white ivy wreath	6	6	0
1352. Do. ivory ground & green & gold ivy wreath	7	7	0
1353. Do. biscuit blue thumb stripe & gold	7	7	0
1354. New gadroon, biscuit blue ground 3 shell panels ivory & gold Baden gold daggers inside	8	8	0
1355. [Renumbered 1346] New gadroon, morone blue ground 3 shell panels white & gold Baden gold daggers inside	8	8	0
1356. New gadroon, Imperial, blue with 3 compartments white currants etc.	7	7	0
1357. New Hambledon, Imperial blue band & 3 gold ornaments with lines	5	15	6
1358. Do. biscuit grey with gold lines & bell drops	5	15	6
1359. Do. gadroon Imperial blue border inside cup & gold vine & gadroon dotted gold & gold vine centre	6	6	0
1360. New Hambledon flute, & gold seaweed striped gold on flute	10	10	0
1361. Do. do. strong fawn & green ivy leaf with gold berries etc.	6	6	0
1362. Do. do. pink thistle & biscuit green	3	3	0
1363. New do. green & gold weed	8	8	0
1364. Do. do. blue & gold weed [ordered April 1830]	8	8	0
1365. Do. biscuit blue ground & gold in panels antique gilt on ivory. R. Williams pattern	10	10	0
1366. New gadroon, purple blue curtain & ivory as 1349 gold sprig in centre	6	6	0
1367. Baden gadroon, Imperial blue antique border gold festoon & simple [?] roses	10	10	0
1368. Royal gadroon, Chester in colours Dinner Service	26	5	0
1369. Green curtain border scroll centre Dinner service	36	15	0
1370. Royal Chantilly gadroon, Chrome green & gold lines with groupe of flowers Dessert service	21	0	0
1371. Chantilly Imperial blue & ivory band with gold gold [sic] lines etc. Dessert service	18	18	0
1372. Chantilly, morone & ivory Dessert service	18	18	0
1373. New Hambleton, blue border & ivory 3 fans with gold star etc.	8	8	0
1374. New Hambleton, blue & gold Japan flowers with red etc.	5	5	0
1375. New shape beaded edge plate, Japan flower pot Dinner Service	36	15	0
1376. Royal Chantilly gadroon, blue curtain ivory & gold as 1333			

Dessert service	18	18	0
1377. Do. do. blue curtain & India red & gold flowers Dessert service	16	16	0
1378. Do. do. blue & ivory border with printed flowers color'd Dessert service	14	14	0
1379. Baden gadroon, 3 shells cup 4 stand & ivory with daggers inside cups	8	8	0
1380. Gadroon, printed blue groupes with gold lines Dinner Service	31	10	0
1381. New gadroon, Imperial blue & tooth border as 1119	5	5	0
1382. Do. blue weed & red berries basket gadroon gilding	5	5	0
1383. Dark chrome green on ground 3 shell panels (as 1354) and gold daggers inside cups etc.	8	8	0
1384. New embossed, red & green sprigs & brown line			
Dinner Service 25gs			
1385. Royal Chantilly gadroon, curtain border & stock centre Dinner service	36	15	0
1386. Pink & 3 shells & ivory with daggers inside cup	8	8	0
1387. Pink & white hawthorn flowers, Imperial flute	6	6	0
1388. Marone & white hawthorn flowers, Imperial flute	6	6	0
1389. Gilding green gold Mills pattern, Imperial flute	6	6	0
1390. Do. do. gilt & white spot in centre	5	15	6
1391. Ivory & blue scroll from the edge (Mills)	5	5	0
1392. Ivory & biscuit blue roses (as 1327) (Mills)	7	7	0
1393. New gadroon, 3 birds & gold (Taylor)	6	6	0
1394. New fluted, pink border [?] & print from 976 & printed flowers breakfast			
1395. New Chantilly gadroon, purple Leeds Dinner Service	36	15	0
1396. New gadroon, green sprigs in the Dresden style printed			
1397. New embossed, red & green sprigs & brown line	1	10	0
1398. Pink band wreath of flowers Royal flute	12	12	0
1399. Gadroon, blue printed border & groups in compartments	4	4	0
1400. Gadroon, green tree underglaze & gold Dinner Service	36	15	0
1401. Hambleton, pattern as 1119 chrome green	5	5	0
1402. Do. pattern 1119 Imperial blue	5	5	0
1403. Do. pattern 1119 marone	5	5	0
1404. Do. pattern 1119 pink	5	5	0
1405. Gadroon, pattern as 844 Imp'l blue	4	4	0
1406. Do. do. as 844 chrome green	4	4	0
1407. Do. do. as 844 marone	4	4	0
1408. Hambleton, pattern as 844 marone			
1409. Gadroon, new India sprigs color'd from Foley bowl			
1410. Embossed, plate color'd draggons			
1411. New Royal gadroon, green shamrock border & centre sprigs & gold line	2	12	6
1412. New gadroon, blue groupes printed & gold line	2	12	0
1413. Baden gadroon, blue printed weed & red berry with gold line	3	3	0

1414. Gadroon, chrome green & star
Dinner Service   52 10 0
1415. Do.   do.   do.   with hawthorn flowers
Dinner Service   63 0 0
1416. Gadroon, marone & star   6 6 0
1417. Do.   do.   with white hawthorn flowers
Dinner Service   63 0 0
1418. Do.   Imperial blue & star
Dinner Service   52 10 0
1419. Do.   do.   star with white hawthorn
flowers   6 6 0
1420. Do.   drab border & stars with white hawthorn flowers
Dinner service   63 0 0
1421. Ditto, drab border & stars only
Dinner Service   52 10 0
1422. Do.   as 1318 only biscuit blue & the rosets
ivory ground   8 8 0
1423. New Hambleton, green printed border round
with line & zig zag centre
Dinner Service   31 10 0
1424. Chrome green round with centre group only
plain edge   36 0 0
1425. [Crossed out & illegible]   8 8 0
1426. Chrome green pattern as 1399 plain edge, new
Chantilly
1427. [Crossed out & replacement illegible]   8 8 0
1428. New concave Chantilly, as 1217 in green &
gold & rose colour
Dinner Service   26 5 0
1429. New Hambleton, Green dropping weed & gold
stripe between   5 5 0
1430. Baden, 982 in enamel green & rose colour
without gold knobs & handles gilt
1431. Do.   green groups & small sprigs as 1276
without gold
1432. Baden, chrome green border & slight star
centre with fine gold lines
Dinner service   26 13 0
1433. Do. marone   do.   do.   do.   do.
Dinner service   26 13 0
1434. Do.   same as 1428 with fine gold line
1435. China new Chantilly, blue print with D of
Kent 4 panels & frog in panel with high flower
& star centre
Dinner Service   36 15 0
1436. Do.   do.   glaze kiln green same pattern
Dinner Service   36 15 0
1437. New gadroon, morone & gold antique border   6 6 0
1438. New Chantilly, blue printed border Gold
drops border & gold star in centre
Dinner Service   31 10 0
1439. Do. do. Drab weed red berry & gold lines
Dinner   26 5 0
1440. New concave Chantilly, blue japan from rich
jar
Dinner Service   36 15 0
1441. Do.   do.   do.   same pattern & green
instead of blue
Dinner Service   36 15 0
1442. Baden gadroon, D of Gloster panels prints
gold & ivory panels high flower as 1627   8 8 0

1443. New Chantilly, green weed & berry & green
line
Dinner Service   21 0 0
1444. Baden gadroon, white as 1307 but rich rais'd 10 10 0
1445. Baden gadroon, & panels as 1427
1446. New Chantilly, drab weed red berry & drab
line
Dinner Service   21 0 0
1447. Baden gadroon, drab print without gold   2 2 0
1448. Do.   do.   same pattern with gold as
1423   3 3 0
1449. New Hambleton, drab print without gold   2 2 0
1450. Do.   same pattern with gold as 1423   3 3 0
1451. New Chantilly, rose colour & black with fly in
centre. Wm. Wood's pattern
Dinner Service   31 10 0
1452. New Hambleton, fawn & gold border   5 5 0
1453. New Chantilly, drab print round without gold
Dinner Service   21 0 0
1454. New Chantilly, blue sprigs & fine blue line
glaze kiln no gold
Dinner Service   21 0 0
1455. New Chantilly, drab print round gold drops
border & star centre
Dinner Service   31 0 0
1456. New Chantilly, gown print in blue & Ivory.
Mills.
Dinner Service   31 0 0
1457. Berlin concave Chantilly, green & white jassamine sprigs (Taylor)
1458. Berlin   do.   do.   fuschia border glaze
kiln
1459. Berlin do. do. from 1451 with fine
gold line slight pattern
1460. Baden gadroon, Kings blue as 1308 but not
rais'd   12 12 0
1461. Chantilly Coburg plate, Drab print & hanging
weed gold on knobs and handles
Dinner Service   26 5 0
1462. Royal gadroon, Dist Drab curtain rose colour
& gilt (Mills)
1463. Berlin, narrow grey border & five black lines &
other centre
1464. New Hambleton, drab print & gold border   3 3 0
1465. New Hambleton, drab vermicelli & gold border   3 3 0
1466. New Chantilly, drab ground & hanging weed
& gilt
Dinner Service   36 15 0
1467. New Hambleton, drab vermicelli not gilt   2 2 0
1468. Coburg plate, rose colour & brown leaves full
pattern
Dinner service   36 15 0
1469. New tea pattern chrome green & gold lace
border & flowers (Ashcroft)
1470. Baden gadroon, gilding green Baden border &
gold rosettes not raised gadroon gilt open
1471. Berlin, chrome green & rose color flowers
jassamine sprigs
1472. Ditto   dove leaves & rose flowers ditto do.
1473. Ditto   drab tree pattern with rose color
flower in centre

1474. New tea pattern biscuit blue & lace gilding & flowers (Ashcroft)

1475. Ditto ditto biscuit curtain & ivory rosettes (Ashcroft)

1476. Ditto   drab festoon & orange rosettes (do.)

1477. Ditto   light & dark blue Ivory oak leaf & flowers (do.)

1478. New Chantilly, best 982 red & gold (Wm Woods)
      Dessert Service   31 10 0

1479. New Hambleton, duck weed only no gold   2 2 0

1480. Coburg plate, enamel chrome green vermicelli & hanging weed as Mortlocks no gold
      Dinner Service   26 5 0

1481. Baden gadroon, light and dark blue fawn & gold rich solid edge (Mills)

1482. New Chantilly, green weed & red berries & gold line
      Dinner Service   26 5 0

1483. New Hambleton, marone curtain, rosettes & single flowers (Ashcroft)

1484. New shape, pattern dove color ground

1485. Ditto   ditto   gilding chrome green

1486. Ditto   Imperial blue curtain orange rosettes & gold star centre   5 5 0

1487. Coburg plate, chrome green & white jassamine as Skey's

1488. Ditto   blue green & hanging weed & star in centre
      Dinner Service   36 15 0

1489. Ditto   ditto   & flower in centre

1490. Berlin, biscuit blue 982 pattern rose color ground etc. (Mills)

1491. Ditto   India pattern   ditto   (Mills)

1492. Ditto   salmon ground purple Vandyke border & gold (Mills)

1493. Coburg plate, chrome green & hanging weed & gilt

1494. Kent shape, green curtain & orange gilt lace work (Ashcroft) with star centre

1495. Coburg plate, blue oak leaf red poppy rose color etc. (Wood)

1496. Kent shape, plain fawn etc. as 1483 (Ashcroft)

1497. Kent shape, new drab ground & union sprigs

1498. Do. do. blue green orange rosettes & roses as 1486 (Ashcroft)

1499. Do. do. new drab fruit & ivory as 1456 (Mills)

1500. Do. do. blue fawn festoon & 3 [chrome?] rosettes & gilt union sprigs (Ashcroft)   7 7 0

1501. Baden gadroon, drab hanging weed & gold as 1363

1502. New Hambleton, drab hanging weed as 1429

1503. Kent shape gilding chrome green orange roses, shells & flies (Ashcroft)

1504. Do.   do.   lace border & chrome green (Ashcroft)

1505. Coburg plate, new blue green & red berries & gold line

1506. Coburg plate, new blue green and red berries and green line

1507. Coburg plate, Chelsea pattern in drab rose color gold etc. with line

1508. Coburg plate, new drab curtain rose color & gold line
      Dinner service   31 10 0

1509. Kent shape, bell border with chrome green spots as 1323

1510. Do. do. gold & chrome green Jessamine border (Wood)

1511. New Hambleton, blue border & outside border as 66 pattern

1512. Coburg plate, new drab curtain with ivory rose colour & gold
      Dinner service   31 10 0

1513. Do.   do.   biscuit blue & ivory curtain border & star centre with rose color & green flowers in Ivory (Mills)
      Dinner service   47 5 0

1514. Do.   do.   printed drab weed & drab flowers moss rose

1515. Do.   do.   printed green weed & drab rose in centre

1516. Do.   do.   do.   drab print & do.do.

1517. Hambleton, drab rose & sprigs

1518. Do.   green weed & drab view

1519. Do.   green rose & sprigs

1520. Do.   drab weed & drab view

1521. Coburg plate, drab dagger border & star centre sprigs in drab

1522. Kent shape, dagger border & star centre in drab

1523. Berlin, green weed & drab rose centre

1524. Hambleton, drab views and sprigs between in drab

1525. Kent shape, blue dagger border & star centre

1526. Coburg plate, blue dagger border & sprigs all biscuit blue light color

1527. Kent shape, green sprigs & rose colour flower

1528. Kent shape, shamrock border as 1411 no gold

1529. Do. do. gilding chrome green and orange rosettes with ivory (Mills)

1530. Coburg plate, drab ground hanging weed & gilt as 1466

1531. Berlin, jassamine rose colour & green

1532. Coburg plate, blue chrome green & gold in 982 style (Ashcroft)

1533. Kent shape, chrome green & gold lace work and wild flowers

1534. Kent shape, bisque blue & gold (Mills)

1535. Coburg plate, drab dagger border & sprigs printed with gold [ordered October 1833]

1536. Baden gadroon, marone rich

1537. Kent shape, light & dark blue with ivory (Ashcroft)

1538. Kent shape, fawn curtain and purple sprigs (Wood)

1539. Berlin marone as 1433 with gold drop border

1540. Coburg, breakfast cup drab stripes & gold lines

1541. Coburg plate, drab dagger border & color'd sprigs

1542. Kent shape, drab scollop from edge chrome green & ivory drops (Ashcroft)

1543. Coburg, breakfast green stripes & gold lines

1544. Kent shape, celeste broad border & one gold key border at the edge

1545. Coburg, breakfast blue stripes & gold lines with sprigs from Lily pattern
1546. Kent, drab curtain & rose color (see 1508)
1547. Kent, blue & ivory lace border
1548. Kent, blue drab & ivory
1549. Kent, shape blue ivory & drab scroll
1550. Kent, drab print & ivory cornucopia
1551. Berlin, narrow pink border & star centre with lines (black)
1552. New Hambleton, blue & gilt
1553. New gadroon, as 1323 the bell in blue
1554. Kent shape, jasmine chrome green & dove colour flowers glaze kiln & gold line   3 3 0
1555. Baden gadroon, blue & ivory & gold the gadroon gilt no flowers
1556. Coburg, breakfast vermicelli in drab ground & gold lines
1557. Coburg, breakfast blue chrome green same pattern
1558. Do.   do.   light blue same
1559. Do.   do.   bisque or king's blue same
1560. Baden gadroon, green & gold lace border rich
1561. Coburg, breakfast grey stripes & gold lines
1562. New Hamilton, green & gold & flowers
1563. Baden gadroon, lace cornucopia gilding & flowers
1564. Hambleton, printed vermicelli inside only with gold lines
1565. Antique embossed, dessert green vermicelli & flowers & gilt
1566. Coburg plate, glaze kiln grey band gold lines & printed star centre
1567. Coburg, breakfast chrome green stripes & lines in gold
1568. Coburg, dessert marone & hanging weed & single flower in centre & gilt
1569. New flanged, painted vermicelli in drab ground & gilt
1570. Do.   do.   do.   same glaze kiln grey
1571. Do.   do.   do.   bisque blue
1572. Kent shape, light & dark blue ivory oak leaf flowers etc. rich (Ashcroft)
1573. New flang'd, blue & drab scrowl & single flower (Ashcroft)
1574. Plain Baden, blue stripes glaze kiln & different single flowers
1575. Kent, chrome green & cornelian red berries & green line
1576. Old Chantilly, 1567, as 1030
1577. Coburg plate, marone painted vermicelli
1578. Coburg plate, blue & chrome green painted vermicelli
1579. Kent, drab print & ivory sprigs with gold
1580. Baden gadroon, raised gold chrome green Helmes pattern
1581. Coburg plate, blue & flowers
1582. Baden Gadroon, Salway green stripes & gold border inside cups & lily flower in green
1583. Baden gadroon, Salway green finger stripes & gold & different style flowers
1584. New flanged, drab & gold stripes ivory edge etc.

1585. New flanged, green gothic border only ivory edge & centre flower painted
1586. Do.   do.   drab gothic do. do. do. do.
1587. Coburg plate, (As 1466) but with single flower in centre see 1653
1588. Coburg plate, drab print & ivory scrowl as 1456
       Dinner service   31 10 0
1589. Baden gadroon, ivory band & gold lines
1590. Coburg plate, Barr's border bisque blue ivory rose colour gold etc.
1591. Flanged gadroon, chrome green & chased cornucopia with flowers rich
1592. Coburg plate, Salway green band & centre star
1593. Hambleton, ivory & small flower & border gilt only outside
1594. Coburg, as 1065 but with new centre
1595. Coburg, dessert blue scrowl & ivory
1596. Hambleton, drab Gothic only
1597. [No pattern recorded]
1598. Coburg, drab gothic only
1599. Hambleton, same pattern chrome green
1600. Do.   same light blue glaze kiln
1601. Leaf edge, gold scrowl & ivory edge
1602. Coburg, fawn striped & gold lines
1603. Coburg, blue & chintz India flowers
1604. Coburg, blue gothic ivory & gilt
1605. Do.   in drab ivory & gilt
1606. Do.   marone vermicelli & star
1607. Coburg, blue chrome green & star
1608. New flanged, celeste green & gilt with white spots in ground
1609. Do.   do.   gold sprigs orange & red edge
1610. Broad stripes marone
1611. Do.   do.   same stripes Imperial blue
1612. Ridgway's shape dessert, marone hawthorn & gold star centre
1613. Coburg, vermicelli print ivory scrowl
1614. Ridgways shape, dessert Light blue painted vermicelli & single flowers
1615. New flanged, drab print ivory & gilt
1616. [No pattern recorded]
1617. Coburg, breakfast pea blossom & gold line
1618. Gadroon, yellow green & hawthorn flower in border & single flower in centre
1619. Gadroon, Imperial blue band & single flower in centre (1834)
1620. Hambleton, new drab wreath no gold
1621. Gadroon, dessert lace gilding & group of birds in centre varied (Ashcroft) [see Plate 185]
1622. Gadroon, Imperial blue & hawthorn flower & single flower in centre
1623. Coburg, red & blue japan no gold (Mills)
1624. New flanged, (as 1427) Imperial blue ivory etc.
1625. Hambleton, (as 1620) with gold line
1626. Gadroon, yellow green & hawthorn & centre star
1627. Coburg, drab ground & gilt scrowl
1628. Hambleton (as 1620) with gold line & spot in border
1629. Coburg, breakfast, Chinese figures in glaze kiln drab & fine double line

1630. Hambleton (as 1620) in light blue
1631. Coburg plate, grey band & printed star & gold lines
1632. Gadroon, as 1329 with rose color ivory etc.
1633. Ridgways dessert, Imperial blue & ivory & single flower in centre
1634. Coburg dessert, blue & gold sprigs
1635. Do. T. plate, red band & star centre (Mills)
1636. New plain Chantilly, (as 1466) with single flower in centre all rose color
1637. Ridgways dessert, (as 1614) no centre sprig *quite plain*
1638. Coburg T. set, Chinese figures gilt
1639. Baden gadroon, lace gilding & flowers (Wood)
1640. Plain Baden, chrome green spots & gold line
1641. Gadroon dessert, drab prints & group flowers in centre
1642. Hambleton, (as 1630) with gold line
1643. Do. breakfast, drab ground and painted vermicelli with ivory gilt edge
1644. Coburg, Barr's border (as 1590) but yellow in lieu of gold fawn edge
1645. Do. McAlpine's pattern with chinese centre
1646. Do. red & blue Japan with rose colour rosettes in border
1647. Coburg T. plate, painted slight from 1623
1648. Hambleton, London chrome green stripes & gold line
1649. Do. drab, print with ivory gothic & gold compartments alternately print
1650. New Adelaide shape, drab ivory & gold
1651. Coburg plate, rich red & blue Japan fawn edge no gold
1652. New Gadroon, (as 1329) green & ivory curtain rich
1653. Coburg T. plate, (as 1466) with different single flowers
1654. Coburg T. plate (as 1652)
1655. Coburg, breakfast celeste spots & gold line plain inside
1656. Baden gadroon, pea green gothic gateway & flowers rich
1657. Hambleton, blue & green hanging weed & gilt
1658. Coburg, woodbine border & gold line
1659. Do. blue tree pattern yellow in lieu of gold blue line
1660. Adelaide, breakfast grey & slightly gilt (as Daniel's Fawn)
1661. Ridgways shape dessert, celeste green & drab views & color'd birds
1662. Coburg, blue spots & gold line
1663. New flanged, celeste stripes & gold & gilt ivory edge
1664. Do. do. blue and gilt rich with ivory
1665. Adelaide shape, blue & gilt rich with flower
1666. New flanged, blue & gold stripes alternately
1667. Ridgways shape dessert, celeste ground & drab views
1668. Adelaide shape, blue, gold, ivory & flowers
1669. Coburg, light blue Chester & blue line
1670. Plain Baden, D [Duke] Gloster not rais'd & groupes in panels

1671. Coburg, celeste band & gold star & lines
1672. Coburg, narrow blue border & gilt
1673. Coburg, chrome green & red sprigs & gold line
1674. Hamilton shape, drab ground & hanging weed
1675. New flanged, celeste ground & gilt
1676. Coburg dessert, celeste band gilt border & single flower in centre
1677. Coburg dinner, blue tree & gilt & blue line
1678. New flanged, light blue & dark scrowl
1679. Adelaide, as Daniel's fawn & gilt slight
1680. Coburg, dinner 5 Dresden sprigs & gold line
1681. Do. do. blue & ivory rock gilt
1682. Do. breakfast fawn & gilt in & out of cups (Mills)
1683. Adelaide shape, new drab & gilt
1684. Coburg, dinner fawn & gilt views (Mills)
1685. Adelaide tea, marone, ivory & gilt rich [see Plate 429]
1686. New flanged, drab & gilt view under (as Coalport)
1687. Baden gadroon, blue & white enamell'd spots
1688. Adelaide breakfast, gilt sprays & yellow green
1689. Gadroon, dinner blue band & star
1690. Baden gadroon, celeste ground ivory & gilt rich
1691. Adelaide, fawn & gilt as Daniels
1692. Ridgways shape dessert, green & gilt flowers
1693. Adelaide tea fawn & gilt (Mills)
1694. Coburg, breakfast pink stripes & gold lines
1695. Adelaide tea, grey as 1683
1696. Gadroon dessert, French gilding & flowers gilt rich
1697. Hamilton, drab band & berries & gold stems & lines
1698. Adelaide, garden scenes or birds & gilt
1699. Adelaide, blue & gilt rich
1700. Coburg dinner as 1627 but in blue
1701. Adelaide breakfast grey vermicelli & gilt as 1465
1702. Coburg dessert, chrome green rich rais'd & gilt & single flower
1703. New flanged, grey & vine border ivory & gilt
1704. Adelaide, tea, pink & Spode's gilt
1705. Do. tea, blue ground ivory & gilt
1706. Do. blue & fawn & ivory
1707. Coburg, maroon patch & hawthorne flowers
1708. Coburg, blue print gold lines & stars
1709. Coburg, green pannels & hawthorn flowers
1710. Adelaide, fawn as Pattern no. 1695
1711. Do. fawn & gilt
1712. Coburg, yellow green & ivory & gilt
1713. Coburg, green dragon
1714. Stone colour tree no gold
1715. Coburg, as 1627 in green china
1716. Adelaide, drab tree & gilt
1717. Do. do. as 1665 pink no blue
1718. Do. celeste Tea
1719. Gadroon, table, blue lines, 35 gs. Nov. 27th 46. [This date was probably added at a later period]
1720. Coburg, Drab weed
1721. Celeste curtain & star
1722. Same but with diff't stars

429. A trio of 'Adelaide' shape decorated in maroon and ivory with 'rich' gilding. Unmarked except for pattern number 1685. Diameter of saucer 6 in. *c.* 1840. *Geoffrey Godden, chinaman*

1723. Same but diff't stars
1724. Adelaide, green vermicelli & gold border
1725. Coburg, blue red & yellow Barr's sprigs
1726. Do.   do.   & gold red line
1727. Do.   drab & blue border dragon gilt
1728. Coburg, drab & blue border dragon gilt
1729. Baden gadroon, celeste & groups
1730. New flanged, blue & flowers
1731. Coburg plate, & green as 1684
1732. Adelaide, blue (as 1688)
1733. Adelaide, dessert (as 1695) but pink & flower
1734. Gadroon, blue & green sprigs blue line
1735. Coburg, red & blue sprigs no gold
1736. Do.   chrome green patch & ivory
1737. Do.   green dragon
1738. Adelaide, green zig zag & gilt
1739. Coburg, drab dragon flower centre
1740. Adelaide, blue vermicelli & ivory & gilt
1741. Adelaide, blue net & star
1742. Coburg, red & bisque Chester no gold
1743. Adelaide, tea blue net & gilt (Boys)
1744. Adelaide, tea rose & blue gilt
1745. Coburg, blue & gold rock no ivory
1746. Do.   bird pattern
1747. Do.   bird Japan
1748. Do.   blue dragon bird & flower centre
1749. Do.   green patch ivory & star
1750. Do.   blue dragon & star centre
1751. Do.   blue Chester & gilt
1752. Adelaide, grey scroll & flowers as Daniel's
1753. Adelaide, drab feather sprigs blue & gilt
1754. Coburg, Chinese figures coloured
1755. Coburg, blue gothic & gilt no ivory
1756. Bisque, blue dot & wreath

1757. Adelaide, bisque blue scroll as 1752
1758. Coburg, drab gothic no ivory gilt
1759. Adelaide, green flowers ivory & gilt
1760. Coburg, dragon border red & star
1761. Adelaide, blue feather sprigs & gilt
1762. Coburg, green stripes
1763. Ivory & gilt
1764. Royal plate, blue & gold scroll
1765. Coburg, drab Virginia blue & gilt & gold line
1766. Adelaide, green net & gilt
1767. Coburg, blue scratch edge & gilt
1768. Coburg, blue net & gold & star printed
1769. Adelaide, blue edge & gilt
1770. Adelaide, green & gilt sprigs etc.
1771. Coburg, drab fish tail & gilt
1772. Do.   blue net & pannels
1773. Coburg, green net & pannels
1774. Do.   blue dots & gilt border & star
1775. Coburg, drab fish tail & panels
1776. Adelaide, dessert blue spot & flower
1777. Baden gadroon, white rais'd & gilt
1778. Coburg, drab dot & gilt & star
1779. Adelaide, white & gold
1780. Adelaide, white & gilt leaf
1781. Do.   new blue scroll [ordered February 1841]
1782. Adelaide, marone & gilt & Dresden flowers as Daniel's
1783. Brown gadroon fawn & gilt & flowers
1784. Adelaide, fawn & flowers as Daniel's
1785. Victoria plate, blue & fawn curtain
1786. Victoria plate, blue Imperial & cypher
1787. Victoria plate, blue & gilt
1788. Coburg plate, blue & star

1789. Adelaide dessert, cross bar & single flower
1790. Victoria plate, blue & gilt scroll
1791. Victoria plate, marone & yellow
1792. Adelaide, tea, white & gold
1793. Adelaide, drab scroll as Daniel's
         [see page 157]
1794. Coburg, enamel green dots & gilt
1795. Coburg, color'd sprigs & black line
1796. Victoria, blue cross bar & gilt
1797. Do.   marone & ivory (Ashcroft)
1798. Victoria, chrome green band & printed star
1799. Adelaide, tea, white & gilt
1800. Baden gadroon, Baillies Sc [scroll?]
1801. Victoria plate, & flowers & gilt
1802. Coburg plate, new India, no gold
1803. Adelaide, blue vine leaf & ivory & gilt
1804. Coburg (as 1802) but in red
1805. Adelaide, lace gilding & flowers
1806. Adelaide, green & gold on edge as 1769
1807. Coburg, green & purple
1808. Victoria plate, marone & gilt on edge
1809. Victoria plate, Imperial blue & do.
1810. Do.   narrow blue border as 1672 & printed
         stars
1811. Adelaide, tea, Imperial blue scroll & groups
         (As Daniel's)
1812. Do.   yellow green   do.   do.
1813. Do.   blue & green on edge & star
1814. Baden, French pattern with flowers & laurel
1815. Coburg, breakfast fill'd (as 1802)
1816. Victoria, tea drab (From Daniel's 5940) slight
1817. Victoria, mat blue same
1818. Victoria, yellow green same
1819. Adelaide, blue & rose colour
1820. Adelaide, blue privet border & gold border
1821. Adelaide, bisque blue ribbon border & gilt
1822. Baden gadroon, blue over gilt
1823. Victoria, tea, green & gilt on edge & line green
1824. Do.   tea, blue sprigs & ivory & gilt
1825. Coburg, blue border gilt. Dresden groups
1826. Adelaide dessert, Dresden group gold & blue
         on edge
1827. Victoria, blue panel & grape vine & Taylors
         scroll
1828. Coburg, Major Strode's [pattern] in blue
1829. Victoria, blue panels & scroll
1830. Adelaide, fawn & white ribbon
1831. Coburg, fawn border & Dresden groups
1832. Baden gadroon, Imperial blue ivory leaf &
         grape rich
1833. Do.   do.   scroll gilding similar to 1563
1834. Coburg, old jar fill'd in as 1802
1835. Chantilly gadroon, blue hawthorn sprigs & star
1836. Adelaide dessert, green band & view & gilt
1837. Coburg, drab privet border & jar border gold
         line
1838. Adelaide, printed & fill'd in groups, blue &
         gold edge
1839. Adelaide, drab feather & gold edge
1840. Adelaide, drab & blue feather & gold edge
1841. Coburg, fawn bands and drab privet & gold
         lines

1842. Coburg, drab Charlemont border blue bands
         & gilt star & lines
1843. Dessert [?], drab Charlemont border & green
         bands & gilt star & lines
1844. New Royal, blue lily & gold, tea ware
1845. Plain gold Royal vermicelli, teas
1846. Plain Royal gold vermacilla
1847. Do.   rich cornucopia gilding & flowers
1848. Drab vermicelli & gilt teas
1849. Blue Victoria edge gilt
1850. Royal, blue webb & gold
1851. Royal, green webb & gold
1852. Royal, blue & gold
1853. Royal, white & gold
1854. Royal, blue & gold drops
1855. Coburg, printed groups green & gold
1856. Coburg, painted group & sprigs in green
         pannels & gold
1857. Royal, fawn & blue shading
1858. Adelaide, blue edge gilt & do.   star &
         border drab
1859. Coburg, boy's India rose color & green
1860. Royal plate, India rose color gold edge
1861. Do.   green & gold borders with painted
         sprigs between
1862. New shade teas & red flower & green etc.
1863. Adelaide, blue edge & fawn ground gilt
1864. Coburg plate, Japan branch gold line
1865. Do.   do.   without gold line
1866. Coburg plate, green ground & white dots, gold
         outside border & star
1867. Coburg, as 1802 without border & fill'd in in
         new style gilt
1868. Dessert Adelaide, with geranium sprigs gilt
1869. Coburg, do.   green spots & flowers
1870. Coburg, French green ground & flowers
1871. Coburg, do.   blue scroll & fawn pannel with
         wild flowers
1872. Tea Royal, Green French pannel with painted
         groups
1873. Tea Royal, celeste & painted groups
1874. Tea Royal, celeste above pink sprigs in lieu of
         painted
1875. Tea Royal, pink & gold
1876. Tea Royal, French green stems & flowers
1877. Breakfast Royal, drab geranium sprigs gilt
         with gold lines
1878. Breakfast Royal, red & green branch, gilt
1879. Breakfast Gotha green studs & gold
1880. Breakfast Coburg   do.   do.   & star
1881. Do.   do.   French green & gold
1882. Royal, stone as 1874

[Pattern numbers restart at 2000. Some of these patterns, because
of their low price, may be of Stone China, not porcelain. See page
146.]

2000. Flowing blue shells & scroll and outer fine gold
         line and centre line
         Dessert Service   3   13   6
2001. Do. do. do. do.
         Dinner Service   11   16   6

2002. Rich flowing blue shell & gold trellis, fine gold wave & gold lines

2003. [No pattern recorded]

2004. Flowing blue gothic print gold centre line & touched on edge
Dessert Service   3 13 6

2005. [No pattern recorded]

2006. Flowing blue shells etc. as 2000 with the addition of gold cross bars
Dessert Service   4 14 0

2007. Flowing blue 1802 [? jar centre] slightly gilt the border of plate & fine gold line
Dinner Service   10 10 0

2008. Do.   do.   Shamrock spot & blue line

2009. Do.   do.   do.   do. with red berry, gilt & gold edge

2010. Do.   rustic spray with gilt & gold line [mentioned in an order dated 24 September 1844]

2011. Celeste ground gold pannels & flowers. Tea ware royal

2012. Parke's green do.   do.   do.   do.

2013. Scarlet & blue cove pattern & gold line
Dessert Set   4 4 0

2014. Flowing blue mistletoe gilt & gold edge. Excellent breakfast ware

2015. Do.   do.   no gold & blue line.   do.

2016. Do.   rosebud gilt & gold edge. Gotha do.

2017. Do.   do.   gold line only

2018. Do.   Blue wreath, scarlet ground & gilt & gold line Coburg   do.

2019. Malta shape tea ware gold coral gilt border inside cup, star & gold line

2020. Flowing blue rosebud richly gilt & gold edge [mentioned in an order dated 9 October 1844]
Dessert Service   7 17 6

2021. Marone ground richly gilt & flowers
Dessert Service   10 10 0

2022. Do.   gilt & gold star & ivory
Dessert Service   10 10 0

2023. Green ground & gilt (Royal tea ware)   4 4 0

2024. Blue ground & gilt etc ivory ground (Royal tea ware)   3 3 0

2025. Celeste ground new printed scroll & filled in sprigs & gilt (Dresden do.)   3 3 0

2026. Blue coral & gold line (Gotha breakfast ware)

2027. Blue stripes & gold lines with sprigs from Lily pattern (1545) (Gotha breakfast ware)

2028. Blue & gold reed edge (Plumtree tea & breakfast)   2 15 0

2029. Blue tulip, lily border & gilt (Plumbtree tea & breakfast)   3 3 0

2030. Flowing blue chintz border & sprigs no gold (do.)

2031. Blue & scarlet coral & gold line (Gotha tea & breakfast)

2032. Blue coral no gold   (do.)

2033. Dresden green coral & gold edge

2034. Dresden blue & gold coral

2035. Drab Chester filled in and gilt & gold line (Royal tea)

2036. Do.   festoon filled in & gilt & gold line (Coburg)
Dinner Service   14 12 6

2037. Do.   rustic birds pattern & gold line (Coburg tea)

2038. Dresden print (drab) & gold cross bar & line (Gotha)

2039. Flowed blue tile pattern & gold line   (do.)

2040. Flowing blue band & shell patch & gold & gold line

2041. Drab thistle gilt & gold line (Gotha) [mentioned in an order dated 5 February 1845]
Dessert Service   4 4 0

2042. Drab rustic spray gilt & botanical in centre
Dessert Service   6 6 0

2043. Flowed blue scroll panels filled in flowers, orange & *touched* with gold
Dessert Service   4 14 6

2044. Scarlet ground broad white band gold lines & botanical
Dessert Service   6 6 0

2045. Green ground broad white band gold lines & botanical
Dessert Service   6 6 0

2046. Peacock Japan blue filled in gilt etc. (Coburg)
Dinner Service   18 13 6

2047. Flowed blue music pattern scarlet ground & gilt (Coburg)
Dinner Service   14 12 6

2048. Green (light chrome) band fine gold lines & star (do.)
Dinner Service   11 16 6

2049. Flowed blue painted pattern & gilt (Coburg)
Dinner Service   13 14 6

2050. Blue Dresden fruit [?] & gold line (Coburg tea)

2051. Drab rosebud & gilt (Royal tea)

2052. Coburg biscuit blue stripes no gold

2053. Green printed rustic birds pattern & gold line

2054. Drab festoon gilt & gold line (Royal tea, Gotha breakfast)

2055. Drab weed, blue spots & gold line (do.)

2056. Green vermicelli gold border at top & gold line (Royal tea)   1 10 0

2057. Drab rosewreath gilt (Royal tea)   1 17 6

2058. Dresden print no gold (Coburg tea)

2059. Blue   do.   do.   (do.)

2060. Flowed blue mistletoe no gold (Excellent)

2061. Do.   rosebud   do.   (Gotha)

2062. Flowed blue rustic spray no gold (Coburg)

2063. Do.   do.   & gold line only

2064. [Crossed out – drab rustic bird pattern in a gold line]

2065. Blue do.

2066. Stone rustic spray gilt & gold line (Gotha breakfast)

2067. Green coral & gold line [crossed out] See 2133

2068. Blue ormolu & gilt as 2024 but Plumptree shape (Plumptree)

2069. Blue scrolls pannels gilt & filled in flowers (do.)

2070. Do.   do.   ivory ground & filled in sprigs (or sprays) (Plumptree)

2071. Do.   do.   gilt (Gotha)

2072. Peacock Japan blue filled in & gilt as 2046 but blue scroll on part of border instead of green sent to Stuart. Coburg dinner.
2073. Curtain border drab printed 880 centre filled in blue etc. red line
2074. Drab curtain partridge spots & curtain or flag red line (do.)
2075. Flowed blue red edge gilt gold line on shoulder of plate & printed & filled in group
     Dinner service   16 17 6
2076. Blue scrolls & gilt & as 2071 but orange shape. Breakfast ware
2077. Green Dresden print & gold drop bar, & line
2078. Blue leaves tendrils red flowers & gilt (Adelaide)
2079. Drab rush border gilt & gold feather edge (Adelaide)   1 17 6
2080. Do. thistle do. do. do. do.   1 17 6
2081. Marone scroll & gilt (Gotha)
2082. Mat blue do. (do.)
2083. Marone ground panels gilt & botanical
     Dessert Service   7 7 0
2084. Chelsea Dessert embossed, green ground white shaded & lines
     Dessert Service   9 9 0
2085. Coburg, pink band gold lines & star [illegible writing above price seemingly relating to earthenware]   3 13 6
2086. Coburg, green do. do. French green
2087. Coburg, marone do. do. two coats
2088. Coburg, F. B. & B. blue & gold branch (modern) & gold line
2089. Coburg, coloured festoon fill'd in Japan blue & red line (Gotha breakfast)
2090. Coburg, all over japan border & sprig in centre
2091. Coburg, marone ground as Hicks' pannels flowers & gold stars as Hicks
2092. Coburg, celeste ground light pannels flowers white red & rose & dontells & gold star
2093. Barr's gadroon marone ground
2094. Coburg, blue pannels gold scroll trellis work & centre star
2095. Royal Lindsay edge, & Sèvres groups
2096. Coburg, marone slight inner scroll border & centre star gold line
2097. Coburg, marone band ormolu & gold reed edge
2098. As Hicks see no 2091 (green)
2099. Coburg, blue & gold grap edge & centre ring
2100. Celeste as 2093 only solid gadroon edge
2101. Coburg, blue reeds & blue line
2102. Coburg, blue festoon
2103. Barr's gadroon green ground gold scroll inner leaf border & solid edge
2104. Marone with solid fish tail on ground with group in centre. Dessert Ware as 2012
2105. Dessert ware green ground flowers & gold
2106. Parke's green ribbon scroll gold dontelle & centre flowers. Dessert
2107. Parke's green or biscuit blue pannels broad white & gold edge & centre flowers
     Dessert service   7 7 0
2108. Stone do. do. do. do.
2109. Celeste ground 3 pannels print & flowers gold scroll centre

2110. Marone ground scroll gilding & flowers
2111. Maroon harp pannel & centre flowers
2112. Biscuit blue ground pannels & sprigs
2113. Gotha, drab rustic birds no gold
2114. Gotha, drab festoon no gold
2115. Gotha, blue rush birds no gold
2116. Do. do. gilt slightly & gold line
2117. Gotha F. B. & B.'s green & gold branch & gold line
2118. Gotha, biscuit blue leaves cut up with gold & gold line
2119. Gotha, blue & gold scroll
2120. Coburg, do. with ivory & fill'd in sprigs
2121. Windsor, green ground pannels & flowers & gold edge as Hicks
2122. Coburg, green band fine broad white & gold lines edge
2123. Orange shape, green & gold trellis work & pannels of flowers
2124. Windsor, blue & gold scroll pannels & Sèvres sprigs [mentioned in an order dated 19 June 1845]
2125. Coburg, Imperial blue bands two coats gold lines & star
2126. Do. grey band gold lines & star
2127. Drab birds no gold (Gotha breakfast)
2128. Chrome green band plate two coats. Coburg shape, gold line & star
2129. Flowed blue reed edge gilt in & new filled in sprig groups
2130. Coburg, narrow blue band gold lines & fine blue line (Earl of Ulster, Regent China)
2131. Royal blue gadroon bar scroll gilt (and badge of 24th reg't)
2132. Coburg, blue shells scroll ivory ground & gilt & gold star (china)
2133. Coburg, china marone ground 3 panels flowers & gilt
2134. Do. do. Mat blue as 2091 (rather slighter)
2135. Do. Cove band & red line plain centre
2136. Do. china gold coral & French outside border & painted groups
2137. Reed edge, gilt light blue tulip sprigs
2138. Do. do. blue leaves and two gold lines on shoulder of plate
2139. Do. marone & gilt groups
2140. Coburg, celeste ground 3 panels & single flowers (similar to 2092) gilt slight, slight star & line
2141. Gotha, gold vine wreath & gold line
2142. Do. pink band broad white band 3 gold lines above
2143. Do. green do.
2144. Do. marone do.
2145. Do. drab weed red berry & gold line
2146. Coburg, drab vine leaf & tendrils gilt & gold line
2147. Do. do. festoon filled in & gilt (as 2036)
2148. Gotha, marone & purple grapes edge gold line
2149. Gotha, F. B. & B.'s blue & gold branch & gold line

2150. Do.   do.   green & brown branch & brown line
2151. Do.   dark Blue tulip lily border & gilt
2152. Do.   Sidmouth filled in & gold line (blue red green etc.)
2153. Coburg, blue dagger border gilt (as 844)
2154. Hambleton, drab 1620 Drab hanging & gold line
2155. Dresden, blue band tooth border gold edge & Dresden flowers
2156. Adelaide, new drab festoon filled in & gilt & feather edge
2157. Coburg, drab weed and gold line
2158. Dresden, shaded blue edge Gold dontelle painted Dresden groups
2159. Royal, on foot drab sea leaf [?] all over & gilt
2160. Harpers [?] stone shell & scroll & gilt Royal on foot
2161. New Windsor, blue scrolls gilt & flowers
2162. Adelaide, stone ground & hanging weed gilt & flower (plain shape dessert)
2163. Drab leaf all over gilt & painted fancy bird exactly same thing as 1201
      Dessert service   7 7 0
2164. Blue ground ivory & gold French outside border & gold star
2165. Pink bands gold lines & star china
2166. Reed edge, slightly gilt biscuit blue leaf & gilt
      Dinner Service   26 2 6
2167. Coburg, blue as above only gold line
      Dinner Service   23 13 0
2168. Reed edge, slightly gilt pink band gold line on shoulder & star in centre
      Dinner Service   18 3 6
2169. Do.   do.   green band gold line on shoulder & star in centre
      Dinner Service   19 17 0
2170. Do.   green lines on edge slight gold leaves line on shoulder and star centre
      Dinner Service   16 17 6
2171. Coburg, green band 3 pannels of flowers gilt as Hicks 2091
      Dinner Service   36 11 6
2172. Coburg, marone pannels slight gilding & star centre as Bond St. order
      Dinner Service   34 6 0
2173. Coburg, blue scrolls & gilt & gold star, no star in tea ware Windsor
      Dinner Service   19 17 0
2174. Coburg, green scrolls & gilt & gold star. No star in tea ware
      Dinner Service   19 17 0
2175. Do.   four pink lines on edge & gold leaves as reeds edge shoulder line star centre
      Dinner Service   15 17 6
2176. Do.   three lines on edge & gold leaves the middle line pink & two outside ones blue, gold shoulder line and star as above
      Dinner Service   15 17 6
2177. Do.   green scrolls shell [?] work gold line slight gilt in pattern and gold star
      Dinner Service   19 17 0

2178. Do.   blue scrolls   do.   do.
      Dinner Service   19 17 0

[A large section is torn from the book here, making nos. 2179-84 incomplete.]

2179. Do.   3 pannels single flowers gilt [...] scroll gilding & star centre
      Dinner Service   31 15 0
2180. Do.   3 pannels single flowers [...] do.
      Dinner Service   31 15 0
2181. Dessert, stone leaf [...] edge or scollop
      Dessert Service   7 7 0
2182. Dessert, best blue leaf [...] light & color'd bird
      Dessert Service   7 7 0
2183. Dessert, blue scroll [...]
      Dessert Service   9 9 0
2184. Dessert, best blue [...] small groups of flowers on the [...]
      Dessert Service   6 16 6
2185. Dessert new vine emboss'd, marone band the leaves ivoried & gilt & tendrils white & gilt gold lines & star
      Dessert Service   6 16 6
2186. Dessert new vine, pink band white vine leaves & tendrils gilt & star
      Dessert Service   6 16 6
2187. Do.   do.   green bands white shaded leaves & tendrils gold lines & Dresden group & sprigs
      Dessert Service   8 8 0
2188. Do.   do.   green leaves & tendrils the shade at side of leaves light gold edge & Dresden group & sprigs
      Dessert Service   7 19 6
2189. Do.   do.   white & gold leaves & tendrils white shade under leaves Dresden groups gold line
      Dessert Service   7 17 6
2190. Dessert, 3 pannels of simple flowers centre group pink band & gold fish tail outside gold edge etc.
      Dessert Service   14 14 0
2191. Dessert, three pannells of simple flowers only drab instead of pink
      Dessert Service   14 14 0
2192. Dessert, mat blue scroll edge slightly gilt gold line & botanical
      Dessert Service   7 7 0
2193. Do.   gold leafage edge shoulder fine line & Dresden group & sprigs
      Dessert Service   10 10 0
2194. Do.   light gold edge shoulder line & botanical in centre
      Dessert Service   5 5 0
2195. Table ware, black printed sprigs & partially filled in green and red line
2196. Bowl & saucer half orange [shape], celeste band gold edge & gilt as matt & embossed   4 4 0
2197. Bowl & saucer half orange shape, pink band as above only that the fleur de lys is in gold   4 4 0
2198. Do. do. F. B. & B.'s border & gold edge
2199. Do.   do.   new print border only pink over the print gold line

2200. Do. do. do. & fill'd in & groups & sprigs – one group in & one outside cup, group in saucer

2201. Do. do. mat blue shaded border & edge gold fill'd in groups

2202. Do. Gotha shape, new blue print border & wreath & gold line

2203. Do. do. drab & gilt in pattern & gold line

2204. Do. Windsor shape, new gold wreath & fill'd in [. . .] groups 4 14 6

2205. Do. do. fill'd in groups as pr[. . .] 1 group on cup one on saucer

[The page is torn at this point and a piece is missing.]

2206. Do. do. celeste returned edge & gold [. . .] sprigs

2207. Do. do. marone [. . .]

2208. Do. do. new Imperial blue print [. . .] gold line

2209. Half orange shape, blue [. . .]

2210. Do. blue [. . .]

2211. Do. blue ribbon [. . .]

2212. Tea ware half orange shape, biscuit blue & gold pannels & white diamond work in the blue small groups 8 8 0

2213. As 2191 Baden gadroon, solid gold edge biscuit blue & gold fish tail panels & 3 small painted flowers between 8 8 0

2214. Tea Windsor shape, white & gold fish tail & small pannels of flowers inside cup as above only no ground 7 10 0

2215. Do. do. pink & gold tooth border & painted Dresden groups and gold edge 7 10 0

2216. Do. do. new green over the black print border gold lines and printed groups as 2208 2 7 5

2217. Do. do. new print drab wreath only & gilt in pattern & gold edge 1 10 0

2218. Blue pannels broad white gold lines & botanical gold edge
Dessert Service 7 7 0

2219. [?] dry Medium black & green sprigs & red line

2220. Blue thistle border & gold lines

2221. Dessert, marone band gilt etc. as Lady Valentine's with view in centre
Dessert Service 14 14 0

2222. Dessert, blue & gold & red coral solid gadroon edge the red in between the coral
Dessert Service 16 16 0

2223. Dessert ribbond wreath of flowers & birds & gold leaves gold edge & low shoulder blue & gold ring round a fancy bird in centre
Dessert Service 14 14 0

2224. Bowl & saucer half orange, green returned edge & gold lines & fill'd in groups 1 slight sprig inside cup

2225. Scotts rich Japan on Windsor shape (by Mills 9 9 0

2226. [No pattern recorded]

2227. [No pattern recorded]

2228. Embossed, rose bud scarlet ground white & shaded & gilt
Dessert Service 9 9 0

2229. Tea ware as 2196, half orange

2230. Half orange shape, teaware, celeste stripes & gilt wreath of flowers 7 10 0

2231. Do. only biscuit blue & that the wreath of flowers are on ivory ground 7 10 0

2232. Adelaide, gold traced edge marone ground ivory leaves & gilt 4 0 0

2233. Same as 2197 without the fleur de lis pink band, breakfast & tea 3 3 0

2234. Same as 2173 only brown & gold 3 3 0

2235. Brown Sidmouth see 880, slightly gilt & gold line

2236. [No pattern recorded]

2237. [No pattern recorded]

2238. Half orange shape, two pannels of flowers on each saucer & cup, marone ground gilt etc. marone & gilt inside cup

2239. Windsor shape, two pannels of flowers on each cup & saucer marone ground gilt etc. Marone inside cup gilt

2240. New Windsor shape, two pannels of flowers on ea cup & saucer pink ground gilt etc. Pink inside cup & gilt

2241. Half orange shape, two pannels of flowers on cup & saucer, pink ground gilt etc. Pink inside cup & gilt

2242. Half orange shape, two pannels of flowers on each cup & saucer blue ground gilt etc. Blue inside cup & gilt

2243. New Windsor shape, two pannels of flowers on cup & saucer blue ground & gilt. Blue inside cup & gilt
[No pattern number 2244]

2245. New Windsor shape, blue scrolls in mat. blue & festoons of flowers gold edge & foot line etc.

2246. New Windsor shape, brown new print wreath & gold edge & foot line

2247. Do. do. drab, new print & touched with gold & gold edge & footline

2248. Half orange shape, gold dontelle edge & gilt border & flowers below rose forget me knot & pansy

2249. New Windsor, brown rose wreath gold lines etc.

2250. New registered embossed, plate form [registered on 6 June 1846] Fawn on embossed richly gilt & gold star

2251. [Pattern crossed out and 'See 2259' put in]

2252. New registered embossed, celeste band on gilt on white embossed inner line & tooth border & star (see 4000 added later)

2253. New registered embossed, marone band on gilt on white embossed inner line & tooth border & star (see 4000 added later)

2254. Do. do. Parke's green do. do. etc.

2255. Do. do. biscuit blue do. do. on ivory embossed

2256. Do. do. white & richly gilt on embossed

2257. Do. do. blue & gold traced edge blue & gold star

2258. Do. do. do. & filled in Dresden group & sprigs

2259. Do.   do.   marone on embossed slight on embossed & gold star
Dessert Service   5   5   0

2260. Do.   do.   celeste   between   embossed richly gilt
Dessert Service   5   5   0

2261. Do.   do.   mat blue do.   do.   & gold star

2262. Coburg, rich gold trellis work & Dresden flowers

2263. Windsor, celest band & gold lines (as B333. Feb 3rd, 1846)

2264. Reed edge, marone & gilt on edge Dresden group & sprigs

2265. Blue tulip & lily border gilt, Coburg

2266. Blue scrolls gilt & gold star (5 of these around plate gold edge and line on rim & star)

2267. Blue Rush birds & gold line, Coburg 22 ware

2268. Coburg, brown Sidmouth gilt & gold line

2269. Scroll embossed, fawn & gilt on embossed gold edge & star (china)

2270. Coburg, mat blue band gold lines & star (as 2087)

2271. Do.   China, Parke's green Hardy's scroll &

2272. Barr's gadroon, celest band scroll border (Macclesfield's) etched edge & star

2273. Do.   marone solid edge & line inner raised gold scrolls

2274. Coburg, marone & gold trellis work & gold star (as B189 1845)

2275. Barr's gadroon, solid edge & fine blue eagle richly gilt & star and baskets of flowers

2276. Scroll embossed, blue & gold scroll on embossed blue & gold star & gold edge

2277. Coburg, drab rush birds & gold line

2278. Do. china, blue tulip & gold line

2279. Do.   do.   blue & gold grape edge blue & gold star & line around star

2280. Dessert, marone panels gold scroll & marble 3 baskets of flowers & single flower in centre

2281. Do.   blue ground white leaf outer & inner border three panels of flowers

2282. Do.   green ground 4 white panels with trellis work ivory & gold scrolls bottle of flowers on centre

2283. Do.   Chelsea rosebud scarlet ground white shaded & gold edge

430.   A drawing from the Chamberlain design book showing pattern 2292, one illegible in the written list. *c.* 1845. *Worcester Royal Porcelain Co. Ltd*

2284. Do.   celest band chaples wreath 2 outer & 2 inner gold lines
2285. Do.   vine leaf embossed lightly Dresden & gilt Dresden group & sprigs broad & fine line
2286. Do.   do.   green ground white shaded gold lines light Dresden group & sprigs
2287. Do.   do.   marone ground & ivory leaves white tendrils gilt gold lines & white star
2288. Do.   Dresden green & gilt scroll (3) panels flowers & group in centre gold dontelle edge
2289. Do.   do.   scrolls butterflies & group of flowers gold edge
2290. Do.   Parke's green & gold trellis gold edge & group of flowers 5 panels in plate
2291. Do.   pink band gold worked edge & border
2292. [Pattern illegible – perhaps torn out. See Plate 430.]
2293. Blue ivory & gold harp panels botanical. Dessert
2294. Gotha, Blue thistle gilt & gold line
2295. Half orange, pink band
2296. Coburg, blue dagger border blue & [?] geranium & gilt
2297. Windsor, marone & gold marble scroll panels & flowers gold edge
2298. Half orange, green returned edge filled in Dresden groups & sprigs
2299. Gotha, blue scrolls & filled in sprigs ivory & gold line (as 2070)
2300. Plumptree, blue broad & fine lines gold edge & under line
2301. Do.   green bands gold edge & lines filled in wreath between the bands
2302. Gotha, mosaic border in copper black & gold line
2303. Do.   broad & blue edge & gold line
2304. Do.   do.   pink do.   do.
2305. Besborough, blue & gold thing [sic]
2306. Windsor, blue & gold all over
2307. Do.   celest band gold edge & outside dontelle gold scroll under Dresden group & sprigs
2308. Do.   blue scrolls gilt gold edge & small flowers as 2070 but no ivory, painted sprigs under each scroll, flower & sprigs inside
2309. Do.   Dresden, green scrolls gilt gold edge & flowers (as 2289)
2310. Old Windsor, Barr's rich rock Japan gold edge etc.
2311. Half orange, gold scroll dot & dontelle border small single flowers under (2248)
2312. Do.   blue ground gold scroll under gold edge
2313. New Windsor, gold japan & flowers wreath & gold edge
2314. Dresden & blue & gold reed edge
2315. Half orange, brown & gold gold [sic] edge
2316. Gotha blue leaf gilt & gold line
2317. Royal, on foot green ground slight French outside border & shell
[This and some twenty preceding patterns were mentioned in an order dated 24 July 1846.]
2318. Malta shape, blue & gold wreath dentele edge

2319. Do.   blue & gold wreath dentele edge
2320. Gotha shape, blue edge & gold line
2321. Windsor shape, two blue lines gold edge & gold lines under the blue one
2322. New embossed shape, fawn & gilt richly on embossed
2323. Malta shape, 4 pink lines & gold rope gold dontelle & gold drop border under the lines
2324. Malta shape, rich white & gold fish tail & gold edge
        Dessert Service   9 9 0
2325. Malta shape, blue scollop & painted roses richly gilt etc. etc. (as Bond St)
        Dessert Service   10 10 0
2326. Malta shape, pink band & rich gold fish tail
        Dessert Service   10 10 0
2327. Malta shape, stone ground blue scrolls & gold flowers etc.
2328. Narrow marone band scollops & gold lines, plain centre, pink
2329. Do.   green   do.
2330. Do.   pink   do.
2331. Enamel blue scollops & group centre – 5 small sprigs
2332. Do.   do.   coral gold edge & gold line – coral deep 2½ inches
2333. Do.   do.   scroles scroll shape
2334. New registered embossed, blue tracings only. China
2335. New registered   do.   blue on emboss'd & white studs & gilding between blue scroll & gold star
2336. Coburg, Green scrolls & white studs on edge finished as new embossed China
2337. Coburg, biscuit blue scrolls & richly gilt. China
2338. New reg'd emboss'd, pink band gilt on white embossed inner line & tooth border & star
2339. Dessert, Green border gold flowers & painted flowers on gold wreath
        Dessert service   10 10 0
2340. Do.   do.   (only), celeste   do.
        Dessert Service   10 10 0
2341. Malta shape, blue line gold Sèvres style & pink flowers   6 6 0
2342. Do.   fawn & gilt registered scrolls   5 10 0
2343. Minton's embossed shape, gold on emboss'd and blue tracings   4 4 0
2344. Do.   do.   gold on emboss'd blue tracings   3 11 6
2345. Gotha shape, key border
2346. Malta shape, gold & flower wreath. Dontele edge   10 0 0
2347. Malta shape, celeste scrolls & flowers   3 2 6
2348. Malta shape, green band & gold spot, wreath   4 4 0
2349. Gotha registered, blue & gilt
2350. Gotha Registered,   do.   & gilt stripes in Vandyke, spots in scrolls
2351. Dessert new registered embossed, gilt celest band line & tooth border & botanical [?]
2352. Do.   do.   & gold scrolls & botanical
2353. New registered embossed, enamel blue slight scroles

2354. Coburg, green border & line & gold line on edge
Dinner Service ... 11 16 6

2355. Do. blue do. do. do.
Dinner Service ... 11 16 6

2356. Coburg, Four green lines on rim of plate with a black one on each side, green line on shoulder and black line just above gold edge
Dinner Service ... 15 19 4

2357. Coburg 3 blue lines & 5 bunches of vine leaves and fine gold shoulder line to imitate Charles Meigh's, as 2423

2358. Enamel blue Elizabethan scroll cut up with black & gold edge
Dinner Service ... 17 17 8

2359. Celeste band & registered embossed, slightly gilt & gold star
Dinner Service ... 21 16 0

2360. New registered edge, blue & gilt on embossed & botanical
Dessert Service ... 14 14 0

2361. New registered edge, marone & gilt & group of flowers
Dessert service ... 16 16 0

2362. Blue chain New registered shape, blue & fawn edge chain & star
Dessert service ... 12 12 0

2363. New registered edge, do. celeste between embossed gilt brown
Dessert service ... 12 12 0

2364. Do. fawn & gilt border & botanical
Dessert Service ... 15 15 0

2365. Do. white & gold edge & botanical
Dessert Service ... 16 16 0
[See Plate 431 for border designs for patterns 2365–7.]

2366. New registered edge, green & gold edge & botanical
Dessert Service ... 16 16 0

2367. New registered edge, green & gold on embossed & botanical
Dessert Service ... 16 16 0

2368. Same as 2362 only with botanical
Dessert Service ... 15 15 0

2369. New registered edge, fawn & blue on embossed
Dessert Service ... 16 16 0

2370. Drab same as 2045
Dessert Service ... 6 6 0

2371. Pink do.
Dessert Service ... 6 6 0

2372. White & gold on registered embossed & simple flowers
Dessert Service ... 12 12 0

2373. New registered embossed, gilt scrolls, Barr's border & grey band & star
Dessert Service ... 12 12 0

2374. Malta shape, same as 2341 only that the edge is dontille, the line pink & flowers blue
Teaset ... 6 6 0

2375. Minton's shape, Gold edge blue spots & blue drop filled in wreath
Teaset ... 3 3 0

2376. Malta shape, pink ribbon & gold gold inside cup ... 6 6 0

2377. Malta shape, blue scrolls drab ground richly gilt do. ... 10 5 0

2378. Celeste on Malta shape, same as dessert 2340 ... 6 14 0

2379. Green do. 2339 ... 6 6 0

2380. Malta shape, marone as 2342 ... 5 10 0

2381. Do. glaze-kiln green 2342 ... 5 10 0

2382. Do. gilt roses as Rollasons [see Plates 179 and 180] ... 14 14 0

2383. Do. gold dontelle & gold border ... 4 14 0

2384. Malta shape, brown & gold border few strokes of brown & black ... 7 1 0

2385. Do. green leaves & gold vine border ... 6 14 0

2386. Do. gold fish tail ... 9 9 0

2387. Besborough shape, grey & figures shaded in white & richly gilt ... 14 14 0

2388. Besborough shape, bat-printed figures in gold pannel richly gilt ... 7 17 6

2389. Do. views & richly gilt ... 17 17 0

2390. Do. fawn & richly gilt & flowers ... 11 11 0

2391. Windsor shape, blue narrow band & groups of flowers gold line border & blue band ... 9 9 0

2392. Do. do. & wreath & flowers hanging in festoon ... 6 6 0

2393. Do. Pink lines & gilt ... 4 14 0

2394. Do. biscuit blue narrow band & flowers ... 9 9 0

2395. Half orange shape, Kerr's pattern

2396. Windsor shape, gold edge

2397. Dessert Chelsea rose bud painted flies, leaves etc. ... 9 9 0

2398. Malta plate, & green scrolls ... 6 6 0

2399. Royal shape, white & gold shells ... 3 3 0

2400. Royal, vine wreath ... 3 3 0

2401. Royal shape, blue & gold edging ... 3 3 0

2402. Marone ground Royal shape, – gold –

2403. Melon shape, blue & gold edge & stripes ... 2 7 3

2404. Green do. ... 2 7 3

2405. Pink do. ... 2 7 3

2406. Coburg, blue dagger border & geranium & white studs

2407. Melon shape, new color'd key border, green pink & black ... 2 15 7

2408. Baden gadroon, gold traced gadroon pink lines & fine pink & gold stripes

2409. Melon shape, blue & fawn chain as part of border of 2369 & gold ... 3 11 6

2410. Royal shape, same as celeste 2348

2411. Do. same as green 2339 ... 6 6 0

2412. Coburg, blue line & gold line as Sharpus

2413. Do. green & gold do.

2414. Baden gadroon, same as 2409 only the gadroon is gilt

2415. Melon shape, gold band & gold line as Daniels 7000 Mr. W. H. Kerr

2416. Gotha shape, blue edge & gold line inside cup

2417. Do. pink do. do. do.

2418. Baden gadroon, gold traced edge & blue stripes ... 3 3 0

2419. Royal shape, green as 2045. Dessert Ware ... 4 10 0

2420. Do. pink as 2371 do. ... 4 10 0

2421. Melon shape, pink as Charles Meigh's in blue only grapes etc. ... 3 3 0

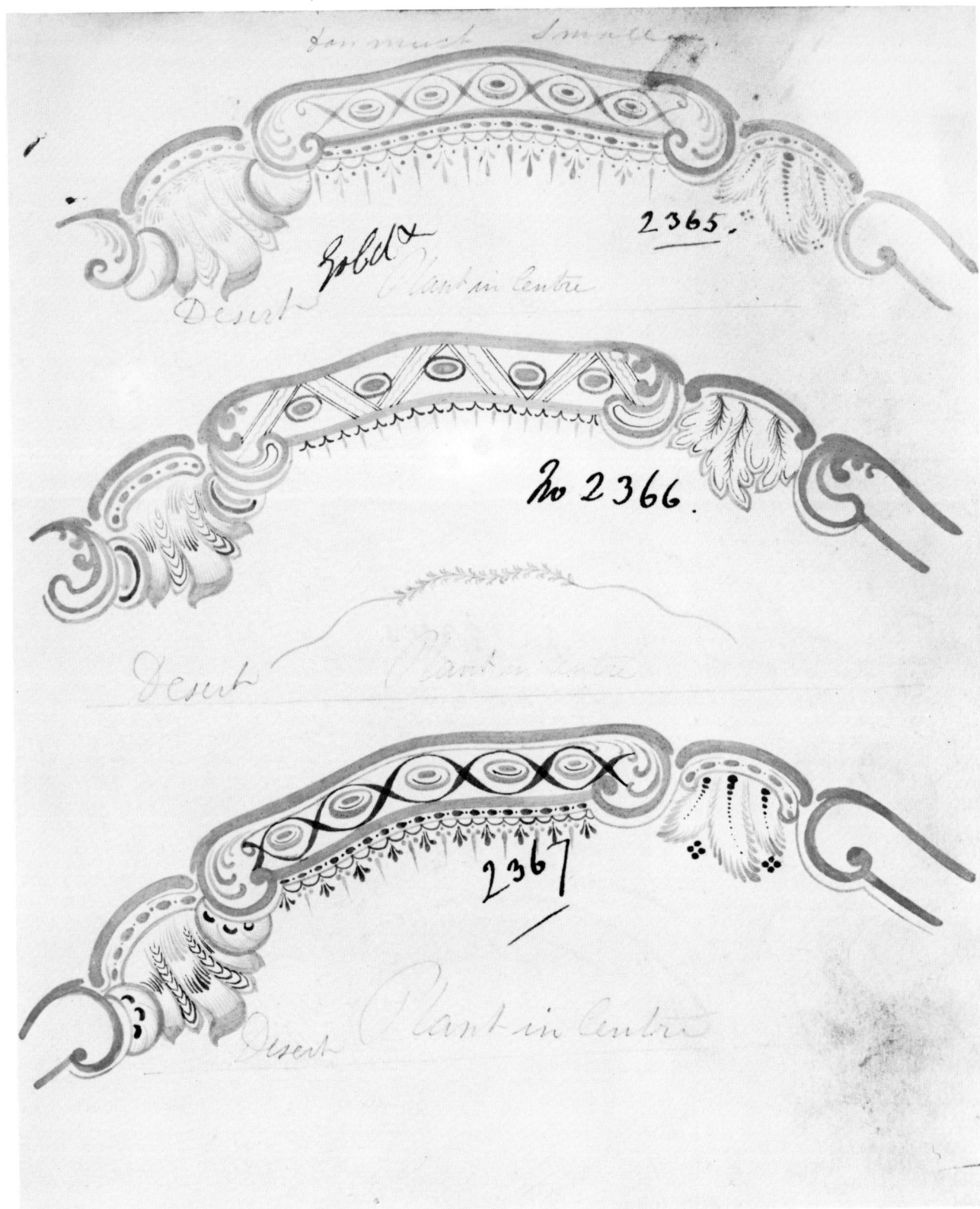

too much Smaller

2365.

Desert Gold &
Plant in Centre

No 2366.

Desert *Plant in Centre*

2367

Desert Plant in Centre

431. Three drawings of dessert service designs, 2365, 2366 and 2367, priced at £16 16s. 0d. for each complete service. c. 1846.
Worcester Royal Porcelain Co. Ltd

2422. Melon shape,   green (as Charles Meigh's in
blue only grapes etc.)   3 3 0
2423. Do.   blue   3 3 0
2424. Do.   marone leaves tendrils in gold as
Daniels 8844   2 7 0
2425. Do.   green do.   do.   2 7 0
2426. Do.   blue   do.   do.   2 7 0
2427. Do.   gold edge narrow band ivory &
gold marble & dontell edge
2428. Melon shape, Scotch plaid border gold dontelle
edge   4 4 0
2429. Coburg, 22 body, pink lines vine leaves in gold.
Meigh's style
2430. Do. do.   blue do. do. do.
2431. White & gold edge
2432. Dontelle edge lines tooth border & dontelle
2433. Melon shape, gold edge coral [drawing] Coral
about an inch wide
2434. New registered embossed, mat blue band same
as no. 2252 only mat blue
2435. Melon shape, rich white & gold border out &
inside cup   9 9 0
2436. Plain round shape, celeste band gold dontelle
edge line on shoulder & tooth border & star

[Patterns 2437–43 inclusive also bear the note: 'Patterns sent to
Grindley & Co. 15 June 1847'.]

2437. As done on fawn edge service for Bond St
[crossed out]
2438. Plain round shape, Parke's green band as above
only Ridgway's star
2439. Plain round shape, biscuit blue band gold
dontelle etc. as above & star
2440. Plain blue band Dontelle edge & star & gilt on
blue & star as 2436
2441. New registered embossed, gilt on emboss'd
marone band inner tooth border & star as 2438
2442. New registered   do.   do. Imperial
blue   do.   & star
2443. Do.   as 2256 with lion crest as finished for
Rigg & Son
2444. Melon shape, celeste narrow band gold edge &
line & wreath under band
2445. Embossed scroll gilt & gold edge & shoulder
line
2446. Melon shape, celeste band with gold stars in
band (9 gs nett)   14 14 0
2447. Do.   mat blue (9 gs nett)   14 14 0
2448. Do.   biscuit blue narrow band richly gilt
with border of No. 2435 under in every other
respect the same   10 10 0
2449. Gotha shape, breakfast ware red lines ivory &
lilac as Daniel's Pompei without figures or key
border [see page 150]
2450. Melon shape, blue key border gold edge
2451. Melon shape, biscuit blue leaves & gilt as the
blue in 2426
2452. Besborough shape, blue enamel & gold scrolls
[see page 152]
2453. [No pattern recorded]
2454. [No pattern recorded]
2455. [No pattern recorded]

[The following six entries relate to the openwork pieces, see pages
168–70.]

2456. Bottle 5⅜ inches high 3 compartments pierced
& 3 solid with painted birds, canary finished
(see pattern book) [see Plate 209]   1 5 0
each
2457. Do.   do.   do.   do.   with painted
flowers, biscuit blue ground & pearls & gilding
[see Plate 209]   1 3 0
each
2458. Small pierced chalice two handles Dresden
blue work solid gold inside.   1 6 0
each
2459. Cup & stand pierced canary finished (see
pattern book)   2 5 0
each
2460. Cup & stand & cover blue finished (see pattern
book)   3 5 0
each
2461. Pierced ivy white & gold raised gold round
neck   2 2 0
each
2462. Melon shape, blue tulip & gold edge
2463. Do.   do.   do.   & tulip gilt
2464. Do.   blue heath   do.
2465. Do.   blue seaweed do.
2466. Do.   black tulip & gold edge
2467. Do.   black thistle & gold edge
2468. Do.   black groups & gold edge
2469. Coburg shape, enamel blue narrow band to
follow shape of Coburg plate gold line & pink
line   11 16 6
2470. Do.   pattern to follow the shape,
Orange band & red lines   6 14 6
2471. Coburg shape, grey band red lines   6 14 6
2472. Do.   ivory band black lines   6 14 6
2473. Do.   narrow green band red do.   6 14 6
2474. Do.   pink band green lines   6 14 6
2475. Do.   green scroles blue & gold blue
shoulder line   7 16 6
2476. Do.   blue do. pink & do.
pink do.   7 16 6
2477. Coburg, enamel blue narrow band & green
lines   6 14 6
2478. Coburg, same as 2355 only pink lines

[The page is badly torn here and part is missing. Patterns 2479–83
are illegible but designs 2483 and 2484 are drawn in one of the
pattern books, see Plate 432.]

2484. Besborough shape, blue scroles on embossed
richly gilt
2485. Coburg, fawn leaves 3 gold lines fawn on
shoulder & gilt
Dinner Service   19 16 6
2486. Do.   green leaves   do.   do.
2487. Do.   narrow celest band & brown lines
2488. Dessert
2489. Candlesticks, green ground & flowers black top
& bottom & gold marble   10 6
each
2490. Candlesticks Imperial blue & do. do. do.   10 6
each

Gilding 5

Celeste Band 1½ inch wide
On cup and Saucer

No. 2483.

2484

Gilding 4½/2

4014
Mat Blue on White Ground
x left arch
+ left oval.

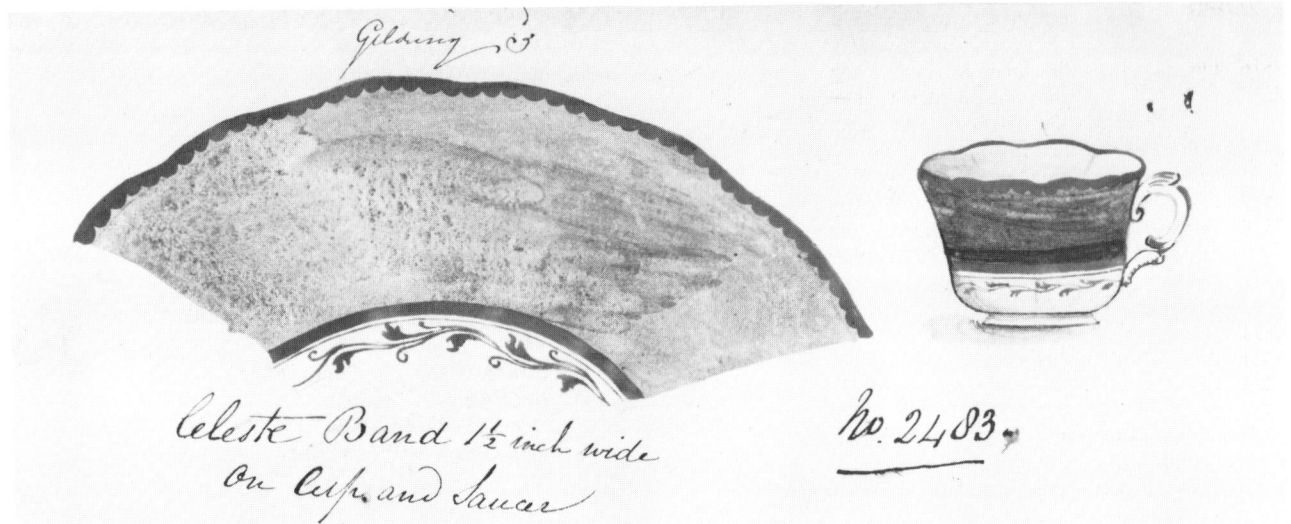

432.   Two teaware patterns, 2483 and 2484, and the different cup shapes. These designs are missing from the written list. *c.* 1846.
Worcester Royal Porcelain Co. Ltd

2491. Do. red ground & figures do. do.	10 6 each		
2492. Do. imperial blue ground & figures do.	10 6 each		
2493. Melon shape, gold wreath gold wreath & color'd bell	2 13 0		
2494. Blue border gold & roses			
2495. Blue lines & gold vine leaves & botanical in centre			
Dessert Service 5 gs			
2496. Melon shape, enamel blue line Gold line & gold vine wreath & edge	2 7 3		
2497. Coburg shape, new asparagus handle enamel blue edge & gold line			
2498. New Royal, enamel blue narrow band gold edge lines tooth border & botanical			
Dessert Service	5 5 0		
2499. Do. green line & stripes gold scroll & botanical			
Dessert Service	5 15 6		

2500. Melon shape, narrow fawn band gold scroles	2	12	6
2501. Do. gold scroll green berry. Boys	2	2	0
2502. Do. blue & gold stripes or lines	2	2	0
2503. Scroll shape, same as 2445 only the scroll in blue no shoulder line & gold only			
2504. Melon shape, blue edge & fine gold line			
2505. Do. do. green			
2506. Do. do. pink			
2507. Royal shape, blue & pink forget me not '& gold leaves' Gold Vandyke etc.			
2508. Melon shape, as 2340 with gold star bottom			
2509. Royal, buff leaves traced in black & gold lines as 2485			
Dessert Service	5	5	0
2510. Melon shape, new convolvulous border drab gilt & gold edge			
2511. Do. do. gold edge only			
2512. Coburg shape, gold line & narrow blue band			
2513. Coburg shape, gold line & narrow pink band			
2514. Do. do. green do.			

2515. Do.   fine blue & gold lines on edge
      & rim of plate
2516. Do.   fine green & do.   do.
2517. Do.   gold line on edge & blue line
      gold line & blue line on rim & centre gold line
2518. Coburg shape, gold line on edge & pink line
      gold line & pink line on rim & centre
2519. Do.   do.   & green do.   green
2520. Coburg shape, green & gold line. 3 lines on
      rim & two gold lines centre green & gold line
2521. Do.   only blue
2522. Do.   only pink
2523. Do.   3 green lines
2524. Do.   3 pink lines
2525. Do.   3 brown lines
2526. Do.   3 blue lines
2527. Melon shape, gold dontelle edge green shading
      & slight painted groups   4 10 0
2528. Melon shape, gold dontelle edge blue shading
      & slight painted groups   4 10 0
      [No pattern number 2529]
2530. Do.   do.   purple do.   do.   4 10 0
2531. Do.   gold dontelle pink & green
      scroll pannels   4 10 0
2532. Do.   gold line Elizabethan in gold
      only   2 7 3
2533. Do.   green band & white lines
2534. Do.   pink   do.   do.
2535. Do.   white & gold rose thistle &
      shamrock border & dontelle
2536. Coburg shape, peacock Japan filled in as
      pattern book
2537. Do.   red Sidmouth filled in with
      enamel blue leaves
2538. Scrole shape, Scrolls in faint chrome green cut
      up with black
2539. Do.   do. in pink   do.
2540. Do.   do. in blue   do.
2541. Melon shape, fawn band blue scroles & fill'd
      in sprigs
2542. Melon shape, new convolvulous border drab
      & gold line
2543. Do.   do.   do.   do.   & gilt in
      pattern
2544. Melon shape, new convolvulous border blue &
      gold line
2545. Melon shape do.   do.   do.   & gilt in
      pattern
2546. Melon do. celeste band & gold etching   4 10 0
2547. Do.   do.   do.   4 10 0
2548. Coburg shape, blue jar & green brown lines
2549. Do.   pink jar   do.
2550. Coburg shape, pink Sidmouth brown lines
2551. New Grass edge, plate finely traced with green
2552. Do.   pink
2553. Do.   blue
2554. Do.   brown
2555. Do.   blue scroles & cut up with black
2556. Do.   green do.   do.   do.
2557. Do.   pink   do.   do.   do.
2558. Melon shape, gold vermicelli   5 2 6
2559. Coburg shape, narrow blue enamelled band as
      2512 but no gold line

2560. Granite Coburg shape, blue line on rim &
      shoulder of plate
2561. Do.   do.   green do.   do.
2562. Do.   do.   pink   do.   do.
2563. Do.   do.   blue line & fine line on rim &
      same on shoulder
1564. Do.   do.   green do.   do.
2565. Do.   do.   pink   do.   do.
2566. Do.   do.   broad blue band on rim
2567. Do.   do.   green do.
2568. Do.   do.   blue line & 2 fine red lines
2569. Granite dessert, 3 pink lines & gold line on rim
      pink & gold line on shoulder & gold centre ring
2570. Granite dessert, 3 blue lines do. blue & gold
      line do.
2571. Do.   do.   green do.   green do.
2572. Green band & gold scrolls & gold line on
      shoulder & gold star
2573. Pink do.   do.   do.
2574. Pink band gold reed edge in gold & leaves &
      gold scrolls in band & centre stone
2575. Green do.   do.   do.   do.
2576. Pink band & brown lines
2577. Pink grass edge (slight)
2578. Gold line green band & gold line on rim &
      shoulder of plate & botanical
2579. Do.   blue   blue   do.
2580. As 2573 only grey
2581. As 2574 only grey
2582. Melon, blue & gold Elizabethan
2583. Blue scroll on grass edge plate (no etching)
      Mrs. Clun's slight scroll
2584. Blue do.   do.   do.   do.
2585. Pink do.   do.   do.   do.
2586. Brown do.   do.   do.   do.
2587. Grass edge, as 2551 only white & gold
2588. Melon (after French style), two blue lines on
      line gold dontelle & foot line
2589. Do.   do.   two pink lines do.   do.
2590. Do.   do.   two green lines do.   do.
2591. Melon, Narrow blue band. Gold wreath under
      gold edge & foot line
2592. Coburg granite, 3 bluelines & 5 gold vine
      leaves & grapes on rim Gold shoulder line
2593. Do.   3 green lines do.   do.   do.
2594. Do.   3 pink lines do.   do.   do.
2595. Melon China, blue enamelled res'd edge Red
      line & gold toothing under inside & arch gold
      foot line outside & line above
2596. Do.   do.   do.   with gold lines only
      (the red & toothing)
2597. Do.   do.   do.   do.   do.
      [2598–600 all crossed out: 'See 1/2. 3. & 4' inserted]
2601. Melon [china?], three blue lines Gold edge &
      foot line only
2602. Do.   do.   Pink   do.
2603. Do.   do.   Green do.
2604. Melon, Gold scrole edge & leafage Gold foot
      line & ring in saucer
2605. Melon, Gold scroll same pattern but X blue
      introduced
2606. Do.   do.   pink   do.
2607. Do.   do.   green do.

2608. Coburg, Printed Royal lily & gilt & gold border
  & brown edge   3 3 0
2609. Coburg, printed gold lines only   3 3 0
2610. Do.   do.   plain no gold
2611. Do.   painted as 2608 brown edge
2612. Coburg, as 2609
2613. Coburg, painted no gold as 2610
2614. Melon, mat blue ground all over same as
    dessert gold scrolls
2615. Do.   green
2616. Melon, mat pink ground all over same as
    dessert gold scrolls
2617. Pink bands, gold spots & group – flower border
    gold dontelle
    Dessert Service   30 0 0
2618. Celeste ribbon & flower border gold dontelle
    Dessert Service   30 0 0
2619. Melon pink returned edge on cup ½ ret'd on
    saucer two gold lines
2620. Dessert Coburg, blue band & panels of flowers
    painted in scroll gilding gold dontelle & flower
    sprig centre
    Dessert Service   14 14 0
2621. Dessert Coburg, pink band 5 panels of flowers
    painted in French style gold edge inner scroll
    border & red group centre
    Dessert Service   25 4 0
2622. Dessert Coburg, blue band 6 panels of painted
    flowers in same style as 2621 – group centre &
    gold dontelle
    Dinner Service   42 0 0
2623. Melon, Red edge on cup ½ ret'd on saucer gold
    & red line
2624. Dessert, as 2620 blue 6 panels of flowers on
    scrole gilding and group centre

[There is a large gap in the sequence from 2625 to 3000. It would appear that no patterns were issued, as the previous number (2624) does not come at the end of the page.]

3000. New registered edge, new red band & gold star
3001. New registered edge, biscuit blue on embossed
    & white pannels & gilt star in centre
3002. Melon shape Granite, 3 blue lines
3003. Do.   do.   3 green lines
3004. Do.   do.   3 brown lines
3005. Do.   do.   3 pink lines
3006. Melon shape, China, gold scrolls & gold edge
    (Toulouse pattern) & star inside cup
3007. Melon shape, China, 3 pink & gold edge
3008. Melon shape, China, 3 blue & gold edge
3009. Do.   do.   3 brown do.
3010. Do.   do.   3 green do.
3011. Dessert Coburg, grey band gold scrolls &
    botanical as 2045
3012. Dessert Coburg, blue pannels round the plate
    & ivory running round & gold
3013. Dessert Coburg shape granite, 5 blue lines on
    plate
3014. Albert shape, blue [?] & flowers dontelle edge   4 14 0
3015. Do.   fawn   do.   do.   4 14 0
3016. Do.   grey   do.   do.   4 14 0

3017. Do.   fawn bands & gold lines & flowers
    between bands   3 3 0
3018. Do.   rose, violet & forget me knot & gold
    dontelle   3 3 0
3019. Albert shape, Sèvres group & slight sprigs   3 3 0
3020. Do.   blue ribbon & bows spotted in gold &
    wreath of flowers
3021. Do.   green   do.   do.
3022. Worcester ['Albert' crossed out] shape, blue
    bands & gold lines with running wreath
    between & rose coloured spots
3023. Chelsea, rose bud, fawn on the embossed & gilt
    Dessert Service   8 8 0
3024. Do.   white & gold – on embossed
    Dessert Service   7 17 6
3025. Do.   coloured natural, no flies
    Dessert Service   7 7 0
3026. Do.   new red ground white shaded leaves
    & gold edge   8 18 6
3027. Do.   chrome green   do.   8 18 6
3028. Royal shape, ivory band & gold lines &
    botanical in centre   5 5 0
3029. Royal shape, ivory band & gold scroll & gold
    dontelle edge & botanical   6 16 6
3030. New registered edge, slightly gilt & botanical
3031. Royal shape, fawn ribbon & wreath of flowers
    & centre group dontelle edge   10 10 0
3032. Do.   fawn band & ivory with gold line &
    Dresden flowers   8 18 6
3033. Do.   fawn & ivory bands & dog rose
    between & in centre [see page 157]
3034. Do.   fawn leaves gilt & dog rose & gold
    dontelle edge   8 18 6
3035. New registered edge, gilt & double roses in
    each compartment, rose in centre   10 10 0
3036. Melon shape, fawn leaves & gilt & dog rose
    between
3037. Melon shape, fawn & ivory bands & gold lines
3038. Melon as 3017
3039. Royal dessert, fawn band apple blossom [see
    Plate 433]   10 10 0
3040. Do.   green do.   as 3039   10 10 0
3041. Do.   blue   10 10 0
3042. Granite Coburg shape, 3 lines in coral, centre
    of the blue
3043. New leaf edge, slightly gilt 3 lines in green
    coral
3044. New leaf edge [illegible]
3045. Melon, blue heath & [green?] bands on edge &
    shoulder 4 gold lines
3046. Granite [?] celeste bands four gold lines &
    wreath   7 7 0
3047. Royal shape, chrome green   do.   do.   9 9 0
3048. Do.
3049. Granite, pink line on edge & shoulder of plate
3050. Do.   blue   do.   do.   do.
3051. Granite green line on edge & shoulder of plate
3052. Registered edge, green coral & slightly gilt
    edge & gold ring coral centre   4 14 6
3053. Do.   blue   do.   do.   do.   4 14 6
3054. Melon shape, green coral gold edge gold foot
    line

3055. Registered edge, blue between embossed Ridgway star only blue as 2240

3056. Royal shape, celeste band ivory & gold French border outside & gold star

3057. Granite two blue ring lines

3058. New registered edge, heath sprigs fine brown line

3059. Granite, narrow (green Parke's) line & outer gold line to join straight lines

3060. Do.   (blue) do.   do.   do.

3061. China outer blue line following shape of plate & inner gold line with white space between & blue shoulder line

3062. [Crossed out and 'See 3082' inserted] [No pattern recorded nor any number]

3064. Melon shape, blue roses gilt etc.

[The following seven patterns are affected by a tear in the book.]

3065. Do.   drab [page torn]

3066. Do.   [?] gold edge foot line etc.
3067. Do.   pink   do.   do.
3068. Do.   green   do.   do.
3069. Do.   blue   do.   do.
3070. Do.   drab   do.   do.
3071. Do.   do.   filled in Sheriff [prints]
3072. [No pattern recorded]
3073. [No pattern recorded]
3074. [No pattern recorded]
3075. Albert shape, Cross S varied heaths. Gold dontelled edge
3076. Registered edge Dessert, gilt on embossed as 3035 & varied heaths
3077. Do. do. do.   varied heaths in wreath and small sprigs
        Dessert Service   10 10 0
3078. Do. do. do.   three sprigs varied heath & centre bit
        Dessert Service   10 10 0

433. A drawing from the factory pattern book showing the 'Royal' dessert service plate form with pattern 3039, priced at £10 10s. 0d. for the service. c. 1849. *Worcester Royal Porcelain Co. Ltd*

3079. Do. do. do. centre sprig of heath small sprigs round
Dessert Service   10 10   0

3080. Granite Coburg, five leaves in plate in gold & 3 blue lines & gold line on shoulder as 2495 no plant

3081. Coburg, celeste band ivory & gold outer French border inner gold line & tooth border

3082. Coburg Granite, red band gold edge & gold inner line gold As Lord Ward's March 17 [18]52 Gold & red shoulder line as Phillips

3083. Registered edge, dessert blue & red chain & gilt botanical centre

3084. Coburg, granite peacock Japan. Dinner

3085. Registered edge, as 2255 only gilt on white instead of ivory, blue band

3086. Registered edge, dessert blue band & ivory as 2255 only print in centre

3087. Registered edge, table plate, blue band and gilt as 2255 on white instead of ivory 3/3

3088. Granite, two pink lines handles gilt [tableware] straight

3089. Do. two green lines do. do.

3090. Do. two brown lines do. do. see 3057 for 2 blue lines

3091. Registered edge, Parke's green embossed white, gilt as 2255 & plant centre. 8d. two flies [?]
Dinner Service   12 12   0

3092. Coburg, celeste band & gold lines & star. White space left between gold line on each side of celeste

3093. Do. celeste band & fine brown lines do. do.

3094. Do. celeste returned edge & gold lines do. do.

3095. Scroll emboss'd, blue tracing etc. on emboss'd gold edge & gold star centre (Arch scroll)

3096. Registered edge, ivory embossed gilt with Vandyke only & fine line under the leafage. Gold star as 2440

3097. Granite dessert. Five enamel'd blue vine leaves on rim & 1 in centre, gold tendrils & brown grapes similar to 2426

3098. Albert shape, 4 gold lines gold chain border & gold studs. Gold foot line

3099. Drab festoon filled in with colours only & printed line. Dinner Worc Coburg

[The sequence ends here and restarts without a break at 4000. It appears that the pattern writer made a mistake and thought that the previous number was 3999 instead of 3099.]

4000. New registered embossed, celeste band etc. as 2252 but with Ridgway's star

4001. Do. do. Parke's green as do. but with do.

4002. Do. do. chrome yellow green as do. but do. do.

4003. Do. do. celeste on embossed & gilt white studs

4004. Do. do. best blue do. do.

4005. Do. do. white ground gold scroll on edge blue fish scale under and gold spikes

4006. Melon, green stripe from top to bottom on each flute with gold edge & gold line at bottom of stripes in saucer but not in cup, only foot line & edge

4007. Do. pink do. do. do. etc. do.

4008. Do. blue do. do. do. etc. do.

4009. Melon, green band & green riggle stripe with gold line on each side of line & gold line & foot line. Gold edge

4010. Melon, pink band & green riggle stripes with gold line on each side of stripe & gold line & foot line, gold edge

4011. Melon, blue do. do. do. do.

4012. [No pattern recorded]

4013. Gotha shape, two gold lines inside cup & blue between & gold foot line

4014. Besborough, mat blue scroll as 2484 but slighted

4015. Melon shape, green coral & gold edge & foot line

4016. Registered embossed, as 2252 but grey band

4017. Do. as 2260 but blue

4018. Do. green band edge as usual & Barr's gold scroll inner border [This design is inscribed 'India Septr 1850' in the pattern books]

4018. Do. do. as 2254 with botanical centre. Dessert [There are two patterns numbered 4018.]

4019. Registered emboss'd shape gilt regular way botanical in centre & 3 slight sprigs on rim – Sheriff   14 14   0

4020. Do. do. biscuit blue band with sprig of print in centre

4021. Do. do. celeste etc. exactly as 2260 but with Ridgway's star

4022. Granite Coburg, green band & white space on rim gold lines & gold star

4023. New registered, edge gilt & picked out with pink [This design is inscribed 'Septr 1850' in the pattern books]

4024. Albert shape, gold lace border festoon & gold dontelle

4025. Albert shape, blue studs in gold chain & gold lines forming a serpentine ribbon Gold edge & foot line

4026. Do. do. do. gold dontelle

4027. Do. do. do. in green gold dontelle etc.

4028. Do. do. do. gold edge

4029. Melon shape, blue band & fawn scroles & stars

4030. Registered edge, dessert exactly as 3091 only celeste instead of green

[No patterns are recorded in the list under numbers 4031–4.]

4035. Coburg, dessert, biscuit blue oak leaves & ivy oak leaves & gold sprigs. Single botanical centre

4036. Granite table ware, Parke's green lines & dinner gold line & tooth

4037. Do. enamell'd narrow blue band outer gold line & inner gold line and tooth

4038. Do.   green lines with gold wreath between outer gold & inner gold line

4039. Worcester shape, chain border 'blue green' studs, gold foot line & gold dontelle border about an inch from edge of cup

4040. London embossed, dessert ware celeste spots etc. & gilt & Sheriff's flowers in centre

4041. Amherst Japan fill'd in rose colour used & gilt – Copeland

4042. Gold weed in a wreath, Worcester shape

4043. Melon shape, gold weed in sprigs

4044. New embossed leafage plate, (granite) no gold, traced blue on embossement

4045. Do.   do.   traced gold on embossed 2 blue lines

4046. Do.   do.   similar to 4044 only all gold

4047. Albert shape, precisely as 2623

4048. Coburg, granite – narrow ivory band & birch blue broad band on rim, gold lines & gold star

4049–52. [No pattern recorded]

4053. As 4035 with buff leaves etc. introduced dessert

4054. Worcester shape, dark & slight blue leaves & fawn flowers & gilt

4055. Do.   drab leaves & fawn flowers

4056. Amherst Japan as 4041 only orange instead of gold

4057. Albert shape, yellow band gold outer line & dontelle. Inner blue spot & gold

4058. Do.   2 yellow bands, gold edge & lines & blue & gold border between bands

4059. [No pattern recorded]

4060. Granite table ware same as 4045 but green in lines

4061. [Pattern crossed out]

4062. Granite table ware white & slightly gilt with gold star

4063. Coburg, celeste band. Ivory & gold outer French border & toothing & star as Lord Wards but slightest

4064. Worcester shape, border & roses etc.

4065. Gotha, gold lace border inside & dontelle inside line outside & foot line

4066. Melon, enamelled blue scroll $\frac{1}{4}$ inch. Gold edge & gold trees 6 on cup & 6 on saucer

4067. Do.   green do.   do.   do.

4068. Melon, white & gold & gold edge

4069. Worcester, enamelled blue & gold convolvulous border

4070. Worcester, blue spot & gold border & dontel edge

4071. Granite. Pheasant Japan brown edge

4072. Granite. Japan sprigs & flies

4073. Granite. Japan Mulberry

4074. New London embossed celeste studs & gilt flowers in centre Dresden style

4075. Granite, red coral border & bird [or band] centre

4076. Albert or Worcester shape, blue rose colour & gold neat border & circle

4077. Kerr's print filled in

4078. Do.

4079. Do.

4080. Do.

4081. [Pattern crossed out]

4082. Dessert Ward shape, gold dontille painted butterflies & insects & 3 small sprigs centre & rim of plate

4083. Dessert Ward shape, green coral mat blue edge & centre ring Granite

4084. Melon, new Antwerp glaze-kiln blue neat wreath & dots on cup & inside saucer & sprigs under wreath

4085. Melon, new Antwerp glaze-kiln blue heath

4086. Do.   do.   do.   rose buds (Chelsea)

4087. Do.   do.   do.   Royal lily

4088. Do.   do.   do.   vine wreath & grapes

4089. London embossed, as 4074 tooth border & line instead of shoulder spots

4090. Worcester shape, pink hawthorn blossom border dontelle & botanical

4091. Worcester shape, blue   do.

4092. Do.   white   do.

4093. Double rich gold scroll & dontil

4094. Worcester shape, drab shamrock all over

4095. Worcester shape, gold dontelle blue lines & gold cable

4096. Dessert London embossed, celeste band white & gold edge & gold circle, 1 gold line & toothing

4097. Melon, gold stripe gold line bottom & line gold edge

4098. Green shamrock border & gold edge – the shape to be specified in orders

4099. Melon, black & blue sprigs & gilt cross sprigs

[The numbers jump here to 5000.]

5000. Melon, neat shamrock border green & gold dontel

5001. Worcester shape, pink band yellow & gold feather under band, gold scroll on pink, gold foot line & edge

5002. New Hawthorn edge table plate, hawthorn painted naturel & rope gilt with line

5003. New Hawthorn Table, Matt blue border with scroll under blue & hawthorn flowers (Coronet in centre for Lord L)

5004–18 [No pattern recorded]

5019. Fluted shape (Tea ware) Blue & gold bell border Gold edge & gold (Barr's) line inside cup & gold foot line

At this point the pattern numbers in the available list jump to number 6000. I believe that this break signifies the end of the Chamberlain & Co. period and that the later numbers were introduced by the Kerr & Binns partnership from 1852 to 1862, and were then continued by the Royal Worcester Company.

However, it would seem likely, if not certain, that the numbering did continue from 5019 onwards in the post-1852 period, as an invoice to a Bristol retailer in October 1856 includes references to patterns 5546, 5596 and 5646. This invoice serves to pin-point the Worcester pattern numbers of the mid 1850s, and Henry Sandon has noted that pattern 7247 had been reached by 10 July 1862 (see *Royal Worcester Porcelain from 1862*, 1973, 3rd edition 1978).

APPENDIX: A DAY AT THE FACTORY, 1843

From *The Penny Magazine*, February 1843

Tours around porcelain factories have always been entertaining and instructive. Nowadays such sight-seeing is very well organized and parties have to book months in advance. Henry Sandon, Curator of the Dyson Perrins Museum, has recorded how at one time before the war the company made more money supplying teas to the visitors than it did from making and selling its fine Royal Worcester porcelain. Today both play their part and details of the 'Connoisseur's Tours' are given on page 370.

This Appendix reproduces a report of a visit made to the Chamberlain factory presumably late in 1842. As well as the text, the Victorian engravings are of great interest as they show that the basic methods of preparation and manufacture were principally the same as those employed at the first Worcester factory in the middle of the eighteenth century, and identical to those Robert Chamberlain would have known before he left to commence trade on his own account. As can be seen from the first engraving, the potter's wheel was still being worked by a young lad turning a wheel his own size. This Victorian visitor also observed that the different painters were specialists in their own field – 'one man takes flowers, another foliage, a third animals, a fourth landscapes, a fifth figures, a sixth heraldic bearings and so forth . . .'.

One wonders how many readers of *The Penny Magazine* were later to buy examples of Worcester porcelain to decorate their homes or to drink their tea from. Whatever the result, this account gives an impressive view of the basic manufacturing processes and some idea of life within the factory in the middle of the last century. It is interesting to compare these with present-day methods: certainly there are no longer any lads of tender age turning the wheel or 'wedging' the clay, and gone too are the old coal-fired kilns.

A DAY AT THE ROYAL PORCELAIN-WORKS, WORCESTER.

[Potter's Wheel—' Thrower, ' Ball-maker,' and Wheel-turner,' at work.]

THOSE among our readers who may have witnessed the remarkable "Chinese Exhibition" near Hyde Park (and well would it be if the price of admission permitted all classes to visit this singular memento of a singular nation), cannot fail to have observed the sumptuous specimens of *porcelain* there deposited—the vases, jars, cups, and other vessels; and may then have conjectured whether or not England can produce specimens equal to these. China has, by a sort of pre-scriptive right, been deemed the land of porcelain, the country whose inhabitants occupy the first rank in the production of this most delicate, chaste, and elegant semi-transparent material. Thanks to the inquiries and ingenuity of travellers, manufacturers, and men of science—who have discovered the nature of the prin-cipal substances employed by the Chinese, the localities in which they may be found in Europe, and who have employed the services of painters far more skilful than any to be found in China—our country now produces specimens of porcelain possessing all those claims to admiration which the " Celestial Empire " has put forth for its manufacture, and—in respect to pictorial embellishment—others in which our Asiatic friends cannot for a moment share.

The " good city of Worcester" is one of the spots in England where the manufacture of the higher kinds of porcelain is located. Those topographers and local historians who love to trace the steps of royalty, have recorded the visits of King George and Queen Char-lotte to the " Royal Porcelain-works " at Worcester, as one of the most marked features in the district ; and indeed the high fame which Worcester porcelain has acquired gives the town reason to be somewhat proud in the possession of such a manufacture. For

a long period two eminent firms among others, viz., Messrs. Flight, Barr, and Barr, and Messrs. Chamber-lain, carried on this branch of manufacture inde-pendent of each other : but these two firms have now merged into one, which combines the resources of both ; and the " Royal Porcelain-works " of Messrs. Chamberlain and Co.—an extended firm—are now the representative of both. To the courtesy of these gentle-men, then, our thanks are due for permission to view and describe the processes conducted in this highly in-teresting establishment.

Everybody knows that porcelain is the same ma-terial as that which is commonly termed ' China ' (a name which in itself does homage to the original producers of the substance), but the meaning of the name is not so well known. One authority* says —"The Portuguese traders were the means of in-troducing the fine earthenwares of China into more general use in Europe ; and the name assigned to the fabric, as distinguishing it from the coarser descriptions of pottery of domestic manufacture, was most pro-bably given by them—*porcellana* signifying, in the Portuguese language, a cup ;" while another authority† states—" It has been satisfactorily shown by Marsden, that the word porcelain, or *porcellana*, was applied by Europeans to the ware of China, from the resemblance of its fine polished surface to that of the univalve shell so named ; while the shell itself derived its appellation from the curved or gibbous shape of its upper surface, which was thought to resemble the raised back of a *porcella*, or little hog." Leaving the reader to select between the ' cup,' and the ' little hog,'

* ' Lardner's Cyclopædia.'
† Davis : ' The Chinese,' chap. 17.

as the forerunner of the name, we will quit this matter by stating that the manufacture to which our attention will be directed is strictly that of porcelain in its most highly finished form, and does not include the commoner kinds of produce classed under the general name of *pottery*.

The factory is situated near the cathedral of Worcester, and not far from the Severn, which flows through the city; and from the upper windows a glance across the Severn shows the blue outline of the Malvern Hills in the distance. In this as in many other large factories there is a central court or area, surrounded by buildings of various forms and dimensions, suited for the processes of manufacture. The general arrangement of these may be indicated by following the processes in their natural order.

First, there is the building in which the crude materials are brought into a plastic or working state. Here we see a ponderous circular stone, nearly four tons in weight, working round in a circle on its edge, and crushing beneath it the stony ingredients of the porcelain. Then, in another part of the building, is a circular vessel, provided with a stirring apparatus, for further preparing the substances by the aid of water. The mixing-room, in another place, contains the vessels in which the pounded ingredients are worked up into a smooth kind of clay, fitted for the purposes of the workman.

Following the prepared material to the hands of the workman, we visit the 'throwing-room,' where the remarkable process of forming circular vessels is conducted. This is a long and busily occupied shop, containing a great number of men employed as we shall describe presently. Kilns in great number are disposed conveniently, with respect not only to the 'throwing-room,' but to the other workshops; for there are 'biscuit-kilns,' 'glaze-kilns,' and 'enamel-kilns,' according to the state of the process in which heat has to be applied to the ware.

Various rooms, called 'placing-room,' 'dipping-room,' 'white-ware room,' 'modelling-room,' 'moulding-room,' 'pressing-room,' &c., are disposed round the open area, for the prosecution of various processes in the course of the manufacture; to which succeed others known as the 'painting' and 'burnishing' rooms, in which those elaborate decorations are given to the manufactured article which form one of the most marked features of distinction between it and common pottery-ware. Then we come to the warehouses in which the finished product is stored. Lastly, there are shops, drying-rooms, and kilns, for the manufacture of the 'tessellated tiles,' which are now becoming so extensively used.

We have glanced at the buildings, and now let us glance at the workmen, and the remarkable processes by which the costly specimens of porcelain are produced. The rough ingredients, too, must have a passing notice.

The ingredients to form porcelain may to many persons seem rather strange. They consist of common flint, flint in the calcined state, Cornish stone, Cornish clay, and calcined bone, all ground and mixed together with water, so as to form a beautifully fine and plastic clay. Numerous and intricate have been the researches into the respective value of different kinds of material, and the particular quality which each one gives to the porcelain. The clay employed, as its name imports, is brought from Cornwall, and is found to possess qualities wanting in most other kinds of English clay. For the commoner kinds of pottery, clay brought from Dorsetshire and Devonshire is largely employed; but for the more exquisite specimens of porcelain this Cornish clay is preferred. Until about a century ago, the strangest views were entertained in Europe respecting the composition and nature of Chinese porcelain; and it was not till after many researches that Reaumur found that the mixture of the two peculiar kinds of earth found in China, called *pe-tun-tse* and *kao-lin*, produced porcelain. It then became an object to discover whether any earths similar to these existed in Europe; and at length Mr. Cookworthy, about seventy years ago, discovered in Cornwall two kinds of earth which nearly answered the desired character. From that time to the present various improvements and additions have been made in the ingredients employed, with a view to produce a porcelain possessing hardness, strength, firmness of texture, whiteness of colour, and a capacity of receiving and retaining colours and gilding on its surface. The Cornish clay is by far the most costly clay employed in such works; but for the finer porcelain it is deemed indispensable. We may perhaps say, in accounting for the respective value of the ingredients, that the clay gives the plastic or working quality, the flint imparts the vitreous or strengthening quality, and the bone aids in producing the semi-transparency for which porcelain is so deservedly admired.

The ingredients have different degrees of hardness, but all must be reduced to an impalpable powder before being mixed. They are laid on a circular bed, as represented in the cut, and ground by the pressure

[Grinding the Flint, Clay, &c.]

of the bulky and ponderous stone roller. They are then transferred to a large circular vessel containing water, and by means of stirrers, sieves, and other appliances, brought into the condition of a creamy liquid, totally free from any gritty particles. It is astonishing to see the degree of fineness thus produced, as manifested by the extreme minuteness of the meshes or interstices of the sieve through which everything must pass before being deemed fitted for the manufacture.

Various depositories or receptacles are provided, in which the ingredients are placed separately during the course of their preparation; and from these they are conveyed to the 'mixing-room,' where they are combined together. Here the experience and judgment of the manufacturer are brought into operation: he has to determine not only the number and kind of ingredients which will produce a ware fitted for service, but also the proportions in which these ingredients are to be combined. It is not improbable that each eminent firm has a recipe peculiar to itself, as is known often to be the case in the glass manufacture, and many other manufactures in which several ingredients are employed. Without making any guess then, as to the proportions used in the establishment to which our details relate, we may proceed to state that the ingredients are mixed together in large square vessels, the utmost attention being paid to the intimate union of all the different kinds. The mixture presents the appearance of a kind of drab-coloured liquid, which is then evaporated to a certain degree of thickness or stiffness by heat applied beneath it. In short it is by the agency of heat that the cream-like liquid becomes a plastic workable clay, fitted for the hands of the potter. Constant attention is necessary throughout this process, to equalize the rate of evaporation and to retain the ingredients in perfect combination while it is going on.

To the 'throwing-room' and the 'potter's wheel' we now direct our attention, where a process is conducted which has never failed to excite the astonishment of a spectator who witnesses it for the first time; nay, there are many who find the comprehension of the process almost as difficult after many visits as after the first. Never does any one agent appear a more complete master over another than the potter is of his clay: he seems as if he could do anything, everything, with it. At one moment his mass of clay is a shapeless heap; at another a circular cake; then a ball; then a pillar or cylinder, hollow or solid; then a jug; then a basin; a sudden turn converts it into a bottle, or a plate, or a saucer. His hands work and form the plastic material with a rapidity almost inconceivable; and we often doubt where the clay seems to come from, and whither it goes, when one form is being exchanged for another. It is true that, in practice, the potter does not give all these several forms to one individual mass of clay; but a visitor has frequently an opportunity to see that the man *can* do so. What a pity, some may say, that such an elegant process (for such it assuredly is) should be thrown away upon wet dirty clay; but in truth the peculiar state of the clay is the very circumstance which gives to the potter such a command over it. But let us look at the arrangements of the potter's shop before we describe his operations.

Why such a room should be called a 'throwing-room,' or why the formation of circular vessels should be called 'throwing,' it does not seem very easy to determine. There is a circular motion in pottery-throwing and also in silk-throwing; but why the same term should be applied in both cases, or why applied at all, we do not see. We believe, however, that 'throw' is a provincial name for a lathe; and if so, an explanation is easily provided, by considering the potter's wheel as a lathe or throw. The throwing-room, however, be its appellation good or bad, is an oblong room, containing a great number of benches and pieces of apparatus, at which men are employed making circular articles of soft porcelain.

Our frontispiece shows one of the most ancient working tools, or machines, which any branch of manufacture can exhibit—the 'potter's-wheel.' Scarcely any other machine has lived so long and undergone so little change. On the Egyptian monuments and on other records of antiquity there are representations of the potter's-wheel similar in all the essential particulars to those of our own day; indeed nothing can be more simple than the construction. In the potter himself, and not in the wheel, lies the merit of the work executed. The potter sits on a kind of stool or bench, immediately behind a small circular whirling-table. His knees are placed one on each side of the central support of the machine, so as to give him a command over it. This, which we have called the whirling-table, is simply a circular piece of wood, whose breadth is sufficient to support the widest vessel that is to be made: it is fixed on the top of a vertical stem or shaft, so that if the shaft be made to rotate, the piece of wood must rotate likewise. The apparatus is rather below the height of a common table. The clay which is to be formed into a vessel is put upon the circular board, and there remains till fashioned; the board and the shaft beneath being made to rotate horizontally, while the potter with his hands gives the form to the mass of clay.

Every potter, or 'thrower,' is attended by two boys, who are called the 'ball-maker' and the 'wheel-turner.' The former of these has before him or near him a mass of prepared clay, having precisely the quality and consistence required for the potter's operations. He separates the clay into smaller masses, each suited to the manufacture of one particular kind of vessel, and works it up into a rude kind of ball, convenient to be handled by the thrower. He is in every way the servant or helper to the thrower. The services of the 'wheel-turner' depend on the manner in which the circular piece of wood is made to rotate. In the early state of the porcelain manufacture in England, the perpendicular shaft beneath the board was put in motion by a wheel provided with spokes, which the 'thrower' moved with his foot; the labour however was so great, that this method became unsuited to the production of large articles. Another method in past times was, to have a crank in the middle of the shaft, with a long rod working upon it, and motion was given to the lathe by the rod being pushed backward and forward. The customary mode at the present day is, however, to have a rope passing from a pulley upon the perpendicular shaft to a large wheel at a distance, which wheel is turned by a boy under the directions of the 'thrower.'

With this very simple kind of lathe, and with a few small tools still more simple, does the workman proceed to fashion all those articles of porcelain which are circular in their form, whether cups, basins, or vessels of any other kinds. When the shape is too diversified to be deemed circular, other modes of formation must be adopted, of which more hereafter. Let us suppose, as an example, that a hemispherical basin is to be formed. The man places a mass of clay, in size and consistence suited for the purpose, upon the bed of his lathe or wheel, striking it down rather forcibly as a means of making it hold firmly to the wood during the process of formation. He gives directions to his 'wheel-turner' to set the machine in motion, and then forms the shapeless mass into a vessel, chiefly by his hands. With his hands, wetted in an adjacent vessel of water, he presses the clay while rotating, and brings it into a cylindrical form; this cylinder he forces again down into a lump, and continues these operations—squeezing the clay into various shapes—until he has pressed out every air-bubble from the body of clay, a precaution of very great importance. Then pressing the two thumbs on the top of the mass, he indents or hollows it, as a first germ of the internal hollow of the vessel. Once having the least semblance of a cavity within, he proceeds with a rapidity almost marvellous to give both the outward and the inward contour to the vessel. With the thumbs inside and the fingers outside, he so draws, and presses, and moulds the plastic material, as to give to the outside a convexity, to the inside a concavity, and to the whole substance an uniform consistency, without breaking the clay or disturbing the circular form of the vessel. It will be seen on a moment's consideration that this circular form is due to the rotation of the clay, while the fingers and thumbs are stationary, just as a turner

THE PENNY MAGAZINE

holds his cutting-chisel stationary while the piece of wood is rotating.

During the pressure of the hands upon the clay, a minute change in the amount or direction of the pressure would transform the basin into a saucer, or into any other vessel whose degree of curvature is very different from that of a basin. The oddness of these transformations might often make a spectator smile, were not his admiration excited by the cleverness and dexterity of the workman who produces them. According to the shape and size of the vessel, the 'thrower' requires the wheel and the mass of clay to rotate with varying degrees of velocity, in which he instructs his 'wheel-turner.'

The general contour of the vessels, inside and out, is given by the thumbs, fingers, and palms of the hands. But as this could not insure accuracy sufficient, the workman is provided with small pieces of wood called 'profiles,' or 'ribs,' each of which is shaped in accordance with either the exterior or the interior of some particular kind and form of vessel. Holding one of these 'ribs' in his hand, and applying it to the surface of the clay, the workman scrapes off the superfluous portion at any protuberant or misshapen part, and makes the whole circumference conform to the shape of the rib. The fragments thus removed, technically called 'slurry,' he throws aside among the unused clay. If a number of vessels are to be exactly the same size, the workman sometimes fixes pegs in the stand on which the clay is placed, which act as a guide to him in regulating the diameter to which the clay is to be expanded, and beyond which it must not reach. When the vessel, by the aid of the hands and the small working tools, is formed, it is cut from the supporting piece of clay or from the board by means of a piece of brass wire, much in the same manner as barrelled butter is cut into slices, and the newly-formed vessel is placed on a board or shelf to dry.

In this manner vast varieties of vessels are formed, comprising all those which present, both on the exterior and the interior, an uniform circularity. And indeed not only are vessels thus formed, but masses of clay are similarly brought into a cylindrical form, as a nucleus from which ornamental articles may afterwards be produced at the turning-lathe. Within the last few years the use of porcelain has greatly extended, in relation to articles both useful and ornamental. Candlesticks, taper-stands, fancy baskets, door-handles, finger-plates, and a host of other articles, are now made of this material; and if the form is such as can be given by the lathe, a mass of clay is first worked by the hand into something like a cylindrical shape, as a preparative for the operations of the turner. The floor of the 'throwing-room' at the factory under notice was filled with these cylindrical masses, technically called 'solids,' some of which were to be turned at the lathe into banister-rails for staircases, and others into articles of various other kinds.

The operation of turning these articles is effected very much in the same manner as the turning of wood. The 'solids' are allowed to remain until, by the evaporation of moisture from the damp clay, they have acquired a degree of dryness which is known among the workmen as the 'green state,' in which state the shaping and smoothing of the surface are better effected than when the clay is either damper or drier. As a turner in wood can produce an internal cylindrical cavity as well as a circular exterior, so can the porcelain-turner; and it is in this way that candlesticks and similar articles are brought to the required shape.

We have now, in supposition, made circular vessels, and turned them to the required shape and smoothness. But before we follow them through their subsequent progress, it is desirable to witness the production of those articles which neither the potter's wheel nor the lathe will produce; articles which exhibit in an especial degree the magnificence and delicacy of the finer kinds of porcelain. This will take us to the workshops of the 'pressers,' the 'mould-makers,' and the 'modellers;' for the decorated articles are produced by pressing or by pouring clay into moulds, which moulds must previously be made from models, and which models must have been before formed by hand. Hence the modeller is the all-important workman whom we must first visit.

In an upper room of the factory are the operations of the man of taste, the 'modeller,' conducted. Here, whatever our Schools of Design, or education, or natural ability could afford, in the development of a knowledge in elegance of form, is important and valuable. The modeller, from drawings made either by himself or by others, has to build up in clay the exact representative of the article to be formed in porcelain. From the handle of a tea-cup up to the most elaborate combination for a piece of drawing-room porcelain furniture, the modeller has to prepare an accurate original in soft clay. Provided with a supply of clay, especially prepared for this kind of work, and with a few simple tools, he elaborates the various parts of his design, whether animals, fruit, flowers, foliage, architectural ornaments, arabesques, or any of the countless varieties of decorative devices; building up his model piecemeal, and carving or cutting out the parts as he proceeds. It has been aptly observed by Mr. Porter, that "the taste of the modeller is put in requisition; calling for the execution on his part of a high degree of skill and ingenuity in forming patterns, and adapting to them appropriate ornaments. To be a perfect modeller, in the higher branches of the art, a man should have an acquaintance with the best productions of the classic climes of Greece and Rome; he should be master of a competent knowledge of the art of design; his fancy glowing with originality, tempered and guided by elegance and propriety of feeling, and restrained by correctness of taste and judgment. To a man thus gifted, the plastic and well-tempered material wherewith he works offers little of difficulty in the execution of his conceptions."

When we visited the *studio* of the modeller at these works, he was engaged upon an elaborate model of a kind of tripod or stand, comprising a vast number of parts, all highly decorated. It is only in the costly articles which require *casting* that the model is thus elaborate: when it can be produced by *pressing*, the preparation of the model is generally more simple. The difference between these two modes of manufacture is this:—that, in pressing, the shallowness of the mould is such that clay, in its usual plastic state, can be pressed into all the minute devices of the mould; while, in casting, the mould is so deep and elaborate that the clay has to be poured into it in the state of a cream-like liquid. Plates, saucers, oval vessels, lids, spouts, handles, and a large variety of articles which are too irregular to be produced at the potter's-wheel and the lathe, and yet not so complex as to require casting, are produced by pressing. But both for pressing and for casting moulds must be made, and these moulds are reversed copies of models produced by the modeller; so that this workman's services are required for all.

Plaster of Paris, prepared in a particular way, is the substance of which the moulds are made. The making of the moulds is quite a distinct occupation from that of modelling, and is carried on in a different part of the factory. A casing of clay is first formed and securely fixed round the model, leaving sufficient space between it and the model for the substance of the mould. The plaster of Paris, being mixed with water to a cream-like liquid, is then poured into the vacant space. In a very short time, in virtue of the well-known qualities of this substance, the plaster solidifies into a compact mass, which is easily separable from the model. The interior of this mould is then found to give a perfect counter-representation of the exterior of the model, in all its minuteness of detail. The model is lastly dried, to prepare it for further use.

For pressing, the mould is sometimes made in two parts, one half of the figure being on one side, and the other half on the other; the two being made to fit accurately together. Clay is pressed into each half of the mould, and cut off flush, so as to have no superfluity; and the two halves of the mould being brought closely together, each piece of clay receives its impress from the half of the mould in which it lies, and the two pieces are at the same time joined together: so that one piece is produced, presenting a fac-simile of both halves of the mould. This mode is adopted in the preparation of a large diversity or variety of articles. Another arrangement, for the production of plain handles, spouts, &c., is to force clay through an orifice in the bottom of a cylinder, the orifice having that shape which is to be given to the clay. A third arrangement, where one surface of a shallow vessel, such as a saucer or a plate, requires to be moulded, while the other can be formed without a mould, is to lay a flat piece of clay on the mould, press it down with a wet sponge, and give a proper form to the exposed surface by a profile or gauge applied to the wet clay while the latter is revolving. The annexed cut represents a few ornamental articles which required to be produced by pressure, and the moulds used in the pressing.

Many a tea-drinker has probably marvelled how the handle of a tea-cup is produced; whether it is fashioned by hand out of the same piece of clay which forms the cup, or cast in a mould with it, or fixed on separately. The preceding details will have prepared us to understand the real state of the matter,—that the cup, if not too elaborate in form, is 'thrown' at the wheel; that the handle is pressed in a mould, and that the one is afterwards affixed to the other. Handles, spouts, knobs, and small raised ornaments are all attached to the vessels in a similar way, and when the latter are in the 'green state,' between wet and dry. The cement employed is simply a creamy mixture of clay and water, technically termed 'slip,' which is applied to the two surfaces to be joined together, and which enables them to adhere permanently. The clay handle or spout is in such a soft state, that considerable neatness and dexterity are requisite, especially in curving the strip of pressed or moulded clay which is to form the handle—a process represented in the annexed cut. The raised or relief orna-

[Moulds for Porcelain, and Casts.]

[Fixing Handles.]

So varied and numerous are the articles now made of porcelain, that it would be utterly impracticable to classify them all in respect of the mode of manufacture; but it will suffice to say that all are produced by one or other of the modes above noticed, viz., throwing at the wheel, aided by profiles or gauges; turning at the lathe; pressing through an orifice in a cylinder; pressing one side on a mould, while the other side is fashioned by a gauge; pressing between two moulds, or the two halves of a mould; and casting while the clay is in a liquid form. In the last-mentioned mode of proceeding, the plaster of the mould quickly absorbs water from the liquid clay which lies in contact with its surface, and brings it to a solid state; and a hardened shell having been thus produced, the subsequent arrangements are such as to make the cast either hollow or solid, according to its form and dimensions.

ments seen on articles of porcelain are made separately in a mould, and cemented on the vessel by the aid of 'slip,' except when the vessel is of such a kind as to require to be cast or pressed, in which case the ornaments are generally made as part of the pattern itself in the mould. Some of the workmen at the factory were engaged in preparing elegant little taper-stands, the construction of which illustrates conveniently the combination of the different modes of manufacture: for the lower saucer or dish had been pressed in a mould; the nozzle had been made into a 'solid' at the wheel and then turned at the lathe; the handle had been formed in a double mould; and lastly, all these were joined together with 'slip.'

Let us suppose, then, that we have traced all the various kinds of porcelain articles to a finished state in respect of their form and decorations: the tea-pots furnished with handles and spouts, the cups with handles, the jugs with lips, and the more highly decorated articles provided with all which the ' thrower,' the ' turner,' the ' presser,' and the ' caster' can do for them. We shall next be prepared to follow them through the subsequent processes which impart that exquisite appearance so especially belonging to porcelain.

Adjacent to the buildings where the early stages of the manufacture are carried on are four ' biscuit-kilns,' in which the ware is exposed to an intense heat. These kilns are probably about fourteen feet high, and nearly as much in diameter. They are heated by fires ranged round the circumference, each kiln having eight fire-places. The whole interior capacity is fitted for the reception of the articles to be ' fired,' or ' baked.' Very great precautions are necessary in this process ; for, if the smoke or flame from the fire attacked the porcelain, it would discolour it at once, and spoil it. To prevent this mischance, all the manufactured articles are put into receptacles called ' seggars,' such as are here represented · these

[Putting manufactured articles into ' Seggars.']

are made principally of a kind of fire-clay capable of resisting an intense heat; and so important are they, that the acquisition of the sort of clay fitted for the purpose has always been deemed a momentous point on the part of the manufacturer. The seggars are of various sizes, shapes, and depths, to suit the different pieces they are to contain. According to the size and shape of the articles, they are either enclosed one in each seggar, or several in each ; but in the latter case precautions are taken that they should not adhere together, nor touch each other at more than two or three points: powdered flint is placed at the bottom of the seggars, and pieces of hard fire-clay are so placed within the seggar, that the articles may be supported with as little contact as possible one with another.

The piling of the seggars in the ' biscuit-kiln ' is a singular arrangement. The whole interior is filled with them. The top and bottom of each seggar (the former open and the latter closed) being flat, they may be piled one on another, so that each one forms a cover for the one underneath. As the heat cannot be perfectly equalized throughout the kiln, care is taken that the larger articles shall be exposed to a higher temperature than the smaller. Thus seggar is laid upon seggar, and pile after pile built up within the kiln, till the whole is filled. Every aperture is then carefully closed—of which the main one is, of course, the door through which the men enter the kiln—and all is ready for the fires to be lighted beneath. The general appearance of the kiln while being filled is here represented.

[Placing the ' Seggars' in the ' Biscuit-kiln.']

We do not know whether it is a customary arrangement in porcelain factories generally, or whether it merely applies to the one which is the object of our visit ; but here the kiln-fires are lighted at a very early hour on Friday morning, and the articles are kept exposed to a fierce white heat throughout Friday and Saturday, forty hours being about the length of time during which they are thus exposed. The precise amount of ' firing' necessary is a delicate point, to be determined only by experience : it must be sufficient to expel all the moisture, and to convert the clay into a kind of semi-vitreous earth, but not beyond this point.

The baked articles are allowed to cool gradually before being drawn from the kiln ; and when so drawn they have acquired the state which is called ' biscuit.' Every article shrinks considerably while in the kiln, and the weight is very materially lessened. The biscuit-ware has a peculiarly delicate, soft, and white appearance, presenting many points of striking difference compared with its unbaked state. Every article, as taken out of the seggar, is nicely cleaned, to remove all symptoms of flint-dust, &c. ; and it is then ready for the process of ' glazing,' by which the dead· and unpolished surface of the biscuit is converted into a beautiful glassy surface.

One of the most important steps in the progress of the porcelain manufacture has been the discovery of substances fitted to impart this 'glaze' to porcelain. Any of the substances which will make glass will afford a glaze to pottery; and these substances comprise various alkalies, various oxides of metals, and flint in a variety of forms: but what is the best combination to form a glaze for the more delicate kinds of porcelain is a question which has occupied much attention, not only among manufacturers, but among chemists also. In the commonest kinds of earthenware or pottery the cheapest ingredients are those most resorted to; but in costly porcelain a totally different system is pursued, the excellence of the material being a much more important matter than the smallness of the price. We believe that in this, as in the choice of clays for making the porcelain, each large establishment has a recipe of its own, derived from the experience of the proprietors.

In one part of the factory is a room called the 'dipping-room,' adjacent to four 'glaze-kilns.' In the dipping-room are troughs or wooden vessels containing the glaze, a whitish creamy liquid. The room is kept at a moderate warmth, and is provided with conveniences for placing the porcelain articles, both before and after being dipped. The pieces of 'baked' or 'fired' porcelain being brought into this room, a workman takes them up one by one, holds them in such a manner that there shall be the smallest amount of contact between them and his fingers, and dips them into the trough of glaze. By one of those manipulations which are peculiar to most occupations, he turns the vessel about, on removing it from the glaze, in such a manner that, while every part shall be coated, none shall have any superabundance but what may easily be drained off. The vessels are put down out of his hand, one by one, on a board, which is thence carried to the 'glaze-kiln placing-room.' In this latter room they are piled up in seggars, nearly in the same way as before, but with certain modifications to suit the peculiarity of the circumstances.

The glaze-kilns, like the biscuit-kilns, are each heated by eight fires, and are each filled up with piles of seggars; but in the glaze-kilns the slight opening between the several seggars of each pile is stopped with clay, to prevent more effectually the entrance of smoke and flame into the seggar. The heat for vitrifying the glaze is much less intense than for biscuit-firing, and is continued for a much smaller number of hours. The operation consists in driving off the watery parts of the glaze, and melting the vitreous part, which, in a vitreous state, combines firmly with the biscuit. Where we find, in the cheaper articles of manufacture, the glaze to become discoloured, or the ware discoloured under the glaze, or the glaze intersected by myriads of minute cracks, this always indicates either that a bad choice of ingredients was made, or that the management of the glaze-kiln was injudicious; and this is one of the many points in which first-rate porcelain shows its excellence.

We have now brought the porcelain to what might be deemed a finished state, so far as regards the actual service demanded from it: but it is very rarely that such porcelain as we are now considering leaves the hands of the manufacturer in this state; it is nearly always decorated either with painting or gilding, or both, before it passes into the hands of the customer. We follow it therefore to one of the largest and most interesting rooms in the factory, known as the 'painting-room.' This is a long room, provided on both sides with rows of windows, through which an ample supply of light is obtained. Close to the windows are a range of tables, at which the painters are seated, each one with his side to the light. At the time of our visit a large number of persons were thus engaged, each one holding in his left hand some article or other of porcelain which he was painting with his right. The odour indicated that various mineral colours, mixed up with oil and turpentine, formed the material of the paint. Each man had a pallet of colour before him, which he laid on the porcelain with a camel-hair pencil, much in the same manner as a miniature-painter would do.

In China this branch of manufacture is so subdivided, that one man paints blue, another red, another yellow, &c., so that each article goes through a great number of hands during the process of painting. But in England the subdivision is more rational. One man takes flowers, another foliage, a third animals, a fourth landscape, a fifth figures, a sixth heraldic bearings, and so forth; confining themselves mainly to that which their taste and studies have enabled them to effect artistically. Consequently, in walking from one part of the painting-room to another, we witnessed in succession the labours of all these classes of artists. Each painter holds the piece of porcelain against a projecting part of his table, so as to retain it firmly; or else, if a circular ornament is to go round it, he rests it on a support which may enable it to rotate with facility. The colours employed in this process are chiefly oxides of various metals, worked up to a liquid state with spirits of tar and of turpentine, and amber oil. Those ornaments which are subsequently to present the brilliant golden appearance so familiar to us on the better kinds of porcelain, are effected by a preparation of refined gold mixed up with some of the liquids just mentioned into a dark brown colour, which has no semblance to a golden hue until after it has been burned in a kiln.

Some of the articles of porcelain have a white or unpainted ground, decorated with coloured ornaments; while others are painted over the whole surface with a ground colour, the laying on of which is the work of a particular set of painters, who show great art in the uniform tinting produced. For instance, we saw some of the painters engaged on a costly service of porcelain for the distinguished Hindoo who has recently visited England—Dwarkanauth Tagore, in which the ground was a delicate tint of green, produced by a different manipulation from that which imparts the decorative devices. In some parts of the room there were herald-painters engaged on articles of porcelain for the mess-rooms of some of our regiments and for noble families, the arms of the regiment or of the family being painted in more or less detail on each piece of porcelain. Not only are vessels for table-service thus painted, but the side slabs for fire-places and a large variety of decorative furniture are now made in porcelain, and then subjected to the taste and skill of the painter. This is one of the branches of the porcelain manufacture in which the English have made very rapid progress within the last few years.

Conveniently placed with respect to the painting-room are the 'enamel-kilns,' in which the painted articles are exposed to a heat sufficient to make the colours adhere to the porcelain. These kilns are a kind of arched oven, having a door at one end, and gratings within on which the articles are placed. The most scrupulous care and delicacy are displayed in managing these kilns, as to the temperature and length of exposure. Sometimes the painter requires to partially heat the porcelain two or three times during the process of painting, to ascertain the effect of his colours, and to combine them well with the porcelain. Indeed the care required in this process is very little less than in the exquisite one of enamel-painting.

We next follow the costly results of all the preceding labours to the 'burnishing-room,' a large apartment occupied by women and girls employed in burnishing those parts which have been gilt in the painting-room. The burnishers are formed of blood-stone and agate, brought to a very smooth surface, and variously shaped to adapt them to the curvatures of the porcelain. Each workwoman is seated at a bench with her face towards a window, holding the porcelain in the left hand, and the burnisher in her right, with which she rubs the gilded parts until they are brought to a brilliant gloss. The warehouses of the firm—of which there is one in the High Street of Worcester, and two in London, in Coventry Street and in Bond Street—illustrate in a striking degree the progress made by our manufacturers in the production of those luxurious articles for which Sèvres and Dresden obtained, in past times, such celebrity

TESSELLATED TILE MANUFACTURE.

We must in closing say a few words respecting a branch of manufacture which promises to be much extended in England, viz. *tessellated tiles* for pavements, &c. Whoever has seen the Temple Church since it has been renovated, will have noticed the beautiful pavement which it displays, formed of a vast number of rectangular tiles about six inches square, glazed on the upper surface. The establishment to which this 'visit' relates is one of those wherein tiles of this kind, a specimen or two of which are here depicted, are made.

[Tessellated Tiles.]

The tessellated tiles are formed of two differently coloured clays, one imbedded in the other, and disposed so as to form an ornamental device. The tile is first made in clay of one colour, with a depression afterwards to be filled with clay of the other colour, and this depression is formed by the aid of a mould. In the first place, the modeller models in stiff clay an exact representative of one of the tiles, about an inch thick, cutting out to the depth of about a quarter of an inch the depression which constitutes the device. When this is properly dried, a mould is made from it in plaster of Paris, and from this mould all the tiles are produced one by one. The ground-colour of the tile is frequently a brownish clay, with a yellow device; but this may be varied at pleasure. Let the colour be what it may, however, the first clay is mixed up very thick, and pressed into the mould by the aid

of the press seen in the next cut. On leaving the press it presents the form of a damp, heavy, uncoloured square tile of clay, with an ornamental device formed by a depression below the common level of the surface.

[Making the Tiles.]

The second-coloured clay, so far from being made stiff like the first, has a consistence somewhat resembling that of honey; and herein lies one of the niceties of manufacture, for it is necessary to choose clays which will contract equally in baking, although of different consistence when used. The tile being laid on a bench, the workman plasters the honey-like clay on it, until he has completely filled the depressed device, using a kind of knife or trowel in this process. The tile, in this state, is then allowed to dry very gradually for the long period of eight weeks, to accommodate the shrinking of the clays to their peculiar natures. After this, each tile is scraped on the surface with an edge-tool, till the superfluous portion of the second clay is removed, and the two clays become properly visible, one forming the ground and the other the device. In this state the tiles are put into a 'biscuit-kiln,' where they are baked in a manner nearly resembling the baking of porcelain, but with especial reference, as to time and temperature, to the quality of the clays. From the biscuit-kiln they are transferred to the 'dipping-room,' where they are coated on the upper surface with liquid glaze by means of a brush. Lastly, an exposure to the heat of the 'glaze-kiln' for a period of twenty-four or thirty hours causes the glaze to combine with the clay, and the tiles are then finished.

The substance of which these tiles are made cannot be called *porcelain*, but the care required in their manufacture is such as to remove them from the rank of common pottery, and to form a sufficient reason for their being made at the very interesting establishment here described, and of which we now take our leave.

SELECTED BIBLIOGRAPHY

Primary Sources

First and foremost I must list the most important source of information on the history of the Chamberlains and their productions – the original account books, many of which are still preserved at the present factory or in the Dyson Perrins Museum adjacent to the Royal Worcester Works. These are listed here in their chronological order. The number given on the left appears on the spine of each book and refers to a later check-list.

23	Invoice book	1788
25	Cash, stock book	1788
26	Cash book	1789
34	Order book	1789–91
36	Invoice book	1789–91
48	Journal	1789–93
5	Order book	1791 +
13	Mr Turner's order book	1791 +
32	Stock book	1792
65	Cash book	1792 +
66	Cash and order book	1792–9
79	Wages book	1793–5
94	Order book	1793–9
27	Journal	1793–6
35	Order book	1793–5
2	Journal, wholesale and retail	1796–1800
8	Cash book, wholesale and retail	1796–1806
9	Wages book	1796–8
30	Contingent book	1796–1804
47	Wages book	1796–1800
91	Ledger	1796–1806
46	Painters' wages book	1799–1804
77	Order book	1799–1808
70	Journal	1800–4
93	Wages book	1801–9
7	Journal	1804–6
14	Cash book	1804–11
15	Cash book	1804–14
50	Journal	1808–19
90	Journal	1811–16
24	Bond Street cash book	1814–25
63	Journal	1817–24
39	Wholesale order book	1817–25
93	Order book	1819–24
47	Journal	1822–4
16	Journal	1824–6
57	Bond Street cash book	1825–33
83	Journal, Bond Street	1838–42
21	Accounts with other manufacturers	1840–2
38	Private journal	1840–8
37	Invoice book	1841–3
69	Journal, Worcester	1844–6
29	Letter book	1848–57

The earliest books are in general the most detailed, but many are in a bad condition, several appear to be incomplete and others seem to have been lost or destroyed. Nevertheless these original Chamberlain account books probably represent the best documented records of any eighteenth- or nineteenth-century British porcelain factory. Without these archives knowledge of Caughley porcelain and the history of the Chamberlain factory would have been almost non-existent.

Books

Very few modern reference books give more than a passing mention of the Chamberlain productions. The great exception is R. W. Binns's mid nineteenth-century work, *A Century of Potting in the City of Worcester*, written less than fifteen years after the Chamberlain partnership gave way to Messrs Kerr & Binns. It was published by B. Quaritch of London in 1865, with a second edition in 1877.

Thomas Turner's Caughley porcelains, which Robert Chamberlain originally traded in and to a large extent decorated, are dealt with in my *Caughley and Worcester Porcelains 1775–1800* (published by Herbert Jenkins, London, 1969). A fresh edition of this book, with a new illustrated introduction, was published in a limited, numbered edition by the Antique Collectors' Club, Woodbridge, Suffolk, in 1981.

The early Worcester porcelains produced before the Chamberlains left this factory are ably covered by Henry Sandon's standard book *The Illustrated Guide to Worcester Porcelain* (Herbert Jenkins, London, 1969, 3rd edition 1980). The later products are very well illustrated in the same author's works *Flight and Barr Worcester Porcelain 1783–1840* (Antique Collectors' Club, 1978) and *Royal Worcester Porcelain* (Barrie & Jenkins, London, 1973, 3rd edition 1978).

Those readers who may wish to view the Chamberlain porcelains in comparison with the various other British makes of the period may usefully consult my general book *British Porcelain: An Illustrated Guide* (Barrie & Jenkins, London, 1974).

Collections of Chamberlain porcelain

Unfortunately it is at the moment difficult to see and handle Chamberlain porcelains apart from the selection of mainly decorative examples in the Victoria & Albert Museum and at the Dyson Perrins Museum at Worcester. The latter is open Monday to Saturday 10.00–13.00 and 14.00–17.00 from April to September, and 10.00–13.00 and 14.00–17.00 Monday to Friday during the months October to March. Admission is free.

The 'Connoisseur's Tours' at the Dyson Perrins Museum enable the visitor to take a closer look at Royal Worcester porcelain works. An introductory talk is followed by a special tour of the Worcester Royal Porcelain factory, including visits to departments not normally seen by the general public. The standard factory tour gives the visitor the opportunity to see Worcester craftsmen in their own surroundings creating many of the items associated with the company. Further information concerning both tours may be obtained from: Dyson Perrins Museum, Severn Street, Worcester. Telephone Worcester (0905) 23221 or 20272. To avoid disappointment visitors must make prior bookings.

The reader will no doubt spot Chamberlain examples as he tours the stately houses in Britain; these, few as they may be, are at least seen in their original setting, but I do not know of any one specialist collector or collection of Chamberlain-Worcester porcelain.

Many of the pieces illustrated in this book and credited to 'Godden of Worthing Ltd', 'Geoffrey Godden, chinaman', and particularly 'Godden Reference Collection' are available in my collection at my business premises, 17–19 Crescent Road, Worthing, West Sussex; a prior appointment should be made. The telephone number is Worthing (0903) 35958, but please note that these premises are not open on Saturdays or Sundays.

INDEX